FAREWELL *the* Derry Road

A history of the railway line from 1847 to 1965 with photographic memories from the past

In memory of my Mother, Harriet Florence Challoner (nee Kilpatrick), a Tyrone girl from Cavenacaw, Pomeroy. It was she who first took me, as a child in her arms, to 'see the railway' at Pomeroy station, and later in life, nurtured and supported my desire to preserve a record of our transport heritage for future generations to enjoy.

ERIC T CHALLONER

First Edition
First Impression

Designed by Colourpoint Books, Newtownards
Printed by W&G Bairds Ltd

ISBN 978 1 906578 76 3

Colourpoint Books
Colourpoint House
Jubilee Business Park
Jubilee Road
NEWTOWNARDS
County Down
Northern Ireland
BT23 4YH

Tel: 028 9182 6339

Fax: 028 9182 1900

E-mail: info@colourpoint.co.uk

Web: www.colourpoint.co.uk

The publishers regret that they cannot supply copies of any of the photographs in this book.

Whilst every effort has been made to trace copyright holders of the photographs used in this book, many of the pictures in private collections bore no clues as to the photographer's identity.

Pictures by A Donaldson appear by courtesy of WT Scott.

Pictures by EM Patterson, HB Priestley and GR Stone appear by courtesy of CP Friel.

The author, who was born in 1947, has been a keen Irish railway transport historian and researcher for many years. Though currently living in Wellington, Shropshire, Eric has strong family ties in County Tyrone and spent most of his childhood summer holidays on and around the Derry Road line, chiefly at Pomeroy where he and his parents used to stay at the family home in Cavenacaw. Less happy and far more poignant were his continued visits to the line after February 1965, when details of the gradual return to nature were faithfully recorded. Eric is also a life member of several societies, including the RPSI and Donegal Restoration Group. His other great love in life are trolleybuses, and following the release of his first book in 2007, *Trolleybus Memories - Wolverhampton*, released to celebrate the 40th anniversary of the closure of that system, he has now passed out and qualified as a trolleybus driver at the Black Country Living Museum, where he is often to be found (appropriately) driving Belfast No 246 around the three-quarter mile route.

Cover pictures

Front: S class 4-4-0 No 171 *Slieve Gullion* waits to depart from Omagh with the 4.30pm to Belfast on 6 July 1963.

Author

Rear: A departing down train passes under the bridge at the west end of Pomeroy on a wet July day in 1964. Soon such sights will be in the past.

Author

Rear: S class 4-4-0 No 174 *Carrantuohill* enters Victoria Bridge with an up train on a sunny Tuesday 11 August 1964. The leading carriage is AEC-fitted L13 Brake Third No 593, followed by a brace of K11 Thirds.

Sam Williamson

Title page: Mogul No 99 *King George VI* takes water at Pomeroy on 28 July 1964.

EM Patterson

Contents

S class 4-4-0 No 171 *Slieve Gullion* arriving at Omagh with an up express on 22 June 1956. The signalman can be seen returning to his cabin after the staff exchange.

BKB Green

Preface

When researching information for a new book, there is something not altogether unpleasant about exploring an abandoned railway line, on a still, warm day in June or September, deep in the countryside and wandering along the remains of a trackbed, surrounded by fields and verdant hedgerows, alive with the sound of bird song, only one's own thoughts and the clouds for company as they frame the distant purple-tinted hillsides. It is a different, though equally enjoyable, sensation to watching driving rain alternating with dappled sunlight, as it crosses rising ground on the far side of a valley, for example, and a sensation that is hard to define or explain to a person not interested in such things. In the case of the railway line, however, along with the exploration there is a often an intense sense of nostalgia, coupled with sadness and an inner anger for something now beyond reach; a way of life somehow lost forever because those in authority thought they knew better – invariably, time has proved they did not.

To this day, the 'Derry Road' is still held with a strong affection by all who knew it. It was a country railway in the fullest sense of the word, as a single-track secondary route running through the countryside of Northern Ireland. It journeyed from the lush green apple orchards of County Armagh in the south to the banks of the River Foyle at the line's northern terminus. Between these two varied settings, it traversed the archetypical scenery of County Tyrone, with its low slate-roofed whitewashed cottages dotted across the slopes of gently rolling hills. Its winding roads and hedges of hawthorn formed a patchwork quilt across the green fields of Mid Ulster. The rivers Blackwater, Camowen, Strule, Mourne and Foyle were crossed en-route by a variety of bridges, both stone and steel.

The line also carried express trains linking the two most important cities in Northern Ireland, managing all this whilst faithfully serving the local community. The line carried a charisma that cannot easily be explained and projected an image that identified it with a less frenetic and generally better, more gentle, way of life, now sadly beyond reach, being held in the same high esteem and awe that is usually reserved for other lost railways of national importance, such as the Somerset & Dorset, in England, or the 'Port Road' from Dumfries to Stranraer, in south west Scotland.

It is doubtful whether there are many other places in the British Isles where the loss of a line has been felt quite so keenly, or mourned so deeply, with a passion that can be startling to those not of a railway persuasion. When still in existence, it was held in high regard, not just by the people who lived within its reach and used the services, but also by professional railwaymen who had a deep and abiding respect for the sometimes wild and unpredictable nature of the route. Crews often pitted their wits against the elements as they battled to work within the public timetables and provide a service to the community that they could justifiably take pride in.

The sensation of being part of a large, protective family is evident throughout the history of the GNR, and nowhere more apparent than on the 'Derry Road'. This feeling was constantly found when talking to ex-GNR employees, as were the happy memories of the people I met, still living in the houses they occupied when the railway was operational, and an important part of their everyday life. Many were the evocative and haunting memories encountered, whilst wandering along the silent, weed-encrusted and overgrown trackbed, far into the countryside and miles from anywhere. The only distraction was the sound of a far-off tractor working in the fields, as I picked my way through derelict stations with roofless abandoned signal boxes, and the remains of rusting railwayana scattered all around, my mind going back to another time and place.

Memories of life become a journey that is forever homeward bound.

Acknowledgements

Though every effort has been made to ensure accuracy, the passing of time, coupled with fading memories and conflicting dates in a number of other sources, has resulted in areas of uncertainty, with some details open to question. The author would be pleased to accept any new information.

I want to specifically thank Charles Friel and Des Fitzgerald for giving me access to their extensive photographic archives. Whilst all photographs have been credited where known, it has not been possible to identify or contact all copyright owners, and it is hoped that any owners recognising their photographs will accept this statement in lieu of a full acknowledgment.

All reference to money is shown in pounds sterling eg £1 3s 6d, as indeed the currency was prior to decimalisation.

I am indebted to friends and relatives for all their help, and though it would perhaps be invidious to single out any one person, I would like to place on record my grateful thanks to everyone for all their help in dealing with my many queries during the preparation of this book, thus ensuring that a permanent record is put down in print, before such information is lost forever. I hope that the result will give readers a glimpse into the fascinating world of Irish railway operation that was the epitome of the Great Northern, and in particular show how the Derry Road helped to shape, and indeed was shaped to some extent, by both the countryside it ran through, and by the people it served in the towns and villages along its route.

The author, as a young man, contemplates the remains of Omagh station after the lifting of the Derry Road in 1966-67.
Author's camera

Introduction

Sunday 14 February 1965, is a date that will live in the minds of working men and railway enthusiasts alike in Northern Ireland, for on that day, a heavily biased Stormont Government, totally obsessed with road transport and with a barely veiled mandate to remove all forms of rail traction in Northern Ireland, closed the 75½ mile railway line between Portadown and Londonderry, together with the Dungannon to Coalisland branch, in the process bringing to an end 118 years of travel in County Tyrone. Nominally closed by the Ulster Transport Authority – in reality another arm of the Government – this completed a move first proposed as far back as 1957.

Known to all as the 'Derry Road' and one of the most important secondary lines in the province, it provided both a social service and a transport feeder for the local economy that was an essential lifeline for the wellbeing of the market towns and rural communities that it served along its route; its platforms and halts had become important meeting places, with much social significance and importance to the community. Stations like Dungannon and Omagh, that bustled with the sounds of porters' cheerful banter, wicker baskets and sacks being loaded with the slamming of carriage doors, fell strangely silent. The often-played-out scenes of heartfelt 'hellos' and desperately poignant 'good-byes' would not be seen again. Passing places like Trew & Moy or Beragh, and distant Pomeroy, high upon the slopes of the Sperrin foothills, suddenly seemed more remote than before.

Wherever your heart lies, there your feet will surely follow.

The final day's UTA workings were operated by ex-Great Northern men in the true spirit of their previous employer. Strong in their beliefs, the timetable was operated faultlessly with the crews determined to go out in style – if they could not stop the closure, they could at least show what they stood for and believed in. The closure, bitterly fought against by Tyrone County Council, and originally planned for 4 January, was postponed following a second attempt by the County Council to force a rethink; their concern regarding the proposed action by the Government was so great that they had taken the unprecedented step of going to the High Court twice in a desperate attempt to stop the closure, stating that they had "lost all confidence in the Government's ability to deal with their objections in a way which was objective, fair and, in the circumstances, adequate".

Despite the Stormont Government's claim that the line was uneconomic, prodigious amounts of freight continued to be worked along the Derry Road, even in its final years: their subversive and, at times, completely false media statements, contrasted sharply with traffic movements on the line itself. With much of the route being single line, it was necessary to move the bulk of the freight at night, with lodging turns being the norm and signal boxes manned 24 hours a day; such was the volume of traffic on a line alleged to be unprofitable. Strabane, as always, had continued to handle a considerable amount of heavy transhipment freight for the County Donegal Railways network, right up to the end (via their road vehicle fleet after December 1959) and there was a steady stream of 'Free to Free' traffic originating in the Irish Republic and destined for one of the three County Donegal stations between Strabane and Londonderry.

One consequence of the closure was that the redundant Derry line BUT railcar sets were redeployed, enabling the elimination of the remaining steam worked diagrams on the ex-GNR lines and thus ensuring an early demise of the steam engines.

In a further move that irrevocably damaged railway services, the Government, through the UTA, withdrew all general freight services with the closure of the Derry Road. The substantial block traffic between Dublin and Donegal, formerly routed over this line, was transferred to overnight fitted trains using CIÉ diesel locos from Dublin as far as Lisburn. From there, totally unsuitable UTA 275 hp multi-purpose diesel railcars (MPDs) replaced the locos, the trains having to reverse at this point and run via the Antrim branch, thence using the ex-NCC main line to Londonderry (Waterside).

Derry Road Route Map

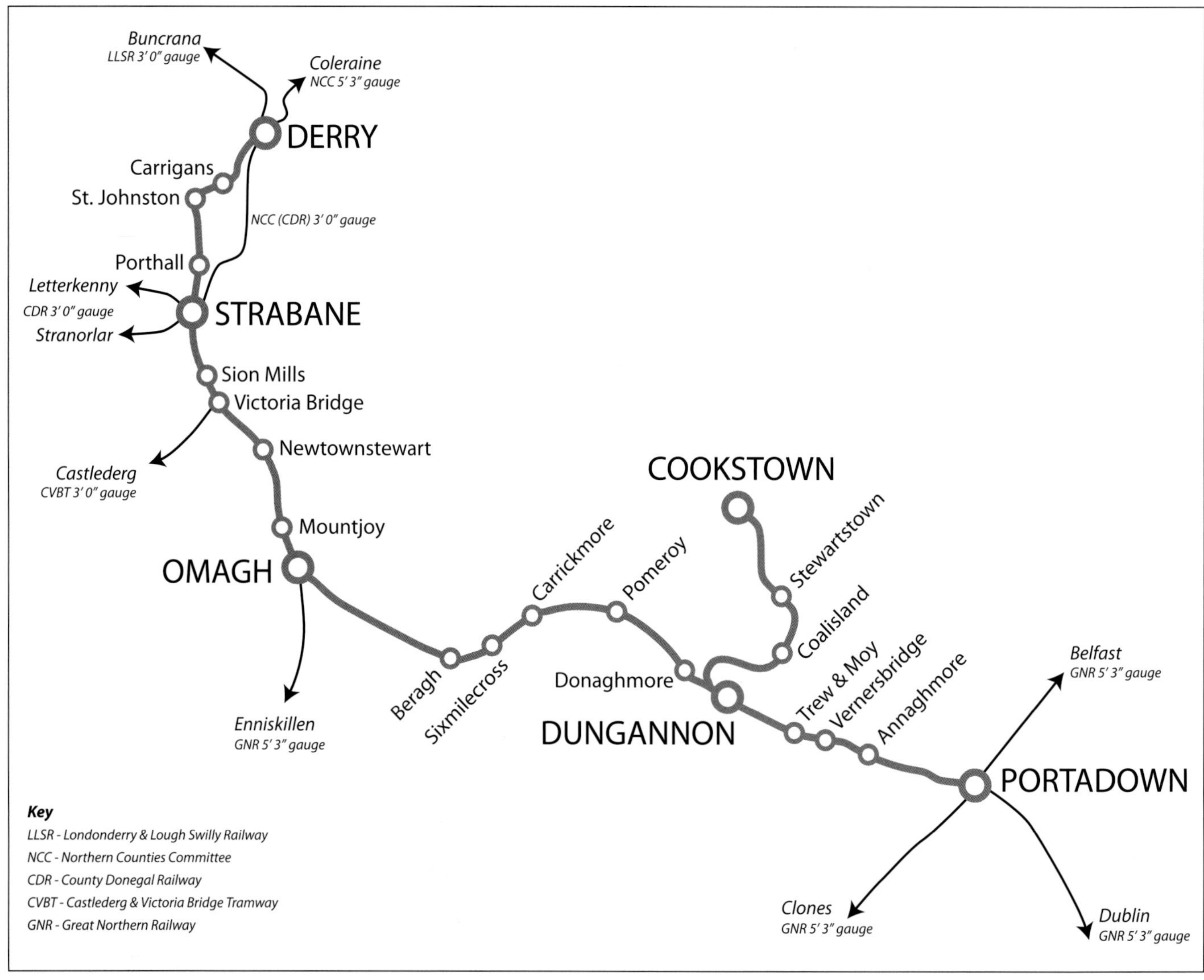

HISTORICAL BACKGROUND

The origins of the Great Northern Railway (Ireland) railway line from Portadown to Londonderry – the 'Derry Road' – lie far back in the mists of time. In common with the construction of many lines across the country, it was the end result of the promotion, construction and eventual amalgamation of several smaller constituent lines, as indeed was the Great Northern itself. Creation of the line was in piecemeal fashion over an extended period of time, starting in the north of the province. To fully understand just how the line came into being, we must first take a brief look at the early individual attempts to build railway lines in that part of the north of Ireland, together with the convoluted manoeuvring and horse trading that took place between the various companies involved.

Londonderry & Enniskillen Railway

First surveyed in 1837 by George Stephenson and incorporated by an Act of Parliament in 1845, with the intention of constructing a railway along the west side of the River Foyle, between these two towns, the line was subsequently surveyed by Sir John Macneill. However, there was disagreement over the recommended route between Strabane and Omagh, the directors being unhappy with the situation. Eventually, George Stevenson's son Robert was called in and retained as a consultant to complete the job. Built to the standard Irish gauge of 5ft 3ins, the contractor, Leishman, started work on the first section of the 60-mile line in October 1845 and the line was opened between Londonderry and Strabane on 19 April 1847. Canal competition was severe and receipts poor during the first year of operation, so much so that the directors tried, in 1848, have the Omagh to Enniskillen section abandoned. The Marquis of Abercorn, across whose lands much of the extension would be laid, blocked this move.

Londonderry had a poorly sited initial terminus on the west bank of the River Foyle, in the old cattle market in Gallows Strand. In 1850, a short extension brought the line some three quarters of a mile closer to the city centre at Foyle Road, alongside what was then known as the Carlisle Bridge (rebuilt in the late 1920s as the Craigavon Bridge) which connected the two halves of the city. Though the railway company could never be described as prosperous, it endeavoured to stimulate agricultural trade in the district it served.

Leaving Derry. An early lineside shot of a passenger train composed mainly of six-wheelers leaving the Maiden City at low tide. The J class 4-4-0, No 17, was built in 1885 and withdrawn in 1924.

LGRP

It erected a market house at Newtownstewart for local farmers, with a similar building constructed at Omagh and incorporating a Corn Exchange.

It took until 9 May 1852 to reach Newtownstewart, with the 19 miles from Strabane to Omagh not being completed until 13 September. Completion of the line was achieved quite slowly, with an extension to Fintona, a distance of 7½ miles, opened on 15 June 1853 and the final goal, Enniskillen, a further 19 miles, not being reached until 19 August 1854. The Newtownstewart to Omagh section was doubled in 1853, only to be singled again in 1869 in an attempt to ease the Company's financial plight. The extensions beyond Omagh were, strictly speaking, on what would later become known as the Irish North Western line and we need not concern ourselves unduly with them at this stage, other than to assist in illustrating the beginnings of the Derry Road line.

The initial section of line to Strabane was laid with 75lb wrought iron double-headed Barlow rails, carried on, and held by, cast iron support chairs, designed and invented by Peter Barlow, a board member and named after him. There were three to each rail, with one common to neighbouring rails being larger and weighing 2 cwt each, the intermediate ones being held by wrought iron tie bars to maintain the gauge. The chairs were in two halves, bolted together, thus avoiding the need for keys. There could be up to five per rail length depending on the terrain. The section from Strabane to Enniskillen however, was laid using 20 foot long 60lb double-headed rails.

The Londonderry & Enniskillen continued to struggle financially throughout its short life, briefly leasing the line to a debenture holder and creditor, Mr McCormick, by an Act of 23 July 1885, before staving off ruin in 1856 by an Act on 21 July, allowing the issue of further preference stocks and debentures. This served to hold the situation until the timely arrival, in Enniskillen, of the Dundalk & Enniskillen Railway in 1859.

Incorporated on 21 July 1845, the Dundalk & Enniskillen Railway succeeded an earlier endeavour, the abortive Dundalk & Western Railway, an enterprise that fell by the wayside shortly after the first sod was turned at Dundalk in May 1839. Construction was slow, beginning at Dundalk on 15 October 1845, and finally reaching Enniskillen on the 15 February 1959.

It became quickly evident to the Board of the LER that the entire line from Dundalk to Derry would be better run a single concern. Accordingly, the necessary Act was raised and, following discussions between the two companies and commencing on 1 January 1860, their line was leased to the DER on a 99 year lease. The initial rental was set at £26,000 pa, increasing after three years to a figure based on 20% of the gross receipts of the combined line on any amount above £95,000 a year until the rental reached £33,000 per year.

A further Act of Parliament on 11 July 1861 enabled an additional 35½ mile line to be constructed by the independent Enniskillen and Bundoran Railway, to Ballyshannon and Bundoran. This opened on 13 June 1866 and was also worked by the DER. Now part of a through route between Dublin and Londonderry, a name change of the DER to the Irish North Western Railway, by an Act of 7 July 1862, reflected its extended influence across the country.

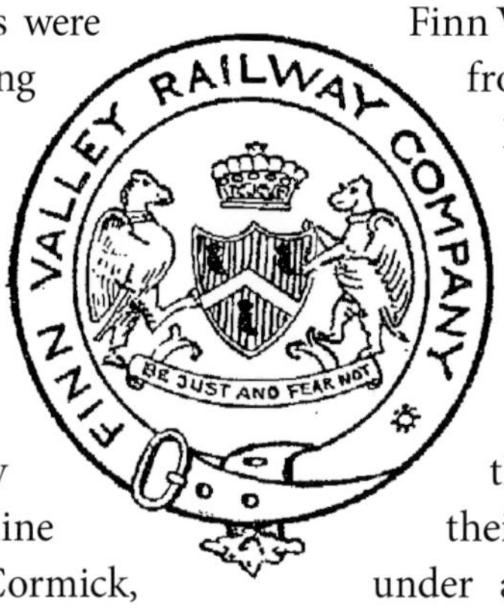

Following Parliamentary legislation in May 1860, the Finn Valley line, 13½ miles in length and running from Strabane to Stranorlar in County Donegal, was opened independently on 7 September 1863. Local landowners, Lord Lifford and Sir Samuel Hayes, had been instrumental in promoting this railway, which joined the LER at a point some 30 chains south of Strabane station. Both of these lines were worked by the INWR using their own rolling stock and motive power, under a separate leasing agreement. The Finn Valley, unhappy with the operating conditions and the high rental charges levied by the INWR, provided its own carriages and wagons under a new agreement that came into effect on 1 November 1872. The INWR continued to supply the motive power and access to their station at Strabane.

This arrangement continued into Great Northern

Strabane station some time after 1894 with CDR narrow gauge stock in the background.

JD FitzGerald collection

days but ended in 1894, when further disagreements about rental charges for the use of Strabane station resulted in the Finn Valley line being rebuilt to three-foot gauge with the track diverted into a separately constructed station alongside the original INWR one, complete with a second bridge across the River Mourne and opened on the weekend of 13-15 July 1894. From this point on, the Finn Valley provided their own locomotives and rolling stock, the diverted line and second station eventually becoming part of the County Donegal Railway narrow gauge system.

The Ulster Railway Company

Following a meeting of merchants in Belfast, a prospectus was issued in November 1835, resulting in a bill being laid before Parliament. An Act, incorporating the 'Ulster Railway Company' became law on 19 May 1836 and allowed for the building of a 36 mile line from the ***Town*** of Belfast to the ***City*** of Armagh. Work commenced on 3 March 1837, and the line opened to Lisburn on Monday 12 August 1839. Construction continued at a steady pace, with the railhead reaching Lurgan on 18 November 1841 and Seagoe, near Portadown, on 31 January 1842. A little later that year, the first train reached Portadown when the line opened to that station on 12 September. The station at Belfast was a solid and pleasing structure, constructed in a classical style and fronting Glengall Place (now Great Victoria Street), with the offices built in Ardrossan stone and the platform area located immediately to the rear of the main building.

From the start, the Company had endeavoured to conform to accepted standards wherever possible and had adopted a wide track gauge of 6ft 2ins. This was in response to guidance given by the Royal Commission of 1836, appointed to consider the system of railways in Ireland, including the track gauge to be used. The track itself consisted of longitudinal American pine timbers with cross sleepers underneath them every 10-15 feet. The rails were bridge type supplied by the Dowlais iron works. The gauge was narrowed to five foot three inches in the late 1840s, following the recommendations of the Royal Commission on the gauge of Irish railways in 1844.

The Portadown & Dungannon Railway

The initial proposal was laid out in an Act of 1847, for a 13½ mile line between Portadown and Dungannon, using £154,775 of share capital and £51,585 of loans. No further movement was made with this and in 1853 a re-enactment was necessary to proceed. With the English firm of Fox, Henderson & Co charged with construction, work finally started in 1855. The Ulster Railway, perhaps viewing the longer term benefits to be had, agreed to sponsor the construction by offering some financial assistance. The line was constructed throughout using bridge rails. By October 1856, the contracting firm had collapsed and William Dargan was brought in to finish the line. In November of that year, the Directors applied for an extension of the line to Omagh and then approached the UR with a view to leasing the entire line to them upon completion, the Act of 1857 allowing the lease to take effect.

Dungannon was reached and the line formally opened on 5 April 1858, though the first station was in Gortmerron townland, a mile to the east of the town. The Board of Trade inspection expressed dissatisfaction with the signalling arrangements at Portadown, at the junction with the Ulster Railway. A temporary platform was installed near Bow Lane (now Curran Street) on 4 May 1858, just onto the Derry line so that working could begin. Passengers had to walk the 40 yards or so to the Ulster's Woodhouse Street station. Through running to the Ulster Railway finally commenced on 4 July 1858.

The amended bill, incorporating the newly titled Portadown, Dungannon & Omagh Junction Railway Company, was finally given Royal Assent in August 1858. Share capital of £100,000 and £33,000 in loans were provided for the 27 additional miles needed to reach Omagh. The route included a 814 yard single bore tunnel from Cunningham's Lane, east of Dungannon, through Windmill Hill. This was at the insistence of Lord Northland, the owner of Northland Demesne, who was very much against any intrusion of the railway upon his property. On the credit side, this did result in a new station to the north-west of the tunnel that was much more conveniently situated for the townsfolk of Dungannon. The new station opened in 1861.

An Act of 12 June 1861 allowed for a branch line from Dungannon to Aughnacloy but, in the event, this was not built. With the railway now operational and bringing in much needed capital, construction of the extension continued to progress up to Pomeroy and on over the bleak moorland summit of the Sperrin foothills towards Carrickmore. That station was built

Above: QLs class 4-4-0 No 156 bursts from Dungannon tunnel with the 1.50pm Belfast-Londonderry in June 1958.
A Donaldson

Right: A distant and very early view of Dungannon station from the Aughnacloy Road probably in the 1890s. The engine, partly obscured by a cattle wagon, is an ex-Ulster Railway 2-4-0 (No 123 or 128) and the second carriage, a First, is also ex-UR.
JD FitzGerald collection

in the townland of Tirooney, close to Termon house and some distance from the village it purported to serve. Skirting the town to the west, the construction reached a junction with L&E at Omagh and the line opened to traffic on 2 September 1861. A second platform was added to the existing LER station to accommodate the additional PDOJR traffic. Sixmilecross station, between Carrickmore and Beragh, opened one year later. With bridge rails now out of fashion, the extension had been laid with wrought iron flange rails.

Above: Omagh station, looking south in the early 1930s, with six-wheel stock from a Strabane local in the bay platform.

JD FitzGerald collection

A 999 year lease of the nominally independent PDOJR was granted to the UR in return for 55% of the profits, with a half mile market branch to a separate PDOJR goods station being constructed three quarters

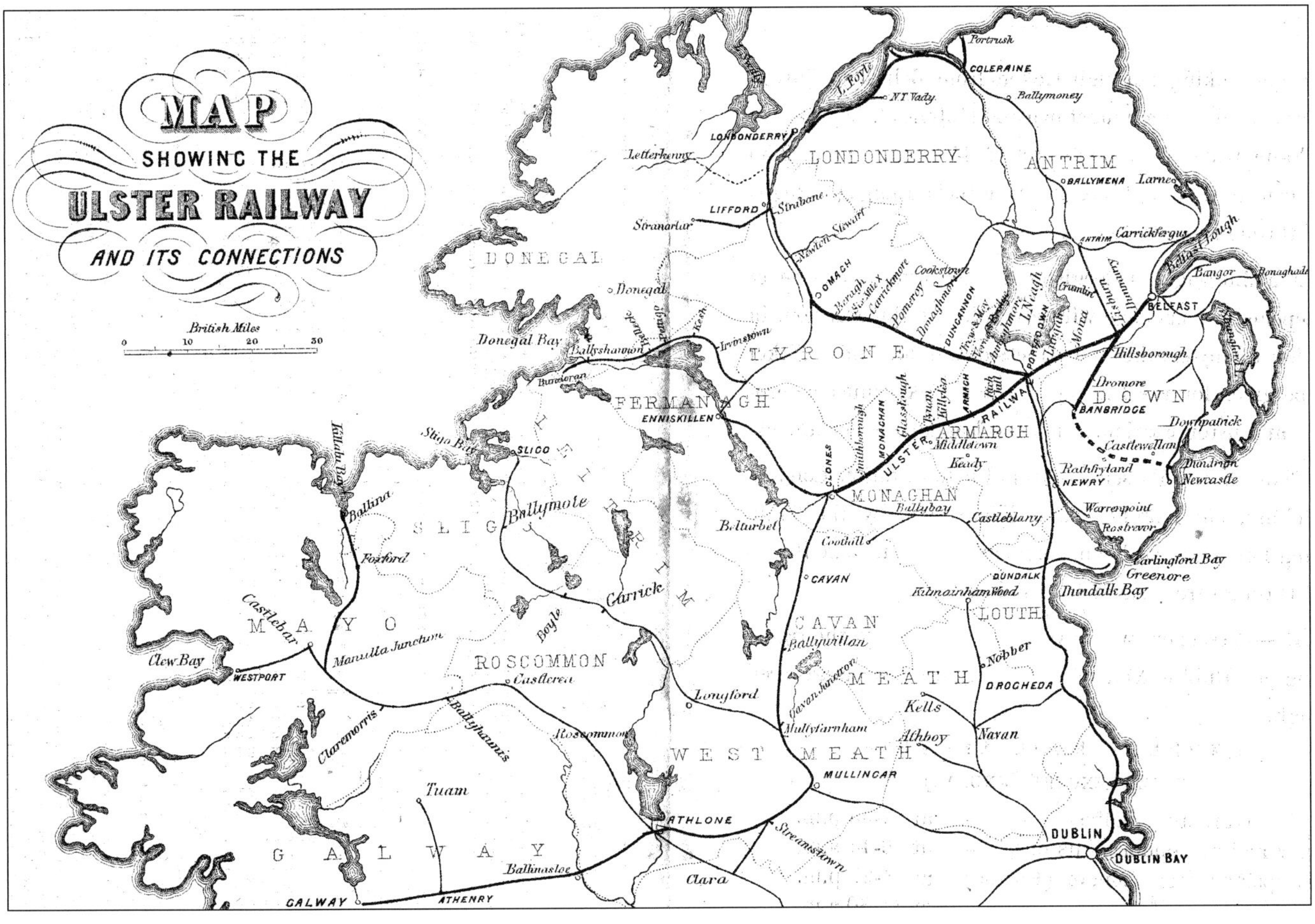

MAP SHOWING THE ULSTER RAILWAY AND ITS CONNECTIONS

UP TRAINS.—Belfast to Banbridge, Antrim, Portadown, Dublin, Armagh, Clones, Dungannon, and Omagh.

Passenger Fares from Belfast.

Stations	Single Tickets.* 1st Clas.	Single 2nd Clas.	Single 3rd Clas.	Return Tickets.* 1st Clas.	Return 2nd Clas.	Return 3rd Clas.	Miles from Belfast.
	s. d.	s. d.	s. d.	s. d.	s. d.	s. d.	
BELFAST dep.	...	...	...	...	...	...	
Balmoral	0 6	0 4	0 2	0 10	0 7	0 4	2½
Dunmurry	0 9	0 6	0 4	1 2	0 11	0 7	4½
Lisburn	1 3	0 10	0 7	2 0	1 6	1 0	7½
Bbridge Branch. Hillsborough	2 0	1 6	1 0	3 0	2 6	1 9	12
Dromore	2 11	2 2	1 5½	4 6	3 4	2 8	17½
Mullafernaghan	3 8	2 8	1 9	5 8	4 3	3 0	21
Banbridge	4 2	3 1	2 0½	6 8	5 0	3 6	24½
Antrim Junct. Line. Brookmount for Magheragall	1 11	1 4	0 11	3 1	2 4	1 6	11½
Ballinderry	2 6	2 0	1 3	4 0	3 2	2 0	14½
Glenavy	3 0	2 3	1 5	4 9	3 7	2 3	18
Crumlin	3 2	2 4	1 6	5 0	3 9	2 4	20½
Aldergrove	3 2	2 5	1 6	5 4	4 0	2 6	22½
Antrim Junc. arr.	3 2	2 5	1 6	5 4	4 0	2 6	28
Moira	3 7	1 11	1 2½	4 3	3 2	2 1	14½
Lurgan	3 6	2 8	1 8	5 9	4 4	3 0	20
Portadown arr.	4 7	3 4	2 1½	7 6	5 7	3 9	25½
Dub. Connection D. & B. J., D. & G., & D. & D. R. Portadown dep.							
Goragh Wood arr.	7 7	5 7	3 4	12 8	9 4	5 10	40¾
Newry M. L.	7 11	5 10	3 7	13 2	9 9	6 3	44
Dundalk	10 11	8 2	4 10	18 2	13 8	8 6	58½
Greenore	13 5	10 1	6 1	21 11	16 6	10 4	71½
Drogheda	15 1	11 6	6 10	25 2	19 2	11 10	80¾
Balbriggan	16 9	12 9	7 8	27 8	21 2	13 1	90¾
Malahide	18 10	14 4	8 9	30 8	23 8	14 10	103¾
DUBLIN	20 0	15 0	9 6	33 4	25 0	15 10	112¼
Omagh Branch. Portadown dep.							
Annaghmore	5 7	4 2	2 7½	9 4	7 0	4 8	31¾
Vernersbridge	6 1	4 7	2 10½	10 0	7 6	5 0	34¼
Trew & Moy	6 3	4 9	3 0	10 5	7 10	5 3	35¾
DUNGANNON	7 0	5 3	3 4	11 8	8 9	5 10	40
Donaghmore	7 6	5 7	3 6½	12 6	9 3	6 3	42¾
Pomeroy	8 7	6 5	4 1	14 3	10 8	7 2	49
Carrickmore	9 5	7 1	4 5½	15 9	11 9	7 10	53¾
Sixmilecross	10 2	7 8	4 9½	16 11	12 6	8 6	57¼
Beragh	10 5	7 9	4 11	17 0	12 6	8 6	59¼
OMAGH arr.	11 8	8 8	5 6	18 4	13 9	9 2	66¼
L. N. W. & F. V. R. Omagh dep.							66¾
Strabane arr.	15 5	11 8	7 4	24 1	18 3	12 0	86
Stranorlar	17 9	13 5	8 6	27 7	21 1		99½
Londonderry	17 0	12 6	7 11	27 0	20 0	13 0	100¾
Portadown dep.							
Richhill	5 6	4 2	2 7	9 4	7 0	4 5	31½
Armagh	6 3	4 8	2 11½	10 3	7 8	5 3	35¾
Killylea	7 0	5 3	3 4	11 6	8 9	5 10	40¼
Tynan & Caledon	7 6	5 8	3 6½	12 6	9 5	6 3	42¾
Glasslough	8 3	6 2	3 10½	13 8	10 3	6 10	46¾
Monaghan	9 3	6 10	4 4	15 2	11 5	7 7	52
Smithboro'	10 3	7 8	4 10	16 8	12 8	8 6	58¼
CLONES arr.	11 0	8 3	5 3	17 0	12 6	8 6	64¾
Clones dep.							
Enniskillen arr.	15 4	11 7	7 2	24 3	18 0	11 8	87
Clones dep.							
Cavan arr.							79¾
Mullingar							115¼
Galway							191¼

* Tickets issued at these Fares will not be available for the Limited Mail Train.

WEEKDAYS.

Stations	1, 2, 3 class	1, 2, 3 class	1, 2, 3 class *	1, 2, 3 class.	1, 2, 3 class	1, 2, 3 class	1&2 to Pdwn 1, 2, 3 Pdwn to Cln'es	1, 2, 3 class †	1 class	1, 2, 3 class	1, 2, 3 class	1, 2, 3 class.	1, 2, 3 class	1, 2, 3 class	1, 2, class
	a.m.	a.m.	a.m.	a.m.	a.m.	p.m.	p.m.	p.m.	p.m.	p.m.	p.m.	p.m.	p.m.	p.m.	p.m.
BELFAST dep.	7 0	7 45	9 0	...	10 30	12 15	1 45		2 55	3 45	5 0	5 15	6 45		9 30
Balmoral	...	7 52	...	...	...	12 21	...		...	3 52	...	5 21	6 53		9 38
Dunmurry	...	7 57	9 8	...	10 40	12 27	...		...	3 57	...	5 27	7 0		9 46
Lisburn	7 14	8 8	9 18	...	10 50	12 38	2 0		...	4 8	5 18	5 38	7 8		10 0
Bbridge Branch. Hillsborough	...	8 25	...	...	...	12 57	...		...	4 23	...		7 24	...	...
Dromore	...	8 45	...	...	...	1 18	...		...	4 43	...		7 43	...	...
Mullafernaghan	...	9 5	...	...	...	1 29	...		...	4 55	...		7 54	...	...
Banbridge	...	9 15	...	...	...	1 40	...		...	5 5	...		8 5	...	...
Antrim Junct. Line. Brookmount for Magheragall	...	...	9 38	...	...	...	...		...	4 23	...		7 23	...	...
Ballinderry	...	...	9 47	...	...	...	...		...	4 32	...		7 32	...	...
Glenavy	...	...	9 56	...	...	...	...		...	4 41	...		7 41	...	...
Crumlin	...	...	10 5	...	...	...	...		...	4 50	...		7 50	...	...
Aldergrove	...	...	10 15	...	...	...	...		...	5 0	...		8 0	...	...
Antrim Junc. arr.	...	...	10 30	...	...	...	...		...	5 15	...		8 15	...	...
Moira	...	...	9 35	...	11 7	...	‡		...	...	5 35	...			10 21
Lurgan	7 35	...	9 48	...	11 22	...	2 24		...	...	5 48	...			10 45
Portadown arr.	7 48	...	10 3	...	11 37	...	2 35		3 40	...	6 8	...			11 5
	c			c			c				c				c 1&2 cl
Dub. Connection D. & B. J., D. & G., & D. & D. R. Portadown dep.	7 50			10 15		...	2 38		...	...	6 10	...		...	1 35
Goragh Wood arr.	8 23			11 20		...	3 10		...	...	6 48	...		...	...
Newry M. L.	...			11 40		...	...		...	...	6 56	...		...	2 30
Dundalk	9 0			12 30		...	3 48		4 41	...	7 30	...		...	3 15
Greenore	9 35					...	5 0		...	...	8 10	...		...	...
Drogheda	9 53			2 10		...	4 37		5 20	...	8 35	...		...	4 10
Balbriggan	10 15			2 54		...	5 0		...	...	8 59	...		...	4 37
Malahide	...			3 40		...	5 24		...	...	9 40	...		...	5 5
DUBLIN	11 0			4 20		...	5 45		6 15	...	10 15	...		...	5 25
	c				c			c			c				c
Omagh Branch. Portadown dep.	7 52				11 48	..	...	3 0	...	...	6 15	...		...	11 20
Annaghmore	8 6				12 6	...	...	3 18	...	...	6 32	...		...	...
Vernersbridge	8 13				...	...	...	3 24	...	...	6 38	...		...	...
Trew & Moy	8 17				12 13	...	...	3 29	...	...	6 42	...		...	...
DUNGANNON	8 29				12 27	...	...	3 42	...	...	6 56	...		...	12 10
Donaghmore	8 36				12 37	...	...	3 52	...	...	7 5	...		...	...
Pomeroy	8 53				12 55	...	...	4 15	...	...	7 21	...		...	...
Carrickmore	9 8				1 10	...	...	4 30	...	...	7 35	...		...	...
Sixmilecross	9 18				1 21	...	...	4 40	...	...	7 45	...		...	...
Beragh	9 25				1 28	...	...	4 47	...	...	7 50	...		...	...
OMAGH arr.	9 45				1 48	...	...	5 10	...	...	8 15	...		...	2 5
L. N. W. & F. V. R. Omagh dep.	...		...	...	2 2	...	...		...	...	8 27	...		...	2 15
Strabane arr.	...		...	...	2 41	...	...		...	...	9 32	...		...	3 7
Stranorlar	...		...	...	5 55	...	...		...	...	...	...		...	...
Londonderry	...		...	...	3 10	...	...		...	...	10 15	...		...	3 50
			c		c		c				c			c	c
Portadown dep.	8 0		10 8		11 55	...	2 40		...	...	6 18	...		8 15	1 35
Richhill	8 15		10 21		12 10	...	2 55		...	...	6 32	...		8 29	...
Armagh	8 25		10 33		12 20	...	3 5		...	...	6 43	...		8 40	2 1
Killylea			10 50		...	...	3 22		...	...	7 2	...		...	...
Tynan & Caledon			10 58		...	...	3 30		...	...	7 9	...		...	...
Glasslough			11 8		...	...	3 40		...	...	7 19	...		...	2 39
Monaghan			11 23		...	...	3 52		...	...	7 34	...		...	2 55
Smithboro'			11 38		...	...	4 10		...	...	7 47	...		...	...
CLONES arr.			11 55 noon.		...	...	4 25 p.m.		...	...	8 5	...		...	3 25
Clones dep.	...	...	12 9			...	6 5		...	...	10 25	...		...	...
Enniskillen arr.	...	...	1 0			...	7 5		...	...	11 45	...		...	...
Clones dep.	...	...	12 10		...	...	4 30		...	...	...	...		...	...
Cavan arr.	...	...	12 50		...	...	5 5		...	...	...	...		...	...
Mullingar	...	...	2 46		...	...	...		...	...	...	...		...	...
Galway	...	...	7 22		...	...	...		...	...	...	...		...	...
	a.m.	a.m.	p.m.	p.m.	p.m.	p.m.	p.m.	p-m.	p.m.	p.m.	p.m.	p.m.	p.m.	p.m.	a.m.

SUNDAYS.

Stations	1, 2, 3 class	1, 2, 3 class	1, 2, 3 class	1, 2, 3 class	1, 2, 3 class	1, 2, class
	a.m.	a.m.	p.m.	p.m.	p.m.	p.m.
BELFAST dep.	8 0	9 0	2 30	4 0	6 15	9 30
Balmoral	8 6	9 7	2 36	4 5	6 21	9 38
Dunmurry	8 12	9 13	2 42	4 13	6 27	9 46
Lisburn	8 20	9 23	2 50	4 23	6 35	10 0
Hillsborough	8 35	...	3 5	...	6 50	
Dromore	8 54	...	3 24	...	7 8	
Mullafernaghan	9 5	...	3 35	...	7 20	
Banbridge	9 15	...	3 45	...	7 30	
Brookmount for Magheragall						
Ballinderry						
Glenavy						
Crumlin						
Aldergrove						
Antrim Junc. arr.						
Moira	...	9 43	...	4 40	...	10 21
Lurgan	...	10 0	..	4 55	...	10 45
Portadown arr.	...	10 13	...	5 10	...	11 5
				c		c
Portadown dep.		...	...	5 15	...	1 35
Goragh Wood arr.		...	...	6 0	...	...
Newry M. L.		...	...	6 9	...	2 30
Dundalk		...	...	6 46	...	3 15
Greenore		...	...	...	...	...
Drogheda		...	...	7 55	...	4 10
Balbriggan		...	...	8 30	...	4 37
Malahide		...	...	9 12	...	5 5
DUBLIN		...	...	10 0	...	5 25
				c		c
Portadown dep.		...	...	...	...	11 20
Annaghmore		...	...	...	...	...
Vernersbridge		...	...	...	...	...
Trew & Moy		...	...	...	...	...
DUNGANNON		...	...	...	...	12 10
Donaghmore		...	...	...	...	...
Pomeroy		...	...	...	...	...
Carrickmore		...	...	...	...	...
Sixmilecross		...	...	...	...	...
Beragh		...	...	...	...	...
OMAGH arr.		...	...	...	...	2 5
Omagh dep.		...	...	...	...	2 15
Strabane arr.		...	...	...	...	3 7
Stranorlar		...	...	...	...	...
Londonderry		...	...	...	...	3 50
						c
Portadown dep.		10 17	...	5 20	...	1 35
Richhill		10 32	...	5 35	...	...
Armagh		10 43	...	5 45	...	2 1
Killylea		11 2	...	...	...	...
Tynan & Caledon		11 12	...	...	...	...
Glasslough		11 22	..	...	...	2 39
Monaghan		11 36	...	...	...	2 55
Smithboro'		11 55	...	...	...	...
CLONES arr.		12 15	...	...	...	3 25
	a.m.	p.m.	p.m.	p.m.	p.m.	a.m.

*Stops at Balmoral on Saturdays. ‡ Stops at Moira on Tuesdays. † Runs on Saturdays only.

Third Class Tickets will not be issued by the 1-45 p.m. and 9-30 p.m. Up Trains from Belfast, or by the 1-35 a.m. and 11-50 a.m. Down Trains from Portadown.

DOWN TRAINS.—Dublin, Clones, Armagh, Omagh, Dungannon, Portadown, Antrim, & Banbridge to Belfast.

Passenger Fares from Clones.

Stations	Single Tickets.* 1st Clas.	Single 2nd Clas.	Single 3rd Clas.	Return Tickets.* 1st Clas.	Return 2nd Clas.	Return 3rd Clas.	Miles from Clones.
Galway dep.							
Mullingar							
Cavan							
Clones arr.							
Enniskillen dep.							
Clones arr.							
CLONES dep.	s. d.	s. d.	s. d.	s. d.	s. d.	s. d.	
Smithborough	1 2	0 11	0 6½	1 11	1 6	1 0	6½
Monaghan	2 3	1 8	1 0½	3 8	2 9	1 10	12½
Glasslough	3 2	2 5	1 6	5 3	4 0	2 8	18
Tynan & Caledon	3 11	2 11	1 10	6 5	4 10	3 3	22
Killylea	4 4	3 3	2 0½	7 2	5 5	3 8	24½
Armagh	5 1	3 10	2 5	8 6	6 4	4 3	29
Richhill	5 11	4 5	2 9½	9 10	7 4	4 11	33½
Portadown arr.	7 0	5 3	3 3½	11 8	8 9	5 10	39¼
L. N. W. & F. V. R. Londonderry dep.							
Stranorlar							
Strabane							
Omagh arr.							
Omagh Branch. Omagh dep.							80¼
Beragh							73
Sixmilecross							71½
Carrickmore							67
Pomeroy	10 0	7 6	5 0	16 8	12 6	8 9	62
Donaghmore	9 0	6 9	4 0	15 0	11 3	7 6	56½
DUNGANNON	8 7	6 5	4 3	14 3	10 8	7 0	53
Trew & Moy	7 6	5 7	4 0	12 6	9 4	6 9	49½
Vernersbridge							48¼
Annaghmore							45½
Portadown arr.							39¼
Dub. Connection D. & G., D. & B. J., & D. & D. R. DUBLIN dep.							
Malahide							
Balbriggan							
Drogheda							
Greenore							
Dundalk							
Newry M.L.							
Goragh Wood							
Portadown arr.							
Portadown dep.							39¼
Lurgan	7 10	5 10	3 10½	13 0	9 9	6 6	44½
Moira	8 9	6 7	4 2	14 7	10 11	7 4	50
Antrim Junct. Line. Antrim Junc. dep.	13 3	9 10	6 3	22 0	16 6	11 0	77¼
Aldergrove							72
Crumlin	11 10	8 10	5 9½	19 8	14 9	10 2	69¾
Glenavy	11 3	8 6	5 7	18 9	14 2	9 10	67¼
Ballinderry	10 9	8 2	5 4	17 10	13 6	9 4	64
Brookmount for Magheragall							60½
Bbridge Branch. Banbridge	10 4	7 9	5 0	17 3	12 10	8 6	74
Mullafernaghan	11 6	8 6	5 6	19 2	14 3	9 8	70½
Dromore	10 6	7 10	5 0	17 6	13 3	8 9	67
Hillsborough							61½
Lisburn	10 0	7 6	4 9	16 8	12 6	8 4	56¾
Dunmurry	10 8	7 11	5 0½	17 0	12 6	8 6	60¼
Balmoral							62¼
BELFAST arr.	11 0	8 3	5 3	17 0	12 6	8 6	64½

* Tickets issued at these Fares will not be available for the Limited Mail Train.

WEEKDAYS.

Stations		1, 2, 3 class	1, 2, 3 class	1, 2, 3 class	1, class	1, A[illegible] P[illegible] 1, [illegible] to	1, 2, 3 class	1, 2, 3 class	1, 2, 3 class	1, 2, 3 class	1, 2, 3 class	1, 2, 3, class §	1, 2, 3 class	1, 2, 3 class	c 1 & 2 class.
	a.m.	a.m.	a.m.	a.m.	a.m.		p.m.	a.m.	p.m.	p.m.	a.m.	p.m.	p.m.	p.m.	p.m.
											c			c	
Galway dep.	...	...	...	...	...		...	...	...	...	7 0	...	...	...	...
Mullingar	...	...	...	...	...		...	...	...	...	11 0	...	...	...	...
Cavan	...	..	...	6 15	...		...	11 0	...	...	245pm	...	...	5 15	...
Clones arr.	...	...	...	7 0	...		...	11 50	...	...	3 30	...	...	5 55	...
Enniskillen dep.	...	...	...	4 0	...		...	9 30		...	1 20	...	..	4 30	...
Clones arr.	...	...	...	5 15	...		...	10 40	...	...	2 8	...	...	5 25	...
				c				c			c			c	
CLONES dep.		...	..	8 10	...		...	12 45	...	...	3 45	...	...	6 5	9 15
Smithborough		...	...	8 23	...		...	12 57	...	...	4 0	...	...	6 21	...
Monaghan		...	...	8 34	...		...	1 10	...	...	4 13	...	...	6 36	9 45
Glasslough		...	...	8 49	...		...	1 28	...	...	4 29	...	...	6 55	10 0
Tynan & Caledon		...	...	8 59	...		...	1 38	...	...	4 40	...	...	7 7	...
Killylea		...	...	9 5	...		...	1 46	...	...	4 48	...	...	7 14	...
Armagh		7 15	...	9 24	...	11 [illegible]	...	2 2	...	...	5 5	...	...	7 31	10 42
Richhill		7 27	...	9 34	...	11 [illegible]	...	2 15	...	...	5 19	..	...	7 44	...
Portadown arr.		7 40	...	9 50	...	11 [illegible]	...	2 30	...	...	5 33	...	...	8 0	11 12
L. N. W. & F. V. R. Londonderry dep.	...	...	...	6 15	...		...	11 5	...	...	1 50	...	...	...	8 40
Stranorlar	...	...	...	...	...		...	8 10	...	...	1 0	...	...	...	8 0
Strabane	...	...	...	7 0	...		...	11 36	...	...	2 25	...	...	...	9 12
Omagh arr.	...	...	...	8 0	...		...	12 16	...	...	3 17	...	...	...	10 10
				c				c 1,2,3			c				c
Omagh Branch. Omagh dep.	...	...	...	8 5	...		...	12 15	...	...	3 30	5 40	...	...	10 20
Beragh	...	...	...	8 23	...		...	12 32	...	...	3 50	6 0	...	...	10 45
Sixmilecross	...	...	...	8 27	...		...	‡	...	...	3 55	6 5	...	...	...
Carrickmore	...	...	...	8 37	...		...	12 43	...	...	4 5	6 15	...	...	...
Pomeroy	..	...	...	8 52	...		...	12 58	...	...	4 20	6 30	...	...	...
Donaghmore	...	...	...	9 4	...		...	1 15	...	...	4 38	6 42	...	...	11 50
DUNGANNON	...	†6 0	...	9 10	...		...	1 24	...	...	4 47	6 52	...	...	12 5
Trew & Moy	...	6 20	...	9 24	...		...	1 45	...	...	4 58	7 10	...	...	...
Vernersbridge	...	6 30	...	9 26	...		...	...	...	...	5 2	7 15	...	...	...
Annaghmore	...	6 45	...	9 33	...		...	1 56	...	...	5 8	7 25	...	...	...
Portadown arr.	...	7 15	...	9 55	...		...	2 25	...	...	5 30	7 45	...	...	1 20
Dub. Connection D. & G., D. & B. J., & D. & D. R. DUBLIN dep.	...	...	...	...	8 10	8 [illegible]	...	9 0	...	...	1 55	...	...	5 0	7 30
Malahide	...	...	...	...	...	8 [illegible]	...	9 23	...	...	2 20	...	...	5 18	7 52
Balbriggan	...	...	...	...	...	9 [illegible]	...	10 6	...	...	2 53	...	...	5 38	8 18
Drogheda	...	...	...	...	9 7	9 [illegible]	...	11 5	...	...	3 19	...	...	6 7	8 45
Greenore	...	...	...	7 50	...	9 [illegible]	...	...	...	...	2 0	...	...	6 0	...
Dundalk	...	...	...	8 25	9 46	10 [illegible]	...	12 25	...	...	4 18	...	...	6 55	9 40
Newry M.L.	...	...	...	8 55	...	...	...	1 15	...	...	4 48	...	...	...	10 19
Goragh Wood	...	..	...	9 2	...	11 [illegible]	...	1 35	...	...	4 56	...	...	7 32	...
Portadown arr.	...	...	...	9 45	10 47	11 [illegible]	...	2 35	...	...	5 43	...	...	8 7	11 10
		c		c		c		c			c			c	c
Portadown dep.	..	7 45	...	10 0	...	11 [illegible]	...	2 40	...	...	5 45	...	...	8 10	1 35
Lurgan	...	7 53	...	10 10	...	12 [illegible]	...	2 52	...	...	5 57	...	...	8 20	1 55
Moira	...	8 5	...	...	...	12 [illegible]	...	3 6	...	...	6 11	...	...	...	...
Antrim Junct. Line. Antrim Junc. dep.	...	8 0	...	...	...	11	...	...	...	...	...	...	5 45	...	...
Aldergrove	...	8 12	...	...	...	11 [illegible]	...	...	...	...	...	...	5 55	...	...
Crumlin	...	8 22	...	...	...	11 [illegible]	...	...	...	...	...	...	6 3	...	...
Glenavy	...	8 35	...	...	...	11 [illegible]	...	...	...	...	...	...	6 12	...	...
Ballinderry	...	8 45	...	...	...	11 [illegible]	...	...	...	...	...	...	6 21	...	...
Brookmount for Magheragall	...	8 55	...	...	...	11 [illegible]	...	...	...	...	...	...	6 30	...	...
Bbridge Branch. Banbridge	...		8 30	9 40	...	...	...	...	2 50	...	...	...	5 55	...	...
Mullafernaghan	...		8 39	9 49	...	...	...	...	3 2	...	...	...	6 4	...	...
Dromore	...		8 50	10 1	...	...	...	...	3 15	...	...	...	6 15	...	...
Hillsborough	...		9 8	10 16	...	...	...	...	3 34	...	...	...	6 33	...	...
Lisburn		8 24	9 21	10 35	...	12 2[illegible]	1 30	3 21	3 50	5 55	6 26	...	6 46	8 43	2 55
Dunmurry		8 33	9 30	10 45	...	...	1 40	...	4 0	6 5	...	...	6 56	*	...
Balmoral		8 40	9 37	...	...	...	1 45	...	4 5	6 10	...	...	7 1	...	...
BELFAST arr.		8 50	9 45	11 0	11 30	12 4[illegible]	1 55	3 45	4 15	6 20	6 45	...	7 10	9 0	3 40
		a.m.	a.m.	a.m.	a.m.	p.m.	p.m.	p.m.	p.m.	p.m.	p.m.	p.m.	p.m.	p.m.	a.m.

SUNDAYS.

Stations	1, 2, 3 class	1, 2, 3 class	1, 2, 3 class	1, 2, 3 class	1, 2, 3 class	c 1 & 2 class
	a.m.	a.m.	p.m.	p.m.	p.m.	p.m.
Galway dep.	...	...	...	...	...	...
Mullingar	...	...	...	...	...	...
Cavan	...	...	...	...	...	...
Clones arr.	...	...	...	...	...	...
Enniskillen dep.	...	...	...	...	...	...
Clones arr.	...	...	...	...	...	...
CLONES dep.	...	...	...	5 40	...	9 15
Smithborough	...	...	...	5 53	...	...
Monaghan	...	...	...	6 8	...	9 45
Glasslough	...	...	...	6 25	...	10 0
Tynan & Caledon	...	...	...	6 35	...	...
Killylea	...	...	...	6 40	...	...
Armagh	9 0	...	...	6 55	...	10 42
Richhill	9 12	...	...	7 10	...	...
Portadown arr.	9 25	...	...	7 25	...	11 12
Londonderry dep.	...	...	...	...	...	8 40
Stranorlar	..	...	...	...	...	...
Strabane	...	...	...	...	...	9 15
Omagh arr.	...	...	...	...	...	10 10
						c
Omagh dep.	...	...	...	...	...	10 20
Beragh	...	...	...	...	...	...
Sixmilecross	...	...	...	...	...	...
Carrickmore	...	...	...	...	...	...
Pomeroy	...	...	...	...	...	...
Donaghmore	...	...	...	...	...	...
DUNGANNON	...	...	...	...	...	12 5
Trew & Moy	...	...	...	...	...	...
Vernersbridge	...	...	...	...	...	...
Annaghmore	...	...	...	...	...	...
Portadown arr.	...	...	...	...	...	1 20
DUBLIN dep.	...	...	...	3 0	...	7 30
Malahide	...	...	...	3 27	...	7 52
Balbriggan	...	...	...	4 6	...	8 18
Drogheda	...	...	...	4 45	...	8 45
Greenore	...	...	...	...	...	...
Dundalk	...	...	...	5 52	...	9 40
Newry M.L.	...	...	...	6 35	...	10 19
Goragh Wood	...	...	...	6 44	...	...
Portadown arr.	...	...	...	7 30	...	11 10
				c		
Portadown dep.	9 30	...	...	7 35	...	1 35
Lurgan	9 40	...	...	7 50	...	1 55
Moira	9 53	...	...	8 5	...	...
Antrim Junc. dep.	...	...	...	...	...	...
Aldergrove	...	...	...	...	...	...
Crumlin	...	...	...	...	...	...
Glenavy	...	...	...	...	...	...
Ballinderry	...	...	...	...	...	...
Brookmount for Magheragall	...	...	...	...	...	...
Banbridge	...	9 40	4 30	...	8 15	...
Mullafernaghan	...	9 50	4 40	...	8 25	...
Dromore	...	10 0	4 50	...	8 35	...
Hillsborough	...	10 18	5 8	...	8 53	...
Lisburn	10 9	10 35	5 25	8 25	9 8	2 55
Dunmurry	10 18	10 45	5 35	8 35	9 18	...
Balmoral	...	10 50	5 40	...	9 25	...
BELFAST arr.	10 30	11 0	5 50	8 50	9 35	3 40
	a.m.	a.m.	p.m.	p.m.	p.m.	a.m.

†This Train does not run on Mondays. ‡ Stops at Sixmilecross on Fair Days. § Runs on Saturdays only. * Stops at Dunmurry each Thursday.

Third Class Tickets will not be issued by the 1-45 p.m. and 9-30 p.m. Up Trains from Belfast, or by the 1-35 a.m. and 11-50 a.m., Down Trains from Portadown.

of a mile to the south-east of Omagh station in June 1862. The lease arrangements pertained until, under an Act of 1875, the PDOJR was effectively amalgamated with the UR on 1 January 1876.

Jumping forward slightly, it is worth noting that the UR and the PDOJR cooperated to promote the 14¼-mile long Dungannon & Cookstown Railway in 1874, ostensibly to tap potential traffic in coal deposits.

The Northern Railway (Ireland)

Amalgamation as a means of improvement had been considered as far back as 1847, when the Dublin & Belfast Junction Railway's Meath branch was transferred to the Dublin & Drogheda Railway Company. The Act that authorised this also allowed for the DDR to merge with the Dublin & Belfast Junction Railway, the Ulster Railway and the Dundalk & Enniskillen Railway, as and when circumstances made it appropriate. In 1873, the DDR applied for a regrant of the old powers covering amalgamation and, at a special meeting held on 27 February 1875, a full merger with the DBJR was agreed. This became effective on Monday 1 March 1875 under the new name of the Northern Railway Company (Ireland) and paving the way for an eventual through line between Dublin and Belfast. The Ulster Railway stood back, its shareholders unhappy at the prospect of their shares being depreciated by amalgamation with less financially sound companies. This was not an unreasonable stance as the DBJR had its share capital and stock reduced by 22½% as a consequence of the 1875 merger.

By 30 June 1875, the fortunes of the Irish North Western Railway had waned to the point where their Company accounts showed a substantial debt after payment of charges and interest had been met. With the agreement of the shareholders, they moved to merge with Northern Railway (Ireland) and this took effect on 1 January 1876. On joining with the Northern Railway, the INWR brought with them some baggage in the form of the LER lease; that Company remaining a separate and nominally independent concern until bought out by the GNR(I) in 1883.

Great Northern Railway (Ireland)

In 1844, following an investigation into the gauges of Irish railways by the Board of Trade Inspector-General of Railways, Major-General Paisley, RE, it was recommended that a gauge of 5ft 3ins be used in Ireland. The was subsequently enforced by 'An Act for Regulating the Gauge of Railways', passed on 18 August 1846. The Ulster Railway was understandably unhappy about the cost that would be involved in conversion of their existing 6ft 2ins lines, but realised that this would be inevitable in time. By then, powers had also lapsed for construction of the Portadown-Armagh section and the new Armagh Extension Act of 1845 stipulated, as expected, that this section would have to conform to the findings of the Report and be built to 5ft 3ins gauge.

Some comfort was taken by the UR from the fact that

Opposite: Ulster Railway timetable from 1874 showing Derry Road connections with the INWR north of Omagh.
J Topley collection

Right: Ex-Ulster Railway 2-4-0 No 114 *Lagan* approaching Derry with a train of six-wheelers sometime between rebuilding in 1897 and 1904, when it became 114A. It was scrapped in 1913.
JD FitzGerald collection

four neighbouring companies had to make contributions to the conversion of the Belfast-Portadown line to 5ft 3ins, though it took long-drawn-out court action to enforce some of the payments, the Newry & Enniskillen Railway withholding payment of their £3997 until 1856. Full conversion to 5ft 3ins gauge was completed by the end of 1847.

If the creation of a unified Belfast-Dublin line was to become a reality, it was essential that the UR join the newly formed Northern Railway. After considerable negotiation over the value of shares and other issues, the Ulster Railway directors held a final half yearly meeting at 1pm on 29 February 1876, at which they declared a comfortable dividend of 7½%. This was followed at 2pm by an Extraordinary General Meeting at which the necessary approval to merge was obtained and this became effective on 1 April 1876. The amalgamation gave UR shareholders a 24½% premium on their shares, no bad deal.

The NR and the UR joined forces under the amended title of Great Northern Railway (Ireland).The UR brought with it the Portadown, Dungannon & Omagh Junction Railway, already absorbed and vested in the UR from 1 January 1876, by an Act passed during the previous Parliamentary session.

The lease for the LER that the Irish North Western Railway brought with them on merging with the NR(I), was in turn taken over by the GNR(I), who agreed to pay the still nominally independent LER a rent of £32,500 for 1876, increasing by £100 per year until £33,000 was achieved. This arrangement continued until 1883 when a Bill for amalgamation with the GNR(I) was put up by the LER and the GNR(I) became the sole owner of the line to Londonderry.

Driver Tommy Hastings of Derry and fireman Roy Ferguson of Belfast pose on No 62 at Strabane on 8 August 1962.

EM Patterson

The Derry Road in Colour

A busy scene at the south end of Portadown station on 28 May 1957. From left to right are U class 4-4-0 No 196 at Platform 4, an unidentified S class 4-4-0 with a van at Platform 3, Qs 4-4-0 No 132 coming off a train at Platform 2 and T2 4-4-2T No 142 waiting in the Bann Siding.

AD Hutchinson, ColourRail

Strabane North Cabin on 22 May 1956 with well-cleaned Qs class 4-4-0 No 136 about to depart for Derry.

Eric Russell, ColourRail

Early BUT days at Dungannon. No 704 arrives at the head of an up three-car set on 1 August 1958, trailing an ancient clerestory bogie coach. The second vehicle is a D5 Brake First.

Eric Russell, ColourRail

U class 4-4-0 No 66 *Meath* (ex-GNR 201), freshly repainted in UTA black, detaches vans from the rear of a Derry-Belfast BUT railcar at Platform 3, Portadown in May 1963.

JG Dewing, ColourRail

S class 4-4-0 No 174 *Carrantuohill* emerging from the west end of Dungannon tunnel with the 3.00pm Belfast-Derry on Friday 28 August 1964.

JD FitzGerald

S class 4-4-0 No 174 pauses at Dungannon with the 3.00pm Belfast-Derry on Saturday 29 August 1964. Her GNR blue livery struggles to push through the grime.

JD FitzGerald

SG class 0-6-0 No 44 at Dungannon's down platform with the 4.40pm (SO) local to Portadown on 30 June 1962.

JD FitzGerald

UG class 0-6-0 No 47 at Dungannon with a train for Belfast on 18 August 1962.

JD FitzGerald

An AEC railcar set arrives at Dungannon with a train from the Portadown direction on 21 July 1964. Note the heavy parcels and mail traffic awaiting an up train at Platform 1. Meanwhile a relief goods for Omagh sits in the Cookstown bay. Its locomotive is SG3 No 33 and the same train was later photographed at Pomeroy by EM Patterson (p74 & 122). *Author*

A train timer checks his stopwatch as a grimy S class 4-4-0 No 170 *Errigal* gets the starting signal at Dungannon with a Derry train on Saturday 25 July 1964.

Author

The up platform at Pomeroy from a passing train on a sunny 3 June 1963.

JD FitzGerald

An unidentified S class 4-4-0 approaches Pomeroy with the heavy 10.15am train from Derry in July 1964.

Author

S class 4-4-0 No 174 at the top of the bank above Pomeroy on the 2.00pm Belfast-Derry on 14 August 1964. Someone has taken the trouble to clean the GNR crest on the tender; No 174 was the last engine to carry one.

Sam Williamson

The same engine is seen a month earlier, on 13 July, climbing Carrickmore bank with the 10.15 Londonderry to Belfast.

JD FitzGerald

A GM on the Derry Road. No B153 approaches Pomeroy with the Omagh to Dublin up 'Pilgrim Train' on Friday 14 August 1964. The fifth carriage is a dining car.

Sam Williamson

The same working is seen a year earlier at Beragh on 3 June 1963, this time with green Metrovick Co-Co No A51. The UTA crew member who accompanied these trains is picking up the staff for the section to Sixmilecross.

JD FitzGerald

The Omagh South signalman receives the Beragh staff from the driver of Ex-NCC W class 2-6-0 No 91 *The Bush* as it arrives at Omagh in June 1962.

RF Whitford, ColourRail

On the same occasion as the front cover photograph, now-preserved S class 4-4-0 No 171 *Slieve Gullion* is seen from Omagh South Cabin with the 4.30pm to Belfast on 6 July 1963. This locomotive, with sisters 170 and 174 had been purchased from CIÉ the previous month and was still in clean blue livery.

JD FitzGerald

No 171 is seen again, this time from Omagh North cabin and in rather more careworn condition, departing with a down train in August 1964. By this date, the UTA had the last inside-cylinder 4-4-0s operating in the British Isles.

JG Dewing, ColourRail

S class 4-4-0 No 174 arrives at Newtownstewart with the 3.00pm Belfast-Derry, on Wednesday 12 August 1964, the signalman having just received the staff from the fireman.

Sam Williamson

The same train is seen again at the Strabane end of Newtownstewart, with the signal already off for departure as the crew pose for the photographer.

Sam Williamson

In its last year of operation, the popular WT class 2-6-4Ts began to appear on the Derry Road. Here No 53 arrives at Newtownstewart, with a return Apprentice Boy's Special on 12 August 1964.

Sam Williamson

The railway followed the valley of the River Mourne between Newtownstewart and Victoria Bridge. The attractive scenery near Victoria Bridge is seen from a passing railcar on 3 June 1963.

JD FitzGerald

Victoria Bridge looks busy as the same train stops there on 3 June 1963. Parcels have just been unloaded and newly arrived passengers greet their families. Guard Andy Lawlor walks towards the train.

JD FitzGerald

The gate leading to the footbridge at the north end of Sion Mills provides a prop for the small boy watching the departing train. Where is he now, 47 years on?

JD FitzGerald

Blue-liveried S class 4-4-0 No 170 *Errigal* makes a splendid sight waiting to depart for Belfast at the south end of Strabane with the 4.30pm up train on Saturday 27 July 1963.

JD FitzGerald

The ex-NCC Moguls were a common sight on Derry Road goods workings in the early 1960s. Here No 98 *King Edward VIII*, still with its original small tender, has a long southbound goods at Strabane Platform 2.

JD FitzGerald

The approaches to the Derry were along the banks of the River Foyle. The Maiden City can be seen in the background, with the spire of St Columb's Cathedral marking the city centre, as the BUT railcar nears journey's end on 3 June 1963.

JD FitzGerald

S class 4-4-0 No 170 reposes outside Derry shed on 27 July 1963, with the running lines in the background. The terminus was to the right beyond the signal cabin.

JD FitzGerald

Ex-NCC W class 2-6-0 No 99 *King George VI* at Foyle Road station in July 1964 with a short local for Strabane. The engine had worked up from Portadown with the overnight goods and will return with the up goods at nightfall. Although over-powered for a one-coach train it is the only engine available. Derry's other terminus, Waterside, can be seen across the river.

R Owen, ColourRail

Looking in the opposite direction to the previous picture, we see how Foyle Road station was overshadowed by the Craigavon Bridge. BUT railcar 135 heads a Belfast train awaiting departure in 1964.

Author

Here the photographer has walked beyond the bridge to capture S class 4-4-0 No 171 with a full head of steam, waiting to depart with the 11.55 to Belfast on Monday, 29 July 1963. The steps on the right lead to the lower deck of the bridge, once used for railway traffic and later to become a road.

JD FitzGerald

The Derry Road in the Great Northern and GNR Board Years 1876 - 1958

Expansion in the Early Years

The Great Northern was Ireland's second largest railway and enjoyed a zenith of prosperity in the early years of the 20th century, with the system extending to well over 600 route miles at its peak in 1922. Its social impact was large; people knew few other means of transport at that time, most families living, working and dying within a 20-mile radius of their homes. Innovative in many areas, it was the first railway in the British Isles to employ electric lighting in all its carriages, beating the English companies by several years. Gas was never used for lighting, though introduced for cooking in the restaurant cars in 1933, when it replaced coke and coal.

The 28 July 1879 saw the opening of the Cookstown branch by the Great Northern, running for 14½ miles from Dungannon Junction. This had been promoted by the Ulster Railway and PDOJR back in 1874 as the Dungannon & Cookstown Railway. It was still incomplete upon formation of the GNR on 1 April 1876, but the newly formed GNR bought out the concern in 1877. Cookstown station was built alongside the Belfast & Northern Counties Railway (later NCC) station, itself on a branch from Magherafelt on the Derry Central line. There was no direct connection but it was possible to exchange wagons via interchange sidings.

During the period 1875-1885, the line between Portadown and Dungannon was re-laid with double-headed rails; the original bridge rails no longer being considered suitable. Similar work was carried out by the GNR on the old Londonderry & Enniskillen permanent way, with the iron flange rails, installed by the INWR, being replaced after 1880 with steel flange rails. In time, a degree of track uniformity was achieved across the GNR empire, with the rails on secondary main lines being eventually brought up to 85 lb weight, using cast iron chairs and bullhead rail profile, with 60ft lengths being introduced after 1933. One interesting aspect, peculiar to the GNR, was the use of inside wooden keys in the chairs, a practice instituted by W H Mills, the chief engineer, on the basis that it would assist and speed up daily track inspections, especially on single track.

Railway expansion was to continue across Ireland and of direct relevance to the GNR was the opening, on 10

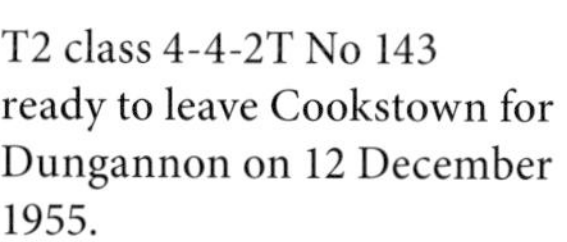

T2 class 4-4-2T No 143 ready to leave Cookstown for Dungannon on 12 December 1955.

EM Patterson

Left: Bullhead rail is much in evidence at the western end of Dungannon as Nos 124 and 174 double-head the 3.50pm Londonderry-Belfast on 26 August 1953.

W Robb

Right: The old CVBT platform at Victoria Bridge on 10 August 1963. The main line is out of view to the left.

J Langford

Below: Double track and two platforms at St Johnston, though by the time of this picture it has become single track with a passing loop. The locomotive is PPs 4-4-0 No 12.

WT Scott

Opposite: The exterior of Foyle Road station on a wet 26 July 1961. The classic cars include a Standard Vanguard Phase II, an MG Magnette ZB, a Ford Zephyr Six and a Humber Snipe – all pretty thirsty, so plenty of money in Derry then!

EM Patterson

July 1884, of the three foot gauge Castlederg & Victoria Bridge Tramway. From a starting point on a curved platform, behind the GNR down platform buildings at Victoria Bridge, the line ran for 7¼ miles to Castlederg. It was a roadside tramway and stayed close to the River Derg for most of its length, serving the communities of Fyfin, Crew and Spamount on the way.

Also in 1884, a Travelling Post Office service (TPO), initially known as a railway post office, was introduced between Portadown and Londonderry, running in tandem with a day mail service on the Belfast to Dublin line. By 1899, nets for automatic collection and delivery of mail pouches had been installed at Trew & Moy, Donaghmore, Pomeroy, Carrickmore, Sixmilecross, Beragh, Newtownstewart and Sion Mills.

The single line Derry Road was doubled in three places. The 10½ mile section from Portadown Junction to Trew & Moy was dealt with between 1899 and 1902, followed by the section between St Johnston to Londonderry in 1902-1907 and finishing with the three mile stretch from Dungannon to Donaghmore in 1905-1906. The total cost for these works was in the region of £110,900.

At a Board meeting in 1890, under the chairmanship of James Gray, the question of Third class carriages with bare board seats was raised. These were still in use on the main line trains, including those to Londonderry and it was agreed to provide cushioning for some of the carriages, as the Board felt that the lack of such amenities did not compare well with the competition.

During 1899, work was undertaken at the northern end of the line, when the GNR embarked on a programme of remodelling for Londonderry's Foyle Road station, which enhanced the original Italianate design provided for the INWR by Thomas Turner.

On 1 August 1900, the County Donegal Railway's three-foot narrow gauge system was enlarged by the opening of a further section, from Strabane to Londonderry (Victoria Road), despite stiff opposition from the adjacent GNR. The GNR were understandably alarmed at the prospect of this incursion into their territory and argued that the new line would duplicate existing services and take valuable traffic away from the Foyle Road route. In reality, the Donegal Railway's line would provide more healthy competition and save a considerable amount of transhipment at Strabane for Londonderry-bound goods. Not only this, the narrow gauge line was in a different county for most of its length and located on the opposite bank of the river, thereby serving a wholly different population group.

The extension passed over the GNR line on a bridge shortly after leaving Strabane and continued along the east bank of the River Foyle, to terminate in Londonderry, virtually opposite the Great Northern station. The CDR station at Victoria Road was adjacent to the Craigavon Bridge, where mixed gauge railway tracks on the lower deck connected all four of the city's stations – two narrow gauge and two broad. Wagons were moved across the bridge by cable and capstans, as locomotives were not allowed to cross.

Meanwhile, in 1903, the BNCR had been purchased by the Midland Railway, in England, who were looking to expand their operations into northern Ireland. With the Donegal finances now in a somewhat parlous state, they had been approached initially by the Midland with a view to takeover. The GNR(I) objected quite strongly to

Left: Mixed gauge pointwork set in the cobbles near Foyle Road station on 19 August 1959.

EM Patterson

Right: Mixed gauge LPHC weighbridge beside Foyle Road station (right) on the same date. This view shows the lower deck of the Craigavon bridge which was used for wagons. A small wagon turntable facilitated the 90° turn.

EM Patterson

Left: A class 0-6-0 No 33 *Belfast* leaves Derry with an up goods about 1900. The engine shed can be seen on the right. No 33 was built in 1891.

LGRP

this move but agreement was eventually reached with the MR for a joint takeover. This took effect On 1 May 1906, the management of the Donegal Railway being by the County Donegal Railways Joint Committee with representatives of both owning companies. The section from Strabane to Londonderry was to be owned exclusively by the MR(NCC) to avoid accusations that the GNR had a monopoly on this stretch, though, in practice, Londonderry-Donemana-Strabane was always worked as part of the CDRJC.

In addition to existing daytime Dublin-Derry through coaches, from 1908 through coaches for First class passengers were also attached to the night mails between Dublin and Belfast/Londonderry, those using the service being provided with blankets and pillows in otherwise ordinary compartments. This service was withdrawn during World War One.

During 1909, the bridge across the River Mourne, just to the south of Strabane station, was reconstructed and the track realigned with the South Cabin, a little to the east of its previous position and on the other side of the tracks.

The Ulster Towns Directory for 1910 offers a glimpse of Edwardian life at this time, with a fascinating, if patchy, list of names, addresses and occupation. Of interest here are the towns and villages served by the Derry Road, with several persons shown as being in employment with the Great Northern Railway or located there: -

PORTADOWN
J Irwin, Watson Street, *Stationmaster.*
Samuel W Willis, Atkinsons Avenue, *Locomotive Superintendent*

ANNAGHMORE
W Tubman, Annaghmore Station, *Spirit Dealer*

MOY
Patrick Toner, Trew & Moy station, *Stationmaster*

DUNGANNON
Phillip Magee, *Stationmaster*
S Hodgett, Mark Street, *Occupation not shown*

COALISLAND
F W Wilson, *Stationmaster*

DONAGHMORE
J Thompson, *Stationmaster*
P McBride, *Clerk*
P McPeak, Tullynure, *Head Porter*
J Quinn, *Signalman*

POMEROY
Mr Lanktree, *Stationmaster*
J Carr, *Signalman*
Bernard Rafferty, *Porter*
Henry Sinnamon, *Porter*
Peter Rafferty, *Night Signalman*

SIXMILECROSS
J McDonnell, *Stationmaster*

BERAGH
R Brown, *Stationmaster*
James Canavan, *Occupation not shown*
William Fowler, Cooley, *Occupation not shown*
John White, *Occupation not shown*

OMAGH
J Irvine, *Stationmaster-Junction Railway Station*
W A Scott, Gortmore House, *District Superintendent*
O R Morris, *Clerk-District Superintendent's Office*

NEWTOWNSTEWART ** (Additional information shown)
James Patterson, *Signalman*
??? Patterson, *Porter*
** Belfast Railway Post Office, Dublin, Holyhead and Kingstown Packet (English and Scotch letters) leave at 3.30pm. Second mail departs at 9.45pm. Incoming railway mail received at 5.00am and again at 10.55am.

STRABANE
A Moore, *Stationmaster GNR*
W Boyle, *Stationmaster BD (CDRJC ?)*

The First World War and Partition of Ireland

With the commencement of World War One, on 4 August 1914, rising costs and shortages of materials began to take their toll. Railways across the British Isles were to feel the effects of war, and a subsequent Government emergency Order in Council, on 22 December 1916, placed all railways under the direct control of the Government which, in the case of Ireland, was exercised through the Irish Railways Executive Committee (IREC) with effect from midnight on 31 December 1916.

This measure was to last well beyond the end of the war (11 November 1918) and, in common with other concerns, control of the Great Northern Railway was not

Left: First World War scenes at Omagh, taken by a local dentist. Cheery troops departing from Platform One in a rake of six-wheelers. They are destined for the Western Front, but will they still be alive in six months?

N Holland

Right: Boarding the same train, probably, but this time viewed from the Derry end of Platform One.

N Holland

Below: Soldiers supervise the loading of ammunition at the goods yard.

N Holland

Opposite: Q class 4-4-0 No 136 *Minerva*, built in 1899, approaches Newtownstewart with the 5.00pm ex-Derry around 1913.

Sir Cecil Smith

handed back to the management until 17 August 1921. In January 1919, the IREC enforced a new, eight-hour, working day for railwaymen, resulting in most railway companies having to take on additional staff. On 31 December 1919, the IREC was wound up and its powers transferred to the newly created Ministry of Transport, with whom negotiations were to continue, as the railways sought to regain control from the Government. The Irish railways as a whole received the sum of £3,000,000 in compensation for their use made during the war and for arrears in maintenance.

There were several changes to the locomotive stock during the war years. In 1915, the first of the U class 4-4-0 tender engines arrived, and some of these graceful engines found themselves working north of Omagh as they covered duties on the Irish North route. At Londonderry, they joined one of the new T class 4-4-2 tank engines that have been allocated to the shed, sharing company with the Q class 4-4-0 tender express engines, now handling regular trains from Belfast. They were to hold sway on the Derry Road for the best part of thirty years.

One very evident area of change, as a result of the country being on a war footing, showed itself at Trew & Moy station. The Moy Horse Fair was internationally famous and the volume of horse wagons being despatched from this station rose dramatically, as hundreds of animals were shipped off to engage in army war work abroad.

There had been continuing political unrest in Ireland as a whole for many years prior to, and during, the war. Acts of sabotage further complicated rebuilding of the railway system and its rolling stock after the war's conclusion. There have been many good tracts written about the national Irish struggle for independence and, as an essentially railway-orientated work, this book is not really the place in which to air them. It is necessary, however, to touch briefly upon the subject in order to set the scene and give some continuity to the history.

The Irish people had long held what many would see as a justly felt wish for self-determination and political freedom from control by England. Over the centuries, this had manifested itself in a number of demonstrations and acts of rebellion, culminating in the proclaiming of the Irish state during the Easter Rising (Irish: *Eiri Amach na Cásca*) which lasted from 24 April (Easter Monday) to 30 April 1916, the most significant rising in Ireland since 1798. Organised by the Irish Republican Brotherhood, it was eventually suppressed after many days of bitter fighting in and around Dublin, and a number of its leaders subsequently executed. The executions were politically counter-productive for the English Government of Herbert Asquith, Liberal Prime Minister from 1908 to 1916, and helped to turn many peaceable Irish men and women into fervent nationalists.

During the Rising, a number of strategic and important locations in and around Dublin were taken and held by the Irish Volunteers and Irish Citizen Army, including Boland's bakery, a high building between Great Canal Street and Grand Canal Quay, which overlooked the Dublin and South Eastern Railway line from Kingstown (now Dun Laoghaire) to Westland Row station. Several volunteers occupied Westland Row station and succeeded in stopping the 12.15pm to Kingstown from

The south end of Strabane around 1914. The locomotive appears to be a Q class 4-4-0 but what is going on to the left? It is possible this is some sort of political gathering, possibly a rally of Irish Volunteers.

JD FitzGerald collection

departing. The line leading out of the city was dislocated, with rails ripped up and signalling equipment smashed, in an attempt to disrupt railway traffic.

A number of minor localised actions also took place across Ireland and of relevance here are events in County Tyrone. At Dungannon several hundred Irish Volunteers had assembled on Saturday 22 April ready to move, only to be stood down in some confusion. A countermanding order had been issued that Sunday by Professor Eoin MacNeill, President of the Irish Volunteers, who regarded the Rising as unwise and wanted to stop it. Faced with conflicting orders, the Tyrone Volunteers decided to disperse rather than take isolated action.

In 1916, David Lloyd George succeeded Herbert Asquith as Prime Minister of a British wartime coalition government. Two years later, at the end of the war, he was faced with the unpalatable facts of the 1918 election, the last all-Ireland one, when the Sinn Féin (in English *We Ourselves*) Party took 75 of the 105 seats. Following this, the proclamation of the Irish Republic in 1916 was re-affirmed by Dáil Eireann (House of Representatives) in January 1919. With Sinn Féin's policies of Irish independence and abstention from Westminster, it became clear to the British Cabinet that some form of Home Rule would need to be re-enacted sooner rather then later. The continuing unrest and violence of the guerrilla campaign was later called the Irish War of Independence and was destined to continue until 1921.

Back in 1912-14, Ulster Unionists had campaigned against the proposal to give Ireland Home Rule. They were led by Sir Edward Carson and had signed a document called the Ulster Covenant. Carson, supported by a recommendation in the House of Lords, had steered through an Amending Bill on 8 July 1914, for the 'temporary exclusion of Ulster' from the workings of the Home Rule Bill. Following the outbreak of war in August, the (Third) Home Rule Bill was passed, but implementation was postponed and the Act never took effect.

With the Easter Rising and its aftermath, the Home Rule Act was clearly unworkable. The end of the war in 1918 was followed by the establishment of Dáil Eireann and more military action by the Volunteers. In response, Westminster passed the Government of Ireland Act 1920. This partitioned the country, with effect from July 1921, and six of the Ulster counties, including the City of Belfast, were reconstituted as 'Northern Ireland'. Partition was seen by the British Government as a necessary compromise but it was controversial and has remained a thorn in the side of Nationalists ever since, though it probably avoided even more bloodshed. Within this six county area there was an overall Protestant majority, in the main loyal to England and the Crown.

During the period of violence leading up to July 1921, railways across Ireland were still liable to receive the unwanted attention of the disaffected, being easy targets for their acts of sabotage and destruction. The Derry Road was as likely as anywhere to be affected, as it passed through several areas with a strong Catholic population who, in many cases, had Nationalist sympathies.

The evening of 17 July 1920 was a good example of sabotage. The Belfast to Londonderry night goods was held up at Donaghmore by a gang of 40 armed men and official and police mail was taken by the self-styled Irish Republican Army, no doubt to see who might be on the British security lists.

Again, in July 1921, at Gortavoy between Donaghmore and Pomeroy, a Londonderry-bound goods train was again held up by armed members of the IRA. That night, 17 wagons were set on fire, and there are still people alive who can remember the smell of burning loaves of bread, drifting for miles across the Tyrone countryside as the wagons blazed, the taint of destroyed foodstuffs reaching as far as Pomeroy.

Direct British rule in Ireland was finally coming to an end and, in December 1921, with the conclusion of the negotiations between the British Government and Eamon de Valera's Republican Government, the Anglo-Irish Treaty was narrowly approved by Dáil Eireann in Dublin. With the position of Northern Ireland already settled by the Government of Ireland Act 1920, the remaining 26 counties, mainly in the south of Ireland formed the new Irish Free State.

The country was effectively split over the Treaty and Partition, as were the volunteers of the IRA, many feeling that they had received short measure and wanted nothing less than a completely independent island. Although in the far northwest geographically, County Donegal became part of the new, Irish Free State, with the result that the Derry Road line now briefly entered the Free State for about nine miles, between Londonderry and Strabane, and it was perhaps inevitable, that this area would cause problems. This proved to be the case and trouble raised its ugly head when, on 12 May 1922, the down Londonderry goods was stopped at St Johnston by a party of armed men. A quantity of foodstuffs including butter and bacon were removed from the vans and stolen.

Internal strife prevailed and across the country and a bitter Irish Civil War was to follow, lasting from June 1922 until April 1923. The Civil War arose from a split in the IRA over the decision to accept the Treaty, and the two opposing factions fought for their beliefs. The Free State army eventually managed to restore a degree of normality as they gained control of the country and the two halves of Ireland settled into an uneasy peace. The Irish railway network, as a whole, continued to suffer from sporadic attacks during this period, with a bomb blast at Amiens Street station in Dublin representing the last such incident for the GNR.

Sadly, the hard-line IRA movement continued to make its presence felt down the years, with acts of pointless destruction, often involving the loss of innocent life, whilst declaring its intention of overthrowing both the Free State and Northern Ireland governments by any means possible, and re-establishing the 32-county Irish Republic declared in 1916.

The Great Northern suffered its share of these malicious incidents, though partition did, by default, ensure that the it would retain its independence for another 31 years, as we shall see shortly.

The Company now found itself it the unique position of having a railway system that crossed the newly-created inter-state border in 17 places, with customs staff and potential problems at 14 stations, seven on each side of the border. The line to Derry briefly crossed the border between Strabane and Londonderry, with Porthall, St Johnston and Carrigans stations all situated in County Donegal in the Irish Free State. Through services operated under special arrangements, with stopping trains being examined by customs men at Strabane and St Johnston.

The partition of Ireland had placed the GNR in an almost impossible position, operationally, and without parallel in the United Kingdom. It was a situation that, over the years, only served to add to the complications of working, as border customs examinations and longer journey times became the norm. The GNR though, as ever, rose to the challenge and continued to provide a wide and excellent service, throughout its independent years, corridor trains of up to nine coaches being introduced on the Derry Road around 1920 with buffet cars appearing on the main trains at the same time.

Financial Consolidation and Political Strife

During 1924, a decision was taken to close the Market Junction signal box, a little to the south of Omagh station, leaving six sections between Dungannon and Omagh. For a while, this was to leave Dungannon Junction as the only box with switching out equipment, the junction box being switched out at 7pm each evening after the departure of the last Cookstown train and opened again at 6.30am for the branch goods train. In time, both Donaghmore and Annaghmore were given this important facility, the essential and heavy nightly

Left: The Market Junction signalbox at Omagh was closed in 1924. It is seen here about 1914 with PP 4-4-0 No 106 *Tornado* approaching on a down train. The short platform was used for ticket checking before entering Omagh.
N Holland

Opposite: P class 4-4-0 No 52 *Snowdrop* at the Omagh end of Newtownstewart about 1914. This engine was built in 1892 and rebuilt as shown in 1906.
Inspector A Johnston

Below: The coalmines at Coalisland, opened in 1924.
Courtesy M Pollard

goods service ensuring the line was in operation 24 hours a day.

The possibility of further traffic on the Cookstown branch came with the opening of a coal mine in 1924 near Coalisland, a new seam having been discovered. The mines, a mile to the north of Coalisland, were connected briefly to the railway system but, sadly, the coal extracted proved to be of poor quality and the resultant traffic was of little benefit to the branch revenues.

Coal was again in the news in 1926, when miners in England went on strike following several years of unrest. The resultant struggle to find suitable supplies pushed the price up five-fold from the regular price of around ten shillings a ton. The Great Northern reserve coal dumps at Adelaide yard, which contained around 35,000 tons, rapidly depleted, even with drivers using on average 36 to 42 lbs per mile. Killochan colliery in Scotland, the usual source of supply for the Great Northern, was unable to supply, following an earlier strike in 1919 for a 40-hour working week. Numerous loco failures resulted, due to the poorer quality coal being obtained elsewhere. In many cases the GNR had to purchase the only coal supplies available at the time, often of indifferent quality.

In 1925, the majority of railway companies within the Irish Free State were amalgamated, to form the Great Southern Railways (GSR). The Great Northern, operating in both jurisdictions, was excluded from this arrangement, in common with all other cross-border railways, and continued to operate independently.

The 1920s saw another threat to the railways emerge, in the form of increasingly competitive road transport. Profits were inevitably affected as the railway companies across Ireland, and indeed the UK in general, fought back with everything they had. The GNR instituted their own passenger and freight road services, as feeders to the rail network, on both sides of the border. Moves were also made to buy out competitors in an effort to form an integrated transport system. In North Ireland, surplus army vehicles and second-hand buses could be bought for a song and this allowed cut throat competition to flourish, to the detriment of the railways. By 1932, net

profit for the GNR had fallen to a mere £29,000 and by 1933 this had turned into a loss of £72,000.

Drastic, if unpopular action was needed to reduce expenditure and, at Dundalk Works, 200 people were given final notice and a further 600 advised that they would only be working (and paid) one week in every three. With the support and backing of the National Union of Railwaymen, all 800 employees went on strike from 1 August 1932. Clearly, it was not a good time for the Great Northern Railway as a whole, with the continuity of supply and attendant risk to maintenance, on both the Derry Road and elsewhere under threat. That strike was finally been resolved after three weeks, following negotiations that included Dundalk Urban District Council and Government Minister, Sean Lemass.

When the Great Northern Railway had been formed in 1876, the various locomotive works owned by the absorbed companies had also merged, but it was not until 1885 that overall control was taken by Dundalk Works, under the direction of Locomotive Superintendent James Crawford Park. Formerly Patrick Stirling's chief draughtsman on the English Great Northern, Park became Locomotive Superintendent on the opening of the new Locomotive, Carriage and Wagon Works at Dundalk in 1880. He is credited with bringing the Doncaster image to the Irish GNR, evident in the general appearance of motive power and coaching stock, including the apple green livery on locomotives up to 1914. He died at Dundalk on 27 May 1895, and was succeeded by Charles Clifford, who was already at Dundalk, having joined the Irish North Western Railway in 1861.

The works at Dundalk were to take care of the Great Northern's requirements for 80 years, with locomotives built and rebuilt and virtually all the coaching stock and wagons completed there. The well-known grained mahogany paint finish was applied from around 1900, carriages prior to that being varnished. Buses were also dealt with between 1929 and the late 1950s, with a total of 53 Gardner-engined vehicles being constructed between 1937 and 1942. In many ways, Dundalk was the Swindon Works of Northern Ireland, with several generations of the same families to be found within its gates. It was generally held that, if there was an item that the GNR needed, Dundalk Works either had it or they could make it.

The 1933 Strike

The spectre of recession was never far away from the Irish economy as a whole, with 7000 workers in the Belfast engineering industry already out of work by 1932. Despite the best attempts by railway companies across the country to reduce costs and improve efficiency, it was perhaps somewhat inevitable that wage reductions would be imposed on railwaymen across the country. Whilst these were reluctantly accepted by those railwaymen in the south, including the GNR, railway employees in the north declared their intention not to cooperate when, in August 1932, the Northern Ireland Government announced that it would apply a similar strategy. Railwaymen had already seen cuts of around 4% in May 1931, in an attempt at achieving solvency and this further cut in pay packets proved to be too much to stomach.

Following an announcement that station masters and clerical staff were to have their wages cut by approximately 16%, railways across the province came to a standstill as drivers, firemen, signalmen and porters all downed tools, with the full support of the National Union of Railwaymen, and stopped work at noon on 31 January 1933. Traffic on the Derry Road and elsewhere across the northern half of the GNR effectively ground to a halt. The only people not to strike were members of the Railway Clerks Association and railway workers on the already financially shaky BCDR.

This action had come hard on the heels of an earlier strike at the Dundalk locomotive works in July 1932. The 1933 strike, covering the majority of employees, lasted until Friday 8 April with many staff, including all of the cleaners and a percentage of the firemen at Adelaide being dismissed as a direct result of the action. The remaining staff and crews returned to their duties, joining their non-striking colleagues two days later, with most, but not all of those dismissed, being gradually re-employed over a period of time, though it was to take until 1940 to complete the reintegration.

In addition to the bitterness that remained between strikers and non-strikers, who had accepted an eventual 10% reduction in wages, the action had caused considerable disruption to services across the country, driving yet another nail into the coffin of the Company which now posted a trading loss, both engine miles and income being reduced by a third.

There were a number of malicious incidents perpetrated during the period of the strike including one in March, involving the 8.25am Belfast to Omagh train, derailed at Omagh Market Branch Junction, when the points were deliberately set half open. The engine, Q class No 122, took itself and two coaches onto the branch and the couplings broke. The rest of the train derailed and continuing some distance along the main line, wreaking havoc to the track in the process, fortunately without any loss of life. Disenfranchised employees with a working knowledge of the system were thought to be responsible, but it could not be proved, and no one was ever brought to account. This was possibly the first occasion on which passenger stock has ever ventured onto the Market Branch, however unintentional. However, PPs class 4-4-0 No 42x took an IRRS enthusiast's special down the branch in 1962.

In a further urgent move to economise on maintenance expenditure and get costs under control, in 1933 the double track section between St Johnston and Londonderry was singled by the removal of the up line. By now, the Derry Road was the only line on the GNR still using line-side staff exchange apparatus. The nets were fitted to locomotive tenders on the drivers side, ensuring that trains could pass through stations at anything up 30mph, as the heavy staff, securely held in a pouch, was mechanically transferred to and from the locomotive. Several trains used the equipment each day.

The Castlederg & Victoria Bridge Tramway

One victim of the strike was the little narrow gauge Castlederg & Victoria Bridge Tramway. Always running on a shoestring budget with very little cash to spare, it did not recover from the effects of the strike and closed on 17 April 1933 after a relatively short life of only 49 years. Several items of rolling stock were to find new homes and an afterlife elsewhere.

The CVBT paraffin-engined railcar, condemned in March 1928, had lain out of use and derelict in the open behind the running shed at Castlederg for some time. Its engine had been removed in September 1929 and sold to a local saw mill owner.

Some three years later, on 15 December 1932, the redoubtable Henry Forbes of the CDRJC was in Castlederg and, after inspecting the remains of the home made railcar, discussed the possibility of purchase with GT Glover, Great Northern Locomotive Engineer at Dundalk Works.

Always with an eye for a bargain, Forbes had already purchased an Atkinson-Walker steam locomotive (or 'tractor' as Atkinsons termed it), which had been supplied on approval in September 1928 to the Clogher Valley Railway and, despite all attempts, had failed miserably to live up its expectations. Several requests by the CVR to have it removed were ignored and Atkinson-Walker eventually went into liquidation at the end of 1929, the 'tractor' appearing to have been written off by them. Forbes subsequently took his purchase back to Donegal, where, fitted out with a Gardner diesel engine and re-named *Phoenix*, it performed satisfactorily at Strabane as a shunter and trip engine, until the end of the system in 1959, after which it moved to the Belfast Transport Museum and is now at its successor, at Cultra.

Returning to the Castlederg railcar, after some haggling, a purchase price of £25 was eventually accepted

Right: The malicious derailment at Market Junction, Omagh in 1933.

N Holland

Left: The same scene viewed from the Dublin Road bridge looking east. The curious vehicle in the foreground is the permanent way lorry, a road vehicle converted to run on rails. There is a story that one of the passengers lived in the house on the left. He was able to scramble up the embankment and over the fence, commenting "That's what I call service!" The station was at the other side of the town.

N Holland

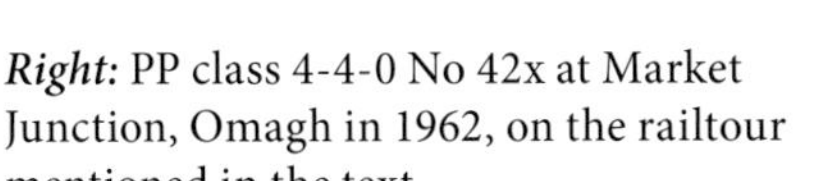

Right: PP class 4-4-0 No 42x at Market Junction, Omagh in 1962, on the railtour mentioned in the text.

CP Friel collection

by the CVBT directors. After being towed to Victoria Bridge on 1 January 1933, the now engineless railcar was loaded onto a GNR wagon and taken first along the Derry Road to Strabane, and thence by CDRJC metals to Stranorlar, where the workshops refurbished the body and fitted it with a six-cylinder REO FA engine. It became the second Railcar No 2 on the Donegal system and worked until 1941. After lying cannibalised and out of use at Glenties for nearly three years, it was decided in April 1944 to rebuild it once more. It became unpowered trailer No 2 and continued in service until the closure of the CDRJC in December 1959, a definite survivor!

After closure of the CVBT, the rolling stock, rails and maintenance equipment were purchased for scrap by Arnott, Young and Co Ltd, of the Fullerton Ironworks in Glasgow. However, Forbes had his eye on the situation and before 2-6-0T locomotive No 4 could be dismantled, Mr DN McClure, Manager of the Clogher Valley Railway, together with Henry Forbes, went to inspect the 30-year old engine with a view to purchasing it for use on the CVR. The CVR Committee waited for nearly two months before making a decision, nearly missing the boat, but managed to secure the locomotive for their own railway by the simple expedient of offering two of their own worn out engines, No 1 *Caledon* and No 7 *Blessingbourne*, in an exchange deal.

In October 1934, with two steam cranes assisting, the Castlederg engine was loaded onto a GNR bogie well wagon at Victoria Bridge, where five men from the Aughnacloy workshops removed the fittings and wheels, before the whole ensemble proceeded to Maguiresbridge station, via Omagh and the INW line, where the procedure was reversed, the locomotive being gently lowered onto the adjacent CVR tracks. A total of 19 cattle wagons were also purchased.

When everything was ready, Driver John Girvan and Fireman Joe Irwin, accompanied by chargehand fitter Joe Robinson, went down to light up No 4 and coupled up to the newly-acquired wagons. They took the whole train slowly up the narrow gauge line to the workshops at Aughnacloy, the journey giving a clear indication that the valve timing required some serious re-setting. After remedial work and some rebuilding, the engine went on to become a good, reliable workhorse, lasting until the closure of the line, on New Year's Day, 1942.

Conversely, the wagons, having arrived on the CVR, never turned a wheel in revenue earning service. Though purchased for only £10 each, they proved a bad bargain. Fourteen had Westinghouse brakes and five had hand brakes only. These would have needed replacing and the buffer beam heights altered to match the CVR stock. In the event, they lay unwanted and unloved for eight years at the side of Aughnacloy yard and were never listed or numbered with the CVR stock.

The Craigavon Bridge

The very first bridge across the River Foyle, at Londonderry, had been a wooden structure with a built in drawbridge to allow boats from Strabane to pass under, as the inhabitants there possessed ancient navigational rights. It was constructed in America and sent to Londonderry, where it was erected around 1790, about 100 yards north of the present bridge. It was replaced by the Carlisle Bridge, erected in 1863 100 yards

Craigavon Bridge, Londonderry, on 29 July 1961, showing the tracks of the Londonderry Port and Harbour Commissioners in the foreground. Foyle Road station is on the right.
EM Patterson

to the south. In 1933 the Carlisle Bridge in its turn was replaced by the present Craigavon Bridge, almost on the same site. Construction had begun in the late 1920s and was finished in 1933.

Formation of the NIRTB

Although the Dublin Government did what it could to protect railways in the Irish Free State from unfair road competition, no such help came from the Stormont based Northern Ireland Government until 1934. There, the situation had become so bad that the railway companies appealed to the Government to assist them in their plight, and a commission was set up, chaired by Sir Felix Pole from England (General Manager of the Great Western Railway from 1921-1929) to investigate all transport operations in the province.

In his report, published in July 1934, he recommended the creation of a Northern Ireland Road Transport Board, with a mandate to take over all road passenger and freight services in Northern Ireland, merging the passenger and road freight operations of HMS Catherwood, the Belfast Omnibus Company, the BCDR, and the LMS(NCC). The Road & Rail Traffic Act (Northern Ireland) of 1935 was passed, making the recommendation effective from 1 October, and included the absorption of fifty road vehicles from the GNR(I) fleet.

By 1 January 1936, the NIRTB had acquired 687 buses as a result of swallowing up 56 smaller bus operators, as well as the five main ones, whilst the freight side swelled to the point where they controlled around 2000 lorries. The NIRTB was cumbersome to operate and this, coupled with a distinct lack of expertise at managerial levels, did little to alleviate the railway's plight. Its creation simply fudged the issue, the Government allowing the NIRTB to compete with the railways, rather than cooperate with them.

One area of freight that continued to be sent in prodigious quantities across Ireland by rail was stout and 'porter', the product of Arthur Guinness, Son & Co and made at the famous St James's Gate Brewery, in Dublin. Regular deliveries of casks would arrive at stations such as Beragh, with the empties being consigned back a few days later, via the first available train.

The pooling of receipts however hid the real problem, which continued to blight the Great Northern, and the net effect only served to weaken the railway's overall position, having now lost their profitable road services. Included in the Pole Report had been a suggestion to absorb the Belfast Corporation bus and tram services. Although the Belfast Corporation Act (NI) 1930 gave legal authority for the operation of trolley buses, these were not included in the Report, as they did not arrive on the scene until 28 March 1938. At the opening ceremony, The Lord Mayor, Sir Crawford McCullough drove the last tram from Castle Street to Queen Street and then the first trolleybus from there to Falls Park. The Belfast trolleybus network expanded considerably, becoming the largest in the British Isles outside of London, and it was to have a considerable impact on economy of the Corporation's finances.

The electrification of the Belfast and County Down line to Bangor was also mooted, but in the event (some would say fortunately), neither this, nor the proposals to take over the Corporation bus and tram services were ever implemented. To all intents, the Government made a fragmented and lamentably tardy approach to the Report's findings.

The Mid-1930s

As well as seeing the formation of the NIRTB, the year 1935 had seen the Northern Ireland Government take an unusually charitable stance. Since opening in 1882, the independent Sligo, Leitrim and Northern Counties Railway, running from Enniskillen, on the Irish North, to Sligo, had always struggled financially. It was an extremely useful feeder of cattle traffic onto the GNR at Enniskillen and thence via Clones to Belfast, with some also going to Londonderry via Omagh and the Derry Road. The economic decline in cross-border trade following partition in 1921, and the politically motivated 'Belfast Boycott' of that period had hit the cross border lines hard, particularly the little SLNCR.

At the end of 1934, the debit balance for the Company was £13,989 and a Northern Ireland Government subsidy, known as Grant-in-Aid was awarded to the Sligo Leitrim on the basis that some of the line's financial difficulties could be attributed to the Government's economic dispute with the Irish Free State. The grant was awarded each year from then on, to compensate for the loss of traffic, though there is no doubt that it also helped to ensure continuing stimulation of trade with the GNR and commerce in Northern Ireland generally.

Following the end of the 1933 strike, economies continued to be looked for with renewed urgency and one area was track where, in 1936, the line between Dungannon and Donaghmore was singled, removing the down line, though the line through Donaghmore station would, in time, be slewed and realigned to the down platform. Also, after three attempts to keep it open, Mountjoy halt, three and a half miles north of Omagh, finally succumbed and closed in 1935, having successively been in business from March 1853 to November 1859, August 1870 to December 1878 and October 1928 to September 1935.

One unanticipated benefit of the newly created border between Northern Ireland and Free State came in the form of the illegal smuggling of goods and foodstuffs from one country to the other, its direction depending on who had a shortage of what. There was always a risk to life and limb when this took place close to a railway line, and one morning in January 1936, tragedy struck when, at McKinney's Bridge, where the Derry Road line from Strabane to Londonderry crosses the River Foyle, a goods train struck a herd of 16 cattle being driven across the border, using the railway bridge between County Tyrone and County Donegal.

Though no blame could be attached to the locomotive crew, who did all they could to avoid a collision, sadly, two of the animals were killed, and the other, less injured animals, by now highly stressed, turned on the train, wrecking five wagons. The surviving cattle were eventually rescued and taken away by the Royal Ulster Constabulary, but the perpetrators quickly faded away into the countryside, and were never caught.

Diesel Railcars

Railcars had been introduced to the Derry Road in 1935 and during 1936-37 were timetabled to stop at certain level crossings, thus providing a much-needed service to the rural population and increasing the Company's income at the same time. Development of a lightweight and cheaper means of rail transport had been taking place since the early 1930s and, in July 1932, the first railcar appeared on the GNR. Rather practically designated 'A' and 40ft long, it was powered by an AEC six-cylinder engine. The railcar was carried on two bogies and could transport 32 passengers at 50mph on the level, reducing to 40mph when towing a wagon. It was an immediate success and proved to have considerable longevity, surviving until 1964, only being withdrawn then due to accident damage caused by a heavy shunt at Londonderry.

Within a few months of the launch of 'A', a second railcar, arrived. Railcar 'B' was two feet longer than 'A' and, though similar in appearance, ongoing experience with this new form of technology produced a very different type of transmission in the form of a diesel-electric unit, with a 120bhp Gleniffer engine and a Tilling Stevens generator driving an electric motor powering one axle of the leading bogie. (Tilling Stevens were better and more famously known during the early 20th century for their work in the trolleybus field, Wolverhampton's fleet in particular benefiting from many of their motors). Railcar 'B' weighed in at 21 tons and had a 1ft 6in longer wheelbase on the power bogie, at 8ft. Proving equally

Donaghmore station with the single track now slewed to the down platform. This photograph was taken in 1965 some months after the closure.

Stations UK

Railcar A working on the Derry Road later in her career. She is seen at Newtownstewart on 5 August 1958 on a local from Strabane.
EM Patterson

successful, it joined 'A' in revenue earning service in the Portadown area, not being withdrawn until 1949.

Railcar A initially spent some time in the Dungannon area before moving to Banbridge, Railcar B taking its place. One of its more unusual daily runs, around school time each morning, was a short trip out to Donaghmore and back, extended to Pomeroy on Tuesdays.

The first two cars were quickly followed by Railcar C in November 1934. It was based on the success of the County Donegal Railway's narrow gauge articulated railcar 12 (itself produced at Dundalk). The railcar was just under 49ft in length, with an articulated driver and engine unit at one end, much in the style of the Donegal stock.

The logical progression from this was a two-car set made up of railcars C2 and C3 in June 1935 (C became C1). These articulated units were coupled back to back, each railcar having a Gardner 6LW engine rated at 102 bhp and capable of 48 mph. This was slightly higher than Railcar C1 which had a similar engine, but rated at 92 bhp. When in use, only the power unit from the leading car was used, as there was no facility for controlling both engines from one cab. There was no corridor connection between the vehicles, their ends being flat, in the manner of mainline coaching stock.

The two-car set was not considered a success and from August 1937 they were separated and spent the rest of their days operating separately, often trailing small purpose-built 2½ton luggage trailers behind them. Unlike railcars A and B, the C designated cars required the use of a turntable at the end of each trip but, as they were used on the Irish North, they occasionally ran on the Derry Road.

One unexpected result of the introduction of the railcars, was the number of narrow escapes experienced by staff in the early years of operation, largely due to the quiet running qualities possessed by the vehicles. So concerned were the management, that an *Appendix to the Working Timetable*, issued in June 1939, exhorted all staff, especially crossing gate keepers and permanent way men to be vigilant, and keep a sharp look out at all times, for the approach of these units –

> *There have been some instances where Gate-keepers and others have had narrow escapes from being run over by the Rail Cars. This is partly brought about by the fact that the Cars run much more quietly than an ordinary train, and a sharp lookout is therefore essential. There is also a great danger to trespassers as well as other members of the Staff whose duties are in connection with the Permanent Way or movement of trains.*
>
> *Station Masters and others must therefore warn all Gatekeepers in their districts where these Cars operate of the necessity for a sharp lookout in addition to warning trespassers of the risk. Shunters and all others engaged in train working and Permanent Way men to be specially alive in this respect.*

A Youth Rally was held at the Balmoral Show Grounds outside Belfast, on 28 July 1937 to celebrate the Coronation Year visit of George VI and Queen Elizabeth, the Coronation having taken place on 12 May that year. Many extra train services were provided for youngsters across the province for the event, and special trains to transport them to Balmoral were operated along the Derry Road from both Cookstown and Londonderry, with Enniskillen also providing a fully packed train via Omagh. Five specials also arrived at Balmoral from the NCC and two from the BCDR. The arrival of the Royal couple was slightly marred by an act of terrorism, with the IRA showing their disapproval at the visit, in the traditional way, with a bridge being blown up and a border customs post being burnt down.

Whilst the intention of the 1935 Road and Rail Traffic Act (NI) had been to abolish unnecessary competition by co-ordinating road and rail transport, it failed lamentably in this respect, to the point where ongoing losses and the methods of operation continued to militate against the railway Companies. Representations were made again to the authorities, this time resulting in the Government-generated Thompson and McClintock Inquiry of 1938. In answer to the railways pleas, His Honour Herbert Thompson KC headed the Inquiry into rate and fares, whilst Sir William McClintock was charged with looking into the organisational and financial structure of the NIRTB. The two reports were complementary and inevitably overlapped in some areas.

The combined reports were published in late 1938 and concluded that there was evidence of deliberate, internally organised competition by the NIRTB in an effort to damage the railway freight services. The report went on to recommend the creation of a single authority to replace the NIRTB, with a mandate to control the NCC, BCDR and all road transport, the GNR to be excluded because of the international nature of its operation. The Northern Ireland Parliament then appointed a Select Committee to review the conclusions. They reported back to the government in mid-1939, with a recommendation that the railways and the NIRTB should be made to coordinate their operations, yet another example of the Government fudging the issue and neatly side-stepping their responsibilities. However, the international climate in the late summer of 1939 was such that no further action was taken and the unsatisfactory transport situation was to continue, with the railways left to struggle on as best they could.

The Second World War

In 1939, hostilities again presented their unwelcome appearance, with the commencement of the Second World War on 3 September effectively shelving any likelihood of the Select Committee's report ever being implemented. Although the railways of Great Britain immediately came under Government control, this did not happen in Northern Ireland on this occasion, though railway companies there were expected to play their part in the war effort without the safety net of guaranteed revenue. The Great Northern, along with a number of other lines, had the additional burden of an international border to contend with in their daily operations, the Irish Free State deciding to take a neutral stance during the war.

An early casualty was the TPO service, withdrawn from the Derry Road in 1940. Much integrated movement of trains took place with both the NCC (Northern Counties Committee) and the BCDR (Belfast & County Down Railway), servicing the many military personnel movements and the supply depots that rapidly sprang up as the war progressed. The War Department bought the frames from several GNR wagons and converted them into mobile trolleys, with diesels engines and steel sided armour plating. Externally, they were disguised as cement wagons and located at Magherafelt and Whitehead, on the NCC lines, their purpose being to patrol the lines in the event of an invasion.

In 1940, two ambulance trains were also created to cover the anticipated requirements of incoming wounded war personnel. Similar trains had been created in World War One. Each train was made up of eleven coaches, three (re-gauged) from the LMS, plus four each from the NCC and GNR, with both sets initially positioned at Whitehead on the NCC. One was moved later to the GNR and out-stationed at Broomhedge, south of Lisburn, with mains electricity supply for battery charging and fresh water supplies laid on, adjacent to the siding holding the train. Fortunately, the trains saw little use (with far lower casualty levels than in 1914-18) and in 1944, the coaches were returned their respective owners.

Notwithstanding the seriousness of the overall situation, the GNR bravely continued to provide excursions for its customers whenever possible. One suspects that there may have been an element of Government approval here, in an attempt to keep morale up and ease the effect of wartime conditions. Certainly the money was there to take advantage of such offerings, in part due to the massive extra industrial output needed for the war effort, and the resulting overtime worked by many people. People living in villages along the Derry Road line were not overlooked, and excursions on offer that year included:

(1) A special day trip to Bundoran on Sunday 15 September. Third class returns were at 4s 6d from stations on the Cookstown branch, including Dungannon, and 4s 0d from any station between Donaghmore and Beragh. The train started from Cookstown at 7.30am, reversing at Dungannon, arriving Bundoran at 10.50am, and leaving again for the return run at 7.00pm.

(2) Cheap afternoon fares to Belfast on Saturdays, starting from September. Third class return was at 5s 0d from any station between Omagh and Donaghmore, leaving Omagh at 1.50pm and arriving in Belfast at 3.55pm. The return trip departed Belfast at 8.40pm. This train would most likely have found favour with those visiting their relatives in the city.

At Londonderry there was a substantial naval base and though the GNR station lay alongside the War Department berths, it was necessary to send railway wagons on a circuitous route to avoid travelling through neutral Southern Irish territory between there and Strabane. Goods in wagons destined for Omagh, some 34 miles away, would be capstan-hauled across the Craigavon Bridge, over the River Foyle, to the NCC station at Waterside and then worked over the Derry Central line via Magherafelt to Cookstown (NCC), From there they would be shunted across to the adjacent GNR station, from which they would be forwarded, via Dungannon, to Omagh, a total journey of some 121 miles.

The German Luftwaffe made three concerted attacks on Belfast during 1941, the first raid being on the night of 7-8 April. The main concentration was in the docks area, causing considerable damage to Harland and Wolff's shipyard and destroying the Short Brothers aircraft factory. Fortunately, this was well away from the GNR terminus at Great Victoria Street, although a small amount of blast damage was suffered by the NCC with windows and doors being blown out at York Road. The raid on the night of 15-16 April was a different matter altogether, with York Road station taking a direct hit and the facade being badly damaged. A number of offices were burned out, as was the general stores department.

The final raid, on 4/5 May, was concentrated on the shipyard and docks, the NCC suffering again due to its proximity to this area. The severity of the damage put York Road Station out of action, with the overall roof and virtually all the remaining offices gutted by fire, as was the Midland Hotel. There was considerable loss of equipment and stores with several workshops completely burned out, and both goods sheds were destroyed. The bombing had also cut the running lines in two places between York Road terminus and Whitehouse. Rolling stock suffered badly with more than 250 wagons and 20 coaches destroyed, but surprisingly (and very much in the style of St Pauls Cathedral during the London blitz), in the middle of all this devastation, by a minor miracle, the signal box and locomotive sheds stood virtually undamaged.

Across the River Lagan, in the East Belfast area of County Down, the Belfast & County Down Railway suffered a number of fatalities amongst its employees. Signalman William Wiseman was working in the cabin at Queens Quay station and guard Jess Hutton was manning the ticket barrier. Both remained at their posts during the air raid, and sadly lost their lives as the bombs rained down upon the city.

The NCC reacted swiftly to re-establish some form of normality, with other transport concerns moving to lend a hand in this national emergency, thus avoiding both the City of Belfast and the transport network grinding to halt. The stations at Whitehouse and Whiteabbey, just north of Belfast, were set up as temporary termini, and the NIRTB provided a shuttle bus service from these points into Belfast. On the heel of this, the GNR made space and equipment available across the city at their Grosvenor Road goods yard, to handle the displaced NCC freight traffic.

On the civil engineering side, military personnel worked closely with the railway's own staff to demolish the now-dangerous structures and clear away mountains of debris. York Road station was able to reopen to passengers on 8 May with goods services being resumed shortly afterwards. To help with the rolling stock shortage, the GNR and Great Southern Railways, between them, built and repaired a total of 250 wagons for the NCC. The parent LMS in England shipped twenty ex-Midland Railway coaches dating from 1922-23 across to Belfast, where they were quickly re-gauged.

RAF Coastal Command and Flying Boats

During the conflict, the Derry Road assumed strategic importance as a line of communication for the transfer and movement of both military personnel and equipment. An added concern was the nearness of the railway line to the border with the nominally neutral Irish Free State, a potential weak point in national security during times of conflict. As a result, the RAF, to ensure its integrity, regularly patrolled the full length of the line as part of their defence protection duties, and the daily flights became a familiar and reassuring sight to villagers and farmers working in the fields, with locomotive crews becoming accustomed to the practice of planes passing low over their trains, as they plied the length of the Derry Road.

Responsibility for this lay with Coastal Command's Group 15, using Squadrons 422 and 423. The former was equipped with PBY Catalinas, made by Consolidated Aircraft, and 423 Squadron with Short Sunderland Flying Boats. These squadrons were based at Castle Archdale, on the shores of Lower Lough Erne near Irvinestown in County Fermanagh, about ten miles north west of Enniskillen. Formed at Lough Erne on 2 April 1942, 422 Squadron was initially supplied with Saro Lerwick aircraft. Manufactured by Saunders Roe for the re-equipment of Coastal Command, the Lerwick appeared first in 1938, with the last of 21 aircraft delivered in May 1941.

They were found to be inherently unstable, both on the water and aerodynamically, and the type was declared obsolete as early as 1942, but the reason for their withdrawal was never officially given. The Catalinas then replaced them, and 422 Squadron also received Sunderlands in November of that year. On 3 November 1943 it was joined by 423 Squadron, formed at Oban on 18 May that year.

Less well known is 202 Squadron, exclusively Catalina operated, which arrived for the final eight months of the war from the North African campaign. This squadron was disbanded on 12 June 1945, but not before gaining its moment of glory, sighting and shadow escorting a German U boat, U1058, spotted on the surface heading towards Londonderry to give itself up, following the unconditional surrender of Germany to the allied invasion forces on 7 May.

As they attempted to seek out the U Boat menace, the aircraft would make regular anti-submarine patrols along the western seaboard and out over the North Atlantic, to meet incoming allied convoys of ships from North America. Southern Ireland's neutral stance emphasised the fact that the country's western flank was exposed. The extensive naval base at Londonderry was also at constant risk from attack, as indeed were the adjacent War Department berths and the GNR Derry Road terminus at Foyle Road, the railway lines being in the likely target area of any carpet bombing. This was an additional headache for the flying boat crews and a watchful eye was always kept on their charges, when on operations.

In July 1945, the Sunderlands were given up and 422 Squadron moved down to RAF Bassingbourn in Cambridgeshire, where it was to become re-equipped with Liberators, as a transport squadron, the intention being to join 'Tiger Force' for operations in the Far East. The previous month, 423 Squadron had transferred to Transport Command, moving to Bassingbourn in August, also to receive Liberators. With the end of the war in the Far East, both squadrons were disbanded on 3 September 1945.

The crews did much good work through the war years patrolling the Derry line to keep it safe from attack, though sadly 30 Catalinas and 28 Sunderlands were lost in defending British shores, with 320 brave crewmen perishing in the process. Several reminders of the flying boats' stay can still be seen to this day on Lower Lough Erne, including the remains of the concrete boat docks, the generator room and a landing stage. On a more poignant note, the graves of eight airmen, at Irvinestown cemetery, are still tended and maintained by a grateful local population.

Closure of the Clogher Valley Railway

On New Year's Day, 1942, the little 3ft gauge Clogher Valley Railway, which ran for 37 miles from Tynan, on the Armagh to Clones line, to Maguiresbridge, on the INW Clones to Enniskillen line, finally closed down, having been in existence since 1887. Like many railways of its kind, it had struggled for years with rising operating costs and trade falling away. The management committee of the railway had, for many years past, relied on the expertise of the GNR repair works at Dundalk and the sage advice of Henry Forbes, manager of the County Donegal Railway narrow gauge network, to keep them afloat, but even they could not stave off the inevitable. This was, of course, in the days before the word 'preservation' had been heard of, and all the benefits that come with it.

On 19 April 1942, an auction was held at Aughnacloy on instruction of the liquidator, and Henry Forbes was quite busy, spending over £4,500 on behalf of his Donegal employers, purchasing several vans and wagons, plus a quantity of sleepers and rolling stock spares. But the jewel in the crown of his purchases was the CVR railcar. It was the most modern piece of rolling stock on the line, a short, articulated railcar built by Walker Bros of Wigan in 1932. Quite innovative and well ahead of its time, it was built in the style of the later, highly successful railcars that served the CDRJC for so many years.

The railcar and a diesel tractor (effectively a second railcar cab unit with a demountable open van body attached) were taken, along with the other purchases, by train down the Derry Road to Strabane, where they were transferred onto narrow gauge metals and taken up the Finn Valley to the CDRJC workshops at Stranorlar, to join the growing number of railcars. As Railcar No 10 in the County Donegal fleet, it became a determined survivor, running a total of 348,977 miles and lasting until the end of service on 31 December 1959. Even then, she continued working demolition trains, before finding a safe home in the Belfast Transport Museum and, like *Phoenix*, is now at the Ulster Folk and Transport Museum, Cultra.

S2 class 4-4-0 No 191 *Croagh Patrick* drifts through Carrickmore with a down train while the staff exchange is carried out.

RM Arnold

Freight During the War

The year 1942 also saw the steady introduction of S Class locomotives onto the Derry Road, working alongside the more familiar and resident Q Class, that had held sway for many years. The shallow frames of the Q Class were generally more tolerant of the pounding received when working the switchback nature of the Derry Road.

Through the war years, the 'Free to Free' traffic – goods from the Irish Free State to stations in County Donegal, continued to be sent from Dublin to Strabane via the Derry Road, in customs-sealed vans. From 1943 the times were changed to 9.00am down, with the corresponding up return service leaving Strabane at 4.25pm.

The wartime conditions had also produced a new traffic in the form of turf trains, originating from Strabane and St Johnston. These ran through to Dundalk, the trains reversing direction at Portadown. Some workings diverged at Omagh onto the Irish North to go via Clones, in an effort to relieve the congestion on the Derry Road created by the wartime conditions.

Despite the restrictions imposed by being on a war

A double-headed goods train pounds up towards the summit of Pomeroy bank with an SG3 0-6-0 leading an SG or SG2 class.

A Donaldson

footing, the GNR continued to make improvements to its services wherever possible and one area that received attention was bread distribution by rail. Small, purpose-made containers were produced, capable of being carried two at a time on four-wheel flat trucks, although securing mechanisms allowed for the transport of just one per truck if needed. All but one of the main Belfast bakeries promptly adopted the new system. The branded containers from Inglis, Hughes Bread and William McCombs Snugville bakery, would be loaded up at the various bakery yards each evening and taken to Maysfield and Grosvenor Road good yards, often by Scammell three-wheel mechanical horses with flat trailers, where they would be placed onto the aforementioned flat wagons, and secured before departure via the correct goods train. A number of wagons were vacuum fitted and could be attached to passenger trains.

The destination points were all within Northern Ireland, as requirements in the Irish Free State were generally covered by a plethora of local bakeries and not so dependent upon rail borne distribution services. The two biggest bakeries in Londonderry, Stevensons and Brewsters, also made use of the system, with despatches of bread from Hugh Stevenson & Company travelling as far south as Dungannon. Deliveries to stations on the Derry Road became an daily occurrence. It would be very unusual to see the likes of Annaghmore goods yard without its regular, light red Inglis container. The container system was also taken up by the NCC system, but there the Inglis-branded containers were painted a dark red to distinguish them. NCC bread containers never migrated onto the GNR lines.

In an effort to stimulate traffic, a further halt was opened on the Cookstown branch during 1943, serving Killymoon Golf Links, north of Stewartstown. The war years were to see the best ever service on the branch, with seven trains on weekdays, supplemented by two trains on Sundays.

By 1943, the additional requirements that had been placed on the GNR resulted in the workforce rising to 6,888 persons.

Towards the end of 1943, yet another Report was presented to Parliament, this time as a result of a Wartime Agricultural Inquiry Commission. Of relevance here is the recommendation that the Government should take over the BCDR, the NCC and the NIRTB. The suggestion was also made that, though the GNR would need to remain independent as a result of its cross-border operations, it might like to take part in a pooling of receipts, etc. It is unlikely that there was much enthusiasm on the part of the GNR management for a further dilution of its profits. However, any possible action was deferred, pending the ending of the War.

During 1943, the Southern Irish Government had announced its intention to restructure the transport network within Southern Ireland. After one failed bill, Transport Bill No 2 was received by the Dáil on 29 November 1944, becoming law by the end of the year. It effectively merged the Great Southern Railways and the Dublin United Tramways Company, covering the trams and buses. The name of the newly formed Company was Córas Iompair Eireann (Irish Transport Company). Once more, the GNR was excluded from the bill, due to its cross-border sphere of operation.

Although this guaranteed its continued independence, it was at the cost of any financial protection offered as part of a Government network.

As a result of the vastly increased traffic created by being on a wartime footing, gross income for the Great Northern had risen in 1944 to £3.4M, as compared with £1.3M in 1938. This, in turn, allowed a small dividend to be paid to shareholders, covering the years 1941-1947. The ending of the war on 8 May 1945 saw some return to normality possible but there were other problems now looming close on the horizon.

Post War Contraction and the end of the Great Northern Railway

With the years of austerity out of the way, the newly formed Labour Court had awarded workers a pay increase of 2s 10d per hour, and this would have to be found from the GNR coffers. Much money would also need to be spent on new rolling stock and clearing the backlog of urgent track repairs. Notwithstanding the welcome additional income generated during the war years, there would be precious little to cover all the expenditure now required and, with the return to peacetime operating, revenue was already rapidly falling away again. Labour costs had effectively risen by 142% in less than a decade.

To the west of the province, the SLNCR, in common with other railways, found their artificially boosted returns rapidly slipping away now that the war was over. This, coupled with a reduction by the Northern Ireland Government of the grant-in-aid paid to them, to £1500, made for a lean future and prompted talks with the Government. The GNR were able to show a slight increase in receipts on the Derry Road but, notwithstanding this, the Government would not move from the reduced figure. However, the GNR kept a watchful eye on the situation and, from 1950, despite the own financially precarious position, increased the payment of through traffic receipts to the SLNCR, by £2000 per half year.

A bad washout occurred in September 1946, damaging a culvert at Gortavoy, between Donaghmore and Pomeroy, with services being disrupted for some time. An empty cattle train from Londonderry to Trew and Moy was derailed on the unstable embankment. The engine fell 50 feet into a cornfield bringing the leading five cattle wagons with it. The driver, Samuel Maginness, was thrown clear but the fireman, 19 year old James Hutton from Derry, was sadly was crushed to death by coal cascading forward from the tender.

During reconstruction work, only one through train per day was allowed, with all other services terminating at Dungannon and Pomeroy, passengers being transferred between these stations by bus. Pomeroy briefly enjoyed higher status as a much busier terminal station but, fortunately, the track layout was well suited to facilitate this. Additionally, the mid-day train was worked via Clones and the INW line, handling through parcels and passenger luggage, the 'Free to Free' traffic following the same route with Tynan and Newtownbutler being used as customs sealing points.

During the severe winter of early 1947, the Derry Road suffering badly with its many exposed stretches of line, particularly between Donaghmore and Beragh, with several villages cut off from road access for days at

Press photograph of the spectacular derailment at Gortahoy on 6 September 1946. The engine was an SG3.
CP Friel collection

a time.

During 1946, the Northern Ireland Government published a White Paper, proposing a merger of all public transport in the province and, following in the steps of the 1943 Inquiry, announced that it was intending to bring the Northern Ireland Road Transport Board (NIRTB), the Belfast & County Down Railway (BCDR) and Northern Counties Committee lines (NCC) under one roof, with the formation of a single new body, to be known as the Ulster Transport Authority (UTA), thus ending the independence of the railway companies. Fortunately, or otherwise, for the GNR they were once again to be exempted from the proposals, by virtue of their cross-border operation.

The Bill was published in 1947 and passed by the Northern Ireland, Stormont Parliament, as the Transport Act (NI) on 10 August 1948, an inauspicious date, if ever there was one. The UTA was authorised to raise capital of up to £10 million. It was given powers to take over the concerns listed, and authority to "co-operate with or acquire" the GNR if needed. The UTA officially came into operation on 1 October 1948, acquiring both the Belfast and County Down Railway, and the NIRTB. They were to show their hand quite early with the closure of most of the County Down system in 15 January 1950, and the Donaghadee line three months later, leaving just the Bangor branch intact.

The English ownership of the NCC had caused a delay in its absorption. The railways in Britain had been nationalised on 1 January 1948 so, in the interim, the NCC came under the BR Railway Executive. The UTA took over the NCC on 1 April 1949, following its purchase by the Stormont Government for a little over £2½ million pounds. The Authority now controlled within its empire some 340 miles of broad gauge railway line and 28 miles of narrow gauge. This was serviced by more than 90 steam locomotives, four diesel locomotives, four railcars, about 340 carriages and some 3000 goods wagons. The 2,517 miles of Northern Ireland roads were covered by 1000 buses and over 1000 lorries.

Diesel Railcars

Experience gained by the GNR during the 1930s with home-produced railbuses and articulated railcars, designed and constructed at Dundalk works, both for their own use and on the County Donegal Railway's network, had convinced the GNR of the benefits and economies to be accrued by operating a number of their lighter trafficked services by this means. Railcar C1 was a regular performer in the Omagh area. Further development at the time had also resulted in the construction of four larger, articulated, units. Each had a small central van which held the engine compartment and guard's area, articulated at each end to a railcar coach with driving compartment, thus obviating the need for turning at the end of each journey. However, these distinctive units seldom strayed onto the Derry Road.

In 1947, orders were placed by the GNR for a total of fifteen new steam locomotives, five each of Classes U, UG and VS, which were delivered during 1948. In the early months of 1948, the decision was taken to purchase twenty diesel railcars for use on both main and secondary lines and, towards the end of the year, an order was placed with AEC Ltd. Each railcar would be powered by two 9.6 litre six-cylinder under-floor diesel engines, giving an output of 125bhp per engine. Transmission would be by a fluid flywheel and five-speed, pre-selector epicyclic gearbox coupled to a two-speed auxiliary gearbox, producing a maximum speed of 70mph in high ratio and 46½mph in low ratio.

Park Royal provided the bodies and the full-width cab bore a marked family resemblance to their four-wheel railbus later built for the English market. Two saloons were provided for passengers, a First class area immediately behind the driver's cab, giving an unrestricted view of the line ahead for the twelve passengers within, behind which 32 passengers were provided for in the Third class area, the guard's compartment backing onto this.

With the first of the AEC units entering service on the Derry Road in 1951, the railcars proved to be an immediate success. They initially covered the 2.10pm ex-Belfast and 6.40pm ex-Londonderry workings. Numbered 600–19, their distinctive Oxford blue and cream livery proved popular with the travelling public. Several coaches from the steam-hauled stock, including buffet coaches, were wired to run between the railcars as trailers, thus forming three-coach sets. The use of two intermediate trailers allowed four-car sets to be formed but the railcars were not wired for full multiple

Right: Five U class 4-4-0s were built for the GNR by Beyer Peacock in 1948 and were the last inside cylinder 4-4-0s built in the world. No 202 *Louth* is seen on Omagh turntable in the late 1950s.
WA Richards

Left: AEC railcar No 607 leads a down three-car set at Victoria Bridge on 12 October 1956.
EM Patterson

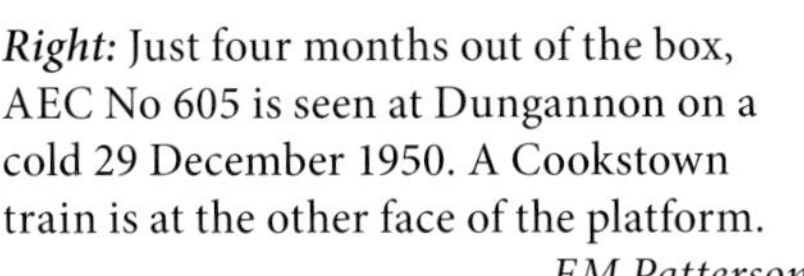

Right: Just four months out of the box, AEC No 605 is seen at Dungannon on a cold 29 December 1950. A Cookstown train is at the other face of the platform.
EM Patterson

operation – unlike the similar CIÉ cars of 1952-54 – so six and eight-car formations could not be formed. The clear view through the drivers cab at each end of the railcar set proved to be very popular with the travelling public and an excellent, if unexpected, marketing tool.

To maximise flexibility of the new AEC railcars and allow one railcar to continue operating even if its twin was withdrawn for maintenance, two unpowered trailers were built new during 1954 and were the last new coaches built at Dundalk. These were classed K31 and were Nos 8 and 9. They had a half-cab in the manner of the later BUT railcars. One is now preserved by the RPSI, but without the cab.

In time, they would be seen operating both the prestigious cross border *Enterprise* service from Belfast to Dublin and in due course, workings to Londonderry, usually with a van or two in tow behind a three-coach set, a trade mark of operations on the Derry Road. At the time of their introduction, they were the first and, for a time, the largest fleet of diesel multiple units operating anywhere in the British Isles, although in Ireland, they were always known as 'railcars', never as 'DMUs'. Within a year or two, senior staff from the British Railways' works at Derby were beating a path to the GNR (and to the UTA Bangor line) to observe the new phenomenon. The experience gained from their visits eventually led to the introduction of the 'Derby Lightweight' DMUs on British Railways in 1954.

In an attempt to stimulate further traffic and ride on the back of the success and popularity of the AEC railcars, an additional set was introduced on the Derry Road in 1955. It travelled out of Londonderry as the second morning train, and back again from Belfast at 4.55pm. Initially, no catering facilities were provided, but a K23 buffet car was soon attached to the set to improve the service.

The Last Years of Independence

On Easter Monday, 1949, the Prime Minster, John Costello, had taken the Irish Free State out of the British Commonwealth, re-naming it the Irish Republic, and proclaiming that it was now a fully independent nation, in the process severing many of the political links that had tied Britain and Ireland together.

Railways, by their very nature, can on occasion be a dangerous place to work and, sadly, another tragic accident occurred on the morning of Friday 24 November 1950 when five permanent way men were killed at Omagh by the engine of the 9.25am Londonderry-Belfast train. They were working on the up line, between the platforms, with the 10.17am arrival from Enniskillen standing at the down platform. There was thick fog that day, reducing visibility down to a few yards and the presence of the Enniskillen train probably masked the sound of the approaching train, which, when it arrived, caught them unawares. The curved layout of the station would also have made it difficult for the trackmen and engine crew to see each other. A memorial plaque to these men was erected at the site in the 1990s.

In a further attempt to modernise and drum up more income, Second class travel was abolished from 1 January 1951, effectively removing what had been something of an anachronism with three classes available to the travelling public. At the same time, First class fares were slightly reduced to just above the old Second class rate.

The financial climate since the war had steadily deteriorated and, notwithstanding the boom in passenger and freight traffic during the war years, general costs had risen alarmingly for the GNR. The small dividends paid out to shareholders during the war were fast becoming a distant memory. Gross receipts were about £3,500,000 in the late 1940s but expenditure exceeded £3,000,000 in 1946 and the Company went into a loss-making situation in 1949 when expenditure finally exceeded income by £118,000. During the Annual General Meeting held at Amiens Street Station on 26 February 1949, the Chairman, Lord Glenavy, stated, "the curtain was about to be rung down on the GNR". The directors relayed this news to the shareholders when the financial reserves finally ran out in November 1950. Faced with such a *fait accompli*, on 6 December the shareholders gave authority for the board to close the railway as soon as was practical.

Faced with a dramatic situation that would have wiped out about a quarter of Ireland's railway system in one blow, the two governments entered into discussions with the Great Northern about what could be done to assist them. In what would be the first official visit to the South since partition in 1921, the Northern Ireland Minister of Commerce, WV McCleery, travelled to

Right: Although taken some five years after the tragedy, this view of a track gang at Omagh in 1955 shows how vulnerable the men were if there was a train at the adjacent platform.
GR Stone

Left: In a photograph taken from the footbridge, a train from Derry drifts round the curve towards Platform 1, while a down train waits at Platform 2. It was the combination of this scenario with a dense fog that led to the tragedy.
GR Stone

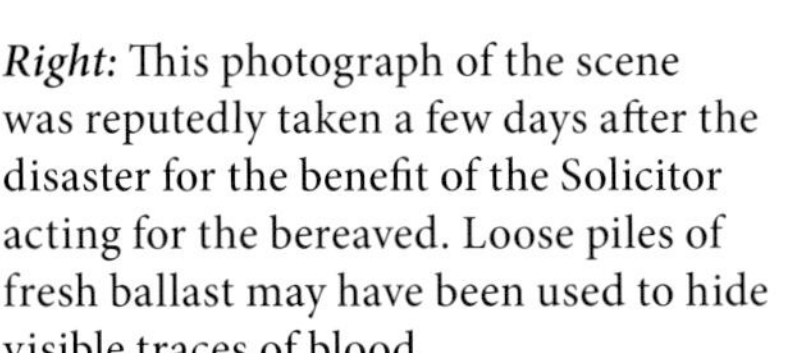

Right: This photograph of the scene was reputedly taken a few days after the disaster for the benefit of the Solicitor acting for the bereaved. Loose piles of fresh ballast may have been used to hide visible traces of blood.
CP Friel collection

Dublin to discuss the crisis situation with his opposite number in Dáil Eireann.

Meanwhile, the Company issued notice on 6 January 1951 of it intention to discontinue all services in Northern Ireland about five weeks later and this was followed two days later by one weeks notice being given to around 1200 employees. Thankfully, this was withdrawn the next day, after receipt of an offer by the two governments to meet the mounting deficit. An offer of £3,900,000 was received from the two governments but was initially rejected by the shareholders. Further hard negotiating increased the offer to £4,500,000 to be divided equally between the two Governments and this was accepted.

With this security in hand, the railway was able to continue operating, albeit on a very fragile basis. On 1 October 1951, the two governments also agreed to finance any continuing deficit, pending outright purchase of the Company. The deficit had reached £1,900,000 by the end of 1952.

It was evident to all that the Great Northern as a business was unlikely to ever be self financing in the foreseeable future and two Acts were passed; one by the Parliament of Northern Ireland and the other in the Republic of Ireland by the Oireachtas. These effectively created a new body, the Great Northern Railway Board, to be run by ten members, five appointed by the Northern Ireland Minister for Commerce and five by the Republic's Minster for Industry and Commerce.

The two Governments, through the GNRB, took possession of 543 miles of running lines, together with an annual wage bill of £2.9M for the 6,490 employees. Unknown to many people, the Act also contained powers allowing the Republic's Government to effectively take over running of the Irish North Western line, in the event of a closure move by the Northern Ireland Government, and it is regrettable that these powers were not exercised in 1957. If they had, the map of railways in the north west of Ireland would perhaps look less barren today.

Life under the Great Northern Railway Board

The new Board took over all running of the railway from 1 September 1953 and the Great Northern's 78 years of independent existence as Ireland's second largest railway company came to an end. Mr GB Howden of the UTA and Mr AP Reynolds of CIÉ initially covered the Chairman and Vice-Chairman's office, respectively. These would alternate each year. Regrettably, the Acts by the two governments securing the continued existence of the Great Northern, had no teeth. Whilst the Republic was prepared to invest money into the enterprise on a like for like basis, in an attempt to modernise the system, the Northern Ireland Government were plainly not prepared to do likewise and did all they could to frustrate any attempt to improve the lot of the railway company and fund as little as they could, for their part.

A surprise visitor made a brief appearance on the Derry Road in June 1953. Along with WT Class 2-6-4T No 57, NCC U2 Class 4-4-0 No 81 *Carrickfergus Castle* had been hired in by the GNR in 1952, and the U2 locomotive spent a short period working services such as the 3.50pm ex-Londonderry, before being transferred to Belfast-Cavan trains. The tractive effort of No 81 proved to be lower than the GNR U class, introduced in 1948 and regularly used on the Strabane-Londonderry section and over the Irish North road through Enniskillen.

Further down the Derry Road at this time, GNR railcar C2, one of the early articulated units introduced in 1935, continued to cover local workings between Dungannon and Omagh, with sister unit C3 often working through from Portadown to Omagh.

One of the first signs of the Board getting to grips with the situation was a decision, after a little over nine months, to increase the railcar stock and a further batch of 24 vehicles were ordered at an estimated cost of £528,000. The modernisation scheme was further extended in April 1954 when the Board invited tenders for the supply of diesel locomotives in three power ranges; 350-400hp, 800hp and 1000hp, the first for shunting and the others for goods haulage. Maschinenbau A-G, based in Kiel, Germany, offered to construct and ship at their own expense, an 800hp diesel-hydraulic locomotive for evaluation. Needless to say, the Board accepted the offer and the MAK locomotive arrived at North Wall docks in Dublin on 14 December that year.

Weighing 57½ tons and with a maximum speed of 53mph, it ran on four coupled axles and power was provided via a Voith transmission unit. Five days before the vessel docked, floods washed away the Tolka bridge, just one mile north of Amiens Street, thus leaving the main line unusable. The MAK had to run inland via

Navan Junction and Drogheda, to reach Dundalk. After extensive testing throughout 1955, and with experience gained on both the GNR and UTA networks, purchase was made, for £29,500, with the engine becoming No 800 in the GNR(B) fleet.

Of interest here are the test runs made along the length of the Derry Road. These were handled by Banbridge man Sandy Gibson, one-time fireman on the Derry Road, and based progressively at Belfast, Portadown and Omagh. He was eventually promoted to driver, his usual charge being a railcar which worked between Scarva and Banbridge, with off-peak workings to Newcastle.

Sandy was selected to take the MAK on a trial run from Londonderry to Portadown, and his reports indicate a high level of overall satisfaction with the performance of the unit, the locomotive being able to maintain a steady 50mph on the 'vertical curves' across the Sperrin foothills, Sandy commenting, "It could have kept going for a week without refuelling". Though this may well have been a slightly exuberant comment, it could certainly operate for extended periods on a full tank of fuel, and its hauling capabilities were excellent, with 65 wagons being regularly worked between Belfast and Portadown. Sadly, the Board's recommendations for continuing modernisation of this kind were not followed up, and this was to prove the only purchase of its kind.

An early sign of Board economies that would directly affect the Derry Road, came on 20 September 1954 when the station at Vernersbridge closed to all traffic. It had seen precious little custom in the preceding years and was quite vulnerable to any act of retrenchment. Despite all attempts by staff and employees on the GNRB to halt the decline, the railway company continued to haemorrhage money and by 1955 was losing over a £1 million a year, escalating to £1.25 million in 1956.

Alarmed at the widespread closure of unprofitable lines elsewhere, and the obvious risk to the Works – the town's biggest employer – the Dundalk Chamber of Commerce organised a meeting to voice their concerns at the current economic climate (and no doubt, their frustration at being able to do so little about it).

It was evident that such losses could not be sustained indefinitely. Since coming under the new regime, the Great Northern had appeared much the same to the casual observer (The word 'Board' replacing 'Ireland' on the company crest was not very noticeable) and the apparent calm on the surface of day to day operations belied the reality. Behind the scenes, the politicians were rapidly approaching panic mode, though some rationalisation was both necessary and inevitable. In the event, rationalisation was not dealt with in a sensible manner.

A shock announcement in 1956 by the Northern Ireland Ministry of Commerce, proposed to withdraw all services within the province on the Portadown to Clones and Irish North lines, thus rendering those stretches of these lines within the Irish Republic isolated stubs ending in the middle of farmland and effectively unworkable. It was obvious to everyone that some modernisation would be needed to ensure the survival of the erstwhile Great Northern, but here again the mandate of the road lobby in the Northern Ireland Parliament was now too evident to be misunderstood by anyone. A year later, in June

Vernersbridge station was closed in September 1954. It still looks in fair condition four years later, on 10 May 1958, as PPs class 4-4-0 No 44 passes on a Dungannon-Belfast train. This locomotive had hauled the Fintona horse tram to Belfast after closure of the Irish North (see page 66) and was now shedded at Adelaide.

A Donaldson

1957, came the statement by the Minister of Commerce that the agreement with the Southern Irish Government for the joint operation of the GNR would be terminated unilaterally. This plan had obviously been brewing for some time at Stormont.

There followed a huge outcry against the idea, north and south of the border. The Government in the Republic vehemently opposed the proposals, as did the majority of the population, The GNR was quite happy to continue working the lines, suggesting the situation was not quite as dire as the Government implied. But it was to be of no avail. The Minister insisted that £14,000 a year could be saved by the closures and, following the Public Enquiry, the report issued in September 1956 confirmed that the closures would go ahead, and the Transport Tribunal chairman rejected the GNR Board's evidence in favour of retention *en bloc*. The bleak situation was not helped by the deficit of £1 million for the year ending 1955. The fact that this figure was spread across the entire GNR network, and that retention of many of the lines was essential for social and economic stability, was ignored.

Fortunately, the Derry Road had so far avoided the eye of the Ministry of Commerce. The fact that it had a very healthy traffic flow would probably not have helped its case if the Ministry had decided it was to go. Such was their autonomy! One economy measure put through in 1956 was the closure to passenger traffic of the Cookstown branch on 16 January. The UTA had already closed their ex-NCC branch from Cookstown Junction back in August 1950, leaving just the GNR(I) passenger service to the town.

The Cookstown branch was the haunt of the T2 class 4-4-2T locomotives and, in the afternoons, one the engines, No 69, would often be seen waiting on the outer face of Dungannon's island platform, with two elderly coaches, waiting for the connecting train from Portadown before working the 3.15pm service to Stewartstown and Cookstown. On rare occasions, sister locomotive No 30 would also appear. Goods traffic was still quite healthy at this time and the line continued to operate for this valuable source of income.

A new IRA campaign, directed against the Northern Ireland Government, began in 1956, with attacks on police stations and customs posts. Attacks were soon directed against other targets. Dislocation on the Derry Road was to occur four times in 1957. On the 17 February an overbridge and underbridge were both damaged by malicious explosions on the section between Pomeroy and Carrickmore, almost certainly caused by the IRA and closing the line for four days.

Then on the night of 2 March 1957, a stormy black night, heavy with rain and thunder, the Enniskillen to Londonderry goods was brought to a stop, and interfered with, shortly after leaving Strabane station. The train was the 9.40pm from Enniskillen. It arrived at Strabane around 2.46am, some 16 minutes down on schedule. Jimmy McGillian was on duty in the North Cabin at Strabane that night and Paddy Campbell, on the footplate, advised Jimmy that 39 wagons were to be detached. Shunter Willie Morris placed the 39 wagons in the Platform 3 road and then had a further eleven wagons, destined for Derry, uplifted from the marshalling yard by the train engine. After the train had been re-formed, the fireman, Lexie Lynch, topped up the water in the tender and, after making the fire up, joined everyone else for a quickly snatched cup of tea. Then it was time for the off.

Jimmy handed the staff for St Johnston up to Paddy, and the train disappeared into the darkness, heading for Derry. He then telegraphed Tommy Dillon, the signalman at St Johnston to inform him that the train was now entering the section, before entering in the register that the train had left Strabane at 3.31am, 3 March 1957. At this point, both Jimmy and Willie stopped for a bite to eat. At 3.52am, Jimmy looked at the clock, saying that it was taking the train a long time to clear the section. Running time for a goods to St Johnston was usually only 18 minutes.

At 4.30am, Tommy Dillon rang Jimmy to say that the train had just passed him, running at speed and although the staff had been exchanged, he had the distinct impression that there were several men on the footplate, with their faces partially covered. Prudently, and in the best tradition of a professional railwayman, Tommy immediately telephoned Derry to ensure that his opposite number there knew what was coming his way.

Then, to Jimmy's surprise, three figures appeared out of the darkness, walking into Strabane station along the ballast from the direction of Derry. Into the cabin came the guard, Sammy McKnight, together with the train crew Paddy Campbell and Lexie Lynch. They related

Right: Cookstown on 25 August 1950 with ex-NCC U2 class 4-4-0 No 75 Antrim Castle shunting the daily UTA goods train. The GNR station is in the left background.

EM Patterson

Left: The GNR branch train is seen crossing Ballinderry Bridge on 29 December 1955. T2 4-4-2T No 143 has the 1.45 to Dungannon, consisting of an ex-LNWR side-corridor Composite and a former railmotor.

EM Patterson

Right: On this occasion QGs class 0-6-0 No 152 has the Cookstown branch train at Dungannon on 13 April 1948, as Qs 4-4-0 No 132 in clean condition pauses with a down Derry train.

HC Casserley

how, after travelling three miles, as far as McKinney's Bridge, detonators went off underneath the train and Lexie saw a red light being waved at them. He shouted across to Paddy who immediately made an emergency brake application, believing that the weather had caused damage to the track. Lexie simultaneously started one of the injectors. On stopping, three armed men with blackened faces appeared by the cab, ordering the crew to abandon the train, telling them to "Get off and walk back to Strabane."

At the other end of the train, the guard, Sammy McKnight, received similar advice. The red lamps and detonators had been used by someone who very obviously knew what they were doing, and as the crew started to walk back, the raiders climbed aboard the engine, SG3 class No 13, turning off the injector, which had sensibly been put on the fireman who was looking after his charge, and set off towards Derry. Although they had slowed at St Johnston to exchange the staff (further evidence of someone with a working knowledge of the railway), the signalman's suspicions were aroused when the regular crew did not appear on the footplate.

At the wayside station of Carrigans, the train appeared to slow down, with several persons dismounting. It then accelerated as the last person to leave pushed the regulator wide open, leaving the train to run on, out of control, towards the maiden city. At Derry, Norman Ballard, the signalman, having already been alerted by Tommy Dillon at St Johnston, was ready for the runaway. Confirming it was driverless as it passed by, he quickly diverted it into a vacant arrival platform, covering his ears and standing helpless as 400 tons of train crashed into and demolished the buffers, with a noise that could be heard clear across the city.

When the dust had settled, it was clear that it could have been much worse. Seven wagons had telescoped into each other, with the station offices and forecourt being wrecked but, miraculously, there had been no loss of life. Over the next two weeks, the station buildings and track were restored and, though the damaged wagons, having taken the brunt of the impact, were beyond economic repair, the locomotive was soon back in traffic, having suffered little damage, apart from a bent vacuum pipe.

The Derry unit of the IRA eventually admitted to taking the train, but the names of the saboteurs were never revealed. In what was seen as a concerted and linked action, the offices in the goods yard at Londonderry were also set on fire that night. In a final act of untoward action, the IRA, by now well aware of the much reduced presence of railway personnel on the branch, proceeded to blow up the signal cabin at Coalisland on 11 June 1957, thankfully with no loss of life or injury. It was rebuilt later that year in a utilitarian style.

An act of nature caused the fourth incident when, on another dark, storm laden evening, the appalling weather blew a large and heavy tree across the mouth of Dungannon tunnel at the station end. It lay there in the dark, resting on the stone abutments across the tunnel entrance, unsuspected by anyone. The last through train of the day from Belfast to Londonderry, headed by S2 class No 62 '*Lugnaquilla*' (ex-GNR No 190), came out of the tunnel at some speed and immediately collided with the tree. The impact stove in the smokebox door but caused no serious injury to passengers.

June 1957 saw the arrival of more new railcars with delivery continuing until October 1958. Pleased with the obvious success of the AEC units ordered back in 1948, the GNRB had, following a nine month wait for authority from the two Governments, placed a further order for 24 railcars, at a cost approaching £528,000, with the British United Traction Company (BUT), which included the previous supplier, AEC. They were fitted out by BUT and finished off at Dundalk Works, work commencing in September 1956.

Although similar in many respects to the earlier AEC cars, there were significant design differences. Each power car had two 150 bhp AEC engines and four-speed gearboxes, although these were not pre-selective. The top speed was now 85mph. They were split into two body styles. Sixteen power cars, numbered 701-716, had small half cabs, toilets and corridor connections at each end, with accommodation for 56 Third class passengers in an open saloon. The remaining eight units, numbered 901-908, seated twelve First class and 44 Third class passengers, but had a traditional full width cab. These cars were intended to be at the front and rear of trains and looked remarkably like their earlier AEC cousins. The two types were different electrically, however, and the original AEC units could not be worked in multiple with their later BUT cousins.

The BUT railcars entered service on the Derry Road in 1958 and provided the ideal type of train for the line. One of the Composite driving cars heads a down service in UTA days at Dungannon on 24 July 1961.
EM Patterson

The Northern Ireland Government showed its teeth and made its intentions crystal clear when, in June 1957, the Minister of Commerce confirmed his decision to end the agreement made under the 1953 Act for joint operation of the GNRB with the Southern Irish Government. In a further statement the Minister added that, as far as he was concerned, the line between Portadown and Londonderry had 'no long term future'. This comment, more than anything before, gave the game away and showed the long-held intentions of the men in Stormont, despite their comments on many occasions to the contrary.

It also showed, for the first time, that the Derry Road was in danger from Government intervention and its survival no longer assured. The Government in the South was, despite their protests, virtually forced into accepting the decision and it was agreed that both the assets and staff of the GNRB would be divided between the two existing nationalised companies, the Ulster Transport Authority and Córas Iompair Eireann.

The closure axe then fell with a ferocity not seen before when, on Monday 30 September 1957, despite considerable local opposition, almost a quarter of the GNR system was removed. Closure came to Portadown to Glaslough, Omagh to Clones and the Bundoran branch as far as Ballyshannon.

Deprived of its connections, the sections in the Irish Republic quickly followed. Ballyshannon to Bundoran closed the same day as the Northern Ireland sections. Passenger services on the Glaslough to Clones, Clones to Cavan and Belturbet and Clones to Dundalk sections lasted only to 14 October 1957, though goods services were retained until 31 December 1959 on some lines, including the goods-only Carrickmacross branch. However, the Monaghan-Glaslough section succumbed as early as 2 June 1958 and the Belturbet branch closed on 1 April 1959, on the same day as the connecting CIÉ-operated Cavan and Leitrim line.

The casualties including the famed *Bundoran Express*, running from Dublin, via Dundalk and the Irish North line through Enniskillen, before branching off at Bundoran Junction. The last express had run on Saturday 31 August. Although the two main lines were still intact, this left the Derry Road as a whole in a precarious and dangerous position politically, with its flank now exposed. It also meant the loss of the nightly Belfast-Enniskillen goods, together with the daily 'shipper' to Belfast, via Clones, and the nightly Enniskillen-Londonderry goods train.

The railway company had made a determined last ditch effort to attract passengers and stave off closure by the introduction of a fast daily Enniskillen-Belfast train using a single BUT railcar, No 705, with an elderly GNR coach, D3 type No 396, as a trailer. The service ran via Omagh, necessitating a reverse in both directions. It had been hoped that any traffic stimulated as a result would see the retention of the Irish North line between Omagh and Enniskillen at the very least. However, it was not to be and the initiative did not sway the minds of those in power at Stormont.

Passengers for bound for Fermanagh would now have to change to buses on arrival at Omagh, and information boards to that effect, were soon erected on the platforms. Following the withdrawal of services on the Irish North

BUT twin cab railcar No 705 with Brake Composite 396 approaching Bundoran Junction with the up Enniskillen-Belfast express in August 1957.
NC Simmons

line, there was a recast of motive power on the Derry Road and a BUT railcar set took over a double daily round trip working. The sealed van service to Strabane remained, six-wheel vans replacing bogie vehicles, and could often be seen attached to the rear of the railcar set. However, the switch to diesels meant the end for the through carriage working from Dublin. A further re-casting of services saw the down mail departure from Belfast set back almost one hour and now handled by an AEC railcar set. With just six stops, the service was accelerated to complete the journey in 2½ hours, producing the fastest ever timing between the two cities.

The three-quarter mile long horse-worked Fintona branch was closed by default, as the Irish North line closure meant that it no longer had a connection at Fintona Junction. This was quite ironic, as the branch, terminating in the town centre, almost certainly turned in a healthy profit. The GNRB determined that the horse drawn tram should be preserved without delay or the risk from souvenir hunters, and on Tuesday 1 October, the day after closure, PPs class 4-4-0 No 44 was despatched light from Enniskillen to collect the tram. At 10.15am they set off for Omagh at a stately 20mph with the tram in tow, where, upon arrival, the tram was parked in the little used bay platform at the Derry end of the station, whilst the engine went to be serviced and turned. One or two very small items were removed by Great Northern employees as mementoes, but it did not detract overall, and who can blame them, knowing how they felt towards authority at that moment.

No 44 then collected the tram once more and set off along the Derry Road for Belfast, by necessity still travelling quite slowly and resting briefly in turn at Pomeroy and Dungannon to check that all was well. The ensemble arrived at Belfast at 3.35pm. From there, it was transferred via the Belfast Central Railway line to Queen's Quay, for housing in the Transport Museum, then in the former railmotor shed there. (The tram currently resides in the splendid Ulster Folk and Transport Museum at Cultra, surrounded by many other fascinating railway items from the past.) One wonders if there was much delay to traffic on the main line from Portadown to Belfast. Perhaps it was placed in a siding at some stations to allow service trains to pass.

As for the motive power of the Fintona Tram, 'Dick' the horse was not forgotten. The Ulster Society for the Prevention of Cruelty to Animals stepped forward, taking him under their wing (some previous 'Dicks' were actually mares, but the last 'Dick' was a gelding) and appealing for subscriptions to look after him now that he was both jobless and homeless. Over £66 was raised (worth more than £1000 today) and numerous offers made to home him. The USPCA accepted an offer from nearby Seskinore village, where he lived on a farm for two years before moving to another farm near Comber, where he was to spend the autumn of his life happily grazing in the fields of County Down. As might be expected, the authorities made no effort to help.

The closures ended the GNR's claim to fame of using four different forms of motive power on their railway – steam, diesel, electric (Hill of Howth Tramway) and horse. The Hill of Howth electric trams survived only for a while longer, the system closing on 31 May 1959.

A secondary casualty of the closure was the Sligo,

Leitrim & Northern Counties Railway, Ireland's last independent and privately-owned common carrier railway, running from Enniskillen to Sligo. It had eked out a precarious existence since opening in 1879 and it was never in a strong position financially. A joint take-over had been mooted as far back as 1894, when, with the Board of Trade being owed a considerable amount of money, the Great Northern and Midland Great Western Railway, had considered purchasing the line. However, the negotiations fell by the wayside, and the SLNCR was left to manage on its own, with annual grant aid from Governments on both sides of the border for the last few years. However, in a move with obvious political intentions, the Northern Ireland Government declared in 1955 that their grant for that year would be the last.

The Dublin government, alarmed at this cavalier act of betrayal and the prospect of closure, stepped into the breach and, together with the West of Ireland Cattle Trader's Association, managed to come up a financial package worth £15,000 that would provide a breathing space and keep the railway operating.

Despite this, the closure announcement of the Irish North line sounded a death knell for the little SLNCR, effectively leaving it no connections for the regular eastbound cattle trains, virtually its only real source of income. However, the SLNCR closure had little impact on the Derry Road, as most of the traffic passing onto the GNR at Enniskillen travelled via Clones on its way to the port at Belfast, with only a small percentage going to Londonderry.

The famous 'Bundoran Express' had been run primarily to give pilgrims an easy route to Lough Derg (near Pettigo) from Dublin, Drogheda and other points in the Irish Republic. It ended with the 1957 closures but, for the 1958 pilgrim season, and subsequent ones, a replacement service was routed via Portadown, terminating at Omagh, from where buses took the pilgrims to Lough Derg.

The GNR introduced container wagons for bread deliveries. Half containers were the norm. These could be transferred to CDRJC narrow gauge wagons at Strabane. Note the five retaining clips; if only one container was on the wagon, it was placed centrally using the second and fourth clips from the left.

Harry Mulholland collection

The Derry Road in the Ulster Transport Authority Years 1958 - 1965

The GNRB was to continue until 1958 when, as a result of the Irish Republic's GNR Act 1958, dated 16 July and the Transport Act (100 NI) 1958, dated 29 July, division was effected by joint agreement. It ceased to exist at midnight on 30 September 1958, with the assets fairly equally divided between the two Governments after 82 years of unified existence. CIÉ took over the operation south of the border, in the process acquiring 130 lorries and 158 buses, while the UTA was now in charge of everything that was left in the north.

The main GNR Works at Dundalk were now effectively surplus to requirements, CIÉ having two good establishments at Inchicore and Limerick. Engineering and maintenance requirements for the Portadown to Londonderry line would, in future, almost certainly be dealt with by existing facilities within the UTA structure. All the Dundalk employees received notice of redundancy in January 1958, eventually resulting in the loss of 1000 jobs.

To avoid unnecessary hardship, and cushion the effects of redundancy, the Southern Irish Government helped to create the Dundalk Engineering Works Limited, to take over and run the old works, as from 10 January 1958. Other companies were also set up in the former workshops, including Heinkel Cabin Scooters Limited, Frank Bonser & Co, Dealgan Steel Founders Limited and Commercial Road Vehicles Limited, all subsidiaries of the Industrial Engineering Company Limited.

The theory was that both CIÉ and the UTA would continue to use the Dundalk Engineering Works for maintenance work, while the new engineering company looked outside for additional work. In practice, this did not really happen, as the UTA did not send work to Dundalk after existing jobs were completed. CIÉ used the Works up to 1960 to repair ex-GNR locomotives. Frank Bonser manufactured the Agrotiller range of agricultural machinery, whilst Heinkel assembled mini-cars, ceasing production in October 1960, disposing of its manufacturing and selling rights, to an English based Company in August 1961. Many years later, in June 1969, the Dáil Eireann voted to write off accrued debts of £3,273,115 incurred over the years by the failing Industrial Engineering Company.

As a result of the division, the UTA gained 173 route miles of ex-Great Northern line plus 83 steam locomotives and 28 diesel railcar units. It also now had the task of running the Great Northern Hotel at Rostrevor, a premier hotel to add to the ex-BCDR Slieve Donard at Newcastle and the Northern Counties, Portrush. These would later be sold off into private ownership, thus ending a long-established tradition of railway hotels. It had been a marriage of necessity and whilst there had been many and varied disagreements as to how the enterprise should have been run, the creation of the GNR Board had, at least, kept the old GNR alive for a few more years. There were not many that would doubt the sense in that.

The down side was that the Northern Ireland Government now had the remaining railways in the province under one control, just where they wanted them, with a free hand to continue with their intended reign of destruction. The GNR lines in the Irish Republic came under the more compassionate and railway-minded Córas Iompair Eireann (CIÉ).

At the time of the division of the GNRB between CIÉ and the UTA, the letters 'UT' or 'CIÉ ' had been stenciled on the bufferbeams of locomotives and the sides of rolling stock. Carriages transferred to CIÉ had the letter 'C' prefixed in front of the number (and 'N' suffixed), but otherwise GNR rolling stock was not renumbered. In contrast, the UTA took the opportunity to renumber all their carriage stock in 1959, including the ex-NCC and ex-BCDR ones. The ex-GNR locomotives were renumbered into gaps in the NCC series. The UTA crest made its appearance, replacing the GNRB one and, on carriages, UTA or CIÉ green steadily replaced GNR mahogany.

On CIÉ, the GNR locomotives were neither renumbered nor given CIÉ livery. On the UTA there was a mixed pattern. The most useful locomotives were renumbered into the NCC series. Older locomotives were to be withdrawn as soon as major work was needed on them. These had their former GNR running number suffixed with an 'x', eg – T2 class No 30 (30x) withdrawn in December 1961.

Most of the locomotives that were renumbered by the UTA survived long enough to be overhauled and were repainted into UTA black. Some of them ended their working days still in GNR livery, with the coat of arms and initials still proudly visible through the accumulated grime.

One of the first moves made by the UTA to directly affect the Derry Road was the singling, in 1959, of the double track section between Portadown and Trew & Moy. The former down line was lifted. This left the entire stretch from Portadown to Londonderry as a single track main line. This was followed by the closure of Carrickmore station. The sidings and passing loop were removed and the running line centred between the redundant platforms.

Around this time the traditional signalling staffs on the Derry Road were replaced by lighter NCC-style tablets that could be carried in pouches. Although the actual tablets were newly cast, it is probable that the actual tablet instruments and pouches were recycled from closed signal boxes on the Derry Central and Cookstown lines of the NCC.

There was also an immediate reduction of one through train per day between Belfast and Londonderry, the Portadown-Omagh local working ceasing, as did the remaining steam worked Omagh-Belfast passenger train. Railcar 101 (ex-GNR 'A') found itself transferred to Londonderry, where it continued to cover local services to Strabane and Omagh. The regular Cookstown engine, T2 4-4-2T No 69 (GNR 148 until 1948), did not survive the branch closure by long and

Above: AEC railcar No 603, still in GNR livery but renumbered 111 by the UTA, heads a down train at Strabane in 1959.
EM Patterson

Right: Bearing the letters 'UT' on its buffer beam, blue U class 4-4-0 No 67 *Louth* (ex-GNR 202) is assisted by 4-4-2T No 30x as it climbs out of Pomeroy with a troop train for Omagh on 11 October 1960. Apart from the Cookstown branch, the Glover tanks were a rarity on the Derry Road.
JD FitzGerald

Left: Railcar A (now UTA 101) was based at Derry in the late 1950s and early 1960s and proved very useful on short workings to Strabane. On 8 August 1962 it was about to work the 5.45 train.

EM Patterson

Right: The second view shows the same train at Porthall, where four adults and two children detrain after enjoying a day's shopping in Derry.

EM Patterson

Left: The daily GNR goods to Cookstown shunts a brake van and bread container on NCC tracks at Cookstown on 7 August 1957. Just over a year later the service was cut back to Coalisland.

EM Patterson

was withdrawn from service in August 1959.

The freight service on the Cookstown branch continued to operate but was progressively cut back, with Stewartstown having already closed on 1 August 1958 and services beyond Coalisland ceasing in January 1959. The line officially closed to all remaining freight on 5 October 1959, but the section to Coalisland continued to be worked as a 5½ mile siding until 1965 to extract the sand traffic, using the old up line as a lengthy siding running from Dungannon station through the goods yard, with no physical connection at Dungannon Junction. Also from 5 October 1959, Donaghmore became a request stop only.

Following the closure of the Irish North lines in 1957, and commencing with the 1958 season, the famed Lough Derg pilgrimage trains now ran via the Derry Road to Omagh, where the pilgrims had to suffer the indignity of being transferred to waiting UTA buses for the final part of the journey to the island site.

These were CIÉ trains and used ex-Great Northern AEC or BUT railcars working throughout, though after a few years locomotive-hauled sets were substituted. The A class Metrovick's were an unusual sight (and sound) on Pomeroy bank. When the train was operated by a railcar, the driver, at some point beyond Dungannon, was usually served with a complementary tray lunch by the buffet car staff – such was life on the Derry Road.

The train was booked out of Dublin at 8.45am and, after collecting additional passengers en route north and at Portadown, also stopped at Dungannon and Pomeroy, waiting ten minutes at the latter to cross the 10.00am from Londonderry, before terminating at Omagh, at 12.35pm.

The return journey left Omagh at 1.15pm, taking pilgrims back from a previous day's working. This train crossed the 11.15am from Belfast at Carrickmore (something which could not be done after closure of the station in 1959) before arriving back at Dublin at 3.45pm. In 1959, this weekday service ran from June until August 15th, traditionally the closing date for the island, and continued to operate until the end of the 1964 season. By 1963, the General Motors 141 class held sway on all pilgrim trains providing a sad and all too brief glimpse

Above: The down Pilgrim train at Dungannon on 22 July 1962, comprising a seven-car CIÉ railcar set in a variety of liveries. The driving cars are in the new black and tan scheme and the first trailer in silver. The dining car on this train was a very ancient vehicle and is fifth in the consist.

EM Patterson

Left: Two weeks later, on 9 August, No 2635 is still at the head of the train but the intermediate coaches are now in reverse order, with the elderly arc-roofed dining car third. The Pilgrim train is crossing the 10.20 ex-Omagh AEC at Trew and Moy.

EM Patterson

on what could have been if the line had not been closed in 1965.

Closure of the County Donegal

The last day of 1959 sadly saw the closure of the once great 124½ mile County Donegal narrow gauge network. Formal application for closure of the complete system was made in May, in the face of continuously rising costs and the urgent need for track renewal that could not be afforded. The branch to Glenties had already closed in March 1952 and the UTA had ended services on the Strabane to Londonderry section in December 1954. This section, though owned by the UTA, had continued, as always, to be worked as part of the CDRJC network.

By the mid-1950s, even the most loyal employees could sense that the days were numbered for the railway and that it was dying a slow death. In 1958, the Joint Committee had applied to the Transport Tribunal for permission to close the Ballyshannon branch, which was losing over £3400pa. The order was granted on the basis that necessary road improvements had to be made prior to the closure.

At the end of May 1959, and with no reserves left to fall back upon, formal application to close the entire system, was made and granted. The Ballyshannon branch was actually still open, pending the road improvements and hung on to the end.

The common bond between railwaymen of the CDRJC and GNR(I) stretched back 106 years, to when the original Finn Valley Line had been worked by the GNR and its predecessor, the INWR, but was now to be sundered. It had been built up over many years and cemented by part ownership by the GNR(I). Dundalk had offered much help to their 'little cousin' in the form of heavy repairs to locomotives and pioneering work on the development of the articulated railcars, of which the County Donegal was justifiably proud.

Efficient and caring to the end, a poster was put up by the CDRJC, listing several extra workings for the Christmas period, including an additional round trip, by railcar of course, from Letterkenny on the evening of 31 December. During the penultimate day of CDRJC existence as a railway entity, *Erne*, the last of the Baltic tanks, worked a sizeable goods train of almost 30 wagons, including nine coal wagons, out from Strabane. It was driven, as usual, by the McMenamin brothers, with James at the regulator, and Francis firing to him. This would be the last goods train to work over Barnesmore Gap to west Donegal.

On the last night of operations, Thursday 31 December, railwaymen on the broad gauge platforms stood and watched with sadness as colleagues across the tracks performed their final duties with stoical faces, bringing the narrow gauge operation to a close. Earlier that evening, Pat Monteith, on duty at his post in Stranorlar West cabin had seen the last railcar for Strabane, No 12, driven by Christie Kennedy, worked out of Killybegs and brought safely over Barnesmore Gap, from Donegal town.

So strong was the feeling by the people of the Finn Valley for their railway, that they turned out in force at Stranorlar, and Railcar 12, normally due to run through

Photographs of Co Donegal trains working alongside UTA-renumbered rolling stock at Strabane were only possible between May and December 1959. In September that year GNR No 172 *Slieve Donard* has become UTA No 60 as it sits beside the North Cabin.
JA Anderson

Left: After the closure of the CDRJC at the start of 1959, stored Co Donegal locomotives and stock became a well-known background to photographs of Strabane in the last five years of the Derry Road. U class No 66 *Meath* takes water about 1964.

CP Friel collection

Below: On 24 July 1961 a shunter uses his pole to brake a fly-shunted van at Strabane North. The narrow gauge tracks are in process of lifting.

EM Patterson

to Strabane, was halted there, while a special, composed of Class 5 loco No 5 *Drumboe* and five coaches, was quickly assembled for a final run to Strabane, where it was greeted with applause. It arrived back at Stranorlar at 8.21pm, through the driving rain and darkness, to a fusillade of detonators placed on the rails.

From the beginning of 1960, the CDRJC became a bus and lorry operator and the once-busy interchange at Strabane presented an increasingly sorry and unkempt state, as tracks were torn up and the station building fell into disrepair. Two Class 5 locomotives, *Meenglas* and *Drumboe*, together with a number of carriages, were left at Strabane on isolated pieces of track, having been purchased at auction by an American dentist, Dr Cox, for further use at a working museum in the USA.

The deal eventually fell through due to the high cost (£35,000) of transportation across the Atlantic and they began to suffer the ravages of time with both the weather and vandalism taking its toll. They were to see the Derry Road out, still being there when it closed, though thankfully they have all now passed into somewhat safer local hands and are in various stages of restoration.

The Derry Road had still considerable goods traffic in 1960, and the 12 September issue of the Working Time Table contained the following workings:

1.00am – Londonderry-Portadown (Mondays only)

1.15am – Portadown-Strabane

2.15am – Strabane-Belfast (Mondays only)

3.15am – Portadown-Omagh

4.20am – Portadown-Dungannon (works to Coalisland as required)

4.30am – Omagh-Portadown

5.30am – Strabane-Sion Mills (Mondays excepted. 4.30am light engine ex Derry)

6.45am – Coalisland-Dungannon (Runs as required. Ex 4.20am from Portadown)

8.20am – Strabane-St Johnston (Mondays excepted. Runs as required)

10.30am – Londonderry-Strabane (Mondays excepted. Mixed service)

Opposite: Omagh South Cabin on 4 July 1961 provides a useful viewpoint to photograph No 98 *King Edward VIII* at the head of an empty carriage working to Belfast. The first carriage is an L11 Brake Third, with slightly different panelling to most GNR coaches.

JD FitzGerald

Above: Goods traffic remained healthy on the Derry Road in the early 1960s. SG2 class 0-6-0 No 38 passes an abandoned Donaghmore on 23 June 1964 with the 7.15am down goods to Derry (altered to 5.05am).

JD FitzGerald

Right: On 21 July 1964 SG3 No 33 passes below Pomeroy village on its way to the summit. Freshly made hay stacks add to the atmosphere.

EM Patterson

Left: Three days later, a thirsty Mogul (No 99 *King George VI*) draws water from the tower at the west end of Pomeroy as it works the 11.30am empty carriages to Omagh to operate the 4.30pm up.

EM Patterson

12.40pm – Strabane-Londonderry (Runs at 9.15am on Mondays)

2.50pm – Portadown-Omagh

7.00pm – Omagh-Portadown

7.55pm – Londonderry-Belfast

8.50pm – Belfast-Londonderry

9.50pm – Belfast-Londonderry

9.55pm – Londonderry-Belfast

Circulars are issued weekly by all railways, to update the current and temporary train movements. On 14 October 1960 Great Northern section circular No 4239 was issued by the UTA. This concerned the use of NCC moguls and stated that:

Commencing Monday 17 October, NCC mogul engines will be permitted to work goods trains between Portadown and Londonderry. The maximum speed for these engines between Portadown and Londonderry will be 30mph. These engines must not be double headed over any portion of that line. These engines are prohibited owing to their outside cylinders from working into the following sidings and stores:

Annaghmore – Cabin siding

Sixmilecross – Store siding

Omagh General – Goods store

Omagh Market – Goods store and branch (weight restriction)

Victoria Bridge – Transhipment shed

Newtownstewart – Goods store

Strabane – Transhipment shed and goods store

Londonderry – Goods store

Drivers must exercise care when entering other goods stores and sidings.

This marked the beginning of a long relationship between this class of engine and the Derry Road. Moguls appeared not only on the goods trains but on some passenger services.

During 1960, the UTA created an internal committee to investigate how the railway system, then in their hands, might be rescued from a loss-making situation and be better placed to operate on a profitable basis. This included the former GNR Derry Road and by early 1961 the committee came back to the UTA board with their findings. The *Blue Book Report*, as their plan became known, was a final attempt to recover the once efficient railway system across Northern Ireland and recommended complete dieselisation of the GNR system with railcars, at a figure of £2½ million.

They were unable to find a way to make the railways profitable but suggested the losses of £497,956 in 1961, could be cut to £87,000 by the closure of the Coalisland and Warrenpoint lines. Bearing in mind the political relationship between the UTA and their road transport biased governmental masters in Stormont, it is not surprising that the UTA Board rejected the findings outright. In a move that was to add fuel to the fire and, perhaps, show the Government's true intentions before they wished it, the Northern Ireland Minister with responsibility for transport, William Craig, commented less than tactfully that, in his opinion, railways would soon be as obsolete as the stagecoach!

As if the political situation was not enough to contend with, on 16 September 1961, having crossed the Atlantic ocean from the USA, Hurricane Debbie arrived off the north west coast of Ireland and proceeded to do considerable damage to the surrounding area and the Western Isles of Scotland. Lerwick Observatory recorded mean wind speeds of 60mph, gusting up 90mph.

On that Saturday afternoon, the hurricane struck with a ferocity not previously experienced. The roof of the footbridge at Strabane was blown down and wrecked, with the twisted remains lying across the main tracks. Willie John Carlin, signalman in the North Cabin, could see the ballast being lifted in the air by the strength of the wind. By 3.00pm, with conditions still deteriorating, Station Master Fred Tutty sent the platform porter out along the line to see just where the 9.15am train from Belfast might be. It transpired that it had only just reached Victoria Bridge, after a difficult journey down from Portadown, and it was now standing in the loop, sheltering alongside an earlier up arrival from Derry.

The guard on the up train joined the signalman at Victoria Bridge, Patsy McGarrigle, as did the guard of the 9.15am down from Belfast. There was no likelihood of its moving forward as there were trees across the line at Sion Mills. All traffic on the line was held at the various stations for several hours, as trains sheltered from the storm between the platform faces, until the winds abated. The lines were cleared a little after 6.00pm, and services then resumed, although trains for the rest of that day and, indeed, throughout the weekend were run on something of an ad hoc basis, as efforts were made to reposition stock to its correct location for the working timetable. Work went on for several weeks following the storm, to re-build and restore the damaged infrastructure.

The Benson Report and its Aftermath

Following on from the UTA's 1961 internal committee report, and with one eye on the modernisation and rationalisation that was being carried out across the water on British Railways, the Stormont Government decided that a detailed research into the future of railways in Northern Ireland would be the way forward. In 1962, John Andrews, the Minister of Commerce, commissioned an enquiry. He announced this in Stormont when replying to a debate on the second reading of the Transport (Finance) Bill, stating that the said enquiry would be carried out by Colonel Henry Benson, a member of Cooper Brothers, a London firm of Chartered Accountants.

Henry Alexander Benson was born in South Africa on 2 August 1909, later moving to London where, in 1926 at the age of 17, he was articled to LH Weatherley Esq, a partner in Cooper Brothers. He joined the City of London accountancy firm, which was quite appropriate as Benson's mother was the daughter of Francis Cooper, the third of the four Cooper brothers who founded the firm in 1854. The Second World War interrupted his employment with the firm and he served from 1940-45 with the Grenadier Guards. He became a member of the Special Operations Executive and served with distinction in the Middle East, eventually attaining the rank of Colonel.

After the War, he made his name in the steel and coal industries. He worked alongside Dr Richard Beeching in 1960 on the Stedeford Committee, with a brief of putting nationalised industries, including the British railway system, on a profitable footing – a portent perhaps, of things to come! Dr Beeching, who had been approached by the Northern Ireland Government for his professional opinion, had recommended Benson. Beeching was shortly to become infamous for his own report, *The Reshaping of British Railways*, resulting in wholesale closure of over 8,000 miles of track on the British Railways network.

On his recommendation, Henry Benson was appointed in 1962 with a remit to look into the financial future of the UTA railway system in Northern Ireland. Full use was made of the ex-Great Northern Directors' Saloon, No 150 (GNR 50), by Mr Benson, as he travelled around Ulster, making spot inspections of operating methods and steadily gathering information from which to draw his conclusions. Although a man of integrity, it has to be fairly said that Benson had not the experience, or mandate, to consider the railway system from any perspective other then that of pure profit and loss.

In April 1963, responsibility for transport in Northern Ireland was transferred to Brian Faulkner, Minster of Home Affairs. Some thought his overall remit was to steer through more closures.

If Stormont had only been concerned with cost saving and efficiency, many improvements could, and should, have been made by this point. UTA lorries could have been used to deliver goods to and from freight trains, instead of attempting to compete with and replace them. Then there was the negative practice of running buses in direct competition with passenger trains, often timed to depart just a few minutes in front of the scheduled train service, one such example being UTA bus service 72, from Portadown to Dungannon via Moy. Equally, no attempt was made to reduce overheads by automating any of the crossings; some saw so little use that they could have been closed without any inconvenience to the population.

The Benson Report, as it came to be known, was published on 17 July 1963, right on the heels of the Beeching Report in Britain. It recommended a much reduced system of a set of suburban lines radiating from Belfast. It was perhaps inevitable that the question of two railway lines serving Londonderry would come to the fore and it was decreed that one line would have to go, that serving Tyrone.

The NCC line to Londonderry was to be retained for around ten years until life expired, and the line to Dublin 'possibly' retained on political grounds. He qualified this further by stating, in a typical accountant's style of approach which made no account for social necessity or deprivation, that there was no requirement for two railway lines from Belfast to Londonderry. The fact that the two lines served widely differing population groups in the east and west of the province, with the terminal stations the only population centres served by both lines, was of no import to him.

Strong emphasis was placed, in the typical language style of an accountant, that the staff numbers could be reduced from 3000 to 1300 persons and, by transferring all freight operation to the Authority's road vehicles, goods traffic by rail could be discontinued. The UTA, by now barely bothering to conceal their anti-rail stance, were quick to seize upon the findings, holding it up as the way forward for the future of transport in the province.

Many years later, in his retirement, Henry Benson stated that, when commissioned in 1962 by the Northern Ireland Government to investigate and make his report, he clearly believed that he was expected to recommend complete withdrawal of all railway services in the province, on the grounds that there appeared to be no likelihood of making the railways economically viable. In the event, some 61% of Northern Ireland's railways were lost in the twenty years up leading up to the disbanding of the UTA in 1968.

A separate report, by Sir Robert Matthew (1906-1975), had been commissioned around this time, again by the Northern Ireland Government, with a view to introducing a modern, regional planning system for Northern Ireland. Sir Robert, a prominent Scottish architect and Professor of Architecture at the University of Edinburgh from 1953, was destined, in 1966, to take a leading role in the planning of Northern Ireland's only new university, at Coleraine.

Regarding trends and movement patterns in the population, the report identified certain towns that should be built up as centres of population and industry, and needing a reliable railway system to transport both materials and workers. It considered that the current network was already at its minimum size for operational effectiveness and should not be reduced. Interestingly, the towns listed included a number served by the Derry Road and adjacent Irish North Western line: Londonderry, Enniskillen, Omagh and Dungannon.

This advice, from a learned man who was being paid for his knowledge and advice, was effectively in complete contradiction to the contents of the Benson Report. However, the Government was more concerned (rather short-sightedly) with the immediate cost savings that could be made. They failed to take into account the boost to the local economy that would have resulted in the long term by investing in the railway infrastructure. This has been dramatically shown over the last 40 or so years in the NIR era.

Indeed, to this day, anyone who wishes to see how life was lived back in 1965 has only to visit the more remote parts of County Tyrone, pretty to enjoy but little changed since the railway closure.

As a direct result of the Benson report, the stage was now set for the final act in the life of the Derry Road. Though the decision to do away with it was fundamentally flawed, its swansong would continue for a few more years. Passenger traffic had inevitably fallen away somewhat towards the end of the 1950s with the increased use of the private motorcar, but the summer timetables continued to see a heavy influx of tourists. Goods traffic by comparison continued to hold up quite well and in 1962 there were still 15 sets of footplate staff plus two extra firemen based at Foyle Road.

Daily passenger services on the Derry Road around this time were:

- Four Belfast-Londonderry workings in each direction by BUT railcars, three with buffet cars
- One Belfast-Omagh round trip by either a BUT or AEC railcar.
- One Londonderry-Strabane round trip by railcar A (UTA 101).
- One Londonderry-Omagh round trip by railcar A (UTA 101).
- One Portadown-Omagh evening round trip by either BUT or AEC railcar.
- One Dungannon-Belfast trip using steam haulage.
- One Empty stock working Portadown-Dungannon to the balance above working.
- Two Portadown-Dungannon round trips by railcar, extended to Pomeroy in school terms.
- One Omagh-Belfast steam train (the relief boat train) with the stock worked down as Empty Carriages.

Railcar 101 went into the maintenance shops briefly during 1962. It was re-engined and whilst there, repainted, emerging in UTA dark green livery as it returned to its Londonderry base. The Portadown-Dungannon railcar workings were usually extended as far as Pomeroy during the school season. In the 1950s local journeys from either end of the line had often been covered by railcars C2 and C3, invariably towing a small luggage trailer, though they had gone by 1962.

Goods services each day were equally impressive and reflected the high volume of traffic still offering between Portadown and Londonderry:

- Two Belfast-Londonderry workings in each direction, 8.50pm and 9.50 pm ex-Belfast.

- One Portadown-Omagh afternoon working.
- One Portadown-Dungannon working in each direction, extended to Coalisland as required.
- One Londonderry-Strabane local trip working.
- Two Strabane-Sion Mills local trip workings.
- At least two Omagh General-Omagh Market Branch transfer workings.

To support the services listed above generally required the use of three railcar sets, one single-unit railcar and eight steam locomotives. This would, of course, be supplemented by additional passenger trains during the summer season, if there was heavy traffic, invariably hauled by S or S2 class steam locomotives. The Q class had held sway for many years on the Derry Road passenger services, being rated to take seven bogie coaches, and were generally regarded as being more tolerant of the many curves (vertical as well as horizontal) that abounded along the line. In more recent years the S class had become well established, putting in many fine performances time-wise and in the summer of 1963 the erstwhile GNR's blue livery made a reappearance on the Derry Road, when S class Nos 170, 171 and 174 were purchased from CIÉ, retaining their GNR numbers and livery. The diminutive, but very attractive, U class had even been seen on occasion between Portadown and Omagh.

Additionally, there were the summer-only Lough Derg pilgrimage trains, running since 1958 from Dublin

Right: UG class 0-6-0 No 47 stops at Annaghmore with a Portadown-Dungannon local.

EM Patterson

Left: Articulated railcar No 104 (GNR 'F') is a rare visitor to Dungannon on a service train. In 1966 she would become a more familiar sight, as she was used by the lifting contractor.

CP Friel collection

Below: S class 4-4-0 No 170 takes water at Pomeroy before setting off for Omagh on 23 July 1964. The first carriage is a J4 Tricompo-Brake dating from 1920.

EM Patterson

Opposite: An AEC railcar pauses at Trew and Moy on 10 August 1962. The shadows of the lattice girder footbridge give the impression that the 'wasp' warning stripes have been applied to the roof!

EM Patterson

Left: SG2 class 0-6-0 No 40 takes the tablet at Dungannon as it passes with a down goods.

Author's collection

Right: An unidentified S class crossing the Mourne at Sion Mills with the 3.00pm ex-Derry on 28 July 1964.

A Donaldson

Left: Two S class 4-4-0s at Londonderry shed on 10 August 1963, probably after hauling Apprentice Boy specials to the Maiden City. Blue No 174 *Carrantuohill* (with nameplates removed by CIÉ in 1963) flanks black No 60 *Slieve Donard*.

DA Idle

to Omagh, where pilgrims were transferred to waiting buses, since the erstwhile line to Enniskillen and Bundoran was now a sad and distant memory. A BUT set was normally used up to about 1961, with a Dundalk driver working through from that town, but from about 1961 the train was usually a CIÉ diesel locomotive-hauled train. On two known occasions a steam-hauled train was used on the Derry Road section to provide extra accommodation from Portadown.

The line had also seen incursions by the UG class 0-6-0s, occasionally on excursion work to Bangor or Orangemen's specials. Lastly, but by no means least, there had been increasing and regular use of both the Mogul 2-6-0 tender engines and Jeep 2-6-4 tanks which migrated from NCC metals, the latter type being much preferred by GNR crews. Both types were originally supplied by the LMS, with 15 Moguls arriving between 1933 and 1942 and 18 Jeeps between 1946 and 1950. The first four Moguls, and all the Jeeps, were built at Derby, most of the Moguls being assembled at the NCC York Road workshops, in Belfast, from parts sent over from Derby.

Apart from the Moguls, the freight services were generally the preserve of the SG2 class (power class C) or SG3 ('Big D') engines, with No 33 being a regular on the line. The wagon limit for down trains between Portadown and Omagh was 45 vehicles for power class D, reduced to 38 for Class C (Moguls and SG2), 33 for B class (UG) and just 27 for passenger engines (ie 4-4-0s).

With closure of the Derry Road now very likely, on 13 March 1964 Tyrone County Council's Planning and Highway's Committee issued an invitation to Mr William Craig (now the Minister of Commerce and Home Affairs) to attend a meeting and answer questions on the pending closure and the Governments proposed replacement road programme. The Council were desperate to avoid the impending closure and all the deprivation and hardship that would surely follow, and the County Council's own solicitor, Mr AF Colhoun, was instructed to prepare a case and brief counsel to

Above: WT class 2-6-4Ts were kept off the Derry Road until 1963. As older types went out of service, the shortage of engines led to a change of heart but lack of tender brakes still kept them off goods trains. No 53 heads away from Portadown with a local to Dungannon. *CP Friel collection*

Left: The powerful SG3 class 0-6-0s remained the first choice for goods work right to the end. No 33 drifts into Dungannon on 21 July 1964. *EM Patterson*

appear at the Transport Tribunal.

Omagh Urban District Council decided that it was in their best interests to make their own protest, and simultaneously instructed their solicitor to lodge an objection to the intended closure, instructing three of its members, Mr Norman Wilson, Mr James Hamilton and Mr Joseph Cunningham, to represent then at the Tribunal. Strabane Urban and Rural District Councils, in turn, joined them at the enquiry, represented in the form of solicitor, Willie Moodie. In Londonderry, political differences were put to one side, as the Unionist Mayor, Albert Anderson, and the Nationalist MP, Eddie MacAteer, joined forces in their protest to the Stormont Government.

As might be expected, the Minister was totally inflexible in his attitude and determination to close the railway line. This was not altogether unexpected, in view of his earlier, blinkered comments about railways being virtually as obsolete as the stagecoach, stating that he intended to replace them with a network of motorways, dual carriageways and trunk roads. In order to try and gain some support from his audience (which was not forthcoming), he also gave an absolute assurance to Strabane Council that a by pass would be in place within five years of the railway closing. By 1992 it had still not happened, though by then, if not much earlier, people had come realise just how they had been duped by the Stormont Government.

Tyrone County Council continued to have a number of intense and, on occasion, heated meetings throughout the year, with the Government at Stormont. However, it was evident from the start that there was no intention on the part of the Northern Ireland leaders of deviating in the slightest from their stated intention of ridding the province of all forms of rail transport in favour of yet more roads, Any pleas about the hardship that would inevitably follow such action and demonstrable proof of this, fell on deaf ears. The Government were simply not interested in the well-being of the people that elected them, preferring instead to push through their own road-based transport policy. In today's hopefully more enlightened world, such high-handed and reckless ministerial action, coupled with a 'Pontius Pilate' attitude when faced with their misdeeds, would surely be regarded as the transport equivalent of ethnic cleansing, with all the distaste that accompanies such events.

Exhausted, and at a complete impasse, Tyrone County Council then issued an open public announcement, stating that they had "lost all confidence in the Government's ability to deal with their objections in a way that was objective, fair, and in the circumstances, adequate". They followed this by an unparalleled move in history, taking the Government, effectively their employers, to the High Court twice in a last ditch attempt to stop the closure, to no avail however, as, on both occasions, the judge presiding over the judicial review, ruled against the application for a suspension of the closure, concluding that correct procedure had been followed by the UTA (they were much too wily to fall foul of that potential thorn in their corporate sides), though the judge made no comment of the likely social implications that would follow such a momentous and devastating decision, contenting himself on the first occasion by confirming the closure for 4 January 1965, though this was deferred as a result of the second High Court hearing, to 14 February

The Last Defiant Stand

So it was that the final glorious summer of 1964 came. Along with the rest of the erstwhile Great Northern System, the Derry Road was operated much as it always had been. Bright summer days, complemented by pale blue skies, almost devoid of fluffy white cumulous clouds, framed the picture as a succession of trains, many of them steam-hauled extras, made their way from Portadown to Londonderry, taking a little over three hours for the full journey from Belfast, as was the norm.

On 8 July, the Railway Manager's Operating Office in Belfast issued a working notice, running to 28 pages, covering the popular industrial holiday period from Saturday 1 August to Friday 14 August. This superseded any weekly train working circular for this period. Alterations and extra services of direct relevance to the Derry Road were listed on no fewer than 16 pages. They were wide and varied, including such interesting gems as:

Saturday 1st – Accommodation reserved on 5.08 pm train from Omagh to Belfast (the Relief Boat Train)for

The north end of Omagh on 28 July 1964. Mogul No 99 has just arrived with the 11.30am empty carriages from Belfast (see also page 74).

EM Patterson

four officers and 20 cadets from Omagh, plus two officers and 20 cadets from Dungannon.

Wednesday 5th – Goods services 6.05 am and 6.10 pm to Sion Mills plus return workings at 7.18 am and 6.34 pm, both cancelled.

Saturday 8th – Derry to Belfast 4.20 pm service will call at Sion Mills to set down Boys Brigade party of 18 persons.

Wednesday 12th – Additional services operating between Belfast and Londonderry (the full list was shown in the publication). "Beragh and Pomeroy signalmen to watch running of 8.05 pm goods (altered) and 8.50 pm goods and if necessary give preference to 8.50 pm at Beragh."

Wednesday 12 August 1964

The annual Apprentice Boys demonstration took place in Londonderry on Wednesday 12 August. A Protestant Society founded in 1814 to commemorate the 105 day siege in 1689, it draws in many thousands of people each year from across the province and beyond, to see and join in the colourful spectacle.

Many heavily loaded steam specials were run that day from Belfast to the maiden city. As always, the trains were operated in an efficient and competent manner throughout. First away from Great Victoria Street, was W class No 97 *Earl of Ulster* with the 6.00am departure. Close behind this, another train left at 6.20am, hauled by sister engine No 91 *The Bush*. These trains were followed by WT class 2-6-4T No 55 with yet more participants, intent on spending the day in Derry.

Later that morning, another Jeep, No 53, worked an additional Apprentice Boys special up from Portadown to join several other trains now arrived and berthed in the sidings at Foyle Road. These trains were all in the dark green livery of the UTA, though they largely comprised ex-GNR wooden bodied coaches, with their distinctive beading on the external panels. These elderly vehicles had been kept beyond their normal life for just such occasions, when extra sets were needed at short notice to cope with the traffic offered.

Despite the intensity of movement and organisation required by railway staff to handle these extra workings in the limited space available at the Londonderry terminus, it was still very much business as usual for southbound services. The first ex-GNR steam working away was the 10.15am to Omagh and Belfast, with S class No 60 *Slieve Donard* in charge. Later in the day, one of the regular service workings to Portadown used Jeep No 53, hastily commandeered after arrival with the morning special from that town (see photograph on p27).

Amongst the many engines on shed at Derry that evening, S class 4-4-0 No 171 *Slieve Gullion* and SG3 class 0-6-0 No 35 could be seen taking some well earned rest as they were serviced for their next turn of duty, some of which were the return Apprentice Boys specials.

This last, 'Indian Summer' of steam on the Derry Road produced many regular turns of duty on the line, with some recorded examples shown in the table overleaf. Ex NCC Moguls shedded at Portadown or Adelaide now handled the majority of the goods workings on the Derry Road, when not otherwise engaged on passenger and goods turns between Belfast and Dundalk. The usual engines were 91, 94, 97, 99 and 104. By now, the Moguls

LOCOMOTIVE	LOCATION	TRAIN	DATE
SG2 class No 38	Pomeroy	Down Freight	23 June
SG3 class No 35	Dungannon	Down Freight	23 June
SG2 class No 40	Dungannon	Down Freight	3 July
CIÉ 141 class No B159	Carrickmore	Down Passenger	13 July
S class No 170 ***Errigal***	Dungannon	Down Passenger	25 July
SG3 class No 33	Dungannon	Down Freight	25 July
W class No 99 ***King George VI***	Pomeroy	Down Passenger	28 July
W class No 99 ***King George VI***	Dungannon	Down Freight	8 August
SG2 class No 40	Mountjoy	Down Passenger	8 August
S class No 62 ***Slieve Donard***	Sion Mills	Down Passenger	8 August
CIÉ 141 class No B153	Pomeroy	Up Passenger	14 August
U class No 67 ***Louth***	Dungannon	Up Empty Carriages	19 August
WT class No 54	Dungannon	Up Passenger	19 August
SG2 class No 40	Omagh	Down Freight	22 August
UG class No 48	Trew & Moy	Down Passenger	22 August
S class No 174 ***Carrantuohill***	Dungannon	Down Passenger	28 August
WT class No 57	Omagh	Up Passenger	31 August
S class No 174 ***Carrantuohill***	Strabane	Up Passenger	1 September
S class No 171 ***Slieve Gullion***	Omagh	Down Passenger	5 September

and Jeeps were subject to an overall 30mph restriction along the Derry Road, with several local limits in force:

- 25mph from milepost 40½ to Omagh
- 20mph from mileposts 101-103 (Victoria Bridge to Sion Mills), 103½-109¼ (Sion Mills to Porthall) and 112½-113 (between Porthall and St Johnston)

Down goods trains were also limited to 5mph over the Camowen River Bridge, No 96, at the foot of a steep bank on the Beragh-Omagh section. The switchback section from Sixmilecross was well known for broken couplings and divided trains.

Railcars were also seen in abundance, the AEC units usually to be found on local Portadown-Dungannon workings, whilst their BUT cousins maintained the long journeys to Londonderry, car No 135 having a regular turn. Observations included CIÉ diesel locomotive B159, seen on Carrickmore Bank on 13 July with the Lough Derg pilgrimage train. As explained earlier, these trains worked through from Dublin to

A five or six-car AEC meets an unusually short three-car BUT at Pomeroy on Sunday 18 March 1962. In the background two UTA PS1 single deckers enjoy a weekend break from their usual school runs.

J Langford

Omagh, where buses waited to take the pilgrims forward. Prior to September 1957, the train had gone by Clones and Enniskillen, terminating at Bundoran.

The sighting of *Slieve Gullion* on 5 September, coincided with the appearance of the last scheduled steam hauled working to Londonderry. The introduction of the winter timetable signalled the end of such trains, as the much reduced requirements could be easily handled by diesel railcars.

The weather was kind to the farmers too and many a smallholder stopped in his labours to rest for a moment in the heat of the noonday sun, leaning on a long-handled pitchfork as he watched the progress of a distant train across the fields. The sheaves of oats, stacked upright against each other and looking like little golden tents, would be there again next year; the railway line would not!

Surprisingly, despite the line having a death sentence hanging over it, buildings and structures along the entire stretch from Portadown to Londonderry had been repainted. This was not as much at variance with the closure policy as might at first be thought. The Government was exercising a well known underhand tactic in that they could show a high, but false, annual maintenance return for keeping the line open. This was a devious practice by those who knew that what they were doing. It was morally indefensible, knowing in their hearts that they had no support from the public for the course that they were taking. In truth, it was simply closure by stealth.

The repainting produced some colourful results; station name boards became bright yellow with black lettering and on many buildings a version of the old GNR(I) Eastern District green and cream spread right along the line, replacing the weather-beaten brown of the old Western District, renowned for its longevity. There were exceptions to the rule, with the wooden station buildings at Victoria Bridge station as a prime example. Finished in a pleasing shade of white, and decked out with red window frames, the red colour also being applied to the window frames on the green and white signal box. In any event, the line appeared to be going out in relatively pristine condition with its head held high, though the poignancy of freshly painted and clean stations would only produce sadness and a feeling of wretchedness in the eyes of those who knew what these signs heralded.

At the end of the summer season, the traditional, reduced autumn timetable was put into effect. The days shortened and the leaves started to fall. The cold winds began to blow, bringing dark skies and rain clouds in from the west, matching the mood of despair felt along the course of the railway. Most people believed that the line had now seen its last summer of operation and in the minds of railwaymen, as they went about their daily routines, the sword of Damocles was never far away. The uncertainty about the future sapped the morale of even the most optimistic.

The mood lifted briefly as December approached; extra train services were laid on, many of them steam worked, as people went home to their families for Christmas, back to the farms and villages where they grew up and once lived. A goodly number arrived in Belfast by overnight boats from England and, in some

Platform staff unloading mails at the south end of Omagh on 9 August 1962. The train, out of shot to the right, is the 8.25am from Belfast. Nelson Hall leans out of the cab of No 38, the resident engine at Omagh that day. It would have worked up on a goods from Portadown overnight and will return in the evening. *EM Patterson*

cases, from as far afield as the USA. This would be the last time they would board the 8.25am train from Great Victoria Street station in Belfast. Those travelling on to smaller stations between Dungannon and Omagh would have a longer journey, changing at Portadown or Dungannon into a local service, that would follow the main train, calling at all the village stations on its way. The last few days before the break saw increasing traffic and on Christmas Eve, Thursday 24 December, the casual observer would have been hard put to realise that anything was amiss.

The larger stations of Omagh and Dungannon were hives of activity, with passengers constantly arriving and spilling out of trains, the station lights reflecting in the puddles of water, and the damp December air carrying the steam down as it leaked from the heating pipes between the coaches and swirled along the platforms. At the smaller country stations, such as Pomeroy and Sixmilecross, the scenes were much the same, and little knots of people, heavy coats on to protect them from the biting wind, were huddled together on the platform, to await the arrival of a son or daughter, home from the city, on the evening train.

A distant whistle would announce the imminent arrival, with smiling faces and waving arms at the lowered carriage door window, as the train drew to a stop. Amidst all the greetings and embraces on the platform, suitcases would be passed out of the carriage, to be carried by willing hands, with everyone making their way out to the waiting vehicle, usually an elderly taxi, as the train left the station and disappeared into the gloom, as it headed up the valley to the next village.

Last Days and the Final Act

Christmas 1964 came and went. For two days there was no railway service and peace reigned, then the winter service restarted. A strange thing happened then, as the uncertainty of the previous months suddenly began to crystallise into a strong and quite defiant mood, slowly at first, and then spreading like a bush fire, through the rural hinterland of Tyrone and Londonderry, as the population determined to stand by their railway and support their lifeline in true style, as it neared the probable end of its days, ensuring that it looked and operated at its best. This, almost tangible, feeling had already permeated through the ranks of railwaymen, many of whom were local men, intent on discharging their daily duties to the surrounding community for as long as they were needed, in a disciplined and professional manner that they could be proud of. They would not allow it to prematurely wither or look untidy if they could help it.

The year turned and the second High Court action took place. Though it was to delay the full closure of passenger services for a few precious weeks, in a continuation of official UTA policy, all remaining goods services on the remnant of the Cookstown branch, still operating to Coalisland, were withdrawn and that line closed with effect from 4 January 1965. The Goraghwood to Warrenpoint line closed to all traffic on the same day.

Despite the mountain of overwhelming evidence in their favour, the decision had gone against the protestors and those who had tried so hard to make those in authority see common sense and the error of their ways. So it came about that, despite an entrenched and bitterly fought battle right to the end, Sunday 14 February 1965 saw the closure of the entire Derry Road from Portadown to Londonderry, at one stroke leaving County Tyrone without any form of rail transport after an unbroken run of 118 years. Fermanagh had already lost theirs back in 1957.

The final weekend's UTA workings were operated by ex-Great Northern men in the true spirit of their previous employer. Strong in their beliefs, the timetable was operated faultlessly, with the crews determined to go out in style – if they could not stop the closure, they could at least show what they stood for and believed in. On Saturday 13th, a cold bright day, steam reigned relatively supreme, with S class locos 170 *Errigal* and 171 *Slieve Gullion* both performing magnificently with the booked services, and use being made of Pomeroy water tank, for what was probably the last time by a service train.

They were supported during the day on passenger workings by ex-NCC W class 2-6-0 No 97, *Earl of Ulster*, the last working Mogul. This engine would, in turn, succumb to withdrawal on 1 December that year. Later that day, No 97 worked a cement special back out of Londonderry and right down the line back to Belfast; it had been sent to Foyle Road in error, with the cement wagons actually meant for the NCC Waterside station on

Right: On the last working Saturday on the Derry Road, 13 February 1965, S class 4-4-0s Nos 170 and 171 did the honours and made the last use of the Pomeroy water tank by service trains. No 170 does just that, six months earlier, on 23 July 1964.

EM Patterson

Below: On the last working Saturday UG No 49 and S class No 60 were busy on local workings at the Dungannon end of the line. Eighteen months earlier, on 31 August 1963, No 60 arrives at Dungannon with the 12.55 from Derry and crosses U class No 67 on the 2.35pm from Portadown.

JD FitzGerald

the other side of the Foyle River. During the afternoon, UG Class No 49 (GN 149) and S Class No 60 *Slieve Donard* (GN 172) were also seen on local workings at the Dungannon end of the line, the three S Class locomotives providing a brilliant swansong for the line and, as events would prove all too soon, for themselves.

On this occasion, the safety rules were relaxed, allowing enthusiasts to obtain many photographic vantage points normally barred to them, at places like Dungannon and Omagh. Strabane even went to the point of organising light engine run-pasts for photographers, set against a back drop of the surviving County Donegal stock, still awaiting the promised rescue by Dr Cox in America. That rescue, happily, has eventually been fulfilled piecemeal by local enthusiast groups.

BBC Television was out in force and recorded many interviews, including one with Dungannon Stationmaster, Jimmy Swarbrigg and several at Omagh, including the Stationmaster, Billy Ross, foreman Billy Kerr and driver Jack Milne. The last evening through working duty from Londonderry to Belfast, was put into the capable hands of 170 *Errigal* and at Strabane she was given a magnificent send-off by the crowds of people thronging the platform. The evening sun glinted on the polished sky-blue paintwork of the loco, as she departed with her train of ex-Great Northern coaches, now in the dark green livery of the UTA.

The train passed over the Lifford Road crossing gates under a darkening red westerly sky, as the lowering sun brought a golden glow to the landscape, and then it slowly rumbled across the Mourne river bridge, as she started her final run, through the wild Tyrone countryside. At Omagh South Cabin, signalman Billy Maguire saw the train safely away, as he handed out the single line tablet to the train crew, watching with sadness as the last steam-hauled passenger train disappeared into the gathering gloom. All along the line, people stood watching, in little groups, as *Errigal* swept through the stations and wayside halts with her train, the driver's hand constantly on the whistle chain, in a final salute and acknowledgement to their loyalty. All too soon, Portadown was reached, and the train swung off the Derry Road for the last time.

Sunday's operations were covered, as usual, by two BUT railcar sets. In a touch of irony that was not lost on objectors to the closure, the engines on the 10.00 am departure from Belfast, Great Victoria Street, refused to start up! There were brief hopes of a steam substitution but the railcars won. A considerable number of enthusiasts made round trips during the day but by the evening the public were turning out in force, in villages and towns all along the line. The 6.30 pm departure from Londonderry was a good example of this; the train departed with 100 souls, rising to 340 at Omagh and 375 by the time Dungannon was reached.

Many of the passengers were local people travelling just one or two stops along the line for sentimental reasons, returning on the last train of the day. The atmosphere at the stations was generally good-natured but, along with the prevailing sadness, there was an underlying and quite intense bitterness toward the Government of the day and the way it had betrayed them by taking away their lifeline, without a thought for the rural economy or hardship to the population, which would inevitably follow the closure.

The very last service train, the 8.05 pm from Belfast, comprised BUT railcar set 123-573-124-594-134 and two vans, the make up being typical of a Derry Road train, with all the rolling stock appropriately of GNR origin. Of the train composition itself, there were three power cars, 123 and 124 were half cab units and 134 a full cab. The intermediate coaches were 573, an F16 side corridor Composite and 594, an L14 Brake/Second open, both ex-steam hauled stock and fitted out for working with BUT sets on January 1958 and June 1958 respectively. The train worked out as far as Portadown without any problems being encountered but, once there, began to lose time, the loss inevitably increasing as it called at each station on the long journey to Londonderry.

It left Portadown just after 9.08 pm, 14½ minutes late, having been delayed by the up train, itself already 12 minutes behind time – evidently the good people of Tyrone and Londonderry were not going to let their railway disappear that easily. More time was lost at every station on the journey as large crowds came to see the trains for the last time and pay their respects, with the strains of 'Auld Lang Syne' heard at several platforms along the length of the line.

As the train pulled into Omagh a band was produced to greet it and further down the line at Strabane station, staff organised an audible reception with suitably placed detonators on the track plus firecrackers and an accordion band on the platform. Although the Royal Ulster Constabulary were in evidence, their duties were not onerous, as the crowds were not intending any vandalism and the only untoward incident recorded was a cord pull as the train approached Derry, arriving some 29½ minutes beyond the official arrival time of 11.16 pm. The two vans were detached and worked into a siding, earning the somewhat dubious honour of being the last non-passenger vehicles to arrive at the station, on a scheduled service.

A short while later, after the last of the passengers had vacated the now deserted platforms and disappeared into the gloom that hung about Londonderry that night, the railcar set slipped quietly out of Foyle Road station, a little after midnight, with the full width cab of BUT unit 134 now appropriately leading the train, as is started on the return journey, empty and unlit, apart from the head and tail lamps. The journey was necessary to clear the line and return both stock and crew to Belfast. As it passed through each station, the lights were put out, signal boxes closed down and the station buildings locked for the last time. At Omagh, where the signalman was still manning the South Cabin signal box, the train stopped briefly for a minute as the crew exchanged sad greetings and said their last farewells to the station staff, before heading out once more across the black Tyrone countryside … and into history.

Post Closure Requiem

The Derry Road had gone down fighting. The 100½-mile journey from Belfast (Great Victoria Street) to Londonderry (Foyle Road) was no more. In the tradition of railwaymen down through the ages, the service had been maintained professionally, right to the very end, and with a dedication that would be hard to match these days. The people of Londonderry, Tyrone and Armagh would not forget the railway line that had served them faithfully for close on 90 years; neither would they forget or forgive a Government that had betrayed them so savagely, and sacrificed the needs of those people across three counties, in the name of so-called progress and modernity.

In an act of thoughtfulness, unlikely to have been that of the UTA, someone thankfully remembered the memorial to those fallen in the First World War and erected by the GNR on the concourse wall of Foyle Road station at Londonderry. It was removed and put into safe storage, parts of it being used ten years later to restore a similar memorial at Great Victoria Street station, damaged in a senseless and stupid bombing act by the IRA in the name of a free Ireland!

Even though the goods service had been officially withdrawn on Sunday 4 January, it still proved necessary to work a number of trips, following the closure, to collect and clear the accumulated rolling stock and motive power, culminating in a final special train on Wednesday 17 February, to collect the remaining wagons stranded along the line. The volume of traffic still offering right up to the end of services had been so great that it was impossible to clear all the goods wagons by the closure date. This, if ever it was needed, was further damning evidence of the Government's duplicity in the whole affair. Locally, people are adamant to this day that a further train passed through Pomeroy on Friday 5 March, its purpose and content remain uncertain.

After the final special had left on Wednesday 17 February, the land fell strangely silent. The empty signal boxes remained – guardians of the Derry Road – once active 24 hours a day and testimony to the traffic that was moved, they now waited along the line like silent, impassive sentinels, for a train that would no longer come. Reading like a roll of honour, they were –

Portadown Junction, Annaghmore, Verner's Bridge, Trew & Moy, Dungannon, Dungannon Junction, Donaghmore, Pomeroy, Carrickmore, Beragh, Omagh South, Omagh North, Newtownstewart, Victoria Bridge, Strabane South, Strabane North, St Johnston, Londonderry South, Londonderry North.

Some of these boxes had already succumbed earlier at the closure of the station they served, but occasionally the box remained, glassless windows staring mutely back at the track. Portadown Junction box would survive a while longer on (much reduced) mainline duties.

On Monday 15 February, the 'new order' was put into effect. At the junction, Portadown shed was closed and silent, still holding the surviving steam engines. Though secure for the time being, with their fires out and boilers cold, they faced a bleak future. Scheduled goods trains were now virtually extinct.

During March, April, May and July 1965, locomotive crews were regularly sent to Portadown, where the remaining steam engines were lit up and one by one, brought up to Adelaide shed. Many of these stalwarts had once worked regularly on the Derry Road. Now, their work done, they were forgotten and cast aside by a Government that no longer cared; some would say it ceased caring back in 1957. Movements were –

- UG 0-6-0 No 48 (ex GN 146) – 2 March
- SG3 0-6-0 No 33 (ex GN 20) – ?? April
- S 4-4-0 170 *Errigal* – 9 April
- S 4-4-0 No 60 *Slieve Donard* (ex GN 172) – 17 April
- S 4-4-0 No 174 *Carrantuohill* – 21 April
- SG3 0-6-0 No 35 (ex GN 41) – 30 April

As mentioned earlier, S Class engines 170, 171 and 174 had originally been bequeathed to CIÉ at the dissolution of the GNRB in 1958, only to be purchased back by the UTA in June 1963, and no change of running number was made by either owner.

The procession east included many old friends such as the well-known and popular goods Class SG3 0-6-0 No 33 (ex-GN 20), making the journey north in April, for scrapping at the end of that month. Another locomotive often seen on Portadown–Dungannon local trains was UG Class No 48 (ex-GN 146). She left Portadown shed for Adelaide on 2 March, having secured a brief reprieve for use on excursion traffic. That summer was pleasantly spent working day excursions over the Belfast Central Railway and out to Bangor, via the notorious 'shaky bridge' over the River Lagan, a duty she shared with sister UG No 49 (ex-GN 149), this engine leaving Portadown on 8 April. After final withdrawn in June 1967, No 48 was cut up in 1968, No 49 having been withdrawn in January 1967 and cut up the following year.

Small reminders would still surface from time to time, pricking the conscience of those in power. On 17 April, S Class No 60 (ex-GN 172) *Slieve Donard*, by now in a

pitiful state of repair and only just able to move under her own power, was steamed at Portadown and slowly made her way east, arriving at Adelaide shed for the last time, where she was condemned and scrapped. Chalked on the engine was the inscription "Derry's gates will close for ever". This had been applied at Londonderry on closure day and the pathos was not lost on the crews present at the shed! They hadn't the heart to remove it.

Some locomotives had already made it to the slightly safer confines of Adelaide shed by the closure date of the Derry Road, including WT Class 2-6-4T No 57 and S Class No 171 *Slieve Gullion*, the latter a determined survivor, withdrawn in December of 1965 and subsequently preserved by the RPSI. For others already there, Adelaide shed was no guarantee of security, and the scrapping continued apace.

It had been intended that U Class No 66 would join the two UG engines working the Bangor traffic (she had been retubed at Portadown shed in late 1964 with this intention), but sadly this never came to fruition. WT Class No 54 was already in the NCC York Road works for the fitting of a new firebox in February 1965, and returned to the GN tracks for a year before heading back to the NCC, from where it was withdrawn in 1967 following discovery of a major fault in the new firebox.

It was the best part of a year before the first lifting trains arrived on the scene with serious intent. Were the UTA uncertain of their legal footing over the closure, or simply hedging their bets, in case they were forced into a subsequent act of reinstatement? Perhaps the line simply refused to die; either way, it poses an interesting question!

In the late autumn of 1965, any lingering doubt about the future was dispelled, when a sign that boded evil, duly appeared on the daily roster board at Adelaide shed indicating the crew rostered to work 'Ballast Adelaide–Strabane'. This portentous announcement heralded the start of track lifting activities.

The lifting train was composed of essentially NCC items – WT Class 2-6-4T 'Jeep' locomotive No 56 (facing Portadown), together with a rake of flat wagons, tailed by ex-NCC 25 ton brake van No 33 (UTA 2033). This performed the last rites, starting from Londonderry, the van being fitted with a winch and metal balcony at one end, to assist in loading sleepers and removing rails. The brake van proved to be a determined survivor, and is currently residing on the preserved Downpatrick & County Down Railway, in largely 1960s condition.

The train was busy in the Strabane area early in 1966 and, as work progressed southwards, track over the River Mourne bridge was lifted, leaving much of track in the station area isolated and still in situ, to be removed locally at a later date. The tall, inner home bracket signal, covering the southern approach, remained, still set at danger, and protecting the now trackless bridge. Lifted rails were worked south to a convenient storage yard, accessible by road, Beragh station yard being used as a consolidation point and becoming quite busy for a time. The water tank at Pomeroy was still functioning, and the lifting train locomotive continued to make use of the facility until removal of the rails prevented this.

On 28 July, No 56 ran away with a loaded train of rails and sleepers while coming down Pomeroy bank and came through Pomeroy station at speed. It collided with some wagons before leaving the road to plunge down an embankment. As No 56 was a tank engine, the driver had only the brake van and driving wheel brakes to hold her and the absence of tender brakes was a factor in the

Opposite top: "Derry's gates will close forever." No 60 *Slieve Donard*, now shorn of its nameplates, lies outside Portadown shed in April 1965, never to be steamed again.

CP Friel collection

Right: Rails from the Londonderry-Strabane section are on the lifting train at Strabane in early 1966.

CP Friel collection

Left: A view of the lifting train at Strabane from Platform 1. County Donegal stock still lies in the background.

CP Friel collection

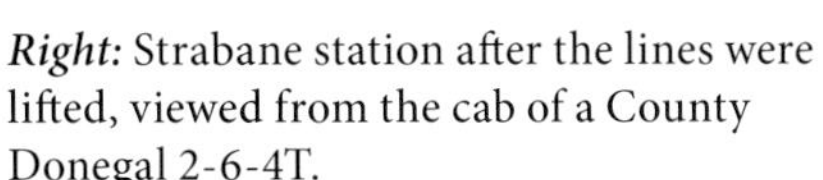

Right: Strabane station after the lines were lifted, viewed from the cab of a County Donegal 2-6-4T.

Author

Left: Omagh about 1968 showing the empty trackbed and derelict buildings.

Author

Right: A redundant sign, still displayed above the down platform at Omagh after the lines were lifted, is a poignant reminder of happier times.

Author

Left: WT class 2-6-4T No 54 on the lifting train at Strabane in 1966.

CP Friel collection

Opposite: The Blackwater, just west of Vernersbridge, marked the boundary between Counties Armagh and Tyrone. S2 class 4-4-0 No 62 *Lugnaquilla* crosses the viaduct about 1964. The second coach is a steel-panelled F16 Composite.

A Donaldson

run away. The front pony truck and smokebox were considerably damaged but later repaired at York Road, so that No 56 enjoyed three more year's service. The crew had a lucky escape from serious injury, whilst a third member of the lifting crew, who was on the footplate, had managed to jump off onto the platform as the train raced through.

With Nos 54 and 55 fully engaged in working specials on the main line to Dublin that summer, there were no spare 'Jeeps' available at Adelaide shed, and 51 was hastily requisitioned from York Road to take her place.

In the autumn, WT Class No 55 became a regular performer on the lifting trains and was another survivor, soldiering on until 23 October 1970. Based at Adelaide during 1965-66, she eventually returned to the NCC in November 1966, after her spell on the Derry Road was completed, along with the damaged No 56. In her twilight years of operation, she and her remaining sister engines saw considerable work on the ex-NCC Larne line, working the spoil trains out of the Magheramorne quarry sidings, in connection with reclaimed land on the shores of Belfast Lough, for the M2 motorway contract. These often involved 20-wagon, 900-ton loads, and thus gained the distinction of hauling the last regular steam-hauled freight trains anywhere in the British Isles on 2 May 1970 – long after such trains had finished on British Rail.

No 55 was also to gain brief notoriety in the Spring of 1965, when the UTA, in their wisdom, made their 'outstanding' contribution to the technical development of the steam locomotive. They attached a small ex-NCC 2500-gallon tender behind No 55, in an effort to ensure it could work trains to Dublin without having to take on water en route. Additional coal also needed to be carried, as stocks were not held at Amiens Street shed after the demise of steam in November 1962 and, in any case, there was no longer a crane.

Needless to say, it looked appalling, and did not work particularly well, suffering from persistent air locks in the maze of connecting pipe work. There was also the problem of moving coal forward from the tender on arrival at Dublin. The experiment was soon abandoned. Instead, use was made of the existing water columns en route and cribs were fitted to the bunker top, enabling more coal to be carried for the return journey.

Over the years, a rumour has persisted regarding the immediate post-closure period to the effect that VS Class 4-4-0 No 207 *Boyne* ventured up the Derry Road. A survivor until withdrawal in December 1965, this was another repatriation from CIÉ in June 1963. It is true that she did proceed onto the Derry Road, at low speed, propelling a permanent way train to recover materials, but it only went as far as Bridge 2, at Corcrain, still within the Portadown town boundary.

Two further lifting trains were also created by the lifting contractor, McGurk. Railcar 104 (GNR 'F'), a lightweight articulated triple unit, powered by two 102 hp Gardner diesel engines in the central section and a product of the Great Northern from 1938, was sold to McGurk and used on the Derry Road, mainly to transfer workers to the lifting site. McGurk subsequently used 104 and 101 (below) in the south of Ireland to lift the West Cork lines and Clonmel–Thurles, where it was noted at Laffansbridge, complete with broken windows, in July 1970, towing a bogie flat wagon (possibly an ex-coach chassis), and loaded with recovered rails, sleepers and chairs. It was scrapped at Clonmel, by

Left: Beragh was used as a storage point for recovered track materials during the lifting. Railcar 101 is on the down track, beside the yard, in this view. The adjacent wagons are on the up line.
Author's collection

Below: Railcar 101 at Annaghmore late in 1966. The far end had been damaged in a collision at Derry and a winch now operated from the damaged end.
Author's collection

then virtually worked to death.

The other 'train' was single-unit railcar 101 (ex-GNR 'A') which could often be seen at Beragh, where the station yard was used as a stockpiling point for recovered materials, prior to them being taken away by road.

Railcar 101 had spent its twilight years on local services along the length of the Derry Road, and had been re-engined and painted in UTA green in 1961. The intention had been that this vehicle should be preserved upon final withdrawal and presented to the Belfast Transport Museum but it was involved in a shunting accident at Londonderry in 1963, and suffered severe bodywork damage.

It was then withdrawn and sold to McGurk, who took it south to the CIÉ network, where it was used during the lifting of the Clonsilla Junction to Navan line. He removed the bodywork from the damaged end and fitted lifting gear and winchs on the bare chassis. It returned to the Derry Road, as described above, in 1966.

Sadly, no attempt was made afterwards to preserve either railcar for posterity, or indeed any of the important artefacts to be found at the abandoned stations. Such was the Government's haste to wash their hands of anything connected with railways, they were simply left to the ravages of weather and vandalism until demolition became the only option left.

EPILOGUE

It is a somewhat sobering thought that if any Government, irrespective of political persuasion, tried to close an important railway today, using similar tactics, they would be unlikely to get away with it. There are regulations in place to stop such desecration of strategic resources and the public as a whole are considerably more streetwise. In recent years, the tide at last appears to be turning, with successive Governments finally realising the error of their predecessors' ways and recognising the need for investment and retention in what is left of the railway system in Ireland as a whole. Tyrone, and indeed County Fermanagh, both now completely devoid of any railway lines, have felt the loss of a good transport and communication network for many years, with the whole area badly in need of revitalisation and the input of considerable finance to redress the years of static investment by successive administrations.

When Henry Benson passed away on 5 March 1995 (He had been made a life peer in 1981), there was, within weeks of his demise, renewed activity in the Council chambers of both Dungannon and Strabane, for a comprehensive feasibility study to be undertaken with regard to re-opening the Derry Road. Councillors are, notwithstanding the passing of the years, quite rightly determined that this most important issue shall not go away. The fundamental mistake of closing the railway line will continue to be debated and haunt the Council meetings until a resolution is agreed.

With the current availability of regeneration funding from the European Union, and the move towards a more integrated public transport system, coupled with an urgent need to reduce greenhouse gases and their effects worldwide, there is now, more than ever, a substantial case for re-opening the Derry Road at the southern end as far as Dungannon at the very least. Looking to the north, if Omagh were reconnected to Londonderry, it would make an ideal railhead for serving Enniskillen and the hinterland of County Fermanagh.

After the closure in February 1965, the UTA continued to operate what was left of the Great Northern system, together with the rest of the lines in Northern Ireland in their care, on a fairly ad hoc basis, with little evident enthusiasm for the task in hand. This situation was to continue until 1968 when Northern Ireland Railways (NIR) was created to take over the remaining lines of the UTA. A drastic and much-needed rolling programme to replace motive power and stock was implemented, and there was a willingness to try and right some of the wrongs of previous years. (Although there was an attempt by the Conservative Government in the mid-1990s to sell the province's railway network off to a private buyer).

This new and welcome approach has been sustained. As recently as 2001, Translink (which has run NIR and Ulsterbus since 1997), showed a positive response to the Northern Ireland Assembly Regional Development Committee report on the future of railways in the province, in which NIR were awarded £20 million for the year to cover new trains and track improvements, on the basis of which investment continues to made on a yearly basis. Translink Managing Director, Ted Hesketh stated "Railways must play a central role for the future, modern, efficient transport system for Northern Ireland".

A pamphlet was also published, outlining their vision for the future of rail services, including proposals to restore a number of closed lines. Of relevance here, is the suggestion that the re-laying of the railway from Portadown "through Dungannon, Omagh and Strabane" to Londonderry was both desirable and viable, as was a connecting line to Enniskillen. This could, in time, form the basis of an improved re-connection with the railway network in the south of Ireland, thus drawing more communities into the public transport arena.

In 2004, a Strategic Rail Review was conducted, essentially an independent review of rail services in the province, to consider economic status and viability, thereby establishing funding requests. The report concluded that lesser-used lines were viable as part of the total operation and should be retained and supported with consistent and continuous investment, rather than with occasional 'knee-jerk' reactions of money injections.

This mood of positive thinking is echoed at the highest level, with the Group Chief Executive of Translink and the Northern Ireland Transport Holding Co (the property-owning element of Translink), Catherine Mason, echoing similar sentiments during a visit to the Railway Preservation Society of Ireland's (RPSI) depot at Whitehead on 30 July 2007. During this she outlined her determination to put Northern Ireland back on the railway map and re-introduce as many (closed) services as she could, noting that the Department for Regional Development had made a major investment in the railway network in recent years. She also praised the way in which the RPSI had nurtured Ireland's railway heritage, noting the scope for increased steam operation and co-operation within the province. She pleasantly surprised those present by revealing her own membership of a preserved railway, the Great Central Railway at Loughborough!

The mood has not been idle across the border either, with Donegal County Council funding a €10,000 survey in 2008, to look at the remaining disused railway lines in and around Letterkenny, Lifford and Londonderry, with a view to assessing the viability of re-establishing rail services. Of interest here are both the ex-GNR and CDRJC lines from Londonderry to Strabane. The report sought to identify trackbeds that remained intact, and those that have been lost to development over the previous 40 years or so. It is perhaps unfortunate the neither the IRRS nor the County Donegal Railway Restoration Limited were consulted, as they could have almost certainly provided this information quickly and quite accurately, at a fraction of the cost to the tax payer.

In June 2008, Brian Guckian, an independent transport researcher from Dublin presented a £460 million proposal to Translink, called the Northern Ireland Network Enhancement. The document includes plans for the reopening of the Derry Road throughout from Portadown to Londonderry plus linking lines into Armagh and Enniskillen. This would transform and revitalise the north and west areas, putting both Tyrone and Fermanagh back on the railway map. Economic and cross-border development would also be given a much-needed boost, with travel between county Donegal and Dublin achievable in a little over three hours.

In recent years, there have been substantial increases in passenger use across the system, stimulated no doubt by the introduction of modern state of the art three-coach 3000-class diesel railcars from CAF in Spain, coupled with vastly improved timekeeping and cleanliness overall. Looking at the wider strategy, NIR is keen to progressively enhance and expand their operation by looking for further, untapped sources of income, as and when other parameters permit this. It has been a long held wish in many official quarters to put County Tyrone, and perhaps even County Fermanagh, back on the railway map. With the new mood of thinking and a positive attitude towards rail travel now pervading the corridors of power, there is real hope that one day a revitalised Derry Road could become a reality.

Sadly, the possibility of a re-built railway line was thrown into question in November 2009, when the Minister for Regional Development, Mr Conor Murphy MP MLA, told the Northern Ireland Assembly, "A business case has not been provided for the extension of the railway system here recently", going on to state that the planned investment in Public Transport over the next ten years had already been set out in the Investment Delivery Plan, and concluding that "The building of a railway link and the necessary services to connect Portadown to Derry, to include links with Dungannon, Enniskillen, Omagh and Strabane is not considered to be feasible at this time".

There is no doubt that an argument could also now be put forward for a vastly improved tourist potential and regenerated rural economy in County Tyrone as a whole, by reconnecting the entire line. It remains to be seen if those in power have the resolve to grasp the nettle and make it happen. Whether the Government in the north will ever admit to the practice of their predecessors in deliberately hiding the truth on the operating costs of railway lines they wished to be rid of, and the wholesale betrayal of loyal railway staff, is a moot point and an issue that will no doubt continue to be debated for many years to come. We can only hope that one day, sanity will prevail within the corridors of power, that the line will return, and the sound of a train on Pomeroy bank, will once again echo across the green fields and drumlins of County Tyrone.

Footnote

There is an interesting postscript to the end of the UTA. Although NIR took effective control of all railways in Northern Ireland during 1968, the ghost of the erstwhile GNR(I) was destined to linger on as a legal entity for some years to come. To understand the rationale behind this odd situation, it is necessary to wind backwards in time and unravel history a little.

Following the take over by the Northern Ireland Transport holding Company (NITHC) in 1968, the UTA's inherited percentage of the GNRB share in the County Donegal Railways Joint Committee (CDRJC) needed to be transferred across to CIÉ, as they were now running the road services formerly operated by the CDRJC. This was achieved by a payment of £3,449 to the NITHC, with the purchase being rubber stamped by the Northern Ireland Ministry of Development on 21 March 1969, and confirmed by the Minster for Transport and Power in the Republic, on 3 April that year.

The CDRJC could now be dissolved by order of the Minister in the Republic. However, agreement was still needed between CIÉ and the British Railways Board (BRB). The BRB was the legal successor to the Midland Railway in England who, in conjunction with the GNR(I), had purchased the Donegal Railway in 1906. Accordingly, in return for a payment of £57,472 by CIÉ, the remaining interest in the CDRJC was transferred by agreement in 1966, thereby absolving the BRB of any further connection or liability. The way was now clear to wind up the CDRJC and the assets of both this and the nominally independent Strabane & Letterkenny Railway were vested in CIÉ with effect from 12 July 1971.

The CDRJC however, was to continue in a state of legal limbo for a further decade. This was due in the main to the presence of pension rights covering existing and former employees of the CDRJC, who would be covered by the British Railway superannuation fund. The Company was kept in existence whilst legislation was enacted to set up a separate fund in Ireland together with an appropriate transfer of monies. An order under the 1971 Act was subsequently made on 13 January 1981 to finally dissolve the CDRJC, becoming effective just three days later.

The GNRB had continued to remain in being all along, due to its notional control of the CDRJC, a situation made more difficult down the years by its own complicated system of ownership. The move to dissolve the CDRJC finally paved the way for the UTA's problem child to be allowed to rest and the last incarnation of the GNR(I), having outlived its fellow railway Companies, also ceased to be from 16 January 1981 – the wheel had come full circle!

Ghosts of the GNR? The author is sitting on his motor bike on the trackbed at Sion Mills station on a visit in 1967. At the time he had an uneasy sense of an unseen train approaching behind him. When the picture was developed there were two white puffs in the photo where the cylinder drain cocks would have been!

Author's camera

LIST OF STATIONS				
STATION	MILES	OPENED	CLOSED	NOTES
Portadown	0	12/09/1842	05/10/1970	A
Annaghmore	6 ¾	05/04/1858	14/02/1965	
Vernersbridge	9 ¼	05/04/1858	20/09/1954	
Trew & Moy	10 ¾	05/04/1858	14/02/1965	
Dungannon	15	02/09/1861	14/02/1965	B
Donaghmore	17 ¾	02/09/1861	05/10/1959	C
Pomeroy	24	02/09/1861	14/02/1965	
Carrickmore	29	02/09/1861	05/10/1959	
Sixmilecross	32 ¾	02/09/1862	14/02/1965	
Beragh	34 ¼	02/09/1861	14/02/1965	
Omagh	41 ¾	13/09/1852	14/02/1965	D
Mountjoy	45 ¼	01/03/1853	01/09/1935	E
Newtownstewart	51 ¼	09/05/1852	14/02/1965	
Victoria Bridge	55 ¾	09/05/1852	14/02/1965	
Sion Mills	57 ½	09/05/1852	14/02/1965	
Strabane	60 ¾	19/04/1847	14/02/1965	
Porthall	63 ¾	01/05/1848	14/02/1965	
Carrickmore	65 ½	19/04/1847	01/02/1853	F
St Johnston	68	19/04/1847	14/02/1965	
Carrigans	69 ¾	19/04/1847	14/02/1965	
Londonderry	74 ¾	19/04/1847	17/04/1850	G
Londonderry	75 ½	18/04/1850	14/02/1965	

COOKSTOWN BRANCH				
STATION	MILES	OPENED	CLOSED (GOODS)	CLOSED (PASSENGER)
Coalisland	5 ½	28/08/1879	04/01/1965	16/01/1956
Stewartstown	8 ½	28/08/1879	01/08/1958	16/01/1956
Cookstown	14 ½	28/08/1879	05/10/1959	16/01/1956

A – The Derry Road starts at Portadown Junction, a half mile south. Portadown station relocated 06/10/1970 to site used by Ulster Railway 01/03/1848-30/06/1863.

B – Original Portadown & Dungannon station located at eastern end of Dungannon tunnel 05/04/1858-01/09/1861.

C – From 05/10/1959 became a request stop only for school journeys.

D – Station reconstructed by L&E in 1863 to accommodate PD&O traffic.

E – Open 1852-01/11/1859, 01/08/1870-01/12/1878, 01/10/1928-01/09/1935.

F – Any early short-lived station, long-forgotten.

G – Original Cow Market terminus, replaced by Foyle Road.

MONDAY 15 FEBRUARY 1965
THE LAST JOURNEY – A DRIVER'S THOUGHTS

It was a little after midnight on the morning of Monday 15 January 1965, at Foyle Road railway station in Londonderry. The sound of a car crossing the upper deck of the Craigavon Bridge broke into the driver's thoughts, bringing him back to reality. He was not enjoying this evening's work knowing, as he did, the outcome at the end of his shift. It was the end of a routine. More than that, it was the end of an era – a way of life down the years, for him and many others like him.

A dull thud caused by the guard closing a compartment door further back along the platform roused him and, with a heavy heart he reached to the control panel on his left and thumbed the starter button, holding it in as the two BUT engines at the rear of his unit roared into life. He repeated the procedure, starting up the engines in the other two power cars, listening for a few seconds until all six engines had settled down to a steady tick over. Satisfied that the air pressure lights to the axle drives were also alight, he relaxed his hand and, sliding down the window, took in a breath of the slightly salty air blowing in from the river. Anticipating departure, he moved the brake handle back for a few seconds, raising the vacuum gauge needle to 12 inches before placing it back in the lap position. Although frowned upon by authority, this move would ensure a relatively quick

Above right: The crew of BUT railcar 121 pose at Derry before departure on 1 January 1965, six weeks before the journey described in this chapter.
EM Patterson

Right: BUT 121 and train await departure from Derry on 1 January 1965. It was an identical train to this that made the last journey in the early hours of Monday 15 February.
EM Patterson

departure if the brakes were at all tardy in coming off.

Two quick notes sounded on his panel buzzer. Repeating them back to the guard, the driver pushed the brake handle fully back into the release position and then selected first on the gear lever. As the transmission engaged, the railcar set nudged forward very slightly and, pulling the power handle two notches towards him, the driver felt the train began to move, the platform sliding out of sight as they passed under the top deck of the Craigavon Bridge. Transferring his right hand to the power handle and raising himself slightly, he put his head out of the window and looked back briefly to satisfy himself that all was well, all the time holding the handle down against the upwards pressure of the safety device, yellow duster in his hand, as drivers everywhere did. The window was slid back up and the driver sat down again, putting his left hand back on the control as he settled down to the journey ahead.

As the train continued to build up speed, the silhouette of the goods shed swept past on the right, the river keeping company close by on the left with the moonlight reflecting back in the water; they would be companions for many miles. The railcar was now in fourth gear and making good time, leaving County Londonderry, some 2½ miles out, as they entered the Irish Republic and travelled rapidly across the north eastern corner of County Donegal through Carrigans, St Johnston and Porthall, before passing over the River Foyle and back into Northern Ireland at McKinney's bridge, as they entered County Tyrone. Soon, the lights of Strabane town came into view.

Passing under the watchful eye of the outer home signal, high on its post, the train slid past the North cabin, its 39 levers in the safe hands of signalman Willie John Carlin, watching its progress from the cabin door, his back warmed by the cabin fire; Willie was working the very last 4.00pm to midnight shift. The guard felt the brakes come on as the train entered the station. It slowed, but did not stop and, clearing the barrow crossing, they coasted through the level crossing gates and over the road to Lifford before rumbling across the Mourne river bridge and powering up the engines again, all under the watchful eye of Station Master, Eugene O'Brien, standing in the shadows under the canopy, together with porter Robert Coyle.

As they disappeared from view, James McGurk, the south box signalman standing in the doorway of his box heaved a sigh of sadness, turning to switch out the light before locking the cabin door and making his way down the steps. Down the road in Strabane town, Clerk to the Council, Jim Bradley, hearing the train passing through, thought to himself, this is a bad day for the north west of Ireland.

The train roared through Sion Mills, past the single

Crossing the River Mourne at Strabane. On this occasion it was No 191 with an Apprentice Boys' Special in August 1957.

A Donaldson

Strabane South Cabin was beside the level crossing. This early view is about 1914. On 15 February, James McGurk was the signalman.

JD FitzGerald collection

Right: "The train roared through Sion Mills, past the single platform . . ." It is seen here a few months later with weeds starting to take hold.
Stations UK

Below: "At Victoria Bridge . . . the redoubtable Patsy McGarrigle (was) manning the signal box and level crossing." This view is also in 1965
Stations UK

platform, the preserve of Jack Latimer, the last Stationmaster to serve there, now totally deserted and in darkness, as was the lane leading down to Herdmans Flax Mill. At Victoria Bridge, Billy Anderson, in charge at the station, was still at his post, with the redoubtable Patsy McGarrigle manning the signal box and level crossing.

Both Victoria Bridge and then Newtownstewart were passed in quick succession. In his house at Newtownstewart, foreman Jack McQuade lay awake in bed, listening to the train as it made its way down the valley and then, before they knew it, the train was at Omagh, and passing Paddy Donaghy in the North signal box. As they entered the curving platform, Stationmaster Billy Ross, surrounded by a small knot of people, including Omagh guard Mickey O'Neil, and foreman Billy Kerr, could be seen gathered at the far end. Drawing to a halt, the cab window was slid down and greetings were exchanged between the driver and the staff that had waited to see the last train through.

All too soon it was time to depart and with a sad exchange of handshakes, the railcar eased forward out of the station. A single salutary note was sounded on the horn as they passed Billy Maguire in the South signal box, the signalman waving back to the train crew. Indifferent to the cold of the night and strangely reluctant to leave, the station staff stood for a moment at the platform end, staring at the sight of the retreating train, its solitary red tail light glowing back at them. The Market Branch junction was passed for the last time and they left the town behind them, climbing all the while, on the steady 1:87 gradient, as the train went through Garvaghy No 1 and 2 crossings.

After slowing for the Camowen River Bridge, speed was once more increased as they passed through both Edenderry and Tattykeernan crossings in quick succession. On the train went, through the dark Tyrone countryside. Though there was little to see outside,

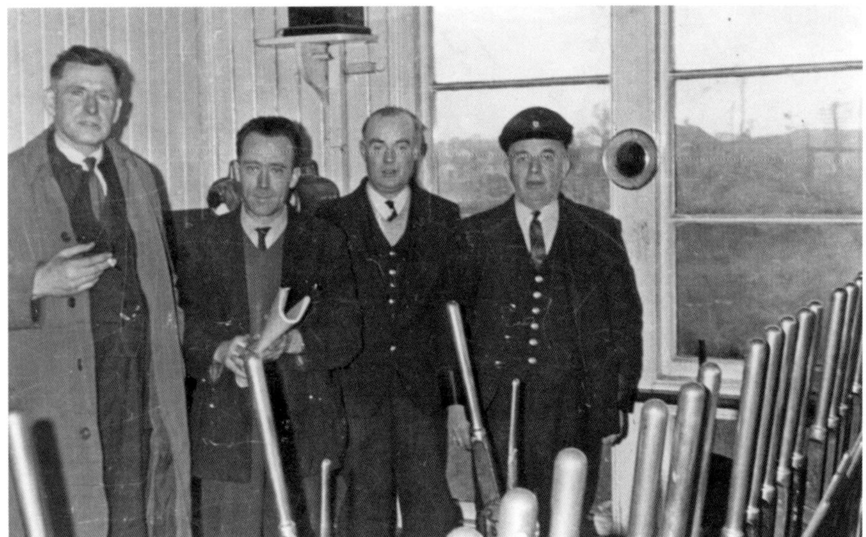

Left: " . . . before they knew it, the train was at Omagh, and passing Paddy Donaghy in the North signal box." This is a posed group a month later, in March 1965, dressed in their uniforms for one last time.
CP Friel collection

Right: At Omagh . . . "greetings were exchanged between the driver and staff that had waited to see the last train through." This BUT set is in a similar position in August 1962 on the afternoon train from Derry.
EM Patterson

Left: "Sitting down on the spare tip-up seat (the guard) poured two steaming mugs of tea, silently passing one to the driver, who acknowledged the mug with a nod, before taking a sip and placing the mug down at the front of the control panel, as he resumed his vigil through the front windows." Driver Barney McGirr of Omagh is at the controls of No 712 on 5 August 1958.
EM Patterson

the Belfast-based driver, whose eyes had now become accustomed to the dark again, was an experienced man, originally from Dungannon. He had worked his apprenticeship many years ago on loose-coupled night freights to Derry and he knew, both by the sound and roll of the train, exactly where he was on the line. The door to the front cab opened and the guard came through, carrying a white billy can and two metal cups, he had used the stop at Omagh to recharge his canister with hot water and give the tea time to mash.

Sitting down on the spare tip up seat he poured two steaming mugs of tea, silently passing one to the driver, who acknowledged the mug with a nod, before taking a sip and placing the mug down at the front of the control panel, as he resumed his vigil through the front windows, the heat from the tea forming a small patch of condensation on the cab window. Each was immersed in their own thoughts, watching the road ahead as the train steadily ate up the miles.

The lights of Beragh station came into view, the high platform-mounted signal box clearly visible against the night sky, with signalman Marcus McKee still at his post, and watching the train's progress through the windows. Under the road bridge they passed, at 40mph, through the curving platforms and away again, leaving a swirl of exhaust spiralling around the tall down home signal. The train headed away across the fields towards Sixmilecross while the public road would go around three sides of the same group of fields to meet the railway again at the next crossing point.

As they swept through the reverse curves between Beragh and Carrickmore, a break in the scudding clouds betrayed the moon. This would be the only February in recorded history not to have a full moon, though there was sufficient light to reflect off the two shining rails of steel streaming away in front of them as they made an ever-lengthening path down the valleys and back towards Belfast. The moonlight added a ghostly appearance to the crossing gates at Sixmilecross, as the train rumbled across the road and past the ancient single wooden platform.

As they rounded one of the more severe curves, the crossing keeper's cottage at Rollingford appeared out of the darkness, the railcar growling through at 30mph, the gates shut firmly against the road traffic for a final time, with the oil lamps flickering brightly on them. Shortly afterwards, the remains of Carrickmore station were glimpsed as the train swept under the road bridge and passing across the embankment, under the lee of Dunmisk Hill, sharply silhouetted against the night sky, a crackle of noise from the six exhaust pipes heralded a change down of gear, as the BUT began the laborious climb to the top of the bank, at milepost 26½. The slowing sound of the train echoed across the bogs as it made its

"The lights of Beragh station came into view . . . Under the road bridge they passed, at 40mph . . ." Railcar 120 passes under the bridge on 22 July 1962.

EM Patterson

". . . through the curving platforms and away again . . ." A driver's eye view of Beragh on 28 July 1964.

EM Patterson

Left: "As they rounded one of the more severe curves, the crossing keeper's cottage at Rollingford appeared out of the darkness . . ." Qs 4-4-0 No 132 passes Rollingford in the summer of 1958.

A Donaldson

Below: "An old man stood on the road bridge at Pomeroy station, in silent vigil, wrapped up in a heavy coat to protect him from the cold night . . ." BUT 125 approaches the same bridge with the up mail on 25 July 1964. This is what the old man would have glimpsed in the darkness.

EM Patterson

lonely way up to the summit and was heard with sadness and regret in many a white-washed hillside cottage that night.

An old man stood on the road bridge at Pomeroy station, in silent vigil, wrapped up in a heavy coat to protect him from the cold night, his faithful and equally silent collie dog crouched against the wall beside him. He had come down earlier to see the last train to Derry, just as his grandfather had, in 1861, to see the first PD&O train through to Omagh; indeed, he still lived in the same house, as he had done all his life. He had not gone down to the platform earlier that night with everyone else, when the northbound train passed through, preferring instead to watch from the lane, keeping his thoughts and regrets to himself, in the shadow of the night. The dog heard the distant sound first, well before his master. His ears pricked up as the train, still some way off, started to descend Pomeroy bank. He knew why they were there; he was faithful and would not leave the man's side that night.

The train appeared out of the night, leaning into the curve and swung onto the quarter mile straight leading to Pomeroy station. In his cab, hunched over the controls, the driver could see the figure standing on the road bridge, silhouetted against the night sky. He knew well who it was and as he neared the bridge, the man's hand was raised in a final salute. The driver, pressing a handle down, sounded a single low note on the horn for several seconds, lifting his hand, palm upwards, in response. The train swept under the bridge, the movement lifting several dead leaves into the air and they tumbled about in the wind before falling to the ground once more. The man crossed to the other side of the bridge, watching with care worn and red-rimmed eyes as the train disappeared out of the station and on down the line towards Dungannon.

All was now quiet again and the collie, head on one side, watched his master with concern. Turning, the man spoke in a quiet, kindly voice to the dog, who came forward and nuzzled the outstretched hand in

Right: This is the bridge described, with S class 4-4-0 No 60 passing under it hauling the 3.00pm Belfast-Derry about 1964.

A Donaldson

Below: A BUT railcar, on the 9.55am Londonderry-Belfast, stops at Pomeroy on 10 September 1961. The second coach is still in GNR livery. In the distance an AEC railcar heads for Omagh.

John Langford

a gesture of love and unswerving trust. Together they started to make their way back up the steep lane to the village, each wrapped up in their own thoughts, on past the doctor's bungalow they went, before turning left at the cross-roads into the main street, to a house where a tilly lamp still burned in the window, waiting their safe return.

In Pomeroy, halfway up the hill, at No 24, Mrs McFarland was with her son and daughter, Billy and Margaret. She looked out of her low, green-framed window onto Main Street, and, hearing the train pass, wondered what would happen now to the village. Earlier that weekend, Margaret and her young man, Leslie Smyth from Cavanacaw, had made a last sentimental train trip down to Portadown, coming back through the dark on the late evening working.

Down on the station, a group of figures watched the train's progress as it streamed through. Alec Ogle, Pomeroy's last Stationmaster, stood on the platform outside the station building, has face impassive and etched with sadness, little swirls of dust formed by the trains progress settling on his shoes. Standing in the doorway behind Alec, was Bobby Moffatt, ticket collector and porter, whilst across the tracks, Hughie McGael, the signalman, stood in his cabin, the light from an oil lamp reflecting off the polished instruments; as always, a yellow duster in his hand.

Dick Hamilton, the other signalman, was outside the box, on the steps. Hughie watched the tail lamp disappear into the darkness for the last time, before ringing 'train out of section' on the bells and placing the duster over the outer home lever as he returned the signal to the danger position. The scrunch of shoe on gravel told him that Alec had gone back into his office to meditate on the days events, before locking up for the night.

From his vantage point on the embankment, the driver saw the long straight Pomeroy to Dungannon road come into view to his left, the two-storey brick-built Orange Hall standing quietly in the dark, a little way back from the road. On the far grass bank below Cavanacaw, Bella McGeary's black cattle stirred uneasily in the sloping

Left: An interesting view of Dungannon station in the 1960s, looking towards the Aughnacloy Road bridge. Here, the crew of the last train shared mugs of tea with the station staff before 'Control' told them to get back on the road.

CP Friel collection

Below: ". . . the train slid under the latticework footbridge and out of the station, gathering speed as it approached Dungannon tunnel." UG No 48 prepares to do just that (apart from the speed bit!) as it leaves with the 4.40pm to Portadown on 29 August 1964.

JD FitzGerald

field as the train passed out of view and continued to descend the gradient, passing through the crossings at Brimmage's, Reynold's and Mullafutherland, before reaching Gortavoy Bridge. A few minutes later they swept through the curving platforms of Donaghmore station, the train banking to the left on the elevated track before continuing the descent to Dungannon Junction, a half mile short of the station itself.

At Dungannon, Stationmaster Jimmy Swarbrigg and the remaining staff were gathered around the stove in the platform-mounted signal box. Some had gone home for a late tea, only to return, still in their uniforms, to see the final train pass through, driven by a desire to be there at the end. Two bottles of Bushmills whiskey were produced, one was put to one side, the other opened and a generous portion poured out into teacups, tin mugs and whatever was to hand. The ancient cast iron stove had been stoked up, giving out a welcome fog of heat against the cold air creeping in under the door.

Without warning, the railcar set appeared out of the dark, coasting in under the Beech Valley Road Bridge. It drew up at the platform, its engines ticking over in unison and pushing plumes of smoky exhaust up into the night sky. The train had made good time since leaving Omagh and, being a few minutes up on the schedule, the crew stepped onto the platform and made their way into the signal box, the driver stopping to stretch his legs and ease the cramp in them, caused by sitting too long at the controls.

Mugs of tea, laced with something stronger, were quickly produced. Though it was against the rules, it was only a very small tot that was put into the cups, something to ward off the cold and there was no real danger. The public had long gone, the staff were all redundant, and the train was effectively an empty stock movement on a line that was all but closed. Somehow, the dictates and regulations of a Government that had sold them down the river did not seem that important anymore. The door swung open as a blast of cold air announced the arrival of a porter: "Control's been on the telephone and your man's wanted out of here as they need to close the section

Right: View from a BUT railcar at Trew and Moy as the guard picks up the staff, though this train is apparently heading *towards* Dungannon.

JD FitzGerald

down". With a wistful look at his colleagues, the driver said, "Indeed, we had best be away" and downed his still scalding hot mug of tea.

With chairs scraping on the wooden floor as they were pushed back, everyone made their way out into the cold night air and along the empty platform to the front of the train. A welcome fan of hot air greeted the crew as the doors were opened. The guard had thoughtfully left the train's heaters running. Last minute wishes for the future were hastily made, along with many handshakes, and a hand pushed through the bodies as the unopened bottle of Bushmills whiskey was passed in through the lowered cab window as a parting gift. A drawn out sigh was heard from the vacuum brakes as they came off and the train slid under the latticework footbridge and out of the station, gathering speed as it approached Dungannon tunnel. As it plunged into the Stygian blackness, the sound of a valedictory blast on the horn echoed back to the staff on the platform watching the tail light disappearing into the gloom.

The train burst out of the south end of the tunnel with a great rumbling roar of power, streaming southwards through Shaw's accommodation crossing before reaching Trew & Moy a few minutes later. The crew were both in the cab and the guard noted with a grim satisfaction that the home starter signal had been placed in the on position, not that this would stem their flight; many were the times in the past he had waited with the mid morning train from Dungannon to Portadown whilst young mothers had pushed their prams over the barrow crossing to board the train. Minutes later, the train left the cover of nearby trees and crossed between open fields, before rattling across the latticed Blackwater Bridge as it entered the rich, fruit growing countryside of County Armagh, still clothed in darkness.

It sped past the long closed Vernersbridge station, slumbering unused since 1954, and on across the flat Armagh fields, the trackbed of the former down line, lifted back in 1959, still visible in the moonlight. Speed was reduced as they cleared Derrycoose crossing and approached Annaghmore. The station was in darkness, save for a solitary platform bulb, lighting a wall-pasted UTA notice of closure for the line. The passing loop was entered for the last time and, leaning into the left hand curve, the train passed through the station and under the road bridge, silhouetted against the night sky.

Leaving the station, power was again applied for the final sprint across relatively level countryside towards Portadown. The final crossing was passed at Annakeera, and a few minutes later, the outskirts of Portadown came into view. The brakes went on sharply for the final approach. As they did so, the guard made his way back to sit in the van portion of the train. Even at the end there was an instilled sense of pride in a job done correctly with everyone at their allotted post – just as it should be. As the railcar slowly approached the 15mph curve and junction at Portadown, the driver was minded to recall the words from AE Housman's poem 'A Shropshire Lad':

Into my heart an air that kills
From yon far country blows:
What are those blue remembered hills,
What spires, what farms are those
That is the land of lost content,
I see it shining plain,
The happy highways where I went
And cannot come again

With these thoughts uppermost in his mind, the driver eased his train around the tight curve, flanges squealing in protest as the wheels followed the shining bend of the rails. Once clear of the junction points, the driver selected second gear, and opening the power handle again, accelerated away, past the goods yard, on across the Bann River Bridge towards the half mile distant twinkling lights of Portadown station … and into history.

The signalman in the Junction box, having observed all this, sighed heavily as he moved the levers back, re-setting the points for the main line and putting the branch outer home signal back to danger for the last time. He put on his greatcoat and a flat cap to keep his head warm. Stepping out onto the veranda, he took one last look round and quietly said to himself "Aye, well, that will be it now", before turning round to lock the door and descend the steps, as he headed off into the ground mist along a well worn and rutted path towards the welcoming lights and warmth that beckoned from the station.

Left: A busy scene at Omagh on 9 August 1962 as SG2 No 38 detaches Y6 van No 649 from the rear of the 8.25am Belfast-Londonderry diesel railcar after it has been unloaded (see also page 86).
EM Patterson

A Pictorial Description of the Line in the Final Years of Operation

Portadown to Dungannon Junction

The legendary 75½-mile Derry Road starts properly at Portadown Junction, a short way south of the town's station, which lies across the River Bann, on the east side, at Watson Street. The station was opened by the Ulster Railway on 1 July 1863 and was designed by Sir John Macneill. At the three-way junction the main line to Dundalk and Dublin veers to the left with the trackbed of the former Armagh line continuing straight ahead and Portadown shed lying in the 'V' between the running lines. The Derry Road diverges sharply to the right, on a 15 mph restricted curve and gradient, as it passes the Junction cabin, where the tablet is collected for the first leg of the journey, on a short but steep gradient. A warning board, erected in 1961, shows in black letters on a yellow background, the overall speed limits, 45 mph for steam trains and 60 mph for railcars (in Ireland, DMUs were always known as railcars). Because on the GNR(I) 'up' is towards Dublin, trains heading in the Derry direction were 'down' and towards Dublin and Belfast were 'up'.

The first eleven miles from Portadown are relatively flat with a series of short vertical curves and one brief, climb of 1 in 84 at eight miles, with lush farmland and the apple-growing orchards of County Armagh visible on both sides of the line. Annaghmore, the GNR's principal fruit station, is reached at 6¾ miles and is a crossing point with two platforms and block post facilities. The original, Portadown & Dungannon Railway station building, on the down platform, greets the traveller, with a wooden shelter on the up platform. A substantial goods shed with siding accommodation is provided for freight. A store was opened in 1930

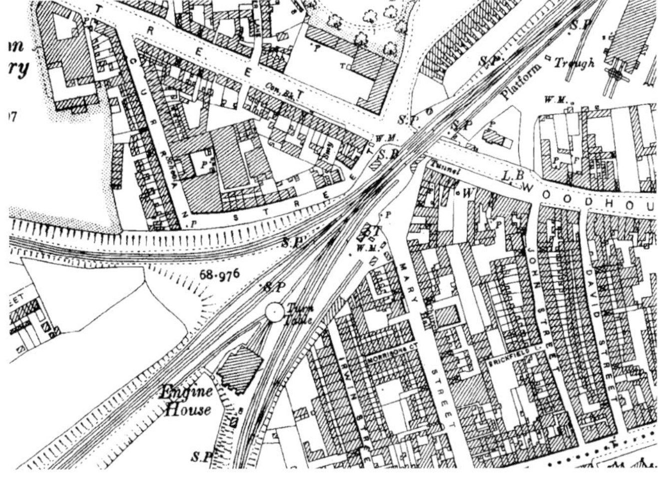

Above right: Portadown Junction layout in 1906, before the well-known roundhouse engine shed was built.

Right: Portadown Junction in May 1957, with the roundhouse between the Dublin and Armagh lines. The Derry Road curves off to the right. This was the only junction in Ireland where a double track line split into three double track routes. Cyril Fry must have scrambled onto the roof of a goods brake van to get this shot.

CL Fry

Left: T2 4-4-2T No 1 takes the tight curve of the Derry Road as it passes Portadown Junction with the 6.03pm to Dungannon on 30 September 1956.

A Donaldson

Below: Annaghmore station, looking east, in August 1962.

EM Patterson

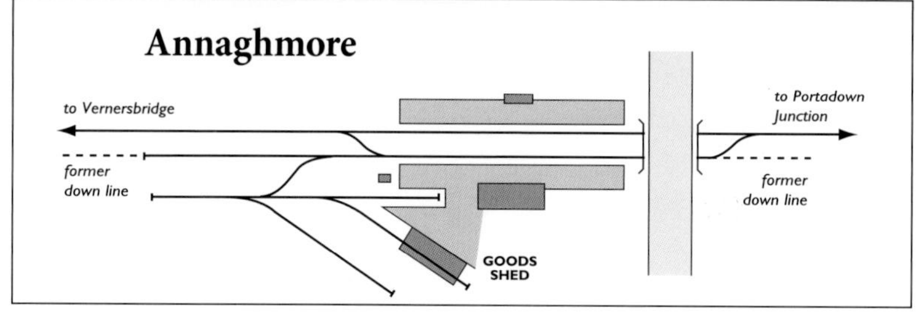

Right: The view looking west from the road bridge on the same date. The bog described in the text is visible beyond the signal cabin.

EM Patterson

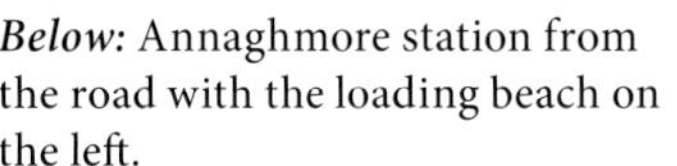

Below: Annaghmore station from the road with the loading beach on the left.

DRM Weatherup

to cope with the burgeoning local traffic in soft fruit. Many special trains of both apples and strawberries are despatched from here to destinations across the province and to the port of Belfast for export.

Adjacent to a road overbridge, the station is set on a curve, restricted to 50 mph, with the staff being exchanged here for another one covering the section to Trew & Moy. All staff exchange is now by hand, though at one time, mechanical staff exchange apparatus, allied to cab-side mounted equipment of locomotives, was in use at nine stations on the Derry Road. To the north, but not visible from the line, lies the Annaghmore Turf Railway. This is a narrow gauge three-foot gauge line, running toward the shore of Lough Neagh at Maghery and used for the extraction of turf from the peat bogs.

Mention must be made at this point of an oft-repeated story of intrigue that occurred at Annaghmore station on the evening of 9 September 1858. The evening train from Portadown to Dungannon had just arrived and there was romance in the air. A Miss Telford, who ran a public house with her sister close to the station, had arranged to elope with the train driver, John Hardstaff. The girl's father, who was against the marriage, arrived at the station and two of the four station staff sided with him. Miss Telford and her luggage were put safely aboard the train from the track side, out of sight of people on the platform, by the remaining staff, including Robert McConner, the Stationmaster. But this was to come to nothing, as Reilly, one of the porters and a close friend of the family, had set the points for a siding, at the insistence of the girl's father, in an attempt to thwart any departure.

The train moved off and Hardstaff, unaware of events, ran the engine through a stop block and into a bog. Miss Telford, in her excitement and trepidation, jumped out of the carriage, and landed in a pond to find herself in a similar situation to the engine. Captain Ross, RE, subsequently issued a Board of Trade report on the whole scenario and it was said that John Hardstaff and Miss Telford later comforted each other after their adventure as they dried out in front of a fire in the station waiting room.

A little beyond Annaghmore, the River Blackwater is crossed on a lattice girder bridge just beyond Vernersbridge station (closed in 1954), as the line

Opposite: Trew and Moy on 9 August 1962. The freshly painted AEC railcar in the loop is the 10.20 from Omagh to Portadown, waiting to cross a down train.
EM Patterson

Above: Vernersbridge in 1956 looking west from the road bridge. The line was very straight at this point.
Stations UK

Right: Vernersbridge about 1915. On the platform are Stationmaster William Topley and Porter David McFarland. The latter had been injured about 1902 at Trew and Moy by the first train on the double track from Annaghmore.
Inspector A Johnston

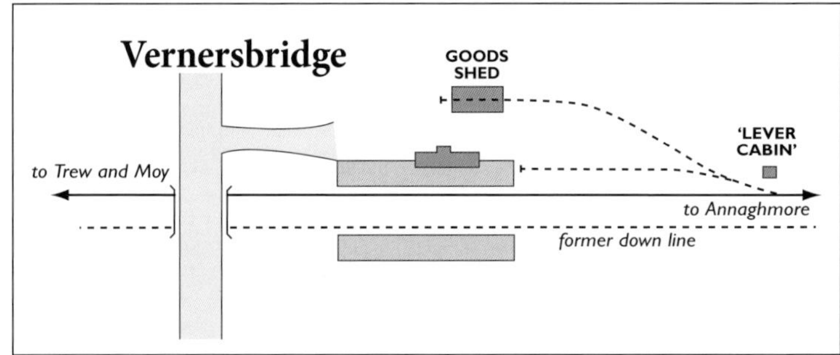

enters County Tyrone, with the remains of early doubling of the tracks, as far as Trew & Moy, still visible, though the second, down line, was removed in 1960. The decision to build Vernersbridge station was heavily influenced by the highly popular and caring local landowner, William Verner, (1st Bart) 1782-1870, with the bridge supporting an access lane, producing the name used!

The station, simply known as Verner until December 1858, possessed two goods sidings and a shed, still in situ, on the up side of the station, along with an attractive single storey building. A ground frame controlled the points and, there being no requirement for a signal box, the key to open the sidings was always kept in the station office. There was no staff to attach it to in the early days, with the track being doubled at the start of the 20th century. Both sidings have long since disappeared and the isolated down platform has all but vanished under the encroaching undergrowth. A stone plaque above the station entrance shows a construction date of 1862. The station now slumbers in the warm Armagh sun, as it has since closure on 20 September 1954.

Once over the Blackwater and county boundary, Trew & Moy is soon reached at 10¾ miles. The name derives from the station being in the townland of Trew, though it serves the village of Moy, some miles away. As with Annaghmore, the station building, of similar design, is located on the down platform with a wood and glass waiting shelter on the up one. This station, another block post and crossing point with goods facilities, once used the GNR automatic staff exchange equipment, with pick-up facilities on the down line. The receiving post and net gear were on the up side at the Portadown end of the platform, though it is now a simple case of exchanging the tablet rather than the large staff. After 1933, the Derry Road was the only GNR line to use mechanical staff exchange apparatus, Trew & Moy being one of the nine stations so equipped between Portadown and Londonderry.

At one time, the annual, week-long Moy Fair was one of the largest horse fairs in Ireland and the railway had much trade in livestock as a result. It was at this station in 1875 that a murder was committed. One Daniel Hagan, whilst returning by a heavily crowded train from a Home Rule demonstration in Dungannon, and in company with many people the worse for drink, was fired on from outside of the train and killed. No one was ever brought to justice for the crime.

The 1932 Northern Ireland Directory listed Williamson's Posting Establishment as providing a car to meet all trains at the station, with the curious exception of the 7.37am and 12.30am!

Once past Trew & Moy, the single line enters an area of wet bog land and poor soil as it begins a steady rise, over bridges originally made suitable for two tracks. It continues on past Shaw's crossing at milepost 14 and into

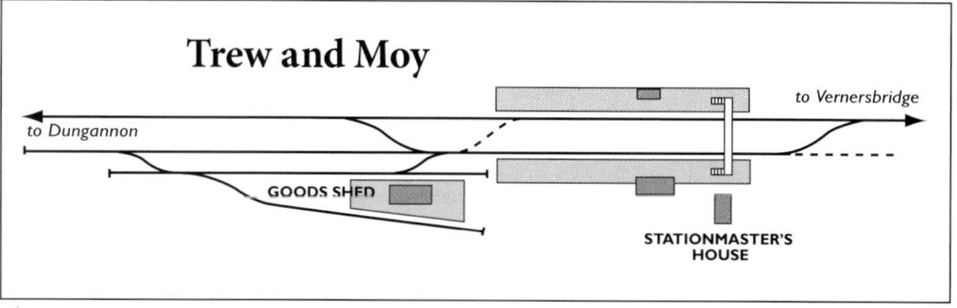

Gortmerron Townland, where the original Dungannon station was sited. This was before the 814 yard tunnel just south of Dungannon was built in the late 1850s at the insistence of Lord Northland, intransigent in his objection to the railway going through his land or at least being visible while doing so!

Emerging from the horseshoe shaped tunnel entrance, the rusty and long disused siding to Dickson's Mill is passed on the left before entering the station. This siding dates back to the late 19th century, and a key attached to the Trew & Moy–Dungannon staff opened the access points. Reached at 15 miles, Dungannon station has the air of an important country town junction, possessing both a main and island platform. The far side of the latter was formerly used for trains on the 14½ mile branch through Coalisland to Cookstown, opened in 1879, though the adjacent siding can often be seen holding elderly ex-Great Northern, wooden-bodied coaches, in their faded and sun-bleached mahogany livery.

There is no engine shed at the station but it does possess a turntable and that prerequisite of the Derry Road, a water tower, in this case somewhat badly located at the Pomeroy end of the station by overbridge 41, causing engines using the facility to foul the approach to the up line platform. Also, crew changing is often carried out here. Unusually, the station building is a little smaller than its rural counterparts at either Trew & Moy or Annaghmore and, with the railway being at a lower level than the road, it has a set of railed stone steps underneath the canopy, leading down from the waiting room and booking hall onto the platform. The waiting room still contains a fireplace complete with an Ulster Railway fender. On the island platform, an out-of-use bookstall still survives and the latticework footbridge has lost its protective roof.

The antecedents of the Derry Road are still much in evidence and show quite clearly that the line was not planned as one railway, but two. On the southern half of the line there is a family resemblance between the station buildings at Beragh, Pomeroy and Trew & Moy. To the north, the structures are quite different and there is a similarity between Omagh and Enniskillen, betraying their Londonderry & Enniskillen Railway ancestry. For many years the line was effectively worked as two sections, Portadown to Omagh and Enniskillen to Londonderry, via Omagh.

Likewise, the track, though standardised over the years by the Great Northern, is a typical mix of 60ft and 45 ft lengths with a few random remaining 26ft and 30ft pieces thrown in for good measure. Portadown–Dungannon is largely comprised of shorter 45ft rails with the Dungannon–Strabane stretch using mixed lengths and the Strabane–Londonderry section virtually all laid with 60ft rails. Some sections in the Annaghmore area have been laid using concrete sleepers, which can give quite a lively ride over the boggy ground, to those travelling in an AEC or BUT railcar on the 15 mile switchback between Portadown and Dungannon!

Dungannon is also a good point at which to show how the two-railway syndrome is carried over into current operational practice. A glance at the timetable will show a goodly number of local services from Portadown to Dungannon, likewise between Londonderry and Omagh with some services

Left: A general view of Dungannon on 13 April 1948. QGs 0-6-0 No 152 is about to depart with a Cookstown train.

HC Casserley

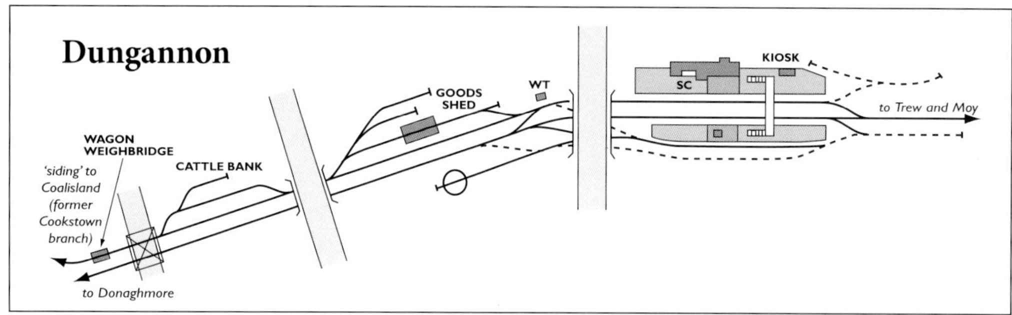

Right: UG 0-6-0 No 145 arrives at Dungannon with a train from Cookstown on 25 May 1953. As was common on many GNR passenger trains, there is a van and cattle wagons on tow. The track on the left leads to the turntable.

DG Coakham

Left: UG 0-6-0 No 45 is turned at Dungannon about 1961. The good shed is in the background.

A Donaldson

The exterior of Dungannon station on 24 September 1963. The Morris Minor and Ford Prefect parked outside are obviously visitors, as they hail from Tipperary and Dublin respectively.

DG Coakham

terminating at Strabane. The central section over the Sperrin foothills however, has to rely on the sparse frequency of through trains. Until the closure of the Irish North Western line in 1957, the District Engineer in Enniskillen was responsible for the line south as far as Dungannon Junction with the Cookstown to Portadown section under the control of the District Engineer in Dundalk, his office moving to Belfast after World War Two ended.

The eventual transfer of the whole line to the Western Engineering District saw the green and cream of the Eastern District on buildings and signal cabins replaced by the more familiar brown and cream of the Western District. The traffic side had a similar division of labour, with the Western District in charge eastward as far as Pomeroy, the last District Superintendent at Omagh, not leaving the post until 1953. The Eastern District covered Donaghmore to Portadown and the Cookstown branch, being under the control of the Traffic Manager in Belfast.

Continuing the journey forward, the Trew & Moy large staff is now replaced by a miniature one and, leaving Dungannon, the turntable is passed on the left and the goods sidings and facilities on the right. In approximately half a mile, Dungannon Junction is reached, as the Cookstown line branches off to the right, with the Junction signal cabin lying just beyond the junction on the branch side of the main line. When first opened in 1879, Cookstown was provided with its own engine shed and turntable, adjacent to the existing one at the BNCR station. The passenger service to Cookstown was withdrawn in 1956 and, in 1959, the goods workings were truncated, leaving a 5½ mile siding to Coalisland. This produced a not inconsiderable amount of traffic, with a daily light engine working from Portadown collecting wagons from both the brickworks and sand pits sidings on the branch.

The branch currently starts from Dungannon station. The main line, once double to Donaghmore, was singled back to the junction in 1932 by removing the down line and to Dungannon station in 1959, by making the up line from there to the station part of the branch line and removing all pointwork at the junction.

The Cookstown branch

At this point, we will explore the 14½-mile long Cookstown branch. On 16 January 1956, this section of line was closed to passenger traffic. The freight

Dungannon Junction from the cab of BUT railcar 712 on 5 August 1958. At this time it was still a full junction with signal cabin.

EM Patterson

The same scene six years later on 28 July 1964, this time from the cab of NCC Mogul No 99. The signal cabin has gone and the truncated line to Coalisland is now worked as a siding from Dungannon..

EM Patterson

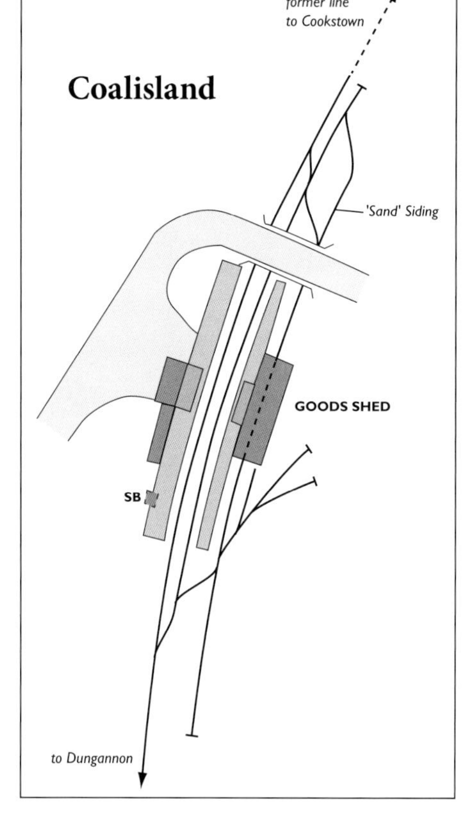

service was progressively cut back, with Stewartstown closing on 1 August 1958 and services beyond Coalisland ceasing in January 1959. The line officially closed to all remaining freight on 5 October 1959, but continued to be worked as a 5½ mile siding until 1965 to extract the sand and brick traffic, a lengthy siding running from Dungannon station through the goods yard, with no physical connection at Dungannon Junction. Many of the station buildings remained intact, but moribund and gently decaying, though for the purpose of this description, we will treat the whole branch as still being accessible.

The route from Dungannon to Cookstown is somewhat circuitous. Though the distance by road from Coalisland to Trew and Moy station is perhaps five miles, the same journey taken by rail, would be over twice that distance. Leaving Dungannon Junction, the line starts on the rise and describes a large clockwise arc around the back of Dungannon town, climbing 60ft in 1½ miles, before descending quite steeply at grades of 1 in 72/90 after passing Old Engine crossing, then turning north east to reach Coalisland at a height of 132 ft, at 5½ miles. Set on a right hand curve, the substantial station buildings, complete with accommodation on the first floor, are on the down (Cookstown) platform, with a goods shed backing onto the Dungannon one. Both platforms possess short canopies, with the Dungannon one boxed in to form an ornate waiting shelter. Both running lines exit under a three-arched road bridge, set at the platform ends. By 1960, only the up line to Dungannon was in use.

There are more brickworks, colliery and sandpit sidings on this section of line than anywhere else on Great Northern system, and they are seldom out view, making the stretch more reminiscent of an English industrial midlands area in the 1930s. Leaving Coalisland, the line passes under a double-arched bridge before clearing Byrne's sand sidings, the last ones to offer traffic, followed by the site of Sir Samuel Kelly's colliery, opened on 25 July 1924, and once home to several trailing sidings.

The climbing now starts in earnest for three miles, passing Annagher Colliery siding and the crossings at Annagher and Lisnastrain, before reaching a summit of 258 ft, at Stewartstown, a little over half way along the branch. As Stewartstown is left behind, an overbridge takes the line across the road to Cookstown.

On the final leg, several descents of 1 in 75/80 follow, punctuated by one short rise, with a level crossing passed at Grange, near the Ballinderry River Bridge,

Opposite: The crew of GNR SG 0-6-0 No 175 and the guard at the end of the GNR platform on 7 August 1957. This locomotive became UTA No 43.

EM Patterson

Left: UG class 0-6-0 No 146 at Coalisland with the 1.50pm goods from Dungannon on 11 May 1957. The second vehicle is a passenger van. Business doesn't seem to be that brisk but then, since Drew was a teacher, this is a Saturday working.

A Donaldson

Right: Cookstown on 25 August 1950, viewed from the signal cabin. GNR station on the left, NCC one in the centre and the NCC goods yard on the right. The GNR goods yard is out of view to the left.

EM Patterson

Below: Viewed from the platform buffers, we now see the GNR goods shed and water tower to the right and the divergence of the lines to Magherafelt and Dungannon.

EM Patterson

(the latter crossing opened as late as 1943 for the golfing fraternity), the line then climbing out of the river valley at 1 in 75/86 past Killymoon crossing. As journey's end is reached, the line curves under three-arched bridge No 32, to enter Cookstown, terminating in the GNR(I) station, adjacent to the NCC one, both of them located in Molesworth Road. The GNR(I) station consists of one platform road to the left of the running line, complete with the usual station buildings and a lengthy canopy. A run-round loop and bay platform for freight, with freight and exchange sidings to the NCC station, are located on the opposite side of the tracks.

Dungannon Junction to Omagh

Returning to the Derry Road proper, from Dungannon Junction the ascent of the line continues to Donaghmore, a further 1½ miles from the junction, attaining a height of 286 ft in the process, the climb running for 16½ miles from Trew & Moy to milepost 26½. A miniature staff, Dungannon Junction–Pomeroy, covers the section. This was subsequently changed to Dungannon–Pomeroy, with provision for switching in Donaghmore though this is rarely, if ever, needed.

Donaghmore is set on a curve. The station once had a reasonable flow of traffic to the soap works but this is now long gone. The sidings have been removed and the single line realigned with the down platform, leaving the up platform and station buildings isolated and out of use. Faded white sighting-patches still adorn both ends of the road bridge, put there to assist drivers of trains from Dungannon in reading the aspect of the semaphore signals that used to grace the station. Presently, the grass covered down platform receives two passenger trains per day, a request stop by a morning up train and an afternoon down train, Mondays to Fridays only, during school term.

Passing under Overbridge 55 as we leave Donaghmore's surviving platform, with fierce gradients ahead, the climbing starts in earnest with almost continuous collar work required by engines on a nine miles plus haul over the Sperrin Mountains watershed, the ruling gradient being around 1 in 72. The vertical curves are now replaced by great sweeping horizontal ones, starting with a 30mph restriction on a half mile of reverse curve leaving Donaghmore. This is followed by running through several cuttings, with Mullafurtherland, Reynold's and Brimage's crossings passed in quick succession. Included in this section is a quarter mile restricted to 45 mph.

A further three quarter mile of reverse curves, situated on a slight fall with a 30 mph limit, heralds the approach to windswept Pomeroy, some 49 miles by rail from Belfast, the highest station on the Great Northern system and a good Irish mile from the village whose

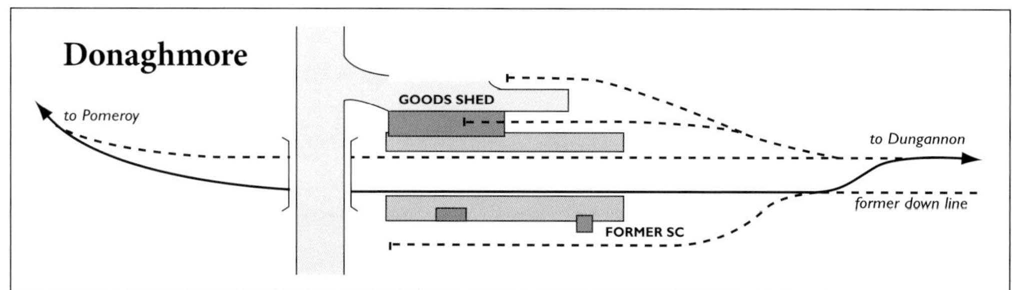

Left: Donaghmore on 24 July 1961, looking towards Pomeroy. The former up platform is on the right, alongside the goods shed.
EM Patterson

Opposite top: Qs class 4-4-0 No 122 stops at Reynold's accommodation crossing on the same date. Note how, in the absence of a platform, a set of steps is used to access the carriages. These stopping points were originally intended for railbus use, the entrance into these being much lower than on carriages.
A Donaldson

Above: Viewed from the overbridge we see the goods shed more clearly as SG2 0-6-0 No 40 pounds through on a down goods..
JD FitzGerald

Left: QL class 4-4-0 No 156 comes through Mullaghfurtherland accommodation crossing on 26 October 1957.
A Donaldson

creamery, once a useful source of traffic and employment locally, but closed many years since.

The goods area is separated from the station building by an outside, open roofed, gents urinal, white painted and redolent with the sensory effects of Jeyes Fluid, the facility being accessed from the platform. This end of the up platform also possesses a jewel from the past, in the form of a working water crane, almost certainly from PD&O days. A rough, stone wall separates the platform from an unsurfaced parking and turning area, with a gate giving access thereto.

name it bears. The village itself, some ten miles by road from both Cookstown and Dungannon, is the highest in Northern Ireland, standing at 564 ft, and lies within an area of oak forest, originally granted to Sir Andrew Chichester by King James I. It was planned out by the Reverend James Lowry in the 18th century. The final few hundred yards lie on an embankment, looking down on the Dungannon road. The line then curves to the left over a trailing point, giving access to a relief siding, before passing the signal box and entering the down platform.

The station is constructed in the traditional style associated with the Derry Road, having two platforms with a passing loop and a road overbridge at the Omagh end of the loop. The main building is on the up platform and adjoins a goods shed and small office, plus a covered dock, with sidings either side of the structure and a third siding running up the back of the goods yard, to terminate just short of the local

The down, northbound platform, contains a well proportioned wooden-fronted waiting shelter, with stone walls, a slate roof and adorned with framed travel posters. White painted oval milepost 24 can be seen beside the shelter. Along the platform, a grassed and bramble strewn earth bank slopes up to a walled lane. The station's water tower, situated at the Derry end of the this platform, is a welcome and well-used

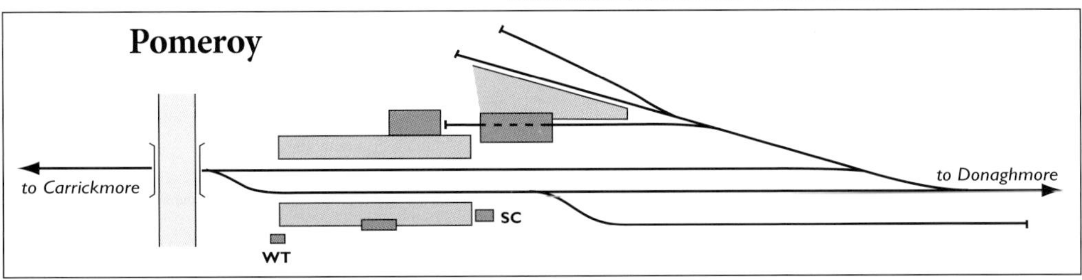

Above: The up platform at Pomeroy about 1915, with the Stationmaster centre. Inspector Johnston was based at Dundalk and was a prolific photographer of GNR stations and locomotives.
Inspector A Johnston

Top: Pomeroy, viewed from the footplate of a U class 4-4-0 as it enters the station with an up train on 29 July 1961. The signalman stands ready for the staff exchange.

EM Patterson

Centre: Pomeroy station looking west in 1965, just after the closure of the Derry Road.

Stations UK

Below: SG3 class 0-6-0 No 33 pulls out of a siding and enters the down platform road on 21 July 1964, while another staff is held in readiness. The goods train had been shunted into the trailing siding to allow the passage of two diesel railcars.

EM Patterson

Opposite: No trains but a pleasant view. This is the panorama at the summit of the bank, one and a half mile west of Pomeroy. It is 21 July 1964 and the farmers have taken full advantage of the glorious weather to mow and stack the hay.

EM Patterson

facility by steam hauled trains. Goods trains invariably set back into the relief siding by the signal box after replenishment, to allow the following passenger trains to pass through, before setting off on their laborious climb up Pomeroy bank and over the 561ft summit at milepost 26½, the highest on the system. On the Pomeroy side of the summit there was once a remote ballast siding on the moorland, and another one down towards Carrickmore, but both have long since disappeared. At night, the station is also the crew changing point for goods trains.

As they leave Pomeroy, trains rejoin the single line at the end of the platform loop and steam engines blast their way under the stone-built road overbridge No 69, blackened with age, shrouded in the smoke and steam that hangs in the air long after the train has gone. The bark of an engine being worked hard echoes across the corn fields as the train lifts into the curve at the foot of Pomeroy bank, the slowing exhaust betraying its location as it disappears from view around the hill and starts the long climb up to the summit. A total of seven speed-restricted curves would be encountered in the next 16 miles.

Once over the top, with the line in a cutting and the Pomeroy to Carrickmore road high above on a sharp bend, the line comes off the bleak moorland and descends at between 1 in 70 and 1 in 80, to the gorse covered Camowen Valley. There it crosses the Pomeroy to Carrickmore road on a skew bridge, before sweeping across a high embankment under the watchful eye of the ancient hill fort of Dunmisk, steeped in prehistoric legend. The bridge, and another one close by, once suffered the attentions of the IRA back in 1957, when an attempted destruction closed the line for five days.

The absolute maximum load over Carrickmore bank is 43 loaded wagons, if hauled by one of the Great Northern's SG3 class, also known as the 'Big Ds'.

The site of the Tyrone County Council siding for the loading of stone from the nearby quarry is cleared and, passing under a traditional stone road bridge, Carrickmore station is entered at the end of the embankment. Close to Termon House and adjacent to the hamlet of Tirooney, the station is some two miles from the village it purports to serve and closed to passenger and goods traffic in 1959. There was once a loop serving a second platform, long since removed, and two trailing sidings, also now gone, accessed by Portadown-bound trains and controlled by a key, the section staff being formerly Carrickmore–Beragh, but since altered to Pomeroy–Beragh.

About three quarters of a mile beyond Carrickmore, a peat moss siding was once to be found, and the line now encounters the traditional Tyrone farmland, the hillsides dotted with small white lime-washed cottages. A series of reverse curves, restricted to 30mph, take us around undulating low lying hills, or drumlins, left by retreating glaciers, through Rollingford's crossing and

Top: Four days later, Edward Patterson was back in the Tyrone countryside and captured this shot, looking in the opposite direction, of Mogul No 99 *King George VI* near the summit.

EM Patterson

Centre: A striking view of Carrickmore looking towards Sixmilecross, taken from the road, at a time when the station was still open.

Author's collection

Bottom: An up AEC railcar set, with 603 leading and a buffet car as intermediate, stops at Carrickmore on a wet day in the early 1950s.

Author's collection

on to Sixmilecross. It was on this stretch in the late 1950s that a driver, in charge of one of the recently introduced BUT railcars, and well known for his amorous activities, was seen to stop his Belfast–Derry train and set down his current companion. She was last seen walking across the fields to her house, as the railcar set pulled away again!

The station at Sixmilecross opened in 1862, a year after completion of the line and is somewhat unusual, but none the less pretty for all that, and is the only station on the 51¼ miles between Portadown and Newtownstewart that adjoins a level crossing. A timber platform, on the up side, greets the would be traveller with a small but neat station building at one end, adjacent to the level crossing and road to the nearby village. Inside the entrance, there is the traditional half moon ticket window set into the office wall, from where tickets may be purchased. Behind the platform, a barn like goods shed, with open sides and ends, gives some protection to the single trailing siding, which splits into two sidings, accessible by up trains only. The Sixmilecross & District Co-operative Society headquarters are alongside the station and they make good use of the railway for the distribution of bread and other products.

A further 1½ miles bring us to Beragh, a more substantial structure altogether, with the signal box set on the main platform, forming part of the station building. Here the station, complete with two platforms and passing facilities, is set on a right hand curve similar to Annaghmore but with the layout reversed. The overbridge lies at the Derry end of the platforms, whilst the yard and large goods shed are entered from the Portadown direction.

After leaving Beragh, the vertical curves reappear, with dips and climbs for the 7½ miles to Omagh through scrub land, with purple heather and the bright yellow of whins or gorse much in evidence. This section is something of a trial for loose-coupled goods trains, always at the risk of separated vehicles as the crews battle to keep the couplings taut between wagons whilst not overstraining them. The Great Northern was one

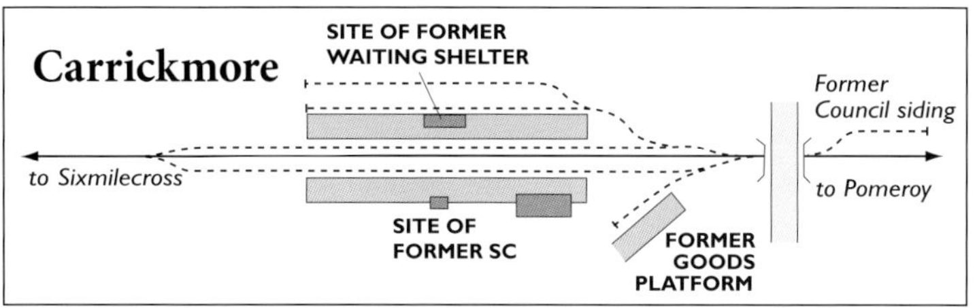

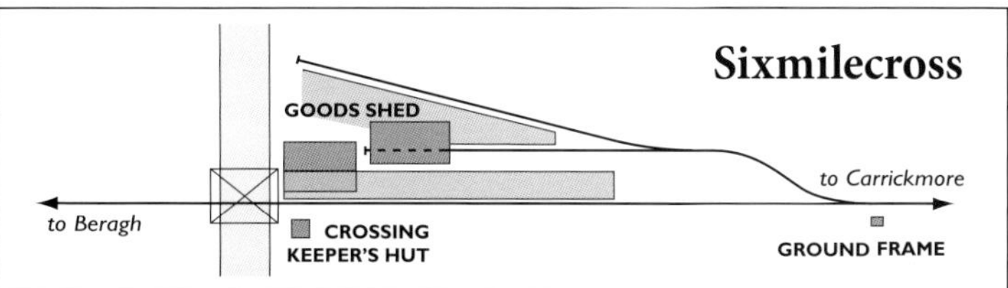

Above: Sixmilecross station on 5 August 1958 showing the wooden platform and goods shed.

EM Patterson

Below: The station building and level crossing. The layout here was very simple and the two-siding goods yard was controlled by a ground frame.

Author's collection

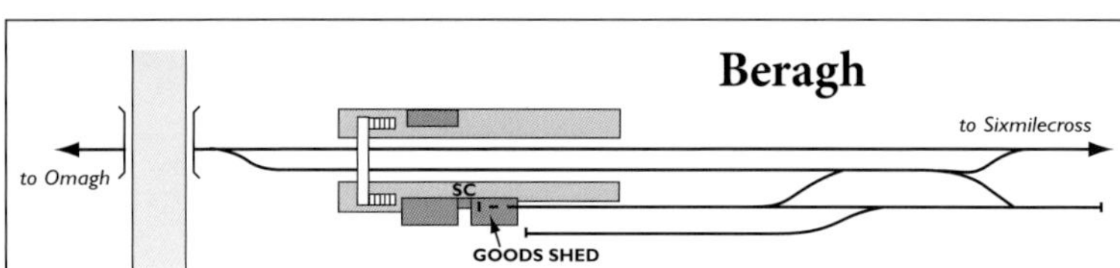

Above: View from the footplate of 2-6-0 No 99 on 25 July 1964 as the 11.30 empty carriages to Omagh approaches Beragh, about half a mile ahead.
EM Patterson

Left: An SG2 0-6-0 crossing the Leap Bridge between Omagh and Beragh with a return Apprentice Boys' Special.
A Donaldson

Opposite bottom: Approaching Omagh Markets station, we see the distant spires of the Sacred Heart church. The nearest building still survives and is now part of Dunnes Stores which occupy the area in the foreground.
EM Patterson

railway that did not routinely fit vacuum brakes to its goods vehicles, the braking equipment in the brake vans being the only assistance that a locomotive could call upon. A short drop brings the traveller down to the Camowen Bridge, with goods trains restricted to 5mph. This is followed by a further crossing bridge (No 100) over the river, on a three-quarter mile long, 40mph curve on a descent of 1 in 87 to reach the facing junction for the Omagh Market branch, on the east of the town, access being covered by a key on the Beragh–Omagh staff.

Omagh Market Branch

Opened in June 1862, the branch is very short, at just half a mile, and drops down on a falling gradient of 1 in 71 through the town to the market yard, where three sidings in a large goods shed handle rail borne traffic from/for the Belfast direction. Generally, there are two to three transfer trains per day between here and the town station (Omagh General), plus a call by one up goods per day, handling all traffic including the gasworks coal supply, the town station goods yard dealing with traffic for Enniskillen and Londonderry. This arrangement was a legacy of the Ulster Railway working the Omagh-Portadown line.

Omagh

Returning to the Market Junction, the main station is encountered after a further three quarter mile run around the town. The journey to the county town

Top: EM Patterson travelled on the footplate of SG 0-6-0 No 44 for a trip down the Omagh Markets branch on Tuesday 28 July 1964. At the junction the fireman has just used the ground frame to set the points for the branch, after the train had run tender first from Omagh General.

EM Patterson

Centre: Part way down the branch, the train is approaching King James Bridge. The shed on the left was owned by the local builder John White, who lived beside the line.

EM Patterson

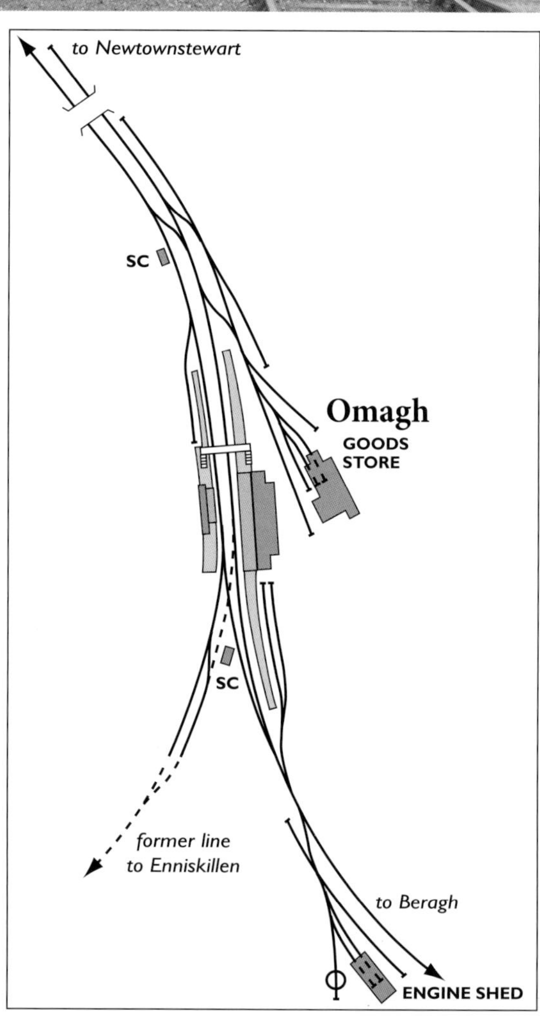

Below: On Easter Monday, 30 March 1964, the local children from Orchard Terrace find amusement in watching S2 class 4-4-0 No 63 *Slievenamon* turning at Omagh shed, by then roofless.

J Langford

Left: In this August 1958 view, a Qs class 4-4-0 is at the shed and railcar C2 or C3 is inside. In the background, Orchard Row can be seen to the left of the shed and newly-built St Brigid's and St Patrick's High Schools are to the left. Children at the schools could enjoy the activities at the shed during breaks, from the vantage point in the middle photograph.

EM Patterson

Opposite top: After arriving at Omagh Markets station, No 44 performed a shunt. The goods store had three roads and there were additional sidings accessed by the two tracks on the right.
EM Patterson

Above: U class 4-4-0 No 197 *Lough Neagh* at Omagh on 11 July 1957, with an AEC railcar at Platform 1. No 197 has Barney McGirr and Peter Judge on the footplate and had just worked the 6.40pm from Enniskillen.
RW FitzHugh

and Omagh General station has brought us 41¾ miles from Portadown and reached perhaps the most important historical point on the line, the location of the meeting and fusing together of the Londonderry & Enniskillen Railway with the Portadown, Dungannon & Omagh Junction Railway, back in 1861. Passing the turntable and the now roofless engine shed on the left, the line swings sharply to the right to join the tracks, set on a sweeping left hand curve through the station, of the erstwhile Enniskillen line, now no more than an extended siding, swinging in from the left to complete the junction, with Omagh South

Below: Two Qs class 4-4-0s at Omagh Junction in 1957. No 120 is arriving in from Belfast and No 123 is waiting on the Enniskillen line. Its train has one of the two GNR W1 clerestory six-wheel brakes marshalled next the engine.
Tom Middlemas

Left: PPs class 4-4-0 No 50 at Omagh with the 3.50 Enniskillen-Londonderry on Thursday 26 May 1955. The Belfast-bound train is due in and has plenty of custom waiting.

BKB Green

Opposite top: The overbridge at the former Mountjoy halt is seen from a Derry-bound railcar on 24 July 1961.

EM Patterson

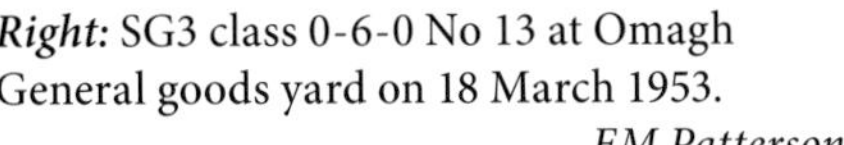

Right: SG3 class 0-6-0 No 13 at Omagh General goods yard on 18 March 1953.

EM Patterson

Below: The signalman of Omagh North Cabin has his coal scuttle filled by the crew of SG3 0-6-0 No 37 on 1 January 1965, six weeks before closure.

EM Patterson

Opposite bottom: U class 4-4-0 No 68 *Down* comes under the road bridge at Newtownstewart with the 4.00pm Omagh-Londonderry on Easter Saturday, 16 April 1960.

A Donaldson

signal box lying between the two routes.

As late as 1961, the lifting train could often be seen stabled on the stub of the Irish North line beyond the platform, as work progressed on the removal of the closed line to Enniskillen and beyond. This was often hauled by SG2 class 0-6-0 No 183, renumbered 42 by the UTA, and itself be withdrawn in May 1961. A multitude of signs now hang from the platform canopy roof girders advising intending passengers of bus connections to destinations once served by rail. A bay platform on our left is hardly ever used now and an extensive and well used goods yard on the right completes the picture.

Omagh to Strabane

North of Omagh, we are now on the old Londonderry & Enniskillen line. A short way out of Omagh, the railway briefly levels as we pass a facing siding on the right, running into the creamery operated by Nestle's and controlled by a key on the Omagh–Newtownstewart staff. A small amount of traffic is still obtained by rail. This is followed by a minor uphill stretch past the site of the long-closed Mountjoy station about three and a half miles north of Omagh, once possessing a siding controlled by Annett's key, and closed in September 1935. The track then falls for almost three miles on a gradient of 1 in 144, with a curved section restricted to 50mph, before following the valley floor, close to the Strule and Mourne rivers. The area is popular with fishermen, often visible from the train as they stand patiently at the salmon leaps. The line will cross the rivers several times before reaching Strabane.

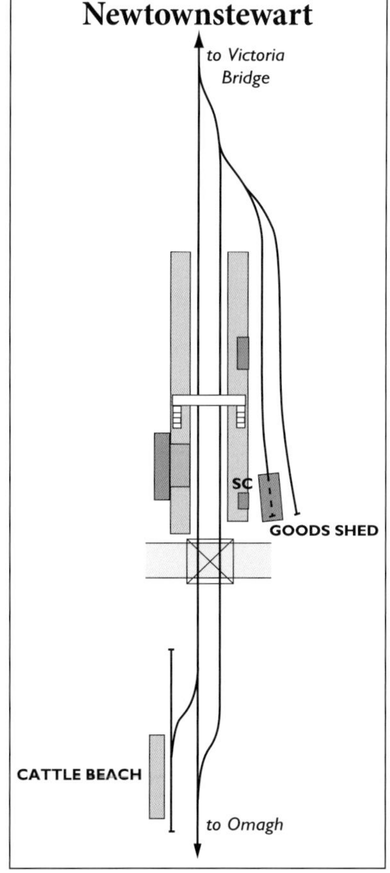

Above: The northern approaches to Newtownstewart are seen from the footplate of 4-4-0 No 68 on 29 July 1961.
EM Patterson

The Blackrock Bridge is crossed before entering Newtownstewart, some ten miles north of Omagh and 51¼ from Portadown. The milepost can be misleading as it reads 97¼, this being the distance from Dundalk, Barrack Street, using the Irish North Western route via Clones and Enniskillen. Set on a gentle curve, Newtownstewart is a crossing point, possessing two platforms with a large goods shed and refuge siding capable of holding 45 wagons, plus engine and van. The station is about half a mile from the town centre and the passenger buildings are constructed in a pleasing Mills style, with yellow brick broken by black, red and purple courses. The family seat of the Abercorns is nearby, at Baronscourt, and members of the family often used the station, especially when the 3rd Duke of Abercorn was Governor of Northern Ireland from 12 December 1922 to 6 September 1945.

With a reduction in local freight traffic, the sidings are now used to store surplus vehicles. Between Newtownstewart and Strabane there are several river bridges including Mulvin Bridge, Breen Bridge and Camus Bridge. Originally constructed in timber by the Londonderry & Enniskillen Railway around 1850-1851, they were replaced by cast iron girder trellis work, only to be rebuilt again by the GNR in 1910-1911 using riveted iron sheets to form enclosed troughs, the whole being supported on steel girders.

Four miles further on we find Victoria Bridge, a block post and crossing point. Arriving over the level crossing, it is still possible to catch a brief glimpse of the remains of the Castlederg & Victoria Bridge Tramway, including staff houses and a transhipment shed. This 3ft gauge

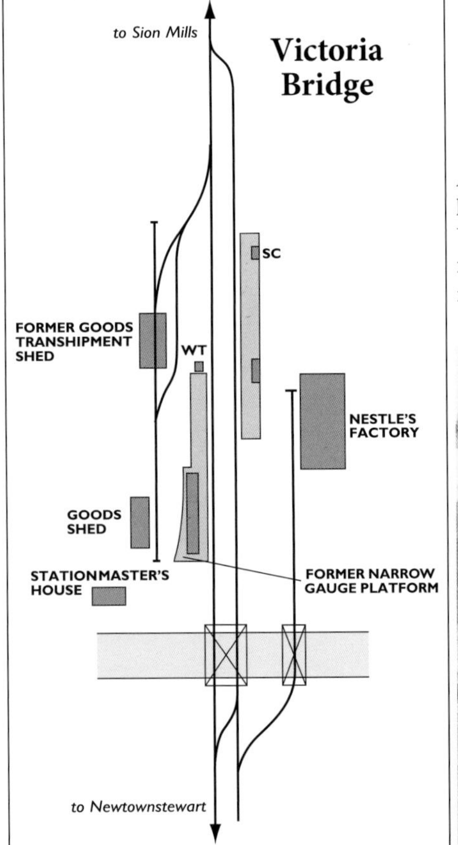

Below: The level crossing at Victoria Bridge from a down BUT railcar about 1963.
Paul Cavanagh

Left: Victoria Bridge station on 13 January 1963, looking towards Newtownstewart.
UTA official

Below: Sion Mills station about 1915 with the station staff and local youths getting in on the picture. Pears soap competes with Brown's Iceberg soap. After a century we know who won! No footbridge when this shot was taken.
JD FitzGerald collection

Bottom: PPs class 4-4-0 No 12 comes through Sion Mills with an up Apprentice Boys' Special in August 1957. Note the footbridge.
A Donaldson

roadside tramway opened in 1884 and ran for seven miles to the town of Castlederg, finishing in the market square. The station name board still exhorts the passenger to 'change for Castlederg'. Although closed as long ago as 1933, there are still remnants of the line to be seen on our left.

The CVBT station building in Castlederg is quite recognisable and still exists, in use as a private dwelling, whilst at Victoria Bridge, the remains of the short, curved departure platform can be seen in the yard behind the GN down platform. Adjacent to this and next to the goods shed, there still exists a single broad gauge siding to cope with any traffic offering. At the south end of the station, there is a single siding through a second level crossing, leading into another smaller Nestle's Milk Factory, the building lying just behind the station's up platform.

Continuing north from Victoria Bridge, the river, having changed its name from the Strule to the Mourne, is crossed again twice before entering the quaintly named Sion Mills, a further 1¾ miles towards Londonderry. The layout here consists of but one platform and a substantial

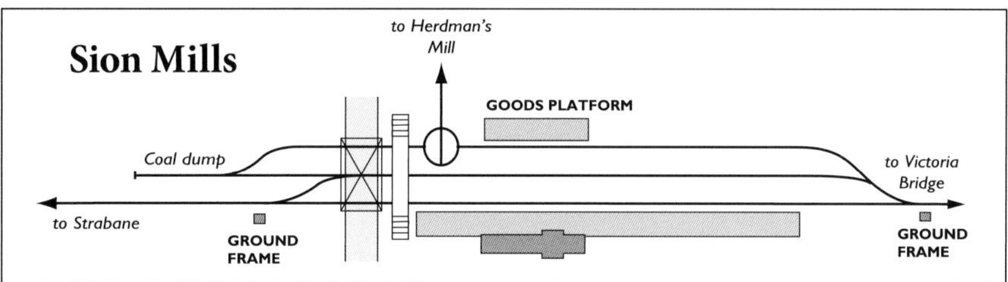

Edward Patterson had an eye for the unusual on his travels and on 12 July 1964 he took the opportunity to record the wagon turntable that gave access to Herdman's Mill at Sion Mills. A BCDR-liveried wagon still in use in 1964 will delight author Des Coakham!
EM Patterson

station building on the down side, the station name set into the bank in large, white painted concrete letters, plus a loop and associated sidings. Constructed in 1883, William Hamilton Mills, the Great Northern's former chief Civil Engineer, is credited with the design of this building, amongst others, constructed in the traditional style associated with the railway and finished in the yellow polychrome brick so beloved of the Company.

The station has regularly come first in its class in the 'best kept station' competitions held by the GNR, with the tradition continued by the UTA. The village, and station, largely owe their existence to the Herdman family, who own and work a large flax mill, producing a not inconsiderable amount of goods traffic for the railway. Siding entry is by staff key, with two local goods working each day from Strabane, propelled in the down direction. A small turntable is set into the goods yard sidings, alongside the goods platform. Wagons are manoeuvred onto this to access the mills own lengthy siding, set at 90 degrees to the running lines. Once horse drawn, the wagons are now pulled into the mill by a tractor with chain attachments. There are three townlands which meet in the centre of Sion Mills, Seein (hill of the fairies) from which Sion takes its name, Liggartown and Ballyfatton. The mill is in Liggartown.

Leaving Sion Mills, there is a steady gradient in a cutting, followed by an equally gentle descent. A short uphill stretch takes us into Strabane as we enter by a bridge over the River Mourne and a level crossing, immediately to the south of the station. At 60¾ miles from Portadown, this is another Mills designed station, this time in red brick, lined with yellow and black, sitting at just 23ft above sea level. It was once a major junction with the adjacent County Donegal Railways Joint Committee station, their 124½-mile narrow gauge empire stretching from Londonderry in the north, to Ballyshannon and Killybegs in the south. There is still a large faded name board on the platform listing the towns in County Donegal that could formerly be reached by changing trains here.

The main and island platforms lie next to the waste ground that was once the busy CDR station, complete with interchange and transfer facilities, right down to a mixed-gauge wagon turntable. The footbridge that once connected all five platforms of both stations now only serves the broad gauge island platform. Despite the exhortations of the station staff, most of the passengers still tend to use the barrow crossing as a more convenient means of crossing the line. The bridge once possessed a fine metal roof, but this was destroyed by Hurricane Debbie in 1961, as mentioned earlier.

The County Donegal station, which lay to the west of the GNR platforms, was built in a pale yellow brick. Latterly housing offices and public accommodation, plus the public search rooms of the British and Irish Customs and Excise Departments, it was originally constructed to a design by James and John Barton of Dundalk, around 1893-1894. Now, the only visible signs of the CDR tenure are the two class 5 locos, *Meenglas* and *Drumboe*, plus a rake of coaches, standing on what were the approach tracks from Stranorlar. The bodies are now badly vandalised and losing what is left of the once pristine geranium red and cream livery, as they wait for a decision on possible preservation. Strabane is still quite busy, with buses from County Donegal now meeting

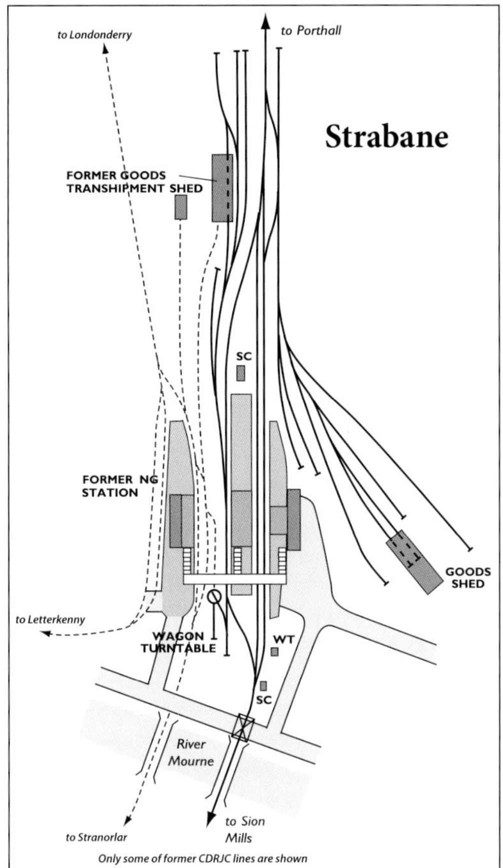

Top: SG class 0-6-0 No 44 arrives at Strabane station on 10 August 1963 with the 8.25am from Portadown. The rear coach is just crossing the River Mourne bridge. Note the whole rake of CDRJC coaches beside the Camel's Hump. *DA Idle*

Centre: The exterior of Strabane station on 24 September 1963 with a Ford Anglia 105E, Austin Somerset, two Morris Minors, an Austin A35 van and an earlier Anglia 100E. *UTA official*

Bottom: Strabane's main platform on 24 September 1963. Note the footbridge, bereft of its roof since Hurricane Debbie in September 1961. *UTA official*

would be passengers from the train.

Following closure of the County Donegal system at the end of 1959, a number of items were rescued and went to the Belfast Transport Museum for historical display. They were carried on transporter wagons but, with the GNR never possessing any, these were ex-NCC vehicles. Two suitable wagons were worked onto the Derry Road and down to Strabane, where various items of rolling stock were loaded onto wagon 3095, plated to carry 20 tons. Then 2-6-4T locomotive *Blanche* was loaded onto wagon 3094, plated at 35 tons. There was a problem since *Blanche* weighed in at 50 tons, as a result of which the wagon bearings constantly ran hot. Progress was inevitably very slow and at Beragh, only 26 miles from Strabane, a very long stop had to be made to allow everything to cool down. Other traffic on the Derry Road suffered much dislocation during this epic journey and Portadown was not reached until the following day, with the locomotive crew on duty for over 18 hours.

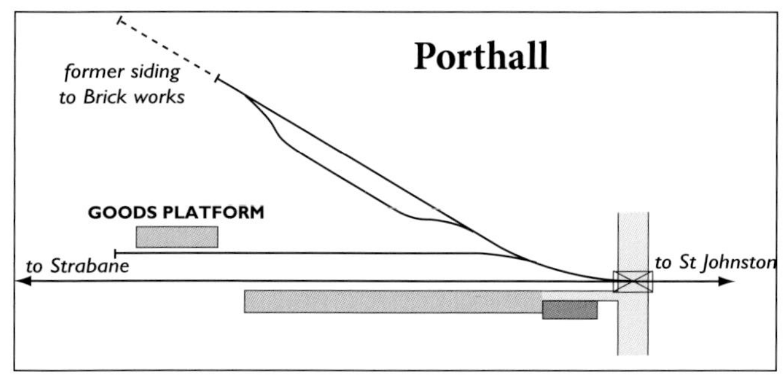

Strabane to Londonderry

As we leave Strabane, it is just possible to pick out the remains of the embankment that took the CDR over the GNR as it headed for the east bank of the river, there to continue its journey into Derry and the Victoria Road terminus. The Derry Road, meanwhile, crosses the Foyle over the metal structure of McKinney's bridge, to reach the west bank of the river, entering County Donegal for nine miles as it passes through the halts of Porthall, St Johnston and Carrigans. The staff at these three stations are clothed in CIÉ uniforms, as befits stations effectively in the Irish Republic and thus uniquely under the control of CIÉ in Dublin, the platforms complete with the obligatory customs posts and huts.

Much 'Free to Free' traffic passes through Strabane on its way from the Republic of Ireland to one of these

Below: Porthall station about 1915 looking south towards Strabane. A double-arm signal serves both up and down directions.

DF FitzGerald collection

Bottom: SG3 0-6-0 No 33 substituting for Railcar 101 on a Strabane local at Porthall about 1963. No 33 will return to Portadown that night on the goods and another SG3 or a Mogul will have arrived next day.

L Hyland

Right: S2 class 4-4-0 No 63 stopped at St Johnston with an up train about 1962. The level crossing is just behind the train.
D Henderson

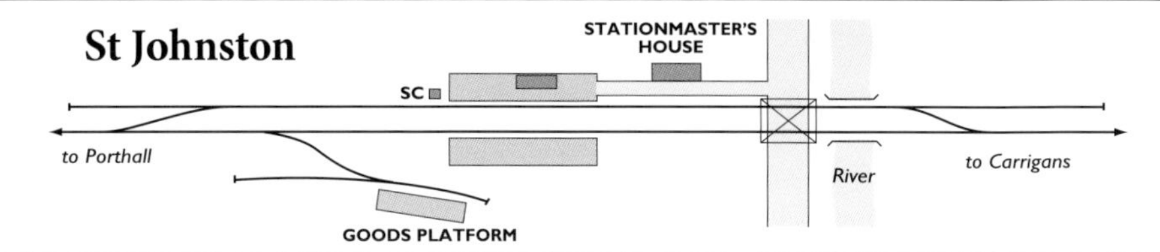

Below: St Johnston station about 1915, looking towards Derry. Note the trailing crossover on the nearside of the level crossing, replaced later by a facing one on the other side of the gates.
DF FitzGerald collection

stations, travelling in wagons sealed by the customs authorities in the Irish Republic, complete with the 'Flying Snail' logo of CIÉ, the lion's share destined for St Johnston. Prior to 1960, sealed containers were also worked into Strabane and transferred by crane to CDRJC narrow gauge flat wagons for delivery within the more remote areas of County Donegal.

The term 'Free to Free' is used to denote freight passing (untouched) through Northern Ireland from one part of the Republic to another, in this case County Donegal in the far north west of the country. The description 'Free to Free' is still in common use by railwaymen although the Free State is now more correctly the 'Republic of Ireland' or Eire.

All three CIÉ stations have siding accommodation, with one platform at Porthall and two at the other stations. The section from St Johnston to Londonderry was singled in 1932, the up line through Carrigans station being removed. The trackbed and up platform now rather wild looking and covered with grass and undergrowth.

Situated a little under two miles from Porthall, between there and St Johnston, lies the site of a second station named Carrickmore. This station had but a brief life from 19 April 1847 to 1 February 1853, and little or no trace now remains of its existence.

It was at Carrigans that a slightly humorous incident once occurred. Derry driver John Breslin was working railcar A out of the maiden city in a bad snowstorm, and left Carrigans for St Johnston without guard Greer on board. The luckless guard started to walk along the track, after the railcar, and was only picked up when the driver, having arrived at St Johnston and realising he had no guard on board, hastily set off back towards Carrigans, to collect the now snow-covered and very unhappy guard from the track side, somewhere between the two stations. Carrigans was also one of the last places on the erstwhile Great Northern system where inside keyed chairs could still be seen, on a section of the old down line now used as a siding.

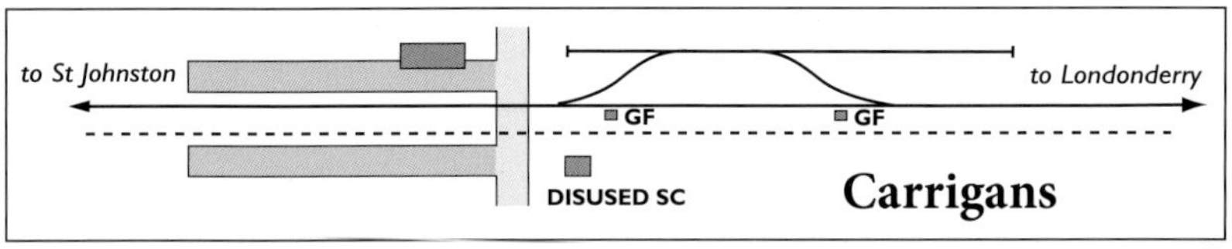

to St Johnston
to Londonderry
GF
GF
DISUSED SC
Carrigans

Right: Carrigans station in late 1965, after the closure, looking towards Strabane.
Stations UK

Left: SG3 0-6-0 No 33 running alongside the goods shed on the approaches to Londonderry on 19 August 1959. The Craigavon Bridge is in the background and the running lines on the right.
EM Patterson

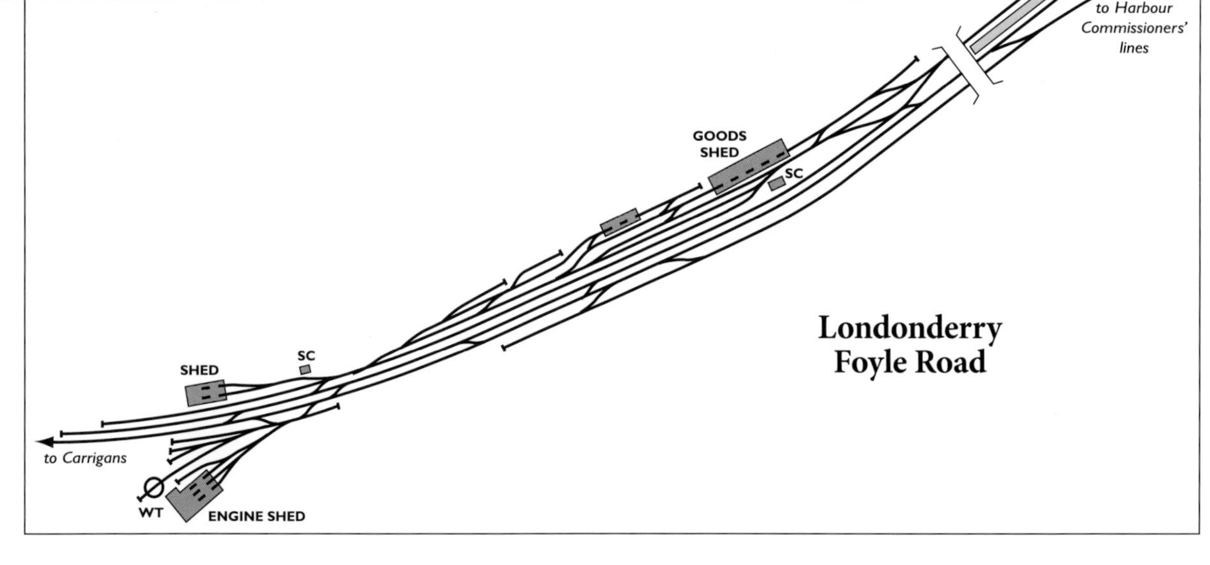

The final 15 miles to Londonderry on the banks of the Foyle are virtually level with slight humps at Porthall and Carrigans, the line losing just five feet in height. Re-entering Northern Ireland, with just 2½ miles to go, the line approaches Londonderry, passing the goods depot, site of the original L&E station from 1847 to 1850, on the left, and the South cabin, closed in 1961. It continues another three quarters of a mile into the terminus at Foyle Road station, sitting alongside the river with just enough room for the Londonderry Port and Harbour Commissioners mixed gauge tracks to pass by on their way to the quayside, once connecting with the erstwhile narrow gauge Londonderry & Lough Swilly Railway.

With a continuing decline in traffic, following the closure of the two narrow gauge lines, the harbour tramway was quietly closed without any fuss, on 31

Above: Londonderry engine shed in 1931 with the River Foyle as a backdrop. The two engines in the yard are PGs 0-6-0 No 103 and C class 0-6-0 No 137. The latter dates from 1872 and was built in Belfast by the Ulster Railway.

LGRP

Below: Foyle Road station viewed from the Craigavon Bridge on 10 August 1936. The locomotive is Ps class 4-4-0 No 27, built in 1892. The platform canopy looks as if it is in process of resheeting with corrugated iron. Good value the job was too – it lasted to 1965!

HB Priestley

Left: The interior of Foyle Road station, looking towards the buffers in early UTA days. SG3 0-6-0 No 33 has a local passenger train and Railcar 101 is still in GNR livery.

L Hyland

August 1962. Foyle Road station is squeezed in between the road and the river on a narrow site. It has a single platform with two faces, the platform ramp finishing hard against the Craigavon Bridge. For many years the bridge was used to transfer broad and narrow gauge wagons from the GNR and the Londonderry & Lough Swilly Railways across the river to the NCC and CDRJC stations This was done by capstan haulage using the lower deck of the bridge. Locomotives were never allowed on the bridge.

The long ‘finger’ platform invariably has attractive baskets of flowers hanging from girders that support the glazed, open-latticed roof. This, in turn, butts onto the main building, the interior of which is in a mix of glazed red brick and fawn tile, with recessed doorways and several stained glass windows incorporating the GNR(I) monogram. The Italianate brick frontage to the station was originally designed and built by Thomas Turner, who was the son of Dublin iron founder Richard Turner and a former assistant to and pupil of Charles Lanyon.

It was built for the GNR in 1899 to replace an earlier structure, the exterior being in a brown brick, and has been subsequently remodelled. The brickwork has darkened with time to give a graceful and weathered appearance, with the entrance giving the casual observer no clue as to the wonderful journey across the hinterland of Northern Ireland that awaits those passing through its portals.

Below: An atmospheric view of Foyle Road station from the concourse about 1963. It is just coming up to 4.00pm and a BUT railcar is at Platform 2.

P Cavanagh

Derry Road Survivors, Buildings and Stock

As is the case with most closed railway lines, many of the stations have vanished without trace and substantial sections of the trackbed have been absorbed back into the adjacent farmland, sometimes without official sanction! The overall picture is varied, with some areas having virtually nothing left that would betray their previous railway ancestry. Fortunately, a few isolated pockets of interest are still to be found where evidence of former occupation is clear to see for anyone with an enquiring mind – especially those of a railway persuasion, with all the delights that can be savoured when a rusting relic of the past is unearthed from the undergrowth, or a gently crumbling structure is encountered upon rounding a curve on the trackbed.

Starting at Portadown, in 1970 the station there reverted back to the site across the River Bann, at Woodhouse Street, that it occupied for 15 years from 1848 when the Armagh line opened, and is now much nearer the centre of the town it serves.

The Derry Road proper started at Portadown Junction, peeling sharply away to the right of the main line and has all but disappeared. A housing estate now encroaches on the trackbed, a short distance beyond the 15mph curve.

In the Armagh countryside at Annaghmore, only the main station building survives, and it is used as offices by Francis Neill Insurance Consultants, the remaining areas having been levelled off, and showrooms erected for Francis Neill Motors. About a mile south of Vernersbridge, the original piers of the railway bridge across the Blackwater River still stand, striding across the water, in isolation. A little further along, the up station building at Vernersbridge is now occupied as a private residence, and has been restored to a very high standard. It can be easily seen from the approach drive or the overbridge without the need to encroach on the property. On the other side of the line, the goods shed still stands forlornly, in isolation.

Trew and Moy has undergone somewhat of a metamorphosis, with the last Stationmaster – Kevin Hughes – taking an entrepreneurial approach to the line's demise. The despatch of mushrooms, in large quantities, was always a good business earner for the station and, following closure, he set up K Hughes and Co Mushrooms and took over the site. The station building now houses the company's offices, with the rest of the station area levelled off for lorry parking and the stone goods shed fully restored and in use as a canteen

Vernersbridge looking east in August 1968. Compare this with the picture on page 112. *Author*

for staff. The nearby Stationmaster's house is now the private home of the Hughes family.

One of the more drastic changes has taken place at the site of the former Dungannon station. The 814 yards long tunnel to the east of the town, under Windmill Hill, can still be found without much effort and is probably passable, though the entrances have long been sealed to dissuade anyone from attempting such a risky manoeuvre. All buildings, including the station, have been demolished and removed. The line of the trackbed around the town now forms a sunken and attractive, if unfulfilling, linear park. (Bear in mind that the real countryside is within feet of this man-made construction.) Some distance beyond the station and linear park, the erstwhile site of Dungannon Junction has disappeared back into the scrubland, but a nearby dwelling (ex signalman's cottage?) helps to pinpoint the approximate location of the signal box and track divergence.

On the Cookstown branch, the three-arched road overbridge, together with the derelict goods shed and crumbling overgrown platforms, can identify the original site of Coalisland station. At the end of the 14½ mile long branch, Cookstown station has been tastefully restored and is now once more in use as commercial premises. Some track has even been relaid alongside the platform. The pleasing proportions of this building betray the very evident GNR origin.

Returning to the Londonderry line trackbed, at Donaghmore, the station building is still standing but any resemblance to a railway use has long disappeared, as have any outbuildings.

Pomeroy, or rather the site of Pomeroy, is the next place to be encountered, and is a sad, though classic, case of gradual but almost total reversion to nature, albeit assisted by the uncaring hand of man. With the distinction of being the highest station in Ireland, Pomeroy was in quite a remote location in the Sperrin mountain foothills. After the closure of the line in February 1965, the station entered a hiatus, with the line appearing to slumber for over a year, a little like Rip Van Winkle in the fairy tale. The lines were lifted during the course of 1966 and, by the middle of 1967, weeds and undergrowth were rapidly taking hold. The station had a sad, deserted appearance with only the track and platform lamp tops missing. Water still dripped from the tank at the end of the Derry platform, and all the signals stood, like silent guardians, their arms still in place and set at danger, where they had been left after the closure.

Gradually, the view from the road overbridge became obscured, as saplings on the trackbed reached higher into the sky during 1968 and filled the cutting. The signal box still stood, bereft of glass, guarding the approach and waiting for a train that would never come. By 1978, some ten years later, little had changed. The ballast was churned up, with evidence of farmers and others using the station area, but otherwise all was just as it had been left all those years ago. Nineteen years on and a different picture presented itself, with the water tank all but out of sight and surrounded by vegetation while, by 1999, all that remained in the station was the roofless waiting shelter on what used to be the Derry platform. The wood and glass front had gone and the track area had been filled up to platform level, with just the edging slabs still visible. The water tank had gone without trace.

To the south there remained just the goods shed, with the skeletal remains of the veranda on the road approach side of the building, and the old toilet block, now roofed over and converted into an amenity waste site, a notice board from Cookstown District Council proudly proclaiming the fact; a sad end to a once useful and important part of life in Pomeroy. Contractors' lorries are now parked on the trackbed. Beyond the road bridge, a local farmer was now using the trackbed to access fields alongside the curve that led out of the site and onto Pomeroy Bank.

The next station to be encountered is Carrickmore. Closed to traffic as long ago as 1959, the goods shed disappeared soon after, the platform and station building remaining until the end even though the track had been slewed away from the platform face and trains no longer called there. Following the closure of the line, rails and chairs were left in piles for collection as track lifting progressed and the scene was one reminiscent of a scrap yard. By August 1968, a local farmer by the name of Anderson was living in the station house, and the station building was being used to house pigs and hay. Beyond Carrickmore, in 1997, horses were regularly being grazed on the trackbed, now overgrown with a lush covering of verdant grass. A little way beyond, the keeper's cottage at Rollingford's crossing remains as a neatly kept private residence. In July 1967 one crossing gate had disappeared completely, with the other one thrown against the hedge; the telegraph poles, shorn of their wiring, still tracing out the former route.

A short way past the crossing is Sixmilecross. The Co-operative Society building has gone and little remains to indicate that there was once a station here. The single-storey station building has been replaced with an attractive bungalow, and only the pinching in of the road gives any clue to the fact that there was once a level crossing here.

Above: The stop block of the goods shed siding beside the ramp the up platform, Pomeroy, in 1968. The projecting whitewashed building is the gents' urinal. In the distance the water tower at the end of the down platform can be seen. *Author*

Below: What was left of Carrickmore in 1968. There is a lot less now. *Author*

After leaving Sixmilecross, we come to Beragh, similar in many ways to both Trew & Moy and Annaghmore. This station has survived almost completely intact, even down the signal box and goods shed, the exact antithesis to Pomeroy. Now in private hands, the trackbed between the platforms has been filled in, landscaped and grassed, to provide a beautiful lawned area. The sloping canopy roof over the down platform still serves its original purpose of keeping people dry whilst they enjoy the (new) view. At the front of the goods shed, the entrance still remains; only the protective canopy for loading and unloading has disappeared.

A small bungalow has also appeared on the left of the entrance drive, but this does not detract from the overall view. The icing on the cake, if you will, is that the whole scene can still be viewed from the road overbridge, set in the surrounding Tyrone countryside, without the need to trespass on what is now private property. If you half close your eyes, it is almost possible to imagine that a train will appear any moment.

At Omagh, there is little left to see, but several clues as to the one-time presence of the railway. The main approach is now a by-pass around the town, appropriately named Great Northern Road. One of the stone built goods buildings has been retained and is now used as a tyre-fitting centre. Adjacent to this is a new structure; a youth club, suitably named 'The Station Centre'. The station proper is now largely under the road and the opposite side of it. The buildings have gone though there is now a memorial plaque to the railwaymen killed at the station in 1950.

Further on, the trackbed still passes alongside the Nestles factory and at one time the line ran through what is now the Ulster-American Folk Park. At Newtownstewart the station, once the haunt of the Dukes

Top: Remains of Sixmilecross station in 1968. The goods shed is then but a skeleton and has long since gone.
Author

Bottom: Beragh station is still lived in and has survived well. This is how it looked not long after the lines were lifted.
Author

of Abercorn, has gone. After closure, the goods shed was used by the Department of Regional Development Roads Service, but demolished in 2001 to make way for a new road. The question has to be asked, could they not have taken the road around the structure and made good use of a well made and sturdily constructed stone building?

At Victoria Bridge, that attractive single storey building, constructed in panelled wood, has disappeared without trace, along with the platform sign 'Victoria Bridge – change for Castlederg'. The adjacent factory, once belonging to Nestles and served by a railway siding, is now a collection of small business units. The only railway building now remaining is the stationmaster's house built by the GNR. It was damaged by a bomb blast in 1972 but subsequently repaired. The station building at Castlederg, once the headquarters of the erstwhile Castlederg and Victoria Bridge Tramway, still survives but is now up for sale, as the local District Council are

Right: Omagh Junction in 1968. The platforms lasted until the 1990s but now a bypass road runs through the site.

Author

unable/unwilling to afford the upkeep any longer, a sad reflection of modern times.

At Sion Mills, the once beautiful station building, designed by Mills and erected by the GNR in 1883, has gone. The rest of the station area is now a car park, serving the 'Riverside Walk' with just a small section of the platform face still remaining and visible, amongst the undergrowth. It is hard to imagine that this area was once a well-kept property that regularly collected the award for the 'Best Kept Station'. Sadly, the nearby Herdman's Flax Mill, part of the railway operation and served by a siding at right angles to the running lines, finally ceased operation 21 May 2004, thus bringing to an end 170 years of flax spinning in Sion Mills.

The site of Strabane station gives one a sense of the unreal. There is absolutely nothing left to show that the hub of a great railway network and interchange ever existed here. Redevelopment and road works have eliminated everything. Famous landmarks like the 'Camel's Hump' on the approach to the CDRJC station would be very difficult to pinpoint now, and the inevitable by-pass uses part of the GNR line from the south. A large traffic island at the junction with the road to Lifford is probably as near to the station site as you are likely to get.

Leaving Strabane, the platform and goods dock at Porthall is covered in scrub and undergrowth, still remain, in splendid isolation, their survival due in part to the fact that the station lay some distance from any habitation. Likewise, at St Johnston, the main building and station master's house both survive as private dwellings. At Carrigans, the concrete building on the down side, one time haunt of the customs men, has been extended and is also a private house.

Finally, we come to Foyle Road station at Londonderry. The station was knocked down and demolished in 1970, as part of a major waterfront development of the former quays from the Guildhall to the Craigavon Bridge. The old GNR water tank south of the bridge still survives. Alongside it, the Foyle Valley Railway and Museum occupy the trackbed, with a large brick-built display building housing ex-County Donegal stock and a three foot gauge track running for approximately two miles along the GNR trackbed back towards Strabane. Derry City Council and the North West of Ireland Railway Society opened the museum in 1989 but is now only open in July and August and working trains are no longer operated.

Across the bridge, Victoria Road terminus station on the CDRJC is almost untouched, and now houses the Foyle Fisheries and a restaurant.

Then and Now

An unidentified S class 4-4-0 coasts past Dunmisk Hill into Carrickmore with an evening train to Derry in 1964. *Author*

An unidentified S class 4-4-0 approaches the road bridge at Pomeroy in 1964. *Author*

Carrickmore bank in 1968, as nature begins to reclaim the scene. *Author*

The view from Pomeroy bridge in 1968 with the signals and telegraph poles still in position. *Author*

Passengers bound for Portadown and Belfast cross the tracks at Trew and Moy to reach their train. Meanwhile, the U class 4-4-0 blows off impatiently as the starting signal is already down. *Author's collection*

Railcar A calls at Pomeroy on a local service from Omagh to Dungannon. *Author's collection*

The remains of Trew and Moy in August 1968. The footbridge has already gone and the lamp on the up platform now sits at a drunken angle. The starting signal will never again fall. *Author*

A derelict Pomeroy station in August 1968 with its windowless cabin and overgrown platform. *Author*

Rolling Stock

Several items of rolling stock have survived both the line closure and the cutter's torch. They include not only ex-GNR and UTA items that would have worked on the line or adjacent to it during their lifetime, often on a regular basis, but rolling stock from companies that adjoined the Derry Road during its life. They are now mostly in the safe hands of the Railway Preservation Society of Ireland, some fully restored and in use, with the rest waiting their turn in the queue. Most are at their Whitehead headquarters, with certain items being out stationed, as needed, at their Dublin area base.

A number of CDRJC items that would have been seen from time to time at Strabane station have also survived, some restored and running once more on preservation sites. These include locomotives, carriages and wagons, under the protection of various bodies, and can be seen at such locations as The Foyle Valley Railway Centre, in Londonderry, The Donegal Railway Heritage Centre in Donegal town, The Finn Valley Railway near Fintown in County Donegal, and the Ulster Folk and Transport Museum at Cultra outside Belfast.

Locomotives

Ex-GNR Qs class 4-4-0 No 131

Built by Neilson Reid at their Glasgow works in February 1901, works number 5727. This locomotive was a regular performer on the Derry Road in the 1920s and 1930s. Following an overhaul in 1958, she passed to CIÉ in October of that year, upon the break up of the GNR, and the locomotive was to remain in service until the end of CIÉ steam in late 1962. After withdrawal, she was retained by CIÉ but lay untended until 1968, when she was moved to Inchicore and given pseudo-GNR blue livery. Towards the end of the 1970s she was repainted black and placed on a plinth at Dundalk station, opposite Platform 2. In June 1984 she was relieved of this indignity, moving to Mallow, to be looked after by the Great Southern Railway Preservation Society.

Unfortunately, this venture failed in the late 1990s, and the locomotive, now with the boiler and firebox out of the frames, was moved to Inchicore Works. She then entered the care of the RPSI and the running frames were moved to Whitehead on 31 May 2003, to be followed in December by the boiler, firebox and cab fittings The locomotive is awaiting suitable funding to enable a restoration to full running order, at which point she will be seen out on the line again.

Ex-GNR S class 4-4-0 No 171 Slieve Gullion

This well-known engine was built by Beyer Peacock at their Manchester works in 1913, Works No 5629, and is named after a high mountain in South Armagh. The engine was initially used for the Belfast–Dublin express service and was renewed by the GNR at Dundalk in 1938, Works No 42. Again, this locomotive was a regular performer across the system and appeared many times on the Derry Road during the final years before closure, including the last weekend. At the division of GNR rolling stock in 1958, *Slieve Gullion* passed to CIÉ, where she continued to work until the end of CIÉ steam in late 1962. She was then sold to the UTA in June 1963, and based for her final two years at Adelaide shed, Belfast, from where she worked trains between Belfast, Portadown and Londonderry until 1965.

The locomotive almost immediately passed to the RPSI, and has being been at the head of many steam specials across Ireland since, in her traditional livery of sky blue (very similar to Caledonian Railway sky blue), with black lining, edged in white. Now one of their flagship engines, she has been out of service since July 2002, awaiting an overhaul. Her last major one was completed in March 1992.

Ex-NCC WT Class No 4

Built by the LMS, Derby Works, to a basically Ivatt design in 1947, for use on the NCC system, this locomotive was assembled from a kit of parts at Belfast, York Road

Workshops, and is now the last surviving member out of a class of 18 locomotives. Popularly know by the crews as 'Jeeps' on account of their all-round capability, she remained in traffic three years after the withdrawal of steam power in Britain on 11 August 1968, based at York Road shed until its closure, in 1970.

On 31 March 1970, No 4 arrived at Belfast with the last main line steam worked passenger train in the British Isles, the 5.25pm local from Whitehead and Carrickfergus. On 2 May, No 4, along with sister engine No 53, brought the last spoil train in from Magheramorne Quarry, to the M2 motorway construction site, at Belfast. Her final duties were a week later, when, in company with No 51, she worked a train of girders out to Ballyclare Junction, followed by a period on pilot duties at York Road until withdrawal in June 1971.

Purchased direct from Northern Ireland Railways on 11 July of that year for £1,275, she then moved to the RPSI headquarters at Whitehead, from where she has been used extensively on tour across the country, often in the company of *Slieve Gullion*. The first stretch of main line running, while in preservation, lasted until 1978. After a general overhaul, return to service in 1984 was accompanied by a week-long stint on NIR permanent way trains, to assist with running in (when available and in steam, No 4 has been known to cover the occasional NIR failed service train – a rare example of cooperation between business and preservation groups). During the late 1990s, No 4 underwent a major overhaul, triumphantly returning to service in August 2002, after a £150,000 rebuild. In her gleaning UTA black livery, lined with red and straw, she is currently in service and hauling excursion trains.

Ex Londonderry Port & Harbour Commissioners 0-6-0ST No 3 'R H Smyth'

Built to a track gauge of 5ft 3ins by the Avonside Engineering Company in 1928, Works No 2021, this locomotive was designed to work on mixed gauge track with both 5ft 3ins and 3ft gauge wagons, facilitated by a large narrow gauge coupling between the draw hook and the left hand side buffer. With its 9ft wheelbase, capable of traversing a 150ft radius curve, this engine spent its entire life until withdrawal in 1959, working on the short, quayside line at Londonderry.

This railway, on the west bank of the River Foyle, ran from a connection with the three foot gauge Londonderry and Lough Swilly Railway at their Graving Dock station, along the quayside to the GNR Foyle Road station. The line continued over the river using the lower deck of the Craigavon Bridge, though all wagons were capstan-hauled, as locomotives were not allowed across the bridge. On the east bank, there were broad and narrow gauge rail connections to the LMS NCC station at Waterside, and the CDRJC station at Victoria Road, respectively.

The loco had been out of use for some time when, in February 1967, the Reverend LH Campbell purchased her for preservation. The loco then remained for some time in the Harbour Commissioners' sheds. In 1972, she was sold to the RPSI so that full restoration to working order could take place, the official handover taking place on 1 May 1972. After a protracted overhaul, No 3 steamed for the first time in preservation in the summer of 1977 and for many years following became the yard shunting engine at Whitehead, a duty which included Santa trains and Easter Bunny rides before such operations became main line events.

Fame beckoned and, in the summer of 2000, contractors Henry Boot hired No 3 to assist with the relaying contract for NIR on the Bleach Green–Antrim line. Neither NIR nor IE were in a position to loan a locomotive for ballast train hauling and, having the ideal motive power available, the RPSI was approached. Between 18 June and 25 November, over 50,000 tons of stone ballast, were hauled and distributed on the main line, at the end of which the locomotive returned in some triumph back to its Whitehead base.

In 2005, the loco was given a major overhaul, as contractors were back, this time on the Bleach Green–Whitehead line and, with its capability now well known, No 3 was formally requested, moving to Greenisland in August. After five months of ballasting duties on the main line again, she finished the job back at her Whitehead base in December of that year. Currently *R H Smyth* is in traffic and based at Downpatrick, where she is on loan to the Downpatrick and County Down Railway Society.

COACHES						
Number	**Origin**	**Built**	**Type**	**Location**	**Acquired**	**Status**
50	GNR	1911 Dundalk Works	A3. 1st Class Directors' Saloon	Whitehead	1973	Out of Use
114	GNR	1940 Dundalk Works	L13. Open Brake Third	Whitehead	1977	Out of Use
9	GNR	1954 Dundalk Works	K31. Open Third	Dublin	1975	*In Use
88	GNR	1938 Dundalk Works	B6. Dining Car	Dublin	1973	**In Use

*Was fitted out as AEC driving trailer in 1954, becoming UTA No N 586 and designated second class.
**Altered in the late 1950s to run as an intermediate (dining) coach with the BUT railcar sets, becoming UTA No 552.
N.B. – The following GNR coaches were also initially preserved, but sadly, subsequently lost through decay and fire damage caused by vandals at Whitehead. 176 (583), 189 (595), 227 (561), 231 (562)

WAGONS						
Number	**Origin**	**Built**	**Type**	**Location**	**Acquired**	**Status**
81	GNR	1945 Dundalk Works	20 ton Brake Van	Whitehead	1985	In Use
504	???	1940 Dundalk Works	20 ton Guinness Grain Van	Whitehead	1965	Out of Use
788	GNR	1934 Dundalk Works	P2. Parcel Van	Whitehead	1979	Out of Use
2518	GNR	???	20 ton Guinness Van	Whitehead	1965	Out of Use
3169	GNR	1912 Cowans Sheldon Carlisle	15 ton Self Propelled Steam Crane	Whitehead	1980	Out of Use
-	GNR	-	4 plank wagon Carrying Steam Crane Jib	Whitehead	-	Out of Use
8112N	GNR	???	20 ton Ballast Wagon	Whitehead	1983	In Use
R5	GNR	1948/1998	30 ton Rail wagon. Ex-Side Corr Brake/ First 231	Whitehead	1975	**In Use
R6	GNR	1948/1998	30 ton Rail Wagon. Ex-Side Corridor First 227			**In Use

** An arson fire destroyed the carriage bodies in 1996. The running gear was salvaged for further use.

Notes on Creamery Traffic and Operation

Freight came in all shapes and sizes to the railways of Ireland and the Derry Road was no exception. Much traffic originated from the many rural Co-operative Society operations. These were often based in a building adjacent to the station, an example being Sixmilecross where there was the attached local creamery. Co-operatives once a common sight across Ireland in the 20th century in most communities of any size, generating a valuable and consistent amount of rail-borne traffic in both directions. To fully understand and appreciate the complex nature of the business and its importance to the railway as a customer, it is necessary to examine how such types of business came into being and we can look at the history and life of the Pomeroy plant as a prime example.

Pomeroy Co-operative Society was formed around the turn of the 20th century, being inspired by the ideas of Sir Horace Curzon Plunkett (24 October 1854-26 March 1932), the third son of Edward Plunkett, 16th Baron Dunsany of Dunsany Castle, in County Meath. Plunkett, an Anglo-Irish unionist and later Irish nationalist. He was a pioneer of agricultural co-operation and reform in Ireland, being a member of the Congested Districts Board, Ireland, from 1891 to 1918 and founder of the Recess Committee and Irish Agricultural Organisational Society (IAOS). He was also MP for South Dublin in the House of Commons between 1892 and 1900.

The stimulus for his farsighted ideas lay in the threat to the dairy market by the Danish butter industry. In this he was ably supported by both George William Russell, an Irish nationalist who wrote under the pseudonym 'AE' and editor of *The Irish Homestead*, the journal of the IAOS, together with Fr Thomas A Finlay SJ, a Jesuit educationalist and social reformer, who was Professor of Economy at University College Dublin and Vice-President of the IAOS. In 1903 there were 146 agricultural societies, 370 dairy societies and 201 co-operative banks, rising by 1914 to over 1000 societies with 90,000 members, all under the auspices of the IAOS.

Pomeroy Creamery was located at 14 Station Road and built at this site for two very good reasons. An abundant supply of clean water could be obtained via a well and, as the address implies, it was adjacent to the railway station, which provided excellent transport facilities for the despatch of its products across the province.

The Pomeroy plant shared its premises with the Pomeroy Mineral Water Company, which produced flavoured mineral water. Known as a central creamery for the making of butter, an auxiliary creamery at Mulnagore separated cream from the milk and sent this across to Pomeroy for churning. The final manager of the creamery was Mr Grant, from Newry. He worked at Pomeroy until the plant's closure in the early 1920s. The village also suffered the loss of the local Agricultural Produce Store, under the managership of John Joe Hurson, around the same time. Members used the store as a central point from which to sell locally-produced agricultural produce and groceries.

When the creamery failed commercially, it was reconstituted as a private concern by Mr Smith, who had gained his previous experience as a onetime manager at the nearby Doons Creamery in Kildress, on the Cookstown to Omagh road. Although part of the creamery complex of buildings, the Mineral Water Company was not taken over at the time and continued to operate independently. It ceased trading a few years later when it was taken over by the Tyrone Mineral Water Company, who acquired the 'good-will' (customer base) but not the machinery or plant, which remained at Pomeroy.

Once installed as owner, Mr Smith made many improvements, including the sinking of an artesian well by Smith, Hayes and Company of The Maze, near Lisburn. Prior to this, dependence had been on an elderly sunken well shared with the Mineral Water Company. This was regularly supplemented by the GNR station supply. This freely-given assistance was conditional that, in times of drought, the railway's requirements naturally had to take priority.

In 1930, a Sabro refrigerator was purchased and installed in the area previously used by the mineral water operation. The ice obtained from this was used to chill the separated cream each morning, removing the need to obtain ice from the Belfast Pure Ice and Cold Storage Company in Great Victoria Street. Previously, ice in two-hundredweight blocks, and wrapped in Hessian sacks, would regularly be sent out from Grosvenor Road goods yard by the late evening Londonderry freight train and, on arrival, would be taken to the creamery's ice house and packed in sand.

By 1933, the coal-burning steam engine that provided power for the creamery was in need of replacement and a 44hp Blackstock crude oil engine was installed. One entrepreneurial benefit of this was the installation of the first-ever electricity supply to Pomeroy village, which previously had total dependence of Tilly pressure lamps, though these were to remain in use on outlying farms for many years to come. Power was made available to village dwellings from 8 am to midnight each day.

Pomeroy Creamery was widely diverse in its output and quite adaptable, producing a range of products including milk, skimmed milk, buttermilk, cream and butter for local consumption, though cheese was never made at the plant. Additionally, butter was sent by rail to numerous shops as far away as Belfast. Imported products were not ignored. Butter would arrive from Australia and New Zealand in 56lb wooden boxes. These would be sent from Belfast docks by rail in eight-ton ventilated Butter Vans, to Pomeroy, for packaging into one pound rolls and delivered to customers the following day. Starting in the late 1920s, this continued through until the mid 1930s with butter being sent by rail to delivery points along the full length of the Derry Road as far as Londonderry.

The creamery at Pomeroy was to continue until April 1935 when Mr Smith went bankrupt and took his own life. The business was sold by the then Belfast Banking Company, now part of the Northern Bank, and acquired by Killyman Creamery, becoming an auxiliary operation to that concern. Pomeroy then operated as an auxiliary unit, sending separated cream to Killyman by rail, via Trew & Moy station. Following the take-over by Killyman, Mr McCormack was appointed manager, a position he was to hold until the creamery's final closure in 1942. During that period, six, eight, 15 and 17 gallon cans were discontinued, although the ten and twelve gallon cans were still in daily use when the creamery closed.

After the closure, the creamery building passed into the hands of Major Alexander of Pomeroy House. He lived there with his uncle, Colonel Lowry, the family having a sizeable land and property base including Termon House, close to Carrickmore station, and much use was made of the GNR railway services at both stations. With the estates having many vehicles and pieces of agricultural machinery, there was a need for good repair facilities locally, and the Major saw both the sense in purchasing the old creamery site and possibilities it opened up for him. He persuaded a local man, James McFarland, to open a garage there, which he ran with his son Billy, a very adept mechanic, for five years. The Ruddy family, who operate a fuel supply business called Pomeroy Fuels, later purchased the premises and the site is now a fuel depot.

Creamery Process

Milk suppliers were given a numbered passbook and a record kept therein of all deliveries to the creamery. Churns, for bringing the milk in, were provided by the creamery, to be paid for by the supplier in instalments deducted from the creamery payment cheques. The churns supplied would be a multiple of either six or ten gallon size, depending upon the amount likely to be brought in and would be marked with the suppliers number.

In time, the churns were standardised on the ten gallon size and the smaller one phased out. Distant farmers used independent carriers to take the milk in and return the empty churns, with those living within a one mile radius bringing their own milk in, often by horse and cart and in time by tractor. With the Ministry of Agriculture eventually providing lorries and dedicated drivers for the movement of churns, the work for independent carriers disappeared.

On arrival, the milk was weighed, recorded and poured into a receiving tank. From there, it was piped into a steam-powered heater and, upon reaching the required temperature, passed into a separator, where it was rotated at high speed to separate the cream. The cream was taken to a chiller before being mechanically churned to produce buttermilk and butter. The remaining liquid, now skimmed milk, was returned to the farmer to be used in animal feed.

The power supply for the creamery was initially a coal-fired steam engine, the steam being used both for heating the milk by passing steam pipes through the milk containment area (effectively a heat transfer unit) and via a driven central power shaft and transmission belts to work the churn and separator. When the steam engine was replaced, the Blackstock diesel engine brought a welcome additional source of revenue with the provision of electric light to the village.

Creamery Employees

Mr Grant. Manager
Mr Smith. Manager
Mr Frank McGurk, Creggan.
Apprentice Manager
Mr Peter Malone, Pomeroy. Apprentice
Manager
Miss Elizabeth Falls (Later Haughey),
Coalisland. Clerk
Miss Molly Falls. Clerk
Miss Mary O'Hagan, Turnabarson.
Dairymaid
(Churning and packing of products)
Miss Power, Dublin. Dairymaid
(Trained at Glasnevin
Agricultural College)
Miss Warnock. Dairymaid
(Churning and packing of products)
Miss Rose Trainor, Pomeroy. Dairymaid
(Churning and packing of products)
Miss McIvor, Pomeroy. Dairymaid
(Churning and packing of products)
Mr Billy Brimmage, Pomeroy. Driver
(Deliveries and collections)
Mr Jimmy Harte, Pomeroy. Driver
(Deliveries and collections)
Mr James McFarlane. Fireman. (Boiler man)
Mr Pearse Kelly, Dungannon. Fireman. (Boiler man)
Mr Frank Kelly. Unknown
Mr Frank O'Hagan, Turnabarson. Engineer
(Maintenance on separator, heater etc)

GNR Butter Van No 847 in 1931. *LGRP*

Railcar Stopping Places at (accommodation) Crossing Points

During the early 1930s, it became evident that spiralling operating costs would have to be seriously addressed, as would the attempts to stimulate more passenger traffic onto the railway and away from the burgeoning competition then being provided by the rising tide of speculative operators, using cheaply purchased second hand, and often poorly maintained, road buses. The prospect of cheap travel often overcame any qualms regarding safety and a way had to be found to encourage people to use the railway system. The Derry Road, with its winding secondary route serving a variety of rural communities, was an excellent example of what could be achieved with a little inventiveness.

With the introduction of railcars and the ongoing improvements in technology, a means was afforded by which some of the potential traffic could be tapped and harnessed. To maximise the use of the lightweight railcars, and even lighter railbuses, then being turned out by Dundalk works, a number of crossing points were identified which, used along with existing halts, could provide a better service for intending travellers. Often, these extra stopping places were no more than public road level crossings, sometimes serving rather isolated communities. In some cases, they would be accommodation crossings. In all cases it would be necessary for an intending passenger to show a hand signal to the driver. Where a signal was also provided, such as Rollingford, this would be placed at danger as an additional indicator to the driver.

Much use was also made of stopping places in more remote areas by the adjacent narrow gauge railway systems, where their systems were ideally suited to a more relaxed style of operation. The Castlederg and Victoria Bridge Tramway had three roadside stopping places, with the nearby Clogher Valley Railway possessing 27 official (and no doubt several unofficial) roadside stops, in addition to the ten stations.

Out of a total of 73 stopping places spread across the GNR, no less than 17 were on the Derry Road. Between Portadown and Omagh, the were two accommodation crossings and ten public road crossings listed as stopping points, with a further five on the Cookstown branch, though virtually all had gone by 1960.

NAME	SECTION LOCATION	OPEN	CLOSED
Annakeera	Portadown – Annaghmore	01/06/1937	01/10/1957
Derrycoose	Annaghmore – Vernersbridge	01/06/1937	01/10/1957
Shaw's **	Trew & Moy – Dungannon	01/06/1937	01/10/1957
Dungannon Junction	Dungannon – Donaghmore	01/06/1937	02/06/1958
Mullafurtherland	Donaghmore – Pomeroy	01/06/1938	13/06/1960
Reynold's	Donaghmore – Pomeroy	27/09/1937	13/06/1960
Brimmage's **	Donaghmore – Pomeroy	01/06/1938	13/06/1960
Rollingford	Carrickmore – Sixmilecross	01/06/1938	13/06/1960
Tattykeernan	Beragh – Omagh	01/06/1938	13/06/1960
Edenderry	Beragh – Omagh	01/06/1938	13/06/1960
Garvaghy No 1 ***	Beragh – Omagh	27/09/1937	13/06/1960
Garvaghy No 2	Beragh – Omagh	01/06/1938	13/06/1960
COOKSTOWN BRANCH			
Old Engine	Dungannon Junction – Coalisland	01/06/1938	01/02/1942
Annagher	Coalisland – Stewartstown	01/06/1938	01/02/1942
Lisnastrain	Coalisland – Stewartstown	01/06/1938	01/02/1942
Grange	Stewartstown – Cookstown	01/07/1938	6/01/1950
Killymoon ****	Stewartstown – Cookstown	1943	16/01/1956

** - Accommodation Crossings. *** - Shown in May 1937 timetable only. **** - Strictly speaking a halt but used by railcars etc.

Railway Employees

With the passing of time, it has become increasingly difficult to identify the names and occupations of persons that once worked on the railway line from Portadown to Londonderry. To have a knowledge of such people provides a fascinating glimpse into the past and is a cameo well worth recording for posterity. Records (sometimes faded and difficult to read) are still being unearthed and the information gleaned to date, although by no means exhaustive, makes interesting reading and is listed below. Where known, the dates applicable are indicated.

TREW & MOY

Patrick Toner	Stationmaster. Circa 1910

DUNGANNON

Phillip Magee	Stationmaster. Circa 1910
J Fagan	Locomotive Department

COALISLAND

F W Wilson	Stationmaster. Circa 1910

DONAGHMORE

See in detail on page 158

POMEROY

Mr Langtree	Stationmaster. Circa 1910
J Carr	Signalman. Circa 1910
Peter Rafferty	Night Signalman. Circa 1910
Bernard Rafferty	Porter. Circa 1910
Henry Sinnamon	Porter. Circa 1910

SIXMILECROSS

J McDonnell	Stationmaster. Circa 1910

BERAGH

R Brown	Stationmaster. Circa 1910

OMAGH

J Irvine	Stationmaster. Circa 1910
W A Scott	District Superintendent. Ditto
O R Morris	Clerk (to above). c1910
S Mulvenna	Inspector
W Ross	Inspector
R Colgan	Foreman
A Aikin	Ticket Collector
H Graham	Signalman
J O'Neil	Signal & Telegraph
J Ewing	Driver
Barney McGirr	Driver
Gerry Donnelly	Fireman
G Donnelly	Guard
Mickey O'Neil	Guard
M Shannon	Restaurant Car Staff

NEWTOWNSTEWART

Jack McQuaid	Foreman
G O'Sullivan	Clerk
Sandy Hempton	Clerk
Bertie Hempton	Ticket Collector
A Arthur	Signalman
James Patterson	Signalman. Circa 1910
F Young	Signalman
Alex Hempton (sen)	Signalman

VICTORIA BRIDGE

B Anderson	Foreman
J Quigley	Porter
J Watson	Porter
M Connolly	Signalman
W Finlay	Signalman
T McKittrick	Signalman
T Morrow	Signalman
Patsy McGarrigle	Signalman
B Black	Permanent Way Man
B Mullan	Permanent Way Man

SION MILLS

J Gorman	Clerk
J Swarbrigg	Clerk
R Coyle	Porter
P Rouse	Porter
Billy Hughes	Porter
J Forbes	Boy Porter

STRABANE

See in detail on page 159

PORTHALL

P Conway	Foreman
J Crawford	Foreman

ST JOHNSTON

W Cole	Signalman
Tommy Dillon	Signalman
T Taylor	Signalman

LONDONDERRY

D Clark	Clerk
C Grimes	Clerk
C McGill	Clerk
B Walsh	Records Clerk
J Armstrong	Ticket Collector
B Bratt	Ticket Collector
J Callaghan	Porter
J Stewart	Parcel Porter
J Downey	Shunter
R Dinsmore	Lamp Man
W Clifford	Locomotive Department
C Pentland	Locomotive Department
T Timmins	Locomotive Department
J Tate	Locomotive Department
J Ballard	Locomotive Department
Paddy McShane	Locomotive Department
W Barton	Locomotive Department
J Turner	Locomotive Department
R Mitchell	Locomotive Department
T Bates	Locomotive Department
D Hagan (sen)	Driver
D Meenan	Driver
D Hagan	Fireman
Von Anderson	Fireman
Norman Ballard	Guard
J McGeehan	Guard
J O'Reilly	Guard
A Young	Guard

DONAGHMORE AND DISTRICT

A more detailed record has emerged for Donaghmore station, and it gives a picture of staffing levels down the years, with successive generations of the same family following each other into service with the GNR.

Stationmasters 1910-1947

Mr J Thompson
Mr Beattie
Mr Eason
Kevin Hughes
Joseph Manelly
Malachy Carron
N.B. – Mr Beattie became Foreman in Charge from 1947.

Head Porter in 1910 – P McPeak
Clerk in 1910 – P McBride

Signalmen 1920-1954

Richard Hamilton
Jimmy Toner
Richard Luke
Sean Gamble
Mick Murphy
Eugene Crilly
Joseph Keough
Alex Ogle
Joseph Quinn
John Kelly
Barry McPeak
N.B. – Alex Ogle eventually became Stationmaster at Pomeroy.

Permanent Way Inspectors 1920-1965

1933-1933 James Donnelly
(Transferred to Enniskillen 1933)
1938-1938 James Bell
1949-1949 Patrick Quinn
1956-1956 Phillip Murphy
1959-1959 James Coulter
1962-1962 George McNally
1965-1965 Robert McKinnon

Sub PW Inspectors 1920-1965

Harold McIntyre
Thomas Devlin
Patrick McGartland
Sam McClear

Permanent Way and Relaying Gangers 1900-1920

Barry McGuigan
James Donnelly
John McGee
John Mc C ???
N.B. – James Donnelly became a Permanent Way Inspector in 1920.

Permanent Way and Relaying Gangs 1900-1920

Bob Little
George Martin
Peter Donnelly
James Hughes
Henry Quinn
Michael Harvey
John McDonald
John Hughes
John McGuigan
John McKeever
Michael Loughran
Michael Quinn
Robert Mallaghan
Barney Toal
John Toal
John McGuirk
John Cobain
George McMaster
Michael Keenan
Dan Donnelly
John Donnelly
Tom Dorne
Patrick Cunningham
Henry Loughran
Ned Gilkinson
Robert Gilkinson
Frank Rafferty
Frank Rafferty (Sen)
Shamous Rafferty
Joseph Carberry
John Carberry
John Cormac
John McCausland
John McGee
Charles McCausland
Thomas Anderson
William Hetherington
Barney McCaughey
Frank McGuigan
Joseph McDonald
Patrick McCallon
James Donnelly
John Steel
Michael Slone
John Joe Donnelly
Patrick Harvey
Michael Murphy
William Hall
Michael McGuirk
John McNally
George Reid
Hugh Brimmage
Percy Cobain
James Dooran

Permanent Way Men 1920-1965

John McGee
Harry Loughran
Joseph Carberry
Frank Rafferty
Michael Quinn
Michael Keeran
Bob Gilkinson (Sen)
Bob Gilkinson
John McGeary
John Carberry
John McCausland
Charles McCausland
William Hetherington
Barry McGaughy
Shamous Rafferty
Frank Rafferty
Michael Loughran
Frank McGuigan
Thomas Anderson

STRABANE

There is a wealth of names recorded and available for Strabane, as befits a joint station of this nature. Inevitably, between documents, there will be some conflict about names, dates and spelling, historical records being prone to variance.

Stationmasters 1900-1965

Until 1905	M Creighton
1905-1910	A J Moore *(W Boyle covered the CDRJC station at this time)*
1911-1920	George R Laverty
1920-1932	John Rogers
1933	John Armstrong
1934-1938	W J Brittain
1938-1945	John McCrossan
1945-1954	J McFoster
1954-1959	Harold Revie
1959-1961	George Robinson
1961-1964	Fred Tutty
1964-1965	Eugene O'Brian

Clerks
J Bell
H Ferguson
Edmund Gordon
J Hampson
W Logan
Tom McDevitte
W Maguire
P Little
B O'Hare
F Woodcock

Temporary Clerk
J O'Gorman

Messengers
E Harkin
H Devine
F McCrossan
Jack Alexander

Boy Porters
D Devine
J Gallagher
B Hughes
N McDaid
J McGurk
C Barr

Easons Platform Bookshop
P Feely
Eileen Casey

Timekeeper
J Stewart

Checker
C Cobain

H Duke
H Devine
J McCurdy
G McMenamin
W Magee

Foremen
C Fleming
G Harold
Peter Donnelly

Booking Clerks
Brendan O'Haire
Mickey Madden

Porters
J Vaughan
Billy Canavan
J Allen
J O'Donnell
T Walker
C Barr
J Brown
R Coyle
D O'Connell
H Diver
B Conway
J Casey
P Donnelly
D Donnell
J Garrity
Charles O'Donnell
P Donaghey
J Ellis
T Follis
J Farrell
P Gillespie
J Kelly
J Kenny
T McKean
M McCrossan
T McGinn
M Sands
J McCrea
J McCrory
B Snodgrass
G McGeehan
E Maxwell
D Meehan
F Milligan
E Tinney
J McHugh
J McNeill

T Molloy
Dickie McGinley

Transhipment Porters
W Maguire
Geoffrey Madden
Eugene Gallagher

Parcel Porter
F Stewart

Signalmen
J Wolfe
C Barr
W J Carlin
B Devenney
P Floyd
W Gordon
J Harte
T Kirk
H McGavigan
Jimmy McGillian
A McHugh
S McCay
James McGurk
M Maddow

Lamp Man
E Rouse

Customs Man
Dennis Perry

Firemen
Gerry Donnelly
W Doherty

Guards
W McKean
P Patton

Shunters
Dominic Carlin
J Duffy
D Gallagher
J Nolan
Willie Morris

Gangers
P Duncan
H Duffy
T Devine

J Hamilton
John O'Kane
Sam Thompson

Permanent Way Men
J Boyle
W Canavan
J Lafferty
P McBride
D Smyth
N Gallagher
C Gallagher
John McKenna

Permanent Way Time Keeper
J Stewart

The time sheets for Saturday 16 August 1952 provide a cameo of a moment in time, giving a glimpse into the workings of a busy, well-ordered station. By referring to other records, it is possible to track the progress of employees through the ranks in later years, as they moved from one job to another, often at different stations.

STRABANE GOODS

Yard Foreman
Fred Boggs

Checkers
F McGowan
P Falconer
W McCourt
J McCurdy
J Doherty
F Wilkinson

Checker Office
J McMenamin
J McLaughlin

Porters
P Devine
W J Scott
Willie Falconer
J McCrory
J Gormley
G Madden
P Heaney
J Roulston
G McDermott
W F Caufield
J Duffy
J McNeill
P McGarrigle

Messenger
D Carlin

Transhipment Porters
P McTrearty
J Catterson
C Donnell
J McLaughlin
R Gallagher
J McGrath
G Snodgrass
J Molloy
E McGuinness
B McGinley

Shunter
E L Foy

STRABANE COACHING

Foremen
J J Dunn
W J Anderson
W McCourt

Signalmen
J McGillan
R J McKean
Eddie McGuinness
H McGavigan
J Harte
S J McCay

Shunters
D Gallagher
J Doherty
M A McLaughlin
A J McHugh
W J McMorris

Assistant Shunter
W Kerr

Ticket Collector
P Madden

Guard
F Greer

Leading Porter
P Shearer

Porter
W J Carlin

Boy Porters
R Coyle
J Gallagher.
A A Fletcher

Messengers
J A Campbell
W Duffy
H A Devine

Crossing Keeper
W Bradley

EMPLOYEE DETAILS FOR THE FINAL YEARS (CIRCA 1964-1965)

TREW & MOY

Kevin Hughes	Stationmaster

DUNGANNON

Jimmy Swarbrigg	Stationmaster

POMEROY

Alex Ogle	Stationmaster
Bobby Moffatt	Ticket Collector & Porter
Hughie McGael	Signalman
Dick Hamilton	Signalman

BERAGH

Marcus McKee	Signalman

OMAGH

Billy Ross	Stationmaster
Billy Maguire	Signalman
Paddy Donaghy	Signalman
Billy Kerr	Foreman
Mickey O'Neil	Guard

NEWTOWNSTEWART

Jack McQuade	Foreman

SION MILLS

Jack Latimer	Stationmaster

STRABANE

Eugene O'Brien	Stationmaster
Robert Coyle	Porter
Willie John Carlin	Signalman

Physics
Third edition

Darren Forbes
Editor: Lawrie Ryan

OXFORD
UNIVERSITY PRESS

Great Clarendon Street, Oxford, OX2 6DP, United Kingdom

Oxford University Press is a department of the University of Oxford. It furthers the University's objective of excellence in research, scholarship, and education by publishing worldwide. Oxford is a registered trade mark of Oxford University Press in the UK and in certain other countries

First published in 2016

British Library Cataloguing in Publication Data
Data available

978 0 19 835945 6

10 9 8 7 6 5 4 3 2 1

Paper used in the production of this book is a natural, recyclable product made from wood grown in sustainable forests.
The manufacturing process conforms to the environmental regulations of the country of origin.

Printed in Great Britain by Bell and Bain Ltd. Glasgow

Darren Forbes would like to give huge thanks to his wife Samantha and daughter Emma for their love and patience and to first mate Pliny Harris for his wise words.

Lawrie would like to thank the following people for their help and support in producing this teacher handbook. Each one has added value to my initial efforts: Annie Hamblin, Sadie Garratt, Emma-Leigh Craig, Amie Hewish, Andy Chandler-Grevatt.

Index compiled by INDEXING SPECIALISTS (UK) Ltd., Indexing house, 306A Portland Road, Hove, East Sussex, BN3 5LP United Kingdom.

COVER: Johnér / Offset

Contents

This book has been written for the *AQA GCSE Physics* and *AQA GCSE Combined Science: Trilogy courses,* making them completely co-teachable. Physics only lessons are easily identifiable with their own black-bordered design, and are also formatted in italics in the below contents list for quick access.

Required practicals

As part of the *AQA GCSE Physics* course, students must complete 10 Required practicals. Each Required practical is fully-supported on Kerboodle with differentiated Practical sheets and accompanying Teacher and technician notes.

	Required practicals	Topic
1	**Determining specific heat capacity.** Determine the specific heat capacity of a metal block of known mass by measuring the energy transferred to the block and its temperature rise, and using the equation for specific heat capacity.	P2.4
2	**Investigating thermal insulators.** Use different materials and different thicknesses of the same material to insulate identical beakers of hot water, and measure the change in temperature of the water at regular intervals.	P2.1
3	**Investigating resistance.** Set up circuits and investigate the resistance of a wire, and of resistors in series and parallel.	P4.3 P4.6
4	**Investigating electrical components.** Correctly assemble a circuit and investigate the potential difference-current characteristics of circuit components.	P4.4
5	**Calculating densities.** Measure the mass and volume of objects and liquids and calculate their densities using the density equation.	P6.1
6	**Investigate the relationship between force and extension for a spring.** Hang weights of known mass from a spring and, using the correct apparatus, measure the resulting extension. Use the results to plot a force-extension graph.	P10.8
7	**Investigate the relationship between force and acceleration.** Using a newton-metre, investigate the effect on the acceleration of an object of varying the force on it and of varying its mass.	P10.1
8	**Investigating plane waves in a ripple tank and waves in a solid.** Determine which apparatus are the most suitable for measuring the frequency, speed, and wavelength of waves in a ripple tank, and investigate waves on a stretched string.	P12.4
9	**Investigate the reflection and refraction of light.** Use different substances and surfaces to investigate the refraction and relection of light.	P14.2 P14.3
10	**Investigating infrared radiation.** Determine how the properties of a surface affect the amount of infrared radiation absorbed or radiated by the surface.	P13.2

Introduction

About the series

This is the third edition of the UK's number 1 course for GCSE Science. The student books have been approved by AQA, and our author teams and experts have been working closely with AQA to develop a blended suite of resources to support the new specifications.

All resources in this series have been carefully designed to support students of all abilities on their journey through GCSE Science. The demands of the new specifications are fully supported, with maths, practicals, and synoptic skills developed throughout, and all new subject content fully covered.

The series is designed to be flexible, enabling you to co-teach Foundation and Higher tiers, and Combined and Separate Sciences. Content is clearly flagged throughout the resources, helping you to identify the relevant content for your students.

Assessment is an important feature of the series, and is supported by our unique assessment framework, helping students to track and make progress.

The series is edited by Lawrie Ryan. Building on his vast experience as an author for much-loved titles such as Spotlight Science and the Chemistry for You Lawrie has become one of the best-known authors and editors of educational science books both nationally and internationally. A former Head of Science, Science Advisor, and Ofsted Inspector, he understands the demands of modern education and draws on his experience to deliver this new and innovative course that builds upon the legacy of previous editions

Your Teacher Handbook

This Teacher Handbook aims to save you time and effort by offering lesson plans, differentiation suggestions, and assessment guidance on a page-by-page basis that is a direct match to the Student Book.

With learning outcomes differentiated you can tailor the lessons and activities to suit your students and provide progression opportunities to students of all abilities.

Lesson plans are written for 55-minute lessons but are flexible and fully adaptable so you can choose the activities that suit your class best.

Separate Science-only content is contained within whole topics and clearly flagged from the Combined Sciences content, enabling you co-teach using one Teacher Handbook.

Key Stage 3 and GCSE Catch-up

This table outlines Key Stage 3 knowledge that is a pre-requisite for this section. Later Section Openers will also include GCSE knowledge from earlier in the course. Quick checkpoint activities, to assess students understanding of each statement, are provided

For each statement, a suggestion for how you can help students catch up is also provided, as well as an index of which topic each statement links to.

Section opener

The Section opener provides an overview of the parts of the specification, required practicals, and maths skills covered in the section.

Specification links

This table provides an overview of the specification topics covered in the chapters of the section. It also gives an indication of which Paper each specification topic will be mainly assessed in.

Required practicals

This table indicates which required practicals are covered within this section. It also gives a list of Apparatus and techniques that could be assessed by that practical.

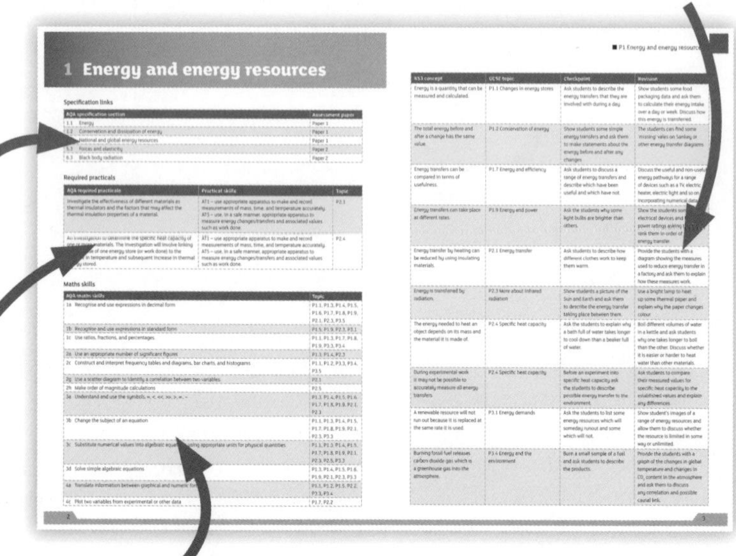
1 Energy and energy resources

Specification links

Required practicals

Maths skills

Maths skills

This table provides an overview of the maths skills covered in the chapters of the section.

Lesson

Specification links

This indicated the area of the *AQA GCSE Physics (9–1)* 2016 specification this lesson covers. Relevant Working scientifically and Mathematical requirements links are also provided.

Differentiated outcomes

This table summarises the possible lesson outcomes. They are ramped and divided into three ability bands. The three ability bands are explained in the Assessment and progress section. Each ability band has two to three outcomes defined, designed to cover the specification content for different ability levels

An index of questions and activities is given for each learning outcome, helping you to assess your students informally as you progress through each lesson

Maths and literacy

These boxes provide suggestions of how Maths and Literacy skills can be developed in the lesson. Where relevant, the Maths skills are linked to the Mathematical requirements of the specification.

Practicals

These boxes provide equipment lists, an outline method, and safety requirements for any practicals in the lesson. Required practicals are flagged with the Required practical icon.

Although safety requirements are given, a fully-comprehensive risk assessment should be carried out before any practical activity is undergone.

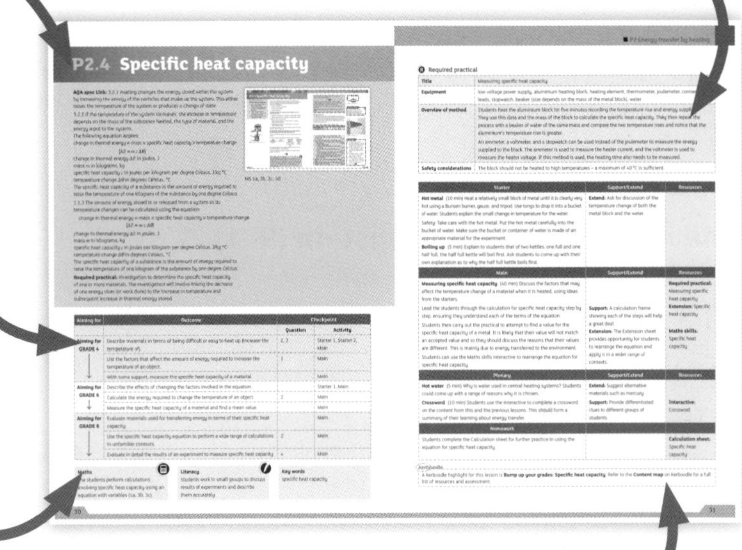

Suggested lesson plan

A suggested route through the lesson is provided, including ideas for support, extension, and homework. The right-hand column indicated where Kerboodle resources are available.

Checkpoint lesson

Overview

The Checkpoint Lesson is a suggested follow-up lesson after students have completed the automarked Checkpoint Assessment on Kerboodle. There are three routes through the lesson, with the route for each student being determined by their mark in the assessment. Each route aims to support students with progressing up an assessment band.

Checkpoint overview

This text provides a brief overview of the chapter, including the key concepts students should be confident with.

Checkpoint lesson plan

This table provides a differentiated lesson plan for the checkpoint follow-up lesson. This includes learning outcomes, starters and plenaries, supporting information for the follow-up worksheets (including any descriptions of relevant practicals), and progression suggestions to support students with progressing up a band.

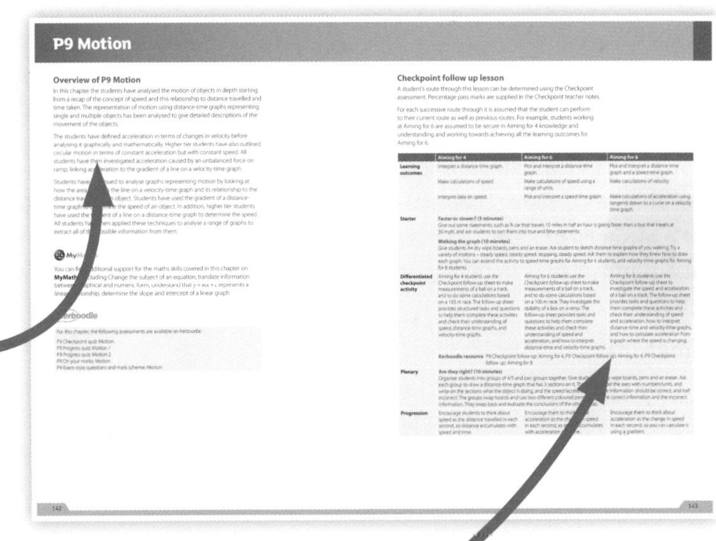

Assessment and progress

Dr Andrew Chandler-Grevatt

To ensure students are fully supported to make progress through the new linear exams, AQA GCSE *Sciences Third Edition* was developed in consultation with assessment consultant, Dr Andrew Chandler-Grevatt. Andrew worked with the team to develop an assessment framework that supports students and teachers in tracking and promoting progress through Key Stage 3 and GCSE.

Andrew is has a doctorate in school assessment, and a real passion for science teaching and learning. Having worked as a science teacher for ten years, of which five were spent as an AST, Andrew has a real understanding of the pressures and joys of teaching in the classroom. His most recent projects include *Activate for KS3 Science*, for which he developed a unique assessment framework to support schools in the transition away from levels.

The new GCSE grading system (9–1)

With the new specifications and criteria comes a new grading system. The old system of grades A*–G, is being replaced with a numerical system with grades 9–1. Grade 9 is the highest, and is designed to award exceptional performance.

The new grades are not directly equivalent to the old A*–C system, although some comparisons can be drawn:

- Approximately the same proportion of students will achieve a grade 4 or above as currently achieve a grade C or above.
- Approximately the same proportion of students will achieve a grade 7 as above as currently achieve an A or above.
- The bottom of grade 1 will be aligned with the bottom of grade G.

A 'good pass' is considered to be a grade 5 or above.

Throughout the course, resources and assessments have been designed to help students working at different grades to make progress.

5-year assessment framework

Purpose

The combination of the removal of levels, new performance measures, a new grading system, and more demanding GCSEs makes it more important than ever to be able to track and facilitate progress from Year 7 and all the way through secondary. Assessment plays a key role in intervention and extension, and these are both vital in helping students of all abilities achieve their potential, and add value to their projected GCSE grade.

In the absence of levels, and as we learn more about the new GCSE grades, it is important that a framework is in place in order to inform learning, teaching, and assessment from Y7-Y11.

Framework

Throughout the 5 years, it is useful to define three ability bands, which can be used to inform the design of learning outcomes, learning resources, and assessments. By defining three bands, realistic and valuable intervention and extension can be designed and implemented to help students of all abilities make progress, and improve their grade projection.

At KS3, the model is designed with the aim of encouraging every student to gain a 'secure' grasp of each concept and topic, so that they are ready to progress. These students will be on track to secure a 'good pass' (grade 5 or above) at GCSE.

In the KS3 course Activate three bands have been defined:

- **Developing**, in which students are able to know and understand a concept, and demonstrate their knowledge in simple and familiar situations.
- **Secure**, in which students are able to apply their knowledge and skills to familiar

and some unfamiliar situations, undertake analysis, and understand more complex concepts.

- **Extending**, in which students are able to evaluate and create, apply their knowledge to complex and unfamiliar situations, and demonstrate advanced use of skills.

Using the framework throughout KS3 helps you to identify which students are ready to progress, and approximately what GCSE grades they should be aiming for.

At GCSE, students can then be differentiated into three bands, aiming for different grades.

- **Aiming for 4** is for students working at the lower grades 1–3, who would have been Developing at KS3, and aspiring to a Grade 4 at GCSE. Resources and assessments for these students are supportive, and focus on developing understanding of core concepts.
- **Aiming for 6** is for students working at grades 4–6, who would have been Secure at KS3. Resources and assessments for these students help to embed core concepts, by encouraging application and analysis, and beginning to explore more complex ideas and situations.
- **Aiming for 8** provides extension for students working at grades 7–9, who are able to grasp complex concepts, and demonstrate higher order skills, such as evaluation and creation in complex and unfamiliar situations.

The framework is summarised in the table below.

<table>
<tr><td rowspan="2">Key stage 3</td><td>Band</td><td colspan="6">Developing</td><td colspan="6">Secure</td><td colspan="6">Extending</td></tr>
<tr><td>Level</td><td colspan="3">3</td><td colspan="3">4</td><td colspan="3">5</td><td colspan="3">6</td><td colspan="3">7</td><td colspan="3">8</td></tr>
<tr><td rowspan="3">GCSE</td><td>Band</td><td colspan="6">Aiming for 4</td><td colspan="6">Aiming for 6</td><td colspan="6">Aiming for 8</td></tr>
<tr><td>Grades</td><td colspan="2">1</td><td colspan="2">2</td><td colspan="2">3</td><td colspan="2">4</td><td colspan="2">5</td><td colspan="2">6</td><td colspan="2">7</td><td colspan="2">8</td><td colspan="2">9</td></tr>
<tr><td>Demand</td><td colspan="6">Low</td><td colspan="6">Standard</td><td colspan="6">High</td></tr>
</table>

Informing learning outcomes

The assessment framework has informed the design of the learning outcomes throughout the course. Learning outcomes are differentiated, and there is a set of learning outcomes for every lesson for each ability band.

The checkpoint assessment system

This series includes a checkpoint assessment system for intervention and extension, designed to help students of all abilities make continuous progress through the course. The system also helps you and your students to monitor achievement, and ensure all students are on-track and monitored through the new linear assessments.

Checkpoint assessments are provided in Kerboodle. These are Automarked objective tests with diagnostic feedback. Once students have completed their assessment, depending on their results they will complete one of three follow up activities, designed for intervention and extension. Students are supported with activity sheets, and lesson plans and overviews are provided for the teacher. The three follow-up routes are:

1. **Aiming for 4** is for students who achieved low score. These resources support students by helping to develop and embed core concepts.
2. **Aiming for 6** is for students who achieved a medium score. These resources encourage students to embed and extend core concepts, and begin to apply their knowledge in more complex or unfamiliar situations.
3. **Aiming for 8** is for students who have achieved a high score. These resources encourage extensive use of more complex skills, in more complex and unfamiliar situations, helping them to reach for the top grades.

Differentiation and Skills

Maths skills and MyMaths

With the introduction of the introduction of the new GCSE competence in maths, the support and development of maths skills in a scientific context will be vital for success.

The Student Books contain a maths skills reference section that covers all the maths required for the specification, explained in a scientific context and with a worked example for reference. Where maths skills are embedded within the scientific content, the maths is demonstrated in a Using Maths feature providing a worked example and an opportunity for students to have a go themselves.

In Kerboodle you will find maths skills interactives that are automarked and provide formative feedback. Calculation sheets provide opportunities for practice of the maths skills and links to MyMaths are shown in the Lesson Player and Teacher Handbook where additional resources exist that can be used to reinforce the maths skill. These include practice sheets and Invisi-pen worked examples.

Literacy skills

Literacy skills enable students to effectively communicate their ideas about science and access the information they need. Though the marks allocated for QWC are no longer present in the new specifications, a good degree of literacy is required to read and answer longer, structured exam questions, to access the more difficult concepts introduced in the new GCSE Programme of Study, to be able to effectively interpret and answer questions.

The student books flag opportunities to develop and practice literacy skills through the use of the pen icon. Key words are identified in the text and a glossary helps students get to grips with new scientific terms.

In Kerboodle, you will find Literacy Skills Interactives that help assess literacy skills, including the spelling of key words. Additional Literacy worksheets are available to reinforce skills learnt and provide practice opportunities.

The Teacher Handbook flags literacy suggestions and opportunities relating to the lesson. All of these features will help to develop well-rounded scientists able to access information and communicate their ideas effectively.

Working Scientifically

Working Scientifically is new to the 2016 GCSE criteria. It is divided up into four areas and is integrated into the teaching and learning of Biology, Chemistry, and Physics. The four areas are:

1. Development of scientific thinking in which students need to be able to demonstrate understanding of scientific methods and the scientific process and how these may develop over time and their associated limitations
2. Experimental skills and strategies in which students ask scientific questions based on observations, make predictions using scientific knowledge and understanding, carry out investigations to test predictions, make and record measurements and evaluate methods
3. Analysis and evaluation in which students apply mathematical concepts and calculate results, present and interpret data using tables and graphs, draw conclusions and evaluate data, and are comment on the accuracy, precision, repeatability and reproducibility of data
4. Scientific vocabulary, quantities, units, symbols and nomenclature in which students calculate results and manipulate data using scientific formulae using basic analysis, SI units, and IUPAC chemical nomenclature where appropriate.

Working Scientifically is integrated throughout the Student Book with flagged Practical boxes, flagged Required Practical boxes, questions. A dedicated Working Scientifically reference chapter is also provided at the back of the Student Book to refer to during investigations, when answering Working Scientifically questions and to enable investigative skills to be developed.

In Kerboodle there are Practicals and Activities resources with their own Working Scientifically objectives, additional targeted Working Scientifically skills sheets as well as other resources such as simulations and Webquests to target specific skills areas. Questions are ramped in difficulty and opportunity to build up to and practise the practical based questions for the exam are provided.

For the required practicals the guidance provided to students acknowledges the differing degrees of support and independence required, with targeted support sheets to the key grade descriptors of Grade 4, 6, and 8, with a view to moving the students over that Grade point onwards.

In the Teacher Handbook lessons will often have a working scientifically focus in mind for the activities in that lesson. Working Scientifically Learning Outcomes, where specified, are differentiated to show the expectations for the differing ability levels.

For the purpose of the practical based questions in the examination, required practicals are flagged and practice opportunities are provided through out the Student Book in the summary questions and exam-style questions.

Differentiation

Building upon the principles of *Activate* at Key Stage 3.

Differentiation using the checkpoint system

The end of chapter Checkpoint lessons will help you to progress students of every ability, targeting the key Grade boundaries of 4, 6, and 8 to enable students to review, consolidate and extend their understanding at each of the grade lesson points.

The tasks focused at students to become secure at Grades 4 and 6 are designed to help them become more secure in their understanding and consolidate the chapter. Teacher input will help them grasp important concepts from the chapter with the opportunity for some extension for Grade 6 students.

The tasks focused at students to become secure and to extend at Grade 8 are designed to develop and challenge. Students will work more independently on these tasks to free up the teacher to be able to focus on those that found the chapter more challenging.

Teacher Handbook

Lesson outcomes are differentiated and suggestions for activities throughout the lesson plans are accompanied by support and extension opportunities.

Student Book

Summary questions per lesson are ramped with a darker shading indicating a more challenging question. In the end of chapter summary questions and exam style questions, ramping occurs within the question (as would be seen in a typical exam question).

Practicals and Activities

All practicals and activities are differentiated. Where more complex areas are covered, additional support sheets may be provided to allow lower attaining students to access the activity.

For all required practicals (compulsory practicals) that may be assessed in an exam, specific support sheets are provided targeting the progression of students across the key Grades 4, 6, and 8.

Additional skills sheets may be used in conjunction with practicals to provide additional support in generic competencies such as constructing a graph etc.

Interactive Assessments

All interactive assessments are ramped in difficulty and support is provided in the feedback directing students where they can improve. In chapters with both levels of content, Higher and Foundation versions of assessment are available.

Written assessments

End of section tests and end of year tests have Foundation and Higher versions.

Kerboodle

AQA GCSE Sciences Kerboodle is packed full of guided support and ideas for running and creating effective GCSE Science lessons, and for assessing and facilitating students' progress. It is intuitive to use and customisable.

Kerboodle is online, allowing you and your students to access the course anytime, anywhere.

AQA GCSE Sciences Kerboodle consists of:

- lessons, resources, and assessment
- access to *AQA GCSE Science* Student books for both teachers and students.

Lessons, Resources, and Assessment

AQA GCSE Sciences Kerboodle offers new, engaging lesson resources, as well as a fully comprehensive assessment package, written to match the *AQA GCSE Science (9–1)* specifications.

Kerboodle offers comprehensive and flexible support for the *AQA GCSE Science (9–1)* specifications, enabling you to follow our suggested lessons and schemes of work or to create your own lessons and schemes and share them with other members of your department.

You can **adapt** many of the resources to suit your students' needs, with all non-interactive activities available as editable Word documents. You can also **upload** your own resources so that everything is accessed from one location.

Set homework and assessments through the Assessment system and **track** progress using the Markbook.

Lessons

Click on the **Lessons tab** to access the *AQA GCSE Sciences* lesson presentations and notes.

Ready-to-play lesson presentations complement every spread in the Teacher Handbook and Student Book. Each lesson presentation is easy to launch and features lesson objectives, starters, activity guidance, key diagrams, plenaries, and homework suggestions. The lesson presentations and accompanying note sections are 100% customisable. You can personalise the lessons by adding your own resources and notes, or build your own lesson plans using your own resources.

Your lessons and notes can be accessed by your whole department and they are ideal for use in cover lessons.

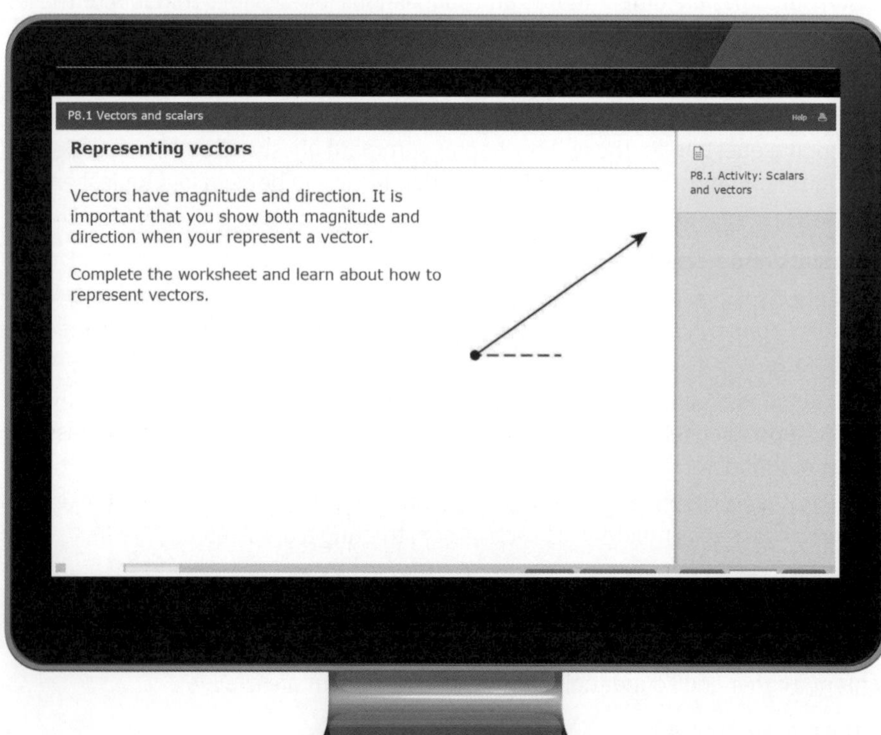

Resources

Click on the Resources tab to access the full list of AQA GCSE Sciences resources. Use the navigation panel on the left hand side to find resources for any lesson, chapter, or topic.

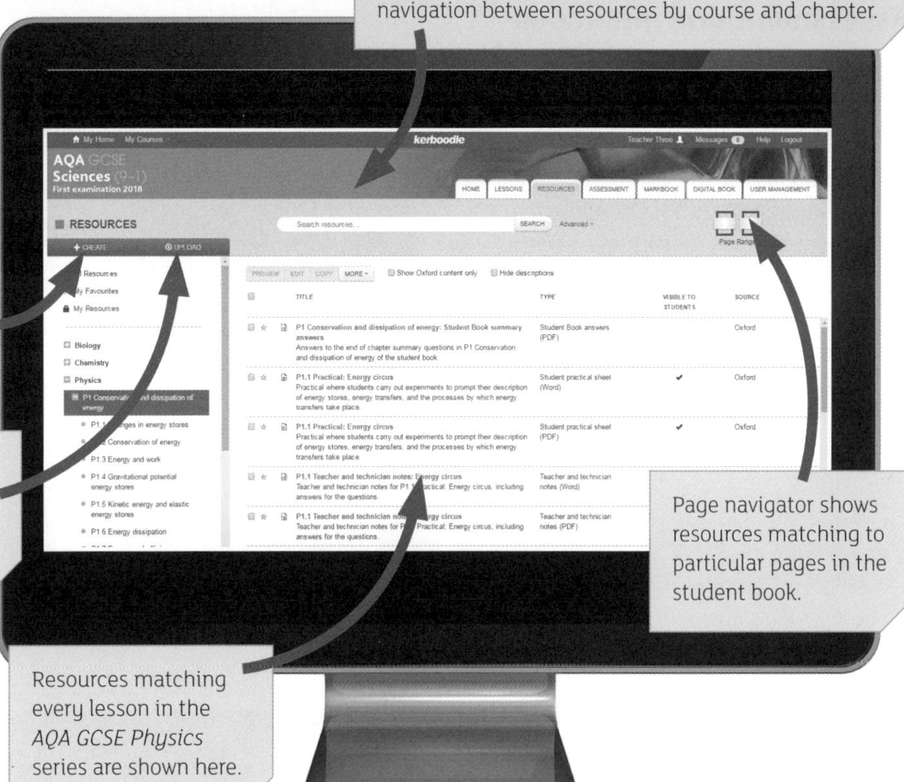

Navigation panel and search bar allow for easy navigation between resources by course and chapter.
Fully customisable content to cater to all your classes. Resources can be created using the create button.
Existing resources can be uploaded on to the platform using the upload button.
Page navigator shows resources matching to particular pages in the student book.
Resources matching every lesson in the *AQA GCSE Physics* series are shown here.
kerboodle
AQA GCSE Sciences (9–1)
First examination 2018
RESOURCES

 **Practicals and activities** Fully-editable resources provided for every lesson to guide students through a practical or activity with fully integrated Working Scientifically skills. Teacher and Technician notes are provided for all practicals and activities to give further ideas on differentiation, answers, example data where appropriate, and a list of resources required by technicians.

 **Interactive starters or plenaries** Accompany each lesson, and can be used front-of-class to maximise student participation.

 **Skills sheets** Editable worksheets that target Maths, Literacy, and Working Scientifically skills. They provide guidance and examples to help students whenever they need to use a particular skill.

 **Skills interactives** Auto-marked interactive activities with formative feedback that focus on key maths and literacy skills. You can use these activities in your class to help consolidate core skills relevant to the lesson, or they can be assigned as homework by accessing them through the Assessment tab.

 **Animations and videos** Help students to visualise difficult concepts or to learn about real-life contexts, with engaging visuals and narration. They are structured to clearly address a set of learning objectives and are followed by interactive question screens to help consolidate key points and to provide formative feedback.

 **Simulations** Allow students to control variables and look at outcomes for experiments that are difficult to carry out in the classroom or focus on tricky concepts.

 **Podcasts** Available for every chapter to help review and consolidate key points. The podcast presents an audio summary with transcript, followed by a series of ramped questions and answers to assist students in their revision.

 **Targeted support sheets** Available for the full ability range and are provided to help students progress as they complete their GCSE. **Bump up your Grades** target common misconceptions and difficult topics to securely move students over the key boundaries of Grades 4, 6, and 8. Extensions activities provide opportunities for higher-ability students to apply their knowledge and understanding to new contexts, whilst **Go Further** worksheets aim to inspire students to consider the subject at A Level and beyond.

 **WebQuests** Research-based activities set in a real-life context. WebQuests are fun and engaging activities that can be carried out individually or within a group and are ideal for peer-review.

 **Checklists and chapter maps** Self-assessment checklists for students of the key learning points from each chapter to aid consolidation and revision. For teachers there is an additional chapter-map resource that provides an overview of the chapter, specific opportunities to support and extend, and information on tackling common misconceptions.

Assessment and markbook

All of the assessment material in Kerboodle has been quality assured by our expert Assessment Advisor. Click on the **Assessment tab** to find the wide range of assessment materials to help you deliver a varied, motivating, and effective assessment programme.

Once your classes are set up in Kerboodle, you can assign them assessments to do at home or in class individually or as a group.

A **Markbook** with reporting function helps you to keep track of your students' results. This includes both auto-marked assessments and work marked by you.

Practice or test?

Many of the auto-marked assessment in the AQA GCSE Sciences Kerboodle is available in formative or summative versions.

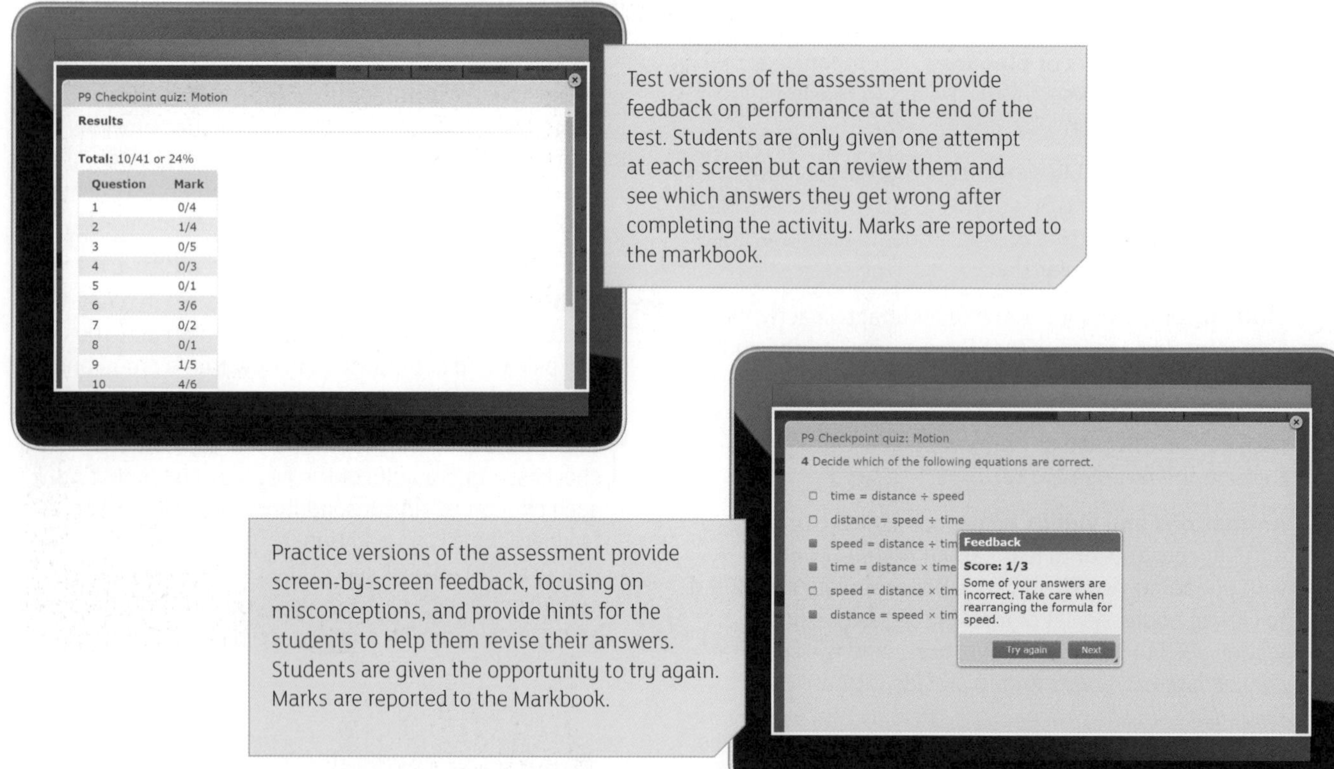

Test versions of the assessment provide feedback on performance at the end of the test. Students are only given one attempt at each screen but can review them and see which answers they get wrong after completing the activity. Marks are reported to the markbook.

Practice versions of the assessment provide screen-by-screen feedback, focusing on misconceptions, and provide hints for the students to help them revise their answers. Students are given the opportunity to try again. Marks are reported to the Markbook.

Assessment per chapter

Through each chapter there are many opportunities for assessment and determining/monitoring progress.

Progress quizzes Auto-marked assessments that focus on the content of the chapters. They are quick, engaging quizzes designed to be taken throughout the course to monitor progress and to focus revision.

Checkpoint assessments Auto-marked assessments designed to determine whether students have a secure grasp of concepts from the chapter. These assessments are ramped in difficulty and can be followed up by the differentiated Checkpoint Lesson activities.

On Your Marks Improve students' exam skills by analysing questions, looking at other students' responses, interpreting mark schemes, and answering exam-style questions.

Homework activities Auto-marked quizzes with ramped questions targeting the key Grades 4, 6, and 8 boundaries designed to help students apply and embed their knowledge and understanding from the classroom.

Formal testing

End-of-chapter tests Provide students with the opportunity to practise answering exam-style questions in a written format. There are differentiated Foundation and Higher versions, with separate options for the combined sciences and the separate sciences. Accompanied by a fully comprehensive mark scheme, data can be entered manually into the Markbook.

Mid-point and end-of-course written tests Provide students with the opportunity to practise answering exam-style questions in a full-length paper. There are differentiated Foundation and Higher versions, with separate options for the combined sciences and the separate sciences. Accompanied by a fully comprehensive mark scheme, data can be entered manually into the Markbook.

Kerboodle Book

The *AQA GCSE Sciences* Kerboodle Books are digital versions of the Student Books for you to use at the front of the classroom.

Access to the Kerboodle Book is automatically available as part of the Lessons, Resources, and Assessment package for both you and your students.

A set of tools is available with the Kerboodle Book so that you can personalise your book and make notes. Like all resources offered on Kerboodle, the Kerboodle Book can also be accessed using a range of devices.

1 Energy and energy resources

Specification links

AQA specification section	Assessment paper
1.1 Energy	Paper 1
1.2 Conservation and dissipation of energy	Paper 1
1.3 National and global energy resources	Paper 1
5.3 Forces and elasticity	Paper 2
6.3 Black body radiation	Paper 2

Required practicals

AQA required practicals	Practical skills	Topic
Investigate the effectiveness of different materials as thermal insulators and the factors that may affect the thermal insulation properties of a material.	AT1 – use appropriate apparatus to make and record measurements of mass, time, and temperature accurately. AT5 – use, in a safe manner, appropriate apparatus to measure energy changes/transfers and associated values such as work done.	P2.1
An investigation to determine the specific heat capacity of one or more materials. The investigation will involve linking the decrease of one energy store (or work done) to the increase in temperature and subsequent increase in thermal energy stored.	AT1 – use appropriate apparatus to make and record measurements of mass, time, and temperature accurately. AT5 – use, in a safe manner, appropriate apparatus to measure energy changes/transfers and associated values such as work done.	P2.4

Maths skills

AQA maths skills	Topic
1a Recognise and use expressions in decimal form.	P1.1, P1.3, P1.4, P1.5, P1.6, P1.7, P1.8, P1.9, P2.1, P2.3, P3.5
1b Recognise and use expressions in standard form.	P1.5, P1.9, P2.3, P3.1
1c Use ratios, fractions, and percentages.	P1.1, P1.3, P1.7, P1.8, P1.9, P3.3, P3.4
2a Use an appropriate number of significant figures.	P1.3, P1.4, P2.3
2c Construct and interpret frequency tables and diagrams, bar charts, and histograms.	P1.1, P1.2, P2.1, P3.3, P3.4, P3.5
2h Make order of magnitude calculations.	P2.5
3a Understand and use the symbols: $=, <, <<, >>, >, \propto, \sim$.	P1.3, P1.4, P1.5, P1.6, P1.7, P1.8, P1.9, P2.1, P2.3
3b Change the subject of an equation.	P1.1, P1.3, P1.4, P1.5, P1.7, P1.8, P1.9, P2.1, P2.3, P3.3
3c Substitute numerical values into algebraic equations using appropriate units for physical quantities.	P1.1, P1.3, P1.4, P1.5, P1.7, P1.8, P1.9, P2.1, P2.3, P2.5, P3.3
3d Solve simple algebraic equations.	P1.3, P1.4, P1.5, P1.6, P1.9, P2.1, P2.3, P3.3
4a Translate information between graphical and numeric form.	P1.1, P1.2, P1.5, P2.1, P2.2, P3.3, P3.4
4c Plot two variables from experimental or other data.	P1.7, P2.2

KS3 concept	GCSE topic	Checkpoint	Revision
Energy is a quantity that can be measured and calculated.	P1.1 Changes in energy stores	Ask students to describe the energy transfers that they are involved with during a day.	Show students some food packaging data and ask them to calculate their energy intake over a day or week. Discuss how this energy is transferred.
The total energy before and after a change has the same value.	P1.2 Conservation of energy	Show students some simple energy transfers and ask them to make statements about the energy before and after any changes.	The students can find some 'missing' vales on Sankey or other energy transfer diagrams.
Energy transfers can be compared in terms of usefulness.	P1.7 Energy and efficiency	Ask students to discuss a range of energy transfers and describe which have been useful and which have not.	Discuss the useful and non-useful energy pathways for a range of devices such as a TV, electric heater, electric light and so on incorporating numerical data.
Energy transfers can take place at different rates.	P1.9 Energy and power	Ask the students why some light bulbs are brighter than others.	Show the students some electrical devices and their power ratings asking them to rank them in order of rate of energy transfer.
Energy transfer by heating can be reduced by using insulating materials.	P2.1 Energy transfer	Ask students to describe how different clothes work to keep them warm.	Provide the students with a diagram showing the measures used to reduce energy transfer in a factory and ask them to explain how these measures work.
Energy is transferred by radiation.	P2.3 More about infrared radiation	Show students a picture of the Sun and Earth and ask them to describe the energy transfer taking place between them.	Use a bright lamp to heat up some thermal paper and explain why the paper changes colour.
The energy needed to heat an object depends on its mass and the material it is made of.	P2.4 Specific heat capacity	Ask the students to explain why a bath full of water takes longer to cool down than a beaker full of water.	Boil different volumes of water in a kettle and ask students why one takes longer to boil than the other. Discuss whether it is easier or harder to heat water than other materials.
During experimental work it may not be possible to accurately measure all energy transfers.	P2.4 Specific heat capacity	Before an experiment into specific heat capacity ask the students to describe possible energy transfer to the environment.	Ask students to compare their measured values for specific heat capacity to the established values and explain any differences.
A renewable resource will not run out because it is replaced at the same rate it is used.	P3.1 Energy demands	Ask the students to list some energy resources which will someday runout and some which will not.	Show student's images of a range of energy resources and allow them to discuss whether the resource is limited in some way or unlimited.
Burning fossil fuel releases carbon dioxide gas which is a greenhouse gas into the atmosphere.	P3.4 Energy and the environment	Burn a small sample of a fuel and ask students to describe the products.	Provide the students with a graph of the changes in global temperature and changes in CO_2 content in the atmosphere and ask them to discuss any correlation and possible causal link.

P 1 Conservation and dissipation of energy

1.1 Changes in energy stores

AQA spec Link: 1.1.1 A system is an object or group of objects.

There are changes in the way energy is stored when a system changes.

Students should be able to describe all the changes involved in the way energy is stored when a system changes, for common situations. For example:

- an object projected upwards
- a moving object hitting an obstacle
- an object accelerated by a constant force
- a vehicle slowing down
- bringing water to a boil in an electric kettle.

Throughout this section on energy students should be able to calculate the changes in energy involved when a system is changed by:

- heating
- work done by forces
- work done when a current flows
- use calculations to show on a common scale how the overall energy in a system is redistributed when the system is changed.

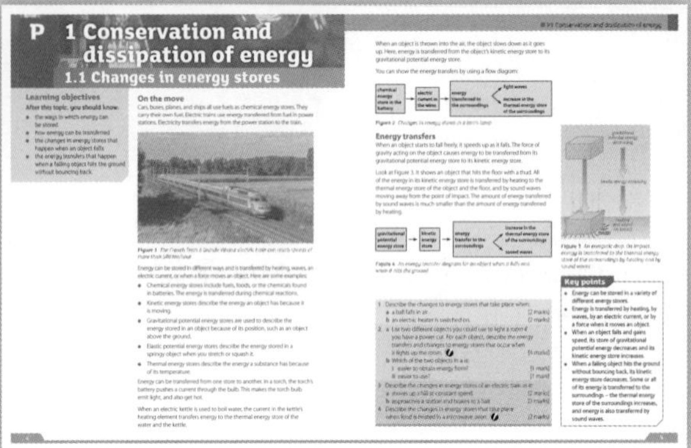
P 1 Conservation and dissipation of energy
1.1 Changes in energy stores

WS 1.2
MS 1a, 1c, 2c, 3b, 3c, 4a

Aiming for	Outcome	Checkpoint	
		Question	Activity
Aiming for GRADE 4	Describe some examples of energy stores.	1	Starter 2, Main 1, Main 2, Plenary 2
	State the processes that can transfer energy from one store to another.	2, 3, 4	Starter 2, Main 1, Main 2, Plenary 2
↓	Identify changes in some energy stores using simple examples.	2, 3	Main 1, Main 2, Plenary 2
Aiming for GRADE 6	Describe a wide range of energy stores in different contexts.	2, 3, 4	Starter 2, Main 1, Plenary 2
	Describe changes in energy stores in terms of the process that causes the change.	2, 3, 4, End of chapter 2	Main 1, Plenary 2
↓	Use quantitative descriptions of changes in energy stores.		Main 2
Aiming for GRADE 8	Describe the nature of energy stores in detail including the relationship between objects.	2, 4	Main 1, Plenary 2
	Explain factors that affect the size of changes in energy stores.	3	Main 1
↓	Represent energy transfers graphically, accounting for changes in all stores.		Main 2

Maths

Energy stores can be represented graphically using bar charts to show how full or empty they are (2c, 4a).

Literacy

The focus should be on language used to describe energy transfers. Pairs of students can describe the changes to each other and make corrections with constructive feedback.

Practical

Title	Energy circus
Equipment	yo-yo, wind-up toy, portable radio, electric torch, electric motor, MP3 player, steel ball bearing, wooden block, candle or spirit burner, matches, remote-control car
Overview of method	Set each piece of equipment up in a different place around the classroom, and label each station. In small groups, students rotate around the stations, investigating the transfers in each station and describing the process that causes changes to the energy stores.
Safety considerations	Take care with the naked flame of the candle or spirit burner, stand them in a sand tray.

Starter	Support/Extend	Resources
Off like a rocket (5 min) Show students a video of a firework. Ask them to draw an energy transfer diagram of what they see happening. Check through their diagrams to discuss the different energy stores. **What is energy?** (10 min) Ask students to express their ideas about what the word energy means. They could produce a visual summary to show their prior knowledge.	**Support:** Produce a partially completed visual summary on the board for students to copy and add additional details to.	
Main	**Support/Extend**	**Resources**
Energy stores and transfers (15 min) Introduce the concept of energy stores and how they can be filled and emptied by energy transfers. Focus on the mechanisms (forces, current, and heating) that cause these changes, avoiding the idea that the energy itself is the cause. Analyse the energy transfers of a falling object, discussing the forces acting at different stages. Remind students that it is the action of unbalanced forces that causes the changes.	**Extend:** Discuss the effect of air resistance, which causes heating during the fall.	
Energy circus (25 min) Allow students to investigate some changes in energy stores using the practical. They should identify which stores are filling and emptying and the process that causes these changes. Ask the students to be specific about the forces – is a frictional or gravitational force acting?	**Support:** Provide the names of the relevant energy stores for each station. **Extend:** The students should discuss all of the stores, including dissipation to the surroundings.	**Practical:** Energy circus
Plenary	**Support/Extend**	**Resources**
What's the transfer? (5 min) Provide students with some examples of simple energy transfers they may encounter regularly (e.g., the ticking of a clock, the growth of a plant, or the ringing of the bell marking the end of the lesson). Students use the interactive to complete a description of what energy transfers are occurring. **Energy links** (10 min) Ask students to draw a large circle with all the different stores of energy listed around the outside. They must then link the stores of energy together with an arrow, labelled with a description of the process that can transfer the energy from one store to another.		**Interactive:** What's the transfer?
Homework		
Ask students to make a list of the energy transfers that take place in devices at home.	**Extend:** Students should produce energy transfer diagrams and find appropriate numerical values.	

kerboodle

A Kerboodle highlight for this lesson is **Working scientifically: Energy analogies**. Refer to the **Content map** on Kerboodle for a full list of resources and assessment.

P1.2 Conservation of energy

AQA spec Link: 1.2.1 Energy can be transferred usefully, stored or dissipated, but cannot be created or destroyed.

Students should be able to describe with examples where there are energy transfers in a closed system, that there is no net change to the total energy.

Students should be able to describe, with examples, how in all system changes energy is dissipated, so that it stored in less useful ways. This energy is often described as being 'wasted'.

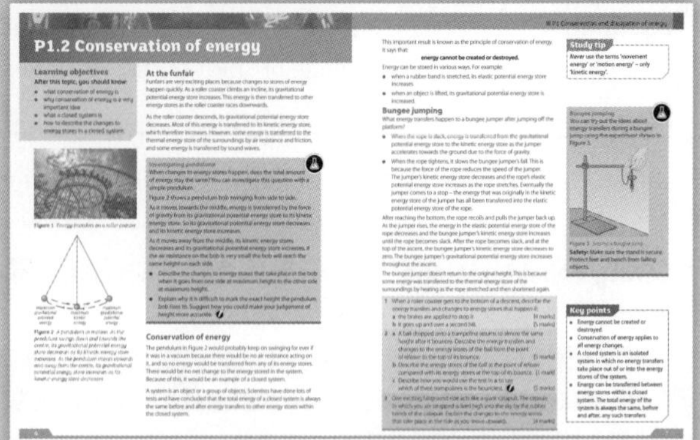

MS 2c, 4a

Aiming for	Outcome	Checkpoint	
		Question	**Activity**
Aiming for GRADE 4 ↓	State that energy is conserved in any transfer.	1, 2	Starter 1, Main 1
	State that energy is dissipated (is no longer useful) when it heats the environment.	2	Main 1
	Investigate the energy transfers in a pendulum and bungee.		Main 1, Main 2
Aiming for GRADE 6 ↓	Apply the law of conservation of energy in straightforward situations.	1, 2, 3	Main 1, Main 2
	Describe changes in energy stores, explaining why energy ceases to be useful.		Starter 1, Main 1
	Describe the energy transfers in a range of experiments and account for energy dissipation to the surroundings.		Main 1, Main 2
Aiming for GRADE 8 ↓	Apply the law of conservation of energy to explain why forces cause heating effects.	1, 2, 3	Starter 2, Main 1, Main 2
	Describe closed systems and the changes to energy stores within them using the principle of conservation of energy.	2	Main 1, Main 2
	Evaluate in detail experiments to investigate energy transfers.	4	Main 2

Maths
Numerical values for quantities of energy can be introduced to allow for discussion of conservation. Bar charts showing energy stores can also be used (2c, 4a).

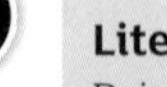

Literacy
Pairs of students should write detailed descriptions of the processes involved in each of the experiments.

Practical

Title	Investigating pendulums
Equipment	retort stand, G-clamp, two small wooden blocks, string with bob (or 50 g mass tied to end), nail (or rod or dowel), graph or squared paper and some reusable adhesive to mount it, torch or lamp (optional)
Overview of method	Students release the pendulum from a fixed height and measure the height it reaches at the end of its swing. They repeat this using a nail to interrupt the pendulum's swing, and observe whether energy is still conserved despite the change in the shape of the swing.
Safety considerations	Only use small pendulum bobs, and restrict swing sizes. Ensure that there is adequate space.

Practical

Title	Bungee jumping
Equipment	retort stand, elastic with mass (or toy tied to end), graph paper and some reusable adhesive to mount it, torch
Overview of method	Students examine the motion of the bungee jumper. A bright light source can be used to cast a shadow onto the graph paper, allowing clearer measurements. Video logging may also be used.
Safety considerations	Do not touch hot filament lamps.

Starter	Support/Extend	Resources
Where does it all go? (5 min) Light a candle with a match and ask students to describe what happens to the chemical store of energy in the wax and the changes in the match.	**Extend:** Expect the students to explain that the store is associated with the wax and the oxygen in the air.	
A plane journey (10 min) Students use the interactive to describe the changes in energy stores at each stage of an aeroplane journey, where the aeroplane lands back at the same place it took off. Ask them what has happened to the energy. Use the ideas that they produce here later in the lesson to discuss the idea that energy cannot 'go away' – it is all accounted for.		**Interactive:** A plane journey
Main	**Support/Extend**	**Resources**
Investigating pendulums (20 min) After a brief recap of changes in energy stores, students should investigate the pendulum. As well as thinking about the processes that remove energy from the system (frictional forces) to explain why the pendulum slows, they will investigate whether energy is roughly conserved over the course of one swing. This allows discussion of energy transfers within a closed system. Discuss the concept of energy dissipation to the surroundings in the initial experiment and emphasise that the total energy is the same at all points in the process. The students must be able to state the law of conservation of energy.	**Support:** Provide some descriptions of the energy transfers for the students to discuss whilst observing the pendulum.	**Practical:** Investigating pendulums
Bungee jumping (20 min) Discuss the energy transfers in a bungee jump and use the experiment to look at the forces, gravitational and tension, and reinforce the idea that energy is always conserved. Make sure that the heating effect in the bungee rope is discussed.	**Extend:** Students should discuss the difficulties in measuring energy transfers quantitatively.	**Practical:** Bungee jumping
Plenary	**Support/Extend**	**Resources**
Measuring the energy in food (5 min) Ask students, as a class or in groups, to discuss some of the issues around designing an experiment to measure the energy in a food sample. Students should aim to minimise energy dissipation to the surroundings.	**Support:** Provide a checklist of energy dissipation that needs to be accounted for, for example, waste gases are hot and the energy in them needs to be measured.	
Evaluate and improve (10 min) Students evaluate the results of their experiments and then design improvements to the experiment.	**Support:** Provide a list of possible improvements and ask the students to explain why they would improve the results.	
Homework		
Students find out how aeroplanes are slowed down on landing, or drag racers stop, and make a booklet or short presentation. Explanations should be in terms of forces and changes in kinetic stores.		

kerboodle

A Kerboodle highlight for this lesson is **Working scientifically: Falling cake cups**. Refer to the **Content map** on Kerboodle for a full list of resources and assessment.

P1.3 Energy and work

AQA spec Link: 5.2 When a force causes an object to move through a distance work is done on the object. So a force does work on an object when the force causes a displacement of the object.

The work done by a force on an object can be calculated using the equation:

work done = force × distance (moved along the line of action of the force)

$[W = F s]$

work done W in joules, J

force F in newtons, N

distance s in metres, m

One joule of work is done when a force of one newton causes a displacement of one metre. 1 joule = 1 newton-metre.

Students should be able to describe the energy transfer involved when work is done.

Students should be able to convert between newton-metres and joules.

Work done against the frictional forces acting on an object causes a rise in the temperature of the object.

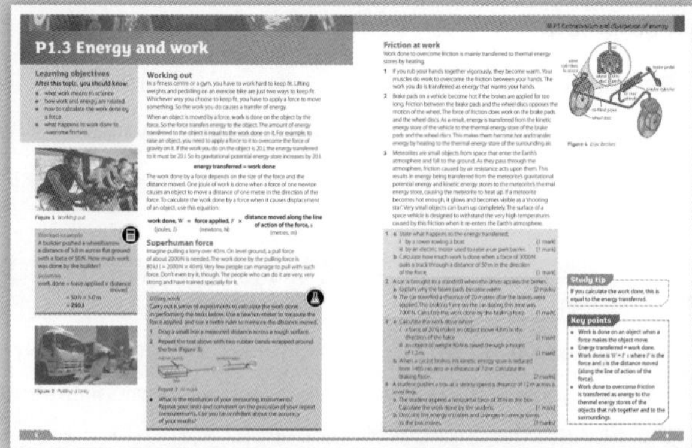

MS 1c, 3a, 3b, 3c

Aiming for	Outcome	Checkpoint	
		Question	**Activity**
Aiming for GRADE 4	State that energy is measured in joules (J).		Starter 1, Main
	Calculate the work done by a force.	2	Main
	Measure the work done by a force experimentally.		Main
Aiming for GRADE 6	Describe the action of frictional forces on objects and the associated heating effect.	1, 2	Main
	Use the equation for work done to calculate distances or size of forces.	2, 3	Main, Plenary 2
	Use repeat values to measure the work done by a force experimentally.		Main
Aiming for GRADE 8	Use the principle of conservation of energy and forces to explain why objects become heated by frictional forces.	1	Main
	Apply the equation for work done in a wide range of contexts.	3, 4	Main, Plenary 2
	Evaluate in detail an experiment to measure work done, explaining why there is variation in the measurements.		Main

Maths
Students perform calculations on work done (3a), including rearrangement of the equations (3b).

Literacy
Descriptions of the action of forces in doing work need to be precise. Students should focus on describing which object is increasing in energy due to work being done on it.

Key words
work

Practical

Title	Doing work
Equipment	newton-meter, small wooden block, elastic bands, metre rule
Overview of method	Students drag the block carefully to measure the force required for both situations and the distance travelled. There will be considerable error involved in these measurements, and so several runs and mean values should be used.
Safety considerations	Ensure that there is adequate space to perform the task. Students should not move the block very quickly, or pull it off the edge of the bench.

Starter	Support/Extend	Resources
Defining work (5 min) Students define the terms work and working as used in common language. Lead them to the idea of a force being involved in working.	**Support:** Provide some example sentences containing the terms.	
Forces and energy (10 min) Ask students to describe some situations where forces cause changes in energy stores. They should explain what factors would affect the size of changes in these stores.	**Extend:** Ask the students to suggest a mathematical relationship between the changes in the stores and the size of forces and distances involved.	
Main	**Support/Extend**	**Resources**
Doing work (40 min) Build on the previous idea of forces causing changes in energy stores to introduce the idea of doing work on something. Be careful with the definition here – it is very specific as opposed to the general term work, with which the students will be familiar. Students should perform a few calculations to embed the equation. Students then carry out the practical, including supporting calculations. There will be considerable errors in the experiments, which the students should discuss. Discuss the heating effect of frictional forces using the examples. These can be supported by practical demonstrations such as hand rubbing, bicycle brakes, and so on.	**Support:** Provide a calculation frame and limit the calculations to the basic form of the equation ($W = Fs$). **Extend:** Differentiate the calculations to stretch the students. **Extend:** Students can use the uncertainty in the measuring instruments in their calculations to find the maximum and minimum work done.	**Practical:** Doing work
Plenary	**Support/Extend**	**Resources**
Working or not? (5 min) Hold a heavy weight but do not lift or drop it. Ask if mechanical work is being done on the weight, and if not, why energy is being transferred as you hold it.	**Support:** You may have to remind students that heating is an energy transfer here.	
Mathematical work out (10 min) Students use the interactive to answer some additional questions involving the equation for work done.	**Support:** Provide a template, and restrict calculations to ones that do not require rearrangement. **Extend:** Include non-base units (e.g., grams) and rearrangement of the equation.	**Interactive:** Mathematical work out
Homework		
Students can describe scenarios where mechanical work is being done in various jobs and show example calculations of the amount of work done. As an alternative, sports can be used.	**Support:** Provide some example scenarios with suggested values for the forces and distances.	

kerboodle

A Kerboodle highlight for this lesson is **Extension sheet: Meteor fall**. Refer to the **Content map** on Kerboodle for a full list of resources and assessment.

P1.4 Gravitational potential energy stores

AQA spec Link: 1.1.1 Throughout this section on energy students should be able to calculate the changes in energy involved when a system is changed by:

- work done by forces
- use calculations to show on a common scale how the overall energy in a system is redistributed when the system is changed.

1.1.2 Students should be able to calculate the amount of energy associated with an object raised above ground level.

The amount of gravitational potential energy gained by an object raised above ground level can be calculated using the equation:

g.p.e. = mass × gravitational field strength × height

$[E_p = m\,g\,h]$

gravitational potential energy E_p in joules, J

mass m in kilograms, kg

gravitational field strength g in newtons per kilogram, N/kg (In any calculation the value of the gravitational field strength g will be given)

height h in metres, m

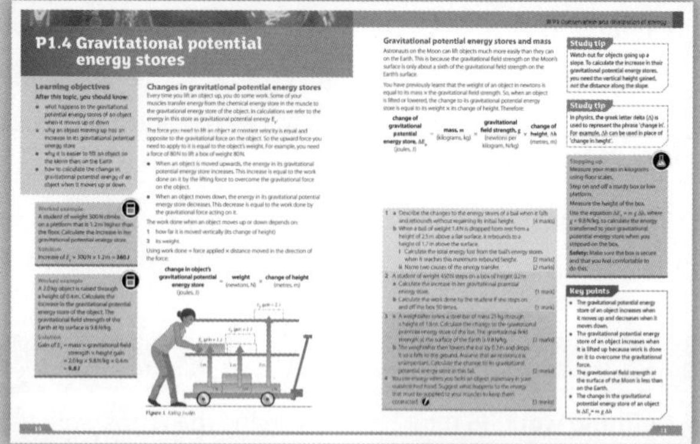

WS 1.2

MS 1a, 1c, 3b, 3c

Aiming for	Outcome	Checkpoint	
		Question	**Activity**
Aiming for GRADE 4	State the factors that affect the change in the gravitational potential energy store of a system.		Starter 1, Main 1
	Calculate the gravitational potential energy store of a system using the weight of an object and its height.	1, 2, End of chapter 4	Main 1
	Measure the gravitational potential energy store changes in a system with a simple practical.		Main 3
Aiming for GRADE 6	Describe the effect of a different gravitational field strength on the gravitational potential energy store changes of a system.		Main 2
	Calculate the gravitational potential energy store of a system using the mass, gravitational field strength, and height.	1, 3	Main 2
	Describe energy transfers that involve a heating effect as opposed to movement of an object.	End of chapter 4	Main 2
Aiming for GRADE 8	Perform calculations using rearrangements of the gravitational potential energy store equations.		Main 1, Main 2
	Apply the gravitational potential energy store equations in a wide range of contexts.	1	Main 2
	Account for all changes of energy during falls or increases in height, including heating effects.	4	Main 2

Maths

Students will perform a range of calculations using the gravitational potential energy store relationship (3c); some students will rearrange the equation to solve problems (3b).

Literacy

Students discuss and develop the concept of energy stores leading to specific calculations for a gravitational potential store.

Practical

Title	Stepping up
Equipment	Scales that measure weight in newtons, objects to step onto. The objects should be robust enough to pose no significant hazards; use steps or benches from the PE department.
Overview of method	The practical should only take a few minutes. Some students may be sensitive about their weight, but you could ask them to move objects onto shelves or up some stairs as an alternative task.
Safety considerations	Any tasks performed should be relatively simple and non-strenuous. Make sure that the students have no medical conditions that could be triggered by the activities.

Starter	Support/Extend	Resources
Lifting work (5 min) Remind students of the idea of work being done by a force when an object moves a distance. Demonstrate lifting things from the floor to a desk and ask them to describe changes in energy stores. Ask them to explain what factors affect the size of energy transfers.	**Extend:** Move on to ask about what affects the weight (mass and the strength of gravity).	
All work (10 min) Give students some scenarios and let them decide if mechanical work is being done. Students use the interactive to explain whether work is being done or not.		**Interactive:** All work
Main	**Support/Extend**	**Resources**
Gravitational potential energy transfers (15 min) Link the equation for work done ($W = F\,s$) to the idea of changing height as the distance. Ask the students to form a simple equation linking change in height to work done. Ask where the energy provided to the lifted object would now be stored, and lead on to the idea of gravitational potential energy stores. Define the gravitational potential energy equation. The students should then perform some simple calculations of work done and changes in gravitational potential energy stores.	**Extend:** Rearrangement of the equation is required.	
Stepping up (25 min) Introduce the idea of calculating weight from $m \times g$ and expand the original GPE equation. As before, students should perform some calculations including some set on different planets. Students can carry out the simple practical to reinforce their use of the GPE equation.	**Support:** Limit the calculations to simple scenarios with no rearrangement. **Extend:** The students should try some rearrangements of the equation.	**Practical:** Stepping up
Plenary	**Support/Extend**	**Resources**
How high? (5 min) Ask students to calculate the E_p of a jumbo jet (400 000 kg) with a cruising altitude of 10 700 m. The E_p is 41 986 800 000 J (~42 GJ).	**Extend:** Students should provide answers in standard form.	
A hard day (10 min) Students estimate the energy they transfer by climbing stairs when moving between lessons during a typical day by estimating the height changes and their weight.	**Support:** Provide some suitable estimates of the numbers – a weight of 500 N and travel upwards through 15 m each day.	
Homework		
Students estimate E_p for three different places they encounter regularly, for example, walking up stairs at home.		

P1.5 Kinetic and elastic stores

AQA spec Link: 1.1.2 Students should be able to calculate the amount of energy associated with a moving object, a stretched spring.

The kinetic energy of a moving object can be calculated using the equation:

kinetic energy = 0.5 × mass × (speed)^2 $[E_k = \frac{1}{2} m v^2]$

kinetic energy E_k in joules, J

mass m in kilograms, kg

speed v in metres per second, m/s

The amount of elastic potential energy stored in a stretched spring can be calculated using the equation:

elastic potential energy = 0.5 × spring constant × (extension)^2

$$[E_e = \frac{1}{2} k e^2]$$

(assuming the limit of proportionality has not been exceeded)

elastic potential energy E_e in joules, J

spring constant k in newtons per metre, N/m

extension e in metres, m

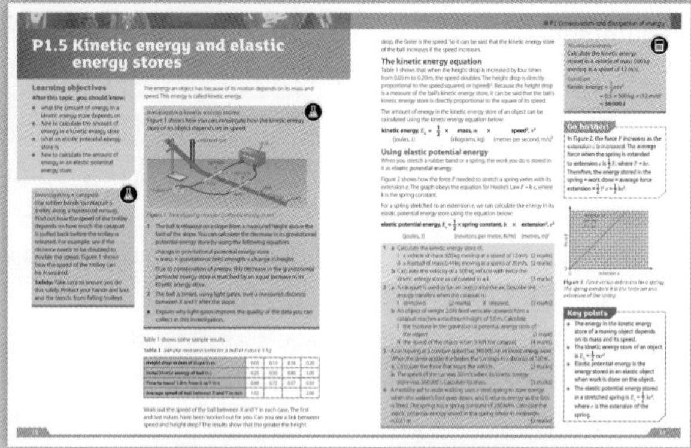
P1.5 Kinetic energy and elastic energy stores

WS 1.2

MS 1a, 1c, 3b, 3c

Aiming for	Outcome	Checkpoint	
		Question	Activity
Aiming for GRADE 4	State the factors that affect the size of a kinetic energy store of an object.		Main 1
	State the factors that affect the elastic potential energy store of a spring.		Main 2
	Describe energy transfers involving elastic potential energy and kinetic energy stores.	2, End of chapter 5	Main 1, Main 2
Aiming for GRADE 6	Calculate the kinetic energy store of an object.	1, End of chapter 1, 6	Main 1, Plenary 2
	Calculate the elastic potential energy store of a stretched spring.	4	Main 2
	Investigate the relationship between the energy stored in a spring and the kinetic energy store of an object launched from it.	2	Main 2
Aiming for GRADE 8	Perform calculations involving the rearrangement of the kinetic energy equation.		Main 1
	Perform calculations involving the rearrangement of the elastic potential energy equation.	4	Main 2
	Perform a wide range of calculations involving transfer of energy.	2, End of chapter 5	Main 1, Main 2

Maths 

Student will perform a wide range of calculations, including those for gravitational potential energy stores, kinetic energy stores, and elastic energy stores (3b, 3c).

Literacy 

Students need to clearly describe the factors affecting changes in kinetic energy stores, including the interpretation of data or graphs.

Key words

elastic potential energy

Practical

Title	Investigating kinetic energy stores
Equipment	ramp (or drainpipe), tennis ball, velocity or distance sensor, balance to measure mass of object
Overview of method	This experiment can be demonstrated with a ball and motion sensor or with a dynamics trolley and light gates.
Safety considerations	Ensure that balls do not fall off desks.

Practical

Title	Investigating a catapult
Equipment	flat surface, elastic bands (fishing-pole elastic works well), a dynamics trolley or wheeled toy
Overview of method	The trolley is pulled back through different distances and fired by the band. The speed (or time taken to cover a distance) is measured and then the changes in kinetic energy stores for the object.
Safety considerations	Ensure that trolleys do not fall off desks.

Starter	Support/Extend	Resources
Mass and velocity (5 min) Using mini-whiteboards, the students must give accurate definitions of mass and velocity and their units.		
Kinetic objects (10 min) Show students various moving objects with the mass and the velocity of the object. Students use the interactive to put them into order from which object has the smallest kinetic energy store to the largest.	**Support:** Identify the factors that affect kinetic energy store beforehand through discussion.	**Interactive:** Kinetic objects
Main	**Support/Extend**	**Resources**
Investigating kinetic energy stores (25 min) Students carry out the practical to investigate the factors that affect the amount of energy in a kinetic store by using the practical. They may need reminding beforehand about gravitational potential energy stores. The data provided in the student book may be used if the experiment does not provide suitable results. Introduce the kinetic energy equation. Demonstrate a set of calculations before expecting students to perform their own.	**Support:** Simple clues for velocity and mass should be used. **Extend:** Calculations involving SI prefixes are very demanding, so try some. **Extend:** Ensure students rearrange this equation.	**Practical:** Investigating kinetic energy stores
Investigating a catapult (15 min) This energy transfer needs careful explanation as there are two linked concepts with corresponding equations. The practical can be used as a demonstration to show how stretching the band further stores more energy.	**Support:** As before, just use simple values for the measurements.	
Plenary	**Support/Extend**	**Resources**
Higher/lower (5 min) Go through a series of objects with different masses and velocities and ask the students to say (or calculate) if the kinetic energy store is higher or lower than the previous one.		
Kinetic cards revisited (10 min) The students now have to calculate the energy of each of the cards used in the second starter to check their order. Use this task to make sure that the students are treating the calculations correctly.	**Support:** Calculation frames can be provided for some of the cards.	
Homework		
Challenge students to build their own elastic-powered vehicles and hold a competition on whose can go the furthest. The vehicles should all have identical elastic bands and could be cars, boats, or aeroplanes.		

kerboodle

A Kerboodle highlight for this lesson is **Calculation sheet: Energy transfers**. Refer to the **Content map** on Kerboodle for a full list of resources and assessment.

P1.6 Energy dissipation

AQA spec Link: 1.2.1 Energy can be transferred usefully, stored, or dissipated, but cannot be created or destroyed.

Students should be able to describe, with examples, how in all system changes energy is dissipated, so that it is stored in less useful ways. This energy is often described as being 'wasted'.

Students should be able to explain ways of reducing unwanted energy transfers, for example, through lubrication and the use of thermal insulation.

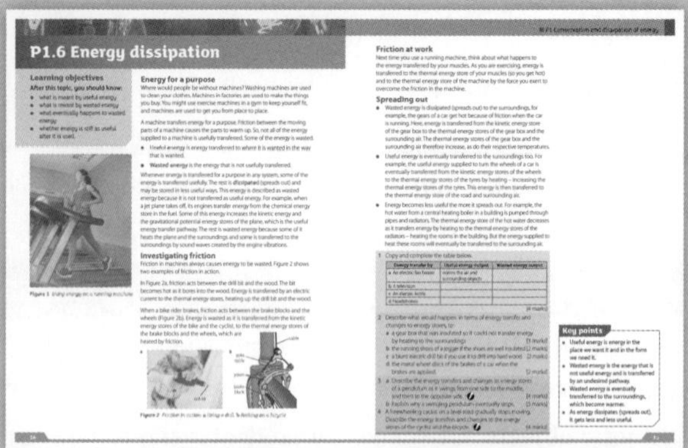
P1.6 Energy dissipation

MS 3a

Aiming for	Outcome	Checkpoint	
		Question	**Activity**
Aiming for GRADE 4 ↓	Identify useful and wasted energy in simple scenarios.	1	Main
	Describe energy dissipation in terms of heating the surroundings.	2	Main
	Measure the frictional force acting on an object.		Main
Aiming for GRADE 6 ↓	Analyse energy transfers to identify useful and less useful energy transfers.	1	Main
	Describe energy dissipation and how this reduces the capacity of a system to do work.	2, 3	Main
	Investigate the factors that affect frictional forces.		Main
Aiming for GRADE 8 ↓	Use a wide range of energy stores and physical processes to decide on wasted and useful energy transfers.		Main
	Apply the concept of energy dissipation in a wide range of scenarios.	2, 3, 4	Main
	Evaluate in detail an experiment to measure the frictional forces acting on an object.		Main

Maths

Students can compare transfers of energy in quantitative terms (3a).

Literacy

Students should discuss different transfers of energy and collaborate to decide which transfers are the more useful ones.

Key words
useful energy, wasteful energy, dissipated

Practical

Title	Investigating friction
Equipment	string, pulley, clamp, selection of masses, 1 kg mass (with hoop), three different surfaces to test (desk surface, carpet tiles, sandpaper)
Overview of method	Students place the 1 kg mass on the surfaces and attach it to a mass holder hanging over the desk by the pulley. They then find out what mass is required to start the 1 kg sliding across the surface. To improve the accuracy of the measurements, encourage students to add smaller masses when they get near to the sliding point of the mass, so several runs will be required.
Safety considerations	Ensure that masses do not fall to the floor.

Starter	Support/Extend	Resources
Useful or useless? (5 min) Show energy transfer diagrams and ask students to use the interactive to identify the useful energy transfers and the useless ones in each case. **Overheating** (10 min) Ask students to explain why humans become hot when they work hard. How is this excess energy transferred from the body? Why do people need to eat less in hot weather? Links can be made to biological processes. This can lead to a discussion about where the energy in food actually ends up.	**Extend:** The specific 'useful pathways' and 'wasteful pathways' can be discussed.	**Interactive:** Useful or useless?
Main	**Support/Extend**	**Resources**
Investigating friction (40 min) Discuss some example energy transfers. Use as many examples as possible until the students are clear on the useful and wasteful transfers. Students then observe or try the practicals, noting that heating of the surroundings is the ultimate effect of most energy transfers. The idea of a force being the pathway by which energy is transferred should be emphasised. Show a video clip of brakes in action – Formula One cars are ideal. Discuss whether the energy in the resulting thermal stores can be reused in any way. Link back to the earlier demonstrations when discussing dissipation. Ensure that the students know that there is still the same amount of energy but eventually it is too spread out to be useful. Ensure that the students can use the term dissipated correctly.	**Support:** A simple set of examples can be used with the key energy stores described. **Extend:** Some braking systems recharge batteries, and these can be described.	**Practical:** Investigating friction
Plenary	**Support/Extend**	**Resources**
Sticky problems (5 min) Ask students to draw a table of the ways friction can be reduced and give examples of exactly where this happens. A table of suggested places can be provided – ask students to complete it to explain how the friction could be reduced. **What's wrong?** (10 min) Ask students to correct some sentences describing energy and friction. This can be used to challenge some misconceptions. Examples can include: 'When a car stops at traffic lights, the speed energy is destroyed by the brakes and is lost.'	**Support:** Video clips of machines operating can be very helpful here. **Support:** Ask the students for ideas about what confuses them in energy transfer.	
Homework		
Students complete the WebQuest activity where they use the Internet to help them answer a series of questions involving energy calculations and comparisons.		**WebQuest:** How many AA batteries?

P1.7 Energy and efficiency

AQA spec Link: 1.2.2 The energy efficiency for any energy transfer can be calculated using the equation:

$$\text{efficiency} = \frac{\text{useful output energy transfer}}{\text{total input energy transfer}}$$

Ⓗ **Students should be able to describe ways to increase the efficiency of an intended energy transfer.**

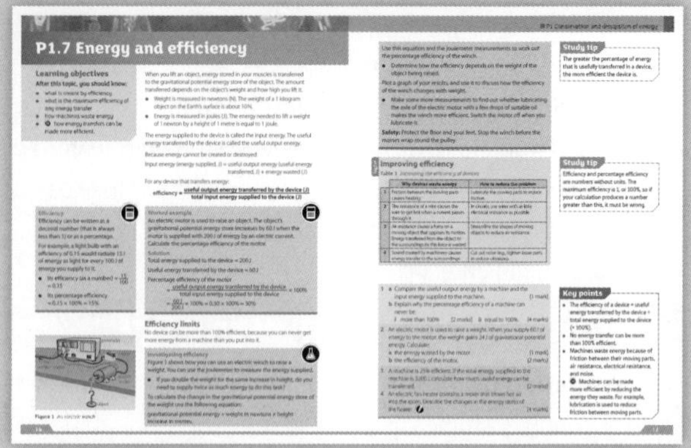

MS 1c, 3b, 3c

Aiming for	Outcome	Checkpoint	
		Question	Activity
Aiming for GRADE 4 ↓	Describe an efficient transfer as one that transfers more energy by a useful process.	4	Starter 1, Main
	State that the efficiency of an energy transfer is always less than 100%.	1	Main
	Calculate the efficiency of a simple energy transfer.	1	Main
Aiming for GRADE 6 ↓	Calculate the efficiency of a range of energy transfers.	2, End of chapter 7	Main
	Use the law of conservation of energy to explain why efficiency can never be greater than 100%.	1, 4	Main
	Investigate the efficiency of a motor.		Main
Aiming for GRADE 8 ↓	Ⓗ **Describe design features that can be used to improve the efficiency of an energy transfer.**		Plenary 2
	Rearrange the efficiency equation to find input or total output energy.	2, 3	Main
	Evaluate in detail an efficiency investigation to justify conclusions.		Main

Maths
Students perform a range of efficiency calculations (1c, 3b, 3c).

Literacy

Students work in small groups to define efficiency, sharing their explanations.

Key words
efficiency

Practical

Title	Investigating efficiency
Equipment	joulemeter, variable low-voltage power supply, connecting leads, small electric winch (motor), five equal masses, metre rule, clamps to secure the winches to benches, cardboard box, or piece of carpet to protect the floor
Overview of method	Students lift a range of masses to a fixed height. A full metre is a good height – if the motor were 100% efficient it would require 0.1 J for a mass on 100 g.
Safety considerations	Protect the floor and keep feet clear from falling masses. Stop motor before masses reach the pulley.

Starter	Support/Extend	Resources
Staying on (5 min) Ask students to explain why some electrical devices of the same type (e.g., two different models of phone) last longer than others even though they use the same batteries. **Efficiency** (10 min) Ask students what is efficiency and why is it wanted? What are the advantages of an efficient device? Form students into groups and ask them to agree on a simple description of what efficiency is and why it is important.	**Extend:** Students link their explanations to the efficiency of the device. They should describe the subtle differences in what the devices do. For example, one phone may have many more applications running than another.	
Main	**Support/Extend**	**Resources**
Investigating efficiency (40 min) Recap the systems used for measuring quantities, particularly the joule and newton as these are required later. Discuss input and output energy in terms of how much energy is transferred from the starting stores into the stores we want it to be. This leads to calculations of efficiency based on these values. Students should try a few of the calculations to ensure that they can do them. Explain the limits to efficiency, linking this to the law of conservation of energy. Students try an efficiency measurement using the practical. Ensure that they are calculating work done correctly and finding the energy supplied to the motor.	**Extend:** Discuss the consequences if a machine was more than 100% efficient – energy could be created. Use Sankey diagrams to represent energy transfers and to find values for energy input and output.	**Practical:** Investigating efficiency
Plenary	**Support/Extend**	**Resources**
Car efficiency (5 min) Show students advertisements for car. Students use the interactive to arrange them in order of energy efficiency, using the fuel consumption figures in the small print. **Improving efficiency** (10 min) (H) Discuss the design features used to improve efficiency of a range of devices, supported by demonstration where possible.		**Interactive:** Car efficiency
Homework		
Students research data on electrical devices, such as laptops or mobile phones, to determine which is most efficient. Students suggest the particular feature that improves the efficiency of the device.		

kerboodle

A Kerboodle highlight for this lesson is **Extension sheet: Using energy conservation**. Refer to the **Content map** on Kerboodle for a full list of resources and assessment.

P1.8 Electrical appliances

AQA spec Link: 1.1.1 A system is an object or group of objects.

There are changes in the way energy is stored when a system changes.

Students should be able to describe all the changes involved in the way energy is stored when a system changes, for common situations. For example:

- bringing water to a boil in an electric kettle.

1.2.2 The energy efficiency for any energy transfer can be calculated using the equation:

$$\text{efficiency} = \frac{\text{useful output energy transfer}}{\text{total input energy transfer}}$$

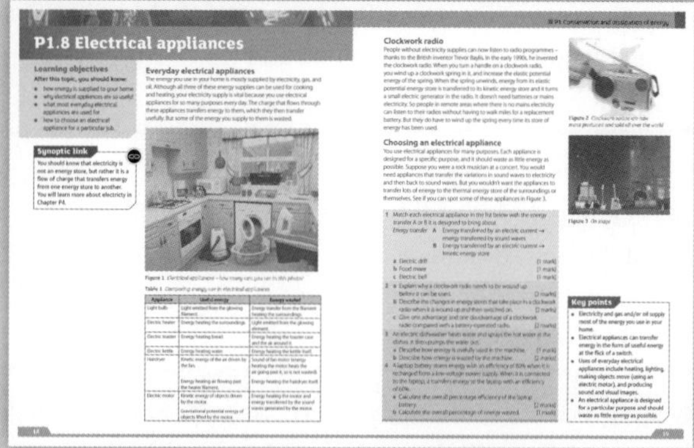

MS 1a, 1c, 3a, 3b, 3c

Aiming for	Outcome	Checkpoint	
		Question	**Activity**
Aiming for GRADE 4	List some example electrical devices.		Starter 1, Main 1
	Survey a range of electrical devices and their operation.		Main 1
	Describe the energy transfers carried out by electrical devices.	1, End of chapter 1	Starter 1, Main 1
Aiming for GRADE 6	Rank electrical devices in terms of their power.		Main 2
	Compare mains-powered and battery-powered devices.	2	Starter 2, Main 2
	Describe the processes that waste energy in electrical devices.	3	Main 2
Aiming for GRADE 8	Compare electrical devices in terms of efficiency.		Main 2
	Calculate the efficiency of an electrical device.	4	Plenary 1
	Explain the operation of electrical devices in terms of forces and electric current.		Main 2

Maths
Students can rank appliances by their power ratings (3a).

Literacy
Descriptions of the operation of devices should be constructed by the students with links to energy transfer.

Practical

Title	Everyday electrical appliances
Equipment	Demo 1: low-voltage power supply (variable), connecting wires, resistance wire, heatproof mat Demo 2: low-voltage motor and power supply Demo 3: loudspeaker and signal generator
Overview of method	For the first demonstration, pass a current through the wire to observe it heating up and glowing. For the second demonstration, observe the motion of the motor. For the third demonstration, observe the motion of the loudspeaker.
Safety considerations	The wire in the first demonstration will be very hot. It should be allowed to cool.

Starter	Support/Extend	Resources
Electricity everywhere (5 min) Ask students to list all of the electrical appliances that they use during the day, including mains-powered and battery-powered. They then describe how their lives would be more difficult if these appliances did not exist.	**Support:** Provide some initial suggestions to get students going.	
Using energy (10 min) Challenge students to design an experiment to compare how much energy is stored in different batteries. Their ideas could include measuring how long a bulb could stay lit or even how long a toy operates.	**Extend:** Ask students to design appropriate results tables.	
Main	**Support/Extend**	**Resources**
Everyday electrical appliances (20 min) Discuss a range of electrical appliances with the students, ideally showing them some examples. The students can then list as many more as they can think of and explain their purpose. Carry out the practical demonstration to show the possible effects of an electric current.	**Support:** Limit the range of devices to simple ones. **Extend:** More complex devices can be used requiring a greater depth of understanding.	**Practical:** Everyday electrical appliances
Mains- or battery-powered (20 min) The students could compare mains- and battery-powered devices, noting that mains devices can transfer energy far more quickly. This can be linked to the voltage and size of the current. Students should also be made aware of clockwork devices and shown one if possible. Students then analyse the different devices mentioned in the student book, discussing how they operate and link this back to the effects of a current from earlier in the lesson.	**Extend:** The electrical power equation ($P = \frac{E}{t}$) can be covered. Look for explanations of the rate of energy transfer using the idea of larger and smaller electrical currents and/or voltages.	
Plenary	**Support/Extend**	**Resources**
Making connections (5 min) Interactive where students complete the paragraph 'Electrical current is a very convenient way of transferring energy because...' and include the words energy, transfer, and current. Students then calculate the efficiency of a series of electrical appliances.		**Interactive:** Making connections
Electrical energy table (10 min) Ask students to produce a table similar to the one in the student book with additional electrical appliances. You could use a mobile phone, projector, vacuum cleaner, and electric fan. For some students, you could add challenging appliances such as a computer.	**Support:** Physical cards can be used to assemble the table.	
Homework		
Students carry out a survey of electrical appliances found at school or at home. Record the useful and wasted energy transfers of each appliance.		

P1.9 Energy and power

AQA spec Link: 1.1.4 Power is defined as the rate at which energy is transferred or the rate at which work is done.

$$\text{power} = \frac{\text{energy transferred}}{\text{time}} \qquad [P = \frac{E}{t}]$$

$$\text{power} = \frac{\text{work done}}{\text{time}} \qquad [P = \frac{W}{t}]$$

power P in watts, W

energy transferred E in joules, J

time t in seconds, s

work done W in joules, J

An energy transfer of 1 joule per second is equal to a power of 1 watt.

Students should be able to give examples that illustrate the definition of power, for example, comparing two electric motors that both lift the same weight through the same height but one does it faster than the other.

1.2.2 The energy efficiency for any energy transfer can be calculated using the equation:

$$\text{efficiency} = \frac{\text{useful output energy transfer}}{\text{total input energy transfer}}$$

Efficiency may also be calculated using the equation:

$$\text{efficiency} = \frac{\text{useful power output}}{\text{total power input}}$$

(H) Students should be able to describe ways to increase the efficiency of an intended energy transfer.

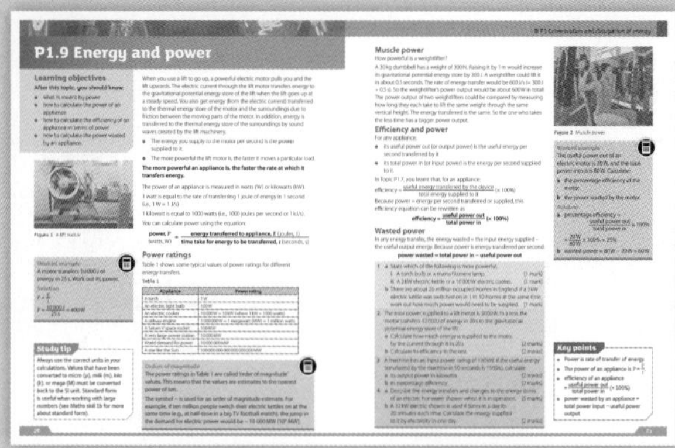

MS 1a, 1b, 1c, 3b, 3c

Aiming for	Outcome	Checkpoint	
		Question	**Activity**
Aiming for GRADE 4 ↓	State the unit of power as the watt and kilowatt.	1	Starter 1, Main
	With support, rank electrical appliances in order of power.	1	Main
	Identify 'wasted' and 'useful' energy transfers in electrical devices.		Main
Aiming for GRADE 6 ↓	Calculate the energy transferred by an electrical device.	2	Main, Plenary 2
	Calculate the efficiency of a device from power ratings.	2, 3	Main
	Find the wasted power of a device.	3	Main
Aiming for GRADE 8 ↓	Compare the power ratings of devices using standard form.		Main
	Apply the efficiency equation in a range of situations, including rearrangement of the equation.	2, 3	Main, Plenary 2
	Combine the electrical power equation with other equations to solve complex problems.	4	Main, Plenary 2

Maths
There is a range of calculations involving power and efficiency that the students need to perform (1a, 1c, 3c). Higher-tier students are also required to rearrange the equations and can also use standard form (1b, 3b).

Literacy
Students discuss the power ratings of devices, linking this to the efficiency and function.

Key words
power

Practical

Title	Efficiency and power
Equipment	low-voltage power supply, low-voltage electrical appliances, joulemeter
Overview of method	Demonstrate the energy use of electrical appliances by connecting appliances to the low-voltage power supply and measuring the energy using the joulemeter. Demonstrate a range of bulbs so that students can link the energy use to the brightness. Then move on to motors, showing larger motors requiring more energy.

Starter	Support/Extend	Resources
Big numbers (5 min) Give students a set of units with SI prefixes and ask them to place the units in order of size. These could be mm, cm, m, km, and another set containing mg, g, and kg. Then add in larger units such as mega (M) and giga (G) that students may not have encountered.	**Support:** Provide examples of the use of each unit to assist students with their ideas of scale.	**Interactive:** Big numbers
Match up (10 min) Ask students to sort a range of electrical appliances into order of energy transfer (power rating). You could do this with real objects or with cards to represent them. The objects could be set up on a long bench and students should add sticky notes for their ranking. Discuss these rankings after everybody has had a go.	**Extend:** Students guess the power ratings then add sticky notes indicating the useful energy transfers and wasted energy on each.	
Main	**Support/Extend**	**Resources**
Efficiency and power (40 min) Carry out the practical demonstration to show the difference in energy use between different devices. Discuss the transfer of energy at different rates leading to the power equation. The students need to try some calculations to ensure that they are performing them correctly and using the correct units. Describe some of the power ratings of typical devices using some of the examples from the student book so that the students understand the stages in the calculation. They should then try an example of their own. A maths skills interactive is available to support students with the calculations and provide some examples for them to carry out themselves.	**Support:** Select appropriate questions for the students. **Extend:** Use numbers with SI prefixes and expect rearrangement of the base equation.	**Practical:** Efficiency and power **Math skills:** Electrical energy
Students then identify the useful and wasted power output of a range of devices and then use this data to find the efficiency. Emphasise careful layout of calculations to avoid mistakes. A support sheet is available where students develop their knowledge of the units of energy and power and also practise using energy terms.	**Support:** Assist students with identifying the useful and the wasted power transfers. **Extend:** Use kilowatts and watts for different examples.	**Support:** Power to the kitchen
Plenary	**Support/Extend**	**Resources**
Matching the power (5 min) Give students a set of pictures of household electrical appliances and a set of power ratings. Ask them to match the ratings with the appliances. For example, kettle 2 kW, washing machine 0.5 kW (average over washing cycle), desktop computer 200 W, dishwasher 1.5 kW, electric clock 1 W, iron 1 kW, CD player 30 W, blender 300 W.		
Calculation loop (10 min) Students match up calculation questions with their numerical answers. There should be a set of calculations and only one card with the correct answer. Students work out the correct answer and then ask the question on that card. Repeat until all of the questions are answered.	**Support:** Differentiate questions according to students' ability.	
Homework		
Students complete the WebQuest where they research how much energy their electronic devices (phone, ipad, mp3 player, laptop) use in a typical day/year, and how this compares with more obvious energy usage such as lighting and heating.		**WebQuest:** Your electronic devices

kerboodle

A Kerboodle highlight for this lesson is **Working scientifically: Working with units**. Refer to the **Content map** on Kerboodle for a full list of resources and assessment.

P1 Conservation and dissipation of energy

Overview of P1 Conservation and dissipation of energy

In this chapter, students developed their understanding of energy and energy transfer, begun in KS3. This included development of an energy stores model and the processes (pathways), such as forces and electrical currents, through which energy can be transferred.

Students have learnt how to measure the work done by a force acting over a distance and how this concept can be used to analyse energy transfers in gravitational stores, through lifting and falling, and elastic potential stores during stretching using the relevant mathematical relationships. The conservation of energy through changes in the gravitational, kinetic and elastic stores was also discussed.

They have considered the dissipation of energy during transfers such as those caused by friction or electrical heating, leading to the idea of efficiency during different energy changes and its calculation. The concept of efficiency has then been applied to the selection of electrical devices.

Finally, the students have learnt about the rate of energy transfer in different systems through the concept of power and how this power rating can be used to determine the total energy transfer over time.

You can find additional support for the maths skills covered in this chapter on **MyMaths**, including recognising and using expressions in standard form, using an appropriate number of significant figures, using of bar charts, and rearranging of equations.

For this chapter, the following assessments are available on Kerboodle:

P1 Checkpoint quiz: Conservation and dissipation of energy
P1 Progress quiz: Conservation and dissipation of energy 1
P1 Progress quiz: Conservation and dissipation of energy 2
P1 On your marks: Conservation and dissipation of energy
P1 Exam-style questions and mark scheme: Conservation and dissipation of energy

Checkpoint follow up lesson

A student's route through this lesson can be determined using the Checkpoint assessment. Percentage pass marks are supplied in the Checkpoint teacher notes.

For each successive route through it is assumed that the student can perform to their current route as well as previous routes. For example, students working at Aiming for 6 are assumed to be secure in Aiming for 4 knowledge and understanding and working towards achieving all the learning outcomes for Aiming for 6.

	Aiming for 4	Aiming for 6	Aiming for 8
Learning outcomes	Name different types of energy store.	Describe processes in terms of energy stores, and transfers.	Explain processes in terms of energy stores.
	Do calculations involving gravitational potential energy, kinetic energy, elastic potential energy, work done, power and efficiency.	Do calculations involving gravitational potential energy, kinetic energy, elastic potential energy, work done, power and efficiency, and change the subject of equations.	Do more complex calculations involving gravitational potential energy, kinetic energy, elastic potential energy, work done, power and efficiency, and change the subject of equations.
	Describe the difference between efficient and inefficient devices in terms of dissipation.		Apply what you know about power and efficiency.
Starter	**Spot the store! (5 min)** Give out cards with pictures of everyday situations, e.g. a camping stove, ball rolling down a hill, and ask students to identify the store or stores where the energy is increasing, and the store or stores where the energy is decreasing. **Guess the question (10 min)** Make packs of cards with the keywords from the energy topic. In groups students take turns to select a card and everyone in the groups writes as many questions as they can think of where the word is the answer. Groups feedback their questions to the class, with a prize for the group with the most questions.		
Differentiated checkpoint activity	Aiming for 4 students use the Checkpoint follow-up sheet to model the transfer of energy between stores, and with help do calculations involving a bouncing ball and electrical appliances. The follow-up sheet is highly-structured to support students with the tasks, and they should work in pairs with input from the teacher.	Aiming for 6 students use the Checkpoint follow-up sheet to design an investigation into bouncing balls, model energy transfers with liquid and coins, and consider the efficiency of different types of light bulb. The follow-up sheet is fairly structured and students should be aiming to work independently.	Aiming for 8 students use the Checkpoint follow-up sheet to design an investigation into craters, model energy transfers with liquid and coins, and calculate the efficiency of different types of light bulb. The follow-up sheet provides minimal support for students and they should be working independently.
	Kerboodle resource P1 Checkpoint follow up: Aiming for 4, P1 Checkpoint follow up: Aiming for 6, P1 Checkpoint follow up: Aiming for 8		
Plenary	**Find the biggest (10 min)** Give out a set of cards with information on each relating to efficiency, work, and power. Students work in teams of three to work out the card in each category that shows the biggest efficiency, work done, or power. Pair the groups up to check the answers. The information on the cards can be differentiated with Aiming at 4 students also being given the equations. **Energy conservation...or not? (5 min)** Show students one of more of three situations that appear to defy the law of conservation of energy: the Gaussian gun, the 'thunder popper' (a rubber hemisphere you turn inside out and drop, which goes higher than you dropped it from), dropping a tennis ball on a football. Ask them to account to the apparent appearance of more energy at the end than at the start. Groups feedback explanations and the class votes for the best one in each case.		
Progression	Students should be able to identify the energy stores involved in a range of energy transfers, and to do calculations involving stores, work, power and efficiency. Encourage students to think about the difference between the energy description of a process and what is physically happening by identifying the stores involved. Putting units in calculations will help them to get more answers correct.	Students should be able to describe a range of processes in terms of the energy stores involved, and to do calculations involving stores, work, power and efficiency, and convert between a variety of units. Encourage students to think about the difference between the energy description of a process and what is physically happening by identifying the stores involved. They should devise a system for remembering the relevant equations for the energy associated with different stores.	Students should be able to use ideas about stores to identify changes in energy in a range of processes, to do more complex calculations involving stores, work, power and efficiency, and convert between a variety of units, and apply what they know about efficiency to a range of situations. Encourage students to differentiate the energy description of a process and what is physically happening by identifying the stores involved, and to think critically about ways of modelling energy transfers.

P 2 Energy transfer by heating

2.1 Energy transfer by conduction

AQA spec Link: 1.2.1 Unwanted energy transfers can be reduced in a number of ways, for example through lubrication and the use of thermal insulation. Students should be able to explain ways of reducing unwanted energy transfers, for example, through lubrication and the use of thermal insulation.

The higher the thermal conductivity of a material the higher the rate of energy transfer by conduction across the material.

Students should be able to describe how the rate of cooling of a building is affected by the thickness and thermal conductivity of its walls.

Students do not need to know the definition of thermal conductivity.

Required practical: Investigate the effectiveness of different materials as thermal insulators and the factors that may affect the thermal insulation properties of a material.

3.2.1 Energy is stored inside a system by the particles (atoms and molecules) that make up the system. This is called internal energy.

Internal energy is the total kinetic energy and potential energy of all the particles (atoms and molecules) that make up a system.

Heating changes the energy stored within the system by increasing the energy of the particles that make up the system. This either raises the temperature of the system or produces a change of state.

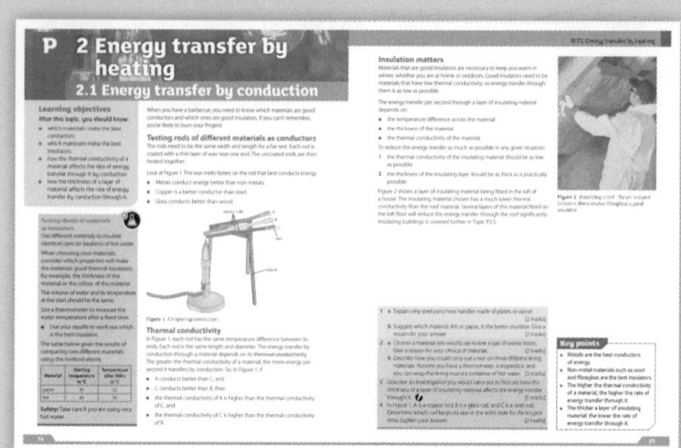

MS 2c, 4a

Aiming for	Outcome	Checkpoint	
		Question	Activity
Aiming for GRADE 4	Describe materials as good or poor thermal conductors.	1	Starter 1, Starter 2
	Compare the thermal conductivities of materials in simple terms.	1	Starter 1, Starter 2, Main
	Relate the thermal conductivities of a material to the uses of that material in familiar contexts.	1	Main
Aiming for GRADE 6	Analyse temperature change data to compare the thermal conductivity of materials.		Main
	Describe the changes in the behaviour of the particles in a material as the temperature of the material increases.	3	Main
	Apply understanding of thermal conductivity in reducing energy dissipation through the choice of appropriate insulating materials.	2, 4, End of chapter 4	Homework
Aiming for GRADE 8	Explain the different thermal conductivities of materials using the free electron and lattice vibration explanations of conduction.	3	Main, Plenary 2
	Evaluate the results of an experiment into thermal conductivity in terms of repeatability and reproducibility of data, and the validity of conclusions drawn from the data.		Main
	Justify the choices of a material involved in insulation or conduction using the concept of thermal conductivity and other data.	4	Homework

Maths

Students draw tables and plot graphs of their results from the practical (2c, 4a).

Literacy

Focus on the precise application of the scientific key terms in descriptions of conduction processes.

Key words

thermal conductivity

Required practical

Title	Testing sheets of materials as insulators
Equipment	containers for water (metals cans, beakers, or boiling tubes), access to hot water (kettle), thermometer (0–100 °C with 0.5 °C divisions), stopwatch, elastic bands or tape, aluminium foil (for lids), range of materials to test (wool, cotton wool, fur, corrugated card, etc.)
Overview of method	Insulate containers using different materials. Pour hot water into the containers and place a lid onto them. Allow the containers to cool for a fixed length of time and compare the temperature drop.
Safety considerations	Kettles can cause burns; a hot water tap may be sufficient as an alternative.

Starter	Support/Extend	Resources
Frying tonight? (10 min) Crack an egg onto a frying pan and a heat-resistant mat and use Bunsen burners to heat them. (Alternatively, show a video of an egg frying.) Students describe the processes that allow energy to reach the eggs and compare the rate of energy transfer. **Spoons** (5 min) Ask students to explain, if a metal spoon and a wooden spoon are put into boiling water, why only the end of one spoon will get hot.	**Extend:** Students should directly link the behaviour of the particles in a material to the material's temperature. **Extend:** Look for descriptions about energy change *within* the materials.	**Interactive:** Frying tonight?
Main	**Support/Extend**	**Resources**
Testing sheets of materials as insulators (40 min) Students complete the practical, focusing on producing results that are as accurate as possible from this experiment by refining the control of variables and eliminating sources of random error. Links should be made to the idea of trapped air in foams or fluffy materials used for insulation and reduction of energy dissipation. For students studying *AQA GCSE Physics* this is a required practical. For students studying *AQA GCSE Combined science: Trilogy* this is **not** a required practical.	**Extend:** Ask students to develop a quantitative test comparing the number of layers of insulation with the temperature change.	**Required practical:** Testing sheets of materials as insulators **Practical:** Testing sheets of materials as insulators
Plenary	**Support/Extend**	**Resources**
Chilling effect (5 min) Explain to students what a defrosting plate is. (You could show students a photo or video of one.) Ask students to explain why an ice cube will melt a lot quicker on a defrosting plate than on a plastic surface, in terms of conduction. (Defrosting trays are made of materials that have a high thermal conductivity and will transfer thermal energy more efficiently than a plastic surface.) **Conduction modelling** (10 min) Ask students to describe a large-scale model of conduction through lattice vibration to provide a visual idea of the process.	**Extend:** Students should incorporate the idea of free electrons into their physical model in some way and evaluate the model.	
Homework		
Students complete a survey of the materials used in their home for insulation or to allow efficient energy transfer. This can include the building materials and the furnishings.	**Extend:** Provide students with some numerical values for the thermal conductivity that they use to justify the choices of materials.	

P2.2 Infrared radiation

AQA spec Link: 6.3.1 All bodies (objects), no matter what temperature, emit and absorb infrared radiation. The hotter the body, the more infrared radiation it radiates in a given time.

A perfect black body is an object that absorbs all of the radiation incident on it. A black body does not reflect or transmit any radiation. Since a good absorber is also a good emitter, a perfect black body would be the best possible emitter.

6.3.2 Students should be able to explain:

- that all bodies (objects) emit radiation
- that the intensity of any emission depends on the temperature of the body

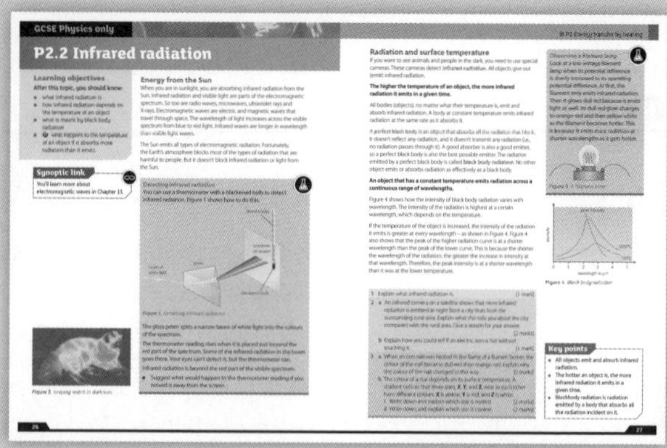
GCSE Physics only

P2.2 Infrared radiation

MS 4a, 4c

Aiming for	Outcome	Checkpoint	
		Question	Activity
Aiming for GRADE 4	State that infrared radiation is radiation of shorter wavelength than red light.	1	Starter 1, Main 1
	State that an object cools by emitting infrared radiation and heats by absorbing infrared radiation.	1	Starter 2, Main 2
	Describe how infrared radiation can be detected.		Main 1
Aiming for GRADE 6	Describe the cooling of objects in terms of the rate of emission of radiation.	3, 4	Main 1, Plenary 2
	Describe how the rate of emission of radiation is related to the temperature of a body.	1, 2	Main 2
	Describe the visible changes in an object's emitted radiation as its temperature is increased.		Main 2
Aiming for GRADE 8	Compare the black body spectra of two objects to identify which is at a higher temperature.		Main 2
	Apply the concepts of absorption and emission of infrared radiation to explain why an object maintains a constant temperature.	1, 2	Main 1, Main 2
	Describe the changes in the black body radiation curve as the temperature of an object changes in terms of change in the radiation emitted.		Main 2

Maths

Students should compare temperatures of objects in degrees Celsius (°C) and use data to plot graphs and find patterns in cooling (4a, 4c).

Literacy

Students should describe the effects of absorption and emission of IR radiation in a range of situations.

Key words

infrared radiation, black body radiation

Practical

Title	Detecting infrared radiation
Equipment	bright white light source (power supply and ray box), sensitive thermometer (to 0.5°C) with bulb painted matt black, clean prism
Overview of method	Shine the light through the prism and produce the spectrum. This could be projected on the wall if this is a demonstration. Position the thermometer just beyond the red part of the spectrum, and the temperature reading will rise.
Safety considerations	The filament lamp will become very hot – allow time for cooling.

Title	Black body radiation
Equipment	6 V filament lamp, 6 V power supply or battery, connecting leads, variable resistor
Overview of method	The students connect the lamp in series circuit with the variable resistor and observe the changes in the filament as the current is increased by altering the potential difference with the variable resistor.
Safety considerations	12 V lamps can become very hot and must not be handled until they cool.

Starter	Support/Extend	Resources
Seeing at night (5 min) Use infrared images and ask students to identify the objects. Can students distinguish the hotter parts of the objects from the colder ones?	**Support:** Use simple images such as animals.	
Hand warming (10 min) Ask students to draw a diagram explaining why holding your hands *in front* of a fire warms them up. Look for key concepts of emission and absorption.		
Main	**Support/Extend**	**Resources**
Detecting infrared radiation (10 min) Discuss the nature of infrared radiation linking this to the electromagnetic spectrum before showing how it can be detected using the simple demonstration.		
Black body radiation (30 min) Students observe the changes in the radiation given out by a filament lamp as it heats up. They should note that the lamp becomes brighter when it is hotter (showing an increase in the total radiation emitted) and also the colour changes of the spectrum (moving from long wavelength to shorter wavelengths). Discuss the nature of a black body and the radiation curves it produces and relate this to the changes in colours they have seen. The changes in the black-body emission graphs (shift in position of the peak wavelength and overall increase in area under the line) should be described.	**Extend:** Link the black body curves to the analysis of light from stars and determination of their surface temperature.	**Practical:** Black body radiation
Plenary	**Support/Extend**	**Resources**
Temperature order (10 min) Show a list of objects or materials (e.g., the Sun's surface, boiling water) and ask students to put them in order of temperature.	**Extend:** Discuss the temperatures and the behaviour of materials in terms of the particle model.	
Choosing the right colour (5 min) Students use the interactive to complete sentences to describe simple scenarios such as the colour of a cup you should us to keep a drink cold on a hot day.	**Extend:** Ask how the answer would change if the scenario was reversed.	**Interactive:** Choosing the right colour
Homework		
Students can research the applications of infrared cameras, including their use in search and rescue and astronomy.		

kerboodle

A Kerboodle highlight for this lesson is **Literacy sheet: Radiation and temperature**. Refer to the **Content map** on Kerboodle for a full list of resources and assessment.

P2.3 More about infrared radiation

AQA spec Link: A body at constant temperature is absorbing radiation at the same rate as it is emitting radiation. The temperature of a body increases when the body absorbs radiation faster than it emits radiation.

The temperature of the Earth depends on many factors including: the rates of absorption and emission of radiation, reflection of radiation into space.

Students should be able to explain how the temperature of a body is related to the balance between incoming radiation absorbed and radiation emitted, using everyday examples to illustrate this balance, and the example of the factors which determine the temperature of the Earth.

Students should be able to use information, or draw/interpret diagrams to show how radiation affects the temperature of the Earth's surface and atmosphere.

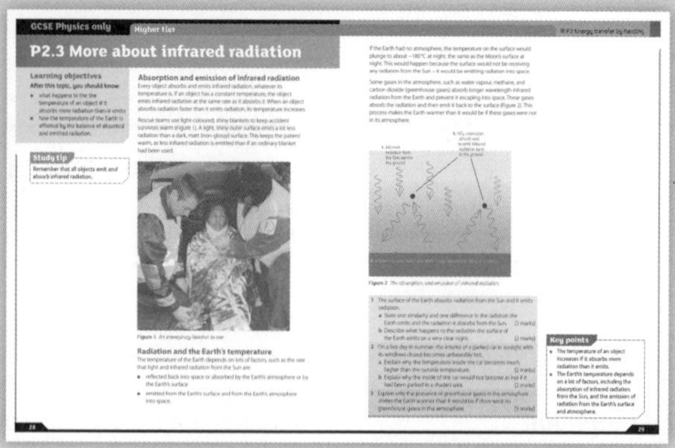
GCSE Physics only Higher tier

P2.3 More about infrared radiation

MS 3a

Aiming for	Outcome	Checkpoint	
		Question	Activity
Aiming for GRADE 6	Compare the emission of infrared radiation from different surfaces (such as shiny and dark).	2	Main 1
	Outline the evidence that changes in the concentration of atmospheric gases are the likely cause of global warming.		Main 2
	Describe the greenhouse effect in terms of absorption and emission of radiation.	1	Main 2
Aiming for GRADE 8	Describe factors that affect the rate of emission of infrared radiation, including surface colour.	2	Main 1
	Apply the concepts of absorption and emission of IR radiation to explain why an object maintains a constant temperature.		Main 1
	Fully explain the greenhouse effect in terms of absorption, emission, and wavelengths of electromagnetic radiation.	1, 3	Main 2, Plenary 1

Maths

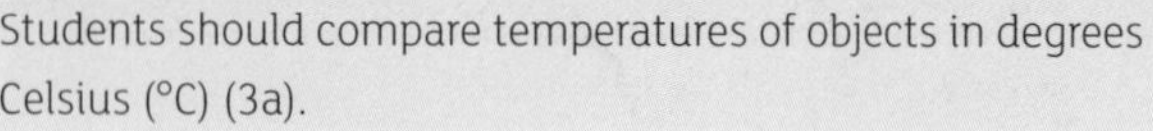
Students should compare temperatures of objects in degrees Celsius (°C) (3a).

Literacy

Students should describe the effects of absorption and emission of IR radiation in a range of situations.

Starter	Support/Extend	Resources
Warm words (10 min) Show the students the famous 'hockey stick' graphs that show marked temperature increase over the past 50 years and a projection of further rapid increases. Students use the interactive to discuss the possible causes and then introduce a graph which also shows changes in the CO_2 concentration of the atmosphere for further discussion. **Spectrum** (5 min) Ask the students to sort a list of the parts of the electromagnetic spectrum into order by wavelength. Ask them to suggest which region in the spectrum causes most harm.	**Extend:** Discuss a more complex graph showing different historical data and predictions and discuss why there is variation in these models.	**Interactive:** Warm words
Main	**Support/Extend**	**Resources**
Radiation and surfaces (10 min) Recap on the emission and absorption of infrared (and other) radiation discussed in the previous lesson. Discuss the effect of surface colour on the emission, linking this to the 'black body' as a perfect emitter and the choice of surface colour for objects such as the emergency blanket.	**Support:** Use a range of photographs of clothing to discuss which one would be suitable for a sunny day.	
The greenhouse effect (30 min) Discuss the heating and cooling of the Earth, focusing on the difference in wavelength of the radiation being emitted by the Sun and that being emitted by the Earth. Relate this to the temperature of the bodies. Discuss the role of greenhouse gasses in maintaining a steady temperature of the Earth over an extended period. Introduce the idea that the concentrations of these gases are increasing and discuss the possible effects. Students should discuss some of the evidence for the changes in concentration and the possible causes.	**Extend:** Present the students with some very long term data for temperate change, before the evolution of humans, and discuss the reasons for the high temperatures. Are these linked to atmospheric changes?	**Activity:** The greenhouse effect
Plenary	**Support/Extend**	**Resources**
Warming worries (10 min) Discuss some of the possible effects of global warming and potential sea level rise. You could show students images and graphs from the Internet that show how carbon dioxide levels have increased, how sea levels have risen, and how glaciers have been affected, to encourage students discussion.	**Extend:** Ask the students to identify regions which face the greatest threat and suggest solutions to the problems faced.	
A world of beauty (5 min) Show the students an image of the planet Venus and discuss the reasons for the very high surface temperature.	**Extend:** Discuss the temperature of a body without an atmosphere such as the Moon.	
Homework		
Students can research the current or proposed legislation or treaties which have been developed to combat the threats posed by climate change.	**Support:** Provide students with the names of some of the protocols as a starting point for their research.	

kerboodle

A Kerboodle highlight for this lesson is **Working scientifically: Explaining the greenhouse effect**. Refer to the **Content map** on Kerboodle for a full list of resources and assessment.

P2.4 Specific heat capacity

AQA spec Link: 3.2.1 Heating changes the energy stored within the system by increasing the energy of the particles that make up the system. This either raises the temperature of the system or produces a change of state.

3.2.2 If the temperature of the system increases, the increase in temperature depends on the mass of the substance heated, the type of material, and the energy input to the system.

The following equation applies:

change in thermal energy = mass × specific heat capacity × temperature change

$$[\Delta E = m\,c\,\Delta\theta]$$

change in thermal energy ΔE in joules, J

mass m in kilograms, kg

specific heat capacity c in joules per kilogram per degree Celsius, J/kg °C

temperature change $\Delta\theta$ in degrees Celsius, °C.

The specific heat capacity of a substance is the amount of energy required to raise the temperature of one kilogram of the substance by one degree Celsius.

1.1.3 The amount of energy stored in or released from a system as its temperature changes can be calculated using the equation:

change in thermal energy = mass × specific heat capacity × temperature change

$$[\Delta E = m\,c\,\Delta\theta]$$

change in thermal energy ΔE in joules, J

mass m in kilograms, kg

specific heat capacity c in joules per kilogram per degree Celsius, J/kg °C

temperature change $\Delta\theta$ in degrees Celsius, °C

The specific heat capacity of a substance is the amount of energy required to raise the temperature of one kilogram of the substance by one degree Celsius.

Required practical: investigation to determine the specific heat capacity of one or more materials. The investigation will involve linking the decrease of one energy store (or work done) to the increase in temperature and subsequent increase in thermal energy stored.

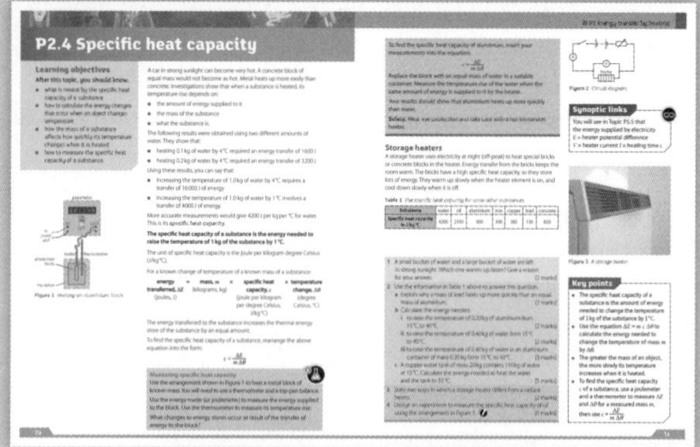

MS 1a, 3b, 3c, 3d

Aiming for	Outcome	Checkpoint	
		Question	Activity
Aiming for GRADE 4	Describe materials in terms of being difficult or easy to heat up (increase the temperature of).	2, 3	Starter 1, Starter 2, Main
	List the factors that affect the amount of energy required to increase the temperature of an object.	1	Main
	With some support, measure the specific heat capacity of a material.		Main
Aiming for GRADE 6	Describe the effects of changing the factors involved in the equation.		Starter 1, Main
	Calculate the energy required to change the temperature of an object.	2	Main
	Measure the specific heat capacity of a material and find a mean value.		Main
Aiming for GRADE 8	Evaluate materials used for transferring energy in terms of their specific heat capacity.		Main
	Use the specific heat capacity equation to perform a wide range of calculations in unfamiliar contexts.	2	Main
	Evaluate in detail the results of an experiment to measure specific heat capacity.	4	Main

Maths

The students perform calculations involving specific heat capacity using an equation with variables (1a, 3b, 3c).

Literacy

Students work in small groups to discuss results of experiments and describe them accurately.

Key words

specific heat capacity

Required practical

Title	Measuring specific heat capacity
Equipment	low-voltage power supply, aluminium heating block, heating element, thermometer, joulemeter, connecting leads, stopwatch, beaker (size depends on the mass of the metal block), water
Overview of method	Students heat the aluminium block for five minutes recording the temperature rise and energy supplied. They use this data and the mass of the block to calculate the specific heat capacity. They then repeat the process with a beaker of water of the same mass and compare the two temperature rises and notice that the aluminium's temperature rise is greater. An ammeter, a voltmeter, and a stopwatch can be used instead of the joulemeter to measure the energy supplied to the block. The ammeter is used to measure the heater current, and the voltmeter is used to measure the heater voltage. If this method is used, the heating time also needs to be measured.
Safety considerations	The block should not be heated to high temperatures – a maximum of 40 °C is sufficient.

Starter	Support/Extend	Resources
Hot metal (10 min) Heat a relatively small block of metal until it is clearly very hot using a Bunsen burner, gauze, and tripod. Use tongs to drop it into a bucket of water. Students explain the small change in temperature for the water. Safety: Take care with the hot metal. Put the hot metal carefully into the bucket of water. Make sure the bucket or container of water is made of an appropriate material for the experiment. **Boiling up** (5 min) Explain to students that of two kettles, one full and one half full, the half full kettle will boil first. Ask students to come up with their own explanation as to why the half full kettle boils first.	**Extend:** Ask for discussion of the temperature change of both the metal block and the water.	
Main	**Support/Extend**	**Resources**
Measuring specific heat capacity (40 min) Discuss the factors that may affect the temperature change of a material when it is heated, using ideas from the starters. Lead the students through the calculation for specific heat capacity step by step, ensuring they understand each of the terms of the equation. Students then carry out the practical to attempt to find a value for the specific heat capacity of a metal. It is likely that their value will not match an accepted value and so they should discuss the reasons that their values are different. This is mainly due to energy transferred to the environment. Students can use the Maths skills interactive to rearrange the equation for specific heat capacity.	**Support:** A calculation frame showing each of the steps will help a great deal. **Extension:** The Extension sheet provides opportunity for students to rearrange the equation and apply it in a wider range of contexts.	**Required practical:** Measuring specific heat capacity **Extension:** Specific heat capacity **Maths skills:** Specific heat capacity
Plenary	**Support/Extend**	**Resources**
Hot water (5 min) Why is water used in central heating systems? Students could come up with a range of reasons why it is chosen. **Crossword** (10 min) Students use the interactive to complete a crossword on the content from this and the previous lessons. This should form a summary of their learning about energy transfer.	**Extend:** Suggest alternative materials such as mercury. **Support:** Provide differentiated clues to different groups of students.	**Interactive:** Crossword
Homework		
Students complete the Calculation sheet for further practice in using the equation for specific heat capacity.		**Calculation sheet:** Specific heat capacity

kerboodle

A Kerboodle highlight for this lesson is **Bump up your grades: Specific heat capacity**. Refer to the **Content map** on Kerboodle for a full list of resources and assessment.

P2.5 Heating and insulating buildings

AQA spec Link: 1.2.1 Students should be able to describe, with examples, how in all system changes energy is dissipated, so that it is stored in less useful ways. This energy is often described as being 'wasted'.

Students should be able to describe how the rate of cooling of a building is affected by the thickness and thermal conductivity of its walls.

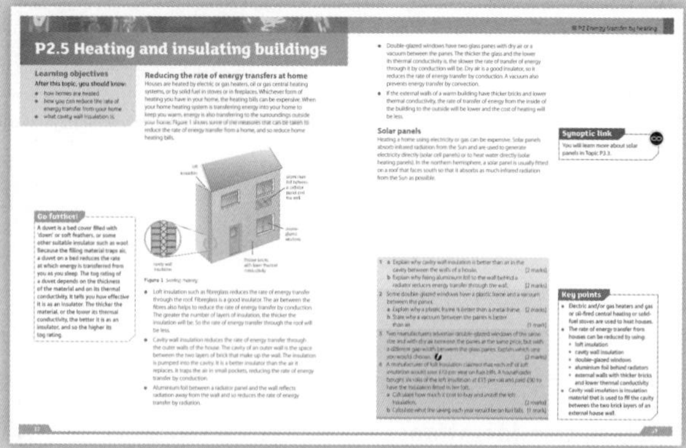
P2.5 Heating and insulating buildings

MS 2h, 3c

Aiming for	Outcome	Checkpoint	
		Question	Activity
Aiming for GRADE 4 ↓	Describe some design features used to prevent energy transfer to the surroundings in the home.	1, 2, 3	Starter 1, Main 1
	Calculate the payback time of a simple home improvement feature.	4	Main 2
Aiming for GRADE 6 ↓	Describe how some design features are used to reduce energy transfers from a home.	1, 2, 3	Starter 1, Main 1
	Compare home improvement features in terms of payback time.	4	Main 2
Aiming for GRADE 8 ↓	Evaluate in detail design features used to reduce energy transferred from the home.	1, 2, 3	Main 1, Main 2
	Decide on home improvement features using payback time and savings beyond the payback time.	4	Main 2, Plenary 1

Maths

Students calculate the payback time for a home improvement feature (2h). Some may also use specific heat capacity calculations (3c).

Literacy

Students work in small groups to discuss energy saving features and their operation.

Starter	Support/Extend	Resources
Worth it? (10 min) Swapping over your mobile phone to a new one will cost you £200 but you will be able to enter a new contract for £10 less each month on a two-year contract. Should you swap your phone? What other factors would you have to consider?	**Extend:** Provide additional information about data tariffs.	
Hot house (5 min) Show students a large diagram of a house showing the various locations where energy can be transferred to its surroundings. Students suggest ways to save energy. Students could copy the diagram, or the diagram could be provided to students for them to annotate.		
Main	**Support/Extend**	**Resources**
Reducing energy transfers in the home (25 min) Discuss the features used to prevent energy transferred in a house one by one. Use example materials (e.g., bricks, insulation foam) if any are available. Provide students with some examples of costs, as these will be useful later.	**Support:** Students work in groups to produce a large, annotated poster describing the features. **Extension:** Students complete the Extension sheet to consider some of the energy transfers from a house and think about some of the best ways to save money.	**Extension:** Energy and buildings
Payback time (15 min) The students compare the payback time of some of the design features, using real data.	**Extend:** Provide more detailed data such as lifetime of improvements.	
Plenary	**Support/Extend**	**Resources**
Energy neutral house (10 min) Students can use their knowledge of energy transfer to design an energy neutral house. They can use all of the design features here and may include some of the developing ideas in electricity generation.		
House analysis (5 min) Provide a set of home improvements costs and savings. Students use the interactive to sequence them in the order in which the improvements should be done.	**Support:** Provide a simple table for the students to complete.	**Interactive:** House analysis
Homework		
Students complete the WebQuest where they research different methods that can be used to improve the insulation of a house.		**WebQuest:** House insulation

kerboodle

A Kerboodle highlight for this lesson is **Bump up your grades: Thermal conductivity**. Refer to the **Content map** on Kerboodle for a full list of resources and assessment.

P2 Energy transfer by heating

Overview of P2 Energy transfer by heating

In this chapter the students have developed their understanding of the heating and cooling processes, which transfer energy within a material or from one object to another. They have investigated thermal conductivity and the differences in the processes of thermal conduction in metals and non-metals.

GCSE Physics students have described the transfer of energy between objects through absorption and emission of infra-red radiation as a part of the electromagnetic spectrum. This included the factors that affect the rate of this transfer such as temperature and surface colour. Higher-tier *GCSE Physics* students have applied this knowledge to the concept of the Greenhouse Effect and its relationship to the wavelength of the radiation penetrating or being absorbed by Earth's atmosphere.

All students have analysed the changes in temperature when a material is heated, leading to the experimental determination of specific heat capacity along with corresponding calculations. The concept of specific heat capacity was then used to explain the choice of materials used in heating systems.

Finally, the reduction of energy transfers to the surroundings by insulation has been studied and applied to the context of reducing the rate of energy transfer in buildings to reduce heating costs including the idea prioritising home improvements in line with payback time.

You can find additional support for the maths skills covered in this chapter on **MyMaths**, including recognising and using expressions in decimal form, solving simple algebraic equations, plotting graphs, using equations and standard form.

Required practical

All students are expected to have carried out the required practical:

Practical	Topic
An investigation to determine the specific heat capacity of one or more materials. The investigation will involve linking the decrease of one energy store (or work done) to the increase in temperature and subsequent increase in thermal energy stored.	P2.4

Students studying *AQA GCSE Physics* are also required to carry out the required practical:

Practical	Topic
Investigate the effectiveness of different materials as thermal insulators and the factors that may affect the thermal insulation properties of a material.	P2.1

For this chapter, the following assessments are available on Kerboodle:

P2 Checkpoint quiz Energy transfer by heating
P2 Progress quiz: Energy transfer by heating 1
P2 Progress quiz: Energy transfer by heating 2
P2 On your marks: Energy transfer by heating
P2 Exam-style questions and mark scheme: Energy transfer by heating

Checkpoint follow up lesson

A student's route through this lesson can be determined using the Checkpoint assessment. Percentage pass marks are supplied in the Checkpoint teacher notes.

For each successive route through it is assumed that the student can perform to their current route as well as previous routes. For example, students working at Aiming for 6 are assumed to be secure in Aiming for 4 knowledge and understanding and working towards achieving all the learning outcomes for Aiming for 6.

	Aiming for 4	Aiming for 6	Aiming for 8
Learning outcomes	Calculate change in thermal energy.	Describe what thermal conductivity depends on.	Calculate specific heat capacity and apply knowledge of specific heat capacity to make predictions.
	Describe what thermal conductivity means.	Describe a variety of ways to keep your house warm.	Apply what you know about thermal conductivity to buildings and other situations.
	Describe how to keep your house warm.	Calculate change in thermal energy and convert between units.	Analyse data in terms of specific heat capacity.
	Describe how the greenhouse effect is affecting the temperature of the Earth.	Describe the greenhouse effect in terms of radiation.	Explain why the temperature of the Earth is increasing.
Starter	**Keeping warm (10 min)** Give students 2 minutes to come up with as many different ways to keep a house warm as they can think of. Then ask them to join with a partner to collate their ideas, and finally join with another pair. Bring the ideas together, and discuss the reasons why these methods would keep a house warm. **What on Earth is happening? (5 min)** Put a big 'True' notice on one side of the room, and a 'False' sign on the other side. Read out true/false statements about the greenhouse effect (what is happening to the temperature, what the greenhouse effect is, what the effects of the greenhouse effect are) and ask students to stand at the True side of the room, at the False side of the room, or somewhere in between.		
Differentiated checkpoint activity	Students use the checkpoint follow-up sheets to complete one of two activities: • investigate into how the volume of water affects the time it takes to heat water • model the greenhouse effect. The Aiming for 4 follow-up sheet provides a structured method for students to follow and guidance on building and interpreting their model. Students should work in pairs with teacher input. The Aiming for 6 follow-up sheet provides limited support for students plan their own investigation. They should be aiming to work independently. Any plans should be checked by the teacher before students carry out any practical work. The Aiming for 8 follow-up sheet provides minimal support and students should plan their own investigation. They should work independently and any plans should be checked by the teacher before students carry out any practical work. All students should also plot given data on different materials' thermal conductivity, and analyse their graph. Students will need graph paper. **Kerboodle resource** P2 Checkpoint follow up: Aiming for 4, P2 Checkpoint follow up: Aiming for 6, P2 Checkpoint follow up: Aiming for 8		
Plenary	**Baked Alaska (10 min)** Give students A4 dry wipe boards, pens, and an eraser. Ask them to do a calculation of the thermal energy required to melt 1 kg of ice cream. Tell them roughly how long it would take a normal oven to transfer this energy. Show a video of a Baked Alaska coming out of the oven and in groups get them to write the best explanation as to why the ice cream does not melt. Display a mark scheme and get them to peer mark the work. **SHC vs SLH (10 min)** On the whiteboards ask students to make a Venn diagram for specific heat capacity and specific latent heat and to compare with the others in their group. Aiming for 8 students discuss how or if thermal conductivity can be added as a third circle.		
Progression	Encourage students to think about specific heat capacity in terms of rise in temperature, and thermal conductivity in terms of time for energy transfer and to apply what they know to keeping a house warm.	Encourage students to think of the link between specific heat capacity and thermal conductivity when choosing building materials, and to describe what is happening in the atmosphere in terms of the absorption and emission of radiation.	Encourage students to think of the link between specific heat capacity and thermal conductivity when choosing building materials, and to explain what is happening in the atmosphere in terms of the absorption and emission of radiation.

P 3 Energy resources

3.1 Energy demands

AQA spec Link: 1.3 The main energy resources available for use on Earth include: fossil fuels (coal, oil and gas), nuclear fuel, biofuel, wind, hydro-electricity, geothermal, the tides, the Sun, and water waves.

A renewable energy resource is one that is being (or can be) replenished as it is used.

The uses of energy resources include transport, electricity generation, and heating.

Students should be able to:

- describe the main energy sources available
- compare ways that different energy resources are used, the uses to include transport, electricity generation, and heating
- understand why some energy resources are more reliable than others.

Descriptions of how energy resources are used to generate electricity are **not** required.

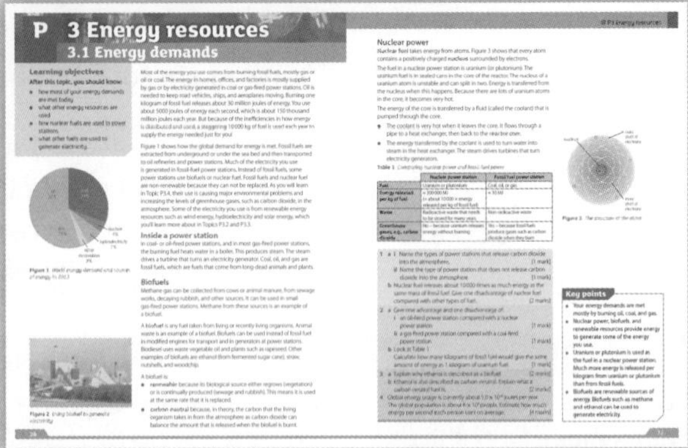

WS 4.4

MS 1b

Aiming for	Outcome	Checkpoint	
		Question	**Activity**
Aiming for GRADE 4 ↓	Identify which fuels are renewable and which are non-renewable.	1	Starter 1, Starter 2, Main 1
	Identify activities that require large energy transfers.	4	Main 1
	Describe biofuels as carbon neutral whereas fossil fuels are not.	1	Starter 2
Aiming for GRADE 6 ↓	Outline the operation of a fossil fuel burning power station.		Main 1
	Outline the operation of a nuclear power station.		Main 2
	Explain why biofuels are considered carbon neutral.	3	Main 1
Aiming for GRADE 8 ↓	Compare energy use from different sources and different societies from available data.	2	Main 1
	Compare fossil fuels and nuclear fuels in terms of energy provided, waste, and pollution.	1	Main 2
	Discuss some of the problems associated with biofuel use and production.	3	Main 1

Maths
Students handle large numbers when discussing energy; some using SI prefixes and standard form (1b).

Literacy
Students describe complex processes in power stations and work together to discuss the advantages and disadvantages of different fuels.

Key words
biofuel, renewable, carbon-neutral, nuclear fuel, nucleus

Practical

Title	Burning fuels for energy
Equipment	heat-resistant mat, small sample of ethanol, spirit burner
Overview of method	Put a small sample of ethanol into the spirit burner, and light the wick.
Safety considerations	Burn the sample on top of the heat-resistant mat and allow the container to cool before handling.

Starter	Support/Extend	Resources
Fossil fuels (5 min) Students use the interactive to put in order statements that describe how coal, oil, and natural gas are formed. **The burning question** (10 min) Students draw a spider diagram or visual summary covering what they know about combustion of fuels. They can do this whilst watching a birthday candle burn, stopping when the candle is finished. Choose a candle that will last for a few minutes.	**Support:** Provide the key stages for the students to put in order. **Support:** Provide example fuels for the students and expect simple word equations. **Extend:** Students should produce some balanced symbol equations for combustion reactions.	**Interactive:** Fossil fuels
Main	**Support/Extend**	**Resources**
Burning fuels for energy (25 min) Begin with an explanation of the very high energy demands of developed countries and ask the students about what they already understand about how these needs are met. Discuss which activities may be responsible for the very large energy demands, such as transport and heating of homes. Show students the structure of a conventional (fossil fuel) power station, supported with animations or video clips where possible. Demonstrate the combustion of a biofuel (e.g., ethanol) whilst discussing how it is produced. Place emphasis on the carbon-neutral nature, identifying photosynthesis and combustion and the key processes. Explain how the process of burning a fuel is used to produce electricity. **Nuclear power** (15 min) Outline the operation of a nuclear power plant, noting the different heating processes taking place in the core with much of the rest of the plant similar to fossil fuel power plants. A quick comparison of nuclear and fossil fuels should be made.	**Extend:** Discuss the additional costs of producing biofuels in terms of land and food shortage, and energy costs and emissions in processing. Ask students to use standard form to represent large numbers.	**Practical:** Burning fuels for energy
Plenary	**Support/Extend**	**Resources**
Anagrams (5 min) Ask students to decipher anagrams of important key words from this lesson. Add a few more about energy resources to see if the students can figure them out. Students then define each key term. **Lightning storm** (10 min) Some people propose harnessing the electricity from lightning strikes for power. Students could discuss the advantages and disadvantages of this idea.	**Support:** Differentiate according to students' abilities by using single words or more complex phrases.	
Homework		
Students complete the WebQuest where they research the differences, of biofuels and fossil fuels, the advantages and disadvantages of biofuels, and the effect biofuels have on the environment. They use their research to prepare a presentation or debate.		**WebQuest:** Biofuels

P3.2 Energy from wind and water

AQA spec Link: 1.3 The main energy resources available for use on Earth include: fossil fuels (coal, oil and gas), nuclear fuel, biofuel, wind, hydro-electricity, geothermal, the tides, the Sun, and water waves.

A renewable energy resource is one that is being (or can be) replenished as it is used.

The uses of energy resources include transport, electricity generation, and heating.

Students should be able to:

- describe the main energy sources available
- distinguish between energy resources that are renewable and energy resources that are non-renewable
- compare ways that different energy resources are used, the uses to include transport, electricity generation, and heating
- understand why some energy resources are more reliable than others
- describe the environmental impact arising from the use of different energy resources.

Students should be able to:

- consider the environmental issues that may arise from the use of different energy resources
- show that science has the ability to identify environmental issues arising from the use of energy resources but not always the power to deal with the issues because of political, social, ethical, or economic considerations.

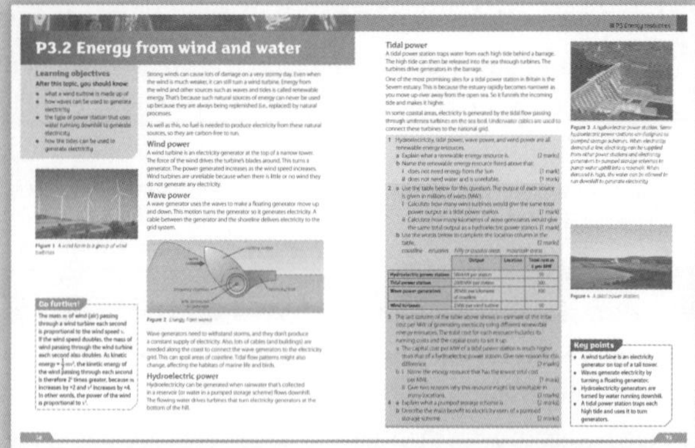

WS 1.3, 4, 4.4

MS 1c, 2c, 4a

Aiming for	Outcome	Checkpoint	
		Question	Activity
Aiming for GRADE 4	State that wind turbines, wave generators, hydroelectric systems, and tidal systems are renewable energy resources.	1	Main
	Describe some simple advantages or disadvantages of renewable energy systems.	End of chapter 4	Main
	Outline the operation of a renewable energy source.	1, End of chapter 3, 4	
Aiming for GRADE 6	Describe the operation of a wind farm.	2	Main
	Describe the operation of a hydroelectric system.	End of chapter 2	Main
	Suggest the most appropriate energy resource to use in a range of scenarios.	2	Plenary 1
Aiming for GRADE 8	Compare the operation of hydroelectric, wave, and tidal systems in terms of reliability, potential power output, and costs.	2, 3, End of chapter 2	Main
	Explain in detail the purpose, operation, and advantages of a pumped storage system.	4	Main
	Justify the choice of an energy resource by using numerical and other appropriate data.	End of chapter 5, 6	Plenary

Maths
Students can use numerical values such as power output to compare different schemes of electricity generation (2c).

Literacy
There are several opportunities for students to discuss in small groups the advantages and disadvantages of energy resources.

Practical

Title	Wind and wave power
Equipment	model wind turbine, desk fan, voltmeter, metre rule, clamp stand, clamp, boss
Overview of method	Attach the voltmeter to the model wind turbine, and use the clamp to hold the turbine at the height of the desk fan. Use the metre rule to measure how far the desk fan is from the turbine. Demonstrate how the number of turbine blades affects voltage output.
Safety considerations	Switch off the desk fan and ensure all parts stop moving before making any changes to the equipment.

Starter	Support/Extend	Resources
Wind and convection currents (5 min) Ask students to suggest the cause of wind in the atmosphere.	**Extend:** Ask students to explain for themselves the causes of the flow of air in terms of expansion, density changes, and pressure.	
Water cycle recap (10 min) Students use the interactive to label a diagram of the water cycle with the key words evaporation, condensation, and precipitation. They then choose the correct words to complete sentences that explain how the water cycle is linked to hydroelectricity.	**Support:** Provide a basic diagram showing an ocean, land, mountains, and a river for the students to annotate.	**Interactive:** Water cycle recap
Main	**Support/Extend**	**Resources**
Wind and water power (40 min) Show a video clip of a wind farm and ask students to explain what is happening. Link back to the idea of a turbine generating electricity. Carry out the simple practical to investigate wind turbines. Discuss the advantages and disadvantages of wind power including its renewable nature. Discuss the operation of a simple system ensuring the students are clear on some of the advantages and disadvantages.	**Support:** Students can complete a simple advantages/disadvantages table for this and other resources discussed this lesson.	**Practical:** Wind and water power
Then explain how a water turbine works and discuss the energy transfers involved, linking back to the idea of gravitational potential energy stores. Include a discussion of a pumped storage system, ensuring that the students know that, although these systems are not efficient, they allow some of the excess power produced at night by the base load of the network to be used usefully. Renewability should be addressed. Tidal power can be linked to the hydroelectric systems but with a different supply of water – the tides.	**Extend:** Students can discuss the efficiency of pumped storage systems, linking this to a graph of base load. Students can also discuss smaller-scale tidal pools, which do not 'block off' whole rivers.	
Plenary	**Support/Extend**	**Resources**
Local solutions (10 min) Give students some example towns and their local environments. Students should decide which of the systems covered today would best suit each town, and determine if the systems are a better solution to local needs than a fossil fuel power station. **Wind farm controversy** (5 min) Ask students to suggest why local communities may campaign against wind farms.	**Extend:** Students analyse their local environment and suggest the best way to generate electricity.	
Homework		
Ask students to design a poster to persuade a local community to allow a wind farm in the vicinity. Other students could design an 'anti' poster. The poster could include information about new jobs, noise, reliability, cheaper or more expensive electricity. Students can then evaluate each other's work.		

kerboodle

A Kerboodle highlight for this lesson is **Working scientifically: Wind turbines**. Refer to the **Content map** on Kerboodle for a full list of resources and assessment.

P3.3 Power from the Sun and the Earth

AQA spec Link: 1.3 The main energy resources available for use on Earth include: fossil fuels (coal, oil and gas), nuclear fuel, biofuel, wind, hydro-electricity, geothermal, the tides, the Sun, and water waves.

The uses of energy resources include transport, electricity generation, and heating.

Students should be able to:

- describe the main energy sources available
- distinguish between energy resources that are renewable and energy resources that are non-renewable
- compare ways that different energy resources are used, the uses to include transport, electricity generation, and heating
- understand why some energy resources are more reliable than others
- describe the environmental impact arising from the use of different energy resources.

Students should be able to:

- consider the environmental issues that may arise from the use of different energy resources.

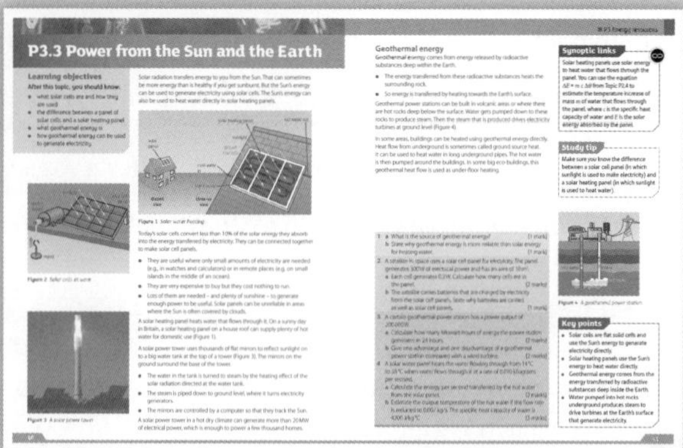

WS 4.4
MS 1c, 2c, 4a

Aiming for	Outcome	Checkpoint	
		Question	**Activity**
Aiming for GRADE 4	Explore the operation of a solar cell.		Main 1, Plenary 1
	Describe one difference between solar cells and solar heating systems.		Main 2
	State that radioactive decay is the source of heating in geothermal systems.	1	Main 2
Aiming for GRADE 6	Compare and contrast the operation of solar cells (photovoltaic cells) with solar heating panels.		Main 2
	Describe the operation of a solar power tower.		Main 2
	Describe the operation of a geothermal power plant.	3, End of chapter 3	Main 2
Aiming for GRADE 8	Analyse the power output of a variety of energy resources.	2, 3	Main 2
	Calculate the energy provided by a solar heating system by using the increase in water temperature.	4	Main 2
	Plan in detail an investigation into the factors that affect the power output of a solar cell.		Homework

Maths
Students compare and evaluate systems in terms of power output (2c). They may use graphical information to assess the effectiveness of a system (4a).

Literacy
There are plenty of opportunities for students to discuss the functions of energy resources and their advantages and disadvantages.

Key words
geothermal energy

Practical

Title	Using solar cells
Equipment	solar cell, motor, bulb, voltmeter
Overview of method	A low-power motor will be required; complete kits containing a matched solar cell and motor are available. Students should be able to investigate how the voltage output of the motor changes with the distance of the bulb from the solar cell. They may like to compare the speed of the motor in bright sunlight to that produced by a bulb. Covering part of the solar cell will reduce the energy output too.

Starter	Support/Extend	Resources
Old Faithful (10 min) Show a video clip of 'Old Faithful' and ask students if they have ever seen a geyser and if they know what causes geysers. Ask them to explain why the water is so hot.	**Support:** Show a video clip of Old Faithful Geyser located in the Yellowstone National Park.	
To the centre of the Earth (5 min) Interactive where students label a simple diagram showing the layers of the Earth (crust, mantle, and core). They then match each layer with its properties. They should be aware that the outer core is a molten layer and that the centre of the Earth is very hot.	**Extend:** Ask for a more detailed description of the properties of the layers, such as the density.	**Interactive:** To the centre of the Earth
Main	**Support/Extend**	**Resources**
Using solar cells (20 min) Students use the practical to investigate the operation of a solar cell. They can measure the effect of reducing the area exposed to light on the current and voltage output, and the effect of increasing the light level by moving a lamp closer or further away.	**Extend:** Students can use some cost data to support discussions of larger-scale solar power schemes.	**Practical:** Using solar cells
Solar and geothermal heating systems (20 min) Remind students about the ideas around heating and the temperature rise caused by absorbing infrared radiation. Discuss the renewable nature of geothermal systems. Students can struggle to remember the heating source in geothermal systems, so emphasise the radioactive decay. Students should compare systems that use high pressure steam with ones that simply provide hot water for direct heating.	**Support:** Place cool water in a black container and a silver container near a lamp at the start of the lesson. Measure the temperature now to remind students of the principles involved. **Extend:** Students should try a calculation such as Summary Question 4. Models of radioactive decay can be used, linking to Chapter P7 Radioactivity later in the course.	
Plenary	**Support/Extend**	**Resources**
Solar car (5 min) Ask students to list the advantages and disadvantages of the design of solar cars.	**Support:** Show students a video clip of a solar car in action, or use a toy one.	
Keep cool (10 min) Ask students to produce a design for a device that keeps them cooler, the brighter the Sun is. A solar-powered fan is a typical design but colour-changing clothing is a possibility with smart materials (white on the side that faces the Sun but black on the opposite side).	**Support:** Show your own design and ask students to evaluate it.	
Homework		
Students can plan an investigation into the power output from solar cells. This could focus on the area of the cells (parts can be covered by black card) or the distance from the light source (moving a lamp closer or further away).	**Extend:** This can form a full investigation over the course of a pair of lessons, allowing students to choose their own independent variable(s) to investigate.	**Working scientifically:** Solar cells

kerboodle

A Kerboodle highlight for this lesson is **WebQuest: Solar panels**. Refer to the **Content map** on Kerboodle for a full list of resources and assessment.

P3.4 Energy and the environment

AQA spec Link: 1.3

A renewable energy resource is one that is being (or can be) replenished as it is used.

Students should be able to:

- describe the main energy sources available
- distinguish between energy resources that are renewable and energy resources that are non-renewable
- compare ways that different energy resources are used, the uses to include transport, electricity generation, and heating
- understand why some energy resources are more reliable than others
- describe the environmental impact arising from the use of different energy resources.

Students should be able to:

- consider the environmental issues that may arise from the use of different energy resources
- show that science has the ability to identify environmental issues arising from the use of energy resources but not always the power to deal with the issues because of political, social, ethical, or economic considerations.

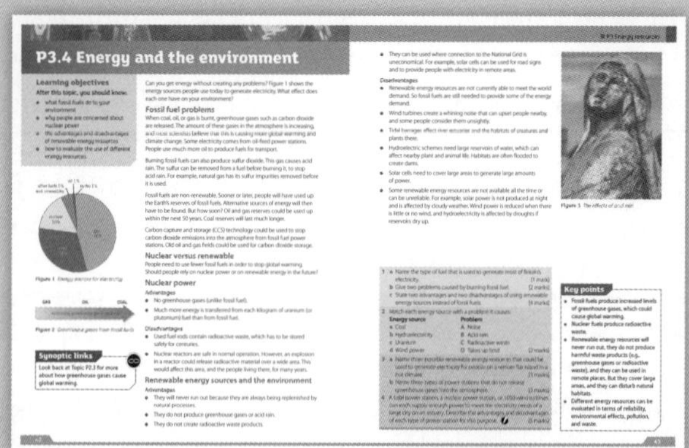

WS 4.4

MS 1c, 2c, 4a

Aiming for	Outcome	Checkpoint	
		Question	Activity
Aiming for GRADE 4	List some environmental problems associated with burning fossil fuels.	2	Main 1
	Identify the waste products of fossil fuels and nuclear fuel.	1	Main 1, Main 2
	Describe simple advantages and disadvantages of a variety of renewable energy resources.	3, End of chapter 1	Starter 1, Main 1
Aiming for GRADE 6	Describe the effects of acid rain and climate change.		Main 1
	Describe techniques to reduce the harmful products of burning fossil fuels.		Main 1
	Compare a wide range of energy resources in terms of advantages and disadvantages.	3, 4	Plenary 1
Aiming for GRADE 8	Evaluate methods of reducing damage caused by waste products of fossil fuels and nuclear fuels.		Main 1, Main 2
	Discuss in detail the problems associated with nuclear accidents and the public perception of nuclear safety.		Main 2
	Evaluate the suitability of an energy resource for a range of scenarios, taking into account a wide range of factors.	3, 4	Main 1, Main 2, Plenary 2

Maths 

Numerical data can be introduced during comparisons of resources (2c, 4a), and a timeline of nuclear accidents can be produced by the students.

Literacy 

There is considerable scope for small groups of students to discuss the issues with each energy resource.

Practical

Title	Acid rain
Equipment	test tubes, universal indicator solution (range pH 4–7), a variety of samples of 'rainwater' (see method) with pH range 4–6, distilled water
Overview of method	Students use the indicator solution to test the pH of the samples. Include real, local rainwater in the samples, but also include a few samples that have been 'doctored' to produce a variety of results to show students that acid rain can have a pH as low as 4.0. Students should note that 'natural' rain has a pH of 5.6.
Safety considerations	Ensure that eye protection is worn.

Starter	Support/Extend	Resources
Renewable or not? (5 min) Give students a list of energy resources and ask them to sort the resources into either renewable or non-renewable. Use coal, oil, natural gas, and uranium for non-renewable resources and tidal, solar, geothermal, wind, wave, and biofuel for renewable resources. **Acid rain** (10 min) Demonstrate the acidity of rainwater with universal indicator and ask students to explain what causes this acidity.	**Extend:** Students should justify their decisions by giving clear definitions of the differences.	
Main	**Support/Extend**	**Resources**
The problems with fossil fuels (20 min) Cover the range of problems with fossil fuels, making sure that the students do not confuse the problems of acid rain and climate change. There is scope here to discuss some of the problems associated with climate change, or this can form a larger part of the debate in Topic P3.5. A simple discussion of the advantages or disadvantages of renewable systems should take place. Students can compile this information in preparation for the debate in Topic P3.5.	**Support:** Students can match problems with explanations by using a simple table. **Extend:** Discuss whether carbon-capture technology is a permanent solution to global warming.	**Activity:** Energy and the environment
Nuclear power (20 min) Recap on the differences between nuclear fuel and other fuels – no combustion and so no carbon dioxide or sulfur dioxide. This leads to discussion of the alternative problems with the waste. Discuss the Chernobyl disaster and its effects but also link to more recent accidents such as Fukushima Daiichi. Emphasise the fact that accidents are rare but very significant.	**Support:** A timeline of serious incidents can be produced. **Extend:** Ask students to evaluate a few possible solutions for the storage or disposal of nuclear waste. Ask students why nuclear power stations are often built on coastlines.	
Plenary	**Support/Extend**	**Resources**
What's the problem? (5 min) Students use the interactive to match environmental problems with their likely causes.	**Support:** Illustrate with photographs of damage and the possible causes.	**Interactive:** What's the problem?
Energy resource crossword (10 min) Students create a crossword that includes all of the key words covered so far in this chapter. They then swap and complete a partner's.	**Support:** Provide a list of the key words. **Extend:** Include more challenging clues, including cryptic ones.	
Homework		
In Topic P3.5 students will debate energy resources. They can be given preparatory materials for this or asked to research relevant information for the discussion.		

kerboodle

A Kerboodle highlight for this lesson is **Maths skills: Energy resources**. Refer to the **Content map** on Kerboodle for a full list of resources and assessment.

P3.5 Big energy issues

AQA spec Link: 1.3

A renewable energy resource is one that is being (or can be) replenished as it is used.

The uses of energy resources include transport, electricity generation, and heating.

Students should be able to:

- describe the main energy sources available
- distinguish between energy resources that are renewable and energy resources that are non-renewable
- compare ways that different energy resources are used, the uses to include transport, electricity generation, and heating
- understand why some energy resources are more reliable than others
- describe the environmental impact arising from the use of different energy resources
- explain patterns and trends in the use of energy resources.

Descriptions of how energy resources are used to generate electricity are **not** required.

Students should be able to:

- consider the environmental issues that may arise from the use of different energy resources
- show that science has the ability to identify environmental issues arising from the use of energy resources but not always the power to deal with the issues because of political, social, ethical, or economic considerations.

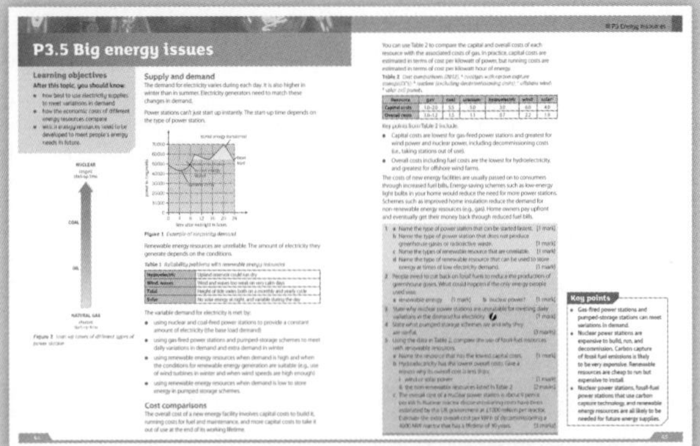

WS 1.3, 4, 4.4

MS 1a, 1c, 2c, 4a

Aiming for	Outcome	Checkpoint	
		Question	Activity
Aiming for GRADE 4	Rank the start-up times of various power stations.	1, 2	Main 1
	Compare some of the advantages and disadvantages of various energy resources.	2	Main 2
	Discuss the construction of a power plant in the local area in simple terms by using information provided.		Main 2
Aiming for GRADE 6	Use base load and start-up time data to explain why some power stations are in constant operation whereas others may be switched on and off.	1, 3	Main 1
	Compare energy resources in terms of capital and operational costs.	4	Main 2
	Debate the construction of a power plant in the local area by using a wide range of information, much of which is provided.		Starter 1, Main 2
Aiming for GRADE 8	Use the capital and operational costs of energy resources to evaluate their usefulness.	4	Main 1
	Form persuasive arguments for and against a variety of energy resources.		Main 2, Homework
	Debate the construction of a power plant in the local area by using a wide range of information, much of which is independently researched.		Starter 1, Main 2

Maths

Students calculate the effective costs of a variety of energy resources (1a, 1c).

Literacy

Students debate significant issues in small and large teams. They write persuasive arguments for and against specific energy resources.

Starter	Support/Extend	Resources
Energy recap (5 min) In preparation for the debate, use the interactive to complete a series of paragraphs to summarise the basic principles of each energy resource studied in this chapter.		**Interactive:** Energy recap
Energy resources (10 min) Students complete the calculation sheet to interpret data about different energy sources, evaluate the data to make conclusions, and calculate cost of energy.	**Support:** Provide tables for students to complete. **Extend:** Ask students to design their own fact sheets.	**Calculation sheet:** Energy resources
Main	**Support/Extend**	**Resources**
Supply and demand (10 min) Discuss the advantages of various resources in terms of reliability and start-up times. Make sure the students are clear on the concept of base load. Students must be able to make comparisons of not only running costs but initial (start-up) and final (decommissioning) costs to judge the cost effectiveness of the different resources.	**Support:** Remind students of the base load graph and the power stations that are in constant operation to provide this power. **Extend:** Students can also consider the decommissioning costs of power stations.	
The big energy debate (30 min) The remainder of the lesson can be centred on a debate about how to meet future energy needs. The debate is relevant because the students will probably not have access to 'unlimited' fossil fuel supplies as the last few generations have. This could be as a result of shortages or commitments to reduce carbon emissions by the government. The result of this is an energy gap that needs to be filled by new resources. Explain the purpose of the debate and the outcomes that are needed (a set of proposals) so that the students know that they have to reach conclusions. Give timings and establish roles within the groups if they are needed. To avoid a chaotic argument, discuss the ground rules for a successful discussion. Rules need to include who can speak and when, who is recording discussions or decisions, and whether roles will be assigned or students will be free to take on any position they want to.	**Support:** Roles can be assigned and partial scripts provided for the students to complete. **Extend:** Students should prepare their own discussions after carrying out research into their chosen areas.	**Activity:** The big energy debate
Plenary	**Support/Extend**	**Resources**
Democracy in action (5 min) Students vote on a range of proposals for energy production. Make this an anonymous vote with ballot papers giving various options. The results can be declared immediately or during the next lesson.		
Cut it out (10 min) Demand for electricity is increasing as more electrical devices are produced. One way to preserve resources is to cut back on waste and to stop using some devices altogether. What are the students willing to cut back on?	**Support:** Provide a list of options for the students to prioritise.	
Homework		
Students write a letter to their MP outlining the decision they have reached in the big debate. They need to explain what they have decided and ask their MP to act on the decision. This should be a formal letter if possible.	**Support:** Provide the basic structure of the letter. **Extend:** Provide clear success criteria about the content of the letter, including how many facts and figures are required.	

kerboodle

A Kerboodle highlight for this lesson is **Literacy sheet: Renewable and non-renewable resources**. Refer to the **Content map** on Kerboodle for a full list of resources and assessment.

P3 Energy resources

Overview of P3 Energy resources

In this chapter the students have examined the different sources of energy that are used to generate electricity or provide heating for homes. They have considered the effect of the production and use of biofuels on the environment along with the concept of carbon-neutrality before outlining the use of nuclear power in comparison to fossil fuels.

Student have described and evaluated renewable resources such as wave power, wind power, hydroelectricity and tidal technology and how these can be used to generate electricity in specific locations. In addition, students have described the operation of geothermal power stations and their links to radioactive decay. The principles of solar cells and both small-scale and large-scale solar heating systems have been outlined.

The students have compared all of the energy resources in terms of local environmental impacts, such as pollution, and global environment impacts, such as acid rain, and their contribution to global warming. Finally, the students have described how the different resources could be applied in combination to meet the base load and changing energy demands throughout a single day before finally considering the capital costs and operating costs over the operational lifetime of the resource.

You can find additional support for the maths skills covered in this chapter on **MyMaths**, including constructing and interpreting frequency tables and diagrams, bar charts and histograms and changing the subject of an equation.

For this chapter, the following assessments are available on Kerboodle:

P3 Checkpoint quiz Energy resources
P3 Progress quiz: Energy resources 1
P3 Progress quiz: Energy resources 2
P3 On your marks: Energy resources
P3 Exam-style questions and mark scheme: Energy resources

Checkpoint follow up lesson

A student's route through this lesson can be determined using the Checkpoint assessment. Percentage pass marks are supplied in the Checkpoint teacher notes.

For each successive route through it is assumed that the student can perform to their current route as well as previous routes. For example, students working at Aiming for 6 are assumed to be secure in Aiming for 4 knowledge and understanding and working towards achieving all the learning outcomes for Aiming for 6.

	Aiming for 4	Aiming for 6	Aiming for 8
Learning outcomes	Describe how current energy demands are met.	Describe how current energy demands are met, including how electricity is generated.	Describe how current energy demands are met, including how electricity is generated and variable demand is met.
	Describe the difference between renewable and non-renewable sources of energy.	Describe how to generate electricity with renewable sources.	Suggest and explain how demand for energy can be met in the future.
	Describe how to generate electricity with renewable sources.	Suggest how demand for energy can be met in the future.	Discuss the issues relating to future energy supply.
Starter	**Sort the resource (10 min)** Give out cards for a pairs matching game that contains the names of renewable and non-renewable energy resources on blue card, with the same number of each card in yellow that has 'renewable' or 'non-renewable' on it. Student put the cards face down, and pick up pairs of different colours, keeping any pairs that match. When they have completed the game they use the names of the resources to make a pyramid with the most important source for electricity production at the top.		
Differentiated checkpoint activity	Students use the Checkpoint follow-up sheet to complete one of two activities: • create a leaflet to describe how our energy demands are met • prepare a presentation about how an island community can meet its energy demands using renewable resources. The Aiming for 4 follow-up sheet is highly structured and students could work in pairs for support. Students should then analyse data to make predictions about future use of resources. Students will need access to graph paper.	Students use the Checkpoint follow-up sheet to complete one of two activities: • create a leaflet to describe how our energy demands are met • prepare a presentation about how an island community can meet its energy demands using renewable resources. The Aiming for 6 follow-up sheet provides some support and students should be aiming to work independently. Students should then analyse data to make predictions about future use of resources. Students will need access to graph paper.	Students use the Checkpoint follow-up sheet to complete one of two activities: • create a leaflet on nuclear power and other ways of generating electricity • devise a method to investigate solar cells and wind turbines. The Aiming for 8 follow-up sheet provides minimal support. Students could work in pairs for support, but should attempt to work independently. Students then analyse data to make predictions about future use of resources. Students will need access to graph paper.
	Kerboodle resource P3 Checkpoint follow up: Aiming for 4, P3 Checkpoint follow up: Aiming for 6, P3 Checkpoint follow up: Aiming for 8		
Plenary	**Mini balloon debate (10 min)** In groups each student selects a resource at random from the cards used in the starter. They prepare a series of 5 points in favour of their resource being included in future plans to meet energy demand. They each share those points, and the others in the group.		
Progression	Encourage students to think about the pros and cons of different energy sources.	Encourage students to think about the pros and cons of different energy sources, including the economic as well as environmental issues.	Encourage students to think about the need to balance the use of energy from a range of sources in the future both to meet baseline requirements and to meet fluctuations in demand.

2 Particles at work

Specification links

AQA specification section	Assessment paper
2.1 Current, potential difference, and resistance	Paper 1
2.2 Series and parallel circuits	Paper 1
2.3 Domestic uses and safety	Paper 1
2.4 Energy transfers	Paper 1
2.5 Static electricity	Paper 1
3.1 Changes of state and the particle model	Paper 1
3.2 Internal energy and energy transfers	Paper 1
3.3 Particle model and pressure	Paper 1
4.1 Atoms and isotopes	Paper 1
4.2 Atoms and nuclear radiation	Paper 1
4.3 Hazards and uses of radioactive emissions and of background radiation	Paper 1
4.4 Nuclear fission and fusion	Paper 1

Required practicals

AQA required practicals	Practical skills	Topic
Use circuit diagrams to set up and check appropriate circuits to investigate the factors affecting the resistance of electrical circuits. This should include: • the length of a wire at constant temperature • combinations of resistors in series and parallel.	AT 1 – use appropriate apparatus to measure and record length accurately. AT 6 – use appropriate apparatus to measure current, potential difference, and resistance. AT 7 – use circuit diagrams to construct and check series and parallel circuits.	P4.3
Use circuit diagrams to construct appropriate circuits to investigate the I–V characteristics of a variety of circuit elements including a filament lamp, a diode, and a resistor at constant temperature.	AT 6 – use appropriate apparatus to measure current and potential difference, and to explore the characteristics of a variety of circuit elements. AT 7 – use circuit diagrams to construct and check series and parallel circuits including a variety of common circuit elements.	P4.4
Use appropriate apparatus to make and record the measurements needed to determine the densities of regular and irregular solid objects and liquids. Volume should be determined from the dimensions of a regularly shaped object and by a displacement technique for irregularly shaped objects. Dimensions to be measured using appropriate apparatus such as a ruler, micrometre, or Vernier callipers.	AT 1 – use appropriate apparatus to make and record measurements of length, area, mass, and volume accurately. Use such measurements to determine the density of solid objects and liquids.	P6.1

Maths skills

AQA maths skills	Topic
1a Recognise and use expressions in decimal form.	P4.2, P4.3, P4.4, P4.5, P5.4, P5.5, P5.6, P6.4, P7.1
1b Recognise and use expressions in standard form.	P7.1, P7.2, P7.6
1c Use ratios, fractions, and percentages.	P7.4, P7.5
2a Use an appropriate number of significant figures.	P4.2, P4.3, P4.4, P4.5, P5.4, P5.5, P5.6, P7.1
2c Construct and interpret frequency tables and diagrams, bar charts, and histograms.	P7.6
2f Understand the terms mean, mode, and median.	P7.6
2g Use a scatter diagram to identify a correlation between two variables.	P6.3, P6.6
2h Make order of magnitude calculations.	P7.9
3a Understand and use the symbols: $=, <, \ll, \gg, >, \propto, \sim$.	P4.2, P4.3, P4.4, P4.5, P5.4, P5.5, P5.6, P6.1, P6.5, P6.7, P7.5

AQA maths skills	Topic
3b Change the subject of an equation.	P4.2, P4.3, P4.4, P4.5, P5.4, P5.5, P5.6, P6.1, P6.4, P6.5, P6.7
3c Substitute numerical values into algebraic equations using appropriate units for physical quantities.	P4.2, P4.3, P4.4, P4.5, P5.4, P5.5, P5.6, P6.1, P6.4, P6.5, P6.7, P7.8
3d Solve simple algebraic equations.	P4.2, P4.3, P4.4, P4.5, P5.4, P5.5, P5.6, P6.1, P6.4, P6.5, P6.7
4a Translate information between graphical and numeric form.	P4.3, P5.1, P6.6, P7.5, P7.9
4b Understand that $y = mx + c$ represents a linear relationship.	P4.3, P6.6
4c Plot two variables from experimental or other data.	P4.3, P6.3, P6.6
5b Visualise and represent 2D and 3D forms including two dimensional representations of 3D objects.	P6.4, P7.2, P7.7
5c Calculate areas of triangles and rectangles, surface areas and volumes of cubes.	P6.1

KS3 concept	GCSE topic	Checkpoint	Revision
There are two types of electric charge.	P4.1 Electrical charges and fields	Ask students to describe why a balloon sticks to a wall when the balloon is rubbed with a cloth.	The students draw a diagram showing the electron transfer from a cloth to or from a plastic rod when it is rubbed.
A cell or a battery pushes electrons round a circuit.	P4.2 Current and charge	Ask the students to describe how a simple circuit using a cell, two leads, and a bulb operates.	The students describe the effect on the current in a simple circuit if additional cells are added and then if a resistor is added.
Potential difference (p.d.) is measured in volts and current is measured in amperes.	P4.3 Potential difference and resistance	Ask the students to draw a circuit diagram showing how current in and p.d. across a bulb can be measured.	Give the students a set of circuit diagrams and ask them identify the voltmeters and ammeters being used.
Power is how much energy is transferred per second.	P5.4 Electrical power and potential difference	Show the students two different light bulbs and ask them to explain why one is brighter than the other.	Students can rank devices in terms of power using data about their operating current and voltage using a card sort or similar.
Mass is the amount of matter in a substance and is measured in kilograms.	P6.1 Density	Ask the students why an object, such as a metal block, has a weight and whether this weight can change.	Students can use data about the weight of objects to sort them in order of mass.
Gas particles move about very fast and collide with the surface of the gas container.	P6.6 Gas pressure and temperature	Ask students to describe why a balloon will 'pop' if you continue to inflate it.	Inflate a balloon, describing the increase in pressure and its cause.
The nucleus of an atom is composed of protons and neutrons.	P7.1 Atoms and radiation	Ask students to draw a diagram showing the components of an atom.	The students can assemble model nuclei from descriptions (some in atomic notation) and small amounts of coloured modelling clay.
Understand that scientific methods and theories develop as earlier explanations are modified to take account of new evidence and ideas.	P7.2 The discovery of the nucleus	Ask students if our understanding of the nucleus has always been the same or if it has changed over time.	Students can sort a timeline of discoveries about atomic structure from ancient Greek ideas to the modern interpretation.
Energy is released when hydrogen nuclei fuse together in the Sun.	P7.8 Nuclear fusion	Ask the students to describe how the sun produced light.	Show the students an animation of a nuclear fusion process and describe how the light reached the Earth.

P
GCSE
Physics
only

4 Electric circuits

4.1 Electrical charges and fields

AQA spec Link: 2.5.1 When certain insulating materials are rubbed against each other they become electrically charged. Negatively charged electrons are rubbed off one material and onto the other. The material that gains electrons becomes negatively charged. The material that loses electrons is left with an equal positive charge.

When two electrically charged objects are brought close together they exert a force on each other. Two objects that carry the same type of charge repel. Two objects that carry different types of charge attract. Attraction and repulsion between two charged objects are examples of non-contact force.

Students should be able to:

- describe the production of static electricity, and sparking, by rubbing surfaces
- describe evidence that charged objects exert forces of attraction or repulsion on one another when not in contact
- explain how the transfer of electrons between objects can explain the phenomena of static electricity.

2.5.2 A charged object creates an electric field around itself. The electric field is strongest close to the charged object. The further away from the charged object, the weaker the field.

A second charged object placed in the field experiences a force. The force gets stronger as the distance between the objects decreases.

Students should be able to:

- draw the electric field pattern for an isolated charged sphere
- explain the concept of an electric field
- explain how the concept of an electric field helps to explain the non-contact force between charged objects as well as other electrostatic phenomena such as sparking.

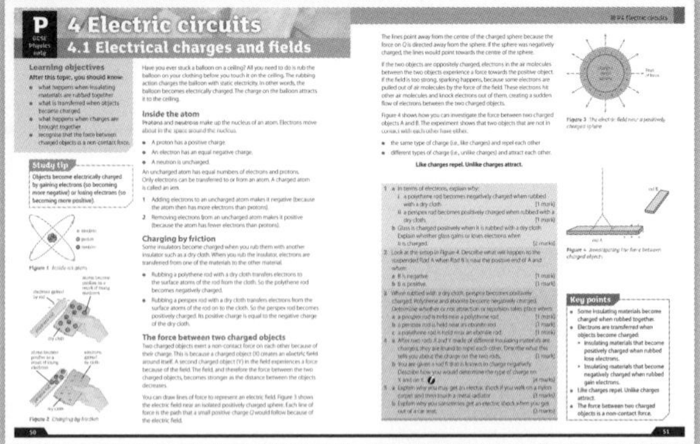

WS 1.2

Aiming for	Outcome	Checkpoint	
		Question	**Activity**
Aiming for GRADE 4 ↓	Label the constituents of an atom (proton, neutron, and electron) on a diagram.		Main
	Describe the interactions between positively and negatively charged objects.	2	Plenary 1
	State that objects can become electrically charged by the action of frictional forces.		Main
Aiming for GRADE 6 ↓	Compare the electrical properties of protons, neutrons, electrons, and ions.		Main
	Use the concept of electric fields to explain why charged objects interact.	3	Starter 1, Main, Plenary 1
	Describe how objects become charged in terms of electron transfer.	1	Main
Aiming for GRADE 8 ↓	Describe the shape of the field and lines of force around a point charge or charged sphere.		Main
	Apply the concept of electric fields to explain in detail why the force between charged objects decreases with increasing distance.	3	Main
	Explain why sparks can be produced by charged materials in terms of charge build-up.	4	Main

Maths

Students use graphical representations in the form of field diagrams and field lines.

Literacy

Students compare results in attraction and repulsion tests to determine the charge on objects.

Key words

neutrons, protons, ions, electric field

Practical

Title	Charging by friction
Equipment	retort stand with boss and clamp, cotton, light card, two Perspex rods, two polythene rods, dry cloth
Overview of method	The students first need to make a hammock from the cotton and light card to suspend one of the rods from the retort stand. They then rub one of the rods vigorously with the dry cloth and place it in the hammock. Next they rub one of the other rods and bring it close to the suspended one and note the interaction – the suspended rod should rotate towards or away from it. Repeat for all combinations of rods.

Title	Charging by friction – Van de Graaff
Equipment	Van de Graaff generator (VDG) and accessory kit
Overview of method	Show the sparks that can be produced by the VDG with a 'discharging wand'. Allow a couple of minutes to build up charge whilst explaining what is happening. Bring the wand close to the dome and explain what is happening during discharge.
Safety considerations	Make sure students do not have any heart conditions. Keep computers (and mobile phones) away from the VDG.

Starter	Support/Extend	Resources
Laws of attraction (5 min) Ask students to draw a diagram of three bar magnets arranged so that they all attract each other. Then ask students to draw another diagram so that all three repel each other. Use real magnets to check the answers.		
Invisible force fields (10 min) Demonstrate magnet rings on a pole if available, and ask the students to explain what is happening. They should reach the idea that there are non-contact forces acting and the size of these forces increases as the distance decreases.	**Extend:** Ask students to state the factors that affect the size of the forces and to consider gravitational forces too.	
Main		**Resources**
Charging by friction (20 min) Recap the structure of an atom, ensuring that the students understand how electrons can be removed from atoms to form ions.	**Support:** Provide a simple diagram for the students to annotate.	**Practical:** Charging by friction
The students should investigate charging by friction using the practical. Students could carry out a series of other electrostatics experiments in a circus activity.		
Then demonstrate the operation of a VDG showing the build-up of charge and discharge during sparks. Use the VDG to discuss the electrical field surrounding it – charged objects brought near to it will experience a force. Move on to the idea of field lines (lines of force) showing the direction that positively charged objects will be pushed.	**Support:** Use additional demonstrations such as lighting fluorescent tubes.	
Plenary		**Resources**
Static force (5 min) Show students a set of diagrams with charged objects on them and force arrows, some correct and some incorrect. Students identify which diagrams are correct.	**Extend:** Students should incorporate the ideas for fields and the relative sizes of the forces.	**Interactive:** Static force
Spark dangers (10 min) Students discuss the potential hazards caused by sparking, including damage to electronic devices and the potential for explosions during refuelling.		
Homework		
Students complete the WebQuest where they research the characteristics of lightning and discuss whether we will ever use its energy.	**Extend:** Expect supporting numerical data such as the size of the current.	**WebQuest:** Lightning

kerboodle

A Kerboodle highlight for this lesson is **Bump up your grades: Static electricity and electric fields**. Refer to the **Content map** on Kerboodle for a full list of resources and assessment.

P4.2 Current and charge

AQA spec Link: 2.1.1 Circuit diagrams use standard symbols.

Students should be able to draw and interpret circuit diagrams.

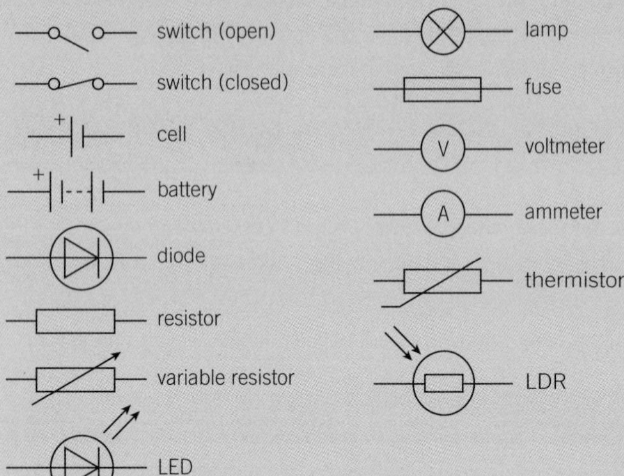

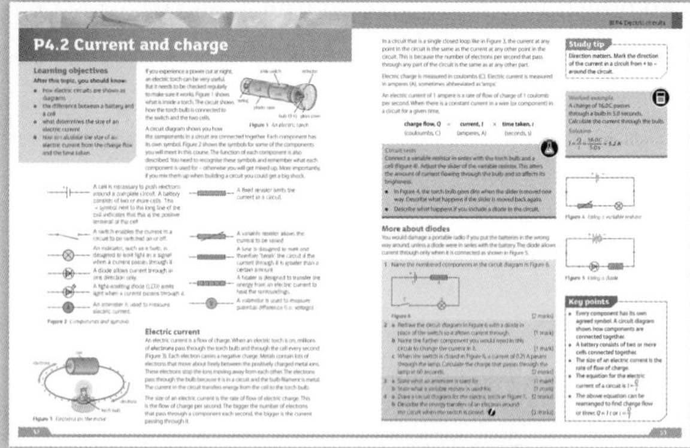
P4.2 Current and charge

WS 1.2

MS 3b, 3c

2.1.2 For electrical charge to flow through a closed circuit the circuit must include a source of potential difference.

Electric current is a flow of electrical charge. The size of the electric current is the rate of flow of electrical charge. Charge flow, current, and time are linked by the equation:

charge flow = current × time

$[Q = I\,t]$

charge flow Q in coulombs, C

current I in amperes, A (amp is acceptable for ampere)

time t in seconds, s

A current has the same value at any point in a single closed loop.

Aiming for	Outcome	Checkpoint	
		Question	Activity
Aiming for GRADE 4 ↓	Identify circuit components from their symbols.	1	Plenary 2
	Draw and interpret simple circuit diagrams.	4	Starter 2
	Construct a simple electrical circuit.		Main
Aiming for GRADE 6 ↓	Describe the operation of a variable resistor and a diode and their effects on current.	2, 3, End of chapter 2	Main
	Calculate the charge transferred by a steady current in a given time.	2	Main, Plenary 1
	Construct an electrical circuit and accurately measure the current.		Main
Aiming for GRADE 8 ↓	Explain the nature of an electric current in wires in terms of electron behaviour.		Main
	Perform a range of calculations, including rearrangement of the equation $Q = It$.		Main, Plenary 1
	Measure the current in a circuit accurately and use it to calculate the rate of flow of electrons.		Main

Maths

Students calculate charge and current with the appropriate equation (3b, 3c).

Literacy

Students need to describe the operation of a variety of electrical components and the nature of a current. They discuss the current model with each other.

Key words

electrons

Practical

Title	Circuit tests
Equipment	For each group: cells (1.5 V), torch bulb (1.5 V), leads, diode, variable resistor, ammeter.
Overview of method	The students set up a simple circuit with the variable resistor and the bulb and explore the effect of altering the resistor. The students then include a diode in the circuit in forward then reverse position. This will show that the diode allows the current in only one direction.

Starter	Support/Extend	Resources
It's symbolic (5 min) Show a set of slides/diagrams to the students containing common symbols and ask them to say what they mean. Use road signs, hazard symbols, washing symbols, and so on.		
Describe the circuit (10 min) Give the students diagrams of two circuits containing cells, switches, and bulbs, one series and one parallel. Ask them to describe both in one paragraph. The students can demonstrate their understanding of circuit symbols, establishing prior knowledge of concepts such as current, voltage, series, and parallel.	**Support:** Use simple circuits with a minimal number of components. **Extend:** Ask students to draw a circuit based on a written description of it.	
Main	**Support/Extend**	**Resources**
Circuit tests (40 min) Construct a 'torch' circuit, showing the students each component and discussing its operation. Demonstrate how circuits should be constructed methodically to avoid problems later. At the same time show some of the other components that will be introduced later. Discuss the nature of a current, with a focus on the rate of flow of charge, leading to the equation $Q = It$. A few example calculations are required to embed the units. Students then construct the circuit described in the practical and test it, with the focus on connecting the apparatus correctly. They can then add the ammeter to collect numerical information and practise using it. Students add a diode to their circuit, note the effect, and discuss its operation ensuring the students link the direction of the arrow on the symbol to the direction of the current.	**Extend:** Provide the charge of an electron and ask the students to find the number of electrons passing through the bulb per second.	**Practical:** Circuit tests
Plenary	**Support/Extend**	**Resources**
Current calculations (5 min) Give the students a few calculations based on the equation to perform.	**Support:** Use relatively simple quantities and calculations requiring no rearrangement.	
Circuit symbols and resistance (10 min) Students work through the interactive to match the circuit symbols and relevant units with their definitions.		**Interactive:** Circuit symbols and resistance
Homework		
Students describe an important development in electronics, such as development of the battery or discovery of the electron.		

kerboodle

A Kerboodle highlight for this lesson is **WebQuest: A short history of electricity**. Refer to the **Content map** on Kerboodle for a full list of resources and assessment.

P4.3 Potential difference and resistance

AQA spec Link: 2.1.3 The current I through a component depends on both the resistance R of the component and the potential difference V across the component. The greater the resistance of the component the smaller the current for a given potential difference (p.d.) across the component.

Questions will be set using the term potential difference. Students will gain credit for the correct use of either potential difference or voltage.

Current, potential difference, or resistance can be calculated using the equation:

potential difference = current × resistance [$V = I R$]

potential difference V in volts, V

current I in amperes, A (amp is acceptable for ampere)

resistance R in ohms, Ω

Students should be able to recall and/or apply this equation.

2.1.4 Students should be able to explain that, for some resistors, the value of R remains constant but that in others it can change as the current changes.

The current through an ohmic conductor (at a constant temperature) is directly proportional to the potential difference across the resistor. This means that the resistance remains constant as the current changes.

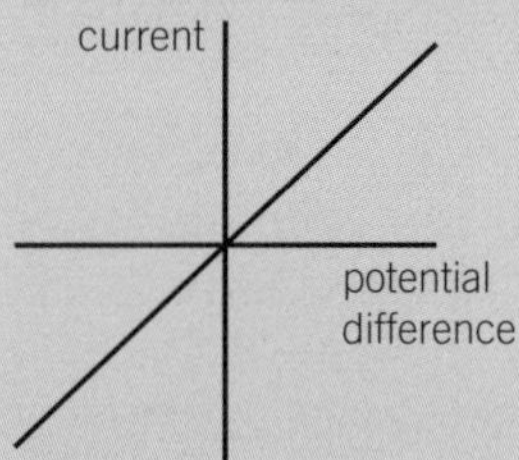

The resistance of components such as lamps, diodes, thermistors, and LDRs is not constant; it changes with the current through the component.

Required practical: use circuit diagrams to set up and check appropriate circuits to investigate the factors affecting the resistance of electrical circuits. This should include:

- the length of a wire at constant temperature.
- combinations of resistors in series and parallel.

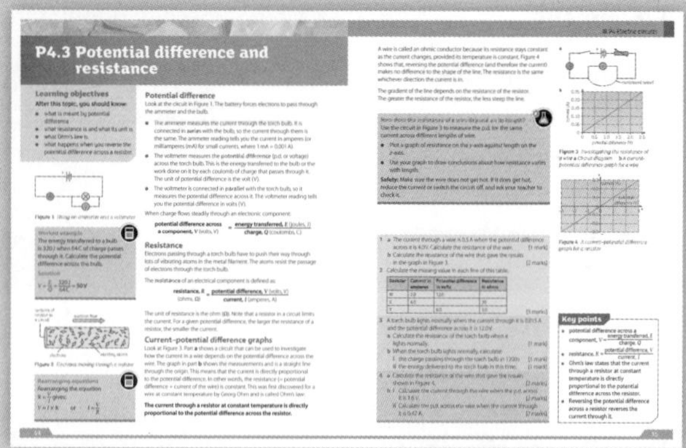
P4.3 Potential difference and resistance

MS 3b, 3c

Aiming for	Outcome	Checkpoint	
		Question	Activity
Aiming for GRADE 4 ↓	State that resistance restricts the size of a current in a circuit.		Main
	State Ohm's law and describe its conditions.	End of chapter 1	Main
	Measure the current and potential difference in a circuit to determine the resistance.		Main
Aiming for GRADE 6 ↓	Calculate the potential difference.	3	Main
	Calculate the resistance of a component.	1, 3, 4	Homework
	Measure the effect of changing the length of a wire on its resistance in a controlled experiment.		Main
Aiming for GRADE 8 ↓	Describe potential difference in terms of work done per unit charge.		Main
	Rearrange equations for resistance and potential difference.	2, 3, 4	Main, Homework
	Investigate a variety of factors that may affect the resistance of a metal wire, such as the current through it, length, cross-sectional area, and metal used.		Main

Maths

The students will use a range of electrical equations and analyse components graphically. They will use the concept of inverse proportionality.

Literacy

Students discuss the factors that may affect the resistance of a metal wire and plan an investigation into these factors.

Key words

series, potential difference, parallel, resistance

Required practical

Title	How does the resistance of a wire depend on the length?
Equipment	power supply or battery pack, connecting leads, switch, crocodile clips, variable resistor, constantan wire (selection of different lengths), heat-resistant mat, ammeter, voltmeter.
Overview of method	Connect the circuit with the variable resistor and test wire in series. Using the variable resistor, control the current through the test wire and measure both the current and the potential difference. Reverse the power supply and repeat the measurements. Use a series circuit with the variable resistor to limit the current to below 0.5 A. Adjust the length of the wire being tested by using the crocodile clips. Constantan or nichrome wire has a high resistivity and gives results that are easier to interpret
Safety considerations	The wire can become very hot – students must not touch it, and the heat-resistant mat should be used to protect surfaces.

Starter	Support/Extend	Resources
Resistors (5 min) Show the students the circuit symbols for all of the different types of resistor and ask them to describe the similarities in the symbols. **Rearranging equations** (10 min) Students use the interactive to identify the three correct arrangements of the equation for charge flow. They then answer an example calculation for each arrangement.		**Interactive:** Rearranging equations
Main		**Resources**
How does the resistance of a wire depend on its length? (40 min) Discuss the nature of potential difference and demonstrate how it is measured in a circuit along with current. Use the Maths skills interactive to give students some practice using the equation. Students then investigate the effect of changing the length of a wire on the resistance. Different groups of students can be given wires of differ diameters or materials to show that the pattern is the same (resistance is proportional to length) and identify some other factors which affect resistance.	**Extend:** Students can discuss interactions between electrons and metal ions and the cause of resistance. **Support:** Provide blank results tables. **Extend:** Students compare several wire characteristics to determine which has the greatest resistance.	**Maths skills:** Potential difference, current, and resistance **Required practical:** How does the resistance of a wire depend on the length?
Plenary		**Resources**
An electron's tale (5 min) Students write a paragraph about the journey of an electron around a circuit containing a bulb and a resistor. They should write about the energy transfers that are going on in the circuit. **Reinforced resistance** (10 min) Additional calculations should be used to reinforce learning, differentiating by student ability as appropriate.	**Extend:** Students complete the Extension sheet on the mathematical relationships of charge, current, potential difference, and resistance.	**Extension:** Electrical quantities
Homework		
Provide students with further resistance and current calculations to complete. The calculations should involve rearranging the equations.		

kerboodle

A Kerboodle highlight for this lesson is **Working scientifically: What's the potential?** Refer to the **Content map** on Kerboodle for a full list of resources and assessment.

P4.4 Component characteristics

AQA spec Link: 2.1.4 Students should be able to explain that, for some resistors, the value of *R* remains constant but that in others it can change as the current changes.

The current through an ohmic conductor (at a constant temperature) is directly proportional to the potential difference across the resistor. This means that the resistance remains constant as the current changes.

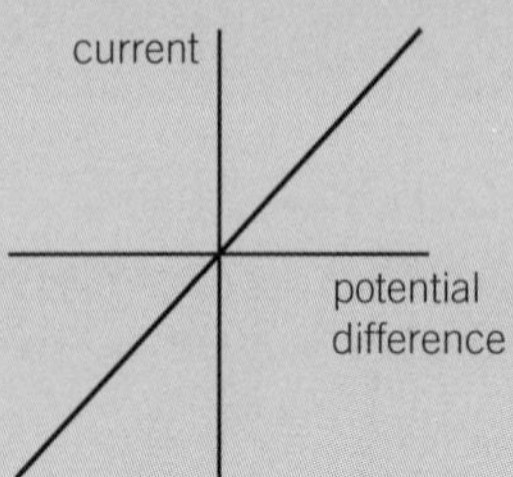

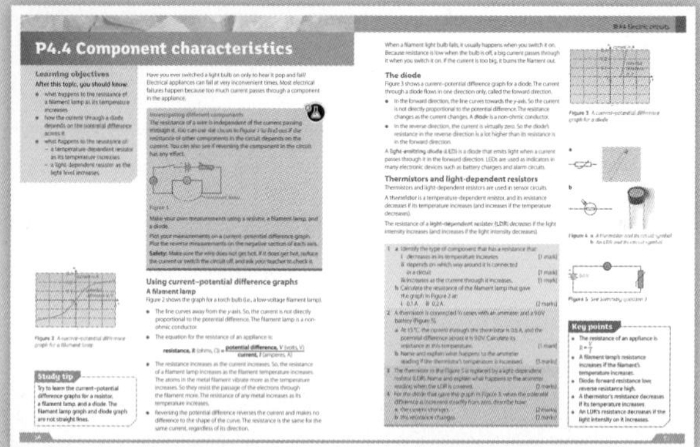

The resistance of components such as lamps, diodes, thermistors, and LDRs is not constant; it changes with the current through the component.

The resistance of a filament lamp increases as the temperature of the filament increases.

current

potential difference

The current through a diode flows in one direction only. The diode has a very high resistance in the reverse direction.

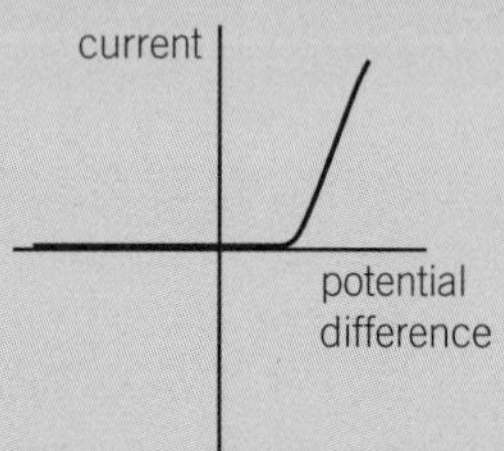

The resistance of a thermistor decreases as the temperature increases.

The applications of thermistors in circuits, for example, a thermostat is required.

The resistance of an LDR decreases as light intensity increases.

The application of LDRs in circuits, for example, switching lights on when it gets dark is required.

Students should be able to:

- explain the design and use of a circuit to measure the resistance of a component by measuring the current through, and potential difference across, the component
- draw an appropriate circuit diagram using correct circuit symbols.

Students should be able to use graphs to explore whether circuit elements are linear or non-linear and relate the curves produced to their function and properties.

Required practical: Use circuit diagrams to construct circuits to investigate the *I–V* characteristics of a variety of circuit elements, including a filament lamp, a diode, and a resistor at constant temperature.

WS 1.2, 1.4

MS 4c, 4d, 4e

Aiming for	Outcome	Checkpoint	
		Question	**Activity**
Aiming for GRADE 4	Identify the key characteristics of electrical devices.	1, End of chapter 1, 2	Plenary 1, Main
↓	Identify components from simple I–V graphs.		Main
	State the operation of a diode in simple terms.	1	Main
Aiming for GRADE 6	Describe the resistance characteristics of a filament lamp.		Main
↓	Describe the characteristics of a diode and light-emitting diode.	3	Main
	Investigate the resistance characteristics of a thermistor and a LDR.	2	Starter 2, Plenary 2
Aiming for GRADE 8	Explain the resistance characteristics of a filament lamp in terms of electrons and ion collisions.		Main
↓	Determine the resistance of a component based on information extracted from a *I–V* graph.	4	Main
	Compare the characteristics of a variety of electrical components, describing how the components can be used.	2	Main

Maths

Students will apply graphical skills in analysis of the behaviour of electrical devices (4c, 4d, 4e).

Literacy

Students translate graphical information into prose.

Key words

diode, light-emitting diode (LED), thermistor, light-dependent resistor (LDR)

Required practical

Title	Investigating different components
Equipment	power supply or battery pack, connecting leads, variable resistor, ammeter, voltmeter, filament lamp, fixed resistor, diode
Overview of method	Connect the circuit with the component being tested in series with the variable resistor and ammeter and a voltmeter in parallel with the component. Using the variable resistor, the students change the p.d. across the component and record the current and potential difference. From the results, the students produce a current–potential difference graph. They should try the circuit with the current in the opposite direction to show that this does not affect the bulb but is very important for the diode.
Safety considerations	Current in the circuits should be kept low.

Starter	Support/Extend	Resources
Comparing wires (5 min) Show the students a graph of the current–p.d. characteristics of three wires. They use the interactive to put the three wires in order of highest resistance to lowest resistance. They then complete a paragraph to describe what characteristics affect the resistance of a wire. **Thermistors and LDRs** (10 min) Introduce thermistors and LDRs briefly. Set up a circuit with a thermistor attached by crocodile clips and place the thermistor into a beaker of hot water. Measure the resistance of the thermistor, and ask students to predict what would happen to the resistance measurement as the water cools.	**Extend:** Students calculate the resistance of each wire by using the graph. **Support:** Provide a brief recap of the effect of high resistance. **Extend:** Students explain in terms of electrons and ions.	**Interactive:** Comparing wires
Main		**Resources**
Investigating different components (40 min) Discuss the results of the investigation into the characteristics of a wire from Topic P4.3. The students then investigate the behaviour of a filament lamp, a diode, and a resistor, as described. Ensure that the students can identify and describe the resulting I–V graphs clearly. Results should be shared so that all students are aware of the characteristics of the components.	**Support:** Students can investigate only one of the components and share their results with a group that has investigated the other component.	**Required practical:** Investigating different components
Plenary		**Resources**
What's in the box? (5 min) An electrical component has been placed inside a black box with only the two connections visible. The students should suggest an experiment to find out what it is. This should involve a detailed analysis of the V–I characteristics. **Thermistors and LDRs – revisited** (10 min) Revisit the circuit with the thermistor from the start of the lesson to see how the resistance of the thermistor has increased as the water cooled. Then ask students to predict what would happen to the resistance of an LDR if it was placed closer to a bright light. Set up the circuit to demonstrate.	**Support:** Suggest some equipment to the students.	
Homework		
Students plan an investigation into the behaviour of a thermistor or LDR.		

kerboodle

A Kerboodle highlight for this lesson is **Bump up your grade: IV graphs**. Refer to the **Content map** on Kerboodle for a full list of resources and assessment.

P4.5 Series circuits

AQA spec Link: 2.2 There are two ways of joining electrical components, in series and in parallel. Some circuits include both series and parallel parts.

For components connected in series:

- there is the same current through each component
- the total potential difference of the power supply is shared between the components
- the total resistance of two components is the sum of the resistance of each component.

$$R_{total} = R_1 + R_2$$

resistance R in ohms, Ω

Students should be able to:

- use circuit diagrams to construct and check series and parallel circuits that include a variety of common circuit components
- describe the difference between series and parallel circuits
- explain qualitatively why adding resistors in series increases the total resistance whilst adding resistors in parallel decreases the total resistance
- explain the design and use of d.c. series circuits for measurement and testing purposes
- calculate the currents, potential differences, and resistances in d.c. series circuits
- solve problems for circuits which include resistors in series using the concept of equivalent resistance.

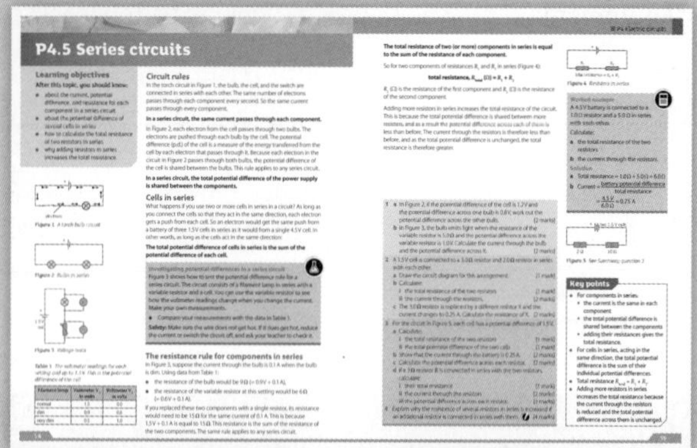

WS 1.4

MS 1c, 3b, 3c, 3d

Aiming for	Outcome	Checkpoint	
		Question	Activity
Aiming for GRADE 4 ↓	State that the current in any part of a series circuit is the same.		
	Calculate the potential difference provided by cell combinations.	3	Main 1
	Calculate the total resistance of two resistors placed in series.	3	Plenary 1
Aiming for GRADE 6 ↓	Find the potential difference across a component in a circuit by using the p.d. rule.	1	Main 1
	Calculate the current in a series circuit containing more than one resistor.	2	Main 2, Plenary 1
	Investigate the resistance of series circuits with several components.		Main 2
Aiming for GRADE 8 ↓	Explain in detail why the current in a series circuit is the same at all points by using the concept of conservation of charge (electrons).		Main 1
	Analyse a variety of series circuits to determine the current through, p.d. across, and resistance of combinations of components.	1, 3, End of chapter 3, 7	Main 1, Main 2, Plenary 1
	Evaluate in detail the investigation of series circuits and explain discrepancies.		Main 1

Maths

Students calculate the sum of resistances and current in series circuits (3b, 3c, 3d).

Literacy

Students describe the current in circuits and explain why it must be the same at all points.

Practical

Title	Investigating potential differences in a series circuit
Equipment	power supply or battery pack (1.5 V), connecting leads, variable resistor, 1.5 V bulb, three voltmeters
Overview of method	The students connect a bulb and variable resistor in series. Connect one voltmeter across the bulb V_1 and one across the variable resistor V_2. When the circuit is switched on, the students should find that $V_1 + V_2 = V_{total}$ when the variable resistor is set to any position.
Safety considerations	Use low potential differences to produce small currents.

Starter	Support/Extend	Resources
Adding wires (10 min) Show the students a circuit with a wire of resistance 2 Ω and ask them what would happen if a second length of identical wire was placed 'in series'. Would the resistance go up or down? What would happen if the wire was placed in parallel with the first?	**Extend:** Students should give numerical values and suggest scientific explanations.	
One way only (5 min) Ask students: In what situation are we allowed only one way through something? Suggest a tour or road system. Discuss the idea of conservation – the same number of people or cars go out and come in.	**Support:** Use an animation of flow to show that the same number of objects must leave as enter.	
Main		**Resources**
Investigating potential differences in a series circuit (25 min) Demonstrate the conservation of current and the addition of potential differences by using ammeters and voltmeters in a series circuit, accounting for any discrepancies. Students then investigate potential difference, discovering that the total p.d. around a branch (summing the p.d.s across the series components) is the same as the p.d. provided by the power supply. There will be some variation in measurements and a discussion of meter precision and error should take place.	**Support:** Use simulations of electron movement in the circuit to show that the electrons pass all the way around the circuit and are not 'used up'. **Extend:** Students should discuss why the meters can sometimes give different readings even though the current is the same at all points.	**Practical:** Investigating potential differences in a series circuit
Resistors in series (15 min) Discuss resistance in series and allow students to confirm the information using fixed resistors in a circuit by constructing a circuit containing fixed value resistors.	**Extend:** The variation in resistance of particular resistors can be discussed.	
Plenary		**Resources**
Controlling current (5 min) Interactive where students are given combinations of cells and resistors and the current they would produce, some correct and some incorrect. Students identify which combinations are correct.	**Support:** Give only simple possibilities.	**Interactive:** Controlling current
Circuit rules (10 min) The students should start making a list of circuit rules to help them work out the currents, potential differences, and resistances in series and parallel circuits.		
Homework		
The students can research the developments in batteries, including the materials used to construct them and the hazards associated with these materials.		

P4.6 Parallel circuits

AQA spec Link: 2.2 There are two ways of joining electrical components, in series and in parallel. Some circuits include both series and parallel parts.

For components connected in parallel:

- the potential difference across each component is the same
- the total current through the whole circuit is the sum of the currents through the separate components
- the total resistance of two resistors is less than the resistance of the smallest individual resistor.

Students should be able to:

- use circuit diagrams to construct and check series and parallel circuits that include a variety of common circuit components
- describe the difference between series and parallel circuits
- explain qualitatively why adding resistors in series increases the total resistance whilst adding resistors in parallel decreases the total resistance.

Students are **not** required to calculate the total resistance of two resistors joined in parallel.

2.1.4 **Required practical:** use circuit diagrams to construct appropriate circuits to investigate the I–V characteristics of a variety of circuit elements, including a filament lamp, a diode, and a resistor at constant temperature.

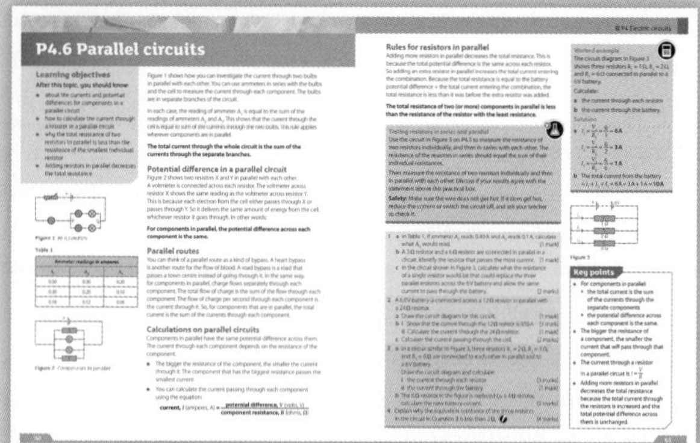

MS 1c, 3b, 3c, 3d

Aiming for	Outcome	Checkpoint	
		Question	Activity
Aiming for GRADE 4	Identify parallel sections in circuit diagrams.	1	Starter 1
	State the effect of adding resistors in parallel on the size of the current in a circuit.		Main 1
	State that the p.d. across parallel sections of a circuit is the same.		Main 1
Aiming for GRADE 6	Measure the p.d. across parallel circuits and explain any discrepancies.		Main 1
	Describe the effect on the resistance in a circuit of adding a resistor in parallel.	1, 4	Main 1, Main 2
	Investigate the effect of adding resistors in parallel on the size of the current in a circuit.		Main 2
Aiming for GRADE 8	Analyse parallel circuits in terms of current loops.		Main 2, Plenary 2
	Calculate the current at any point in a circuit.	2, 3, End of chapter 4	Main 1, Plenary 2
	Evaluate in detail an investigation into the effect of adding resistors in parallel on a circuit.		Main 2

Maths

Students calculate the current in parallel circuits (3b, 3c, 3d).

Literacy

Students discuss the changes in resistance in parallel circuits and how these changes affect the current in the circuits.

Required practical

Title	Testing resistors in series and parallel
Equipment	battery or power supply, connecting leads, two voltmeters, two ammeters, two fixed value resistors (10 ohms)
Overview of method	The students measure the resistance of the individual resistors and then the two resistors in series and finally the two resistors in parallel.
Safety considerations	Ensure the wires do not overheat.

Starter	Support/Extend	Resources
Circuit jumble (5 min) Show the students a diagram of a parallel circuit with three branches and several components on each branch. The wires and components are jumbled up, and the students must redraw the circuit properly.	**Support:** Provide students with a partially completed circuit diagram.	
The river (10 min) Show the students a picture of a river branching and re-joining. Ask them to explain what happens to the current in the river (mass of water passing a point each second) before, during, and after the split. They should compare this to the current in circuits.	**Extend:** At the end of the lesson, students should be asked to identify the limitations of this model of current and p.d.	
Main		**Resources**
Investigating parallel circuits (30 min) Students construct a simple parallel circuit and measure the current in the two branches. Use a conservation model to explain this – electrons are not created or destroyed, so the current into a junction is the same as the current out of it. The students should perform some example calculations on parallel circuits. Students need to analyse a circuit with the worked example in the student book to consolidate the current and p.d. rules. **Resistors in parallel** (10 min) The students should test a pair of resistors in series and parallel using the practical task. Explain this by discussing the new current loop provided by the new branch whilst the old current loop still exists.	**Extend:** Emphasise the formal definition of potential difference. Additional branches can be incorporated. **Support:** Lead the students through the stages methodically.	**Required practical:** Testing resistors in series and parallel
Plenary		**Resources**
Stair lights (5 min) Students design a simple circuit that can be used to turn the lights on and off from the top and bottom of a set of stairs.	**Support:** Demonstrate the circuit and show the diagram, asking the students to explain how it operates.	
Another circuit (10 min) Interactive where students analyse a parallel circuit to determine the current from a battery.	**Extend:** Use more complex resistors such as 1.2 kΩ.	**Interactive:** Another circuit
Homework		
Students explain why thicker wires are used in applications where high currents are needed, using the idea of resistance and heating.		

kerboodle

A Kerboodle highlight for this lesson is **Extension sheet: Analysis circuits.** Refer to the **Content map** on Kerboodle for a full list of resources and assessment.

P4 Electric circuits

Overview of P4 Electric circuits

In this chapter the students described the structure of an atom in terms of charged sub-atomic particles and the process of charging by friction resulting in ions and the transfer of electrons. This led to the concept of an electric field surrounding charged objects causing attractive or repulsive forces between them.

The students then described electric circuits and the components used to construct them using the concept of current as the rate of charge flow through components due to a potential difference between points in the circuit. Resistance was introduced and the cause of a heating effect and corresponding energy transfer. Students then investigated the factors affecting the resistance of a wire and the corresponding current-potential difference graphs. Further investigations of the components and analysis of the current-potential difference graphs have shown ohmic and non-ohmic behaviours for wires, filaments, and diodes. The relationship between the resistance of a thermistor and its temperature along with the relationship between the resistance of a light-dependent resistor and light level have been investigated.

Finally, the students investigated and analysed a range of series and parallel circuits describing the path of current at junctions, the potential difference across branches and components, and the effect on resistance of series and parallel branches.

You can find additional support for the maths skills covered in this chapter on **MyMaths**, including recognising and using expressions in decimal form, using an appropriate number of significant figures, understanding and using the symbols: $=, <, \ll, \gg, >, \propto, \sim$, and solving simple algebraic equations.

For this chapter, the following assessments are available on Kerboodle:

P4 Checkpoint quiz: Electric circuits
P4 Progress quiz: Electric circuits 1
P4 Progress quiz: Electric circuits 2
P4 On your marks: Electric circuits
P4 Exam-style questions and mark scheme: Electric circuits

Checkpoint follow up lesson

A student's route through this lesson can be determined using the Checkpoint assessment. Percentage pass marks are supplied in the Checkpoint teacher notes.

For each successive route through it is assumed that the student can perform to their current route as well as previous routes. For example, students working at Aiming for 6 are assumed to be secure in Aiming for 4 knowledge and understanding and working towards achieving all the learning outcomes for Aiming for 6.

	Aiming for 4	Aiming for 6	Aiming for 8
Learning outcomes	Describe how static electricity is produced.	Explain charging and discharging in terms of electron movement.	Apply what you know about charge to everyday examples of static electricity.
	Describe the attraction and repulsion of charges.	Explain attraction and repulsion using the idea of electric fields.	Explain phenomena using the idea of electric fields.
	Describe and explain what happens in series and parallel circuits.	Apply knowledge of series and parallel circuits.	Apply what you know to a range of problems involving series and parallel circuits.
Starter	**Jumping crumbs (5 min)** Put some crumbs in a saucer and cover it with cling film. Either give each group a saucer and cloth, or demonstrate by rubbing the cling film with the cloth. The crumbs should jump up and down. Display some true/false statements about the movement of the crumbs and ask students to hold up cards of different colours (e.g., red for true, blue for false) to show what they think. **Brightest/dimmest (5 min)** Give students A4 dry wipe boards, pens and an eraser. Ask them to draw a circuit diagram containing 3 bulbs and a battery, where the bulbs are: dimmest, brightest, two bulbs are dim and one is bright. Students compare their diagrams and hold up the best diagram in each category.		
Differentiated checkpoint activity	Aiming for 4 students use the Checkpoint follow-up sheet to do an experiment involving charging rods electrostatically, solve problems involving series and parallel circuits, and practise using the equations involving potential difference, current, resistance, energy, power, and time. The follow-up sheet provides structured tasks and questions to help them complete these activities and check their understanding of electrostatics, series and parallel circuits, and do calculations involving current, charge, time, potential difference, and resistance.	Aiming for 6 students use the Checkpoint follow-up sheet to investigate the link between the type of material in rods and cloths and the charges that rods acquire. They then play a game involving series and parallel circuits, and practise using the equations involving potential difference, current, resistance, energy, power, and time, and identify mystery components by plotting a characteristic curve for each. The follow-up sheet provides tasks and questions to help them complete these activities and check their understanding of electrostatics, series and parallel circuits, do calculations involving current, charge, time, potential difference, and resistance, and revise characteristic curves, and sensor circuits.	Aiming for 8 students use the Checkpoint follow-up sheet to investigate the link between the type of material in rods and cloths and the charges that rods acquire. They then play a game involving series and parallel circuits, and practise using the equations involving potential difference, current, resistance, energy, power, and time, and identify mystery components by plotting a characteristic curve for each, and then produce a calibration graph. Finally, they will apply what they know about measurement circuits. The follow-up sheet provides tasks and questions to help them complete these activities and check their understanding of electrostatics, series and parallel circuits, do calculations involving current, charge, time, potential difference, and resistance, and revise characteristic curves, and the use of LDRs and thermistors in sensor circuits.
	Kerboodle resource P4 Checkpoint follow up: Aiming for 4, P4 Checkpoint follow up: Aiming for 6, P4 Checkpoint follow up: Aiming for 8		
Plenary	**How did you get that? (10 min)** Give students A4 dry wipe boards, pens and an eraser. Display a number and unit, for example, 10 Ω, and ask students to devise a calculation where that is the answer. You can put up different quantities to check the equations involving current, charge, time, and potential difference, current, resistance and steer students towards different calculations depending on the level at which they are aiming. Students swap boards and check their calculations.		
Progression	Encourage students to think about the idea of electric fields when explaining how charged objects behave, and to use the idea of net resistance in series and parallel circuits.	Encourage students to think about the idea of electrons and electric fields when explaining how charged objects behave, and to use the ideas about thermistors and light dependent resistors to make sensor circuits.	Encourage students to think about the idea of electrons and electric fields when explaining how charged objects behave, and to use the idea that potential dividers make sensor circuits.

P 5 Electricity in the home

5.1 Alternating current

AQA spec Link: 2.3.1 Mains electricity is an a.c. supply. In the United Kingdom the domestic electricity supply has a frequency of 50 Hz and is about 230 V.

Students should be able to explain the difference between direct and alternating potential difference.

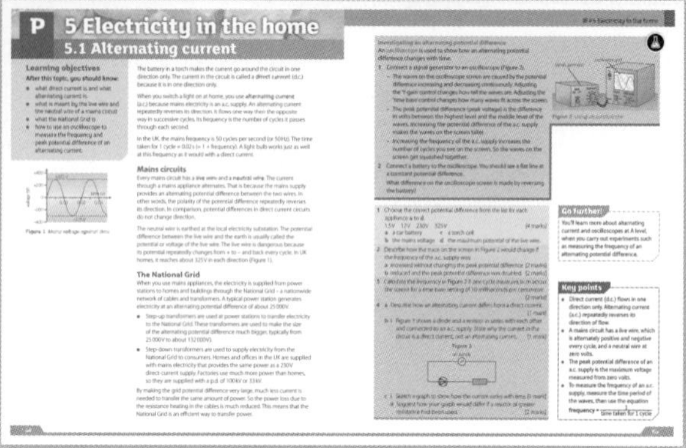

MS 4a

Aiming for	Outcome	Checkpoint	
		Question	**Activity**
Aiming for GRADE 4	State that the UK mains supply is a high-voltage alternating current supply.		Main 1
	State simple differences between a.c. and d.c. sources.	1	Main 1
	Describe how the trace on an oscilloscope changes when the frequency or amplitude of the signal is changed.	2	Main 2, Plenary 2
Aiming for GRADE 6	Describe the characteristics of the UK mains supply.	End of chapter 1	Main 1
	Compare a.c. traces in terms of period and amplitude (voltage).	3, End of chapter 1	Main 2
	Operate a cathode ray oscilloscope to display an a.c. trace.		Main 2
Aiming for GRADE 8	Explain the process of half-wave rectification of an a.c. source.		Main 2
	Analyse a.c. traces with an oscilloscope to determine the voltage and frequency.	3	Main 2, Plenary 2
	Compare and contrast the behaviour of electrons in a wire connected to d.c. and a.c. supplies.		Main 1

Maths
Students read graphical data from an oscilloscope and translate this into numerical data (4a). They also calculate the frequency of a waveform from its period.

Literacy
Students will need to collaborate to describe how an oscilloscope operates and to describe the observed waveforms.

Key words
direct current, alternating current, live wire, neutral wire

Practical

Title	Investigating an alternating potential difference
Equipment	cathode ray oscilloscope (CRO), low-voltage a.c. source (e.g., signal generator), battery, leads
Overview of method	The greatest problem the students will have with this experiment is setting the time base and volts per centimetre (Y-gain) dials on the CRO. If these are incorrectly set, then the students will not get a useful trace. To make things easier, put small blobs of paint on the scale around the dials showing the correct setting for displaying a 2 V, 50 Hz trace clearly. Digital oscilloscopes connected to a computer can be easier to use.
Safety considerations	Ensure that only low-voltage sources are used.

Starter	Support/Extend	Resources
Waveforms (5 min) Show the students a wave diagram (e.g., picture from the student book) and ask them to discuss it. They should recognise the sine wave shape of the wavelength (or period) and the amplitude.	**Support:** Provide a wave diagram for students to annotate.	
Mains facts (10 min) Ask the students some true/false questions about mains electricity to see what they already know. These should include some basic questions that have already been covered on d.c. and some testing of their knowledge of mains electricity.	**Support:** Differentiate by selecting appropriately challenging questions.	**Interactive:** Mains facts
Main	**Support/Extend**	**Resources**
Alternating and direct current (20 min) Discuss d.c. using a simple series circuit and ask students to describe electron movement. Introduce the idea that the electrons can be made to move back and forth rapidly (an a.c. supply), which still transfers energy to devices. Discuss the structure of a mains circuit, outlining the function of the live, neutral, and then earth wires. Emphasise the higher, rapidly varying voltages. The characteristics of the mains (50 Hz and around 230 V) should also be covered, noting that the peak voltage is significantly higher (325 V). Outline the basic features of the National Grid in terms of transformers and changes in voltage.	**Extend:** Introduce the concept that the energy is transferred by a varying electric field within the wire. Discuss electron behaviour in the a.c. wire.	
Investigating an alternating potential difference (20 min) Demonstrate or allow students to use an oscilloscope. They should be able to form a steady trace and measure the key characteristics of a.c. and d.c. sources by using the scales. They should also interpret some additional traces when given the oscilloscope settings in questions. Show students the waveform produced by half-wave rectification by placing a diode in series with a resistor and a low-voltage a.c. source.	**Support:** Teaching assistants or technicians should support students with a CRO as CROs are difficult to access. **Extend:** Ask students to explain the waveform in terms of electron movement.	**Practical:** Investigating an alternating potential difference
Plenary	**Support/Extend**	**Resources**
a.c./d.c.? (5 min) Give the students a set of electrical appliances and ask them to stack them into one of two piles: a.c. operation and d.c. operation.	**Extend:** Include less obvious devices such as laptops and phones.	
Traces (10 min) Show the students a series of oscilloscope traces with settings data (time base) and ask them to extract data from them, such as the peak p.d. and period.	**Support:** Use a single time-base setting for most of the diagrams. **Extend:** Students should calculate frequency from the period.	
Homework		
Students suggest the differences between the European and US mains electric systems. How and why were these choices made by each country?		

P5.2 Cables and plugs

AQA spec Link: 2.3.2 Most electrical appliances are connected to the mains using three-core cable.

The insulation covering each wire is colour coded for easy identification:

live wire – brown; neutral wire – blue; earth wire – green and yellow stripes.

The live wire carries the alternating potential difference from the supply. The neutral wire completes the circuit. The earth wire is a safety wire to stop the appliance becoming live.

The potential difference between the live wire and earth (0 V) is about 230 V. The neutral wire is at, or close to, earth potential (0 V). The earth wire is at 0 V, it only carries a current if there is a fault.

Students should be able to explain:

- that a live wire may be dangerous even when a switch in the mains circuit is open
- the dangers of providing any connection between the live wire and earth.

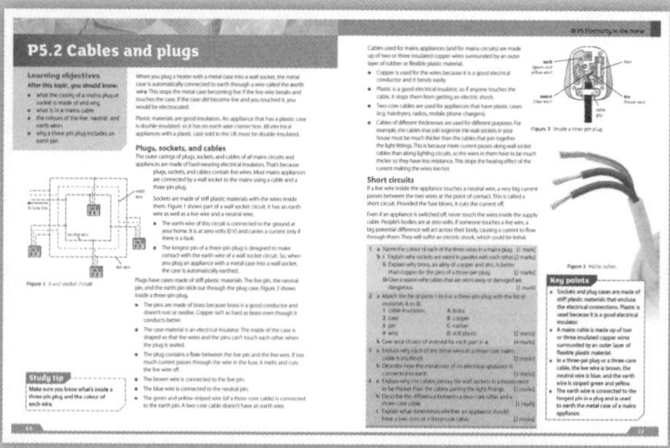
P5.2 Cables and plugs

WS 1.5

Aiming for	Outcome	Checkpoint	
		Question	**Activity**
Aiming for GRADE 4 ↓	Identify the live, neutral, and earth wires in a three-pin plug.	End of chapter 2	Main
	Identify the key components of a typical three-pin plug and socket.	2	Main
	Identify simple and obvious hazards in electrical wiring.	1	Main, Plenary 2
Aiming for GRADE 6 ↓	Discuss the choices of materials used in cables and plugs in terms of their physical and electrical properties.	1, 2	Starter 2, Main, Plenary 1
	Describe why a short circuit inside a device presents a hazard.	3	Main
	Identify a variety of electrical hazards associated with plugs and sockets.	1	Plenary 2
Aiming for GRADE 8 ↓	Explain when there will be a current in the live, neutral, and earth wires of an appliance.	4	Main
	Discuss in detail the hazards associated with poor electrical wiring.	3	Main

Literacy
Students discuss electrical hazards associated with electrical wiring and their potential consequences.

Key words
earth wire, fuse

Practical

Title	Short circuit
Equipment	6 V battery pack or power supply, 6 V bulb and holder, connecting leads, crocodile clips, heat-resistant mat, very thin nichrome or constantan wire
Overview of method	Connect the bulb and battery, showing it illuminated. Use the crocodile clips to carefully connect the wire in parallel with the bulb. The wire will become very hot and could melt.
Safety considerations	Place the apparatus on the heat-resistant mat, and do not touch the wire.

Starter	Support/Extend	Resources
Mystery object (5 min) Place a mains plug in a bag and ask one student to describe it to the rest of the class but only using shape and texture. This can be made more difficult by using a continental plug.		
Material sorting (10 min) Give each group of students a bag containing a range of materials and ask them to sort the materials in any way they wish. They must explain how they sorted them to other student groups in terms of the properties. Ensure that sorting criteria include conductors, insulators, hard, and flexible.	**Support:** Provide a list of properties to use during the sorting process.	
Main	**Support/Extend**	**Resources**
Plugs, cables, and short circuits (40 min) Show the students appliances with three-pin plugs (do not use loose plugs without devices connected). The students discuss the choices of materials and physical design of the pins and socket. Recap the purpose of each of the three wires.		**Activity:** Plugs, cables, and short circuits
Show partially stripped three-core and two-core cables and discuss the materials and design. Compare these to the leads used in low-voltage experiments. Students need to understand that thick cables are less likely to overheat than thin ones. Demonstrate the practical and discuss what would happen if the wire was in contact with flammable materials.	**Extend:** Emphasise the heating effect and the higher resistance of thin wires in this discussion, and ask students to suggest an explanation.	
Plenary	**Support/Extend**	**Resources**
Materials summary (5 min) Students make a table listing the parts of a plug and cable, the materials used, and the reasons for those choices. This should be centred on ideas about good conductors and insulators along with flexibility or rigidity.		
Wonky wiring (10 min) Students use the interactive to match the colour of a wire's insulation with what pin of a plug it is attached to. They then complete a paragraph to describe the hazards associated with plugs and sockets.	**Support:** Ask students to match known problems with particular pictures of plugs.	**Interactive:** Wonky wiring
Homework		
Students complete the WebQuest where they research plug designs from around the world, discussing which they think is the safest and/or best design.	**Extend:** Expect justification of shapes and materials.	**WebQuest:** Plugs

kerboodle

A Kerboodle highlight for this lesson is **Bump up your grade: Mains electricity**. Refer to the **Content map** on Kerboodle for a full list of resources and assessment.

P5.3 Electrical power and potential difference

AQA spec Link: 2.4.1 Students should be able to explain how the power transfer in any circuit device is related to the potential difference across it and the current through it, and to the energy changes over time:

$$\text{power} = \text{potential difference} \times \text{current} \qquad [P = V\,I]$$

$$\text{power} = (\text{current})^2 \times \text{resistance} \qquad [P = I^2\,R]$$

power P in watts, W; potential difference V in volts, V; current I in amperes, A (amp is acceptable for ampere); resistance R in ohms, Ω

2.4.2 Everyday electrical appliances are designed to bring about energy transfers.

The amount of energy an appliance transfers depends on how long the appliance is switched on for and the power of the appliance.

Work is done when charge flows in a circuit.

The amount of energy transferred by electrical work can be calculated using the equation:

$$\text{energy transferred} = \text{power} \times \text{time} \qquad [E = P\,t]$$

$$\text{energy transferred} = \text{charge flow} \times \text{potential difference} \qquad [E = Q\,V]$$

energy transferred E in joules, J; power P in watts, W; time t in seconds, s; charge flow Q in coulombs, C; potential difference V in volts, V

Students should be able to explain how the power of a circuit device is related to:

- the potential difference across it and the current through it
- the energy transferred over a given time.

Students should be able to describe, with examples, the relationship between the power ratings for domestic electrical appliances and the changes in stored energy when they are in use.

WS 1.2, 1.4

MS 3b, 3c

Aiming for	Outcome	Checkpoint	
		Question	**Activity**
Aiming for GRADE 4	State that the power of a device is the amount of energy transferred by it each second.		Starter 1, Main 1
	Describe the factors that affect the rate of energy transfer by a current in a circuit.		Main 1
	Explain why different fuses are required for different electrical devices in simple terms.	1, 3	Main 2, Plenary 1
Aiming for GRADE 6	Calculate the power of systems.	1, End of chapter 6	Main 1
	Calculate the power of electrical devices.	1, 2	Main 1
	Select an appropriate fuse for a device.	2, End of chapter 4	Main 2, Plenary 2
Aiming for GRADE 8	Measure and compare the power of electrical devices and explain variations in readings.		Main 1
	Calculate the electrical heating caused by resistance.	4, End of chapter 5	Main 2
	Combine a variety of calculations to analyse electrical systems.	4	Main 2

Maths

Students use a range of electrical equations in their analysis of electrical power (3b, 3c).

Literacy

Students describe energy transfer in terms of work done on or by electrons in a current.

Practical

Title	Energy and power
Equipment	power supply (12 V), joulemeter (or ammeter and voltmeter combination), leads and a few appliances that operate at 12 V. The appliances could be a lamp, clocks, a small heater
Overview of method	The students connect the power supply to the appliance along with the joulemeter and determine the electrical power by measuring the energy transfer over one minute. Alternatively, they can connect the ammeter in series and voltmeter in parallel and determine the power rating using the electrical equation power = current × potential difference.
Safety considerations	Ensure that devices do not become hot.

Starter	Support/Extend	Resources
Power (5 min) Can the students give a scientific definition (and an equation) for power? Once a formal definition has been made, ask how this could be connected to electrical current where no force is apparently causing anything to move.	**Support:** Provide a definition and ask students to find an equation that matches the definition.	
Electrical units (10 min) Students use the interactive to match up electrical quantities with their definitions, abbreviations, and units. Include current I (amperes), voltage V (volts), resistance Ω (ohms), power P (watts), and energy (E, joules). Can the students provide any definitions for these units?	**Support:** Frame the activity as a jigsaw puzzle that can be assembled to produce a table of the information.	**Interactive:** Electrical units
Main	**Support/Extend**	**Resources**
Energy and power (25 min) Recap the concept of energy and the power equation that was met when studying mechanical power. The students should try some simple calculations to refresh their understanding. Ask students what factors will affect the rate of energy transfer by a current and then introduce the equation $P = IV$. The practical can be used to support this section. As usual, several example calculations will be required to embed this.	**Extend:** Calculations should include units such as kW, mA, and so on.	**Practical:** Energy and power
Fuses, resistance and heating (15 min) The students should apply the power calculation to select fuses for a variety of devices using the mains p.d. of 230 V. Show how the equations $V = IR$ and $P = IV$ can be combined algebraically, and ask the students to perform some heating calculations based on $P = I^2R$.	**Extend:** Combinations of devices can be used (e.g., through an extension lead) Do not exceed the rating of the extension cable. Link the equation back to all of the heating effects mentioned during fuses and electrical safety in earlier lessons.	**Maths skills:** Electrical power and charge
Plenary	**Support/Extend**	**Resources**
Electrical error (5 min) 'I'm sick of all my stuff fusing; I'm going to put a 13 A fuse in all of my things, so that they'll all keep working.' Ask students to discuss the hazards associated with doing this.		
Match the fuse (10 min) The students need to find the correct fuse for an electrical appliance after being told the power rating. This involves calculating the current and then choosing the fuse that is slightly higher. Use 3 A, 5 A, 13 A, and 30 A fuses.	**Extend:** Ask the students to select fuses for circuits where there are several appliances connected (e.g., a four-socket extension).	
Homework		
The students should perform additional calculations using the equations covered in this lesson.	**Support:** Differentiate the questions by students' ability.	

kerboodle

A Kerboodle highlight for this lesson is **Working scientifically: Are you energy smart?** Refer to the **Content map** on Kerboodle for a full list of resources and assessment.

P5.4 Electrical currents and energy transfer

AQA spec Link: 2.4.1 Students should be able to explain how the power transfer in any circuit device is related to the potential difference across it and the current through it, and to the energy changes over time:

power = potential difference × current $[P = V I]$

power = (current)^2 × resistance $[P = I^2 R]$

power P in watts, W; potential difference V in volts, V; current I in amperes, A (amp is acceptable for ampere); resistance R in ohms, Ω

2.4.2 Everyday electrical appliances are designed to bring about energy transfers.

The amount of energy an appliance transfers depends on how long the appliance is switched on for and the power of the appliance.

Students should be able to describe how different domestic appliances transfer energy from batteries or a.c. mains to the kinetic energy of electric motors or the energy of heating devices.

Work is done when charge flows in a circuit.

The amount of energy transferred by electrical work can be calculated using the equation:

energy transferred = power × time $[E = P t]$

energy transferred = charge flow × potential difference $[E = Q V]$

energy transferred E in joules, J; power P in watts, W; time t in seconds, s; charge flow Q in coulombs, C; potential difference V in volts, V

Students should be able to explain how the power of a circuit device is related to:

- the potential difference across it and the current through it
- the energy transferred over a given time.

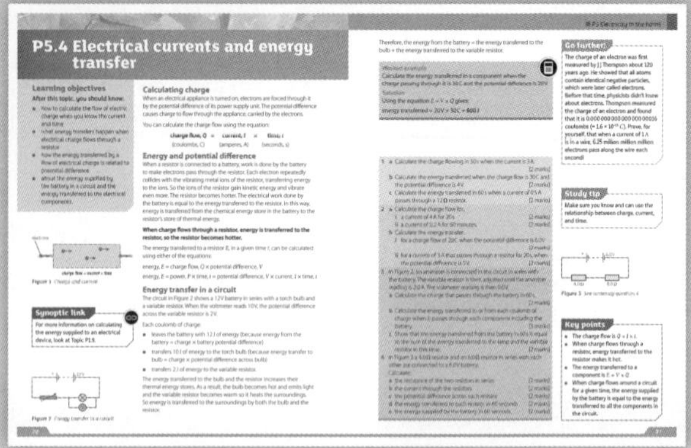

WS 1.2, 1.4

MS 3b, 3c

Aiming for	Outcome	Checkpoint	
		Question	Activity
Aiming for GRADE 4	Describe how an electric current consists of a flow of charge (electrons in a wire).		Main 1
	Identify the factors that affect the energy transfer in a circuit.		Main 2
	State that a battery or power supply provides energy to a current whereas a resistor causes a transfer of energy to the surroundings.		Main 2
Aiming for GRADE 6	Calculate the charge transferred by a current in a given time.	1, 2	Main 1, Homework
	Calculate the energy transferred by a charge passing through a potential difference.	1, 2, 3	Main 2
	Apply the law of conservation of energy in a circuit.	3	Main 2
Aiming for GRADE 8	Perform calculations involving rearrangement of the equations $Q = It$ and $E = VQ$.	2, 4, End of chapter 5	Main 1, Main 2, Homework
	Explain how energy is conserved in terms of current and p.d. during energy transfers by an electric current.	3	Main 2
	Use algebra to combine the equations $Q = It$ and $E = VQ$ to form the relationships $E = VIt$ and $P = IV$.	End of chapter 5	Main 2

Maths
The students will apply the relationships $Q = It$, $E = VQ$, $E = IVt$, and $P = IV$ for a variety of calculations (3b, 3c).

Literacy
Students describe energy transfer by using the various concepts about current in circuits.

Practical

Title	The power of lamps
Equipment	12 V or 6 V lamp, power supply variable resistor, ammeter, voltmeter
Overview of method	The students use the variable resistor to gradually increase the current in the lamp whilst measuring the current in it and p.d. across it. They compare changes in these values to the brightness of the lamp.
Safety considerations	The lamp may become hot – allow time for cooling.

Starter	Support/Extend	Resources
Current and p.d. rules (5 min) Ask the students to describe the rules for current and potential difference in series and parallel circuits.	**Extend:** Students should also describe the idea of conservation of energy.	
Energy transfer (10 min) How many electrical appliances can the students describe energy transfers for? The students can also estimate the electrical efficiency of the appliances after they are clear about which of the energy pathways are useful.	**Support:** Provide simple appliances and possible starting points for the diagrams.	
Main	**Support/Extend**	**Resources**
Charge and current (15 min) Show a simulation or model of an electric current and discuss the movement of electrons around the circuit. Ensure that students understand that the charge is conserved throughout the circuit. Introduce the equation $Q = It$ and ask the students to perform a few calculations with it.		
The power of lamps (25 min) Use the idea of a potential difference to describe energy transfer when charges pass through a resistor. Support this with measurement of the current and p.d. for a lamp with increasing brightness, as described in the practical, so that the students can relate the two factors to energy transfer.	**Extend:** Discuss the similar equation about energy provided *to* the charges (charge field) by a power supply such as a battery.	**Practical:** The power of lamps
Plenary	**Support/Extend**	**Resources**
Electrical spelling (5 min) Hold a spelling competition about electrical words using mini-whiteboards.		
Electric crossword (10 min) Interactive where students complete a crossword with answers based on the key words of the topics covered so far.	**Extend:** Give the students the completed crossword and ask them to write clues.	**Interactive:** Electric crossword
Homework		
Students should complete a range of electrical calculations based on the equations from the chapter so far.	**Support:** Differentiate the level of the questions according to students' ability.	

kerboodle

A Kerboodle highlight for this lesson is **Extension sheet: Electrical power.** Refer to the **Content map** on Kerboodle for a full list of resources and assessment.

P5.5 Appliances and efficiency

AQA spec Link: 2.4.2 Everyday electrical appliances are designed to bring about energy transfers.

The amount of energy an appliance transfers depends on how long the appliance is switched on for and the power of the appliance.

Students should be able to describe how different domestic appliances transfer energy from batteries or a.c. mains to the kinetic energy of electric motors or the energy of heating devices.

Work is done when charge flows in a circuit.

The amount of energy transferred by electrical work can be calculated using the equation:

energy transferred = power × time $[E = P\,t]$

energy transferred = charge flow × potential difference $[E = Q\,V]$

energy transferred E in joules, J; power P in watts, W; time t in seconds, s; charge flow Q in coulombs, C; potential difference V in volts, V

Students should be able to explain how the power of a circuit device is related to:

- the potential difference across it and the current through it
- the energy transferred over a given time.

Students should be able to describe, with examples, the relationship between the power ratings for domestic electrical appliances and the changes in stored energy when they are in use.

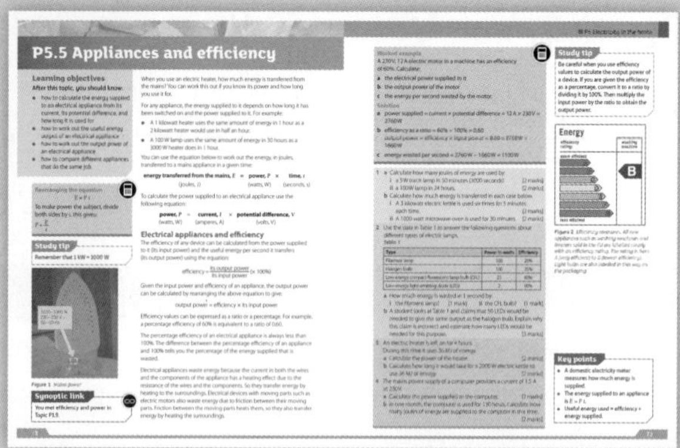
P5.5 Appliances and efficiency

WS 1.4, 1.2

MS 3b, 3c

Aiming for	Outcome	Checkpoint	
		Question	**Activity**
Aiming for GRADE 4 ↓	Describe the factors that affect the cost of using various electrical devices.		Main 2
	Calculate energy transfer in joules.	1	Main 1
	State that energy transfer can be measured in kilowatt-hours.		Main 1
Aiming for GRADE 6 ↓	Calculate energy transfer in kilowatt-hours.	1, 2, End of chapter 4	Main 1
	Convert between efficiencies stated in percentages and those stated in decimal forms.		Main 2
	Calculate the power rating of a device from the energy transferred and the time of operation.	3	Main 1, Main 2
Aiming for GRADE 8 ↓	Convert between relevant units during calculations of energy transfer.		Starter 2, Main 1
	Analyse the use of a variety of electrical devices to determine their costs of operation.	4, End of chapter 4	Main 2
	Compare a range of electrical devices in terms of efficiency using calculations to support any conclusions.	2	Main 2, Plenary 1

Maths

Students calculate the energy transferred by a device and the cost of operation by using data from meter readings and electricity bills. Some students may convert between the units joule and kilowatt-hour (3b, 3c).

Literacy

Students discuss the nature of the units joule and kilowatt-hour and their use in a variety of situations. Students also discuss the idea of cost.

Starter	Support/Extend	Resources
Multiple purchase (5 min) Ask the students to work out the unit cost of an everyday object from a bill (e.g., how much a chocolate bar costs when it is bought in a pack of five for £1.20).	**Extend:** Include special offers such as buy two get one free.	
Conversion factors (10 min) Ask students to convert between some factors such as converting four days into hours then seconds, three miles into kilometres, and so on. Discuss why people use different units for the same quantity.	**Support:** Focus on the conversion of seconds into hours and vice versa.	
Main	**Support/Extend**	**Resources**
Electrical energy transfer (25 min) Replace earlier units with kilowatts as the base for power and hours for time to show that the values can be simpler for everyday devices. Ensure the students understand that the kilowatt-hour is just a different unit for energy, and show them how many joules the kWh represents. The students should try some simple calculations using the kWh to reinforce learning. Recap the energy and power equation ($E = Pt$), finding the energy transferred in joules but use larger values such as 200 W and 40 minutes. Show that using this system can produce large numbers that are difficult to understand. Discuss the idea that using kilowatts and hours as units may be better in some circumstances.	**Support:** Provide a simple calculation frame to develop students' skills. **Extend:** Students should try calculations that involve conversion between units.	**Activity:** Electrical energy transfer
Electrical efficiency (15 min) Recap on the concept of efficiency and the ideas of useful and less useful energy transfers. Describe the power version of the efficiency equation and ask the students to apply this equation to a range of calculations. Students should also discuss the reasons for inefficiency – heating by the current and frictional forces.	**Support:** Show the students some efficiency band labels. **Extend:** Students should also carry out calculations involving rearrangement of the equation.	
Plenary	**Support/Extend**	**Resources**
Comparing kettles (10 min) Provide the students with data about UK and USA kettles including voltage, current, and operating time. Students identify which kettle is the most efficient. They then complete a paragraph to describe what makes electrical appliances efficient.	**Extend:** Include the volume of water each model of kettle can boil to add extra demand to the question.	**Interactive:** Comparing kettles
Big bill (5 min) Ask the students to verify their school's electricity bill or a simplified version of it.	**Extend:** Include data on any standing charge.	
Homework		
The students should produce a summary or visual map of the information about current electricity, mains electricity, and electrical energy calculations. This has been quite a lot of information, so encourage the use of small diagrams on the map to enhance the readability.	**Support:** Provide a partially completed map for students to finish.	

kerboodle

A Kerboodle highlight for this lesson is **Literacy sheet: Electricity**. Refer to the **Content map** on Kerboodle for a full list of resources and assessment.

P5 Electricity in the home

Overview of P5 Electricity in the home

In this chapter the students have compared direct and alternating currents in terms of current direction. An oscilloscope has been used to analyse changes in the potential difference that causes the current and to measure the peak voltage, period and frequency of a low voltage sinusoidal a.c. signal.

The students have described the UK mains supply and the wires used within it, outlining the National Grid and the high voltages associated with it. Understanding of mains circuits, including the function of the neutral and earth wires, has been applied to three pin plugs and a simple ring-main. The choice of materials used for construction of mains circuits such as wires, cables, and plugs was discussed along with the need for a fuse to prevent overheating and insulation for protection from short circuits.

Students have mathematically analysed circuits to determine the power supplied by a current and the relationship between power and the resistance of components. This was linked back to the charge transfer in a circuit and the concept of electrical heating as charges move within or through components.

Finally, students have considered the importance of efficiency within mains powered electrical devices, linking this concept back to energy transfer by a current and to the simplified system of energy efficiency ratings used when considering the purchase of an appliance.

You can find additional support for the maths skills covered in this chapter on **MyMaths**, including recognising and using expressions in decimal form, using an appropriate number of significant figures, changing the subject of an equation, translating information between graphical and numeric form.

For this chapter, the following assessments are available on Kerboodle:

P5 Checkpoint quiz: Electricity in the home
P5 Progress quiz: Electricity in the home 1
P5 Progress quiz: Electricity in the home 2
P5 On your marks: Electricity in the home
P5 Exam-style questions and mark scheme: Electricity in the home

Checkpoint follow up lesson

A student's route through this lesson can be determined using the Checkpoint assessment. Percentage pass marks are supplied in the Checkpoint teacher notes.

For each successive route through it is assumed that the student can perform to their current route as well as previous routes. For example, students working at Aiming for 6 are assumed to be secure in Aiming for 4 knowledge and understanding and working towards achieving all the learning outcomes for Aiming for 6.

	Aiming for 4	Aiming for 6	Aiming for 8
Learning outcomes	Describe the purpose of fuses, earthing, circuit breakers, and plastic casings in electrical safety.	Explain the purpose of fuses, earthing, circuit breakers, and plastic casings in electrical safety.	Explain the purpose of fuses, earthing, circuit breakers, and plastic casings in electrical safety, and how a circuit breaker works.
	Calculate power, charge flow, energy transferred from the mains, and efficiency.	Describe the link between charge, potential difference, current, time, energy and power and do calculations involving those quantities.	Explain the link between charge, potential difference, current, time, energy and power, and do more complex calculations involving those quantities.
		Calculate peak potential difference and frequency from measurements of a trace on an oscilloscope screen.	Take measurements of peak potential difference and frequency from a trace on an oscilloscope screen.
Starter	**Mains danger (5 min)** Show an image of a kitchen with a range of appliances in it. Discuss what mains electricity is, and how large currents can be fatal. Ask students to 'snowball' ideas for preventing that happening when you are in the kitchen. Make a list of the words/phrases on the board (to use in the bingo later). **Efficient or not? (5 min)** Give groups a large piece of paper and ask them to draw a line down the middle. On the left they should write down three situations in real life where we use the word efficient. Then ask them to write three sentences using the word 'efficient' as we use it in science.		
Differentiated checkpoint activity	Aiming for 4 students use the Checkpoint follow-up sheet to produce a safety leaflet for primary school students that explains the purpose of fuses, earthing, plastic casing, circuit breakers, and what is inside a plug. They then practise using equations for power, energy, charge, current, and efficiency. The follow-up sheet is highly structured and students should work in pairs with teacher support.	Aiming for 6 students use the Checkpoint follow-up sheet to produce a safety leaflet for primary school students. They do an experiment with lamps that work on the same potential difference but have different powers. They then practise using equations for power, energy, charge, current, and efficiency. The follow-up sheet is fairly structured and students should be aiming to work independently.	Aiming for 8 students use the Checkpoint follow-up sheet to produce a safety leaflet for primary school students. They do an experiment with lamps that work on the same potential difference but have different powers. They practise using equations for power, energy, charge, current, and efficiency, and make estimates of the use of appliances in a year. The follow-up sheet provided minimal support and students should be working independently.
	Kerboodle resource P5 Checkpoint follow up: Aiming for 4, P5 Checkpoint follow up: Aiming for 6, P5 Checkpoint follow up: Aiming for 8		
Plenary	**Safety bingo (10 min)** Give out grids and ask students to make a bingo card with words related to plugs, wiring, and safety from the starter. You may want to add to the list before you start with the colours of the wires, the potential difference of the wires, and so on. Play bingo. **What's the question? (5 min)** Display the rubric for an exam question that asks for a calculation, and ask students to write down the information from the question that they need, as well as the equation. If time allows, students can select a question and answer it. You can select different questions depending on the level at which the students are aiming, or make a set of cards based on the questions and give them to different groups.		
Progression	Students should be able to identify the wires in a plug, explain what they are for, and how fuses work. They should be able to do calculations involving power, potential difference, and kWh, and describe the impact of using more efficient devices. Encourage students to think about explaining the impact of efficient devices on energy bills.	Students should be able to explain the structure of plugs in terms of safety and to identify other ways of protecting appliances and people. They should be able to do a range of calculations involving power, current, potential difference, energy, time, cost and efficiency, and describe the impact of using more efficient devices. Encourage students to think about explaining the impact of efficient devices on energy bills.	Students should be able to describe and explain in detail features that protect appliances and people in terms of mains electricity. They should be able to apply equations involving electrical quantities in a range of situations, and to explain the impact of efficient devices on energy bills. Encourage students to think critically about issues involving efficiency.

P 6 Molecules and matter

6.1 Density

AQA spec Link: 3.1.1 The density of a material is defined by the equation:

$$\text{density} = \frac{\text{mass}}{\text{volume}} \qquad [\rho = \frac{m}{V}]$$

density, ρ, in kilograms per metre cubed, kg/m^3

mass, m, in kilograms, kg

volume, V, in metres cubed, m^3

Required practical: Use appropriate apparatus to make and record the measurements needed to determine the densities of regular and irregular solid objects and liquids. Volume should be determined from the dimensions of regularly shaped objects, and by a displacement technique for irregularly shaped objects. Dimensions to be measured using appropriate apparatus such as a ruler, micrometer, or Vernier callipers.

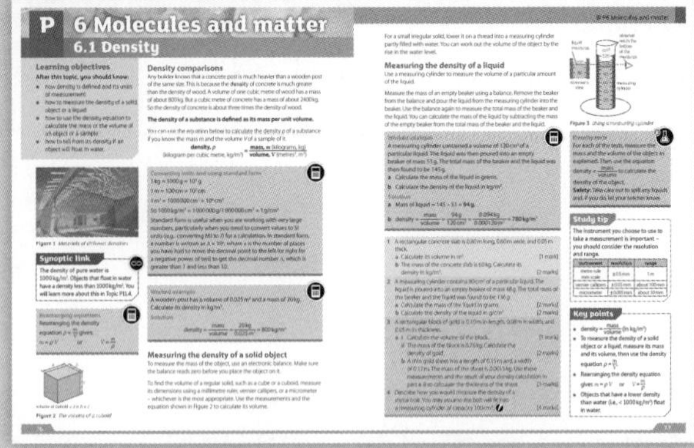

MS 1a, 1b, 1c, 3b, 3c, 5c

Aiming for	Outcome	Checkpoint	
		Question	Activity
Aiming for GRADE 4	Describe density as a property of a material and not a particular object.		Starter 1, Main
	State that the density of a material is the mass per unit volume.		Main
	Calculate the volume of some regular shapes and the density of materials, with support.	1, 3	Main
Aiming for GRADE 6	Explain why some materials will float on water.		Starter 2
	Calculate the density of materials.	1, 3	Main
	Measure the density of a solid and a liquid.	2	Main
Aiming for GRADE 8	Use the density equation in a wide variety of calculations.	3, End of chapter 1, 2	Main, Plenary 1
	Use appropriate significant figures in final answers when measuring density.		Main
	Evaluate in detail the experimental measurement of density, accounting for errors in measurements.		Main

Maths

Students calculate the volume and density of a range of objects (5c).

Literacy

Students use clear scientific language to compare the properties of a variety of materials in a fair way.

Key words

density

Required practical

Title	Density tests – solids
Equipment	variety of regularly shaped objects (cubes, cylinders, etc.), ruler, top-pan balance
Overview of method	The students measure the dimensions of the object and calculate the volume. They then measure the mass and calculate the density.
Safety considerations	Do not use massive objects.

Title	Density tests – liquids
Equipment	measuring cylinders, beakers, top-pan balance, variety of liquids (water, oils, etc.)
Overview of method	Students measure the mass of the cylinder or beaker, add a measured volume of the liquid, and find the increase in mass. These values are used to find the density.
Safety considerations	Clear up spillages immediately.

Starter	Support/Extend	Resources
Material properties (10 min) Interactive where students match a list of material properties with its description (e.g., conductivity: How good a material is it at conducting electricity). Students then identify how the properties are measured.	**Extend:** Ask students to describe how some of the properties could be measured.	**Interactive:** Material properties
Cocktail (5 min) Pour some vegetable oil into a beaker partly full of water. Ask why the oil floats.	**Extend:** Add several immiscible liquids.	
Main	**Support/Extend**	**Resources**
Density tests (40 min) Students should analyse some materials and describe their properties, particularly how heavy they feel. They rank the materials in terms of heaviness. Discuss whether this ranking is fair (some objects are larger than others) and introduce the idea of density. Use the Maths skills interactive to provide students with some mass and volume data to calculate the density of a few sample materials using the equation. Discuss units of kg/m^3 and g/cm^3.	**Extend:** Students should use rearranged versions of the equation.	**Required practical:** Density tests **Maths skills:** Density
Students then carry out the practical to measure the density of some samples. They should focus on the resolution of the instruments and the appropriate use of significant figures in their answers.	**Support:** Provide the equations for volumes and some example calculations. **Extend:** Students should use the resolution of the instruments to estimate the uncertainty in their overall density answers.	
Plenary	**Support/Extend**	**Resources**
Irregular solids (10 min) Students explain a way of finding the density of a rock or other irregular object.	**Support:** Provide a picture showing how this may be done and ask the students to explain it.	
Smoke signals (5 min) Light a candle and blow it out after a few seconds. The students should explain why the smoke rises. Link this to the idea of gasses floating on top of each other due to density differences.		
Homework		
The students should explain how a ship, constructed of a dense metal, can float on water. They can include data on real ship masses and volumes.		

kerboodle

A Kerboodle highlight for this lesson is **Extension sheet: Solving density puzzles.** Refer to the **Content map** on Kerboodle for a full list of resources and assessment.

P6.2 States of matter

AQA spec Link: 3.1.1 The particle model can be used to explain:

- the different states of matter
- differences in density.

Students should be able to recognise/draw simple diagrams to model the difference between solids, liquids, and gases.

Students should be able to explain the differences in density between the different states of matter in terms of the arrangement of atoms or molecules.

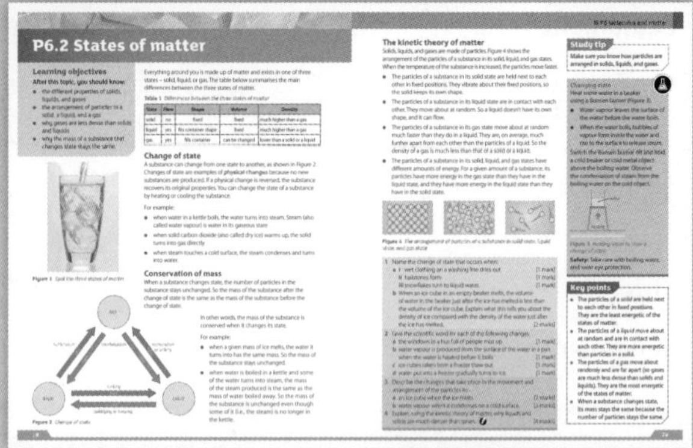
P6.2 States of matter

Aiming for	Outcome	Checkpoint	
		Question	Activity
Aiming for GRADE 4	Describe the simple properties of solids, liquids, and gases.		Starter 1, Main 1
	Name the changes of state.	1, 2	Main 1
	State that there are changes in stores of energy associated with a material when its temperature is increased.	3	Main 1
Aiming for GRADE 6	Describe the arrangement of the particles in a solid, liquid, and gas.	3	Main 1, Main 2, Plenary 2
	Explain the behaviour of a material in terms of the arrangement of particles within it.	3, End of chapter 3	Main 1, Main 2
	Describe the changes in behaviour of the particles in a material during changes of state.	3	Main 1, Main 2
Aiming for GRADE 8	Describe the forces acting between particles in a solid, liquid, and gas.	3	Main 2, Plenary 1, Plenary 2
	Describe the changes in the energy of individual particles during changes of state.	4, End of chapter 3	Main 2
	Explain in detail why the density of a material changes during a change of state, using a particle model.	4, End of chapter 3	Main 2

Literacy

Students use a particle model to describe the changes of state and properties of a material.

Key words
physical changes

Practical

Title	Changing state
Equipment	Bunsen burner, tripod, heat-resistant mat, gauze, beaker (250 cm^3), icy cold spoon or something similar, ice (optional)
Overview of method	Students heat the water in a beaker using a Bunsen burner. They observe the changes of state and think about the idea of changes in energy and particle behaviour. Alternatively, half fill a beaker with ice and heat with a Bunsen burner to demonstrate melting then boiling.
Safety considerations	Clear up spillages immediately. The apparatus and water will become very hot.

Title	Kinetic theory
Equipment	plastic tray, marbles, ping-pong balls or other small balls
Overview of method	Place a few balls in the tray and allow them to roll around – this is similar to a gas – the particles can move freely and are generally far apart. Almost fill the bottom layer of the tray – the particles can still move a bit, but there are few gaps between them, similar to a liquid. Finally, fill the tray so that the particles cannot move – they are closely packed together in a manner similar to the particles in a solid.
Safety considerations	Ensure that no marbles, or similar, are left on the floor.

Starter	Support/Extend	Resources
State the facts (5 min) Ask students to name the different changes of state and say whether energy is gained or dissipated by substances during these changes and where this energy is transferred from or to.	**Support:** Provide a diagram to add the labels to.	
Property match (10 min) Interactive where students sort the properties according to whether they describe solids, liquids, and gases. They then match descriptions of other properties – such as density, fluidity, and compressibility – with solids, liquids, and gases.	**Extend:** Challenge students to give explanations of these properties in terms of particle arrangement and movement.	**Interactive:** Property match
Main	**Support/Extend**	**Resources**
Changing state (40 min) Revise Key Stage 3 work by describing the three states of matter, using water as a simple example, using simple demonstrations in your explanations if appropriate. Ensure that the key properties of the three states are understood and that the concept of conservation of mass is covered. Model the particles of the three states using small balls and a plastic tray. Place a few balls in the tray and allow them to roll around – this is similar to a gas – the particles can move freely and are generally far apart. Almost fill the bottom layer of the tray – the particles can still move a bit, but there are few gaps between them, similar to a liquid. Finally, fill the tray so that the particles cannot move – they are closely packed together in a manner similar to the particles in a solid. Describe the changes in the forces between the particles. The students should use the model to explain the behaviours of solids, liquids, and gases.	**Support:** Demonstrate the conservation of mass when ice melts.	**Activity:** Changing state
Plenary	**Support/Extend**	**Resources**
Particle behaviour (5 min) Students could act out the states of matter. Ask them to behave like particles in a solid, a liquid, and a gas.		
Particle diagrams (10 min) Ask students to make particle diagrams. Provide them with a lot of discs from a hole-punch and let them create a diagram representing the three states and the transitions between them.	**Extend:** Ask student to discuss the limitations of these simple visual representations.	
Homework		
Students can research the evidence for the particle model, including Brownian motion.	**Support:** Provide students with observations of Brownian motion (or from a smoke cell) and ask them to complete a cloze exercise explaining these observations.	

kerboodle

A Kerboodle highlight for this lesson is **Working scientifically: Does melting ice expand?** Refer to the **Content map** on Kerboodle for a full list of resources and assessment.

P6.3 Changes of state

AQA spec Link: 3.1.2 Students should be able to describe how, when substances change state (melt, freeze, boil, evaporate, condense, or sublimate), mass is conserved.

Changes of state are physical changes which differ from chemical changes because the material recovers it original properties if the change is reversed.

3.2.3 Students should be able to interpret heating and cooling graphs that include changes of state.

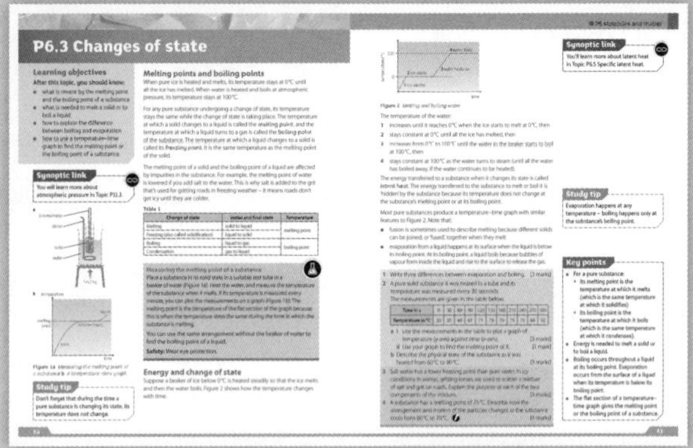

MS 4c

Aiming for	Outcome	Checkpoint	
		Question	Activity
Aiming for GRADE 4	State that the melting point of a substance is the temperature at which it changes from a solid to a liquid and vice versa.	1	Main
	State that the boiling point of a substance is the temperature at which it changes from a liquid to a gas and vice versa.	1	Main
	Describe the process of melting and boiling.	1, End of chapter 3	Main
Aiming for GRADE 6	State that the melting and boiling points of a pure substance are fixed.	3	Main
	Use the term 'latent heat' to describe the energy gained by a substance during heating for which there is no change in temperature.		Main
	Find the melting or boiling point of a substance by using a graphical technique.	2	Main, Plenary 1
Aiming for GRADE 8	Describe how the melting points and boiling points of a substance can be changed.	3	Main, Plenary 1
	Describe in detail the behaviour of the particles during changes of state.	4, End of chapter 3	Main
	Evaluate data produced by a heating experiment to discuss the reproducibility of the measurement of a melting point.		Main, Plenary 2

Maths
Students plot graphs of experimental data and identify their features (4c).

Literacy
Students describe the behaviour of materials and the features of a graph.

Key words
melting point, boiling point, freezing point, latent heat

Practical

Title	Measuring the melting point of a substance
Equipment	heating apparatus, stopwatch, 250 cm^3 beaker, stirrer, water, boiling tube containing a thermometer in solid wax or salicylic acid
Overview of method	The students set up the apparatus as shown in the student book and heat the water. They stir the water and measure the temperature of the solid every 30 seconds until it has completely melted.
Safety considerations	Wear eye protection, and clear up spillages immediately.

Starter	Support/Extend	Resources
Water properties (5 min) Ask the students for the melting and boiling points for water. How can these be altered? **How hot?** (10 min) Provide the students with some important temperatures and ask them to match them to objects or changes (e.g., boiling point of water, temperature of the surface of the Sun).	**Extend:** Select more obscure temperatures to discuss.	
Main	**Support/Extend**	**Resources**
Measuring the melting point of a substance (40 min) Recap the changes in the behaviour of the particles as a material melts and then as it boils. Ask the students to suggest why, when the melting point is reached, all of the substance does not melt at once. The students carry out the practical and produce a temperature–time graph. The region in which the state changes (no increase in temperature) should be clearly identified. Discuss the identified region, emphasising that energy is still being transferred to the substance. This increase in the energy store is not obvious, hence the term latent heat. The terms fusion, boiling, and evaporation should be introduced.	**Support:** A simpler experiment measuring the boiling point of water can be used. Students use the equipment and method from Topic P6.2, measuring the temperature every 30 seconds until it boils, and for 3 minutes after (noting that there is no further increase in temperature). **Extend:** Discuss changes in melting and boiling points when the substances are not pure (e.g., salted water). Students should compare results to help evaluate the reproducibility of the measurements.	**Practical:** Measuring the melting point of a substance
Plenary	**Support/Extend**	**Resources**
Boiling at altitude (10 min) Show the students a graph of the boiling point of water compared with altitude. Students use the interactive to complete a description of this relationship and an explanation of why the boiling point changes. **Melting point** (5 min) Provide the students with a variety of measurements of the melting point for a substance and ask them to find the mean and range.	**Extend:** Students should use the data to discuss the reproducibility of the experiment and the precision and accuracy of their answer.	**Interactive:** Boiling at altitude
Homework		
Students complete the WebQuest where they research unusual materials. These include materials with extreme density values, melting points, and boiling points, and materials that cannot be easily categorised as solid or liquid.		**WebQuest:** Unusual materials

kerboodle

A Kerboodle highlight for this lesson is **Literacy skills: Changes of state**. Refer to the **Content map** on Kerboodle for a full list of resources and assessment.

P6.4 Internal energy

AQA spec Link: 3.2.1 Energy is stored inside a system by the particles (atoms and molecules) that make up the system. This is called internal energy.

Internal energy is the total kinetic energy and potential energy of all the particles (atoms and molecules) that make up a system.

Heating changes the energy stored within the system by increasing the energy of the particles that make up the system. This either raises the temperature of the system or produces a change of state.

3.2.2 If the temperature of the system increases, the increase in temperature depends on the mass of the substance heated, the type of material, and the energy input to the system.

The following equation applies:

change in thermal energy = mass × specific heat capacity × temperature change

$[\Delta E = m\, c\, \Delta\theta]$

change in thermal energy ΔE in joules, J

mass m in kilograms, kg

specific heat capacity c in joules per kilogram per degree Celsius, J/kg °C

temperature change $\Delta\theta$ in degrees Celsius, °C.

The specific heat capacity of a substance is the amount of energy required to raise the temperature of one kilogram of the substance by one degree Celsius.

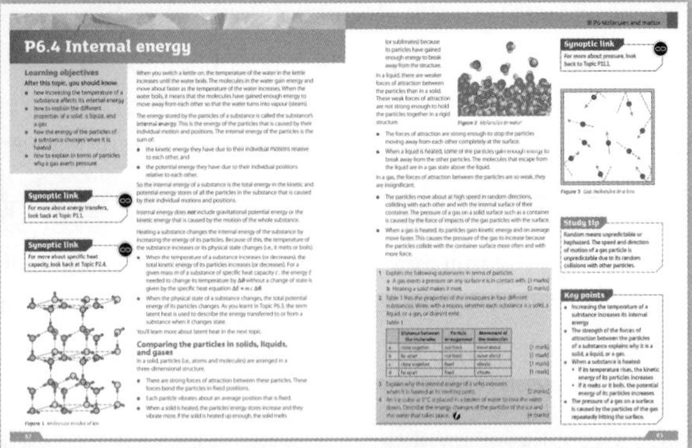

MS 1a, 3b, 3c, 3d

Aiming for	Outcome	Checkpoint	
		Question	Activity
Aiming for GRADE 4	State that the internal energy of a system increases as it is heated.		Starter 1, Main 1
	Identify which changes of state are related to increases in internal energy and which are related to decreases.		Main 1
	Outline the behaviour of particles in solids, liquids, and gases.	2, End of chapter 7	Main 2
Aiming for GRADE 6	Describe how the internal energy of an object can be increased by heating.		Main 1
	Describe how the behaviour of particles changes as the energy of a system increases.	1, 2, End of chapter 7	Main 2
	Describe the energy changes by heating between objects within the same system.	4	Main 2, Plenary 2
Aiming for GRADE 8	Use the concepts of kinetic and potential energy to explain changes in internal energy.		Main 1
	Describe the changes in the size of intermolecular forces during changes of state.	3, End of chapter 7	Main 2

Maths
Students calculate the energy changes associated with heating a material (3b, 3c, 3d).

Literacy
Students apply the particle model to describe changes in the internal energy of an object as it is heated.

Key words
internal energy

Practical

Title	Internal energy
Equipment	heating apparatus, 500 cm^3 beaker, water and crushed ice, thermometer
Overview of method	Place the iced water in the beaker and gradually heat it whilst discussing changes in the internal energy.
Safety considerations	Wear eye protection, and clear up spillages immediately. The apparatus will become very hot.

Starter	Support/Extend	Resources
Specific heat capacity (5 min) Introduce the equation $\Delta E = m\,c\,\Delta\theta$, then students complete the interactive where they work through some example calculations.	**Extend:** Use non-base units such as grams.	**Interactive:** Specific heat capacity
Convection (10 min) Pour some hot water into a beaker and add ice cubes that have food colouring in them. Ask the students to describe the processes taking place.	**Support:** Students can card sort the stages of a convection current.	
Main	**Support/Extend**	**Resources**
Internal energy (20 min) Begin heating the beaker of iced water and discuss the energy transfers involved. Initially there will be no temperature increase, allowing discussion of the latent heat and the repositioning of the bonds of the particles. As the ice melts and the temperature starts to increase, begin to describe the changes in motion for the particles. By the time the water is boiling, the students should have a good understanding of internal energy.	**Extend:** Discuss the processes causing temperature change throughout the liquid – convection and any dissipation to the surroundings.	**Activity:** Internal energy
Particle behaviour (20 min) Describe the behaviour of the particles in a solid, liquid, and gas with a focus on the forces between the particles. Describe the attraction between individual particles and how the motion changes. Additional details about the behaviour of gasses will be covered in the next few lessons.	**Support:** Provide a table for students to summarise the forces and particle separation.	
Plenary	**Support/Extend**	**Resources**
Convection revisited (10 min) Repeat the second starter, but ask the students to describe the changes in particle behaviour for the ice.		
What forces? (5 min) Can the students describe which forces are responsible for attraction and repulsion between molecules and atoms?	**Support:** Students can match up key terms describing the behaviour of atoms and molecules.	
Homework		
The students can describe energy changes in a variety of systems to revise their understanding of energy changes.	**Support:** Provide examples such as making a cup of tea or watching television.	

kerboodle

A Kerboodle highlight for this lesson is **Working scientifically: Assumptions in models.** Refer to the **Content map** on Kerboodle for a full list of resources and assessment.

P6.5 Specific latent heat

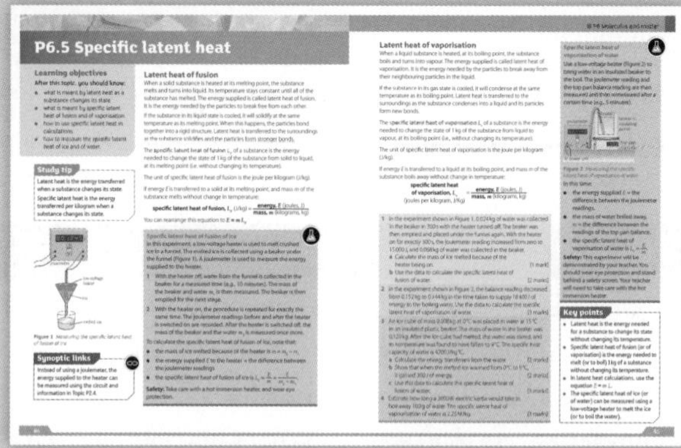

MS 1a, 3b, 3c, 3d, 4a

AQA spec Link: 3.2.3 If a change of state happens:

The energy needed for a substance to change state is called latent heat. When a change of state occurs, the energy supplied changes the energy stored (internal energy) but not the temperature.

The specific latent heat of a substance is the amount of energy required to change the state of one kilogram of the substance with no change in temperature.

energy for a change of state = mass × specific latent heat

$[E = m\ L]$

energy E in joules, J

mass m in kilograms, kg

specific latent heat L in joules per kilogram, J/kg

Specific latent heat of fusion – change of state from solid to liquid

Specific latent heat of vaporisation – change of state from liquid to vapour

Students should be able to distinguish between specific heat capacity and specific latent heat.

Aiming for	Outcome	Checkpoint	
		Question	**Activity**
Aiming for GRADE 4 ↓	State that heating a material will increase its internal energy.		Main
	Describe energy changes during melting and vaporisation.		Main
	Measure the latent heat of vaporisation for water.		Main
Aiming for GRADE 6 ↓	Describe the changes in particle bonding during changes of state.		Main
	Calculate the latent heat of fusion and latent heat of vaporisation for a substance.	2, End of chapter 4, 5	Main, Plenary 2
	Measure the latent heat of fusion for water.		Main
Aiming for GRADE 8 ↓	Perform a variety of calculations based on the latent heat equation.	4, End of chapter 4, 5	Main
	Combine a variety of equations to solve problems involving heating.	1, 2, 3	Main, Plenary 2
	Evaluate the reproducibility of a measurement of latent heat based on collated data.		Main

Maths
Students use the latent heat equation to solve a variety of problems (1a, 3b, 3c, 3d).

Literacy
Students use the particle model to discuss changes in internal energy.

Key words
specific latent heat of fusion, specific latent heat of vaporisation

Practical

Title	Specific latent heat of fusion of ice
Equipment	joulemeter, low-voltage electrical heating element and power supply, beaker, ice, funnel
Overview of method	Put a known mass of crushed ice into a funnel and secure over a beaker. Put the heating element of a low-voltage heater into the crushed ice but do not turn it on. Leave the experiment for a set period of time (e.g., 10 minutes) then measure the mass of water collected in the beaker. Repeat the procedure, this time with the heater on and the joulemeter measuring the energy supplied to the heater.
Safety considerations	Wear eye protection, and clear up spillages immediately.

Title	Measuring the specific latent heat of vaporisation of water
Equipment	joulemeter, low-voltage electrical heating element and power supply, beaker, water, a top-pan balance
Overview of method	Wrap a beaker with some insulating material. Attach a low-voltage heater to a joulemeter and place the heater into the beaker of water. Place on a top-pan balance. Take a reading from the joulemeter and top-pan balance. Switch on the heater. After five minutes, take another reading from the joulemeter and top-pan balance.
Safety considerations	Wear eye protection, and clear up spillages immediately.

Starter	Support/Extend	Resources
Thermal conduction (10 min) Students should describe the process of thermal conduction in solids (metals and non-metals).	**Support:** Provide a diagram for the students to annotate.	
Puddle puzzle (5 min) Interactive where students complete an explanation to explain why a puddle of water disappears over time.	**Extend:** Ask which factors affect the rate and why.	**Interactive:** Puddle puzzle
Main	**Support/Extend**	**Resources**
Specific latent heat (40 min) Recap the energy changes during the heating of a solid substance, with an emphasis on the breaking of bonds during melting. Define the latent heat as the energy change required for 1 kg of a substance to melt (with no change in temperature), pointing out that this is different for different substances. Students complete the Maths skills interactive to practice using the equation.	**Support:** Show several example calculations before asking the students to perform one.	**Maths skills:** Latent heat **Practical:** Specific latent heat
Follow a similar method with vaporisation and energy change checking with a simple calculation before moving to the practical.		
Form students into groups and ask them to complete one of the two practicals. They should share data with another group that completed the same experiment to find a mean value for the latent heat. After this they share conclusions with the groups that completed the other practical.	**Support:** The vaporisation experiment is the simpler of the two. **Extend:** Students use the range of results to discuss the reproducibility of the experiment and the uncertainty in the answer.	
Plenary	**Support/Extend**	**Resources**
Overall heating (10 min) Ask the students to solve a problem involving the latent heat and specific heat capacity by finding the energy change when 2 kg of ice at –4 °C is melted.	**Extend:** A similar task involving heating until the water boils can be used.	
A watched kettle (5 min) Ask the students how long a 3.0 kW kettle would take to cause 1.5 kg of water to evaporate.		
Homework		
The students should write an explanation of why evaporation causes cooling of surfaces, for example, sweating.		

kerboodle

A Kerboodle highlight for this lesson is **Bump up your grade: Specific latent heat**. Refer to the **Content map** on Kerboodle for a full list of resources and assessment.

P6.6 Gas pressure and temperature

AQA spec Link: 3.3.1 The molecules of a gas are in constant random motion. The temperature of the gas is related to the average kinetic energy of the molecules.

Changing the temperature of a gas, held at constant volume, changes the pressure exerted by the gas.

Students should be able to:

- explain how the motion of the molecules in a gas is related to both its temperature and its pressure
- explain qualitatively the relation between the temperature of a gas and its pressure at constant volume.

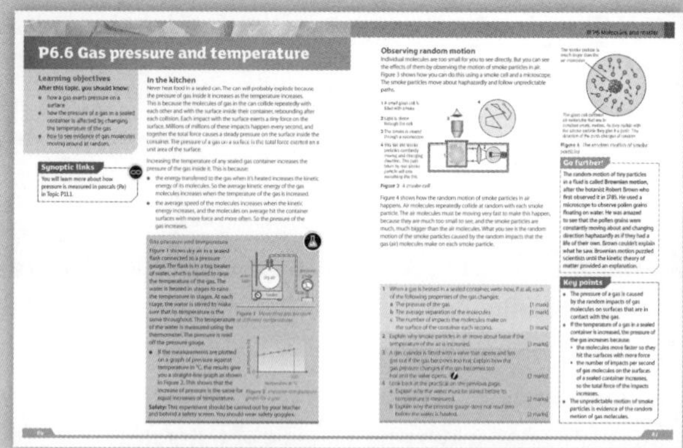

WS 1.2

MS 4b

Aiming for	Outcome	Checkpoint	
		Question	Activity
Aiming for GRADE 4	State that as the temperature of a gas in a sealed container increases, the pressure of the gas increases.	1	Main 1
	Describe a gas as consisting of a large number of rapidly moving particles.		Main 1, Main 2
	Describe pressure as being caused by collisions of gas particles with the walls of its container.	1	Main 1
Aiming for GRADE 6	Describe the behaviour of particles in a gas as the gas is heated.	1	Main 1
	Outline Brownian motion and how this provides evidence for the particle nature of matter.	2	Main 2, Plenary 1
	Describe the relationship between an increase in the temperature of a fixed volume of a gas and the increase in pressure of the gas.	3	Main 1, Plenary 2
Aiming for GRADE 8	Describe the linear relationship between changes in temperature and pressure for a gas.		Main 1
	Explain Brownian motion in terms of particle behaviour and collisions, relating the speeds of smoke particles and air molecules.	2	Main 2
	Describe in detail how the relationship between the pressure of a gas and its temperature can be investigated.	4	Main 1

Maths
Students describe linear relationships between quantities (4b).

Literacy
Students describe the motion of gas particles in detail as part of an explanation of gas pressure.

Practical

Title	Gas pressure and temperature
Equipment	water bath (large beaker of water), round flask, thermometer, heater, pressure gauge
Overview of method	Connect the apparatus as shown in the student book, making sure that the flask is completely submerged. Heat the water gradually, and record the temperature and pressure.
Safety considerations	Do not heat the water above 60 °C. Ensure glass vessels are in good condition and do not have any scratches or chips.

Title	Theory of Brownian motion
Equipment	Brownian smoke cell with integrated light source, low-power microscope with large aperture, power supply, smoke source, pipette
Overview of method	Suck up some smoke from a source with the pipette and blow it into the chamber. Observe the behaviour of the smoke with the microscope. A single smoke cell can be connected to a visualiser so that the whole class can see it at once.
Safety considerations	Take care with the smoke source, and ensure that direct sunlight does not pass through the microscope.

Starter	Support/Extend	Resources
Pressure recap (10 min) Students use the interactive to recap their knowledge of pressure. They carry out some calculations, then complete a paragraph to describe what causes pressure when two surfaces are in contact with one another.	**Extend:** Introduce the idea of forces acting between the individual atoms of the two surfaces.	**Interactive:** Pressure recap
That's a bit random (5 min) Ask the students what the term random means, and discuss how random events can happen.	**Extend:** Ask whether random events are compatible with physical laws.	
Main	**Support/Extend**	**Resources**
Gas pressure and temperature (25 min) Discuss the behaviour of gases and what happens to their particles as they increase in energy through heating. Remind the students of the cause of gas pressure – particle collisions with container walls – and ask what will happen to pressure when temperature increases. Demonstrate the heating of a gas and find the relationship between gas temperature and pressure as outlined in the practical.	**Extend:** Sample data could be provided for students to plot a graph and to determine a pattern.	**Practical:** Gas pressure and temperature
Theory of Brownian motion (15 min) Show Brownian motion with a real smoke cell and discuss the conclusions that can be made using the Working scientifically sheet. Diffusion can also be demonstrated to show the random motion of particles and the gradual spreading effect.	**Support:** Back up any explanation with a simulation of the process. **Extend:** Discuss the relative speeds and masses of the smoke and air particles.	**Working scientifically:** Theory of Brownian motion
Plenary	**Support/Extend**	**Resources**
A random walk (5 min) Students place a counter in the central square of some graph paper. They roll a die (eight-sided ideally) to determine which direction to move the counter. Do this 10 times and compare the final position of the counter with other 'players'.		
Absolute zero (10 min) Show students two pressure–temperature graphs – one with the temperature in kelvin and the other in degrees Celsius. Students discuss why the two graphs are different and under what circumstances temperature is directly proportional to pressure. They then use the data to find the temperature when the pressure reaches zero.	**Extend:** Discuss this state as the lowest possible temperature.	
Homework		
The gas laws were important discoveries – students should find out who discovered them and how these were achieved. Students should also describe the properties of an 'ideal gas' in terms of the particles within it.	**Extend:** Students can describe the ideal gas law, which brings the gas laws together.	

P6.7 Gas pressure and volume

AQA spec Link: 3.3.2 A gas can be compressed or expanded by pressure changes. The pressure produces a net force at right angles to the wall of the gas container (or any surface).

Students should be able to use the particle model to explain how increasing the volume in which a gas is contained, at constant temperature, can lead to a decrease in pressure.

For a fixed mass of gas held at a constant temperature:

$$\text{pressure} \times \text{volume} = \text{constant}$$

$$[p\,V = \text{constant}]$$

pressure p in pascals, Pa
volume V in metres cubed, m^3

Students should be able to calculate the change in the pressure of a gas or the volume of a gas (a fixed mass held at constant temperature) when either the pressure or volume is increased or decreased.

(H) 3.3.3 Work is the transfer of energy by a force.

Doing work on a gas increases the internal energy of the gas and can cause an increase in the temperature of the gas.

Students should be able to explain how, in a given situation, for example a bicycle pump, doing work on an enclosed gas leads to an increase in the temperature of the gas.

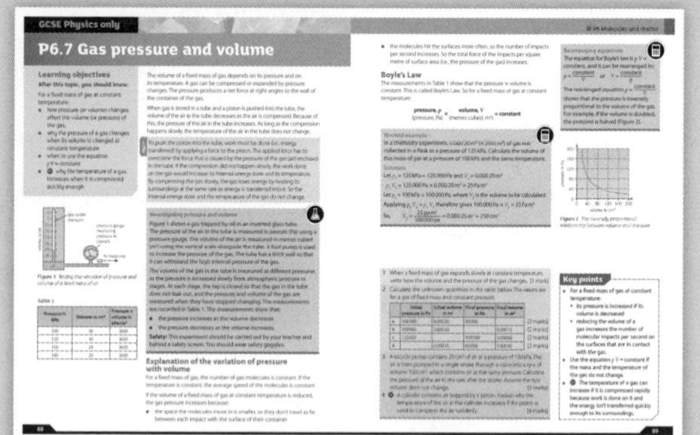

WS 1.2
MS 3b, 3c

Aiming for	Outcome	Checkpoint Question	Checkpoint Activity
Aiming for GRADE 4	State that the temperature of a gas is related to the kinetic energy of the gas particles.	1	Main 1
	State that the pressure of a gas increases when it is compressed (at a constant temperature).		Main 2
	Describe how forces are required to compress a gas.	4	Main 1
Aiming for GRADE 6	Describe how the pressure of a gas can change when it is compressed or allowed to expand.	1	Main 2
	Use the relationship pV = constant to calculate the constant.	2	Main 2
	(H) Explain why the temperature of a gas increases when it is compressed.	4	Main 1
Aiming for GRADE 8	Explain in terms of particle behaviour why the pressure of a gas increases when its volume decreases.		Main 2
	Calculate the pressure or volume of a gas.	2, End of chapter 7	Main 3
	Solve a variety of problems in which gas pressure or volume changes.	3	Main 3

Maths
Students use the relationship pV = constant in a wide variety of calculations (3b, 3c).

Literacy
Students describe the behaviour of particles in a gas and explain how this is linked to the pressure and temperature of the gas.

Practical

Title	Investigating pressure and volume
Equipment	gas pressure apparatus (gas trapped by oil and volume scale), pressure gauge, foot pump
Overview of method	Demonstrate the effect on the volume of the gas when the pressure is changed by operating the pump.
Safety considerations	Do not use excessive force to compress the gas. Ensure glass vessels are in good condition and do not have any scratches or chips.

Starter	Support/Extend	Resources
Work done (5 min) (H) Students describe how a force does work. What is the equation and what does doing work mean? **Squashing solids** (10 min) Ask students to describe and explain what will happen to the temperature of a spring if it is continually stretched and compressed.	**Extend:** Students should use descriptions of intermolecular forces.	
Main	**Support/Extend**	**Resources**
Doing work on a gas (15 min) (H) After reminding students about the concept of doing work, ask them what would happen if work was done on a gas. How could the energy transferred be stored? They should realise that any energy may be transferred to a thermal (internal) store and so there would be a rise in temperature. **Investigating pressure and volume** (25 min) Demonstrate the practical and discuss what would happen to the pressure of a gas if the volume were decreased. The particles would be forced closer together and so there would be more collisions with the container, and the pressure would increase. The students check the data to see there is a linear relationship. Introduce Boyle's law as the formal relationship ($pV =$ constant) and let the students try a few calculations.	**Support:** Differentiate calculations as appropriate. **Extend:** Ensure the students understand that the temperature of the gas is maintained during the experiment.	**Practical:** Investigating pressure and volume
Plenary	**Support/Extend**	**Resources**
Particle summary (10 min) Interactive where students fill in the missing words to complete an outline of the key information about particle behaviour during changes in temperature or energy for a material. **Varying constant** (5 min) Provide data for pressure and volume for a gas. The students must find a mean value for the constant.		**Interactive:** Particle summary
Homework		
Students should find out how air is liquefied into liquid nitrogen, oxygen, and other liquefied gases. They may also describe the potential uses of these gases.		

kerboodle

A Kerboodle highlight for this lesson is **Extension sheet: Gas pressure, volume, and temperature.** Refer to the **Content map** on Kerboodle for a full list of resources and assessment.

P6 Molecules and matter

Overview of P6 Molecules and matter

In this chapter the students have increased their understanding of the concept of density as a property of a material or object by measuring and calculating the density of solids and liquids. This led to a discussion of the states of matter, the properties of matter in these states, and the changes that occur as a material changes from one state to another. The changes in the properties of matter were used to introduce the kinetic theory and to analyse the changes in temperature occurring during heating and the concept of latent heat.

The students moved on to discuss the concept of internal energy in more detail; analysing the behaviour of particles in a solid, liquid or gas as the temperature changed. Students described latent heat of fusion and vaporisation mathematically, calculating energy changes during the appropriate phase changes and attempted to measure the latent heat of fusion for ice using electrical heating.

The students analysed the relationships between the pressure and temperature of a fixed mass of gas, determining that the pressure is proportional to the absolute temperature. They described the cause of pressure in terms of random particle behaviour and impact between the particles and its container, explaining the changes in pressure in terms of changes in the motion of the gas particles as the temperature decreases.

Finally, *GCSE Physics* students investigated the relationship between gas pressure and volume, determining that as the pressure increases the volume of the gas is decreased or vice versa. Noting that this was a linear relationship led to Boyle's law and calculations based on it. The behaviour of the gas during compression was again explained using a particle model. Higher level students also noted that work was done during the compression of a gas and this can have a heating effect.

You can find additional support for the maths skills covered in this chapter on **MyMaths**, including recognising and using expressions in decimal form, understanding and using the symbols: =, <, <<, >>, >, ∝, ~, and solving simple algebraic equations.

kerboodle

For this chapter, the following assessments are available on Kerboodle:

P6 Checkpoint quiz: Molecules and matter
P6 Progress quiz: Molecules and matter 1
P6 Progress quiz: Molecules and matter 2
P6 On your marks: Molecules and matter
P6 Exam-style questions and mark scheme: Molecules and matter

Checkpoint follow up lesson

A student's route through this lesson can be determined using the Checkpoint assessment. Percentage pass marks are supplied in the Checkpoint teacher notes.

For each successive route through it is assumed that the student can perform to their current route as well as previous routes. For example, students working at Aiming for 6 are assumed to be secure in Aiming for 4 knowledge and understanding and working towards achieving all the learning outcomes for Aiming for 6.

	Aiming for 4	Aiming for 6	Aiming for 8
Learning outcomes	Define density.	Calculate density and describe factors that affect it.	Calculate density, including converting between units, and describe factors that affect it.
	Describe the densities of different states.	Analyse data in terms of specific latent heat.	Analyse data in terms of specific latent heat in a range of situations
	Describe the effect of specific latent heat on the change of state of liquid.	Calculate energy transfer to produce a change in state.	Do calculations involving the equation for specific latent heat
	Describe and explain what happens when you increase the temperature or decrease the volume of a gas.	Explain why a gas exerts a pressure.	Use explanations of why a gas exerts a pressure to further explain the relationship between pressure and volume, and volume and temperature
	Describe the relationship between the pressure and volume of a gas.	Explain the relationship between pressure and volume, and volume and temperature.	Apply knowledge of specific latent heat and the behaviour of gases to unfamiliar situations.
Starter	**Melting and boiling (5 min)** Give students A4 dry wipe boards, pens and an eraser. Display or read a description of a material that melts then boils, giving details such as the temperatures and the times, and ask students to sketch the graph and label it with melting, boiling, solid, liquid, and gas, and with temperatures and times on the axes. Ask them to make the line where the density is highest into a zigzag line, and the line where it is lowest into a dotted line.		
Differentiated checkpoint activity	Aiming for 4 students use the Checkpoint follow-up sheet to complete one of three activities: • model density and states of matter using marbles • analyse data from an investigating into evaporation of liquids • investigate gas pressure using a syringe. The Checkpoint follow-up sheet is highly-structured and provides students with simple questions to consolidate their understanding from the tasks. Students will need access to graph paper.	Aiming for 6 students use the Checkpoint follow-up sheet to complete one of three activities: • create a of model density and states of matter using marbles • analyse data from an investigating into evaporation of liquids • investigate gas pressure using a syringe. The Checkpoint follow-up sheet provides limited support for students and includes more open-ended questions for students to consolidate their understanding of the tasks. Students will need access to graph paper.	Aiming for 8 students use the Checkpoint follow-up sheet to complete one of three activities: • design a of model density and states of matter using marbles, including qualitative analysis of their model • analyse data from an investigating into evaporation of liquids • investigate gas pressure using a syringe. The Checkpoint follow-up sheet provides limited support for students and includes open-ended questions for students to consolidate their understanding of the tasks. Students will need access to graph paper.
	Kerboodle resource P6 Checkpoint follow up: Aiming for 4, P6 Checkpoint follow up: Aiming for 6, P6 Checkpoint follow up: Aiming for 8		
Plenary	**What's wrong? (10 min)** Give students A4 dry wipe boards, pens and an eraser. Show a calculation of density and specific latent heat that is incorrect and ask students to write the correct calculation. You can have the wrong numbers, equation, or units. Aiming for 4 students could be given the equations. **Bubbles and bikes (5 min)** Give each group a set of 9 cards which have on them: High pressure/medium pressure/low pressure, small/medium/large bubble, bike on hot day/average day/winter day. They also need 6 blank cards. Ask them to make a grid matching the pressures to the tyre pressure and pressure of air inside the bubble to the pressure cards. Students then write a brief explanation using the particle model to go next to each picture.		
Progression	Encourage students to think about both the arrangement of the particles and the bonds between them when explaining latent heat.	Encourage students to think about the effect on the collisions of particles with a container when about talking the factors affecting gas pressure.	Encourage students to think about the assumptions of the particle model when using it to explain phenomena.

P 7 Radioactivity

7.1 Atoms and radiation

AQA spec Link: 4.1.1 Atoms are very small, having a radius of about 1×10^{-10} metres.

The basic structure of an atom is a positively charged nucleus composed of both protons and neutrons surrounded by negatively charged electrons.

The radius of a nucleus is less than $\frac{1}{10\,000}$ of the radius of an atom. Most of the mass of an atom is concentrated in the nucleus.

The electrons are arranged at different distances from the nucleus (different energy levels). The electron arrangements may change with the absorption of electromagnetic radiation (move further from the nucleus; a higher energy level) or by the emission of electromagnetic radiation (move closer to the nucleus; a lower energy level).

4.2.1 Some atomic nuclei are unstable. The nucleus gives out radiation as it changes to become more stable. This is a random process called radioactive decay.

Required knowledge of the properties of alpha particles, beta particles, and gamma rays is limited to their penetration through materials, their range in air, and ionising power.

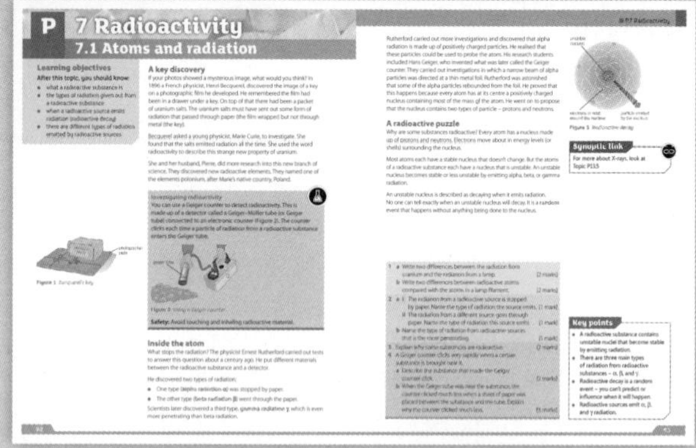

MS 1a, 1b, 2a

Aiming for	Outcome	Checkpoint	
		Question	Activity
Aiming for GRADE 4	Name the three types of nuclear radiation.		Main
	Name the three sub-atomic particles found in an atom (proton, neutron, and electron).		Starter 1, Starter 2, Main
	Identify some sources of background radiation.	3, 4, End of chapter 5	Main
Aiming for GRADE 6	Describe some safety precautions used when dealing with radioactive materials.		Main
	Describe how a Geiger counter can be used to detect radiation.	4	Main
	Identify natural and man-made sources of background radiation.	End of chapter 5	Main
Aiming for GRADE 8	Describe in detail the decay of an unstable nucleus.	3	Main
	Explain the similarities and differences between nuclear radiation and visible light.	2	Main, Plenary 2
	Describe the relative penetrating powers of the three types of nuclear radiation.	1	Main

Maths
Students compare count rates to describe the activity of a source or the level of background radiation.

Literacy
Students describe the operation of a Geiger counter and what the count rate says about the level of radiation present.

Key words
alpha radiation, beta radiation, gamma radiation, random

Practical

Title	Investigating radioactivity
Equipment	Geiger–Müller tube, ratemeter (and possibly high-voltage power supply), large plastic tray, tongs, radioactive sources, laboratory coat
Overview of method	Position the detector in the tray and switch it on. Bring the sources close to the tube window (and above the tray), and the ratemeter should count. If you can find a ratemeter that clicks, the demonstration is a lot more fun. A video camera connected to a data projector can be used to show the demonstrations more clearly.
Safety considerations	Follow local rules on the use of radioactive sources.

Starter	Support/Extend	Resources
Look alike (5 min) Ask students to draw and label an atom and discuss whether it is a realistic model. Show the students some caricatures of famous people to see whether these capture the essence of each person.	**Extend:** Discuss whether a model must look exactly like the object/situation it is meant to be describing.	
Atom models (10 min) Ask students to draw some simple atomic models. Ask them to note any of the properties of the sub-atomic particles that they already know, for example, from studying electricity or from atomic structure in chemistry.	**Support:** Give students a set of cut-out protons, neutrons, and electrons to use. **Extend:** Ask for specific atoms to be constructed.	
Main	**Support/Extend**	**Resources**
Investigating radioactivity (40 min) Discuss the discovery of nuclear radiation, outlining the initial evidence and the efforts made to explain it. Show how the Geiger counter can be used to detect nuclear radiation, starting with a background count. Some sample rocks or salts can be used to show that natural substances are radioactive.	**Extend:** Discuss the operation of the counter, including the need for ionisation.	**Activity:** Investigating radioactivity
Introduce the explanation of the source of the radiation – radioactive decay. Outline that there must be changes to the nucleus itself to produce these particles. Discuss some of the sources of background radiation, differentiating between natural sources and some man-made ones, particularly medical sources.	**Support:** Introduce simple animations of the decay; these will be expanded on in future lessons. Provide a table of the sources of background radiation and relative importance.	
Plenary	**Support/Extend**	**Resources**
Murder mystery (5 min) The body of a press photographer has been found in a sealed room, and all of the film in her camera has gone black even though it hasn't been used. Students explain what they think happened and how they know.		
Comparing locations (10 min) Interactive where students are provided with some data about the sources of background radiation in different locations in a pie chart. They use the pie chart to answer questions that compare the risks in each of the locations.	**Extend:** Provide the data and ask students to draw their own pie chart. **Extend:** Provide extra information, including the actual values, and ask students to calculate percentages from the source information.	**Interactive:** Comparing locations
Homework		
Students should write a report on the work of one of the named scientists in this lesson. As an alternative, the students may research the occurrence of radioactive radon gas in the UK and find out whether there are any links to an increase in lung cancer.	**Support:** Provide some initial research links to websites.	

kerboodle

A Kerboodle highlight for this lesson is **Bump up your grade: Atoms and isotopes**. Refer to the **Content map** on Kerboodle for a full list of resources and assessment.

P7.2 The discovery of the nucleus

AQA spec Link: 4.1.3 New experimental evidence may lead to a scientific model being changed or replaced.

Before the discovery of the electron, atoms were thought to be tiny spheres that could not be divided.

The discovery of the electron led to the plum pudding model of the atom. The plum pudding model suggested that the atom is a ball of positive charge with negative electrons embedded in it.

The results from the alpha scattering experiment led to the conclusion that the mass of an atom was concentrated at the centre (nucleus) and that the nucleus was charged. This nuclear model replaced the plum pudding model.

Niels Bohr adapted the nuclear model by suggesting that electrons orbit the nucleus at specific distances. The theoretical calculations of Bohr agreed with experimental observation.

Later experiments led to the idea that the positive charge of any nucleus can be subdivided into a whole number of smaller particles, each particle having the same amount of positive charge. The name proton was given to these particles.

The experimental work of James Chadwick provided the evidence to show the existence of neutrons within the nucleus. This was about 20 years after the nucleus became an accepted scientific idea.

Students should be able to describe:

- why the new evidence from the scattering experiment led to a change in the atomic model
- the difference between the plum pudding model of the atom and the nuclear model of the atom.

Details of experimental work supporting the Bohr model are not required.

Details of Chadwick's experimental work are not required.

WS 1.1, 1.2, 4.1

MS 1b

Aiming for	Outcome	Checkpoint	
		Question	Activity
Aiming for GRADE 4	Identify the Rutherford (nuclear) model of an atom.	1	Main 1
	Identify the locations of protons, neutrons, and electrons in the nuclear model.	1	Main 1
	State that electrons can move between fixed energy levels within an atom.		Main 2, Plenary 1
Aiming for GRADE 6	Describe the plum pudding model of the atom.	3	Main 1
	Describe the evidence provided by the Rutherford scattering experiment.		Main 1
	Describe the properties of protons, neutrons, and electrons.	4	Main 1
Aiming for GRADE 8	Compare the plum pudding model, Rutherford model, and Bohr model of the atom in terms of the evidence for each model.	3	Main 2
	Explain how Rutherford and Marsden's experiment caused a rejection of the plum pudding model.	2	Main 1
	Describe how the initial evidence for the nuclear model was processed and how the model came to be accepted.	3	Main 1

Maths

Students discuss the size of an atom and that of a nucleus by using standard form (1b).

Literacy

Students discuss how a scientific model is accepted or becomes rejected as new evidence is discovered.

Starter	Support/Extend	Resources
What's in the tin? (5 min) Peel the label off a tin of sponge pudding. Show the unmarked tin to the students and ask them to describe ways they could find out what's inside without opening it. **Believe it or not?** (10 min) What does it take to change the students' minds about something? How much evidence would be needed to convince them that NASA has sent men to the Moon? Discuss how difficult it is to change people's strongly held beliefs, and point out that scientists also find it difficult to change ideas that they may have been working with for many years.	**Support:** Suggest some methods and discuss them (e.g., X-rays, ultrasound). **Support:** Provide a set of cards showing possible evidence and ask students to prioritise them (e.g., photographs, testimony, rock samples, and radio communications).	
Main	**Support/Extend**	**Resources**
The Rutherford model of the atom (25 min) Discuss the atomic model that students will have used in KS3 and ask them what evidence there is for it. Outline Rutherford's work and allow the students to discuss the idea of discovery by firing particles. Emphasise Rutherford's mathematical analysis of the Geiger and Marsden experiment that confirmed the model and how the model matched the behaviour observed during nuclear decay. Compare the Rutherford model briefly with the plum pudding model. **Further changes to the model of the atom** (15 min) Show the students the typical electron arrangement diagram used in Chemistry lessons, and discuss the nature of energy levels using the Bohr model. Ensure the students know that electrons can move between these levels when the electron's energy changes. Explain the need for a neutron as a component of most nuclei, and outline its discovery. The students should now know the key properties of all three sub-atomic particles.	**Support:** Animations and simulations can be very useful here. **Extend:** Students should discuss the relative size of an atom and a nucleus using standard form. They may also discuss the nature of the interaction – electric fields and forces. **Extend:** Discuss the need for specific amounts of energy for electrons to move between energy levels. The students should also explain why neutrons were initially difficult to detect.	**Activity:** The Rutherford model of the atom
Plenary	**Support/Extend**	**Resources**
Not like a solar system (5 min) The students should make a list of similarities and particularly differences between atomic models and solar systems. **I don't believe it** (10 min) Interactive where students choose the missing words to complete a paragraph summarising the evidence that led to the plum pudding model being replaced. Students then use this summary to write a letter to an unconvinced scientist who wants to hold on to the plum pudding model.		**Interactive:** I don't believe it
Homework		
Students finish writing their letter to an unconvinced scientist from Plenary 2 (or start their letter if Plenary 1 was chosen). They should also include the evidence provided by the work of Bohr and Chadwick in their letter.	**Support:** Differentiate by asking for different levels of detail for different students.	

kerboodle

A Kerboodle highlight for this lesson is **Working scientifically: Changing models of the atom.** Refer to the **Content map** on Kerboodle for a full list of resources and assessment.

P7.3 Changes in the nucleus

AQA spec Link: 4.1.2 In an atom the number of electrons is equal to the number of protons in the nucleus. Atoms have no overall electrical charge.

All atoms of a particular element have the same number of protons. The number of protons in an atom of an element is called its atomic number.

The total number of protons and neutrons in an atom is called its mass number.

Atoms can be represented as shown in this example:

$$^{\text{(Atomic number) }11}_{\text{(Mass number) }23}\mathrm{Na}$$

Atoms of the same element can have different numbers of neutrons; these atoms are called isotopes of that element.

Atoms turn into positive ions if they lose one or more outer electron(s).

Students should be able to relate differences between isotopes to differences in conventional representations of their identities, charges, and masses.

4.2.2 Nuclear equations are used to represent radioactive decay.

In a nuclear equation an alpha particle may be represented by the symbol:

$$^{4}_{2}\mathrm{He}$$

and a beta particle by the symbol:

$$^{0}_{-1}\mathrm{e}$$

The emission of the different types of nuclear radiation may cause a change in the mass and/or the charge of the nucleus. For example:

$$^{219}_{86}\text{radon} \rightarrow {}^{215}_{84}\text{polonium} + {}^{4}_{2}\mathrm{He}$$

So alpha decay causes both the mass and charge of the nucleus to decrease.

$$^{14}_{6}\text{carbon} \rightarrow {}^{14}_{7}\text{nitrogen} + {}^{0}_{-1}\mathrm{e}$$

So beta decay does not cause the mass of the nucleus to change but does cause the charge of the nucleus to increase.

Students are not required to recall these two examples.

Students should be able to use the names and symbols of common nuclei and particles to write balanced equations that show single alpha (α) and beta (β) decay. This is limited to balancing the atomic numbers and mass numbers. The identification of daughter elements from such decays is not required.

The emission of a gamma ray does not cause the mass or the charge of the nucleus to change.

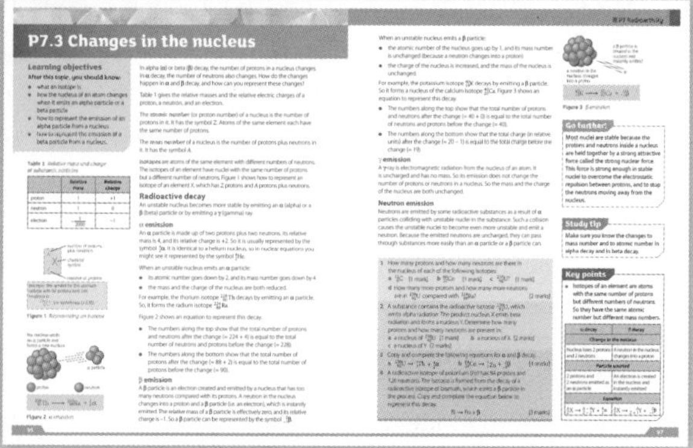
P7.3 Changes in the nucleus

WS 1.2, 4.1

MS 3c

Aiming for	Outcome	Checkpoint	
		Question	Activity
Aiming for GRADE 4 ↓	Identify the mass and atomic number by using nuclear notation.	1, 2, End of chapter 1	Main 1, Plenary 2
	Identify the type of decay taking place from a nuclear equation.		Main 2
	Describe how isotopes are atoms of the same element with different mass numbers.		Main 1
Aiming for GRADE 6 ↓	Calculate the number of neutrons in an isotope by using nuclear notation.	1, End of chapter 1	Main 1
	Describe the differences between isotopes.	1	Main 1
	Complete decay equations for alpha and beta decay.	2, 3	Main 2
Aiming for GRADE 8 ↓	Explain why particles are ejected from the nucleus during nuclear decay.		Main 2
	Describe the changes in the nucleus that occur during nuclear decay.		Main 2
	Write full decay equations, for example, nuclear decays.	4	Main 2

Maths
Students calculate changes in mass and atomic number in nuclear equations (3c).

Literacy
Students describe how a nucleus changes during decay.

Key words
atomic number, mass number, isotopes

Starter	Support/Extend	Resources
Fact or fiction (5 min) Give the students a set of 'facts' about radioactivity and atoms and let them use traffic light cards to indicate whether they agree (green), don't know (amber), or disagree (red).'	**Support:** Differentiate questions as appropriate.	
Chemical change (10 min) Give the students a demonstration of a chemical reaction (magnesium + oxygen $\rightarrow$ magnesium oxide). Ask the students to describe what is happening in terms of particles and see if they understand basic conservation of particles in chemical reactions.	**Support:** Provide simple atom diagrams showing the process and ask students to describe the making or breaking of bonds. **Extend:** Require descriptions of energy changes.	
Main	**Support/Extend**	**Resources**
Nuclear notation (10 min) Show some examples of nuclear notation, ensuring the students can identify the atomic number (proton number) and mass number (nucleon number). Students should calculate the number of neutrons in some examples. Discuss isotopes, showing some in nuclear notation and noting the difference in mass numbers.	**Support:** Students can construct atomic models from cut-out circles to match the notation.	
Alpha, beta, and gamma emission (30 min) Describe an alpha decay and the changes it causes in a nucleus. The students should look at an example and then try to construct a few additional equations by using a periodic table. Move on to beta emission, focusing on the change of a neutron to a proton and how this affects the decay equation. Show a few examples and ask the students to complete a few more. Discuss gamma emission, pointing out that there is no change in the particle structure of the nucleus and so no decay equations are needed. Students then calculate changes in atomic number and mass number of an atom after it emits alpha and beta radiation.	**Support:** A support sheet is available to help develop students understanding on alpha and beta radiation. **Extend:** An extension sheet is available where students write and interpret equations to represent nuclear reactions. **Extend:** The students can be made aware of the production of an anti-electron neutrino during beta emission.	**Activity:** Alpha, beta, and gamma emission **Support:** Nuclear decay equations **Extension:** Nuclear equations
Plenary	**Support/Extend**	**Resources**
Name that isotope (5 min) Students use the interactive to complete a table describing various isotopes. They need to fill in missing details such as element name, proton number, mass number, and number of electrons.		**Interactive:** Name that isotope
Definitions (10 min) The students must give accurate definitions of the terms 'proton', 'neutron', 'electron', 'ion', 'mass number', 'atomic number', 'alpha particle', 'beta particle', and 'gamma ray'.	**Support:** Make this activity a simple phrase- or card-matching task.	
Homework		
Students can each be given a particular isotope to research how it may be useful.		

kerboodle

A Kerboodle highlight for this lesson is **Maths skills: Nuclear reactions**. Refer to the **Content map** on Kerboodle for a full list of resources and assessment.

P7.4 More about alpha, beta, and gamma radiation

AQA spec Link: 4.2.1 The nuclear radiation emitted may be:

- an alpha particle (α) – this consists of two neutrons and two protons, it is the same as a helium nucleus
- a beta particle (β) – a high speed electron ejected from the nucleus as a neutron turns into a proton
- a gamma ray (γ) – electromagnetic radiation from the nucleus
- a neutron (n).

Required knowledge of the properties of alpha particles, beta particles, and gamma rays is limited to their penetration through materials, their range in air, and ionising power.

Students should be able to apply their knowledge to the uses of radiation and evaluate the best sources of radiation to use in a given situation.

4.2.4 Radioactive contamination is the unwanted presence of materials containing radioactive atoms on other materials. The hazard from contamination is due to the decay of the contaminating atoms. The type of radiation emitted affects the level of hazard.

Irradiation is the process of exposing an object to nuclear radiation. The irradiated object does not become radioactive.

Students should be able to compare the hazards associated with contamination and irradiation.

Suitable precautions must be taken to protect against any hazard that the radioactive source used in the process of irradiation may present.

Students should understand that it is important for the findings of studies into the effects of radiation on humans to be published and shared with other scientists so that the findings can be checked by peer review.

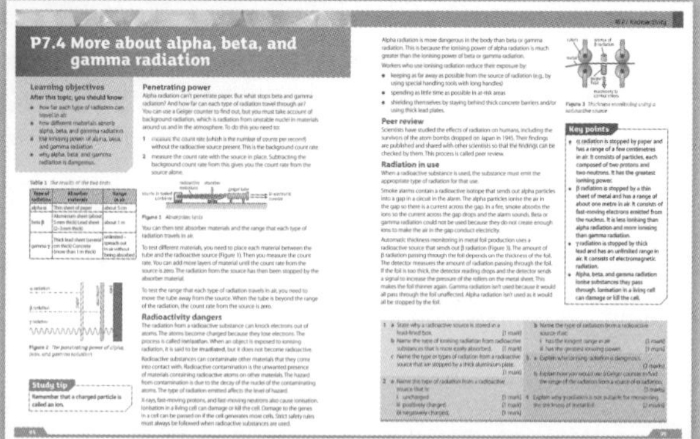
P7.4 More about alpha, beta, and gamma radiation

Learning objectives

Penetrating power

Radioactivity dangers

Peer review

Radiation in use

Key points

Study tip

WS 1.4

MS 1c

Aiming for	Outcome	Checkpoint	
		Question	Activity
Aiming for GRADE 4	Rank the three types of nuclear radiation in order of their penetrating power.	1 End of chapter 2, 5	Main
	Rank the three types of nuclear radiation in order of their range through air.	1, End of chapter 2	Main
	State that all three types of nuclear radiation are ionising.	1	Main, Plenary 1
Aiming for GRADE 6	Describe how the penetrating powers of radiation can be measured.	4, End of chapter 5	Main
	Describe the path of radiation types through a magnetic field.	2, End of chapter 6	Main
	Describe the process of ionisation.	3	Main, Plenary 1, Plenary 2
Aiming for GRADE 8	Describe in detail how the thickness of a material being manufactured can be monitored by using a beta source.		Main
	Compare the ionisation caused by the different types of nuclear radiation.	3	Main, Plenary 2
	Evaluate in some detail the risks caused by alpha radiation inside and outside the human body.	1	Main, Plenary 1, Plenary 2

Maths

Students compare the distances through which the different types of nuclear radiation can travel in different materials.

Literacy

Students discuss the effects of radiation on living tissue.

Key words

ionisation, irradiated

Starter	Support/Extend	Resources
Too many symbols? (10 min) Scientists use a lot of symbols in their work. Students use the interactive to match some symbols they have met so far with what they represent (e.g., elements, equations, the names of things, etc.). Discuss the reasons that scientists use symbols.	**Support:** Give some example symbols and ask students to say what they represent.	**Interactive:** Too many symbols?
X-ray flashback (5 min) The students should explain why X-rays can be harmful and the precautions used to reduce exposure.	**Extend:** Students should describe how X-rays are produced.	
Main	**Support/Extend**	**Resources**
Radiation in action (40 min) Describe how the penetrating power of radiation can be measured by using a Geiger counter. Discuss the safety measures that must be used when measuring radiation. Introduce the different penetrating powers of the three types of radiation – alpha, beta, and gamma. Students suggest how the penetrating power could be used to measure the thickness of a material and how this can be applied to controlling thickness. Students complete the Working scientifically sheet to examine the results from an investigation on beta radiation through cardboard and link it to the measurement and control of cardboard manufacture. Discuss the damage caused by ionisation and some of the precautions that can reduce exposure, emphasising that keeping the sources at a distance is one of the most effective methods. The concept of sharing data about radiation effects should be covered here.	**Support:** The students can fill in a partially completed flow chart showing how thickness is controlled. **Extend:** The deflection of charged particles by magnetic fields can be shown.	**Working scientifically:** Radiation in action
Plenary	**Support/Extend**	**Resources**
Local rules (10 min) The students should make a plan for a poster or booklet explaining how the radioactive sources should be stored and handled and explaining how these precautionary rules reduce harm. They can then produce this booklet as homework. **Protect and survive** (5 min) Ask students to suggest what would need to be done if one of the radioactive sources was dropped and lost.	**Support:** Show the students the rules and ask them to explain how each of the rules reduce risk or harm.	
Homework		
Ionising radiation can be detected by cloud and bubble chambers, spark detectors, and photographic films. The students could find out about these devices and why they are used.	**Support:** Each student is allocated one device to research and share their information in class.	

kerboodle

A Kerboodle highlight for this lesson is **Extension sheet: Radiation hunt!** Refer to the **Content map** on Kerboodle for a full list of resources and assessment.

P7.5 Activity and half-life

AQA spec Link: 4.2.1 Activity is the rate at which a source of unstable nuclei decays.

Activity is measured in becquerel (Bq).

Count-rate is the number of decays recorded each second by a detector (e.g., Geiger–Muller tube).

4.2.3 Radioactive decay is random.

The half-life of a radioactive isotope is the time it takes for the number of nuclei of the isotope in a sample to halve, or the time it takes for the count rate (or activity) from a sample containing the isotope to fall to half its initial level.

Students should be able to explain the concept of half-life and how it is related to the random nature of radioactive decay.

Students should be able to determine the half-life of a radioactive isotope from given information.

(H) Students should be able to calculate the net decline, expressed as a ratio, in a radioactive emission after a given number of half-lives.

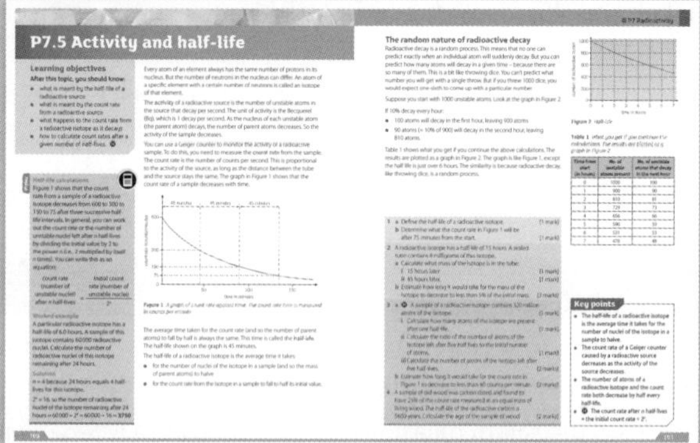

MS 1b, 1c, 3d, 4a

Aiming for	Outcome	Checkpoint	
		Question	Activity
Aiming for GRADE 4	State that the activity of a radioactive sample will fall over time.		Main 1
	Define half-life in simple terms such as 'the time it takes for half of the material to decay'.	1	Main 1
	Find the half-life of a substance from a graph of count rate (or nuclei remaining) against time with support.		Main 1
Aiming for GRADE 6	**(H) Find the ratio of a sample remaining after a given number of half-lives.**	2, 3, End of chapter 4	Main 2
	State that all atoms of a particular isotope have an identical chance to decay in a fixed time.		Main 1
	Plot a graph showing the decay of a sample and use it to determine half-life.	End of chapter 3	Main 1
Aiming for GRADE 8	Compare a physical model of decay with the decay of nuclei, noting the limitations of the model.		Starter 1, Starter 2, Main 1
	Outline how the age of organic material can be determined by using radioactive dating.	4, End of chapter 4	Main 2
	(H) Calculate the changes in count rate or nuclei remaining by using an exponential decay function.	2	Main 2

Maths
Students plot graphs of data and find half-life from them (1c, 4a). They also calculate changes in count rate by using exponential functions (1b, 3d).

Literacy
Students describe the random but predictable nature of decay.

Key words
activity, count rate, half-life

Practical

Title	A decay model
Equipment	set of 60 identical six-sided dice
Overview of method	The students roll the full set of dice, and after each roll, they remove the dice that landed showing one. They record the number of dice 'surviving' and then roll *only these dice*, and so on. They continue this process of elimination for 20 rolls or until no die survives. Plotting a graph of the number of dice remaining (y-axis) against roll number (x-axis) reveals that the dice behave like decaying atoms and a half-life can be calculated.
Safety considerations	Keep dice off the floor.

Starter	Support/Extend	Resources
An exponential decay puzzle (5 min) A farmer has a warehouse with two million corn cobs in it. Every day she sells exactly half of her remaining stock. How long before she has sold every last nugget (not cob) of corn?	**Support:** Use a calculator and just keep dividing by two to see how many steps this would take.	
An exponential growth puzzle (10 min) A philosopher places a grain of rice on the first square of a chess board, two on the next, four on the next, and so on. How many go on the last (sixty-fourth) square?	**Support:** Limit the calculation to the first two rows and then show the graph to see what happens next.	
Main	**Support/Extend**	**Resources**
Activity and count rate (20 min) Recap decay and remind students that some sources seem more active than others. Discuss the concept of activity (decay rate) and then count rate. Students should then try the decay model with dice described in the practical, finding the half-life from a graph.	**Extend:** The students should compare this model with the decay of nuclei, noting that the numbers of dice used is far smaller than the number of atoms in a typical sample.	**Activity:** Activity and count rate
Half-life calculations (20 min) (H) The students try some half-life calculations using the relationship shown. Discuss why the random behaviour of particles can be mathematically modelled whereas individual behaviour cannot. Outline radioactive dating briefly, linking to a decay curve graph.	**Support:** Students can spend this time completing and analysing the graph from the practical. Decay simulations are useful here. Each student can try to guess which of the particles will survive to the end.	**Extension:** Half-lives and radioactive decay
Plenary	**Support/Extend**	**Resources**
Activity and decay (5 min) Show the students a graph with three decay curves on it. Students use the interactive to put the three decay curves in order of longest half-life.	**Extend:** Students should find the half-lives of the three isotopes.	**Interactive:** Activity and decay
Coin toss (10 min) If someone has 120 coins and tosses them all, removing all of the heads after each toss, how many tosses until there are only 15 left?	**Extend:** Ask students to discuss why the real results can diverge from theoretical models.	
Homework		
The students should find out how radioactive carbon dating works and report on one example of its use in dating an object.		

kerboodle

A Kerboodle highlight for this lesson is **Bump up your grade: Half life and the random nature of decay**. Refer to the **Content map** on Kerboodle for a full list of resources and assessment.

P7.6 Nuclear radiation in medicine

AQA spec Link: 4.3.2 Students should be able to explain why the hazards associated with radioactive material differ according to the half-life involved.

4.3.3 Nuclear radiations are used in medicine for the:

- exploration of internal organs
- control or destruction of unwanted tissue.

Students should be able to:

- describe and evaluate the uses of nuclear radiations for exploration of internal organs, and for control or destruction of unwanted tissue
- evaluate the perceived risks of using nuclear radiations in relation to given data and consequences.

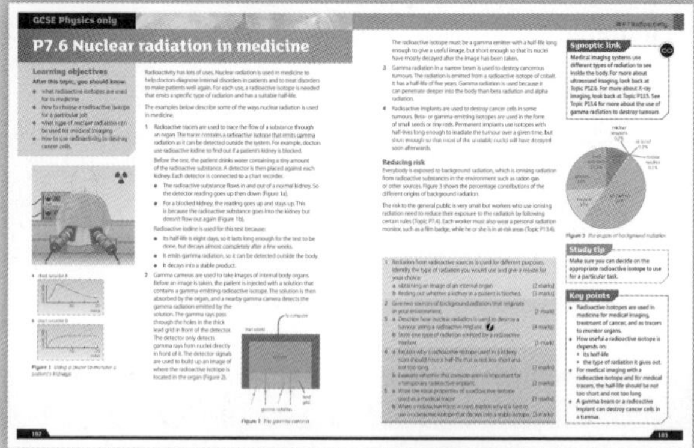
GCSE Physics only

P7.6 Nuclear radiation in medicine

WS 1.5, 1.6

MS 1b, 2c, 2f

Aiming for	Outcome	Checkpoint	
		Question	**Activity**
Aiming for GRADE 4	Name some medical applications for radioactive substances.		Main
	State that the larger the dose of radiation, the more likely harm will be caused.	2	Main, Homework
	Describe some precautions used during diagnoses or treatments involving radioactive substances.	2, 3, 4	Main, Homework
Aiming for GRADE 6	Explain why alpha, beta, or gamma radiation is chosen for a particular medical application.	1	Main
	Describe how gamma rays can be used to destroy cancerous cells and the damage they may cause to healthy tissue.		Main
	Explain how precautions to reduce exposure to patients and medical staff work.		Main, Homework
Aiming for GRADE 8	Describe the use of radioactive implants and the hazards associated with the technique.	2	Main
	Discuss the factors that need to be taken into account when selecting a medical tracer for a diagnostic test.	3, 4	Main
	Explain how a medical tracer is used including the function of a gamma camera.	4	Main

Maths

Students can look at success data for various treatments (2c, 2f).

Literacy

There is great scope for discussion of various medical treatments.

Starter	Support/Extend	Resources
A three pipe problem (10 min) A plumber has found an outlet pipe in a block of flats but does not know which apartment it comes from. How can he find out? **Tumours** (5 min) What are tumours, are they all dangerous, how do they arise, and how can they be treated?	**Extend:** Students should describe as many ways as they think are possible to solve this.	
Main	**Support/Extend**	**Resources**
Nuclear radiation in medicine (40 min) Discuss the idea of using radioactive tracers in the body, balancing the risks and benefits clearly. Ensure that the reasons alpha sources cannot be used are discussed. Show some gamma camera images and outline the operation of a detector. Images can be compared with X-rays in terms of resolution. The purpose of gamma treatment should now be discussed, linking it to ionisation and cell destruction. Damage to healthy cells should also be mentioned. Discuss the need for implants to provide long-term exposure to tumours. These are often in regions where a gamma ray beam would cause too much damage to healthy tissue (e.g., the brain). Summarise the benefits of each treatment and the risks to the patient, along with the precautions taken by medical staff.	**Extend:** Students can be provided with information about tracers other than iodine and discuss why they are suitable. **Support:** Animations and videos showing how this treatment is performed are available with an Internet search.	**Activity:** Nuclear radiation in medicine
Plenary	**Support/Extend**	**Resources**
Radiation and medicine (5 min) Interactive where students match up the type of radiation with its medical use. They then explain why each type of radiation is used for that particular medical use.		**Interactive:** Radiation and medicine
Informed consent (5 min) Students discuss who should have the final say about medical diagnosis and treatment. How much information should be provided to the patient?	**Extend:** Expand the discussion to include children and those unable to actually give consent.	
Homework		
Students complete the WebQuest to find out information on radioactive tracers. They use their research to write a leaflet on radioactive tracers for young patients.	**Support:** Search for a brochure and print it for the students as a starting point.	**WebQuest:** Radioactive tracers

kerboodle

A Kerboodle highlight for this lesson is **Working scientifically: Radiation risks and benefits.** Refer to the **Content map** on Kerboodle for a full list of resources and assessment.

P7.7 Nuclear fission

AQA spec Link: 4.3.2 Radioactive isotopes have a very wide range of half-life values.

Students should be able to explain why the hazards associated with radioactive material differ according to the half-life involved.

4.4.1 Nuclear fission is the splitting of a large and unstable nucleus (e.g., uranium or plutonium).

Spontaneous fission is rare. Usually, for fission to occur the unstable nucleus must first absorb a neutron.

The nucleus undergoing fission splits into two smaller nuclei, roughly equal in size, and emits two or three neutrons plus gamma rays. Energy is released by the fission reaction.

All of the fission products have kinetic energy.

The neutrons may go on to start a chain reaction.

The chain reaction is controlled in a nuclear reactor to control the energy released. The explosion caused by a nuclear weapon is caused by an uncontrolled chain reaction.

Students should be able to draw/interpret diagrams representing nuclear fission and how a chain reaction may occur.

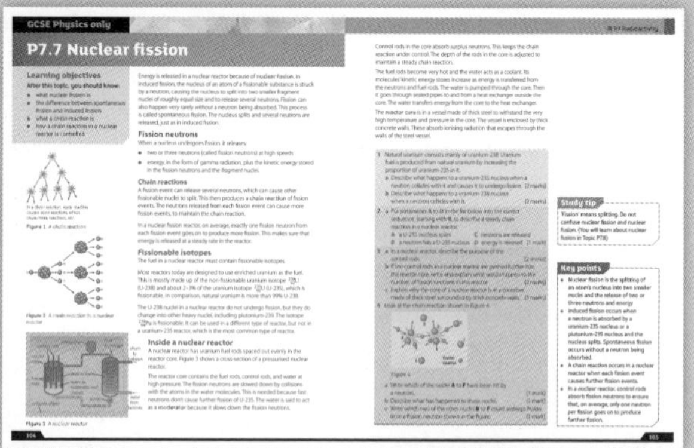

MS 1b

Aiming for	Outcome	Checkpoint	
		Question	Activity
Aiming for GRADE 4	Describe how nuclear fission is the breaking of a large nucleus to form two smaller nuclei.	4	Main
	Distinguish between induced fission and spontaneous fission.		Main
	Label the key components of a nuclear reactor.		Main
Aiming for GRADE 6	Describe induced nuclear fission in terms of neutron impacts and release.	1, End of chapter 7	Main
	Explain how an escalating induced fission reaction occurs.	4	Main, Plenary 2
	Outline the function of the moderator, control rods, and coolant.	3, End of chapter 7	Main
Aiming for GRADE 8	Explain how a steady-state induced fission reaction can be maintained.	2	Main, Plenary 2
	Explain the differences between naturally occurring isotopes and enriched nuclear fuels.		Main
	Explain the operation of a nuclear fission reactor, including the choices of appropriate materials.	2, 3, End of chapter 5	Main

Maths
Students can model the number of fission processes taking place in each stage of a chain reaction.

Literacy
Students describe chain reaction diagrams and explain each stage in the process.

Key words
nuclear fission, chain reaction

Practical

Title	Domino model
Equipment	large set of dominoes
Overview of method	A chain reaction can be demonstrated using dominos. Set up a simple chain where one domino knocks over another – this represents a critical reaction where the rate stays constant. To show an increasing reaction, simply set up the dominoes so that one knocks over two, two knock over three, and so on.
Safety considerations	Keep the dominoes off the floor.

Starter	Support/Extend	Resources
Protection from radiation (5 min) The students describe the penetrating powers of the three types of radiation and explain how people can be protected from them.		
Power station basics (10 min) Interactive where students put in order a simple flow diagram showing how a fossil fuel power station operates, including the furnace, boiler, turbines, generators, and transformers. They then complete an explanation of what each part does.	**Support:** Provide a diagram and ask students to describe the processes at each stage. **Extend:** Ask students to draw a Sankey energy transfer diagram indicating energy dissipation.	**Interactive:** Power station basics
Main	**Support/Extend**	**Resources**
Chain reactions and the fission process (25 min) Use the domino model to introduce a chain reaction. Students should note that the reaction must be started off but then rapidly snowballs. Introduce the fission process, including the fission neutrons so that the next stage in the chain reaction can be discussed. Describe what would happen if the process was uncontrolled (as in a nuclear weapon) and how this is prevented in a reactor by absorbing excess neutrons. Discuss the fact that only a few isotopes will undergo fission in a reactor and that these are fairly rare and difficult to enrich, making the technique expensive.	**Extend:** Calculations of the number of nuclei splitting after each stage can be performed. Mention breeder reactors in which more fissionable isotopes are produced in the reactor.	**Working scientifically:** A domino chain
Reactor design (15 min) Compare the design of a nuclear power plant to a non-nuclear one. Bring the focus onto the reactor and then the roles of the moderator, control rods, and coolant. Suggest some example materials for these and their properties.	**Extend:** Students should discuss why the fission neutrons need to be moderated. The role of delayed neutrons released by unstable fission products can also be mentioned.	
Plenary	**Support/Extend**	**Resources**
The China syndrome (5 min) If a nuclear core melts down, it gets so hot that it can melt the rock beneath it and start sinking into the Earth. What stops it sinking all the way through?		
Chain reaction (10 min) The students should be asked to develop a physical model to show a chain reaction.	**Extend:** Ask students to calculate how many nuclei would be splitting after five stages if each split releases an average of 2.5 neutrons.	
Homework		
Students should identify the locations of nuclear power plants and explain why the plants have been constructed at these locations.		

kerboodle

A Kerboodle highlight for this lesson is **Working scientifically: Nuclear threat.** Refer to the **Content map** on Kerboodle for a full list of resources and assessment.

P7.8 Nuclear fusion

AQA spec Link: 4.4.2 Nuclear fusion is the joining of two light nuclei to form a heavier nucleus. In this process some of the mass may be converted into the energy of radiation.

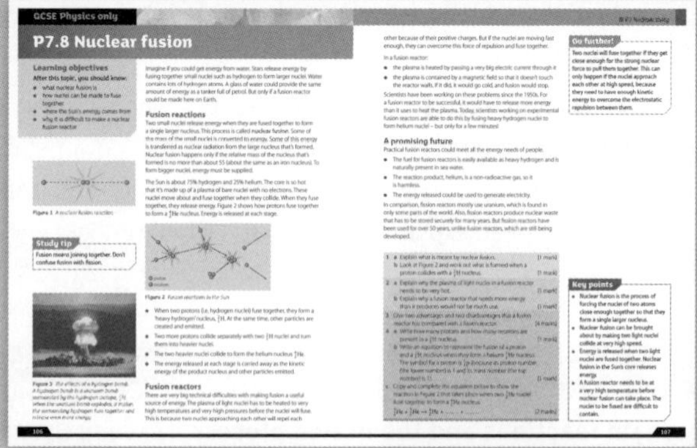
GCSE Physics only

P7.8 Nuclear fusion

Learning objectives

Fusion reactions

Study tip

Fusion reactors

A promising future

Go further!

Key points

MS 3c

Aiming for	Outcome	Checkpoint	
		Question	Activity
Aiming for GRADE 4	State that nuclear fusion is the energy releasing process in the Sun.		Starter 2, Main
↓	State that the Sun fuses (joins together) hydrogen nuclei into helium nuclei.		Main
	Describe how very high temperatures and pressures are required for fusion to take place.		Main
Aiming for GRADE 6	Outline the process of nuclear fusion.	1, End of chapter 8	Main
↓	Complete a nuclear equation showing simple fusion processes.	4	Main
	Describe the key design features of a nuclear fusion reactor.		Main
Aiming for GRADE 8	Explain why it is difficult to carry out controlled nuclear fusion on Earth.	2, End of chapter 8	Main
↓	Construct a variety of nuclear equations showing nuclear fusion.	4	Main
	Compare the operation of a nuclear fission reactor and a nuclear fusion reactor.	3	Homework

Maths
Students use conservation rules to determine the number of protons and neutrons before and after nuclear fusion (3c).

Literacy
The students describe the process of nuclear fusion in the Sun and the structure of reactors on Earth.

Key words
nuclear fusion

Starter	Support/Extend	Resources
A Sun myth (10 min) The Sun has a lot of mythology based on it and a lot of religions had a 'Sun god'. What stories do the students know?		
Star one (5 min) Ask students where does the Sun get its energy? The students dicuss their ideas and then discuss possible problems with them.	**Extend:** Discuss why it was difficult to explain the Sun's behaviour before the discovery of radioactivity.	
Main	**Support/Extend**	**Resources**
Fusion reactions (40 min) Introduce nuclear fusion, explaining that the mass of the products is slightly less than the mass of the initial nuclei and so there is an energy release. Discuss this process in the Sun, where there is a readily available source of fusible nuclei and the right conditions to cause them to fuse. Students should form some of the nuclear equations for fusion. They can make models of some of the processes.	**Extend:** The concept of binding energy can be introduced to explain why there is an energy release.	**Activity:** Fusion reactions
Discuss the design of a fusion reactor and compare the conditions with those in the core of the Sun. Emphasise how difficult it is to maintain the right conditions for fusion in reactors on Earth. Discuss the future potential for nuclear fusion, but note that progress has been very slow.	**Extend:** Inertial confinement reactors can be mentioned as an alternative to magnetic containment.	
Plenary	**Support/Extend**	**Resources**
A bright future (10 min) Students use the interactive to sort statements according to whether they give advantages or disadvantages of using nuclear fusion as a potential energy source of the future. They then complete a paragraph to compare nuclear fusion and nuclear fission.		**Interactive:** A bright future
Building carbon (5 min) The carbon in the students' bodies was formed in stars through fusion processes. Ask the students to suggest the stages that produce carbon-12 from lighter elements.	**Extend:** Ask for nuclear fusion equations that could produce carbon-12.	
Homework		
The students should make a poster, comparing and contrasting the processes of nuclear fission and nuclear fusion. They need to discuss what happens to the protons and neutrons in each process and why energy is released by both processes. They could outline why one process is easier to achieve than the other.	**Extend:** Students incorporate the ideas of fuel source and how to deal with waste.	

kerboodle

A Kerboodle highlight for this lesson is **Bump up your grade: Nuclear fission and nuclear fusion**. Refer to the **Content map** on Kerboodle for a full list of resources and assessment.

P7.9 Nuclear issues

AQA spec Link: 4.2.4 Radioactive contamination is the unwanted presence of materials containing radioactive atoms on other materials. The hazard from contamination is due to the decay of the contaminating atoms. The type of radiation emitted affects the level of hazard.

Irradiation is the process of exposing an object to nuclear radiation. The irradiated object does not become radioactive.

Students should be able to compare the hazards associated with contamination and irradiation.

Suitable precautions must be taken to protect against any hazard that the radioactive source used in the process of irradiation may present.

Students should understand that it is important for the findings of studies into the effects of radiation on humans to be published and shared with other scientists so that the findings can be checked by peer review.

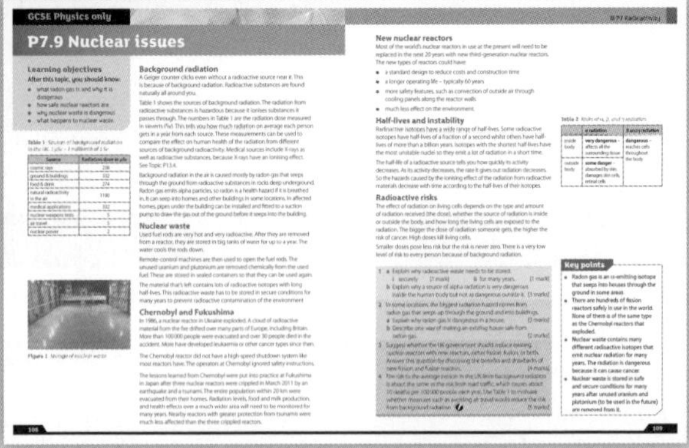

WS 1.5, 1.6

MS 1b, 4a

Aiming for	Outcome	Checkpoint	
		Question	**Activity**
Aiming for GRADE 4	Identify sources of radiation, including medical and background radiation.	2	Starter 1, Main 1
	Describe the type of damage caused by large-scale nuclear accidents.		Main 2
	Describe how nuclear waste is very dangerous and must be stored safely for very long periods of time.	1	Main 2
Aiming for GRADE 6	Compare the risks and damage associated with alpha, beta, and gamma radiation.	1	Main 1
	Describe how damage caused by radioactive material can be reduced.	2, 4	Main 1
	Discuss the difficulties associated with the handling and storage of nuclear waste.		Plenary 2, Homework
Aiming for GRADE 8	Discuss the risks and benefits of nuclear power compared to other methods of electricity generation.	3	Main 2
	Describe and explain the safety precautions that need to take place after a large nuclear accident.		Main 2
	Evaluate in detail a variety of storage or disposal solutions for nuclear waste.		Main 2, Plenary 2, Homework

Maths
Students analyse graphical information and compare dose values (1b, 4a).

Literacy
The students discuss the various issues associated with nuclear power stations and nuclear waste.

Key words
radiation dose

Starter	Support/Extend	Resources
An empty pie (5 min) Show the students a pie chart with all the sources of background radiation and their contribution to an average dose removed. Ask the students to guess what each slice of the pie represents and then compare with the real figures. **Risk awareness** (10 min) All activities have some associated risk but this must be balanced against the benefits. Discuss some activities with the students, such as driving, crossing a road, walking to school, and ask them to assess how risky they think each activity is.	**Extend:** Students should estimate the percentage contributions from the unnumbered chart. **Support:** Provide accident statistics from the Health and Safety Executive website and make a card sort game in which the students rank the risks of different tasks.	
Main	**Support/Extend**	**Resources**
Radiation all around us (15 min) Recap the sources of background radiation, presenting some data for the local region if possible. Compare this with more dangerous locations. Discuss the typical radiation dose and how this is significantly affected by some medical treatments. **Nuclear accidents and waste** (25 min) Show news footage of the two major nuclear accidents and ask the students to compare the responses by the authorities in the short and long term. Discuss the environmental damage caused and casualty numbers. Incorporate a brief discussion of the handling and disposal of the radioactive waste produced by reactors.	**Extend:** Provide some numerical data about the doses from medical treatments and working in a nuclear power station. **Extend:** In the discussion include some data on the number of people killed during coal mining and those at risk from global warming.	**Activity:** Nuclear issues
Plenary	**Support/Extend**	**Resources**
Radioactivity (10 min) Students complete the interactive to summarise what they have learnt about radioactivity, including the advantages and disadvantages of using radiation and nuclear power in the various contexts introduced. **Where's the waste?** (5 min) Show the students maps of the UK and the rest of the world and ask them to decide where nuclear waste should be stored and why.	**Extend:** Ask students what criteria they are using and to prioritise them in order of importance.	**Interactive:** Radioactivity
Homework		
Students complete the WebQuest and research the characteristics needed for radioactive waste storage sites. They use their research to create a leaflet to explain to people what nuclear waste is, why we need to store it, and what the risks are.		**WebQuest:** Nuclear waste – not in my back yard?

P7 Radioactivity

Overview of P7 Radioactivity

In this chapter the students have described how the structure of the nucleus was discovered by the radiation emitted during nuclear decay and how experimentation and developments in our understanding of sub-atomic particles have driven changes in the model used to describe the atom from the plum pudding model, through to the Rutherford model and then the Bohr model.

The students have described the changes in the nucleus which occur during alpha, beta, and gamma decay along with neutron emission in terms of atomic (proton) number and mass number using the appropriate nuclear notation for isotopes. The properties of alpha, beta, and gamma radiation have been demonstrated leading to a discussion of their use in thickness monitoring and then the safety measures required when using radioactive materials.

Students then moved on to discuss the concepts of activity, count rate, and the patterns in radioactive decay that explain half-life and the associated graphs despite the random nature of individual decays. Higher tier students have performed calculations involving the relationship between the initial activity, current activity, and half-life.

GCSE Physics students discussed the application of radioactivity to medical tracers within the body releasing gamma rays detected by gamma cameras and evaluated in terms of risks and benefits. These students have also looked at both nuclear fission and fusion in relation to nuclear power. Chain reactions involving fissionable isotopes have been described along with an outline of a fission reactor, its fuel rods, control rods, and physical construction. The dangers associated with nuclear fission, in particular accidents and the handling of waste have been debated. Nuclear fusion reactions in stars was discussed and compared to the difficulties of producing stable fusion reactions on Earth.

You can find additional support for the maths skills covered in this chapter on **MyMaths**, including making order of magnitude calculations, translating information between graphical and numeric form, visualising and representing 2D and 3D forms including two dimensional representations of 3D objects.

For this chapter, the following assessments are available on Kerboodle:

P7 Checkpoint quiz: Radioactivity
P7 Progress quiz: Radioactivity 1
P7 Progress quiz: Radioactivity 2
P7 On your marks: Radioactivity
P7 Exam-style questions and mark scheme: Radioactivity

Checkpoint follow up lesson

A student's route through this lesson can be determined using the Checkpoint assessment. Percentage pass marks are supplied in the Checkpoint teacher notes.

For each successive route through it is assumed that the student can perform to their current route as well as previous routes. For example, students working at Aiming for 6 are assumed to be secure in Aiming for 4 knowledge and understanding and working towards achieving all the learning outcomes for Aiming for 6.

	Aiming for 4	Aiming for 6	Aiming for 8
Learning outcomes	Describe the structure of the nucleus, how we show what is in a nucleus. The Thomson, Rutherford and Bohr models of the atom, and evidence that led to the model changing.	Describe the Thomson, Rutherford and Bohr models of the atom, the structure of the nucleus and evidence that led to the model changing.	Explain how and why the model of the atom has changed over time.
	Describe what alpha, beta, and gamma radiation is, and their different properties.	Describe what alpha, beta, and gamma radiation are, and their different properties and how to balance equations for nuclear decay.	Use ideas about radiation to balance nuclear equations.
	State what is meant by half-life.	Use ideas about half-life to solve problems.	Use a graph to determine half-life, calculate net decline, and solve problems involving half-life.
Starter	**Radioactive tennis (5 min)** Put students in groups of three. Two students take it in turns to say words relating to radioactivity and they keep going until one person can't go. The third student notes down the words. These are then fed back as a whole class. The words just need to be related to the topic not to each other (as in word association). Leave the words as a list for use in the plenary. **What's the difference? (5 min)** Put up two sets of images: X-ray of healthy/broken bone, gamma camera image of functioning/non-functioning kidney. In groups students to write down as many similarities and differences between the two sets of images as they can, and report back. You could display a series of prompts, such as: how are the images made/what radiation is used/how is the radiation detected.		
Differentiated checkpoint activity	Aiming for 4 students use the Checkpoint follow-up sheet to complete one of three activities: • design a matching game to summarise alpha, beta, and gamma radiation • design an animation to describe fission and fusion • model half-life and radioactive decay using sweets. The follow-up sheet is highly structured and students should work in pairs with teacher support. If the lesson is conducted in a laboratory, marbles or other small objects should be used instead of sweets, or students should be told not to eat the sweets.	Aiming for 6 students use the Checkpoint follow-up sheet to complete one of three activities: • design a cartoon to explain the principles of radioactive decay • design an animation to describe fission and fusion, carrying out some related calculations • model half-life and radioactive decay using sweets. The follow-up sheet provides limited support and students should aim to work independently. If the lesson is conducted in a laboratory, marbles or other small objects should be used instead of sweets, or students should be told not to eat the sweets.	Aiming for 8 students use the Checkpoint follow-up sheet to complete one of three activities: • design a cartoon to explain the principles of radioactive decay • design an animation to describe fission and fusion, carrying out some related calculations • model half-life and radioactive decay using sweets. The follow-up sheet provides minimal support and students should work independently. If the lesson is conducted in a laboratory, marbles or other small objects should be used instead of sweets, or students should be told not to eat the sweets.
	Kerboodle resource P7 Checkpoint follow up: Aiming for 4; P7 Checkpoint follow up: Aiming for 6; P7 Checkpoint follow up: Aiming for 8		
Plenary	**Radioactivity mind map (5 minutes)** Display the words from the tennis starter. Give out a large sheet of paper to each group and ask them to put all the words on a mind map. Each student could be responsible for a separate section of the map (model of the atom, α, β, γ, nuclear medicine, fission/fusion, half-life) and then they can discuss the links between them. **What's the question? (10 minutes)** Give students A4 dry wipe boards, pens and an eraser. Ask or display a series of answers, such as: 'because most of the alpha particles went through but some of them came back', and ask them to write the question. Alternatively give out a list of answers that are tailored to the different levels at which students are aiming.		
Progression	Students should be able to describe the model of the atom that we use now, give some evidence for how the model of the atom has changed, and describe the radiation emitted by unstable isotopes. They should be able state what is meant by half-life.	Students should be able to give an account of the history of the model of the atom and describe evidence that led to the discovery of the nucleus, use nuclear equations to account for the emission of radiation from nuclei. They should be able to do calculations involving half-life.	Students should be able to account for changes to the model of the atom, balance nuclear equations and use ideas about half-life, types of radiation emitted and the effect on tissue to explain the choice of isotopes in nuclear medicine. They should be able to apply knowledge of the processes of fission and fusion to a range of situations including nuclear power stations and the Sun. They should be able to calculate the net decline in activity of an isotope, and do calculations using half-life in a range of situations.

3 Forces in action

Specification links

AQA specification section	Assessment paper
5.1 Forces and their interactions	Paper 2
5.2 Work done and energy transfer	Paper 2
5.3 Forces and elasticity	Paper 2
5.4 Moments, levers, and gears (physics only)	Paper 2
5.5 Pressure and pressure differences in fluids (physics only)	Paper 2
5.6 Forces and motion	Paper 2
5.7 Momentum	Paper 2

Required practicals

AQA required practicals	Practical skills	Topic
Investigate the relationship between force and extension for a spring.	AT1 – use appropriate apparatus to make and record length accurately. AT2 – use appropriate apparatus to measure and observe the effect of force on the extension of springs and collect the data required to plot a force–extension graph.	P10.8
Investigate the effect of varying the force on the acceleration of an object of constant mass, and the effect of varying the mass of an object on the acceleration produced by a constant force.	AT1 – use appropriate apparatus to make and record measurements of length, mass, and time accurately. AT2 – use appropriate apparatus to measure and observe the effects of forces. AT3 – use appropriate apparatus and techniques for measuring motion, including determination of speed and rate of change of speed (acceleration/deceleration).	P10.1

Maths skills

AQA maths skills	Topic
1a Recognise and use expressions in decimal form	P8.1, P8.2, P8.4, P8.7, P8.9, P9.1, P10.1, P10.2, P10.3, P10.4, P10.5
1b Recognise and use expressions in standard form	P9.1, P11.2, P11.3
1c Use ratios, fractions, and percentages	P9.1, P11.4
1d Make estimates of the results of simple calculations	P9.1
2a Use an appropriate number of significant figures	P8.1, P8.2, P8.4, P8.7, P8.9, P10.3, P10.4, P10.5
2b Find arithmetic means	P10.3
2c Construct and interpret frequency tables and diagrams, bar charts, and histograms.	P10.2, P10.3, P10.7
2f Understand the terms mean, mode, and median	P9.1, P10.3, P10.7
2g Use a scatter diagram to identify a correlation between two variables.	P10.2
2h Make order of magnitude calculations	P8.1, P10.3
3a Understand and use the symbols: $=$, $<$, $<<$, $>>$, $>$, $\propto$, $\sim$	P8.1, P8.4, P8.7, P8.8, P9.1, P10.1, P10.2, P10.3, P10.4, P10.5, P10.6
3b Change the subject of an equation	P8.4, P8.7, P8.8, P9.1, P9.2, P9.3, P9.4, P10.1, P10.2, P10.3, P10.4, P10.5, P10.6, P10.8, P11.1, P11.2, P11.3
3c Substitute numerical values into algebraic equations using appropriate units for physical quantities	P8.4, P8.5, P8.7, P8.8, P8.9, P9.1, P9.2, P9.3, P9.4, P10.1, P10.2, P10.3, P10.4, P10.5, P10.6, P10.8, P11.1, P11.2, P11.3, P11.4
3d Solve simple algebraic equations	P8.4, P8.7, P8.8, P8.9, P9.2, P10.1, P10.2, P10.3, P10.4, P10.5, P10.6, P10.7
4a Translate information between graphical and numeric form	P9.1, P9.2, P9.3, P9.4, P10.1
4b Understand that $y = mx + c$ represents a linear relationship	P9.1, P9.2, P9.3, P9.4

AQA maths skills	Topic
4c Plot two variables from experimental or other data	P9.2, P9.3, P9.4, P10.2
4d Determine the slope and intercept of a linear graph	P9.1, P9.2, P9.3, P9.4
4f Understand the physical significance of area between a curve and the x-axis and measure it by counting squares as appropriate	P9.2, P9.3, P9.4
5a Use angular measures in degrees	P8.8
5b Visualise and represent 2D and 3D forms including two dimensional representations of 3D objects	P8.1, P8.8, P8.9

KS3 concept	GCSE topic	Checkpoint	Revision
Force is measured in newtons (N) using a newton-meter.	P8.2 Forces between objects	Ask students to describe how they would measure the force need to lift a chair.	Students can label a range of simple force diagrams using force arrows and approximate values for the forces.
An object is in equilibrium because the forces acting on it are balanced.	P8.3 Resultant forces	Ask students to draw a force diagram showing the forces acting on a car travelling at a constant speed.	Students can determine which objects are in equilibrium by analysing a set of diagrams of objects with a range of forces acting on them.
The turning effect of a force acting on a pivoted object depends on how far the force acts from the pivot.	P8.4 Moments at work	Balance a ruler of the tip of your finger and ask students to explain why it does not fall off.	Student can describe how two different-sized people can balance on a seesaw. This can be supported with a suitable calculation.
Speed is measured in metres per second.	P9.1 Speed and distance–time graphs	Ask students to estimate the speed that you walk around the classroom.	Students should use the speed equation to calculate the speed of some common objects in metres per second.
An object is accelerating if its speed is increasing.	P9.2 Velocity and acceleration	Ask the students to describe the motion of a drag car through the whole race.	Students label the speed–time graph of motion for a drag race noting acceleration and deceleration.
When objects interact, each one exerts a force on the other one.	P8.2 Forces between objects	Ask students to draw a force diagram for a ball falling directly downwards and a second force diagram showing what happens at the moment of impact.	Students should draw diagrams which match up pairs of forces such as the forces between an object and the Earth, a pair of magnets or a ship floating.
The force in a stretched object is called tension and it increases if the object is stretched more.	P10.8 Forces and elasticity	Ask students to describe the forces acting when a catapult is stretched.	Students plot a force–extension graph for a stretching spring and describe the relationship between these variables.
Assess risk in an experiment.	P10.8 Forces and elasticity	Ask students to preform a risk assessment for the spring constant investigation.	The students should assess each other's risk assessments after the experiment and determine which was the most suitable.
The pressure in a liquid acts in all directions.	P11.2 Pressure in a liquid at rest	Ask students to explain why a balloon full of water is stretched in all directions.	Place some tape over parts of a water filled balloon and pin-prick some small holes. Students discuss why the water is forced out and why the flow gradually decreases.

P 8 Forces in balance

8.1 Vectors and scalars

AQA spec Link: 5.1.1 Scalar quantities have magnitude only.

Vector quantities have magnitude and an associated direction.

A vector quantity may be represented by an arrow. The length of the arrow represents the magnitude, and the direction of the arrow the direction of the vector quantity.

5.1.2 Force is a vector quantity.

MS 1a, 2a

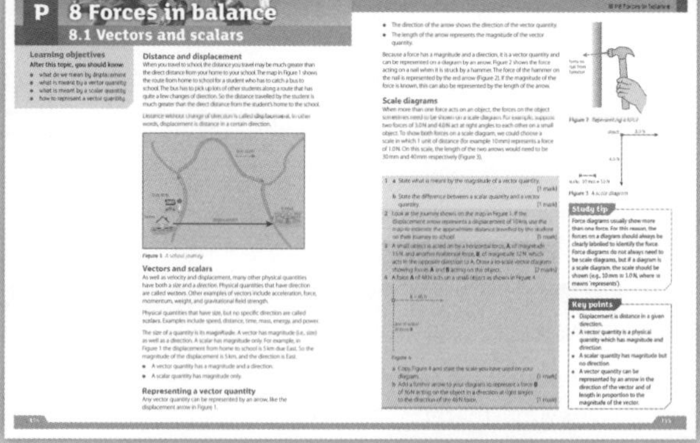

Aiming for	Outcome	Checkpoint	
		Question	Activity
Aiming for GRADE 4	Describe how scalars have size (magnitude) without direction.	1	Starter 1, Main 1
	Describe how vectors have both size (magnitude) and direction.	1	Main 1
	List some common scalars and vectors.		Main 1
Aiming for GRADE 6	Draw a scale diagram to represent a single vector.	3, 4	Main 2
	Categorise a wide range of quantities as either a vector or a scalar.		Main 1
	Compare a scalar and a similar vector and explain how these quantities are different.		Starter 2, Main 1
Aiming for GRADE 8	Interpret a scale diagram to determine the magnitude and direction of a vector.	2	Main 1, Main 2
	Translate between vector descriptions and vector diagrams and vice versa using a range of appropriate scales.	3, 4	Main 2
	Use a scale diagram to add two or more vectors.	4	Main 2, Plenary 2

Maths
Students will add and subtract both vector and scalar quantities including the use of SI prefixes.

Literacy
Students should translate between vector diagrams and accurate descriptions of the vectors shown and vice versa.

Key words
vectors, scalar, magnitude, displacement

Practical

Title	Measuring instruments
Equipment	wide range of measuring instruments such as: rulers, tape measures, trundle wheel, callipers, ammeter, voltmeter, resistance meter, force meter, top-pan balance, scales, measuring cylinder, thermometer, stopwatch, compass, light meter, joule meter, protractor
Overview of method	The students examine and discuss the instruments and how they are used. They note the type of measurements which can be made, including the appropriate units for this measurement. Students can also discuss how the instruments can be used in combination to measure quantities such as speed (a stopwatch and tape measure) which leads on to the idea of velocity (stopwatch, tape measure and compass or protractor).

Starter	Support/Extend	Resources
Measuring instruments (5 min) Students examine a range of measuring instruments and discuss their operation.	**Extend:** Discuss the importance of measurement in physics and the fundamental quantities of length, mass, and time.	
As the crow (10 min) Interactive where students measure the direct distance between two places on a map. They then compare their value to the distance given from an Internet mapping service, choosing reasons for why there is a discrepancy.	**Extend:** Extend this discussion into much longer journeys, for example, How far away is Sydney? Should we measure in a straight line through the Earth?	
Main	**Support/Extend**	**Resources**
The difference between a vector and scalar quantity (15 min) Discuss the similarities and differences between a distance and a displacement. Use plenty of examples such as those in the Starter 2 and the student book. Ensure that the students understand the concepts of magnitude (size) and direction. Link back to the ideas in the first starter and discuss the quantities that the instruments measure in more depth. Discuss whether these quantities are scalar or vector in nature. Can some of the instruments be used to measure both? For example, a measuring cylinder will only measure volume (always scalar) whilst a ruler may be used with a protractor to measure displacement.	**Extend:** Ask the students to categorise all of the measurements they think can be made with the measuring instruments. Discuss the degree of measurement uncertainty associated with each measuring instrument.	
Representing vectors (25 min) Introduce the idea of a scale diagram to discuss how vectors can be represented. Start with further examples of displacements before introducing forces. Students should attempt to draw several scaled vector diagrams from descriptive sentences (e.g., a force of 500 N acting to the left or a force of 3.2 N at an angle of 30 degrees to the horizontal). In addition, they should write a description of a vector by interpreting a diagram. Students can use the activity sheet to examine the relationship between displacement and distance in detail.	**Support:** Using squared paper will make drawing scale diagrams simpler. **Extend:** Students should use a scale diagram to represent a pair of vectors at right angles and then find the resultant. They should also use SI prefixes in their diagrams as appropriate.	**Activity:** Scalars and vectors
Plenary	**Support/Extend**	**Resources**
Vectors and scalars (5 min) Students complete the interactive where they choose the correct words to complete a summary of the key points from the lesson.	**Extend:** Students should explain if any of these measurements are vector or scalar in nature. Are all of the properties *measureable* scientifically?	**Interactive:** Vectors and scalars
The shortest journey (10 min) Use a local map and select six different locations. Ass the students to find the shortest journey that allows them to visit all six. They should estimate the total distance travelled, for example, using string and the appropriate scale.	**Support:** Limit the number of locations to five and provide a clear starting and end point. **Extend:** The students must select the best starting and end points to produce the shortest travel distance.	
Homework		
Students should be asked to draw a range of scale diagrams showing vectors based on the description provided. For example, the forces acting on a moving car or directions on a map.	**Support:** Provide partial diagrams for the students to draw the vectors on. **Extend:** Students should also find the resultant of several vectors using diagrams.	

kerboodle

A Kerboodle highlight for this lesson is **Literacy sheet: Scalars and vectors**. Refer to the **Content map** on Kerboodle for a full list of resources and assessment.

P8.2 Forces between objects

AQA spec Link: 5.1.2 A force is a push or pull that acts on an object due to the interaction with another object. All forces between objects are either:

- contact forces – the objects are physically touching
- non-contact forces – the objects are physically separated.

Examples of contact forces include friction, air resistance, tension, and normal contact force.

Examples of non-contact forces are gravitational force, electrostatic force, and magnetic force.

Force is a vector quantity.

Students should be able to describe the interaction between pairs of objects which produce a force on each object. The forces should be represented as vectors.

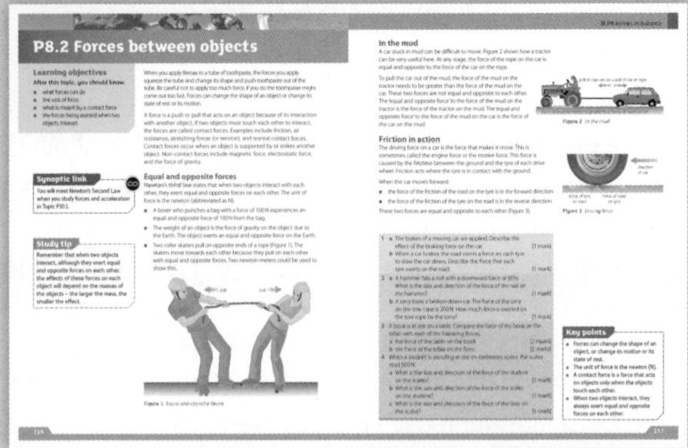
P8.2 Forces between objects

MS 1a, 2a

Aiming for	Outcome	Checkpoint	
		Question	Activity
Aiming for GRADE 4	Use arrows to represent the directions of forces.		Starter 2
	Give examples of contact and non-contact forces.	3	Starter 1
	Compare the sizes of forces using the unit newton (N).	2, 4	Plenary 1
Aiming for GRADE 6	Use scale diagrams to represent the sizes of forces acting on an object.		Starter 1, Main 1
	Describe the action of pairs of forces in a limited range of scenarios.	1, 2	
	Investigate the effect of different lubricants on the size of frictional forces.		Main 2
Aiming for GRADE 8	Use appropriate SI prefixes and standard form to describe a wide range of forces.		Plenary 1
	Explain the pairs of forces acting in a wide range of unfamiliar scenarios, including the nature (contact or non-contact), direction, and magnitude of the forces.	3	Main 2
	Evaluate force measurement techniques in terms of precision and accuracy.		Main 2

Maths
Students compare the size of forces that include SI multipliers.

Literacy
Students describe the action of forces, referring clearly to the objects.

Key words
force, friction, Newton's third law

Starter	Support/Extend	Resources
It's a drag (5 min) Show a video of a drag racer deploying a parachute to assist in braking. Ask the students to explain how the parachute helps to slow the car down. Try and draw out the key concepts of forces and friction.	**Extend:** Show the start of the race, especially if a rocket booster is being used, and ask the students to discuss the forces acting during this part of the motion.	
Force diagrams (10 min) Show a set of diagrams of objects and statements about their motion – standing still, at constant velocity or accelerating and ask the students to mark on all of the forces. Check that the students are using 'force arrows' and that they are marked clearly onto the point at which the force acts.	**Extend:** Expect the students to compare the size of the forces by drawing scale diagrams.	
Main	**Support/Extend**	**Resources**
The nature of forces (15 min) Demonstrate the action of some forces by pushing and pulling some objects to show that there can be different sizes and that the direction of the force is significant. This will establish that forces are vector quantities. Students can drag a few items using a newton-meter to experience different sizes of forces.	**Support:** Students can visualise forces by attaching cardboard 'force arrows' to objects showing weight and reactions.	
Forces between objects (25 min) Students read a passage on high diving describing the heights, times, and the potential risks involved. They use this passage to identify contact and non-contact forces, action and reaction pairs, and to explain changes in motion due to the action of forces.		**Activity:** Forces between objects
Plenary	**Support/Extend**	**Resources**
Pulling power (5 min) Provide students with ten (or more) force strengths of players (50 N, 100 N, 150 N, 200 N, 250 N, 300 N, 350 N, 400 N, 450 N, 500 N). Students assign them to two tug-of-war teams so that the teams are balanced. There may be several solutions.	**Support:** Start with only a small set of forces which can be balanced by placing three on each side. **Extend:** Use SI prefixes and/or standard form for some of the forces.	
Forces between objects (10 min) Students use the interactive to sort examples of contact and non-contact forces. They then identify the action and reaction pairs in the given scenario of a car driving at a constant speed.	**Support:** Limit the forces to simple examples. **Extend:** Use SI prefixes and/or standard form for some of the forces.	**Interactive:** Forces between objects
Homework		
Students analyse the forces acting in a scenario of their choice such as a particular sport or an engineering project. They should include ideas about the size and directions of the forces.	**Support:** Limit the scenarios appropriately. **Extend:** Students should produce a force diagram of a complex scenario such as the forces acting on a bridge with traffic travelling across it.	

kerboodle

A Kerboodle highlight for this lesson is **Go further: The effects of nuclear forces**. Refer to the **Content map** on Kerboodle for a full list of resources and assessment.

P8.3 Resultant forces

AQA spec Link: 5.1.1 A vector quantity may be represented by an arrow. The length of the arrow represents the magnitude, and the direction of the arrow the direction of the vector quantity.

5.1.2 Force is a vector quantity.

5.1.4 A number of forces acting on an object may be replaced by a single force that has the same effect as all the original forces acting together. This single force is called the resultant force.

Students should be able to calculate the resultant of two forces that act in a straight line.

(H) Students should be able to:

- **describe examples of the forces acting on an isolated object or system**
- **use free body diagrams to describe qualitatively examples where several forces lead to a resultant force on an object, including balanced forces when the resultant force is zero.**

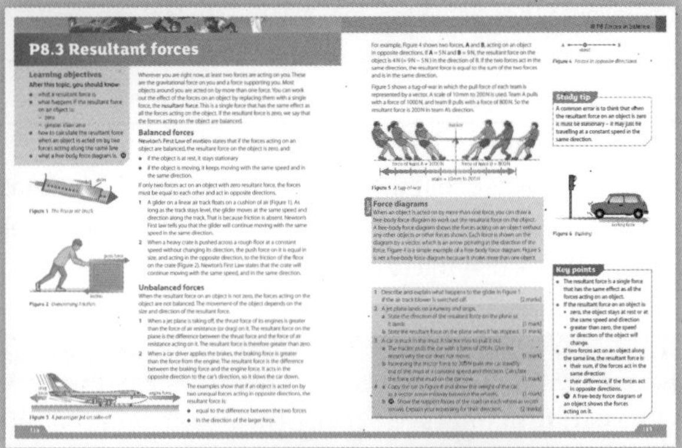

WS 1.2

Aiming for	Outcome	Checkpoint	
		Question	Activity
Aiming for GRADE 4	Label a diagram showing several forces acting on an object.		Starter 2
	Calculate a resultant force from two parallel forces acting in opposite directions.		Starter 1
	State that a non-zero resultant force will cause a change in motion and a zero resultant force will not (Newton's First Law of motion).	2	Starter 2
Aiming for GRADE 6	Draw a scaled diagram of the forces acting in a range of situations using arrows to represent the forces.	4	Main 1
	(H) Calculate resultant force produced by several forces acting on an object in coplanar directions.	3	Main 2
	Describe the effect of zero and non-zero resultant forces on the motion of moving and stationary objects.	1, 2	Main 1
Aiming for GRADE 8	**(H) Draw a scaled free-body force diagram showing forces as vectors and find the resultant force vector.**	4	Main 2
	(H) Calculate resultant forces from several forces acting in coplanar directions using a range of SI prefixes.		Main 2
	Create a detailed plan to investigate the factors that affect the acceleration of objects acted on by a non-zero resultant force.		Main 1

Maths 
Students perform simple vector addition on coplanar vectors. These may be represented by positive and negative numbers.

Literacy 
Students focus on the terminology for forces and the description of their effects.

Key words
resultant force, Newton's First Law of Motion

Starter	Support/Extend	Resources
Vector addition (5 min) Develop students' mathematical skills using addition sums that include negative numbers to check their understanding. Link this to the idea that forces are added together but ones in opposite directions are treated as negative.	**Support:** Use force arrows lying in the same direction to show addition, and in the opposite direction to show subtraction.	
Balanced forces (10 min) Show the students a toy boat floating on water and ask them to draw a diagram of all of the forces on the boat. Add small masses, one at a time, until the boat sinks. Ask them to draw a diagram showing the forces at the time when the boat was sinking.	**Extend:** Ask the students why the upward thrust of the water increases as the load does.	
Main	**Support/Extend**	**Resources**
Resultant forces and their effects (25 min) Discuss with students how an object with zero resultant force will be either moving at a constant velocity or stationary. Focus on an object moving at a constant velocity, using the example of an aircraft cruising to demonstrate. Then show a video of a jet aircraft taking off and discuss the forces involved – the sound of the engines will give an indication of increasing and decreasing thrust. Emphasise the concept that unbalanced forces cause *acceleration*, which can be a change in speed or direction of motion. Students then complete the activity sheet where they apply their knowledge and understanding of zero and non-zero resultant (balanced and unbalanced) forces on three different objects – a motorbike, an aircraft, and a runner – and carry out calculations of resultant forces from forces applied on different objects.	**Extend:** Students should be able to describe the forces acting in all of these situations using vector diagrams. **Support:** Pause at key moments and draw force arrows onto the still frame. Ask the students to describe what will happen to the motion at these key points.	**Activity:** Resultant forces and their effects
Free-body force diagrams (15 min) **H** The activity sheet also gives higher-tier students the opportunity to gain confidence in interpreting free-body diagrams and in describing the effects of force on different objects. They need to focus on individual objects and the forces acting on them when drawing free-body diagrams. Sketch some additional ones at this point, such as the forces acting on a boat resting on the ocean surface or a sprinter leaving the starting blocks. Two versions of each diagram can be drawn – one with all of the forces and one with just the resultant. Emphasise the term *vector* as opposed to *arrow* when describing the forces.	**Extend:** An extension sheet is available for further practice in drawing free-body diagrams.	**Extension:** Free-body diagrams
Plenary	**Support/Extend**	**Resources**
Resultant forces (10 min) Interactive where students identify true and false statements about the forces acting on a cyclist. **H** They then identify the correct free-body diagram for a submarine moving forward and descending.	**Extend:** Students suggest how to correct the false statements.	**Interactive:** Resultant forces
An uphill struggle (10 min) Challenge students to come up with some explanations about forces and link the ideas to energy transfer. For example, why is it harder to push a car uphill rather than on a flat road?	**Extend:** Calculations of work done (studied in KS3) can allow the students to find changes in the energy stores.	
Homework		
Students can find the resultant forces in a range of situations both from prose questions and from simple diagrams. They should describe the effect of the forces on the motion of objects.	**Extend:** Use examples that involve a wide range of forces with SI prefixes.	

kerboodle

A Kerboodle highlight for this lesson is **Bump up your grade teacher: What is the resultant force?** Refer to the **Content map** on Kerboodle for a full list of resources and assessment.

P8.4 Moments at work

AQA spec Link: 5.4 A force or a system of forces may cause an object to rotate.

Students should be able to describe examples in which forces cause rotation.

The turning effect of a force is called the moment of the force. The size of the moment is defined by the equation:

moment of a force = force × distance

$[M = F\,d]$

moment of a force M in newton metres, Nm

force F in newtons, N

distance d is the perpendicular distance from the pivot to the line of action of the force, in metres, m.

If an object is balanced, the total clockwise moment about a pivot equals the total anticlockwise moment about that pivot.

A simple lever and a simple gear system can both be used to transmit the rotational effects of forces.

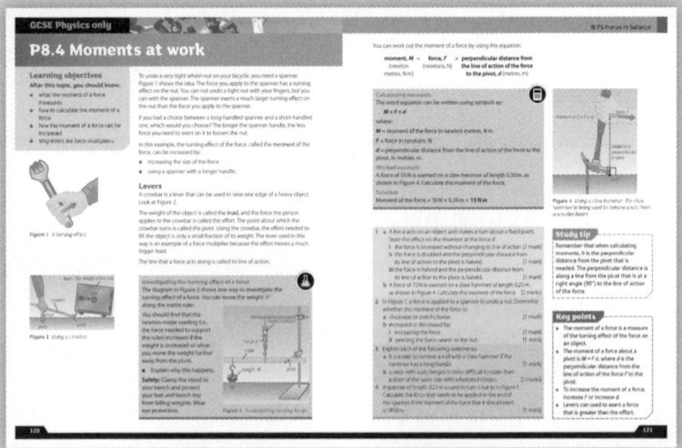
GCSE Physics only

P8.4 Moments at work

MS 3c

Aiming for	Outcome	Checkpoint	
		Question	**Activity**
Aiming for GRADE 4	Give the factors that affect the size of a moment.	1, 2, 3, 4	Main 2
	Calculate the moment of a force using the appropriate equation and base units.	1, End of chapter 2, 3	Main 3
	Record experimental data clearly.		Main 2
Aiming for GRADE 6	Describe the uses of a force-multiplier lever.		Main 1
	Perform calculations involving moments, including rearrangement of the equation.	1, 4	Main 3
	Design a system for recording data and associated calculations clearly.		Main 2
Aiming for GRADE 8	Explain why a force multiplier requires the effort force to move through a larger distance than the load.		Main 1, Main 2
	Apply the equation for a moment in a range of novel contexts including rearrangement and changes to and from base units.	1, 4, End of chapter 2, 3	Main 3
	Evaluate in detail the accuracy and precision of a set of data based on comparison of measurements and a 'true value'.		Plenary 2

Maths
The students will perform calculations of moments using the mathematical equation (3c).

Literacy
Students apply scientific vocabulary to descriptions of the action of forces. Students also interpret diagrams to produce written instructions for putting together flat-pack furniture.

Key words
moment

Practical

Title	Investigating the turning effect of a force
Equipment	retort stand with two clamp arms, 50 cm or 30 cm ruler with a hole drilled towards one end, newton-meter (10 N), 10 g mass holder with four 10 g masses, some cotton

Overview of method	Attach the newton-meter to the arm of a clamp and halfway along the ruler as shown in the student book (Figure 3). Fit a second arm from the stand through the hole in the ruler providing a pivot. The masses are then suspended near the end of the ruler and can be slid back and forth to determine the effect on the newton-meter. Students vary the distance and note the effect on the newton-meter, they then vary the force (by altering the position of the mass) and note the effect. Finally they can combine both conclusions into a statement about the factors that affect the moments in the system.
Safety considerations	Small masses should be used to reduce the chance of injury of falling objects.

Starter	Support/Extend	Resources
Force facts (10 min) Students should draw a quick visual summary to show their prior knowledge about forces from KS3. This should include concepts such as forces acting in particular directions, pivots, size of forces, units, forces causing movement/acceleration, and friction.	**Support:** Key words can be provided to prompt the students' memories.	
Right tool for the job (10 min) Show students tools (e.g., crowbar, screwdriver, spanner) and some jobs that they are used for (e.g., opening a box or paint tin or removing a bolt). Ask the students to match each tool to appropriate jobs, and then ask the students to explain how they work.	**Extend:** Ask the students to show rotations and draw force arrows that are in proportion to the forces that may be used.	
Main	**Support/Extend**	**Resources**
Levers (10 min) Demonstrate the use of several tools that show the application of forces and rotation, for example, removing a nail with a claw hammer, using a crowbar to lift a heavy object, using a spanner to tighten/loosen bolts. Introduce the concept of a moment as the turning effect of the force and suggest factors that will change the size of this moment.	**Support:** Students should sketch the tools and locate where the effort, load, and pivot are for each.	
Investigating the turning effect of a force (20 min) Students should carry out an investigation and clearly identify the factors that affect the size of the moment (force and distance). They design a results table that will allow recording of the force acting on the newton-meter and the weight of the masses and distance from the pivot.	**Support:** Provide a results table for the experiment. **Extend:** The students should record the initial reading on the newton-meter and find the change in values to determine the change in moments.	**Practical:** Investigating the turning effect of a force
Calculating moments (10 min) Students carry out some differentiated calculations to find moments. This can include calculation of moments produced by the moving masses in their earlier experiment and the force recorded by the newton-meter.	**Extend:** Students evaluate the experiment by relating the moments they recorded with the results calculated here.	
Plenary	**Support/Extend**	**Resources**
Moments at work (5 min) Interactive where students calculate the moment applied to turn a nut using a spanner. They then identify the gears from a bicycle that have the biggest moment.	**Support:** Demonstrate a real lever balance as used in, for example, a greengrocer's, instead.	**Interactive:** Moments at work
Weighing machine (10 min) Provide students with some object of unknown weight and ask them to use the apparatus from the investigation to find the weight. Provide the actual masses and discuss the precision and accuracy of the system.		
Homework		
Give the students copies of wordless instructions for flat-pack furniture. Ask them to produce written instructions based on the diagrams that include scientific explanations.		

kerboodle

A Kerboodle highlight for this lesson is **Extension sheet: Using the equation of moments of a force**. Refer to the **Content map** on Kerboodle for a full list of resources and assessment.

P8.5 More about levers and gears

AQA spec Link: 5.4 A force or a system of forces may cause an object to rotate.

Students should be able to describe examples in which forces cause rotation.

The turning effect of a force is called the moment of the force. The size of the moment is defined by the equation:

moment of a force = force × distance

$[M = F\,d]$

moment of a force M in newton metres, Nm

force F in newtons, N

distance d is the perpendicular distance from the pivot to the line of action of the force, in metres, m.

If an object is balanced, the total clockwise moment about a pivot equals the total anticlockwise moment about that pivot.

Students should be able to calculate the size of a force, or its distance from a pivot, acting on an object that is balanced.

A simple lever and a simple gear system can both be used to transmit the rotational effects of forces.

Students should be able to explain how levers and gears transmit the rotational effects of forces.

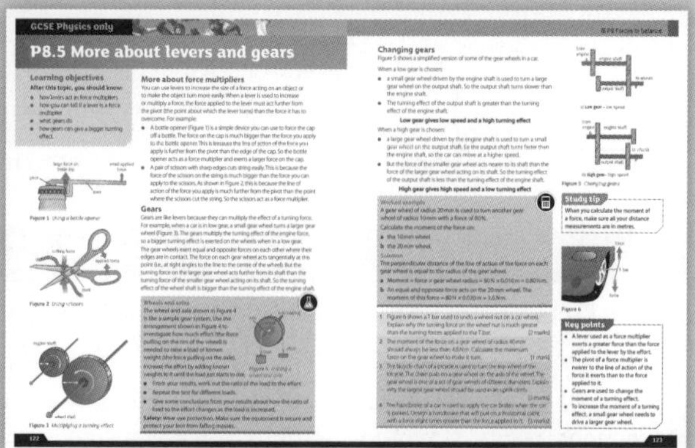

MS 3c

Aiming for	Outcome	Checkpoint	
		Question	Activity
Aiming for GRADE 4 ↓	Identify levers being used as force multipliers.	1	Starter 1, Main 1
	Calculate the forces produced by force multipliers.	2	Starter 1, Main 1
	State that gears can be used to increase or decrease the size of forces.		Main 2, Main 3
Aiming for GRADE 6 ↓	Describe the action of levers being used as force multipliers.	2	Main 1
	Describe the action of a pair of gears in terms of increasing or decreasing the size of forces.	3, End of chapter 7	Main 2
	Investigate the action of a set of two gears.		Main 2
Aiming for GRADE 8 ↓	Describe the action of gears relating changes in the size of forces to the speed of rotation and the number of teeth in the gear.	3, End of chapter 7	Main 2, Main 3
	Analyse systems of gears of different ratios.	3	Main 3
	Evaluate the results of a gear experiment, explaining any discrepancies in terms of the uncontrolled forces acting on the system.		Main 2

Maths

Students calculate moments and the forces produced by gear combinations (3c).

Literacy

Complex descriptions of the action of gears are required for this lesson. Students should explain their ideas to each other clearly using the appropriate scientific terms.

Practical

Title	Wheels and axles
Equipment	wheel and axle combination, small masses and cotton, two mass hangers retort stands and bosses The apparatus can be made by gluing together different sized cork pieces and passing a metal rod through the centre. The load hangers are attached with the cotton.
Overview of method	Suspend the axle from a pair of stands, attach the load and effort holders. Increase the number of masses on the effort until the load rises.
Safety considerations	Use small masses to avoid damage to the floor or feet.

Starter	Support/Extend	Resources
Elephant v. mouse (5 min) An elephant has a mass of 2000 kg, and a mouse has a mass of 10 g. If they sit on either side of a seesaw, and the elephant is 0.5 m from the pivot, how far away should the mouse sit? This can lead to a calculation of the moment from the elephant and then the distance the mouse needs to be away from the pivot (100 km).	**Extend:** Discuss the assumptions or simplifications in this question: could a 200 km-long seesaw be constructed?	
Odd one out (10 min) Interactive where students choose the odd one out of a series of images showing pivots and gears.		**Interactive:** Odd one out
Main	**Support/Extend**	**Resources**
More about force multipliers (10 min) Examine the devices shown in the student book to explain the action of levers being used as force multipliers.	**Extend:** Students should try some example calculations when given appropriate data.	
Simple gears (20 min) Demonstrate the action of a set of gears using equipment or a simulation. Emphasise that the changes in distance from the shaft (pivot) allow changes in the sizes of the force linked to changes in the speed of rotation. Students then investigate the effect of different wheel diameters on an axle with this practical. They should note the additional forces that affect the results (e.g., friction on the axle) for use in evaluating the results.	**Support:** Students should simply note that the larger the wheel, the smaller the effort needs to be. **Extend:** Students should use ratio calculations with the diameter and forces to determine a pattern.	**Practical:** Wheels and axles
Changing gears (10 min) Students study the application of gears in a simple engine, explaining how larger or smaller forces can be produced by differing gear combinations. An engine gear model is exceptionally valuable here, if one is available.	**Extend:** Students can consider the effect of the number of teeth on the gears and discuss ratios.	
Plenary	**Support/Extend**	**Resources**
Rolling on a river (10 min) Show the students a paddle-boat steamer and ask them to explain how the actions of the wheel make the boat move forwards. How might gears be involved with the paddle wheel?	**Extend:** The students should note that the forces from the wheel on the air and on the water are different sizes.	
Distance multipliers (5 min) Can the students identify any levers that increase the size of movement but reduce the size of forces?		
Homework		
The students should research devices that have gear systems and explain how they operate.	**Extend:** Students can support their explanations with example calculations.	

kerboodle

A Kerboodle highlight for this lesson is **Video: The important Moments of an Engineer**. Refer to the **Content map** on Kerboodle for a full list of resources and assessment.

P8.6 Centre of mass

AQA spec Link: 5.1.3 The weight of an object may be considered to act at a single point referred to as the object's 'centre of mass'.

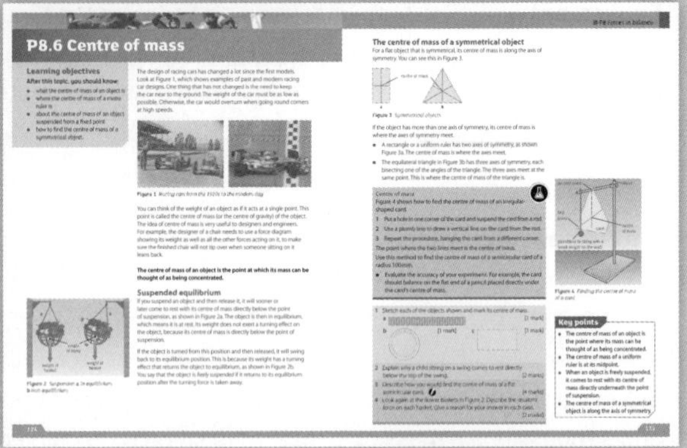

Aiming for	Outcome	Checkpoint	
		Question	**Activity**
Aiming for GRADE 4	Identify the approximate centre of mass of a range of simple shapes.		Main
	State that a suspended object will come to rest so that the centre of mass lies below the point of suspension.	1	Main
	Use lines of symmetry to identify the location of the centre of mass.	1	Main
Aiming for GRADE 6	Describe an experimental technique to determine the centre of mass of an object.	3	Main
	Explain why a suspended object comes to rest with the centre of mass directly below the point of suspension in terms of balanced forces.	2, 4	Main
	Compare the stability of objects to the position of their centre of mass.		Main
Aiming for GRADE 8	Evaluate an experimental technique to determine the centre of mass of an object, identifying the likely sources of error leading to inaccuracy.		Main
	Apply understanding of the particle model and moments to explain why objects have a point at which the mass seems to act.		Main
	Plan a detailed investigation into the stability of three-dimensional objects.		Homework

Maths
Students should apply the concept of symmetry when finding the centre of mass of regular objects.

Literacy
Students should describe why objects will rest with the centre of mass below the point of suspension.

Practical

Title	Centre of mass
Equipment	retort stands, bosses and clamps, string and pendulum bobs (plumb lines), corks, long pins, card, and scissors
Overview of method	Students cut out a range of shapes from the cards – rectangles, triangles, and irregular shapes. Hold the cork in the clamp, so that the pins can be pushed through the card into it. Wrap the plumb line around the pin and push it through a point near the edge of the card into the cork. Students gently press the line against the card (squeezing from both sides) and mark a point near the bottom of the shape. They then remove the card and draw a line from the mark to the pinhole.
Safety considerations	Protect feet, furniture, and the floor, from falling objects.

Starter	Support/Extend	Resources
Force diagrams (10 min) Students label the forces on a car moving at a steady speed along a horizontal road. Discuss why the students have drawn the weight where they have. Does their force arrow show the force coming from the bottom of the car or the middle? Show that the arrows should be coming from the centre of the car, and explain that the lesson will deal with what this centre is.	**Support:** To reduce the complexity, the car can be stationary. **Extend:** Expand the discussion to include the parts of the car – why is only one arrow for the weight used when each individual part has a weight?	
Fearful symmetry (5 min) Give students a set of shapes (rectangle, square, equilateral triangle, isosceles triangle, circle) and ask them to draw on the shapes the lines of symmetry. Discuss whether the point at which these lines cross is the centre.	**Extend:** Ask the students to discuss how to balance the flat shapes. Do not provide any clues about symmetry and centres.	
Main	**Support/Extend**	**Resources**
Centre of mass (40 min) Discuss the concept of the 'middle' of objects in terms of where the mass of an object seems to be. This is a simplification of all of the individual masses of the particles within the object.	**Extend:** Discuss the nature of a centre of mass as result of the individual particles within an object.	**Practical:** Centre of mass
Demonstrate suspending some objects to show that they align themselves in particular ways and that there is a point that is always directly below the suspension point. Secure a clamp to a desk, and students suspend the objects from the stand using string. Suspend the same object from several different points to show roughly where the centre of mass is. Show the students, or allow them to find, the position of the centre of mass of symmetrical objects by drawing the lines of symmetry and lifting the objects at this point.	**Extend:** Students use some objects for which the centre of mass is actually outside the physical object. Emphasise that this point will always be directly below a suspension point when the object hangs freely.	
Students then test various objects to find their centre of mass. Start with simple geometric shapes to confirm that the centre of mass is where they expect, and then move on to irregular shapes.	**Support:** Provide cards with holes pre-cut and lines already drawn on them. **Extend:** Students describe the types of error that lead to inaccuracy in the experiment.	
Plenary	**Support/Extend**	**Resources**
Centre of mass (10 min) Interactive where students decide where the centre of mass is in a series of images, and then decide which item will topple over.	**Extend:** Use complex shapes with portions cut out.	**Interactive:** Centre of mass
Topple (10 min) Students draw a table, listing some objects designed to topple over and some objects designed to be stable. They sketch these shapes and try to describe where the centre of mass is in each of them.	**Support:** Look at simple shapes such as bowling pins. **Extend:** Looking at chairs, tables, and non-symmetrical objects.	
Homework		
Students complete the WebQuest to research stability, the centre of mass, equilibrium, and when objects topple. They use their research to produce a presentation on two or three examples of objects/situations where stability is important.	**Extend:** Students should provide a qualitative measurement which indicates stability for the objects.	**WebQuest:** Stability

P8.7 Moments and equilibrium

AQA spec Link: 5.4 The turning effect of a force is called the moment of the force. The size of the moment is defined by the equation:

moment of a force = force × distance

$[M = F\,d]$

moment of a force M in newton metres, Nm

force F in newtons, N

distance d is the perpendicular distance from the pivot to the line of action of the force, in metres, m.

If an object is balanced, the total clockwise moment about a pivot equals the total anticlockwise moment about that pivot.

Students should be able to calculate the size of a force, or its distance from a pivot, acting on an object that is balanced.

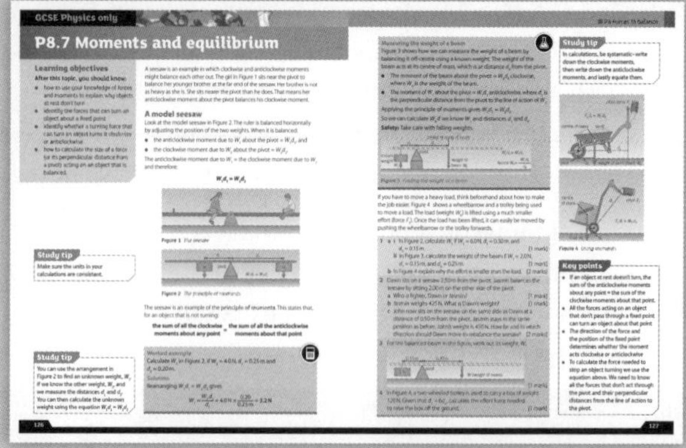

MS 3a, 3c

Aiming for	Outcome	Checkpoint	
		Question	Activity
Aiming for GRADE 4	Calculate moments using the appropriate equation.	1	
	Define the principle of moments.		Main 1
	Find the weight of an object using a balanced beam.		Practical 1, Practical 2
Aiming for GRADE 6	Use calculation of moments to determine if a seesaw is in equilibrium.	1	
	Apply the principle of moments to determine if an object is in equilibrium.	1, 2	Main 1, Main 3
	Establish the possible range of uncertainty of a weight using repeat values.		Practical 1
Aiming for GRADE 8	Use calculations to determine if an object with three or more moments is in equilibrium.	1, 2, 3, 4	
	Describe the application of moments in balance (equilibrium) in a range of contexts.		Main 3
	Evaluate an experiment to determine the weight of objects in terms of accuracy and precision.		Practical 1, Practical 2

Maths
Students will calculate moments through the appropriate equation (3c). Some students will use ranges to establish the uncertainty of a measured value (3a).

Literacy
Students can discuss and describe the application of techniques used to measure weights during their practical tasks.

Key words
principle of moments

Practical

Title	Measuring an unknown weight
Equipment	one uniform beam, pivot (triangular block), ruler, known mass (100 g) and unknown mass and a suitable top-pan balance
Overview of method	Students set up the apparatus as shown in Figure 2 in the student book. They balance the masses and measure the distances, so that they can find the unknown mass. Students should repeat the measurements at least three times using different distances and find the mean value. The top-pan balance is used to check results.
Safety considerations	Protect feet, furniture and the floor, from falling objects.

Practical

Title	Measuring the weight of a beam
Equipment	one uniform beam, pivot (wooden triangular block), ruler, an appropriate mass (about half the mass of the ruler)
Overview of method	Students balance the ruler by placing the pivot and then balancing the beam by adjusting the position of the mass. Repeat the experiment several times with the pivot in different positions.
Safety considerations	Protect feet, furniture, and the floor, from falling objects.

Starter	Support/Extend	Resources
Tipping point (5 min) Place a 50 cm ruler on a triangular pivot 20 cm from one end so that it is unbalanced. Ask the students where they could place a 20 g mass so that the ruler becomes balanced and to explain why this is.	**Extend:** Provide the mass of the ruler and ask the students to show a calculation justifying their explanation.	
Moments: equilibrium (10 min) Interactive where students answer questions on moments and a balanced seesaw. Students are then shown several seesaws with a variety of masses on and determine whether it is balanced or unbalanced. They must explain their reasoning; some will be using moment calculations already whilst others will be using some 'rule of thumb'.	**Support:** Use relatively simple situations (just one force on each side of the pivot). **Extend:** Having a range of forces with different SI prefixes or more than one force acting on each side of the pivot.	**Interactive:** Moments: equilibrium
Main	**Support/Extend**	**Resources**
Seesaws and balance calculations (15 min) Follow up the starters with the formal conditions for balance – equal moments in each direction. The equation and principle of moments follows logically from this.	**Extend:** Expand the equation to include situations where there is more than one object on one side of the see saw.	**Maths skills:** Moments
Lead the students through some differentiated example calculations to ensure they can apply the mathematical techniques to find out if the system is balanced or not.	**Support:** Provide a step by step template. **Extend:** Students should find distances as well as forces.	
Measuring an unknown weight (10 min) Place an emphasis on careful positioning to gain a precise answer in this experiment. The experiment also allows student to gain additional practice with moment calculations.	**Support:** Provide a worksheet with a table for repeat measurements to help in finding a mean value for the weight. **Extend:** Expect the students to express the weight as a range based on the spread of the data.	**Practical:** Measuring an unknown weight
Measuring the weight of a beam (15 min) The second practical links together the concepts of moments and centre of mass, a recap on the second of these ideas is needed. The concept of balance is then applied to the wheelbarrow and luggage trolley.	**Extend:** Discuss whether this technique could be adapted to find the weight of a non-uniform object; this is possible if the centre of mass can be found with one of the earlier techniques.	
Plenary	**Support/Extend**	**Resources**
Odd one out (5 min) Support students by showing a set of diagrams of three balanced seesaws and one unbalanced one. Can they find the odd one out? They will need to perform supporting calculations.	**Support:** Use simple distances and masses to reduce the demand of the questions. **Extend:** Place two people on one side of the seesaw and one on the other.	
In balance (5 min) How can a 10 kg, a 5 kg and a 1 kg mass be balanced on a metre rule? How many combinations can the students come up with in 5 minutes?	**Extend:** Provide additional masses as part of the question.	
Homework		
Ask students to write their own moments calculation question and provide a mark scheme.		

kerboodle

A Kerboodle highlight for this lesson is **Extension sheet: Moments in balance**. Refer to the **Content map** on Kerboodle for a full list of resources and assessment.

P8.8 The parallelogram of forces

AQA spec Link: 5.1.4 Students should be able to:

- use free-body diagrams to describe qualitatively examples where several forces lead to a resultant force on an object, including balanced forces when the resultant force is zero.

A single force can be resolved into two components acting at right angles to each other. The two component forces together have the same effect as the single force.

WS 1.2
MS 5a, 5b

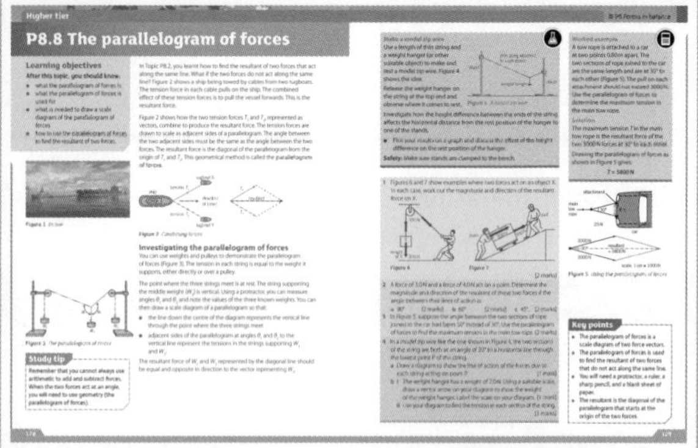

Aiming for	Outcome	Checkpoint	
		Question	**Activity**
Aiming for GRADE 6	Find the resultant of two forces at an acute angle by drawing a scale diagram.	1, 2, 4	Main
	Describe a system in equilibrium in which non-parallel forces are acting.		Main
	Calculate the component of a force using scale diagrams and ratios.		Main
Aiming for GRADE 8	Find the resultant of two forces at an obtuse angle by drawing a scale diagram.	End of chapter 5	Main
	Investigate non-parallel forces acting on a system in equilibrium to verify the parallelogram of forces.		Main
	Analyse a wide range systems of non-parallel forces using a parallelogram technique.	End of chapter 5	Plenary 2, Main, Homework

Maths
The students use scale diagrams to find the resultants of forces. Some may also use trigonometric and geometric approaches to find the resultant forces (5a, 5b).

Literacy
Ensure accurate descriptions of the forces with clear references to direction and magnitude.

Key words
parallelogram of forces

Practical

Title	Making a model zip wire
Equipment	two retort stands with bosses, string, mass holder and masses, protractors, ruler, two G-clamps
Overview of method	Tie the string securely between the retort stands. One side of the string should be lower than the other. Hang the mass onto the top end of the string and release. Observe where it comes to rest. Investigate how the height difference between the ends of the string affects the horizontal distance from the rest position of the hanger to one of the stands.
Safety considerations	The retort stands can be clamped to the desk for additional stability.

Starter	Support/Extend	Resources
Resultant recap (5 min) Provide the students with a few resultant force questions to refresh their understanding of adding forces. Move on to a final question where the two forces are perpendicular (e.g., 4 N at right angles to 3 N) and ask how they would find a resultant in this case.	**Support:** Use the force arrows technique to model forces. **Extend:** The final question can be solved using trigonometry (Pythagoras' theory).	
Shape up (5 min) Provide written descriptions of some shapes and ask the students to draw them using a ruler and protractor. The final shape should be a parallelogram.	**Support:** Simpler shapes can be described.	
Main	**Support/Extend**	**Resources**
Parallelogram of forces (40 min) Recap on the idea that forces are vectors – they have magnitude and direction – by working through a few examples of parallel forces such as the tug of war. The students place a pair of force arrows head to tail so that the second arrow is at an angle to the first. They find the resultant of the two arrows using the metre rule (and the protractor if required). Students then investigate the parallelogram of forces using a zip wire. Ask student to draw force diagrams for their experiment and discuss the changes in the sizes of these forces for differences in height between the ends of the wire.	**Extend:** This activity can be extended by examining the resultant of forces at obtuse angles. **Support:** Each mass can be assumed to represent 1 N and be drawn to a scale of 1 cm to simplify the diagrams.	**Practical:** Parallelogram of forces
Plenary	**Support/Extend**	**Resources**
Finding the resultant force (10 min) Interactive where students order instructions for finding the resultant of two forces.		**Interactive:** Finding the resultant force
Force chain (10 min) Two students call out forces with directions, and the teacher (or nominated student) must find the resultant by drawing a scale diagram on the board. After this, another force is added onto the end, and the new resultant is found. Continue until time runs out. Restart if the resultant goes off the board.	**Extend:** Challenge the students to draw scale diagrams at the same time and find the resultant.	
Homework		
Use additional questions involving finding resultants of a set of forces. This may include the use of graph paper to find components of vectors drawn on the paper and the drawing of resultant vectors from descriptions of their components.	**Support:** Limit the analysis to a single vector at a time. **Extend:** Students should find the perpendicular components of a set of forces, add them, and then find the overall resultant.	

kerboodle

A Kerboodle highlight for this lesson is **Extension sheet: Force vector diagrams**. Refer to the **Content map** on Kerboodle for a full list of resources and assessment.

P8.9 Resolution of forces

AQA spec Link: 5.1.4 Students should be able to:

- use free-body diagrams to describe qualitatively examples where several forces lead to a resultant force on an object, including balanced forces when the resultant force is zero.

A single force can be resolved into two components acting at right angles to each other. The two component forces together have the same effect as the single force.

WS 1.2
MS 5b

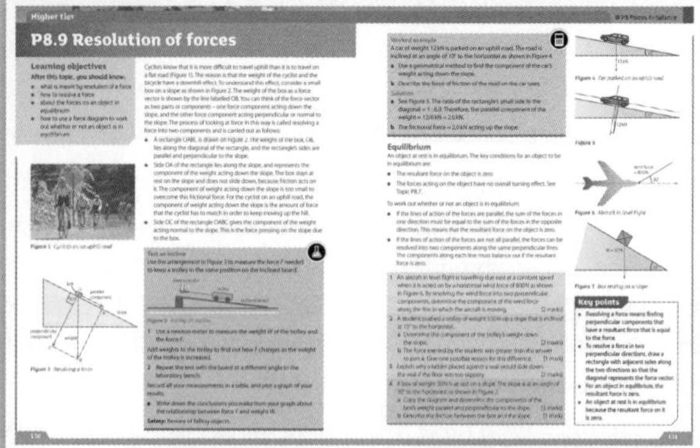
Higher tier
P8.9 Resolution of forces

Aiming for	Outcome	Checkpoint	
		Question	**Activity**
Aiming for GRADE 6	Resolve a single force into two perpendicular components.	1, 2	Main 1
	Determine if an object is in equilibrium by considering the horizontal and vertical forces.	3	Main 3
	Investigate the effect of increasing the weight of an object on a slope on the component of the weight acting along the slope.		Main 1
Aiming for GRADE 8	Resolve a pair of forces into the overall perpendicular components.	End of chapter 5	Main 1, Plenary 2
	Determine if an object is in equilibrium by considering the horizontal and vertical components of forces.	3	Main 3
	Plan a detailed investigation into the effect of increasing the gradient of a slope on the component of the weight acting along the slope.		Main 1

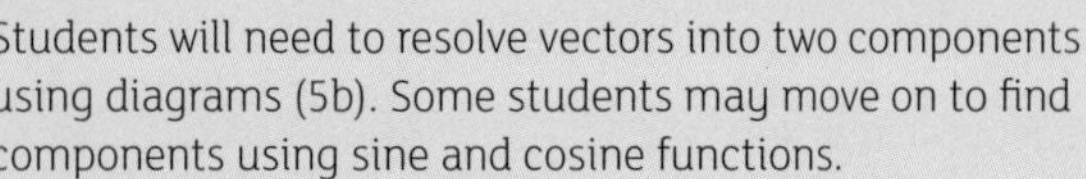

Maths
Students will need to resolve vectors into two components using diagrams (5b). Some students may move on to find components using sine and cosine functions.

Literacy
The focus should be on terms used to describe directions such as 'along the line of the slope' and 'perpendicular to the slope'.

Practical

Title	Testing an incline
Equipment	dynamics trolley (or other low-friction toy car), a set of 50 g masses, newton-meter, string, adjustable slope
Overview of method	The students measure the force required to keep the empty trolley stationary, and then gradually increase the weight of the trolley by adding masses and noting the effect on this force. To extend the students the angle of the slope can be gradually increased instead of the weight. In this version the students could be provided with the suggestion that the force is proportional to either the sine or the cosine of the slope angle, and the students determine which is more likely.
Safety considerations	Prevent the trolley from rolling off the edge of the desk.

Starter	Support/Extend	Resources
Slide (5 min) Show some video footage of various slides, and ask the students to explain the motion of the people on them. Look for explanations about why the people are accelerating (unbalanced forces) and why they reach constant speeds (balanced force) or end up stuck.	**Support:** Pause the video at important points and mark on the forces to allow discussion of the effects.	
Direction sense (10 min) Students should translate prose descriptions of forces (e.g., 'a 20 N force acting at 30 degrees to the horizontal') into figures and vice versa to develop their ability to describe forces precisely.	**Support:** Provide descriptions and figures for the students to match up.	
Main	**Support/Extend**	**Resources**
Resolving vectors (10 min) Demonstrate the idea of breaking down a force into components by showing that any one force can be represented by two forces acting at right angles. Cardboard force arrows can assist with this. Apply this technique to the forces acting on an object on a slope emphasising that the components act at right angles.	**Support:** Limit the discussion to horizontal and vertical components initially. **Extend:** The fraction of the force acting in particular directions can be discussed.	
Testing an incline (20 min) Students can try this experiment to see that the force increases with the weight of the trolley. A simple mathematical model should show that doubling the weight doubles the force. It is likely that this will not be exactly true because frictional effects increase with the weight of the trolley.	**Extend:** Students can investigate the effect of changing the angle of the slope instead of the weight.	**Practical:** Testing an incline
Equilibrium (10 min) Students analyse a system at equilibrium in detail, as shown in the student book, to ensure they are aware of the conditions required for equilibrium. This needs to be a methodical treatment of this demanding situation.	**Extend:** It is possible to discuss the additional condition for moments around any point to be equal as a more formal definition of equilibrium.	
Plenary	**Support/Extend**	**Resources**
Resolving a force (10 min) Interactive where students resolve components of forces acting in different directions.		**Interactive:** Resolving a force
How long is a piece of string? (5 min) Give each student a length of string and ask the student to stick it on to a sheet of squared paper in a random diagonal direction. The students then resolve the string into horizontal and vertical components, writing down these values.	**Extend:** Students place separate two pieces of string head to head and find the components of the resultant.	
Homework		
Students should produce a summary poster of all of the content from this chapter, including a range of figures showing the key ideas.	**Support:** A partially completed template can be provided. **Extend:** The poster must show examples of all of the types of calculation required in this topic.	

P8 Forces in balance

Overview of P8 Forces in balance

In this chapter students have compared vectors and scalars using the examples of distance and displacement along with the nature of forces. Representations of vectors using scale diagrams led to descriptions of the forces acting in a wide variety of situations and the identification of Newton's third law. The concept of balanced and unbalanced forces was used to determine the behaviour of objects and the application of Newton's first law of motion. Higher tier students have produced free body diagrams demonstrating the forces acting on an isolated object.

The *GCSE Physics* students have analysed the rotational effects of forces through the idea of moments using both a mathematical approach and an investigation into the turning effect. These students also examined the application of levers and gears in increasing the size of the available force or the movement of an object.

While all students determined the centre of mass of an object experimentally only the *GCSE Physics* students have gone further with the idea of equilibrium and have used it to analyse the equilibrium conditions in seesaws, and other objects, mathematically using a rigorous approach.

All higher tier students have analysed the forces acting on an object in additional depth using a parallelogram of forces approach to determine the resultant force or a 'missing force' when an object is in equilibrium. In addition, the students have resolved forces at right angles to analyse systems and determine if a system is in equilibrium.

You can find additional support for the maths skills covered in this chapter on **MyMaths**, including substituting numerical values into algebraic equations using appropriate units for physical quantities and using angular measures in degrees.

For this chapter, the following assessments are available on Kerboodle:

P8 Checkpoint quiz: Forces in balance
P8 Progress quiz: Forces in balance 1
P8 Progress quiz: Forces in balance 2
P8 On your marks: Forces in balance
P8 Exam-style questions and mark scheme: Forces in balance

Checkpoint follow up lesson

A student's route through this lesson can be determined using the Checkpoint assessment. Percentage pass marks are supplied in the Checkpoint teacher notes.

For each successive route through it is assumed that the student can perform to their current route as well as previous routes. For example, students working at Aiming for 6 are assumed to be secure in Aiming for 4 knowledge and understanding and working towards achieving all the learning outcomes for Aiming for 6.

	Aiming for 4	Aiming for 6	Aiming for 8
Learning outcomes	Describe what is meant by a resultant force.	Calculate resultant forces.	Use the parallelogram of forces to find a resultant force.
	State how the centre of mass is linked to stability.	Describe why some objects are stable and others topple.	Explain why some objects are stable and others topple.
Starter	**Make the force! (5 min)** Give out diagrams with arrows showing forces on them. The arrows should be recognisably 1 unit, 2 units, and 3 units in length. Call out a force and ask them to hold up two arrows that produce that resultant force.		
	How stable? (5 min) Give out a selection of diagrams of objects that are stable, unstable, and have neutral stability. In small groups, ask students to put them in order of most to least stable. Pair groups together and ask them to compare their orders, and discuss the best explanation for the order.		
Differentiated checkpoint activity	Aiming for 4 students use the Checkpoint follow-up sheet to investigate adding forces to produce a resultant force and to investigate how the stability of a box depends on the mass inside a box. The follow-up sheet provides structured tasks and questions to help them complete these activities and check their understanding of resultant forces and stability.	Aiming for 6 students use the Checkpoint follow-up sheet to find an unknown mass using a seesaw and the law of moments, and to investigate how the stability of a box depends on the mass inside a box. The Aiming for 6 Checkpoint follow-up sheet provides tasks and questions to help them complete these activities and check their understanding of moments, stability, and resolving forces.	Aiming for 8 students use the Checkpoint follow-up sheet to model the stability of a lorry on a slope, and to model removing a fence post from the ground using a tractor. The Aiming for 8 Checkpoint follow-up sheet provides tasks and questions to help them complete these activities and check their understanding of moments, stability, resolving forces, and the parallelogram of forces.
	Kerboodle resource P8 Checkpoint follow up: Aiming for 4, P8 Checkpoint follow up: Aiming for 6, P8 Checkpoint follow up: Aiming for 8		
Plenary	**Make the forces again (10 min)** Use the same arrows from the starter activity. Aiming for 4 students should find as many different resultant forces as they can from the arrows they are given.		
	Against the wall! (5 min) Students should work in pairs. One student should stand against the wall so that they are close enough that their back and legs are touching it. The other student should place a chair in front of them, and ask them to reach down and pick it up. They swap, and then discuss why it is not possible. Discuss the ideas with the class, and the link between moments and stability.		
Progression	Encourage students to review a series of objects and describe their stability.	Encourage students to calculate the components of a force using trigonometry and check their results using a scale diagram.	Encourage students to practise using the parallelogram of forces to find resultant forces.

P 9 Motion

9.1 Speed and distance–time graphs

AQA spec Link: 5.6.1.1 Distance is how far an object moves. Distance does not involve direction. Distance is a scalar quantity.

5.6.1.2 Speed does not involve direction. Speed is a scalar quantity.

The speed of a moving object is rarely constant. When people walk, run, or travel in a car their speed is constantly changing.

The speed at which a person can walk, run, or cycle depends on many factors including: age, terrain, fitness, and distance travelled.

Typical values may be taken as: walking ~ 1.5 m/s, running ~ 3 m/s, cycling ~ 6 m/s.

For an object moving at constant speed the distance travelled in a specific time can be calculated using the equation:

distance travelled = speed × time

$[s = v\ t]$

distance s in metres, m

speed v in metres per second, m/s

time t in seconds, s

5.6.1.4 If an object moves along a straight line, the distance travelled can be represented by a distance–time graph.

The speed of an object can be calculated from the gradient of its distance–time graph.

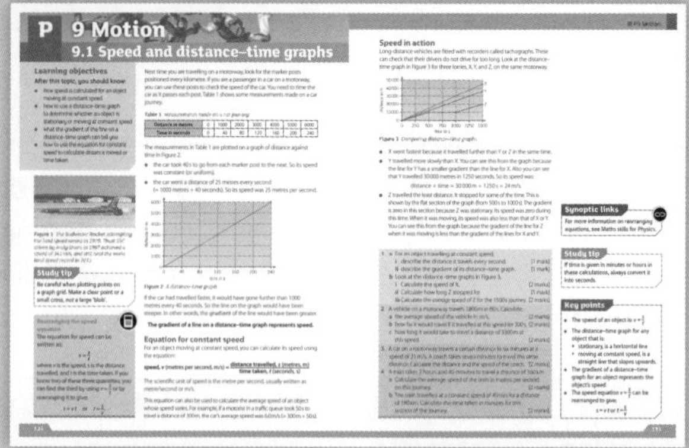

MS 1a, 1b, 1c, 1d, 3b, 3c, 4a, 4b, 4d

Aiming for	Outcome	Checkpoint	
		Question	Activity
Aiming for GRADE 4	Describe how the gradient of a distance–time graph represents the speed.	1	Starter 1
	Estimate typical speeds for walking, running, and cycling.		Main
	Calculate the distance an object at constant speed will travel in a given time.	2	Main
Aiming for GRADE 6	Use the gradients of distance–time graphs to compare the speeds of objects.	End of chapter 4	Main
	Describe the motion of an object by interpreting distance–time graphs.		Starter 1, Main
	Calculate the speed of an object and the time taken to travel a given distance.	2, 3, 4, End of chapter 1	Main
Aiming for GRADE 8	Calculate the speed of an object by extracting data from a distance–time graph.	End of chapter 2	Main
	Extract data from a distance–time graph to calculate the speed of an object at various points in its motion.		Main
	Perform calculations of speed, distance, and time which involve conversion to and from SI base units.		Main

Maths
Students will calculate speed using the appropriate relationship (3b, 3c). Some students will extract the necessary data from a distance–time graph (4a, 4b, 4d).

Literacy
The students will describe the movement of an object based on information extracted from a graph.

Key words
gradient

Starter	Support/Extend	Resources
Speed, velocity, and acceleration graphs (10 min) Ensure the students can interpret a simple graph of motion by matching data with a graph. They should identify the gradient and note that it is constant when the distance is changing by a fixed amount each second. **Speedy start** (5 min) Give students different moving objects, and ask them to put the objects in order from fastest to slowest. Provide data on the objects so that the students can actually work out the speed of the objects using the speed equation. Examples could be a worm (0.5 cm/s), human walking (0.5 m/s), bicycle (5 m/s), car (20 m/s), passenger aircraft (200 m/s), and missile (1 km/s).	**Extend:** Students should discuss what would happen to the graph if the speed was not constant and how this relates to the gradient. **Support:** Focus on base units in the examples. **Extend:** Try some unusual units (e.g., mm/year for continental drift).	**Interactive:** Speed, velocity, and acceleration graphs
Main	**Support/Extend**	**Resources**
Distance–time graphs (40 min) Students try a few example speed calculations based on the equation. Use examples that lead to typical walking (1.5 m/s), running (3 m/s), and cycling speeds (6 m/s) as students are expected to recall these values. Students then complete the activity sheet where they analyse a distance–time graph of a motorbike, describing when it was travelling at the slowest speed, and extracting simple data from the graph to find speed in different phases of motion.	**Support:** A simple calculation frame should be used, especially for rearrangement of the equation. **Extend:** Use examples which require changes to SI base units. **Support:** Students make a set of rules about what different features of the graph represent (e.g., steeper = faster). **Extend:** Ask the students to describe a graph that shows acceleration and deceleration rather than sudden speed changes.	**Activity:** Distance–time graphs
Plenary	**Support/Extend**	**Resources**
Timetable (5 min) Provide the students with a graph and ask them to describe the motion of the object in prose and calculate the speed of the object during each stage of the motion. **A driving story** (10 min) Provide students with a paragraph describing the motion of a car through a town, including moving at different speeds and stopping at traffic lights, and so on. Ask them to sketch a graph of the described motion.	**Extend:** Students use bus timetables and a map to estimate speeds between different stops. **Support:** Give students a graph of the motion and ask them to convert it into prose. **Extend:** Provide numerical information for the students to use in accurately plotting a graph.	
Homework		
Students analyse data about the 100 m sprint records (or other records such as swimming). They can try to find out if there appears to be a continuous improvement in running speeds or if there are leaps where the records change suddenly.	**Extend:** Students should discuss the resolution implied by the measurements and link this to improvements in timing technology.	

kerboodle

A Kerboodle highlight for this lesson is **Extension sheet: Distance–time gradient calculations**. Refer to the **Content map** on Kerboodle for a full list of resources and assessment.

P9.2 Velocity and acceleration

AQA spec Link: 5.6.1.3 The velocity of an object is its speed in a given direction. Velocity is a vector quantity.

Students should be able to explain the vector–scalar distinction as it applies to displacement, distance, velocity, and speed.

H Students should be able to explain qualitatively, with examples, that motion in a circle involves constant speed but changing velocity.

5.6.1.4 If an object moves along a straight line, the distance travelled can be represented by a distance–time graph.

The speed of an object can be calculated from the gradient of its distance–time graph.

H If an object is accelerating, its speed at any particular time can be determined by drawing a tangent and measuring the gradient of the distance–time graph at that time.

Students should be able to draw distance–time graphs from measurements and extract and interpret lines and slopes of distance–time graphs, translating information between graphical and numerical form.

Students should be able to determine speed from a distance–time graph.

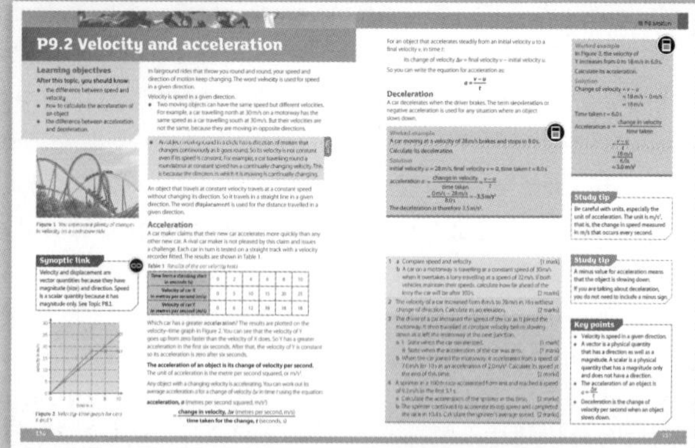

MS 3b, 3c, 3d, 4a, 4b, 4c, 4d, 4f

Aiming for	Outcome	Checkpoint	
		Question	Activity
Aiming for GRADE 4	Describe the difference between speed and velocity using an appropriate example.	1, 3	Starter 1, Main 1
	Give the equation relating velocity, acceleration, and time.	2	Main 3
	Calculate the acceleration of an object using the change in velocity and time.	2, End of chapter 4	Main 3
Aiming for GRADE 6	Identify the features of a velocity–time graph.		Plenary 1
	Rearrange the acceleration equation in calculations.	3	Main 3
	Calculate the change in velocity for an object under constant acceleration for a given period of time.	3	Main 3
Aiming for GRADE 8	Compare and contrast the features of a distance–time, displacement–time, and velocity–time graph.	End of chapter 4	Plenary 1
	Combine equations relating to velocity and acceleration in multi-step calculations.	3	Main 3, Plenary 2
	Calculate a new velocity for a moving object that has accelerated for a given period of time.	3	Main 3

Maths
The students will be performing a series of calculations based on velocity and acceleration equations (3b, 3c, 3d).

Literacy
There are many terms with fine distinctions between them (e.g., *distance* and *displacement*), which the students need to use correctly throughout this lesson.

Key words
displacement, velocity, acceleration, deceleration

Starter	Support/Extend	Resources
Getting nowhere fast (5 min) A racing driver completes a full circuit of a 3 km racetrack in 90 seconds. Ask what is his average speed? Why aren't they 3 km away from where they started? Use this idea to explain the difference between distance travelled and displacement. **Treasure island** (10 min) Provide the students with a scaled map with a starting point, hidden treasure, protractor, and ruler. At first, only give them the times they have to walk for, then the speeds they must go at, and finally the matching directions. See which group can find the treasure first. This shows how important direction is when describing movement.	**Support:** Show an overhead map of the track and discuss the difference between direction and displacement at different points along it. **Extend:** Ask the students to produce a set of instructions to get to a treasure chest whilst avoiding a set of obstacles such as the 'pit of peril'.	
Main	**Support/Extend**	**Resources**
Defining velocity (15 min) Use plenty of examples involving the description of the direction of motion as students can struggle with the difference between speed and velocity. (H) For higher-tier students you will need to discuss circular motion. Showing a conical pendulum, bolas, or a lasso can assist with this.		
Acceleration (25 min) Students will understand acceleration to mean *getting faster*. Use this as a starting point and move towards the idea that it is possible to find out how much faster each second. This leads to the formal equation. The students will need to try several example calculations at this point. Ensure they can identify starting or end velocities of zero in the questions (e.g., at rest, stopped, stationary). Students use the term deceleration in a description of an object slowing down to make sure they understand it.	**Support:** Show partially complete calculations and a methodical method for the students to follow. **Extend:** Students should tackle multi-step calculations where they need to find speeds from distance and time values, and then acceleration using these speeds. **Extend:** Consider an object which is moving backwards and slowing down, and discuss which term would describe this motion best.	**Activity:** Acceleration
Plenary	**Support/Extend**	**Resources**
Comparing graphs (10 min) Ask the students to make a comparison of what a distance–time graph and a velocity–time graph show. They should produce a chart/diagram highlighting the distinctions between what the features of these graphs represent.	**Support:** Provide a pair of simple example graphs for the students to use. **Extend:** Ask the students to sketch a pair of graphs which show the motion of the same object, matching up important points.	
Accelerated learning (10 min) The students should try a few additional acceleration questions. Differentiate these so that there are several stages of calculation in some of the questions.	**Support:** Use more structure in questions to guide students through them.	**Interactive:** Accelerated learning
Homework		
Ask the students to find data on vehicle accelerations (e.g., 0–60 mph in 10 s) and to show this data as a graph. Expand this beyond the typical cars, and ask them to look at sprinters, animals, rockets, and so on.	**Extend:** Ask the students to convert the data into SI units. They need to find how many metres are in 1 mile (1609 metres).	

kerboodle

A Kerboodle highlight for this lesson is **Working scientifically: Acceleration of a trolley**. Refer to the **Content map** on Kerboodle for a full list of resources and assessment.

P9.3 More about velocity–time graphs

AQA spec Link: 5.6.1.5 An object that slows down is decelerating.

The acceleration of an object can be calculated from the gradient of a velocity–time graph.

(H) The distance travelled by an object (or displacement of an object) can be calculated from the area under a velocity–time graph.

MS 3b, 3c, 4a, 4b, 4c, 4d, 4f

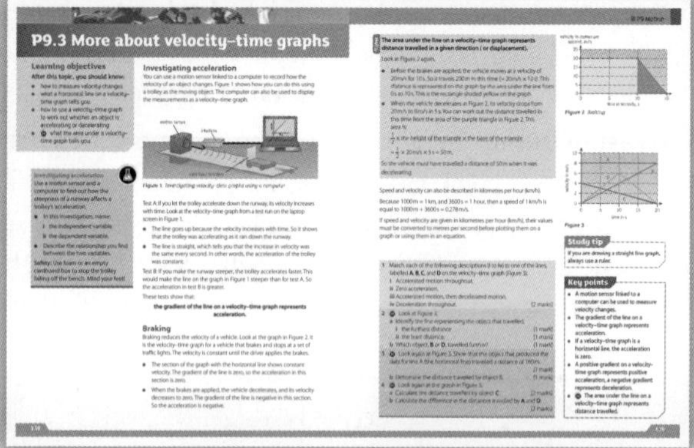
P9.3 More about velocity–time graphs

Aiming for	Outcome	Checkpoint	
		Question	Activity
Aiming for GRADE 4	Identify the feature of a velocity–time graph that represents the acceleration [the gradient], and compare these values.	1, 3	Main 2
	Identify the feature of a velocity–time graph that represents the distance travelled [the area beneath the line], and compare these values.		Main 2
	Measure the acceleration of an object as it moves down a ramp.		Main 1
Aiming for GRADE 6	Describe sections of velocity–time graphs, and compare the acceleration in these sections.	3, End of chapter 6	Main 2
	Calculate the distance travelled using information taken from a velocity–time graph for one section of motion.	3, End of chapter 4	Main 2
	Use a series of repeat measurements to find an accurate measurement of the acceleration of a moving object.		Main 1
Aiming for GRADE 8	Calculate the acceleration of an object from values taken from a velocity–time graph.		
	Calculate the total distance travelled from a multi-phase velocity–time graph.	2, 4, End of chapter 5, 6	Main 2
	Evaluate an experiment into the acceleration of an object in terms of precision based on the spread of repeat measurements.		Main 1

Maths
Students will interpret graphs to extract numerical information (4a, 4d) to use in calculations of distance and acceleration (3b, 3c).

Literacy
Specific scientific language is required to compare displacement, distance, velocity, and speed. The students should ensure that they apply these terms correctly.

Practical

Title	Investigating acceleration
Equipment	dynamics trolley, adjustable slope, protractor, data-logging equipment including a velocity sensor
Overview of method	Set up the equipment so that the angle of the ramp can be adjusted and easily measured. Make sure that the sensor is pointing along the path of the slope as otherwise the velocity will not be measured accurately. The students activate the sensor and then release the trolley. Repeating this for a range of slope angles should give the result that the steeper the slope, the greater the acceleration.
Safety considerations	Make sure the trolley does not shoot off the end of the runway. Protect feet and bench.

Starter	Support/Extend	Resources
Late again? (5 min) Give the students the distance from their last class to where they are now and ask them to work out their speed on the journey to you, using the time it took them to arrive. Provide some example distances from other likely rooms if students have no idea about how far it is between places. **Finding areas** (10 min) Ask the students to calculate the total area of a shape made up of rectangles and triangles or circles.	**Support:** Provide simple data for the calculations. **Extend:** Supply data which requires conversions to SI base units (e.g., distance in km and time in minutes). **Support:** Provide the equation for the area of a triangle, rectangle, and circle as required. **Extend:** Use shapes with cut-out sections (e.g., a square with a circular hole in it).	
Main	**Support/Extend**	**Resources**
Investigating acceleration (25 min) After a brief recap of the concept of acceleration, the students can carry out this investigation depending on the equipment available.	**Support:** The motion sensor apparatus provides the simplest method. **Extend:** The light-gate method requires additional calculations to find the speed of the trolley from which acceleration is calculated.	**Practical:** Investigating acceleration
Braking (15 min) In this activity the students look at what the features of the velocity–time graph represent. They need to clearly identify the acceleration and distance travelled as separate concepts. Summary questions 1 to 4 in the student book will provide additional examples.	**Support:** Limit the complexity of the graphs to two phases at most (and acceleration or deceleration, and a constant velocity section). **Extend:** Students can find accelerations and distance travelled on more complex graphs with several discrete phases of motion.	
Plenary	**Support/Extend**	**Resources**
Rushed off your feet (5 min) Wear a pedometer throughout the lesson, calculate your average step distance, and then ask the students to work out how far you have moved and your average speed. A typical example stride distance is 0.5 m with somewhere between 400 and 600 paces per lesson.	**Extend:** The students could find their average daily speed, based on sensible estimations.	
Matching motion (10 min) Students match velocity–time graphs with the descriptions of a car's motion. They then interpret a velocity–time graph of an athlete during a training session.	**Support:** Take students through the provided examples step by step. **Extend:** Ask the students to read data from the graphs (such as starting speed and final speed) and attempt to calculate the acceleration.	**Interactive:** Matching motion
Homework		
The students can analyse a photocopy of a tachograph disc and describe the motion of the vehicle it was used in.	**Extend:** Students can also research the need for these devices and the replacement technology being introduced (based on GPS).	

kerboodle

A Kerboodle highlight for this lesson is **Bump up your grade: Using motion graphs to decide how things move**. Refer to the **Content map** on Kerboodle for a full list of resources and assessment.

P9.4 Analysing motion graphs

AQA spec Link: 5.6.1.4 The speed of an object can be calculated from the gradient of its distance–time graph.

Ⓗ If an object is accelerating, its speed at any particular time can be determined by drawing a tangent and measuring the gradient of the distance–time graph at that time.

5.6.1.5 The acceleration of an object can be calculated from the gradient of a velocity–time graph.

Ⓗ The distance travelled by an object (or displacement of an object) can be calculated from the area under a velocity–time graph.

The following equation applies to uniform acceleration:

(final velocity)^2 – (initial velocity)^2 = 2 × acceleration × distance

[$v^2 - u^2 = 2\,a\,s$]

final velocity v in metres per second, m/s

initial velocity u in metres per second, m/s

acceleration a in metres per second squared, m/s^2

distance s in metres, m

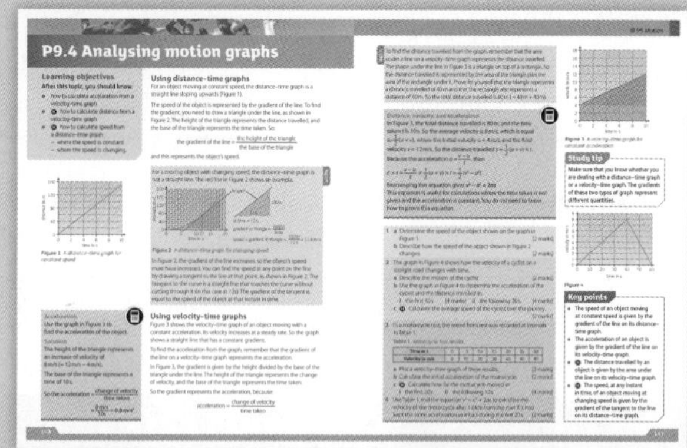

MS 3b, 3c, 4a, 4b, 4c, 4d, 4f

Aiming for	Outcome	Checkpoint	
		Question	**Activity**
Aiming for GRADE 4	Identify a change in speed on a distance–time graph using change in gradient.	2	Starter 1, Main 1
	Identify a change in acceleration on a velocity–time graph using change in gradient.	2	Main 2
	Calculate the distance travelled by an object at constant velocity using data extracted from a graph.		Main 3
Aiming for GRADE 6	Calculate the speed of an object by extracting data from a distance–time graph.	1	Main 3
	Ⓗ Use a tangent to determine the speed of an object from a distance–time graph.		Main 2
	Use the equation $v^2 - u^2 = 2as$ in calculations where the initial or final velocity is zero.	4	Main 3
Aiming for GRADE 8	Calculate the acceleration of an object by extracting data from a velocity–time graph.	3	Main 2
	Use the gradient of a velocity–time graph to determine the acceleration of an object.	3	Main 2
	Apply transformations of the equation $v^2 - u^2 = 2as$ in calculations involving change in velocity and acceleration where both velocities are non-zero.	4	Main 3

Maths

The students will be using tangents of lines to determine gradients leading to speed or acceleration (4a, 4e). They will find the area of shapes to determine the distance travelled (4f). Students will also use equations describing the motion of objects under constant acceleration (3b, 3c).

Literacy

Conversion between graphs and descriptions of graphs is crucial in this lesson, and scientific language development should be focused in this area.

Practical

Title	Cardboard graphs
Equipment	cardboard pieces in rectangles, triangles, and squares (cut from card with a grid pattern printed on)
Overview of method	Students can construct graphs from the cut-out shapes, placing them together in different combinations onto a grid background. This will allow them to analyse the area of the graph, leading to distance travelled for velocity–time graphs.
Safety considerations	None applicable.

Starter	Support/Extend	Resources
Graph matching (5 min) The students have to match the description of the movement of objects with distance–time and velocity–time graphs. Provide three different descriptions of journeys and three graphs that represent the movement for the students to match them with.	**Extend:** Use similar graphs and ensure the descriptions contain similar numerical values.	
Plot (10 min) Give the students a set of velocity–time data for a moving object, and ask them to plot a graph of displacement against time. Check the graphs for accuracy of plotting and clear labelling of the axes.	**Support:** Provide partially completed graphs to add points to.	
Main	**Support/Extend**	**Resources**
Using distance–time graphs (15 min) **H** Lead the students through the process of determining the gradient of a line using tangents. Ensure the students can identify when the object is speeding up and when it is slowing down clearly. Students should find some velocities from example graphs to ensure they have mastered the technique.		
Velocity–time graphs (15 min) Discuss finding acceleration from velocity–time graphs, making sure that students are aware of the difference between this type of graph and the earlier distance–time graph. Ask the students to analyse a few graphs and find acceleration using the gradient.	**Extend:** **H** The tangent techniques can be used to find the acceleration when objects are not accelerating uniformly.	**Activity:** Velocity–time graphs
Velocity–time graphs and distance travelled (10 min) Recap the idea that the area beneath the line on the graph represents the distance travelled. This can now be linked to the mathematical equations which find the area of the shapes, noting that these are a product of the velocity and the time. Then discuss the origin of this equation of motion ($v^2 = u^2 + 2as$). Adding the area of the triangle and the rectangle together will lead to the expression.	**Extend:** The students can be led through the derivation, and this can reinforce their understanding of it.	
Plenary	**Support/Extend**	**Resources**
Dynamic definitions (10 min) The students should provide detailed definitions of speed, velocity, distance, displacement, and acceleration, including how they are represented on graphs.	**Support:** Students should be provided with definitions to match up with the key terms.	
Using graphs (10 min) Students answer true or false statements on velocity, then identify velocity–time graphs.	**Extend:** Students correct the false statements.	**Interactive:** Using graphs
Homework		
The students have completed their look at graphs of motion and so should attempt a series of more formal questions to check their progress and identify areas to develop.	**Support:** Select appropriate levels of questions for the students.	

kerboodle

A Kerboodle highlight for this lesson is **Extension sheet: Non-uniform motion**. Refer to the **Content map** on Kerboodle for a full list of resources and assessment.

P9 Motion

Overview of P9 Motion

In this chapter the students have analysed the motion of objects in depth starting from a recap of the concept of speed and this relationship to distance travelled and time taken. The representation of motion using distance-time graphs representing single and multiple objects has been analysed to give detailed descriptions of the movement of the objects.

The students have defined acceleration in terms of changes in velocity before analysing it graphically and mathematically. Higher tier students have also outlined circular motion in terms of constant acceleration but with constant speed. All students have then investigated acceleration caused by an unbalanced force on ramp, linking acceleration to the gradient of a line on a velocity-time graph.

Students have continued to analyse graphs representing motion by looking at the area beneath the line on a velocity-time graph and its relationship to the distance travelled by an object. Students have used the gradient of a distance-time graph to determine the speed of an object. In addition, higher tier students have used the tangent of a line on a distance-time graph to determine the speed. All students have then applied these techniques to analyse a range of graphs to extract all of the possible information from them.

You can find additional support for the maths skills covered in this chapter on **MyMaths**, including changing the subject of an equation, translating information between graphical and numeric form, understanding that $y = mx + c$ represents a linear relationship, and determining the slope and intercept of a linear graph.

For this chapter, the following assessments are available on Kerboodle:

P9 Checkpoint quiz: Motion
P9 Progress quiz: Motion 1
P9 Progress quiz: Motion 2
P9 On your marks: Motion
P9 Exam-style questions and mark scheme: Motion

Checkpoint follow up lesson

A student's route through this lesson can be determined using the Checkpoint assessment. Percentage pass marks are supplied in the Checkpoint teacher notes.

For each successive route through it is assumed that the student can perform to their current route as well as previous routes. For example, students working at Aiming for 6 are assumed to be secure in Aiming for 4 knowledge and understanding and working towards achieving all the learning outcomes for Aiming for 6.

	Aiming for 4	Aiming for 6	Aiming for 8
Learning outcomes	Plot a distance-time graph.	Plot and interpret a distance-time graph.	Plot and interpret a distance-time graph and a speed-time graph.
	Make calculations of speed.	Make calculations of speed using a range of units.	Make calculations of velocity.
	Interpret data on speed.	Plot and interpret a speed-time graph.	Make calculations of acceleration using tangents drawn to a curve on a velocity time graph.
Starter	**Faster or slower? (5 minutes)** Give out some statements, such as 'A car that travels 10 miles in half an hour is going faster than a bus that travels at 30 mph', and ask students to sort them into true and false statements. **Walking the graph (10 minutes)** Give students A4 dry wipe boards, pens and an eraser. Ask student to sketch distance time graphs of you walking. Try a variety of motions – steady speed, steady speed, stopping, steady speed. Ask them to explain how they knew how to draw each graph. You can extend the activity to speed-time graphs for Aiming for 6 students, and velocity-time graphs for Aiming for 8 students.		
Differentiated checkpoint activity	Aiming for 4 students use the Checkpoint follow-up sheet to make measurements of a ball on a track, and to do some calculations based on a 100-metre race. The follow-up sheet provides structured tasks and questions to help them complete these activities and check their understanding of speed, distance-time graphs, and velocity-time graphs.	Aiming for 6 students use the Checkpoint follow-up sheet to make measurements of a ball on a track, and to do some calculations based on a 100-metre race. They also investigate the stability of a box on a ramp. The follow-up sheet provides tasks and questions to help them complete these activities and check their understanding of speed and acceleration, and how to interpret distance-time and velocity-time graphs.	Aiming for 8 students use the Checkpoint follow-up sheet to investigate the speed and acceleration of a ball on a track. The follow-up sheet provides tasks and questions to help them complete these activities and check their understanding of speed and acceleration, how to interpret distance-time and velocity-time graphs, and how to calculate acceleration from a graph where the speed is changing.
	Kerboodle resource P9 Checkpoint follow up: Aiming for 4, P9 Checkpoint follow up: Aiming for 6, P9 Checkpoint follow up: Aiming for 8		
Plenary	**Are they right? (10 minutes)** Organise students into groups of four or five and pair groups together. Give students A4 dry wipe boards, pens and an eraser. Ask each group to draw a distance-time graph that has three sections on it. They should label the axes with numbers/units, and write on the sections what the object is doing, and the speed/acceleration. Half the information should be correct, and half incorrect. The groups swap boards and use two different coloured pens to circle the correct information and the incorrect information. They swap back and evaluate the conclusions of the other group.		
Progression	Encourage students to think about speed as the distance travelled in each second, so distance accumulates with speed and time.	Encourage them to think about acceleration as the change in speed in each second, so speed accumulates with acceleration and time.	Encourage them to think about acceleration as the change in speed in each second, so you can calculate it using a gradient.

P 10 Forces and motion

10.1 Force and acceleration

AQA spec Link: (H) 5.6.2.1 The tendency of objects to continue in their state of rest or of uniform motion is called inertia.

5.6.2.2 Newton's Second Law:

The acceleration of an object is proportional to the resultant force acting on the object, and inversely proportional to the mass of the object.

As an equation:

resultant force = mass × acceleration

[$F = m\,a$]

force F in newtons, N

mass m in kilograms, kg

acceleration a in metres per second squared, m/s^2

(H) Students should be able to explain that:

- **inertial mass is a measure of how difficult it is to change the velocity of an object**
- **inertial mass is defined by the ratio of force over acceleration.**

Students should be able to estimate the speed, accelerations, and forces involved in large accelerations for everyday road transport.

Students should recognise and be able to use the symbol that indicates an approximate value or answer ~.

Required practical: investigate the effect of varying the force on the acceleration of an object of constant mass, and the effect of varying the mass of an object on the acceleration produced by a constant force.

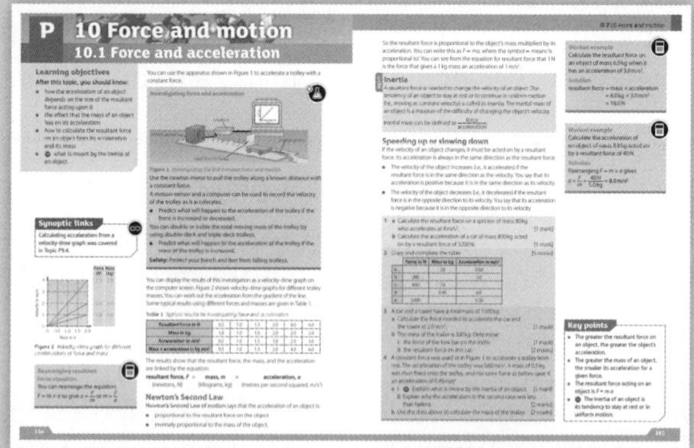

MS 1d, 3a 3b, 3c

Aiming for	Outcome	Checkpoint	
		Question	Activity
Aiming for GRADE 4	State the factors that will affect the acceleration of an object acted on by a resultant force.		Starter 1, Main 1
	Calculate the force required to cause a specified acceleration on a given mass.	1, 3	Main 2
	Investigate a factor that affects the acceleration of a mass.		Main 1
Aiming for GRADE 6	Describe the effect of changing the mass or the force acting on an object on the acceleration of that object.	4	Main 1
	Perform calculations involving the rearrangement of the $F = ma$ equation.	2, End of chapter 3	Main 2
	Combine separate experimental conclusions to form an overall conclusion.		Main 1
Aiming for GRADE 8	**(H) Define the inertial mass of an object in terms of force and acceleration.**		Main 2, Plenary 2
	Calculate the acceleration of an object acted on by several forces.	3, End of chapter 3	Main 2
	Evaluate an experiment by identifying sources of error and determining uncertainty in the resulting data.		Main 1

Maths

Students will investigate factors that are proportional or in inverse proportion (3a). Some will combine these factors to form an overall expression.

Literacy

Students discuss results, combining two different concepts together to produce an overall statement about acceleration, force, and mass.

Key words

Newton's Second Law of Motion inertia

Required practical

Title	Investigating force and acceleration
Equipment	dynamics trolley, track, string, masses (similar to trolley mass), stopwatch, and possibly motion sensor or light gates
Overview of method	Pull the trolley along a track of known distance, attempting to use a constant force by watching the newton-meter. Measure the acceleration. Repeat with at least three different constant forces. Add a mass to the trolley and pull along at a constant force. Measure the acceleration. Add another mass to the trolley and pull along at the same constant force, measuring the acceleration. Repeat for at least three different masses.
Safety considerations	Ensure a clear working area for the trolleys to be dragged.

Starter	Support/Extend	Resources
Accelerator (5 min) Ask the students to describe the function of the accelerator in a car.	**Support:** Animations of the process can be found with an Internet search.	
Lift off (10 min) Interactive where students complete a description on the changes in energy stores during the launch of a chemical rocket, and link the ideas to the action of forces.		**Interactive:** Lift off
Main	**Support/Extend**	**Resources**
Investigating force and acceleration (25 min) Students carry out two investigations. First they investigate the effect that changing the force on an object has on the acceleration. They then investigate the effect that changing the mass of the object has on the acceleration when a constant force is applied. Students use the investigations to reach two conclusions that can then be combined into a mathematical relationship.	**Extend:** Students should evaluate the data and discuss why the relationships are not exact. Ensure the students are familiar with sources of error and uncertainty.	**Practical:** Investigating force and acceleration
(H) **Inertial mass and acceleration** (15 min) Discuss the relationships $a \propto F$ and $a \propto \frac{1}{m}$ and combine them to reach the expression $a \propto \frac{F}{m}$, which leads to the more familiar $F = ma$. Analyse some scenarios involving resultant forces acting on objects to find the acceleration or the force required to cause particular accelerations. Focus on the idea that both the force and the acceleration are vectors in the same direction.	**Support:** Students should try questions that do not require rearrangement of the equation. Limit the calculations to finding the force when the equation is expressed as $F = ma$. **Extend:** Questions should involve rearrangements and some SI prefixes for values.	**Maths skills:** Force, mass, and acceleration.
Plenary	**Support/Extend**	**Resources**
What's wrong? (5 min) Students consider the common misconception *Objects always move in the direction of the resultant force* and write a corrected version.	**Support:** Give examples of where a moving object is decelerating to show why this statement is wrong.	
I'm snookered (10 min) Students draw a series of diagrams showing the forces involved in getting out of a snooker. They draw each of the stages of the movements, showing the forces as the white ball is first hit and the collisions with the cushions.	**Support:** A snooker or pool simulation game can make this more interactive and fun for the students.	
Homework		
Students evaluate the experiment and suggest improvements, explaining why they would make the results more convincing. This should focus on the removal of forces that cause the results to be inaccurate, such as friction.	**Extend:** Expect at least one idea for reduction of friction, for example, compensated (tilted) track.	

kerboodle

A Kerboodle highlight for this lesson is **Maths skills: Force and acceleration**. Refer to the **Content map** on Kerboodle for a full list of resources and assessment.

P10.2 Weight and terminal velocity

AQA spec Link: 5.1.3 Weight is the force acting on an object due to gravity. The force of gravity close to the Earth is due to the gravitational field around the Earth.

The weight of an object depends on the gravitational field strength at the point where the object is.

The weight of an object can be calculated using the equation:

weight = mass × gravitational field strength

[$W = m\,g$]

weight W in newtons, N

mass m in kilograms, kg

gravitational field strength g in newtons per kilogram, N/kg (In any calculation the value of the gravitational field strength (g) will be given.)

The weight of an object may be considered to act at a single point referred to as the object's 'centre of mass'.

The weight of an object and the mass of an object are directly proportional.

Weight is measured using a calibrated spring-balance (a newton-meter).

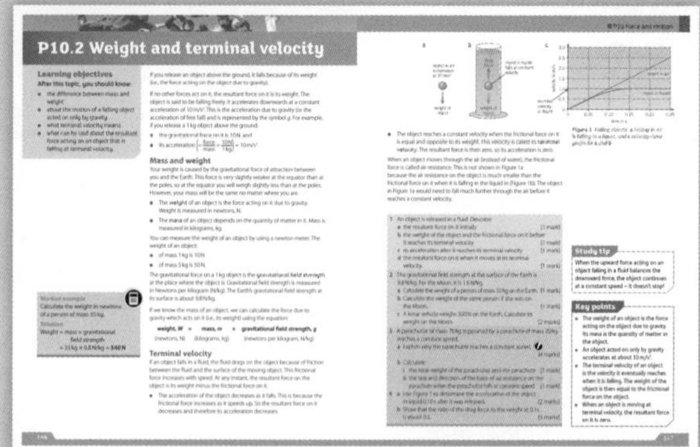
P10.2 Weight and terminal velocity

MS 2c, 2g, 3a, 3b, 3c, 4c

Aiming for	Outcome	Checkpoint: Question	Checkpoint: Activity
		Question	Activity
Aiming for GRADE 4	State the difference between the mass of an object and its weight.		Main
	Describe the forces acting on an object falling through a fluid.	1	Starter 2, Main
↓	Investigate the motion of an object when it falls.		Main
Aiming for GRADE 6	Calculate the weight of objects using their mass and the gravitational field strength.	2, End of chapter 2	Main
	Apply the concept of balanced forces to explain why an object falling through a fluid will reach a terminal velocity.	3	Main, Homework
↓	Investigate the relationship between the mass of an object and the terminal velocity.		Main
Aiming for GRADE 8	Apply the mathematical relationship between mass, weight, and gravitational field strength in a range of situations.	2, End of chapter 2	Main
	Explain the motion of an object falling through a fluid by considering the forces acting through all phases of motion.	3, 4	Main
↓	Evaluate the repeatability of an experiment by considering the spread of each set of repeat results.		Main

Maths 
Students plot a graph of experimental data (4c); this may be a simple bar chart or a scatter graph depending on the experiment (2c, 2g).

Literacy 
Students describe the action of forces and their effect on the motion of an object. Explanations link together resultant forces, weight, frictional forces, and acceleration.

Key words
weight, mass, gravitational field strength, terminal velocity

Practical

Title	Investigating falling
Equipment	two small and different sized masses, string or cotton thread, scissors, approximately 15 × 15 cm square of cloth

Overview of method	Drop the mass from a set height. Then use the string or thread to tie the small mass to the cloth to make a basic parachute. Drop the parachute from the same height. The higher the parachutes are dropped from, the more effective they are, so use somewhere with sufficient height. A wide stairwell can be good if proper supervision can be arranged. Repeat the experiment using a different mass.
Safety considerations	Do not stand on desks or ladders. Drop the object from a safe point. It may be safer to pick one responsible student to perform the dropping, rather than the whole class.

Starter	Support/Extend	Resources
Fluid facts (5 min) Interactive where students match up information (including diagrams) about the physical properties of solids, liquids, and gases with explanations in terms of particle behaviour. This will help them revise the states of matter and the particle theory in particular. **Air resistance** (10 min) Students use their understanding of particles and forces to suggest what causes air and water resistance. They should sketch the movement of objects, label the forces on them, and then try to show the particles being pushed out of the way and pushing back.	**Extend:** Draw out the idea that moving faster through a fluid will require a greater force as more particles will need to be pushed out of the way each second.	**Interactive:** Fluid facts
Main	**Support/Extend**	**Resources**
Investigating falling (40 min) Demonstrate the acceleration caused by the weight of an object when there is no supporting force by dropping some objects. Discuss the unbalanced forces acting whilst they fall and when they stop. Spend a few minutes ensuring that the students are clear on the distinction between these two with some calculations of weight for different masses. Ensure the students are aware that the weight of the objects is due to a gravitational field surrounding masses. Continue with the discussion of forces focusing on drag and how this changes as the velocity increases. Students should realise that, when the drag force matches the weight, then the object stops accelerating and so reaches terminal velocity. Use the animation to describe the changes in the forces experienced by a sky diver. Then carry out the practical to investigate falling using a model parachute. Students should investigate the effect of different masses on the time for descent. If time is limited, individual groups could investigate one mass, and then collate results as a class. As there will be considerable variability in the results, the students should focus on repeat measurements to find mean values, reducing the effects of random error.	**Support:** Limit the scope of the calculations to just finding the weight on Earth. **Extend:** Students work through the extension sheet that uses the gravitational field strength on some different planets in calculations. **Support:** Use simple force diagrams to show the relative sizes of the forces at each stage of motion. **Extend:** Students find the range of each repeat set of results and use this to evaluate the precision of the experiment. They may also use this to draw error bars on any graphs.	**Extension:** Getting to grips with gravitational field strength. **Practical:** Investigating falling **Animation:** Sky diver
Plenary	**Support/Extend**	**Resources**
Top speed (5 min) Show the students a list of top speeds for cars along with some other information such as engine power and a photograph. They can discuss why the cars have a maximum speed. **Falling forces** (10 min) The students draw a comic strip with stick figures showing the forces at various stages of a parachute jump. This should summarise the concepts and demonstrate the changing size of the forces.	**Extend:** Provide data on the power of engines of sports cars and their maximum speeds. **Support:** Provide the images in the correct order and label them. **Extend:** Students should draw the force arrows to scale.	
Homework		
Students can identify aerodynamic design features of vehicles that allow them to reach higher speeds. This can be a study of an individual car or a comparison of several.	**Support:** Provide stimulus material such as images of both older and more modern sports cars.	

kerboodle

A Kerboodle highlight for this lesson is **Bump up your grade: Getting to grips with gravitational field strength**. Refer to the **Content map** on Kerboodle for a full list of resources and assessment.

P10.3 Forces and braking

AQA spec Link: 5.6.3.1 The stopping distance of a vehicle is the sum of the distance the vehicle travels during the driver's reaction time (thinking distance) and the distance it travels under the braking force (braking distance). For a given braking force the greater the speed of the vehicle, the greater the stopping distance.

5.6.3.2 Reaction times vary from person to person. Typical values range from 0.2 s to 0.9 s.

A driver's reaction time can be affected by tiredness, drugs, and alcohol. Distractions may also affect a driver's ability to react.

Students should be able to:

- explain methods used to measure human reaction times and recall typical results
- interpret and evaluate measurements from simple methods to measure the different reaction times of students
- evaluate the effect of various factors on thinking distance based on given data.

5.6.3.3 The braking distance of a vehicle can be affected by adverse road and weather conditions and poor condition of the vehicle.

Adverse road conditions include wet or icy conditions. Poor condition of the vehicle is limited to the vehicle's brakes or tyres.

Students should be able to:

- explain the factors which affect the distance required for road transport vehicles to come to rest in emergencies, and the implications for safety
- estimate how the distance required for road vehicles to stop in an emergency varies over a range of typical speeds.

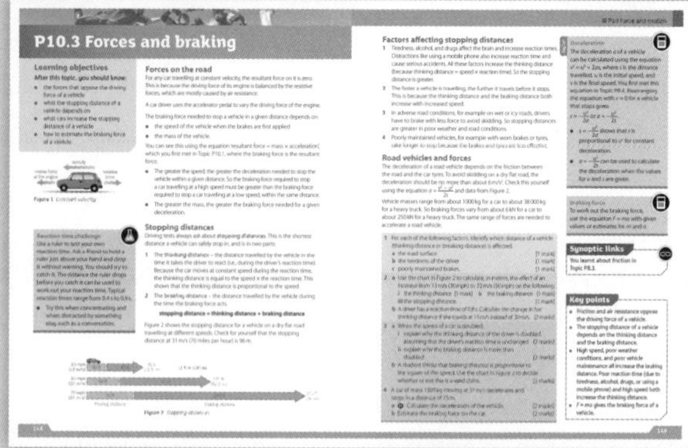
P10.3 Forces and braking

5.6.3.4 When a force is applied to the brakes of a vehicle, work done by the friction force between the brakes and the wheel reduces the kinetic energy of the vehicle and the temperature of the brakes increases.

The greater the speed of a vehicle the greater the braking force needed to stop the vehicle in a certain distance.

The greater the braking force the greater the deceleration of the vehicle. Large decelerations may lead to brakes overheating and/or loss of control.

Students should be able to:

- explain the dangers caused by large decelerations
- **H estimate the forces involved in the deceleration of road vehicles in typical situations on a public road.**

WS 1.5, 2.2

MS 1a, 1c, 1d, 2c, 2f, 2h, 3b, 3c

Aiming for	Outcome	Checkpoint	
		Question	Activity
Aiming for GRADE 4	List the factors which affect the stopping distance of a car.	1, End of chapter 1	Starter 2, Main
	Calculate the thinking distance for a car from the initial speed and reaction time.	2	Main
	Estimate the relative effects of changing factors which affect the stopping distance of cars.	1	Starter 2
Aiming for GRADE 6	Categorise factors which affect thinking distance, braking distance, and both.	1, End of chapter 1	Main
	Calculate the braking distance of a car.	4	Main
	Describe the relationship between speed and both thinking and braking distance.	3	Main
Aiming for GRADE 8	Calculate acceleration, mass, and braking force of vehicles.	4, End of chapter 3, 5	Main
	Calculate total stopping distance, initial speed, reaction time, and acceleration.	4	Main
	Explain the relative effects of changes of speed on thinking and stopping distance.	3	Main

Maths
Students calculate stopping distances and thinking distances (1a, 3b, 3c).

Literacy
Students discuss factors which affect the stopping of a car; working together to reach conclusions.

Key words
stopping distance, thinking distance, braking distance

Practical

Title	Reaction time challenge
Equipment	ruler
Overview of method	Students work in pairs. One student holds a ruler just above the other's hand. They drop the ruler suddenly and the other student has to catch it. The distance the ruler falls before it is caught can be used to work out your reaction time. Repeat multiple times, both when concentrating and when distracted by something else, such as a conversation.

Starter	Support/Extend	Resources
Safety first (10 min) Use information from government safety websites about car collisions in the local area to identify accident hotspots. Link these results to the idea of speed restrictions in the area, especially around primary schools.	**Support:** Research and simplify the statistics in advance to make them more accessible.	
Stop! (5 min) To support students in understanding the wide range of factors that can affect the stopping distance of cars, provide students with a list of factors to sort according to whether they will affect stopping distances or not.	**Extend:** The students should discuss and describe how the factor affects the stopping distance and construct well-formed descriptions.	
Main	**Support/Extend**	**Resources**
Reaction time challenge (40 min) Discuss the forces acting on a car whilst it is moving at constant velocity. Reinforce the idea that the forces must balance. Identify the resistive forces clearly. The students should understand the factors affecting overall stopping distance, but they need to be clear which affect the thinking distance and which affect the braking distance. **H** For higher-tier students, the braking distance should be linked closely to the decelerating forces using $F = ma$ with a few example car masses and maximum braking forces. From this acceleration and the initial speed, the braking distance should be calculated. Formally introduce stopping distance to all students, ensuring that any misconceptions are corrected. Students then carry out the practical to investigate how distractions can affect your reaction times to demonstrate how using a mobile phone whilst driving can affect stopping distances. They should appreciate that the times improve with practice and when they are fully concentrating on the clock. In a real car situation, the driver would not be able to focus on one simple task, so the times would be significantly greater.	**Extend:** Discuss the nature of the force driving the car forwards. This must be a frictional force between the road and tyres. **Support:** Help students with the multiple equations. **Extend:** Students should find total stopping distances. **Extend:** Students complete the Extension sheet where they investigate the circumstances in a fake car collision to identify if the driver was distracted.	**Practical:** Reaction time challenge **Extension:** Finding the stopping distance of a vehicle
Plenary	**Support/Extend**	**Resources**
Stopping distances and motive forces (10 min) Interactive where students consolidate their understanding of stopping distances. Students link together parts of sentences on braking distance, identify true and false statements on stopping distance, reaction time, and braking distance, and put a description of the forces involved as a car stops in the correct order.		**Interactive:** Stopping distances and motive forces
Homework		
Students complete the WebQuest where they research factors that affect stopping distance. They classify these as factors that affect either thinking distance or braking distance. They use their research to select one particular factor and produce a leaflet on their chosen factor.	**Extend:** Students must include graphical information in their reports such a pie charts.	**WebQuest:** Safe driving

kerboodle

A Kerboodle highlight for this lesson is **Extension sheet: Stop that bike!** Refer to the **Content map** on Kerboodle for a full list of resources and assessment.

P10.4 Momentum

AQA spec Link: 5.7.1 Momentum is defined by the equation:

momentum = mass × velocity

[$p = m\,v$]

momentum, p, in kilograms metre per second, kg m/s

mass, m, in kilograms, kg

velocity, v, in metres per second, m/s

5.7.2 In a closed system, the total momentum before an event is equal to the total momentum after the event.

This is called conservation of momentum.

Students should be able to use the concept of momentum as a model to:

- describe and explain examples of momentum in an event, such as a collision.

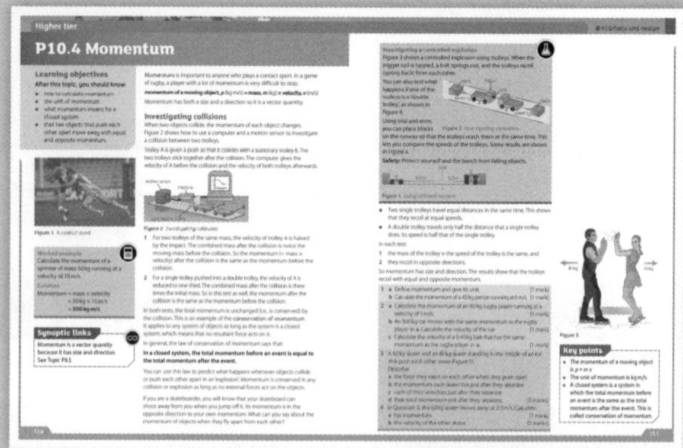

WS 1.2

MS 3b, 3c

Aiming for	Outcome	Checkpoint	
		Question	Activity
Aiming for GRADE 6	Apply the equation $p = mv$ to find the momentum, velocity or mass of an object.	1, 2, 4	Main 1
	Describe how the principle of conservation of momentum can be used to find the velocities of objects.	3	Main 1
	Investigate the behaviour of objects during explosions to verify the conservation of momentum.	3, 4	Main 2
Aiming for GRADE 8	Fully describe the motion of objects after an explosion accounting for any frictional effects.	3, 4	Main 2
	Apply the principle of conservation of momentum to a range of calculations involving the velocities of objects.	3, 4	Main 1, Main 2, Plenary 1
	Evaluate the data produced from an investigation and compare this to a theoretical framework.		Main 2

Maths
The students will perform a range of calculations to find momentum (3b, 3c).

Literacy
The students work in teams to discuss the results of their investigations building clear conclusions.

Key words
momentum, conservation of momentum

Practical

Title	Investigating a controlled explosion
Equipment	two trolleys (one with a trigger and bolt), runway, two wooden blocks
Overview of method	Set the two trolleys on the runway between the two blocks. Press the trigger on the trolley so the bolt springs out. Observe the movement of the two trolleys, then use trial and error to place the blocks on the runway so that the trolleys reach them at the same time.
Safety considerations	Protect feet and bench from falling trolleys.

Starter	Support/Extend	Resources
Trying to stop (5 min) Ask students to explain why it takes a container ship several kilometres to stop but a bicycle can stop in only a few metres, even when they are travelling at the same speed.	**Extend:** The students should also discuss the forces acting in the two scenarios.	
Stopping power (10 min) Students use the interactive to put a list of sport balls (e.g., golf ball, cricket ball, rugby ball, and football) in order of difficulty to stop. They then complete a paragraph to explain what properties make it more difficult for the balls to stop. They should be able to link the stopability to the speed and mass of the balls.	**Support:** Provide typical masses and velocities for the balls.	**Interactive:** Stopping power
Main	**Support/Extend**	**Resources**
Calculating momentum (15 min) Introduce the concept of momentum and the equation for it by discussing a wide range of examples. The students should calculate the momentum of several objects and also the velocities of some objects when given the mass and momentum.	**Support:** Limit calculations to finding momentum without any rearrangement of the equation. **Extend:** Use SI prefixes and standard form in the examples.	**Support:** Understanding conservation of momentum **Extension:** Understanding conservation of momentum
Investigating a controlled explosion (25 min) The students should refine the details of the practical, explaining how it will demonstrate the conservation of momentum in explosions. This will involve an explanation of the different velocities of the trolleys after the collision and hence the distance they will travel in the same time. Once the data is gathered they should compare it to their predictions and suggest explanations for any differences.	**Extend:** Students evaluate their data to see if it supports the law of conservation of momentum and provide reasons why it may not be an exact fit.	**Practical:** Investigating a controlled explosion
Plenary	**Support/Extend**	**Resources**
The skate escape (5 min) Two people are trapped on a perfectly friction-free surface (e.g., an ice rink) just out of reach of each other. They are both 10 m from the edge and all that they have to help them escape is a tennis ball. Ask: how do they both escape? [Throw something from one to the other, this will give them momentum in opposite directions and they will slowly drift to the sides.]	**Support:** Students answer using diagrams. **Extend:** Students estimate the change in momentum when the ball is thrown. This may be conceptually linked to exchange particles in a discussion.	
Boating (10 min) Discuss what happens when somebody steps on to or off of a boat but falls in the water because the boat moves away from the land. Ask the students to explain what happened, perhaps with diagrams. They should understand that the person is actually pushing the boat away. When they move left, the boat will always be forced to the right as a consequence of the conservation of momentum.	**Support:** Students should use diagrams to show the forces involved. **Extend:** Students should provide explanations linked to forces acting and changes in momentum.	
Homework		
Students try some additional momentum calculations for reinforcement and preparation for the next lesson.		

kerboodle

A Kerboodle highlight for this lesson is **Working scientifically: Momentum in action**. Refer to the **Content map** on Kerboodle for a full list of resources and assessment.

P10.5 Using conservation of momentum

AQA spec Link: 5.7.2 Students should be able to use the concept of momentum as a model to:

- complete calculations involving an event, such as the collision of two objects.

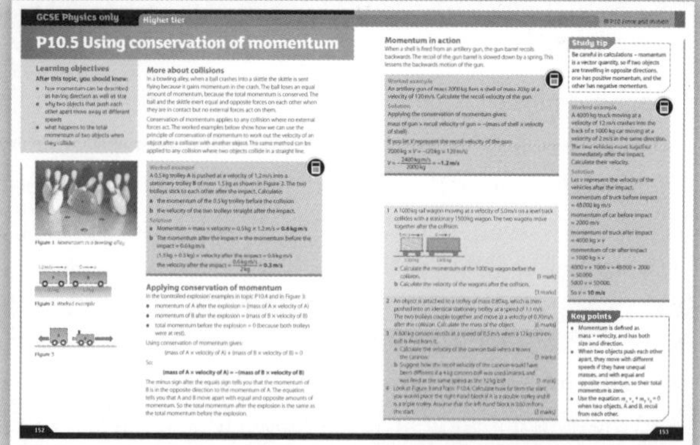

WS 1.2

MS 3b, 3c

Aiming for	Outcome	Checkpoint	
		Question	Activity
Aiming for GRADE 6	Apply the law of conservation of momentum to find the momentum before and after impacts.	1, 2	Main 1
	Calculate the momentum of a combination of objects after an impact.	1, 2	Main 1, Main 2
	Evaluate data used to verify the law of conservation of momentum.		Main 2
Aiming for GRADE 8	Apply the law of conservation of momentum to find velocities of objects after impacts.	1, 2	Main 1
	Analyse the velocities of objects in a wide range of collisions.	1, 2	Main 1
	Evaluate an experimental technique and discuss in detail the factors which lead to differences between experimental data and an accepted law.		Main 2

Maths

The students will calculate the momentum of objects before and after collisions (3c). They will also transpose the relevant equation to find velocities or masses (3b).

Literacy

The students collaborate to describe the behaviour of objects during collisions during an investigation.

Key words

momentum, conservation of momentum, closed system

Practical

Title	Investigating and analysing collisions
Equipment	three dynamics trolleys with velcro on the end, ramp, motion sensor, card
Overview of method	Set the motion sensor up at the top of the ramp. Label the trolleys A and B, and attach the card to the front of trolley A. Push trolley A so that it collides with the stationary trolley B. The two trolleys should stick together after the collision. The motion sensor will measure the velocity of trolley A before the collision and the velocity of both afterwards. Alternatively, a light gate can be used in place of a motion sensor.
Safety considerations	Protect feet and bench from falling trolleys.

Starter	Support/Extend	Resources
Jumping frogs (5 min) Position a few spring-loaded 'jumping frog' toys on the desk and set them off. The students need to account for changes in the energy stores before they all go off.	**Extend:** The students also have to account for the processes and pathways that cause the changes in the energy stores.	
Slow motion (10 min) Show a video of a simple explosion frame-by-frame and ask the students to explain what is happening in terms of forces, mass, and acceleration. They should see the pieces flying off in different directions – some will have greater speed than others.	**Support:** Provide key words or a set of diagrams showing the stages of the explosion. **Extend:** Students must incorporate the idea of conservation of momentum into their descriptions.	
Main	**Support/Extend**	**Resources**
Conservation of momentum (15 min) The students should analyse scenarios where trolleys move apart, performing calculations to find the velocities of the components immediately after the explosion. Students answer the summary questions in the student book for practice.	**Support:** Use a calculation frame to lead the students through the stages of the calculation. **Extend:** Extend the calculations to allow the students to find the distance travelled by components a certain time after the explosion.	
Investigating and analysing collisions (25 min) Students analyse collisions using the practical. Ensure that the students are calculating the momentum before and after the impacts and comparing it. Reinforce the idea of conservation of momentum by performing some calculations supported by the worked examples in the student book. Use some additional examples that incorporate larger masses and objects moving in opposite directions.	**Extend:** Students should describe changes in the energy stores of the system and explain them in terms of acting forces.	**Practical:** Investigating and analysing collisions
Plenary	**Support/Extend**	**Resources**
It's against the frog (5 min) Use a set of quick questions and the jumping frogs again. A student has the time it takes for the frog to go off in which to answer a question.	**Support:** Ask simpler questions that involve some basic calculations.	
Impossibly super (10 min) In many superhero films, cars are thrown and caught easily. The cars stop dead and the costumed hero doesn't budge. Students use the interactive to complete an explanation about the flaws in these films using the conservation of momentum. They can then consider what forces would do to the system (do they think that the friction of the feet on the ground would make any significant difference?)		**Interactive:** Impossibly super
Homework		
Students research car test dummies to prepare for the next few lessons. They can find facts about their introduction and uses including the range of sensors used inside the dummy.	**Extend:** Expect concepts to be clearly linked to forces and changes in momentum.	

P10.6 Impact forces

AQA spec Link: 5.7.3 When a force acts on an object that is moving, or able to move, a change in momentum occurs.

The equations $F = m \times a$ and $a = \frac{(v - u)}{t}$

combine to give the equation $F = \frac{(m\,\Delta v)}{\Delta t}$

where $m\,\Delta v$ = change in momentum

That is, force equals the rate of change of momentum.

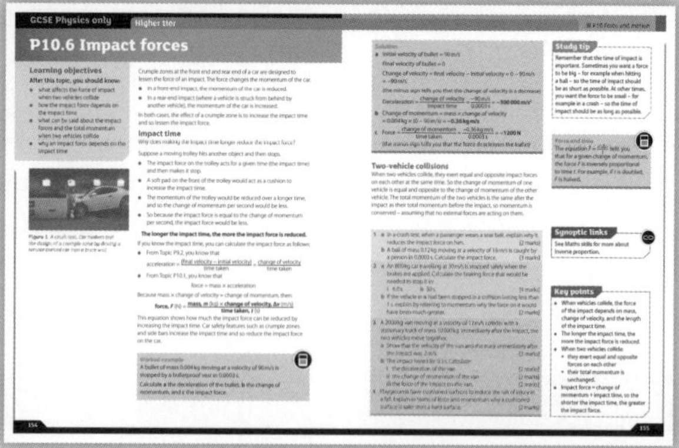

WS 1.2

MS 3a, 3b, 3c

Aiming for	Outcome	Checkpoint	
		Question	Activity
Aiming for GRADE 6	Describe collisions in terms of forces and conservation of momentum.		Main
	Calculate the force involved in an impact from the change in momentum and time.	1, 2	Main
	Design features that will reduce the size of impact forces in a collision.	4	Homework
Aiming for GRADE 8	Apply the concept of equal and opposite forces in collisions to explain why momentum is conserved in impacts.		Main
	Calculate changes in velocity and momentum during impacts using the force involved in the impact and the impact time.	3	Main
	Plan an investigation into the impact forces involved in a collision and how they can be reduced.		Homework

Maths
There are several calculations involved in this lesson, some of which involve multiple steps (3b, 3c). Formal mathematical relationships (inverse proportionality) are also discussed (3a).

Literacy
Descriptions of forces and their effect on acceleration and changes in momentum are needed. These explanations require precise scientific language.

Practical

Title	Investigating impacts
Equipment	dynamics trolley, modelling clay, motion sensor, launch ramp, house brick
Overview of method	The impact between a trolley and a wall or brick can be investigated. The trolley rolls down a ramp from a fixed point, to ensure that the impact velocity will be the same, and collides with the wall/brick. This is then repeated with a cushioning Plasticine cone/ball on the front of the trolley. For a simple test compare the two impacts just by observing the plasticine after the impact. For a more detailed examination use the motion sensor.
Safety considerations	Protect feet and bench from falling bricks and trolleys. Wear eye protection.

Starter	Support/Extend	Resources
Skids (5 min) Why does a car take longer to stop in wet weather? Show students some pictures of cars stopping suddenly and discuss the sizes of the forces. What reduces the forces and why does this mean that the car takes a greater distance to stop?	**Extend:** The students should provide equations for acceleration and then for an equation linking force and acceleration, then link these to change of momentum.	
Sudden impact (10 min) Arrange some bathroom tiles on the floor (inside a tray and wear safety glasses). Drop some objects onto the tiles to see if the tiles (or objects) break. These can include heavy but soft objects and a hammer. Ask the students to explain why the tiles break or why they do not.	**Support:** Provide a list of key concepts for the students to use in their explanations such as the size of the force and the time of the impact.	
Main	**Support/Extend**	**Resources**
Investigating impacts (40 min) Students investigate the effect of crumple zones or similar using the simple practical. This clearly shows that the forces involved in impacts are reduced by using a material that distorts. Link this to the time of impact increasing – if the impact takes place over a longer time period, then a smaller force is required to change the momentum by the same amount. Link this to the relationship $F = \frac{(m\,\Delta v)}{\Delta t}$ or $F = \frac{\Delta p}{\Delta t}$, leading to $\Delta p = F\Delta t$, to show that the relationship between the same change in momentum can be brought about by a smaller force acting over a longer time period.	**Extend:** Use a spring as an 'impact absorber' and observe the motion. Links can be made to changes in energy stores.	**Practical:** Investigating impacts
The calculations here are quite complex and must be broken down into logical stages. Remind the students of some simple acceleration calculations including some decelerations as this is more important in impacts. Recap the calculation of change in momentum ($m\Delta v$) before linking this to the size of the acting force. Students should apply this concept to a collision between vehicles. The focus should be on the equal and opposite forces acting for the same period of time. This demonstrates that the change in momentum of one object is matched by the change in momentum of another during a collision.	**Support:** Focus on the calculation of force from change in momentum, leaving out the acceleration. **Extend:** Try different transpositions of the equations.	
Plenary	**Support/Extend**	**Resources**
Bouncy castles (5 min) Why don't children hurt themselves when they fall on bouncy castles? The students should draw a diagram showing why not. Check that they are identifying the forces and the timings involved.	**Support:** Video clips, paused at key moments, will help in explanations.	
Owwzatt! (10 min) How should cricketers catch fast-moving cricket balls? Students use the interactive to complete instructions explaining the science behind safely catching a cricket ball, including the reasons why gloves are used to 'cushion' the catch.	**Support:** Demonstrate the actions and properties of the ball and glove in the laboratory. Borrow some props from the PE department if possible. **Extend:** Extended explanations should include the motion of the fielders when they catch the ball.	**Interactive:** Owwzatt!
Homework		
Ask the students to design egg safety capsules using cardboard tubes, sponge tape, etc. You can then see which work by dropping eggs or throwing them. These can be tested at the start of the next lesson.	**Support:** Provide some example designs. **Extend:** The students must also describe the rigorous testing regime that will be used to see which capsule is the most effective.	

kerboodle

A Kerboodle highlight for this lesson is **Maths skills: Momentum**. Refer to the **Content map** on Kerboodle for a full list of resources and assessment.

P10.7 Safety first

AQA spec Link: 5.7.3 When a force acts on an object that is moving, or able to move, a change in momentum occurs.

The equations $F = m \times a$ and $a = \frac{(v-u)}{t}$

combine to give the equation $F = \frac{(m\,\Delta v)}{\Delta t}$

where $m\Delta v$ = change in momentum

That is, force equals the rate of change of momentum.

Students should be able to explain safety features such as: air bags, seat belts, gymnasium crash mats, cycle helmets, and cushioned surfaces for playgrounds with reference to the concept of rate of change of momentum.

Students should be able to apply equations relating force, mass, velocity, and acceleration to explain how the changes involved are inter-related.

6.3.1 Students should be able to estimate how the distance for a vehicle to make an emergency stop varies over a range of speeds typical for that vehicle.

Students will be required to interpret graphs relating speed to stopping distance for a range of vehicles.

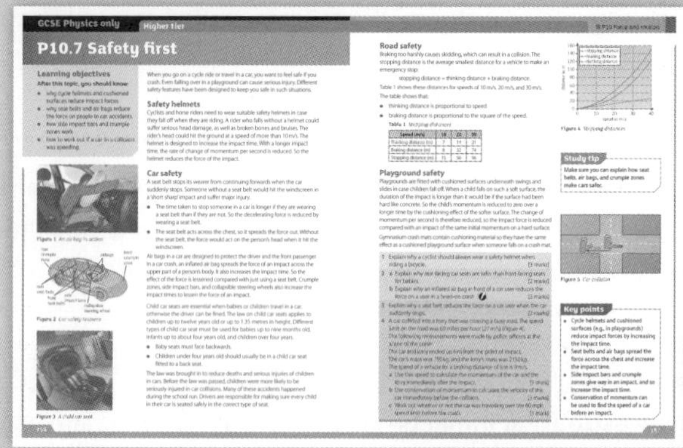

WS 1.2, 4

MS 2c, 2f, 3b, 3c, 3d

Aiming for	Outcome	Checkpoint	
		Question	**Activity**
Aiming for GRADE 6 ↓	Describe the operation of some safety features of a car in simple terms.	1, 2, 3	Starter 2, Main 1
	Report on the differences in safety features between expensive and inexpensive cars.		Main 1
Aiming for GRADE 8 ↓	Use scientific principles such as rate of change of momentum to explain in detail the operation of a range of car safety features.	1, 2, 3	Starter 2, Main 1
	Evaluate a range of optional safety features based on their costs and effectiveness.		Main 1

Maths

Students can consider costs of safety features or explain the statistics about their effectiveness (2c, 2f).

Literacy

The students can produce a written report about a particular safety feature.

Practical

Title	Car safety features
Equipment	eggs, a cloth sheet (about 1 m^2), tray
Overview of method	Drop a raw egg from a height of about 1 m into a tray to show how a sudden impact causes damage. Repeat the experiment but drop the egg on to the sheet which is 10 cm above the tray and being held firmly at the corners but not totally taut. Discuss how the sheet increases the time of impact and compare to the operation of seatbelts.
Safety considerations	Use fresh eggs and clean up any mess immediately.

Starter	Support/Extend	Resources
Crash flashback (5 min) Give the students a momentum problem to solve to refresh the ideas from Topic P10.6. Include cars or other large items as the objects involved in the collision.	**Extend:** To extend other students, provide a more complex situation requiring rearrangement of the basic equation.	
Crumpled cars (10 min) Show the students selected photographs of crashed cars (search the Internet for images) and ask them to describe the damage they see. They should notice the crumpling effect, especially at the front or rear of the car, but may not realise that this is a deliberate design. Students then use the interactive to identify safety features of a car and the reasons why a designer would deliberately want this effect.	**Support:** Refresh students' ideas by linking back to plastic and elastic materials. **Extend:** Discuss the causes of the energy changes involved in collisions.	**Interactive:** Crumpled cars
Main	**Support/Extend**	**Resources**
Car safety features (30 min) Show the students a cycle helmet and discuss its features and the materials used. Link the choices to the 'cushioning' of an impact asking what this term means. Discuss the use of seat belts in cars, linking this concept back to reducing forces by increasing the duration of the force. Use the practical to demonstrate this. Air bags operate in a similar way to seat belts – an increase in the collision time as the passenger pushes through the bag. This can be demonstrated by carefully dropping an egg onto a hard surface then onto a soft surface – the impact of the object on the floor is cushioned slightly. The demonstration can be expanded to include dropping an egg onto balloons inflated by different amounts – to model air bags – and dropping an egg with a crumple zone made of a paper cone. If possible, use a real child car seat to explain the features. The students should see soft materials absorb impacts and strong materials maintain the shape of the seat during a collision. Ensure that you cover the advantages of placing the seat facing backwards. Finally discuss the surface used in playgrounds, showing the students some examples if these are available. **Emergency stop** (10 min) The students should examine and explain some numerical and graphical data on car stopping distances for different speeds.		**Practical:** Car safety features
Plenary	**Support/Extend**	**Resources**
Best car (10 min) Give the students pictures and information about cars through the ages and get them to identify the innovations that have taken place. They can produce a timeline showing the changes. Include information about changes to maximum speeds and road types, such as the introduction of motorways.	**Support:** Provide a blank timeline and some articles (to find information from) to add to the timeline.	
Hard sell (10 min) The students must produce an advertisement for the expensive safety features in a new car. This could be hard-hitting or subtler in its persuasiveness. Most safety features started off as expensive accessories but as their benefits were proven, they became required by law.	**Support:** Provide the students with a car diagram and list of features to 'sell'.	
Homework		
The students can research developments in braking systems in cars such as ABS or the flywheel brakes.	**Extend:** Expect specific numerical information to back up any ideas presented.	

P10.8 Forces and elasticity

AQA spec Link: 5.3 Students should be able to:

- give examples of the forces involved in stretching, bending, or compressing an object
- explain why, to change the shape of an object (by stretching, bending, or compressing), more than one force has to be applied – this is limited to stationary objects only
- describe the difference between elastic deformation and inelastic deformation caused by stretching forces.

The extension of an elastic object, such as a spring, is directly proportional to the force applied, provided that the limit of proportionality is not exceeded.

force = spring constant × extension

$[F = k\,e]$

force F in newtons, N

spring constant k in newtons per metre, N/m

extension e in metres, m

This relationship also applies to the compression of an elastic object, where 'e' would be the compression of the object.

A force that stretches (or compresses) a spring does work and elastic potential energy is stored in the spring. Provided the spring is not inelastically deformed, the work done on the spring and the elastic potential energy stored are equal.

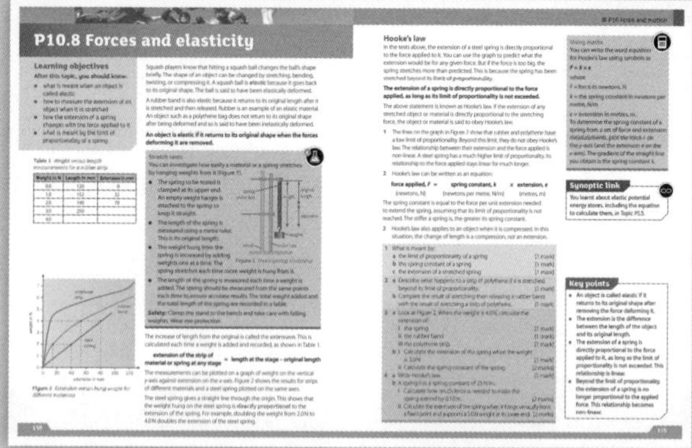

Students should be able to:

- describe the difference between a linear and non-linear relationship between force and extension
- calculate a spring constant in linear cases
- interpret data from an investigation of the relationship between force and extension.

Students should be able to calculate relevant values of stored energy and energy transfers.

Required practical: investigate the relationship between force and extension for a spring.

MS 3b, 3c, 4a, 4b

Aiming for	Outcome	Checkpoint	
		Question	Activity
Aiming for GRADE 4	State Hooke's law.	1, 4	Main
	Calculate the extension of a material using its length and original length.	End of chapter 4	Main
	Compare materials in terms of elastic and non-elastic behaviour.	2	Main
Aiming for GRADE 6	Explain the limitations of Hooke's law including the limit of proportionality.	4	Main
	Calculate the force required to cause a given extension in a spring using the spring constant.	3	Main
	Compare the behaviour of different materials under loads in terms of proportional and non-proportional behaviour.		Main
Aiming for GRADE 8	Find the spring constant of a spring using a graphical technique.	End of chapter 4	Main, Plenary 1
	Apply the Hooke's law equation in a wide range of situations.	3, 4	Main
	Evaluate an investigation into the extension of materials in terms of the precision of the data.		Main

Maths
Graphical skills are emphasised in this lesson along with the tabulated recording of data (4a, 4b).

Literacy
Students organise information in tables and describe the behaviour of materials under load during group work.

Key words
elastic, extension, directly proportional, limit of proportionality

Required practical

Title	Stretch tests
Equipment	set of masses (50 g) and holder, retort stand, clamp, spring, elastic band, strips of plastic, rulers (30 cm, 50 cm, and 1 m are likely to be needed), G-clamp (to hold the retort stand on the bench if needed)
Overview of method	Students set up the equipment as shown in Figure 1 from the student book. The initial length is measured, and then the spring is loaded by placing 50 g masses on it. Students measure the length and find the extension. The results should indicate the relationship for Hooke's law. Students should also investigate elastic (fishing-pole elastic is ideal). Finally, other materials such as strips of plastic can also be investigated.
Safety considerations	Eye protection should be worn in case the spring or elastic snaps.

Starter	Support/Extend	Resources
Distortion (5 min) Get the students to list the basic things that forces can do (cause acceleration, change the shape of the object). Concentrate on the forces in the diagrams that cause objects to compress or stretch, and use these to discuss whether these changes are permanent or can be reversed.	**Support:** Students can draw diagrams showing forces acting on objects that cause these things to happen.	
In proportion (10 min) In this lesson the students will find a relationship that is proportional, so start the lesson by asking the students to use the interactive to compare some graphs and the relationship between them. They then complete a description on the idea of proportionality.	**Support:** Use a simple graph such as one showing the amount of money earned compared with hours worked to show an easily identifiable proportional relationship.	**Interactive:** In proportion
Main	**Support/Extend**	**Resources**
Stretch tests (40 min) Demonstrate a simple elastic band to show a material returning to its original shape showing elastic behaviour. Show the similar behaviour for a spring and then the plastic behaviour of polythene or something similar whilst also stretching a spring beyond the elastic limit to show permanent deformation. Students then test the behaviour of materials under load using the practical. They should focus on accurate measurement of length, well organised recording of the data, and calculation of extension. When the data for the practical has been collected, graphs can be plotted to show the relationships. Identify areas where the relationship is directly proportional, ensuring the students can identify this, and the limits to the behaviour. Use the data for the spring tests to explain Hooke's law and the associated equation. The students should find the spring constant for the spring they tested.	**Support:** Provide a results table, and support students in the calculation of extension. **Extend:** Students should use repeat tests to find ranges for the data, helping to evaluate it. **Support:** Provide simplified data for the graph plotting if required. **Extend:** Use data from the repeat tests to find the possible range of the spring constant. **Extend:** The energy changes can be linked to work done by the force stretching the spring.	**Required practical:** Stretch tests
Plenary	**Support/Extend**	**Resources**
Graphical analysis (5 min) Give the students a graph showing the extension of different springs and ask them to describe the differences. They should look at the limit of proportionality and the spring constants. **Catapult** (10 min) Students can explain how a catapult operates or plan an investigation measuring the energy stored in it.	**Extend:** Provide just the raw data and ask the students to plot the graphs.	
Homework		
Students can research the uses of springs for cushioning and support in seats, cars, and beds.		

kerboodle

A Kerboodle highlight for this lesson is **Working scientifically: Unbreakable laws and powerful theories**. Refer to the **Content map** on Kerboodle for a full list of resources and assessment.

P10 Forces and motion

Overview of P10 Forces and motion

Students began this chapter by experimentally determining the relationships between a force acting on an object and the acceleration, and the mass of the object and the acceleration. The results led to the formulation for Newton's second law of motion and its application. Higher-tier students have also defined the inertial mass of an object.

The students have then compared the concepts of mass and weight, linking them through the idea of a gravitational field before looking at the forces acting on an object as it falls through a fluid and the resulting terminal velocity. The forces acting during stopping a car have been analysed; identifying two phases of the motion; thinking and braking distance and the effects of a wide range of factors on both of these distances. Students have calculated the size of the accelerations experienced during braking with higher tier students deriving an appropriate equation involving the stopping distance.

The higher tier students have investigated the concept of momentum and its conservation. Higher-tier *GCSE Physics* students have used the principle of conservation of momentum to allow them to determine the velocity of objects after collisions or explosion have taken place in a range of scenarios. Further analysis has allowed higher tier students to use the concept of momentum to determine the force acting during collisions and relate this to the duration of the impact. Higher-tier *GCSE Physics* students have also applied their knowledge of impacts to discuss the safety features of a car.

Finally, all of the students have investigated the effect of forces on the stretching of a range of materials identifying both linear and non-linear relationships between the force and extension. Students have applied Hook's law as appropriate and identified its limitations.

You can find additional support for the maths skills covered in this chapter on **MyMaths**, including translating information between graphical and numeric form, substituting numerical values into algebraic equations using appropriate units for physical quantities, determining the slope and intercept of a linear graph.

For this chapter, the following assessments are available on Kerboodle:

P10 Checkpoint quiz: Forces and motion
P10 Progress quiz: Forces and motion 1
P10 Progress quiz: Forces and motion 2
P10 On your marks: Forces and motion
P10 Exam-style questions and mark scheme: Forces and motion

Checkpoint follow up lesson

A student's route through this lesson can be determined using the Checkpoint assessment. Percentage pass marks are supplied in the Checkpoint teacher notes.

For each successive route through it is assumed that the student can perform to their current route as well as previous routes. For example, students working at Aiming for 6 are assumed to be secure in Aiming for 4 knowledge and understanding and working towards achieving all the learning outcomes for Aiming for 6.

	Aiming for 4	Aiming for 6	Aiming for 8
Learning outcomes	Describe the effect of force and mass on acceleration.	Explain the effect of force and mass on acceleration.	Explain the effect of force and mass on acceleration in unfamiliar situations.
	State factors that affect stopping distance.	Describe the factors that affect stopping distance.	Explain factors affecting stopping distance.
		Describe the behaviour of elastic materials.	Explain the behaviour of elastic materials.
Starter	**Safer cars (5 min)** Show images of a range of cars from different times in history, including the most recent and Formula 1, and ask students to come up with as many different reasons as possible for improvements in car safety. **Faster cars (5 min)** Ask students to discuss what would happen if there was a race between a motorcycle, a car, and an aeroplane. Who would win? Why?		
Differentiated checkpoint activity	Aiming for 4 students use the Checkpoint follow-up sheet to model a car using a margarine tub and an elastic band, and investigate the link between force, mass, and stopping distance. The follow-up sheet provides structured tasks and questions to help them complete these activities and check their understanding of the factors affecting stopping distance, and the link between force, mass, and acceleration.	Aiming for 6 students use the Checkpoint follow-up sheet to complete one of three activities: • model a car using a margarine tub and an elastic band, and investigate the link between force, mass, and stopping distance • investigate how the force on an elastic band affects the extension. • model crumple zones using a trolley. The third activity is only appropriate for students studying *AQA GCSE Physics*. The follow-up sheet provides tasks and questions to help them complete these activities and check their understanding of the link between force, mass, and acceleration, and between force and extension, as well as to apply their knowledge of forces to stopping distances and car safety.	Aiming for 8 students use the Checkpoint follow-up sheet to design an investigation. Students studying *AQA GCSE Combined science: Trilogy* design an investigation into force, mass, and acceleration. Students studying *AQA GCSE Physics* design an investigation either into forces, mass, and acceleration, or into the use of crumple zones in cars. The follow-up sheet provides tasks and questions to help them complete these activities and check their understanding of the relationship between force, mass, and acceleration, and between force and extension, as well as to apply their knowledge of forces to stopping distances, and to car safety, by doing calculations involving force, momentum, and time
	Kerboodle resource P10 Checkpoint follow up: Aiming for 4, P10 Checkpoint follow up: Aiming for 6, P10 Checkpoint follow up: Aiming for 8		
Plenary	**Stop the car (10 min)** Give students A4 dry wipe boards, pens, and an eraser. Read out a series of answers to questions about stopping distance and ask students to write the question, for example, 'because the friction between the wheels of the car and the road is less'. **Acceleration race (5 min)** Group students by the level to which they are aiming, and give out a pack of cards. Each card should have a picture of an object with the force acting on it and the mass of the object. Include the motorbike, car, and aeroplane from the Starter. Aiming for 4 students should put them in order of fastest to slowest acceleration, and Aiming for 6/8 students should calculate the acceleration. Aiming for 8 students should also calculate the time that would produce the same force on each object if they are all travelling at 10 m/s.		
Progression	Encourage students to think about acceleration as affected by force and mass, rather than force affected by mass and acceleration.	Encourage students to think about acceleration as affected by force and mass, rather than force affected by mass and acceleration, and similarly to explain the effect of force and spring constant on extension.	Encourage students to think about acceleration and extension as the dependent variables, and to use ideas about time of impact and momentum to explain measures to improve car safety.

P GCSE Physics only

11 Force and pressure

11.1 Pressure and surfaces

AQA spec Link: 5.5.1.1 A fluid can be either a liquid or a gas.

The pressure in fluids causes a force normal (at right angles) to any surface.

The pressure at the surface of a fluid can be calculated using the equation:

$$\text{pressure} = \frac{\text{force normal to a surface}}{\text{area of that surface}}$$

$$[p = \frac{F}{A}]$$

pressure p in pascals, Pa

force F in newtons, N

area A in metres squared, m^2

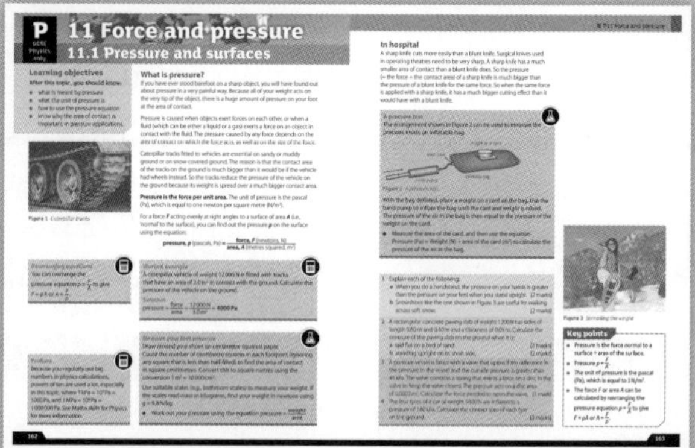
P 11 Force and pressure
11.1 Pressure and surfaces

WS 4.3, 4.4, 4.5, 4.6

MS 3b, 3c

Aiming for	Outcome	Checkpoint	
		Question	**Activity**
Aiming for GRADE 4 ↓	State the factors that affect the pressure acting on a surface.	1	Starter 1, Main, Plenary 2
	Calculate the pressure caused by an object resting on a surface, given the force and area of contact.	2, 3, 4	Main
	Describe how pressure can be caused by the action of fluids (liquids and gases) on a surface.		Main
Aiming for GRADE 6 ↓	Describe the effect on the pressure of changing the area of contact or weight acting on a surface.	1	Starter 1, Main
	Calculate forces or areas of contact.	2, 3, 4	Main
	Use SI prefixes in expressions for pressure as appropriate.		Main
Aiming for GRADE 8 ↓	Apply the concept of pressure in explaining the effect on a surface in a wide range of contexts.		Main, Plenary 2
	Perform pressure calculations including conversion of areas and forces with SI multiplier prefixes.	2, 3, 4	Main
	Estimate uncertainty in values for pressure using experimental data.		Main

Maths

Students will calculate pressure using the appropriate equation (3b, 3c).

Literacy

Students should use scientific terms to describe the action of a force on a surface.

Practical

Title	Measure your foot pressure
Equipment	squared paper (A4), scales (measuring in newtons)
Overview of method	The students weigh themselves in newtons and measure the area of their feet in contact with the floor (measuring one foot and doubling this area) using the squared paper. They then calculate the pressure that they exert on the floor.
Safety considerations	Ensure that there is a suitable amount of space available for the activity.

Title	A pressure test
Equipment	inflatable bag, hand pump, card, 500 g mass
Overview	Arrange equipment as shown in Figure 2 of the student book. Place a weight onto a card on the deflated bag. Use the hand pump to inflate the bag until the card and weight is raised. The pressure of the air in the bag is then equal to the pressure of the weight on the card.
Safety	Use a sturdy bag and do not over-inflate.

Starter	Support/Extend	Resources
Let it sink in (10 min) Use a large tray of damp sand and place objects into it – some with flat surfaces and some spiky. Ask students to explain why some sink into it and others don't. Step into the tray wearing different shoes if it is large enough.	**Extend:** The students should explain why the object eventually stops sinking into the sand.	
Hole in the wall (5 min) Use a darts board, some darts, and some blunt objects to show that some objects will 'stick into things' whilst others do not. Ask the students to explain this effect.	**Support:** The students should examine the area (points) on the objects to help them reach conclusions.	
Main	**Support/Extend**	**Resources**
Measuring pressure (40 min) Use the conclusions of one of the starters to discuss the concept of pressure using plenty of examples such as those shown in the student book. Students will become familiar with the concept of the force acting over an area. Then introduce the equation relating pressure to force and area. Use several examples, some of which can be taken from the summary questions. Ensure that the students are comfortable with the unit for pressure (pascal) and its equivalence to the newton per square metre. Use of the equation can be reinforced by the two practical tasks. These also serve in helping the students convert areas from square centimetres to square metres. Examples of the wide differences in pressure and their effects should now be covered. The action of a sharp blade (e.g., a scalpel) and a blunt one (e.g., a normal cutlery knife) can be demonstrated.	**Support:** Props such as toy models of vehicles can help to reinforce the ideas. Students may need support with the calculation of weight if the scales measure in kilograms. **Extend:** Students should try questions that involve rearrangement of the equation and different SI prefixes. They may also make an estimate of the uncertainty of their weight and the area of contact with the floor. **Extend:** Students can estimate some forces and areas in the contexts described and then calculate example pressures.	**Practical:** Measuring pressure
Plenary	**Support/Extend**	**Resources**
On thin ice (5 min) Interactive where students identify measures that must be taken during a rescue on an ice-covered lake and discuss the measures taken to reduce the pressure on the ice.	**Support:** Show photographs of snow shoes and other methods of spreading the force over large areas.	**Interactive:** On thin ice
If the shoe fits (10 min) Show a range of sports and other shoes discussing their designs and how they would affect a surface. Are they designed to grip or sink into surfaces?	**Extend:** Students can calculate typical pressures produced by the shoes by estimating their area of contact.	
Homework		
The students can research an application of pressure and materials science, such as worktop protectors or bulletproof vests, discussing the materials used.		

P11.2 Pressure in a liquid at rest

AQA spec Link: 5.5.1.2 The pressure due to a column of liquid can be calculated using the equation:

pressure = height of the column × density of the liquid × gravitational field strength

$[p = h\,\rho\,g]$

pressure p in pascals, Pa

height of the column h in metres, m

density ρ in kilograms per metre cubed, kg/m^3

gravitational field strength g in newtons per kilogram, N/kg (In any calculation the value of the gravitational field strength g will be given.)

Students should be able to explain why, in a liquid, pressure at a point increases with the height of the column of liquid above that point and with the density of the liquid.

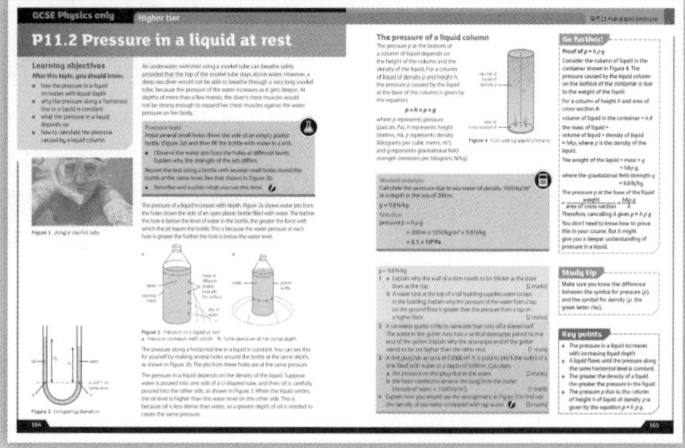

WS 4.3, 4.4, 4.5, 4.6
MS 3b, 3c

Aiming for	Outcome	Checkpoint	
		Question	**Activity**
Aiming for GRADE 6 ↓	Use the concept of force, mass, and volume to explain why the pressure increases with depth in a liquid.	4	Main
	Calculate the pressure at a point in a liquid using $p = h\rho g$.	3, End of chapter 1, 2	Main
Aiming for GRADE 8 ↓	Use algebraic techniques to derive the equation $p = h\rho g$.		Main
	Rearrange the equation $p = h\rho g$ to solve a range of questions involving the pressure in a liquid.	3, End of chapter 1, 2	Main

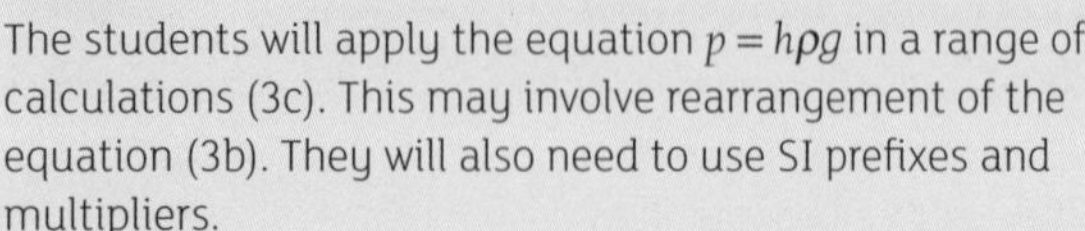

Maths
The students will apply the equation $p = h\rho g$ in a range of calculations (3c). This may involve rearrangement of the equation (3b). They will also need to use SI prefixes and multipliers.

Literacy
Detailed descriptions of concepts and their links to the mathematical expression are needed to explain the changes in pressure in a liquid.

Practical

Title	Pressure tests
Equipment	two large plastic bottles with small holes drilled into them, parcel tape, water, glass U-tube, oil, water
Overview of method	To demonstrate that pressure is the same at a fixed depth, put four holes into a plastic bottle at a fixed depth. Tape up the holes with a strip of easily removed tape and then remove it quickly to show the even spread of the water jets. To demonstrate that the pressure increases with depth, use a similar bottle with holes at different depths. Tape these holes up and fill the bottle before removing the tape again. The jets at the bottom should push the water further out, showing increased pressure. To demonstrate the importance of the density of the liquid, pour water into one side of the glass U-tube and oil into the other. The top of the oil will be at a greater height than the top of the water.
Safety considerations	Ensure that the water does not spill onto the floor.

Title	Pascal's vases
Equipment	set of Pascal's vases filled with water
Overview of method	Demonstrate that the liquid in the vases will settle at the same level. Add additional water to show that the level will remain equal.
Safety considerations	Clean up any spillages.

Starter	Support/Extend	Resources
The deep (10 min) Students use the interactive to describe the conditions deep beneath the oceans and how this relates to the design of submarines. They should realise that the pressure is very large even at fairly shallow depths.	**Extend:** Ask the students to describe the changes in pressure as they travel up a mountain. Why are the changes smaller per metre than the changes in water?	**Interactive:** The deep
Leaky pipes (5 min) Prick some small holes into a rubber Bunsen tube connected to a tap and turn it on. Ask the students to explain why no water comes out of the holes. Block the end of the tube and ask the students to explain why the water is coming out now.	**Support:** Look for simple explanations with ideas of simple forces in the liquid. Provide a diagram to annotate if needed.	
Main	**Support/Extend**	**Resources**
Pressure tests (40 min) Explain the factors that affect the pressure at a specific depth in a liquid using the three simple demonstrations described in the practical. These effects need to be explained by discussing the forces acting at specific points – the weight of the fluid above the holes in the bottle and the pipe. This will lead onto discussion of the calculations.	**Extend:** Include the particle model and specific explanations of density in these explanations.	**Practical:** Pressure tests
Link the factors discussed together to arrive at the pressure equation $p = h\rho g$. Ensure that the students are clear on each of the terms in the equation and how the pressure would change if that factor was changed – they should be able to make statements such as if the density of the liquid increases, the pressure increases. Students should then try some calculations based on the equation.	**Support:** Provide a calculation support frame to lead the students through each of the stages. **Extend:** Students should rearrange the equation and perform calculations.	
Plenary	**Support/Extend**	**Resources**
Pascal's vases (10 min) Demonstrate the behaviour of this equipment and ask the students to provide explanations for it. These should be presented using the idea of equal pressure at equal depth as shown earlier in the lesson.	**Support:** Provide key terms and phrases the students can use in their descriptions.	
Plumbing problems (5 min) Discuss the problems associated with plumbing in tall buildings. Why does the pressure of the water decrease the higher up the building the taps are?	**Extend:** Can the students think of any solutions to this problem?	
Homework		
Students research recorded dives and the design of the submersibles used. This can include manned and unmanned dives and historical records.	**Support:** Students produce a timeline of events and records. **Extend:** Students should focus on the design features of the submersibles and some associated problems (e.g., pressurisation, decompression).	

kerboodle

A Kerboodle highlight for this lesson is **Working scientifically: Liquid under pressure**. Refer to the **Content map** on Kerboodle for a full list of resources and assessment.

P11.3 Atmospheric pressure

AQA spec Link: 5.5.2 The atmosphere is a thin layer (relative to the size of the Earth) of air round the Earth. The atmosphere gets less dense with increasing altitude.

Air molecules colliding with a surface create atmospheric pressure. The number of air molecules (and so the weight of air) above a surface decreases as the height of the surface above ground level increases. So as height increases there is always less air above a surface than there is at a lower height. So atmospheric pressure decreases with an increase in height.

Students should be able to:

- describe a simple model of the Earth's atmosphere and of atmospheric pressure
- explain why atmospheric pressure varies with height above a surface.

5.5.1.2 Ⓗ The pressure due to a column of liquid can be calculated using the equation:

pressure = height of the column × density of the liquid × gravitational field strength

[$p = h\,\rho\,g$]

pressure p in pascals (Pa)

height of the column h in metres (m)

density ρ in kilograms per metre cubed (kg/m³)

gravitational field strength g in newtons per kilogram (N/kg) (In any calculation the value of the gravitational field strength g will be given.)

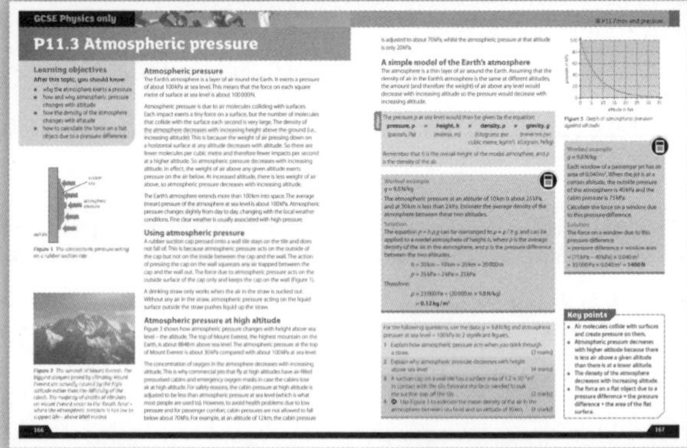
GCSE Physics only
P11.3 Atmospheric pressure

WS 1.2, 4.3, 4.4, 4.5, 4.6
MS 3b, 3c

Aiming for	Outcome	Checkpoint	
		Question	Activity
Aiming for GRADE 4	Describe how the pressure of the atmosphere decreases with height above the Earth's surface.		Main 1
	Describe how the density of the atmosphere decreases with height.		Main 1, Main 2
↓	Describe the cause of atmospheric pressure in simple terms.		Main 1
Aiming for GRADE 6	Calculate the forces produced by pressure differences.	2	Main 2
	Describe the change in pressure at different heights.	3	Main 2
↓	**Ⓗ Use the equation $p = h\rho g$ to determine pressure in a fluid.**	4	
Aiming for GRADE 8	Use the particle model to explain in detail the changes in atmospheric pressure.	3	Main 1
	Explain a range of phenomena in terms of pressure difference.	1	Main 1
↓	**Ⓗ Explain why the relationship $p = h\rho g$ is not suitable for calculating changes in pressure in the atmosphere over a large change in height.**	4	Main 2

Maths

The students will calculate pressure differences using the equation for pressure in a liquid (3c).

Literacy

The students should discuss the effects of pressure differences in the atmosphere and their consequences in terms of weather events. They may also report on extreme weather events.

Practical

Title	Atmospheric pressure and its effects
Equipment	suction cups, pair of Magdeburg hemispheres, vacuum pump
Overview of method	Demonstrate the effect of a suction cup by attaching it to a small metal plate and lifting it. If you have some Magdeburg hemispheres, then demonstrate the effect of removing air from them and attempting to pull them apart.
Safety considerations	Ensure that the students cannot fall or overexert themselves when attempting to pull the hemispheres apart.

Starter	Support/Extend	Resources
Tornado (5 min) Discuss why there are weather characteristics like the wind. Why does air move around the surface of the planet? What is the cause of the pressure differences in the first place? **Atmospheric pressure** (10 min) Students complete the interactive to describe the cause of atmospheric pressure.	**Extend:** Demonstrate the expansion of a gas as it is heated and ask the students to use this concept in their explanation.	**Interactive:** Atmospheric pressure
Main		**Resources**
Atmospheric pressure and its effects (20 min) Link back to Topic P11.2 and the factors that affect the pressure in a liquid, asking students to describe the differences between a liquid and a gas. Include a discussion of density and the motion of the particles. Discuss the motion of the particles and how these produce the forces that cause pressure on surfaces during collisions and link this to atmospheric pressure. Use examples such as a suction through a straw, simple breathing, suction cups, or the Magdeburg hemispheres as described in the practical. **Modelling pressure and altitude** (20 min) Discuss the changes in atmospheric pressure with altitude and use a worked example to show the forces that can result in pressure differences. (H) Higher-tier student should relate the atmospheric pressure to the equation $p = h\rho g$ and discuss where this is a suitable equation to determine the pressure at any height. All students should compare the equation with the pressure graphs and note that that they do not match. The equation would produce a linear relationship between pressure and height. Discuss the changes in density of the air to explain the difference.	**Extend:** Incorporate the idea of reduced temperature when describing the motion of the particles resulting in even lower pressure.	**Practical:** Atmospheric pressure and its effects
Plenary		**Resources**
Suckers (5 min) Stick a suction cup toy on a window and ask student to explain why it shouldn't be called a 'sucker' at all. **Extreme pressure** (10 min) (H) Ask students to find the change in height of a mercury column for the highest (105 360 Pa in Aberdeenshire 1902) and lowest (92 560 Pa in Perthshire 1884) recorded pressures for the UK.	**Extend:** Records from around the world can be used in addition. The highest recorded atmospheric pressure was 108.33 kPa and lowest 87.00 kPa	
Homework		
Students can research pressure records in different countries and the weather conditions that cause these records.		

kerboodle

A Kerboodle highlight for this lesson is **Working scientifically: Initial readings**. Refer to the **Content map** on Kerboodle for a full list of resources and assessment.

P11.4 Upthrust and flotation

AQA spec Link: 5.5.1.2 Students should be able to calculate the differences in pressure at different depths in a liquid.

A partially (or totally) submerged object experiences a greater pressure on the bottom surface than on the top surface. This creates a resultant force upwards. This force is called the upthrust.

Students should be able to describe the factors which influence floating and sinking.

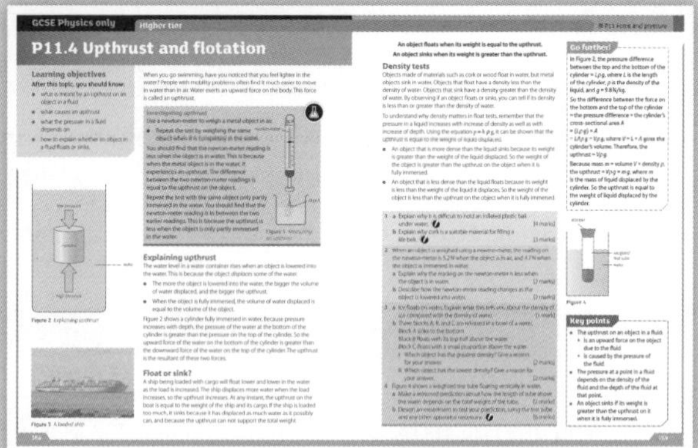
GCSE Physics only Higher tier

P11.4 Upthrust and flotation

MS 1c, 3c

Aiming for	Outcome	Checkpoint	
		Question	**Activity**
Aiming for GRADE 6	Describe the relationship between upthrust and weight for floating and submerged objects.	1, 2	Starter 1, Main 1
	Compare the density of an object with the density of a liquid to determine whether or not the object will float.	3, 4	Main 2
	Plan an investigation into the relationship between the average density of an object and the distance it submerges.	4	
Aiming for GRADE 8	Calculate the upthrust acting on a submerged object by using the pressure difference on the top and bottom surfaces.	2, End of chapter 5	Main 1
	Use algebraic techniques to show that the weight of liquid displaced is equal to the upthrust provided.		Main 2
	Carry out and evaluate in detail an investigation into the relationship between the average density of an object and the distance it submerges.	4	Main 2

Maths
Students will apply the equation $p = h\rho g$ to find upthrust when objects are floating and submerged (3c).

Literacy
Students must apply scientific terms when explaining floating and sinking.

Key words
upthrust

Practical

Title	Investigating upthrust
Equipment	large beaker of water, newton-meter, string, range of metal objects
Overview of method	The students attach the object to the newton-meter by string and weigh them. They then lower the objects into water and weigh them again. They should note the apparent decrease in weight for the object.
Safety considerations	Ensure that water does not spill onto the floor.

Starter	Support/Extend	Resources
Will it float or will it sink? (10 min) Start the lesson by testing whether a range of objects or materials will float or sink in water using a large tank of water (e.g., a fish tank) and objects of your choice. Students should sketch simple force diagrams for both floating and sinking.	**Extend:** Expect diagrams to have an appropriate scale.	
Density recap (5 min) Students should measure the density of a regular object by determining its volume and mass.	**Support:** Provide a reminder of the equation for density. **Extend:** Ask for the density in kg/m^3 to get the students to convert units.	
Main	**Support/Extend**	**Resources**
Investigating upthrust (25 min) Demonstrate a floating object and discuss the forces acting on it. The students should realise that there is a force balancing the weight of the object – the upthrust. Students then use the practical to note that even objects that are sinking will have an upthrust acting on them. The cause of upthrust should be explained with reference to the equation for pressure at a depth in a liquid. Using this, show that the pressure will be greater at the bottom of an object than that at the top. Using a simple object such as a cylinder or cube will make this easier for the students to see that there will be different sizes of forces acting on the top and bottom surfaces and the resultant is the upthrust.	**Support:** Provide a simple results table to help with the recording of results. **Extend:** Ask the students to determine whether the upthrust is always the same for objects of the same volume that sink. Students can try a calculation of the upthrust based on the $p = h\rho g$ equation and the area of the top and bottom surfaces.	**Practical:** Investigating upthrust
Density tests (15 min) Recap the concept of density if the second starter was not used, and then explain floating and sinking objects and describe why they float (or not) in terms of the upthrust provided and the weight of the object. The upthrust can then be linked to the weight of the liquid displaced. Ensure that both cases, floating and being submerged, are covered here. Some students can be led through the proof that the upthrust is equal to the weight of the fluid displaced by using the Kerboodle activity. This is *not* required by the specification, but will allow students to further develop their understanding.	**Extend:** Some calculations of density can be used to test whether an object will float in water before carrying out a real test. **Extend:** An extension sheet is available with qualitative and quantitative problems about flotation.	**Extension:** Floating and sinking
Plenary	**Support/Extend**	**Resources**
Practical planning (10 min) Students design a practical method for showing that the weight of liquid displaced is equal to the upthrust acting on an object floating or submerged in it. This can be shown by measuring the upthrust and comparing it with the weight of water displaced in a displacement can.	**Support:** Provide some equipment for the students to consider in their plan. **Extend:** Expect students to consider accuracy and precision in their plans.	
The pressure is off at last (5 min) Use the interactive to give students a series of true or false statements covering the content from the whole chapter. Students should correct the statements they identify as false.		**Interactive:** The pressure is off at last
Homework		
Students complete the WebQuest where they research the physics of deep sea fish – how they use their swim bladder for flotation and how they withstand the high pressures deep below the surface. Students use their research findings to produce a poster.		**WebQuest:** Surviving in the deep

kerboodle

A Kerboodle highlight for this lesson is **Maths skills: Pressure in fluids**. Refer to the **Content map** on Kerboodle for a full list of resources and assessment.

P11 Force and pressure

Overview of P11 Force and pressure

In this chapter the students have defined pressure as a force acting over a surface before measuring pressure and describing its effects on materials and calculating the pressure acting on a surface. Higher tier students moved on to describe the pressure in a liquid, explaining the change of pressure with depth in terms of particle behaviour, the pressure in a liquid column, and the relevant equation.

Students then discussed the cause of atmospheric pressure in terms of the behaviour of particles in the air, variations in density, and temperature. They described some of the consequences of atmospheric pressure such as the suction cup and how it grips surfaces. Higher-tier students also apply the relationship between pressure, height, density, and acceleration due to gravity to determine pressures at different points in the atmosphere.

The higher-tier students continue with their examination of the effects of particles in fluids by investigating upthrust and then explaining the effect by considering the effects of differences in pressure inside the fluid. They apply the concept to explain why some objects float while others do not.

You can find additional support for the maths skills covered in this chapter on **MyMaths**, including changing the subject of an equation, substituting numerical values into algebraic equations using appropriate units for physical quantities, and solving simple algebraic equations

For this chapter, the following assessments are available on Kerboodle:

P11 Checkpoint quiz: Force and pressure
P11 Progress quiz: Force and pressure 1
P11 Progress quiz: Force and pressure 2
P11 On your marks: Force and pressure
P11 Exam-style questions and mark scheme: Force and pressure

Checkpoint follow up lesson

A student's route through this lesson can be determined using the Checkpoint assessment. Percentage pass marks are supplied in the Checkpoint teacher notes.

For each successive route through it is assumed that the student can perform to their current route as well as previous routes. For example, students working at Aiming for 6 are assumed to be secure in Aiming for 4 knowledge and understanding and working towards achieving all the learning outcomes for Aiming for 6.

	Aiming for 4	Aiming for 6	Aiming for 8
Learning outcomes	Describe how pressure is related to force and area.	Explain, in terms of force, why the atmosphere exerts a pressure.	Explain how and why atmosphere changes with height.
		Describe how and why the pressure in a fluid is related to depth.	Explain how and why the pressure in a fluid is related to depth and density.
Starter	**Going up! (5 min)** Show a picture of a weather balloon and discuss how scientists use the balloons to make measurements of temperature, pressure, etc. in the atmosphere to help us predict the weather. Ask students to write down what they think will happen to pressure readings as the balloon goes up. Keep the description for the plenary. **Big pressure, small pressure (5 min)** Cut an apple in half, and talk about the pressure exerted by the knife blade on the apple. Ask students to sort a series of cards showing different everyday situations into those that require a large pressure (nails, drawing pins, etc.) and those that require a small pressure (bag handles, skis, etc.).		
Differentiated checkpoint activity	Aiming for 4 students use the Checkpoint follow-up sheet to make impressions in modelling clay and do calculations involving pressure. The follow-up sheet provides structured tasks and questions to help them complete these activities and check their understanding of pressure.	Aiming for 6 students use the Checkpoint follow-up sheet to make impressions in modelling clay and carry out calculations involving pressure. Students then investigate the link between pressure and depth in a fluid using a balloon in water. The follow-up sheet provides tasks and questions to help them complete these activities and check their understanding of how to calculate pressure, force and area and how pressure in fluids such as liquids and gases varies with height and depth.	Aiming for 8 students use the Checkpoint follow-up sheet to make impressions in modelling clay and carry out calculations involving pressure, then they plot a graph of atmospheric pressure against height. Then they design an investigation to find the link between pressure and depth in the context of container ships. The follow-up sheet provides tasks and questions to help them complete these activities and check their understanding of pressure, force, and area, and how pressure in fluids such as liquids and gases varies with height and depth.
	Kerboodle resource P11 Checkpoint follow up: Aiming for 4, P11 Checkpoint follow up: Aiming for 6, P11 Checkpoint follow up: Aiming for 8		
Plenary	**What's wrong? (10 min)** Give students A4 dry wipe boards, pens, and an eraser. Show a calculation of pressure that is incorrect and ask students to write the correct calculation. You can have the wrong numbers, equation, or units. Aiming for 4 students could be given the equations. **Going up, going down (5 min)** Return to the descriptions from the starter and ask them to write a 'teacher' comment on the description, and then write an explanation to go with it. Aiming at 8 students could repeat the exercise with a balloon in water being pulled down.		
Progression	Encourage students to put units into calculations to ensure that their answer is correct.	Encourage students to think about pressure in a fluid as related to the weight of fluid above it.	Encourage students to think about pressure in a fluid as related to the weight of fluid above it, and to critically evaluate models of real life situations involving pressure in fluids.

4 Waves, electromagnetism, and space

Specification links

AQA specification section	Assessment paper
6.1 Waves in air, fluids, and solids	Paper 2
6.2 Electromagnetic waves	Paper 2
7.1 Permanent and induced magnetism, magnetic forces and fields	Paper 2
7.2 The motor effect	Paper 2
8.1 Solar system; stability of orbital motions; satellites (physics only)	Paper 2
8.2 Red-shift (physics only)	Paper 2

Required practicals

AQA required practicals	Practical skills	Topic
Make observations to identify the suitability of apparatus to measure the frequency, wavelength, and speed of waves in a ripple tank and waves in a solid and take appropriate measurements.	AT4 – make observations of waves in fluids and solids to identify the suitability of apparatus to measure speed/frequency/wavelength.	P12.4
Investigate the reflection of light by different types of surface and the refraction of light by different substances.	AT4 – make observations of the effects of the interaction of electromagnetic waves (light) with matter. AT8 – make observations of waves in fluids and solids to identify the suitability of apparatus to measure the effects of the interaction of waves with matter.	P14.2, P14.3
Investigate how the amount of infrared radiation absorbed or radiated by a surface depends on the nature of that surface.	AT1 – use appropriate apparatus to make and record temperature accurately. AT4 – make observations of the effects of the interaction of electromagnetic waves with matter.	P13.2

Maths skills

AQA maths skills	Topic
1a Recognise and use expressions in decimal form.	13.5, 14.2, 16.1, 16.2, 16.3
1b Recognise and use expressions in standard form.	12.7, 13.1, 13.2, 13.4, 16.1, 16.2, 16.3, 16.4, 16.5
1c Use ratios, fractions, and percentages.	12.2, 12.4, 12.5, 13.1, 13.2, 13.3, 14.4, 15.8, 16.3
2g Use a scatter diagram to identify a correlation between two variables.	16.4
3b Change the subject of an equation.	12.2, 12.4, 12.5, 12.6, 13.1, 13.2, 13.3, 14.4, 14.5, 15.4, 15.8
3c Substitute numerical values into algebraic equations using appropriate units for physical quantities.	12.2, 12.4, 12.5, 12.6, 13.1, 13.2, 13.3, 14.4, 14.5, 15.4, 15.8
4a Translate information between graphical and numeric form.	12.5, 12.6, 15.5, 15.2, 15.3, 15.6
5a Use angular measures in degrees.	12.3, 14.1, 14.2, 14.4, 14.5
5b Visualise and represent 2D and 3D forms including two dimensional representations of 3D objects.	12.3, 14.4, 14.4, 14.5, 15.2, 15.5
5c Calculate areas of triangles and rectangles, surface areas, and volumes of cubes.	14.1, 14.2, 14.4, 14.5

KS3 concept	GCSE topic	Checkpoint	Revision
Waves are vibrations that transfer energy.	P12.1 The nature of waves	Show the students footage of an earthquake and ask them to describe the energy transfers.	Demonstrate transverse and longitudinal wave motion with a slinky spring.
The top of a water wave is called a crest and the bottom is called a trough.	P12.2 The properties of waves	Students should be asked to label a diagram showing the appropriate parts of a transverse wave such as a ripple.	Students should compare a set of wave diagrams and describe differences in their amplitude and wavelength.
Waves can be reflected by smooth surfaces.	P12.3 Reflection and refraction	Ask students to describe how they can hear an echo of their own voices.	Students should describe the properties of an image reflected in a mirror with a suitable ray diagram.
Sound travels faster in solids than in liquids and faster in liquids than in gas.	P 12.4 Sound waves	Ask students to describe how they could compare the speed of sound in air to the speed of sound in a solid material.	Students should calculate the speed of sound in different materials using distance and time data.
Light waves travel much faster than sound waves.	P13.1 The electromagnetic spectrum	Ask students to explain why we see a flash of lightning before we hear the thunder clap.	Students use distance and speed data to calculate the time taken for a lightning flash and thunder clap to reach them.
The spectrum of white light is continuous from red to orange to yellow to green to blue to violet.	P13.2 Light, infrared, microwaves, and radio waves	Ask students to sketch a labelled diagram of a spectrum.	Demonstrate dispersion of white light by a prism or diffraction grating to produce a spectrum and discuss the colours produced.
The ray model of light can be used to explain images formed by lenses.	P14.4 Lenses	Ask students to give an example of where they would find a lens and explain how the lens operates.	Students should produce a ray diagram showing the image formed by a converging lens.
A magnet lines up with the Earth's magnetic field.	P15.1 Magnetic fields	Ask students to find magnetic north using a magnet.	Students should describe how the magnetic poles of the Earth differ from the rotational poles.
An electric motor is used to turn objects. An electric generator produces an electric current when it turns.	P15.4 The motor effect	Ask students to describe the uses of a small electric motor.	Ask the students to match up the factors which affect the voltage output of a generator with their effects as well as the factors which affect the power of a motor.
Satellites go round the Earth repeatedly above the Earth's atmosphere.	P16.3 Planets, satellites, and orbits	Ask the students to draw the path of a satellite around the Earth and explain why it does not slow down.	Use simple simulation software to show the circular motion of a satellite and what would happen if it sped up or slowed down.
Astronomers use telescopes and other instruments to study light from objects in space.	P16.4 The expanding universe	Ask the students to describe how we observed objects inside and outside of the Solar System.	Students should match up objects with the techniques we use to observe them such as light telescopes, radio telescopes, probes and so on.

P 12 Wave properties

12.1 The nature of waves

AQA spec Link: 6.1.1 Waves may be either transverse or longitudinal.

The ripples on a water surface are an example of a transverse wave.

Longitudinal waves show areas of compression and rarefaction. Sound waves travelling through air are longitudinal.

Students should be able to describe the difference between longitudinal and transverse waves.

Students should be able to describe evidence that, for both ripples on a water surface and sound waves in air, it is the wave and not the water or air itself that travels.

6.2.1 Electromagnetic waves form a continuous spectrum and all types of electromagnetic wave travel at the same velocity through a vacuum (space) or air.

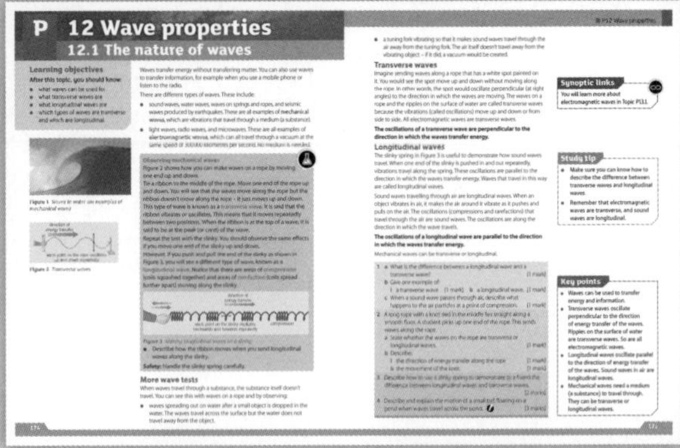
P 12 Wave properties
12.1 The nature of waves

WS 1.2, 2.2

Aiming for	Outcome	Checkpoint: Question	Checkpoint: Activity
Aiming for GRADE 4	State that waves can transfer energy and information without the transfer of matter.		Starter 1, Main
↓	Identify waves as either transverse or longitudinal.	1, 2	Main, Plenary 2
	Identify waves as either mechanical or electromagnetic.		Starter 1, Main
Aiming for GRADE 6	Investigate wave motion through a spring model.	3	Main
↓	Compare transverse and longitudinal waves in terms of direction of vibration and propagation.	1, 2, End of chapter 1	Main, Plenary 2
	Compare electromagnetic and mechanical waves in terms of the need for a medium.	1	Main, Plenary 2
Aiming for GRADE 8	Explain the features of a longitudinal wave in terms of compressions and rarefactions by using a particle model.	3	Main
↓	Discuss the features of a transverse wave in terms of particle or field behaviour.	4	Main
	Compare mechanical waves and their particulate nature with electromagnetic waves and their field oscillations.		Main

Maths

Students apply mathematical terminology such as parallel and perpendicular to describe wave motion.

Literacy

There is a focus here on careful descriptions and explanations of the behaviour and properties of waves. Students should question each other on these descriptions and refine them.

Key words

mechanical waves, electromagnetic waves, transverse waves, longitudinal waves, compression, rarefaction

Practical

Title	Observing mechanical waves
Equipment	slinky spring, piece of ribbon
Overview of method	Demonstrate longitudinal waves by stretching the spring out slightly and then move one end of the slinky spring in and out whilst keeping the other end still. The emphasis should be on the vibrations of the particles without them actually progressing. Sticking a bit of ribbon on a point on the spring can show this more effectively. Transverse waves can be produced by moving the spring from side to side, showing the particles vibrating at right angles to the direction of propagation of the wave.
Safety considerations	Make sure there is sufficient space, and do not move the spring violently.

Starter	Support/Extend	Resources
Aftershock value (5 min) Use video clips of tsunami and recent earthquakes to demonstrate the power of an 'uncontrolled' wave. Point out the regular vibration in earthquakes – shaking buildings and so on. **Wave** (10 min) Ask students to list as many types of wave as possible. Check through a few lists with the class and then ask the students to explain what a wave actually does. Use some of the examples to get them to realise that waves transfer energy but not material.	**Extend:** Ask students to describe why these waves are not simple, by comparing them with the definition in the student book.	
Main	**Support/Extend**	**Resources**
Observing mechanical waves (40 min) Demonstrate mechanical waves in a wire and ripples in water to discuss the movement of particles. This will lead to the students exploring waves in a slinky spring through the practical. Use a light source to discuss electromagnetic waves. The waves act as a pathway to transfer energy (e.g., they can heat surfaces), but they are not transferring material and there are no particles vibrating. Discuss particle behaviour in springs, ropes, and ripples, ensuring that the students can visualise the movement of the particles clearly. Using the spring model again to discuss particle behaviour in longitudinal waves. Make sure that the students understand that forces are acting between the particles causing these vibrations.	**Support:** Provide diagrams so that the students can note the direction of oscillation in the waves. **Extend:** A model of oscillating electric and magnetic fields can be discussed. **Support:** Use the animation to help students with their understanding of longitudinal and transverse waves. **Support:** A support sheet is available to help students with the terminology of this topic.	**Practical:** Observing mechanical waves **Animation:** Transverse and longitudinal waves **Support:** Waves – knowing the words is half the battle
Plenary	**Support/Extend**	**Resources**
The same but different (5 min) Interactive where students match key words from the lesson to their definitions, complete a description of longitudinal and transverse waves, then identify true and false statements about longitudinal and transverse waves. **Mexican brain wave** (10 min) Put the students into three or four rows all seated. Select one student to be the questioner in each row and give them a set of questions and answers about waves. The student asks the first person in the row a question – if they get the answer right, then all of the people who have answered correctly so far stand up, wave, sit down, and the questioner moves on.	**Support:** Use foundation-level questions for appropriate groups. **Extend:** Involve higher-level questions.	**Interactive:** The same but different
Homework		
Students can explore the history of people's understanding of light, from particle models to wave models, and finally mixed models.	**Extend:** Students focus on the evidence that leads to a change in a model.	

kerboodle

A Kerboodle highlight for this lesson is **Bump up your grades: Transverse and longitudinal waves**. Refer to the **Content map** on Kerboodle for a full list of resources and assessment.

P12.2 The properties of waves

AQA spec Link: 6.1.2 Students should be able to describe wave motion in terms of their amplitude, wavelength, frequency, and period.

The amplitude of a wave is the maximum displacement of a point on a wave away from its undisturbed position.

The wavelength of a wave is the distance from a point on one wave to the equivalent point on the adjacent wave.

The frequency of a wave is the number of waves passing a point each second.

$$\text{period} = \frac{1}{\text{frequency}}$$

$$[T = \frac{1}{f}]$$

period T in seconds, s

frequency f in hertz, Hz.

The wave speed is the speed at which the energy is transferred (or the wave moves) through the medium.

All waves obey the wave equation:

$$\text{wave speed} = \text{frequency} \times \text{wavelength}$$

$$[v = f\,\lambda]$$

wave speed v in metres per second, m/s

frequency f in hertz, Hz

wavelength λ in metres, m

Students should be able to:

- identify amplitude and wavelength from given diagrams
- describe a method to measure the speed of sound waves in air
- describe a method to measure the speed of ripples on a water surface.

Required practical: make observations to identify the suitability of apparatus to measure the frequency, wavelength, and speed of waves in a ripple tank and waves in a solid and take appropriate measurements.

MS 1c, 3b, 3c

Aiming for	Outcome	Checkpoint	
		Question	Activity
Aiming for GRADE 4	Identify the wavelength and amplitude of a wave from a simple diagram.	1, 2	Main 1
	Describe how the frequency of a wave is the number of waves produced each second and is measured in hertz.		Main 1
	Measure the speed of a water wave.		Main 2
Aiming for GRADE 6	Outline the derivation of the wave speed equation.		Main 2
	Calculate the period of a wave from its frequency.		Main 1, Plenary 2
	Calculate the wave speed from the frequency and wavelength.	3, End of chapter 2	Main 2
Aiming for GRADE 8	Explain how the wave speed equation can be derived from fundamental principles.		Main 2
	Perform calculations involving rearrangements of the period equation and the wave speed equation.	4, End of chapter 2	Main 1, Plenary 2
	Perform multi-stage calculations linking period, frequency, wave speed, and wavelength.	4	Main 2

Maths

A wide range of calculations take place during this lesson using the wave speed equation and the relationship between frequency and period (1c, 3b, 3c).

Literacy

Students should work in small groups to discuss the movement of waves and the effect of changing frequency on wave speed.

Key words

amplitude, wavelength, frequency, speed

Practical

Title	Measuring the speed of ripples
Equipment	ripple tank, stopwatch, ruler, tray, signal generator, loudspeaker, connecting leads
Overview of method	The practical is as described in the student book. Waterproof trays can be used as an alternative. The students fill the tray to about 1 cm depth – moving the ruler at one end should send a wave along the tray, and this can be measured. Alternatively, a sharp tap on the outside of the tray can initiate a good-quality wave pulse. Students can be extended by using this technique to see whether altering the depth of the water increases or decreases the wave speed. The changes to depth should only be by 1 mm at a time and between 1 and 2 cm overall.
Safety considerations	Clean up any water spills immediately.

Starter	Support/Extend	Resources
Up to speed (5 min) Students use the interactive to perform some simple speed calculations to remind them of this work from KS3. Make sure that they are using the correct units for speed, distance, and time.	**Extend:** The students need to rearrange the equation and use more challenging data.	**Interactive:** Up to speed
Spotlight on knowledge (10 min) Students need to list the properties of light and any other facts that they know about it. They should be able to produce a range of facts from KS3.	**Support:** Students can confirm or refute a set of facts presented to them.	
Main	**Support/Extend**	**Resources**
Describing waves (20 min) Remind students of the basic shape of a transverse wave through a simple demonstration with a rope, and then each of the measureable or identifiable characteristics can be discussed. Particular attention should be paid to the amplitude because this is commonly mislabelled. Continue the analysis by looking at changing the frequency and showing the number of waves passing a fixed point per second on the rope. The relationship between frequency and period needs to be discussed, and the students should perform an example calculation.	**Support:** Provide a diagram for the students to label and measure. Limit calculations to the $T = \frac{1}{f}$ arrangement. **Extend:** The amplitude of a longitudinal wave can be discussed in terms of maximum particle displacement.	
Measuring the speed of ripples (20 min) The wave speed equation can then be introduced, ideally using a ripple tank. Demonstrate that changing the frequency has an effect on the wavelength whilst the speed stays the same. Model a calculation and then ask students to try their own. The students can then use the ripple tanks to investigate the wave equation.	**Extend:** An extension sheet is available where students look at a wave diagram to calculate speed and frequency. **Extend:** Explain the derivation of the wave speed equation. Students may also investigate whether depth of water has an effect on wave speed.	**Practical:** Measuring the speed of ripples **Extension:** Waves
Plenary	**Support/Extend**	**Resources**
Wave taboo (5 min) Split the students into groups and assign each students a key word (e.g., transverse, longitudinal, reflect, speed) and a list of words they cannot use to describe it. Students take it in turns to describe their key word. How many can the group get in a set time limit?	**Support:** Reduce the number of words in the 'banned words' list for each question.	
Kinaesthetic maths challenge (10 min) Provide students with cards labelled 'wavelength', 'wave speed', 'frequency', '×', and '='. Each card has a number on it too. The students must form themselves into 'living equations' by standing in groups of five to make a correct equation.	**Extend:** Provide students with more difficult numbers and questions that require rearrangement.	
Homework		
Students complete the calculation sheet to practise using the wave equation.		**Calculation sheet:** The wave equation

kerboodle

A Kerboodle highlight for this lesson is **Maths skills: The wave equation**. Refer to the **Content map** on Kerboodle for a full list of resources and assessment.

P12.3 Reflection and refraction

AQA spec Link: 6.2.2 Different substances may absorb, transmit, refract, or reflect electromagnetic waves in ways that vary with wavelength.

Some effects, for example refraction, are due to the difference in velocity of the waves in different substances.

Students should be able to construct ray diagrams to illustrate the refraction of a wave at the boundary between two different media.

Students should be able to use wave front diagrams to explain refraction in terms of the change of speed that happens when a wave travels from one medium to a different medium.

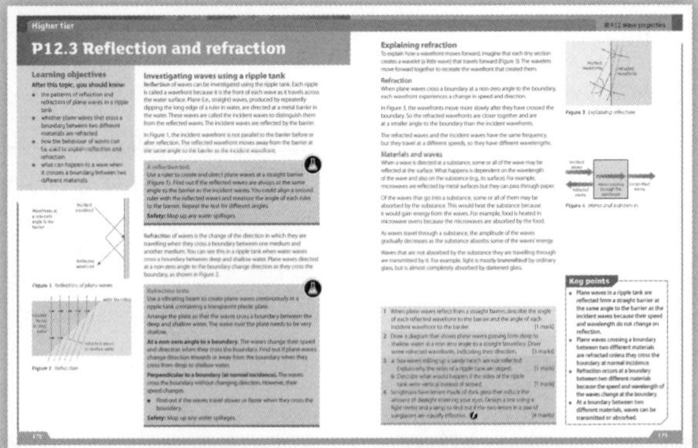

WS 1.2
MS 5a, 5b

Aiming for	Outcome	Checkpoint	
		Question	Activity
Aiming for GRADE 6 ↓	Describe refraction at a boundary in terms of wavefronts.	2, End of chapter 3	Main 2
	Describe refraction including the reflected rays.		Main 1
	Explain partial absorption as a decrease in the amplitude of a wave and therefore the energy carried.	4	Main 1
Aiming for GRADE 8 ↓	Use a wavefront model to explain refraction and reflection.		Main 2
	Describe the relationship between the angle of incidence and angle of refraction.	2, End of chapter 4	Main 1
	Explain refraction in terms of changes in the speed of waves when they move between one medium and another.	2, End of chapter 4	Main 2

Maths
Students measure and describe changes in angle when observing ray and wavefront paths (5a, 5b).

Literacy
The students discuss the wavefront model of reflection and refraction, forming and sharing explanations at different levels of understanding.

Key words
reflection, refraction, transmitted

Practical

Title	A reflection test
Equipment	ripple tank (or a plastic tray), ruler, solid obstacle, protractor
Overview of method	Students investigate the reflection of wave fronts using the ripple tank or water tray by sending a simple wave towards a barrier and measuring the angle of reflection.
Safety considerations	Clean up any water spills immediately.

Title	Refraction tests
Equipment	ripple tank, wave generator, block to alter depth of water
Overview of method	Students investigate the refraction of wave fronts using the ripple tank by allowing waves to pass over submerged obstacles. Simulations of ripple tanks are a simpler, safer, and cheaper alternative but these should be used alongside a demonstration of a real ripple tank to show the real scenarios.
Safety considerations	Clean up any water spills immediately.

Starter	Support/Extend	Resources
It's just a broken pencil (5 min) Place a pencil in a beaker of water. Can the students produce an explanation of why the pencil looks broken? This is quite difficult – make sure that the students see the effect clearly (show a big photograph on the interactive whiteboard if needed).	**Extend:** Ask students to draw a ray diagram explaining the effect.	
Ray diagram (10 min) Ask students to draw a ray diagram showing how they can see a non-luminous object such as the writing in their books. Make sure that the students are using a ruler to draw rays of light and that the rays are reflecting cleanly from the surface.	**Extend:** Ask students to critique each other's work and advise each other how to correct the work to make it the highest possible standard.	
Main	**Support/Extend**	**Resources**
Investigating reflection and refraction (25 min) Demonstrate the operation of the ripple tank focusing on reflection. The students can then introduce the barrier during the practical and find out about the reflection of the wavefronts at different angles. Link this to the simple light reflection experiments that students will have studied in KS3. Some students can also investigate the effect of changing the depth of water in a ripple tank and note the changes in speed of the wavefronts. Students should be able to see that speed changes during the refraction whilst the frequency does not change.	**Support:** Provide a visual set of instructions for the students to follow. **Extend:** Students can devise a method to verify the law of refection.	**Practical:** Investigating reflection and refraction **Bump up your grade:** Wave diagrams
Explaining reflection and refraction (15 min) Discuss the use of wavefronts and wavelets to explain reflection using a series of diagrams or a simulation. Use simulations or the ripple tank to show the behaviour of wavefronts during refraction, altering the angle of incidence to show the changing effect.		
Plenary	**Support/Extend**	**Resources**
Reflect or refract? (10 min) Interactive where students summarise the differences between reflection and refraction. They then identify correct ray diagrams showing reflection and refraction.		**Interactive:** Reflect or refract?
Mirror maze (5 min) Check students' understanding of the law of reflection by asking them to add mirrors to a simple maze diagram so that a light ray can pass through it to the centre.		
Homework		
Students complete question 4 from the student book where they design a test using a light meter and a lamp to find out if the two lenses in a pair of sunglasses are equally effective.		

kerboodle

A Kerboodle highlight for this lesson is **Working scientifically: Spectacle lens options**. Refer to the **Content map** on Kerboodle for a full list of resources and assessment.

P12.4 More about waves

AQA spec Link: 5.6.1.2 A typical value for the speed of sound in air is 330 m/s.

6.1.2 **Required practical:** Make observations to identify the suitability of apparatus to measure the frequency, wavelength, and speed of waves in a ripple tank and waves in a solid and take appropriate measurements.

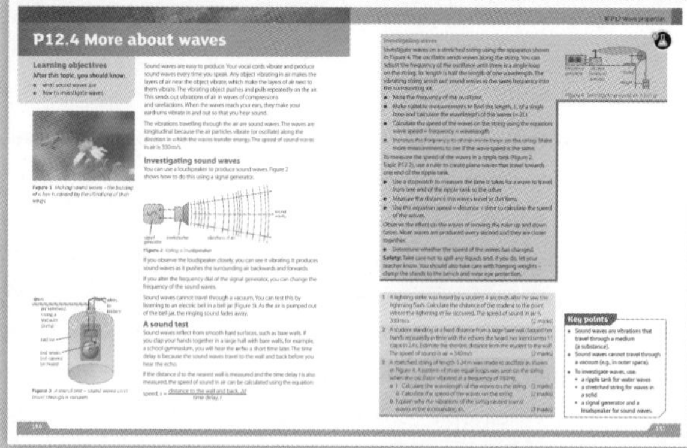

MS 1c, 3b, 3c

Aiming for	Outcome	Checkpoint	
		Question	**Activity**
Aiming for GRADE 4	Measure the speed of a wave in water.		Main
	Describe how sound waves travel more quickly in solid than they do in gases.		Main
	State that sound waves require a medium to travel in.		Main
Aiming for GRADE 6	Measure the speed of a wave in a solid (string).		Main
	Describe the effect that changing the frequency of a wave has on its wavelength in a medium.		Main
	Calculate the speed of waves using the wave speed equation.		Main
Aiming for GRADE 8	Evaluate the suitability of apparatus for measuring the frequency, wavelength, and speed of waves.		Main
	Explain why the wavelength of a wave in a particular medium changes as the frequency changes with reference to the wave equation.		Main
	Evaluate data from speed of sound experiments to discuss the range of possible speeds for sound.		Main, Plenary 2, Homework

Maths
All students calculate the speed of sound, and some use speed and timing data to measure distances (1c, 3b, 3c).

Literacy
The reflection, absorption, and refraction of sound waves are used in descriptions of energy transfers.

Key words
echo

 Required practical

Title	Investigating waves in a solid
Equipment	signal generator, vibration generator, pulley, masses on a mass holder, length of high quality string or wire (at least 1 m in length, preferably over 2 m), tape measure or meter rule
Overview of method	Test the apparatus in advance to ensure that stationary waves can be produced across its length using the vibrating motor. This depends on both the wire material and the tension in it. It may not be easy to set up a single half wave pattern as shown in the student book, therefore the students may need to start with a whole wave pattern depending on the wire and tension chosen. Students set up stationary wave patterns measuring both the frequency (from the signal generator) and the wavelength (with the tape measure) trying to obtain at least four different patterns. They should discover that the wave speed is constant.
Safety considerations	The pulley should be clamped to the desk. Be careful of falling masses.

Title	Investigating waves in a ripple tank
Equipment	ripple tank (or tray of water) and ruler, video camera, squared paper
Overview	Students measure the length of the tank and then produce ripples, timing how long they take to travel the length of the tank. This data is used to determine the wave speed. Placing squared paper beneath the tank and videoing the wave motion can make it easier to see that the wavelength decreases as the frequency increases.
Safety	Clear up any spilled water immediately.

Starter	Support/Extend	Resources
Sound facts (5 min) Give the students a set of 'facts' about sound and let them use traffic light cards to indicate whether they agree (green), don't know (amber), or disagree (red).	**Support:** Select simple 'facts' that are obviously true or false. **Extend:** Select 'facts' that are more open to debate and discussion.	
Good vibrations (10 min) How do different instruments produce sound waves? Students should describe what is going on for five different ways of producing a sound. Demonstrate a drum, guitar, flute or recorder, loudspeaker, and singing. This should show that vibrations are needed to produce sound waves.	**Support:** Video clips can be used to illustrate the vibrations. **Extend:** The vibrations of key areas of acoustic instruments can be analysed.	
Main	**Support/Extend**	**Resources**
Investigating waves (40 min) Students should briefly examine the behaviour of sound waves in air and how a medium is required for these waves to travel. They then move on to investigate waves in solids and liquids using the two practical tasks as outlined. The practicals can be carried out simultaneously. The first practical relies on producing stationary waves which allow the wavelength to be measured. Students do not need to know the details of how these form; they only need to measure their wavelength. The second practical uses simple ripples which can be produced with a ruler or with a vibrating bar in a ripple tank.	**Support:** When investigating waves in a solid, provide students with approximate set of frequencies which will produce stationary waves. **Extend:** When investigating waves in a ripple tank, students can investigate whether changing the tension in the wire has any effect on the wave speed in it.	**Required practical:** Investigating waves
Plenary	**Support/Extend**	**Resources**
Oscilloscope solutions (5 min) Students use the interactive to match a set of problems encountered when using the oscilloscope to appropriate solutions, for example, a trace where the waves' peaks are too close together – the solution is to reduce the time base.	**Extend:** Students should not be provided with potential solutions – they can produce their own.	**Interactive:** Oscilloscope solutions
Let's hear your ideas (10 min) Students need to design a simple experiment that will show that sound travels faster in solid materials than it does in air. This could be either a basic plan or a more detailed one.	**Extend:** The plan must include procedures for measuring the speed.	
Homework		
Students complete the WebQuest where they research the physics of Felix Baumgartner's skydive, where he broke the sound barrier.		**WebQuest:** Supersonic skydive

kerboodle

A Kerboodle highlight for this lesson is **Working scientifically: Measuring sound**. Refer to the **Content map** on Kerboodle for a full list of resources and assessment.

P12.5 Sound waves

AQA spec Link: 6.1.4 Sound waves can travel through solids causing vibrations in the solid.

Within the ear, sound waves cause the ear drum and other parts to vibrate which causes the sensation of sound. The conversion of sound waves to vibrations of solids works over a limited frequency range. This restricts the limits of human hearing.

Students should be able to:

- describe, with examples, processes which convert wave disturbances between sound waves and vibrations in solids. Examples may include the effect of sound waves on the ear drum
- explain why such processes only work over a limited frequency range and the relevance of this to human hearing.

Students should know that the range of normal human hearing is from 20 Hz to 20 kHz.

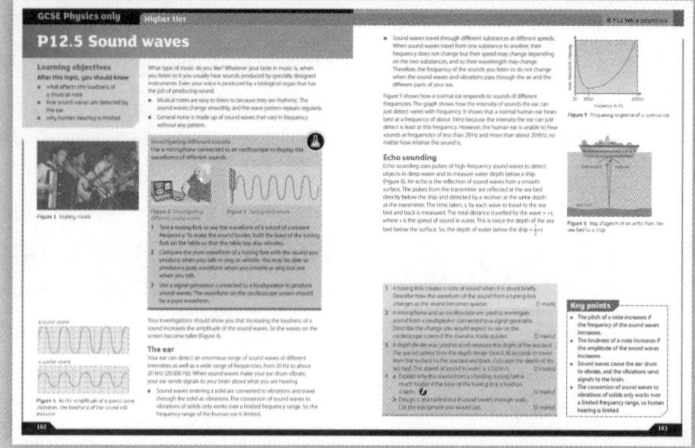

MS 1c, 3b, 3c, 4a

Aiming for	Outcome	Checkpoint	
		Question	Activity
Aiming for GRADE 6 ↓	Describe the properties of a sound in terms of amplitude and frequency.	2, End of chapter 5	Main 1, Plenary 2
	Identify the range of frequencies that humans can hear.	End of chapter 6	Main 1, Main 2
	Measure the frequency of a sound wave using an oscilloscope and the relationship frequency = $\frac{1}{\text{period}}$	3	Main 1
Aiming for GRADE 8 ↓	Outline the structure of the human ear in terms of transfer of waves and vibrations.		Main 2
	Explain why the human ear has a limited range of frequencies it can detect.	4	Main 2
	Compare the propagation of a sound wave in a solid and a gas.	3	Main 2

Maths
Students can compare waveforms in terms of amplitude, frequency, and period, translating from graphs to numerical data (1c, 3b, 3c, 4a).

Literacy
Students work in groups to describe the operation of musical instruments and how the notes they play can be adjusted.

Practical

Title	Investigating different sounds
Equipment	signal generator, loudspeaker, microphone, oscilloscope, tuning forks, some musical instruments
Overview of method	The students use the oscilloscope to produce traces for the range of tuning forks and instruments. The oscilloscopes should be adjusted in advance so that waveforms are clear. The settings should be provided to the students so that they can revert to them as needed.
Safety considerations	Students should not play loud instruments close to their ears.

Starter	Support/Extend	Resources
Music to my ears (5 min) Play some brief extracts of music, from classical to punk, and ask the students to list the instruments they can hear. Ask the unanswerable question 'Which music is the best?' for a discussion. **Intro round** (10 min) Using a personal music player (through headphones on low volume so that the rest of the class cannot hear it), a student listens to the introductions of some songs and has to reproduce them using only his/her vocal skills. The rest of the students guess what they are reproducing.	**Support:** Provide supporting apparatus for any students with auditory problems as appropriate. **Support:** Simple, easily recognisable tunes can be used. **Extend:** Non-musical sounds are far more challenging.	
Main	**Support/Extend**	**Resources**
Investigating different sounds (30 min) Students carry out the practical and find traces for a range of tuning forks so that they can make connections between the frequency and pitch and also the loudness and amplitude. They should note that the forks are producing very simple waveforms. Students should attempt to determine the period of some of the signs and from this the frequency. Discuss the propagation of sound waves in solids as compared to gasses noting that the close packed particles will allow the wave to travel more quickly.	**Extend:** Students can examine the effect of placing the forks on a resonance board or other surface.	**Practical:** Investigating different sounds
Inside the ear (10 min) Students should identify the key features of the human ear. Focus on the idea of absorption and reflection of sound waves at boundaries to explain why not all sounds can be detected. The limitations of the frequency range of the ear should be covered.	**Support:** Provide a clear diagram for the students to annotate.	
Plenary	**Support/Extend**	**Resources**
Perfect pitch (5 min) Which of the students can produce the purest note according to the oscilloscope? Connect a microphone directly to the oscilloscope, and the students can try to see who is best able to produce a sine wave.	**Extend:** Students must find numerical values for each wave.	
Compare traces (10 min) Show three oscilloscope traces. Students use the interactive analyse them in terms of frequency, amplitude, and quality of the note. They then describe the differences and explain how they will sound different when produced by a musical instrument.		**Interactive:** Comparing traces
Homework		
Students research the phenomenon of resonance and report on how this is used in acoustic instruments.	**Extend:** Students can discuss how resonance can be an issue in product or building design.	

kerboodle

A Kerboodle highlight for this lesson is **Extension sheet: Waves**. Refer to the **Content map** on Kerboodle for a full list of resources and assessment.

P12.6 The uses of ultrasound

AQA spec Link: 6.1.5 Students should be able to explain in qualitative terms, how the differences in velocity, absorption, and reflection between different types of wave in solids and liquids can be used both for detection and exploration of structures which are hidden from direct observation.

Ultrasound waves have a frequency higher than the upper limit of hearing for humans. Ultrasound waves are partially reflected when they meet a boundary between two different media. The time taken for the reflections to reach a detector can be used to determine how far away such a boundary is. This allows ultrasound waves to be used for both medical and industrial imaging.

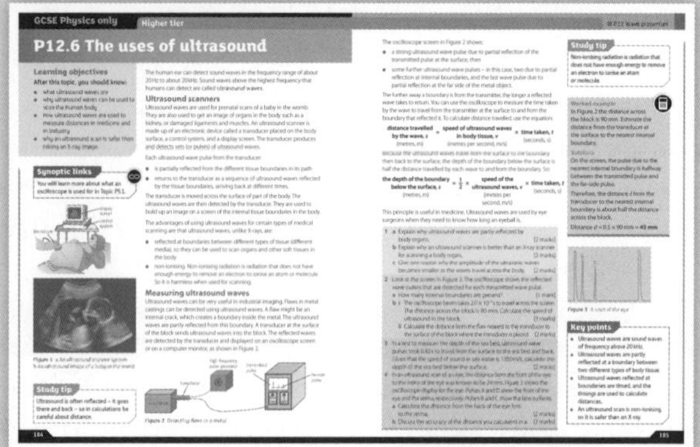

WS 1.4
MS 3b, 3c, 4a

Aiming for	Outcome	Checkpoint	
		Question	Activity
Aiming for GRADE 6 ↓	Compare ultrasound and audible sound waves in terms of frequency.		Main 1
	Outline some uses of ultrasound in distance measurement.	1, 3, End of chapter 8	Main 2
	Describe the operation of an ultrasound transducer in terms of partial reflection.	2, End of chapter 8	Main 2
Aiming for GRADE 8 ↓	Investigate the reflection and absorption of ultrasound waves.	1	Main 1
	Calculate the positions of objects or flaws in metal objects using data from an ultrasound trace.	2, 3	Main 2
	Use an oscilloscope to obtain timing information for an ultrasound pulse.		Main 1

Maths
Students calculate distances using the wave speed equation and the idea of echoes (3b, 3c). Some will look at multiple reflections and extract data from graphs (4a).

Literacy
Students can work in small groups to test the properties of ultrasound and write explanations about the similarities and differences compared with audible sound waves.

Key words
ultrasound waves

Practical

Title	Demonstrating the range of hearing
Equipment	signal generator, loudspeaker
Overview of method	Using a signal generator, demonstrate the range of human hearing. Connect it to a suitable loudspeaker and gradually increase the frequency until the students cannot hear the sound any more. Connect the signal generator to an oscilloscope to show the changes in the waveform as the frequency is increased.
Safety considerations	Do not use large amplitude sounds.

Title	Investigating ultrasound
Equipment	oscilloscope, signal generator, two microphones, loudspeaker, range of thin materials such as an aluminium plate, plywood, rubber sheets
Overview of method	Students should use the oscilloscope and microphone to measure the period and frequency of an ultrasonic wave produced by the signal generator and loudspeaker. If time permits the remaining materials can be used to determine if ultrasound waves can be reflected and absorbed by different materials.
Safety considerations	Avoid high amplitude sounds and those on the edge of human hearing.

Starter	Support/Extend	Resources
Mystery scans (5 min) Show the students some ultrasound scans of objects other than a foetus, and see if they can identify the organs involved.	**Support:** Students can identify simple features of clear objects. **Extend:** Images can be differentiated according to student ability.	
Echo (10 min) Ask the students to work out how far away a cliff face is if, when they shout, the echo takes 4 seconds to arrive and the speed of sound is 330 m/s.	**Support:** Provide a calculation frame including a diagram. **Extend:** Extend the calculation for a sound wave travelling in fat (1450 m/s) or bone (4000 m/s).	
Main	**Support/Extend**	**Resources**
Investigating ultrasound (25 min) Demonstrate the range of human hearing as described in the practical box. Students then investigate ultrasound using the second practical. They compare results and discuss what they have learnt about ultrasound.	**Support:** Limit the investigation to simple qualitative tests. **Extend:** Ask students to investigate a more quantitative variable such as the thickness of the material in relation to reduction of amplitude.	**Practical:** Investigating ultrasound
Ultrasound scanners (15 min) The operation of a transducer should be described, comparing this with a loudspeaker and microphone combination. Emphasise the use in B-scans and compare the safety with that of X-rays. Explain the operation of a depth-measuring ultrasound pulse, linking back to simple echoes with which the students will be more familiar. Students should examine some examples pulse traces and use these to determine the thickness of some material layers. Examples from industrial and medical imaging should be used.	**Support:** Limit analysis to single reflections. **Extend:** Discussions about the piezoelectric effect as used in the transducer can take place.	
Plenary	**Support/Extend**	**Resources**
Comparing light and sound (10 min) Make a detailed comparison of light and sound waves. This should include the nature of the waves (mechanical, electromagnetic) and their interaction with matter.	**Extend:** Ask students for detailed examples and comparisons such as why X-rays are ionising whereas sound waves are not.	
Scan analysis (5 min) Interactive where students calculate the time it would take for an ultrasound pulse to travel through layers of skin, fat, and muscle when given the speed of sound in those materials.	**Extend:** Ask students to find the time for an echo to arrive at the transducer.	**Interactive:** Scan analysis
Homework		
Students can research and report on further applications of ultrasound, which could include industrial use or use by animals.	**Support:** Provide a list of subjects for students to select from. **Extend:** Allow independent research.	

kerboodle

A Kerboodle highlight for this lesson is **Animation: Ultrasound imaging**. Refer to the **Content map** on Kerboodle for a full list of resources and assessment.

P12.7 Seismic waves

AQA spec Link: 6.1.5 Students should be able to explain in qualitative terms, how the differences in velocity, absorption, and reflection between different types of wave in solids and liquids can be used both for detection and exploration of structures which are hidden from direct observation.

Seismic waves are produced by earthquakes. P-waves are longitudinal, seismic waves. P-waves travel at different speeds through solids and liquids. S-waves are transverse, seismic waves. S-waves cannot travel through a liquid. P-waves and S-waves provide evidence for the structure and size of the Earth's core.

Students should be aware that the study of seismic waves provided new evidence that led to discoveries about parts of the Earth which are not directly observable.

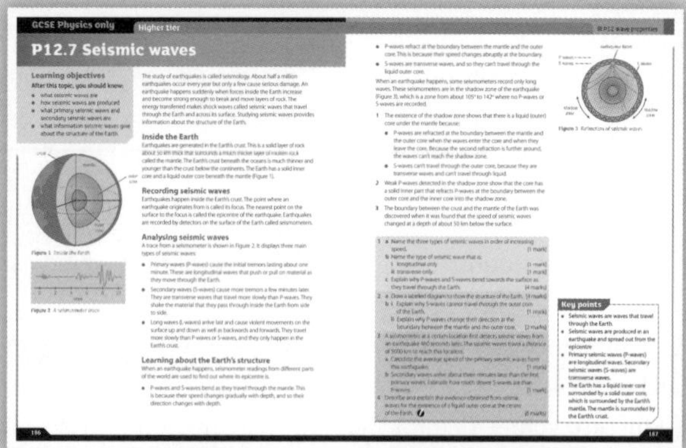

WS 1.1, 1.4
MS 1b

Aiming for	Outcome	Checkpoint	
		Question	Activity
Aiming for GRADE 6 ↓	Describe the internal structure of the Earth.	2	Starter 2, Main 1
	Compare the three types of seismic waves (P, S, L) in terms of the speed they travel and whether they are transverse or longitudinal.	1	Main 2, Plenary 2
	Describe the operation of a seismometer.		Main 1
Aiming for GRADE 8 ↓	Explain in detail how the internal structure of the Earth can be determined by waves passing through it.	2, 4	Main 2
	Calculate the speed of different types of seismic waves.	3	Main 2
	Interpret seismographs to determine the difference in speeds of seismic waves.		Main 2

Maths

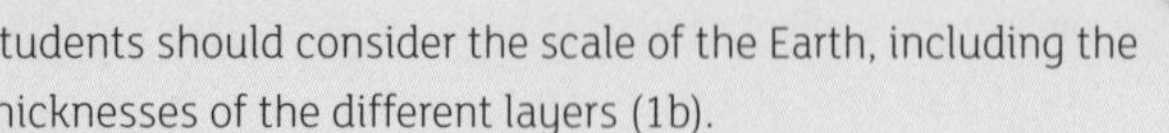

Students should consider the scale of the Earth, including the thicknesses of the different layers (1b).

Literacy

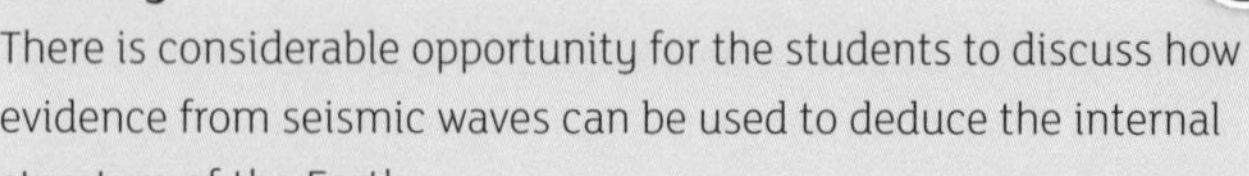

There is considerable opportunity for the students to discuss how evidence from seismic waves can be used to deduce the internal structure of the Earth.

Practical

Title	The seismometer
Equipment	large cardboard box, plastic or paper cup, string, marker pen, gravel or marbles, felt tip pen, sheet of paper
Overview of method	Punch a hole in the bottom of the cup, and push the pen through it so that the tip is a few centimetres below it. Position the box so that the open end is to the side. Suspend the cup inside the cardboard box so that the pen touches a sheet of paper at the bottom of the box, and partly fill the cup with gravel or small stones. Causing vibrations will make the box vibrate a few millimetres, and the cup will swing back and forth slightly. The marker pen should draw a trace on the piece of paper.
Safety considerations	Large vibrations are not required – students do not need to shake objects vigorously.

Starter	Support/Extend	Resources
Earthquake! (10 min) Show students footage of an earthquake and ask them to discuss the causes. This will allow initial assessment of prior knowledge. **Flat Earth** (5 min) Show students an image of the flat Earth model and ask them what evidence there is that this model is incorrect. They should then explain the model they use.	**Support:** Use targeted questioning to help students to refute the model.	
Main	**Support/Extend**	**Resources**
The seismometer (25 min) Outline the structure of the Earth, ensuring that the students can identify the different layers. Discuss the operation of the seismometer in the practical in terms of small vibrations that cause vibration of the pen. The students should discuss the movement of the paper at a regular pace to produce an appropriate displacement–time graph for the tip of the pen, which then links to the vibration of the ground.	**Support:** Provide a simple diagram of the Earth for the students to annotate. **Extend:** Ask the students to discuss the purpose of the heavy weight in the real seismometer and in the model.	**Practical:** The seismometer
Analysing seismic waves to find the Earth's structure (15 min) The students should describe the different types of waves and the media they can and cannot travel through. Link the speed of the wave to the time of arrival at a detector. This evidence can be difficult to understand, and the focus should be on the meaning of the 'shadow zone', which demonstrates the existence of a liquid outer core.	**Support:** Provide the evidence and ask the students to link the explanations to these points. **Extend:** An extension sheet is available where students are guided through an analysis of seismic wave measurements from an earthquake.	**Extension:** What lies beneath?
Plenary	**Support/Extend**	**Resources**
Make waves (10 min) Interactive where students choose the missing words to complete a summary on seismic waves and the evidence they provide for the structure of the Earth. **Balloon waves** (5 min) Demonstrate the transmission of sound waves through a water-filled balloon by placing a loudspeaker on one side and a microphone on the other. Ensure that the balloon is not near mains voltage electricity.		**Interactive:** Make waves
Homework		
Students write a brief report about the safety features of a building constructed in an earthquake zone.	**Support:** Provide some starter links for the students. **Extend:** Students should include the concept of resonance in their report.	

kerboodle

A Kerboodle highlight for this lesson is **Bump up your grade: Inside the earth P- and S-waves**. Refer to the **Content map** on Kerboodle for a full list of resources and assessment.

P12 Wave properties

Overview of P12 Wave properties

In this chapter the students have observed and described the properties of mechanical and electromagnetic waves in terms of energy transfer with or without the need for a transfer medium. They have compared transverse waves and longitudinal waves by examining the relationship between the direction of propagation and the direction of the oscillations.

The students have analysed wave properties such as wavelength, amplitude, and period leading to the relationships between period, frequency and wave speed, frequency, and wavelength. They have also measured the speed of sound in air and the speed of ripples on water.

Higher-tier students have investigated and described both the reflection and refraction of waves describing these effects in terms of wave fronts. The processes of absorption, transmission, and reflection of waves in terms of energy have also been described.

GCSE Physics students have investigated how sound waves are transmitted through a medium in terms of the vibration of particles in the medium. The concept of echoes being used to measure distances in water or other media have been used in calculations. In addition, higher-tier *GCSE Physics* students have investigated the properties of sound waves in more detail using oscilloscope traces, comparing both amplitude and frequency before looking at the ear's response to frequency.

Required practical

All students are expected to have carried out the required practical:

Practical	Topic
Make observations to identify the suitability of apparatus to measure the frequency, wavelength, and speed of waves in a ripple tank and waves in a solid and take appropriate measurements.	P12.4

You can find additional support for the maths skills covered in this chapter on **MyMaths**, including recognising and using expressions in decimal form, using an appropriate number of significant figures, understanding and using the symbols: $=, <, \ll, \gg, >, \propto, \sim$, and changing the subject of an equation.

kerboodle

For this chapter, the following assessments are available on Kerboodle:

P12 Checkpoint quiz: Wave properties
P12 Progress quiz: Wave properties 1
P12 Progress quiz: Wave properties 2
P12 On your marks: Wave properties
P12 Exam-style questions and mark scheme: Wave properties

Checkpoint follow up lesson

A student's route through this lesson can be determined using the Checkpoint assessment. Percentage pass marks are supplied in the Checkpoint teacher notes.

For each successive route through it is assumed that the student can perform to their current route as well as previous routes. For example, students working at Aiming for 6 are assumed to be secure in Aiming for 4 knowledge and understanding and working towards achieving all the learning outcomes for Aiming for 6.

	Aiming for 4	Aiming for 6	Aiming for 8
Learning outcomes	Describe the nature and properties of waves.	Use equations for wave speed.	Recall and use the equations for wave speed and period.
	Describe what happens to waves when they hit a boundary.	Explain why waves are reflected and refracted.	Explain the behaviour of waves at boundaries.
		Describe how ultrasound waves are used to detect structure that we cannot see.	Explain how ultrasound can be used to produce a scan.
		Describe how and seismic waves are used to detect structure that we cannot see.	Explain how seismic waves have given scientists information about the internal structure of the Earth.
Starter	**Articulate waves (10 min)** Give out cards with a wave property/key word on it and ask each student in the group in turn to pull out a card and explain the word to the group without using the word. The groups can keep score, and the student with the most correct answers can get a prize. **How fast? (5 min)** Use cymbals or a fog horn make a short, loud sound. Give each student a piece of card, and ask students to write down: their name, the time for the sound to hit a wall and reach their ear, and the distance that a wall would need to be from them for them to hear an echo after 1 second. Students should put the cards in an envelope with the name of their group on it and give it to you.		
Differentiated checkpoint activity	Aiming for 4 students use the Checkpoint follow-up sheet to make a game about the nature and properties of waves, and practise using equations for wave speed and period. The follow-up sheet provides structured tasks and questions to help them complete these activities and check their understanding of the key words of this topic, use the wave equation correctly and calculate period.	Aiming for 6 students use the Checkpoint follow-up sheet to practise using equations for wave speed and period, model the reflection and refraction of waves as well as the production of an ultrasound image, and consider how seismic waves help scientists to work out the structure of the Earth. The follow-up sheet provides tasks and questions to help them complete these activities and check their understanding of how to use the wave equation, what happens to waves when they interact with surfaces, how to model ultrasound scanning, and how this applies to working out the structure of the Earth.	Aiming for 8 students use the Checkpoint follow-up sheet to devise methods of modelling reflection and refraction, and ultrasound scanning, and investigate how they can use a beaker of water to model what happens when seismic waves go through the Earth. The follow-up sheet provides tasks and questions to help them complete these activities and check their understanding of the processes of reflection and refraction and how to explain refraction, how to produce and ultrasound scan, and how scientists have worked out the structure of the Earth using seismic waves.
	Kerboodle resource P12 Checkpoint follow up: Aiming for 4, P12 Checkpoint follow up: Aiming for 6, P12 Checkpoint follow up: Aiming for 8		
Plenary	**Speed and structure (10 min)** Give students the task of working out the time using speed and distance, and distance using speed and time from the starter question. Work out which student/s were correct, and, if possible give out a small prize. Aiming for 4 students can a set of cards with statements such as 'the period of a wave with a frequency of 10 Hz is 0.1 s into true statements and false statements.		
Progression	Encourage students to describe what happens to waves when they are reflected and refracted.	Encourage students to use changes of direction in refraction in terms of changes of speed and to link ideas about ultrasound and seismic waves.	Encourage students to think about changes of direction in refraction in terms of changes of speed and to link ideas of reflection and refraction to the production of the images of internal structure of people and the Earth.

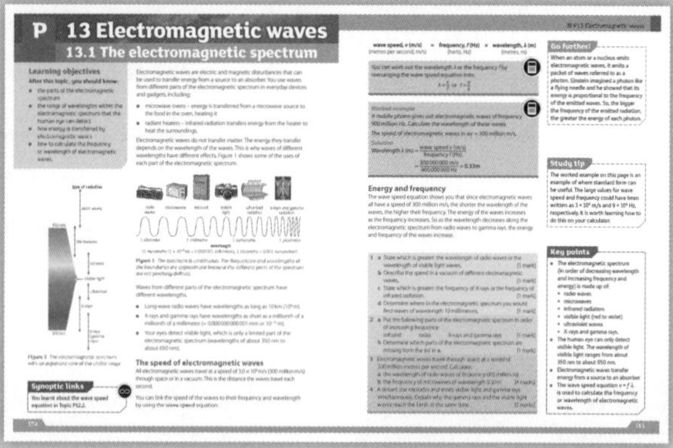

P 13 Electromagnetic waves

13.1 The electromagnetic spectrum

AQA spec Link: 6.1.2 The wave speed is the speed at which the energy is transferred (or the wave moves) through the medium.

All waves obey the wave equation:

wave speed = frequency × wavelength

$[v = f\lambda]$

wave speed v in metres per second, m/s

frequency f in hertz, Hz

wavelength λ in metres, m

6.2.1 Electromagnetic waves are transverse waves that transfer energy from the source of the waves to an absorber.

Electromagnetic waves form a continuous spectrum and all types of electromagnetic wave travel at the same velocity through a vacuum (space) or air.

The waves that form the electromagnetic spectrum are grouped in terms of their wavelength and their frequency. Going from long to short wavelength (or from low to high frequency) the groups are: radio, microwave, infrared, visible light (red to violet), ultraviolet, X-rays and gamma rays.

MS 1b, 1c, 3b, 3c

Long wavelength ——————→ Short wavelength

Radio waves	Microwaves	Infrared	Visible light	Ultraviolet	X-rays	Gamma rays

Low frequency ——————→ Higher frequency

Our eyes detect visible light and so only detect a limited range of electromagnetic waves.

Students should be able to give examples that illustrate the transfer of energy by electromagnetic waves.

(H) 6.2.2 Different substances may absorb, transmit, refract, or reflect electromagnetic waves in ways that vary with wavelength.

Aiming for	Outcome	Checkpoint	
		Question	Activity
Aiming for GRADE 4	State that electromagnetic (EM) waves transfer energy without transferring matter.		Starter 1, Main 1
	Identify the position of EM waves in the spectrum in order of wavelength and frequency.	2, 4	Main 1
	State that all EM waves travel at the same speed in a vacuum.	4	Starter 2, Main 1
Aiming for GRADE 6	Describe the relationship between the energy being transferred by an electromagnetic wave and the frequency of the wave.	1	Main 2
	Calculate the frequency and the wavelength of an electromagnetic wave.	3	Main 1, Plenary 2
	Explain why the range of wavelengths detected by the human eye is limited.		Main 1, Main 2
Aiming for GRADE 8	Apply the wave model of electromagnetic radiation as a pair of electric and magnetic disturbances that do not require a medium for travel.		Main 1
	Use standard form in calculations of wavelength, frequency, and wave speed.	3	Main 2, Plenary 2
	Explain the interactions between an electromagnetic wave and matter.	End of chapter 6	Main 2

Maths
Students calculate wave speed using the wave speed equation (3c). Some students rearrange this equation and use standard form in these calculations (1b, 1c, 3b).

Literacy
Students describe the discovery of different regions of the electromagnetic spectrum in a brief report (Homework).

Key words
wave speed

Practical

Title	Introducing electromagnetic waves
Equipment	small radio, kitchen foil, microwave transmitter and receiver (if available), infrared remote control and device, sheet of paper, sheet of glass, UV source sheet of acetate or OHP sheet, sunscreen, white object
Overview of method	Radio waves: surround a small radio set with kitchen foil and see if it still picks up radio signals. Microwaves: Use a microwave transmitter and receiver. Infrared: Try using a remote control through paper, glass, and a human body. Ultraviolet: Investigate the effectiveness of sunscreen by smearing it onto acetate and seeing if it stops UV getting through and making a white object behind the acetate glow.
Safety considerations	Students must not touch the IR source or stare into the UV source.

Starter	Support/Extend	Resources
The visible spectrum (10 min) Ask students to outline their prior knowledge of the electromagnetic spectrum by asking them to show how light is reflected, transmitted, or refracted.	**Extend:** Move on to see if they can explain reflection from coloured surfaces – this includes reflection and absorption.	
Light speed (5 min) Ask the students to use the following data to determine the speed of light. It takes 1.3 s to travel from the Earth to the Moon, a distance of 390 000 km [300 000 km/s or 300 000 000 m/s].	**Extend:** Use standard form for the numerical values.	
Main	**Support/Extend**	**Resources**
Introducing electromagnetic waves (25 min) Recap the nature of electromagnetic radiation compared with mechanical waves. Focus on the wide range of wavelengths of the waves, linking this to the effects. Show the link between frequency and wavelength. Students need to attempt a few calculations of wavelength and frequency. Outline the link between frequency and energy. Students then carry out the practical. They can either rotate through all of the experiments, or each group carries out one experiment and then they share and discuss results.	**Extend:** Introduce the concept of oscillations in linked electric and magnetic fields to describe the waves. **Support:** Provide examples of how to deal with very large and small numbers which cannot be typed directly into a calculator.	**Practical:** Introducing electromagnetic waves **Maths skills:** Electromagnetic waves
EM waves and matter (15 min) (H) Recap absorption, reflection, and transmission using visible light as an example and ask students if this behaviour will be the same for all electromagnetic waves and materials.	**Extend:** Discuss the effect on temperature when EM waves are absorbed.	
Plenary	**Support/Extend**	**Resources**
RMIVUXG? (5 min) The students may know a mnemonic to give the order of the visible spectrum. Can they think up a method of remembering the regions of the electromagnetic spectrum?		
EM calculations (10 min) Students complete the interactive where they are given further calculations of wavelength or frequency for electromagnetic waves.	**Extend:** Speeds in other materials can be incorporated in examples.	**Interactive:** EM calculations
Homework		
Students can research the discovery of different regions of the EM spectrum to find out how each group of waves was discovered.	**Support:** Assign students a particular region to ensure all are covered.	

kerboodle

A Kerboodle highlight for this lesson is **Working scientifically: Unthinkably small, unimaginably large**. Refer to the **Content map** on Kerboodle for a full list of resources and assessment.

P13.2 Light, infrared, microwaves, and radio waves

AQA spec Link: 6.2.4 Electromagnetic waves have many practical applications. For example:

- radio waves – television and radio
- microwaves – satellite communications, cooking food
- infrared – electrical heaters, cooking food, infrared cameras
- visible light – fibre optic communications.

H Students should be able to give brief explanations why each type of electromagnetic wave is suitable for the practical application.

6.2.2 **Required practical:** Investigate how the amount of infrared radiation absorbed or radiated by a surface depends on the nature of that surface.

WS 1.4
MS 1b, 1c, 3b, 3c

Aiming for	Outcome	Checkpoint	
		Question	**Activity**
Aiming for GRADE 4	Describe how white light is a part of the electromagnetic spectrum and is composed of a range of frequencies.	End of chapter 1	Starter 2, Main 2
	List some simple examples of the uses of light, microwaves, and radio waves.	1, 3, End of chapter 1	Main 2, Plenary 1
	Measure the rate of cooling due to emission of infrared radiation.		Main 1
Aiming for GRADE 6	Describe how a range of electromagnetic waves are used in a variety of scenarios.	1, 3, End of chapter 6	Main 2
	H Explain why a particular wave is suited to its application.	2	Main 2
	Plan an investigation into the rate of cooling of infrared radiation.	4	Main 1
Aiming for GRADE 8	Determine the wavelength of radio waves in air.	3, End of chapter 2	Plenary 2
	Describe the interactions between a range of waves and matter, including the effect of absorption.	2, 4	Starter 2, Main 1, Main 2
	Evaluate an investigation into the rate of cooling of infrared radiation.	4	Main 1, Homework

Maths
Students compare waves in terms of wavelength and frequency and calculate the wavelength of some EM waves (1b, 1c, 3b, 3c).

Literacy
Students work in small groups identifying and discussing the properties of various EM waves and writing up an investigation.

Key words
white light

Required practical

Title	Absorption and emission of infrared radiation
Equipment	kettles or another way of heating water, two drink cans or two beakers (one painted silver and the other matt black), two thermometers (to 0.5°C), aluminium foil (if beakers are used), stopwatch, a measuring cylinder, ice cold water, infrared lamp or sunlight
Overview of method	Add the same volume of hot water to each of the containers and record the temperature every 30 seconds for 5 to 10 minutes as they cool. The containers can be filled with very cold water and placed in sunlight or under an infrared lamp to explore the absorption of infrared radiation.
Safety considerations	Avoid spills and scalds from hot water.

Starter	Support/Extend	Resources
Radio gaga (5 min) Give the students a set of mixed-up sentences about radio waves and ask them to sort the words into the right order to produce correct sentences. **Colour filters** (10 min) Shine a bright white light through a series of filters and ask the students to explain what is happening with a diagram. Ask the students if they think that there will be a similar effect for the non-visible parts of the spectrum. This leads into the absorption of electromagnetic energy as it passes through materials.	**Support:** Remind students that white light is composed of bands of colours, and give an example of the effect of a filter before asking them to try some of their own.	
Main	**Support/Extend**	**Resources**
Absorption and emission of infrared radiation (20 min) Students investigate the absorption and emission of infrared radiation using the required practical task. **Electromagnetic radiation** (20 min) Remind students of the different parts of the electromagnetic spectrum. Then introduce the uses of IR radiation, microwaves, and radio waves. • IR radiation – emphasise the relatively low energy of the waves but explain that high intensity (relate to 'brightness') can mean that large amounts of energy can be delivered by electric heaters and so on. • Microwaves – describe the uses of microwaves, ideally with a phone and a microwave oven as props. Students should note that microwaves are absorbed by water and fat molecules, and this absorption produces the heating effect. • Radio waves – Demonstrate a radio to show that radio waves can penetrate walls. Bluetooth devices such as console game controllers can also be shown. Moving the device gradually further away from its partner will allow the students to check the maximum range. They should use the student book (and other resources if available) to produce a revision summary of the uses of the different parts of the electromagnetic spectrum.	**Extend:** Discuss the reduction in intensity with distance, leading to the idea of an inverse square law. **Extend:** The intensity of the microwaves can be discussed to explain why ovens cook food but mobile phones do not. Discuss the effect of absorption of radio waves in metal wires as part of an explanation about how antennae operate.	**Required practical:** Absorption and emission of infrared radiation
Plenary	**Support/Extend**	**Resources**
EM wave summary (10 min) Students produce a summary about all of the areas of the electromagnetic spectrum they have studied so far. **What's the frequency?** (5 min) Students use the interactive to calculate the wavelengths of some radio stations when given the frequency. They should then calculate the radio station frequency when given the wavelength. This recaps the calculations from earlier.	**Support:** Provide a table for the summary or a partially completed visual summary. **Support:** Use calculation templates to support students. **Extend:** Use standard form and SI prefixes.	**Interactive:** What's the frequency?
Homework		
Students can plan to investigate the penetrating power of microwaves, comparing the density of the material with the stopping power.	**Support:** Provide a framework for the students to use to make their plans.	

P13.3 Communications

AQA spec Link: Ⓗ **6.2.2 Different substances may absorb, transmit, refract, or reflect electromagnetic waves in ways that vary with wavelength.**

Students should be able to construct ray diagrams to illustrate the refraction of a wave at the boundary between two different media.

Ⓗ **6.2.3 Radio waves can be produced by oscillations in electrical circuits.**

When radio waves are absorbed they may create an alternating current with the same frequency as the radio wave itself, so radio waves can themselves induce oscillations in an electrical circuit.

6.2.4 Electromagnetic waves have many practical applications. For example:

- radio waves – television and radio
- microwaves – satellite communications, cooking food
- visible light – fibre optic communications.

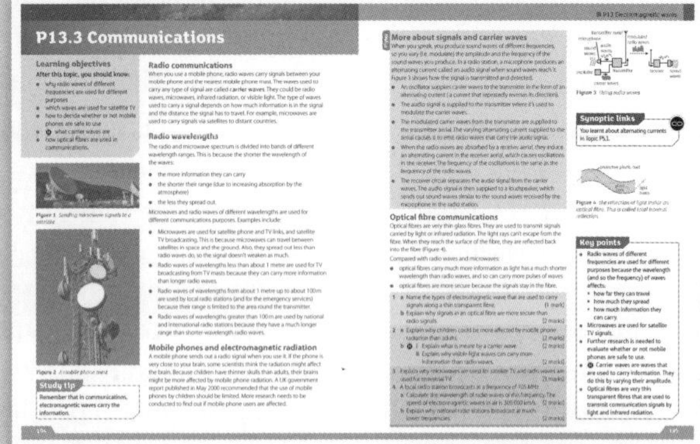

MS 1c, 3b, 3c

Aiming for	Outcome	Checkpoint	
		Question	**Activity**
Aiming for GRADE 4	State that radio waves and microwaves are used in communications through the atmosphere.	1	Main 1
	State that the higher the frequency of a wave, the greater the rate of data transfer possible.	1	Main 1, Main 2
	Describe the sub-regions of the radio spectrum.	3	Main 1
Aiming for GRADE 6	Compare the rate of information transfer through optical fibres and radio signals.	1	Main 1, Main 2
	Outline the operation of a mobile phone network and the waves used.	1	Main 1
	Discuss the evidence for mobile phone signals causing damage to humans.	2, End of chapter 3	Main 1
Aiming for GRADE 8	Ⓗ **Describe in detail how carrier waves are used in the transfer of information.**		Main 2
	Ⓗ **Describe the structure of a radio communication system, including the effect of a radio wave on the current in the receiver.**		Main 2
	Discuss the relationship between wavelength, data transmission, and range to explain why particular frequencies are chosen for particular transmissions.	3, 4	Main 1, Main 2

Maths
Students use the wave equation to calculate wavelength from frequency for electromagnetic waves (1c, 3b, 3c).

Literacy
A wide variety of communication systems can be discussed by the students.

Key words
carrier waves

Practical

Title	Optical fibres for communication
Equipment	length of optical fibre (2–10 m), bright light source (preferably one that can be switched on and off quickly)
Overview of method	Bend the fibre around several objects. Allow one student to observe the distant end whilst demonstrating the flash of a torch into the near end. Even with the thinnest of fibres, the transmitted light should be obvious.
Safety considerations	Ensure that there is adequate space for the activity.

Starter	Support/Extend	Resources
Instant messaging (5 min) How does mobile phone messaging work? Students complete the interactive to explain how a message gets from one phone to another phone in the same room by putting the different stages in order.	**Support:** Provide the stages and ask students to place them into a flow chart.	**Interactive:** Instant messaging
Get the message across (10 min) The students must think up as many ways as possible to communicate with each other and pass on a simple message such as 'I am hungry' or 'I am thirsty'.	**Support:** Provide some unusual examples such as semaphore.	
Main	**Support/Extend**	**Resources**
Radio waves and mobile phones (20 min) Discuss the various regions of the radio spectrum, with a particular emphasis on the position of microwaves within it. Link this to the rate at which data can be transmitted – microwaves provide the greatest rate. Discuss the transmission of signals, particularly the need for transmission towers – the phones do not communicate directly. An older, broken phone may be useful here to show the aerial. No link between mobile phone use and brain effects has so far been found – the intensity of the signals are very low and are unlikely to cause damage. Students then complete the Bump up your grade worksheet to consolidate their understanding of the electromagnetic spectrum and how microwaves and radio waves are used in communication.	**Support:** A flow chart can simplify the explanation.	**Bump up your grade:** Communicate – Stay in touch
Optical fibres for communication (20 min) Demonstrate a simple transition of light pulsed through a fibre with a torch and convoluted path for the cable. Remind students that visible light and IR are much higher frequency than radio and so fibres will transmit data at a higher rate. Students can compare energy and information transfer through a fibre to that in radio transmissions.	**Extend:** Discuss the ray path within the fibre core, showing total internal reflection.	**Activity:** Optical fibres for communication
(H) Higher-tier students also need to discuss signals and carrier waves. The process here is quite complex and students need to be led through the stages carefully.	**Support:** Foundation-tier students can spend this time discussing safety precautions for the use of mobile phones.	
Plenary	**Support/Extend**	**Resources**
Round the bend (5 min) Give the students a diagram of an optical fibre with a curved path and ask them to draw the path of a ray that is shown entering the fibre.	**Extend:** Provide a more convoluted fibre diagram and insist on proper construction of the reflection.	
Broken signal (10 min) Students design a leaflet from a satellite TV company explaining why the television signal has been poor recently. It should explain how the TV signal is transmitted to the house and what factors can affect it (rain, snow, sunspots).		
Homework		
Students complete the WebQuest where they research claims that radio waves from human technologies are making people ill. They use their research to create an information leaflet for people who are worried about this.		

kerboodle

A Kerboodle highlight for this lesson is **Working scientifically: Range of a Bluetooth dongle**. Refer to the **Content map** on Kerboodle for a full list of resources and assessment.

P13.4 Ultraviolet waves, X-rays, and gamma rays

AQA spec Link: 6.2.3 Changes in atoms and the nuclei of atoms can result in electromagnetic waves being generated or absorbed over a wide frequency range. Gamma rays originate from changes in the nucleus of an atom.

Ultraviolet waves, X-rays, and gamma rays can have hazardous effects on human body tissue. The effects depend on the type of radiation and the size of the dose. Radiation dose (in sieverts) is a measure of the risk of harm resulting from an exposure of the body to the radiation.

Ultraviolet waves can cause skin to age prematurely and increase the risk of skin cancer. X-rays and gamma rays are ionising radiation that can cause the mutation of genes and cancer.

6.2.4 Electromagnetic waves have many practical applications. For example:

- ultraviolet – energy efficient lamps, sun tanning
- X-rays and gamma rays – medical imaging and treatments.

WS 1.5
MS 1b

Aiming for	Outcome	Checkpoint	
		Question	Activity
Aiming for GRADE 4 ↓	State that high-frequency electromagnetic radiation is ionising.		Main
	Describe the uses and dangers of ultraviolet (UV) radiation.	2	Starter 2, Main
	Describe the uses and dangers of X-rays and gamma radiation.	End of chapter 5	Starter 2, Main
Aiming for GRADE 6 ↓	Describe the penetrating powers of gamma rays, X-rays, and ultraviolet rays.	1, 2, 3	Main
	Compare X-rays and gamma radiation in terms of their origin.		Main
	Describe the ionisation of atoms in simple terms.	4, End of chapter 5	Main
Aiming for GRADE 8 ↓	Describe in detail the interaction between ionising radiation and inorganic materials.	End of chapter 6	Main
	Compare different regions of the electromagnetic spectrum in terms of their potential harmfulness.	4	Main
	Explain how the process of ionisation can lead to cell death or cancer through damage to DNA.	4, End of chapter 5	Main

Maths
Students may compare electromagnetic waves in terms of wavelength or frequency using standard form (1b).

Literacy
The students describe the effects of radiation on living cells and discuss the safety concerns.

Key words
ionisation

Practical

Title	Ultraviolet waves
Equipment	ultraviolet lamp, samples of different coloured clothing (or fabric) optional: cloths washed in biological washing powder, white paper, real paper money, other UV-responsive objects (e.g., nail-varnish beads)
Overview of method	Demonstrate the effect of UV light on the different clothing whilst explaining that they absorb the UV light and then emit visible light. Optional: demonstrate with the further suggested objects. Discuss the reaction of the paper money compared with that of the white paper.
Safety considerations	Ensure that students cannot look directly into the UV light source as this can cause eye damage.

Starter	Support/Extend	Resources
Mutant mayhem (5 min) 'Mutants' with super powers caused by exposure to radiation are common in films and comics. Do students think that this radiation can have beneficial effects in reality?		
Stellar imagery (10 min) Show a range of images of the Sun, capturing the different parts of the EM spectrum (a visible light image, ultraviolet, infrared, and so on). Discuss how these images are captured and which parts reach the surface of the Earth.	**Extend:** A graph showing the transmission characteristics of the atmosphere can be used.	
Main	**Support/Extend**	**Resources**
UV, X-rays, and gamma rays (40 min) Start by demonstrating the effect of UV radiation on a range of materials to show that it exists using the practical outlined. Emphasise the damage it can cause, particularly to the eyes. Images of skin damage are readily available on the Internet. Move to higher-frequency/higher-energy waves, emphasising the penetrating power through different materials. A few simple non-medical X-ray photographs can be used to outline a use for X-rays, because medical photographs will be used in Topic P13.5.	**Extend:** Discuss the difference in origin of X-rays and gamma radiation.	**Activity:** UV, X-rays, and gamma rays
Outline the key uses of gamma radiation, all of which are linked to high energy causing ionisation and damage to living cells.	**Support:** Simple descriptions, without example bacteria and radioactive sources, can be used.	
Describe the process of ionisation and, in particular, the damage to DNA. The students should understand that the greater the exposure, the more damage is likely. Various control procedures should be discussed, including reducing exposure, protective clothing, and dose measurement. The students should be provided with some data about the risks associated with radiation exposure to analyse.	**Extend:** Describe the process of ionisation in more depth, mentioning the role of the freed electron in causing further damage.	
Plenary	**Support/Extend**	**Resources**
One world (5 min) Interactive where students complete a paragraph to briefly discuss the problem with the ozone layer discovered in the 1980s and the steps taken to reduce it, to show that global problems can be solved when countries work together.	**Extend:** The timescale for recovery can be discussed – the damage will not be overcome until 2050 or later.	**Interactive:** One world
Safety first (10 min) Students design a safety notice for either a sunbed or an X-ray machine.	**Support:** Provide key phrases and images that may be used for the notice.	
Homework		
Students can plan an investigation into the effectiveness of UV sunscreen lotion using a UV detector.	**Extend:** Expect a fully formed plan that can be carried out within the laboratory, including any safety precautions needed.	

kerboodle

A Kerboodle highlight for this lesson is **Bump up your grade: Electromagnetic waves**. Refer to the **Content map** on Kerboodle for a full list of resources and assessment.

P13.5 X-rays in medicine

AQA spec Link: 6.2.3 X-rays can have hazardous effects on human body tissue. The effects depend on the type of radiation and the size of the dose. Radiation dose (in sieverts) is a measure of the risk of harm resulting from an exposure of the body to the radiation.

1000 millisieverts (mSv) = 1 sievert (Sv)

Students will not be required to recall the unit of radiation dose.

X-rays are ionising radiation that can cause the mutation of genes and cancer.

6.2.4 Electromagnetic waves have many practical applications. For example:

- X-rays – medical imaging and treatments.

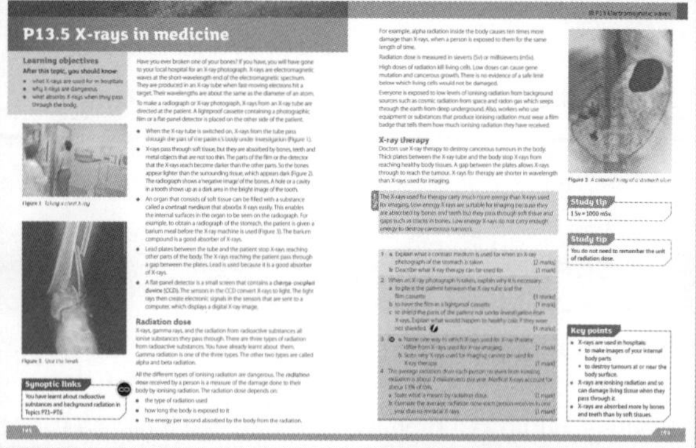

WS 1.5
MS 1a

Aiming for	Outcome	Checkpoint	
		Question	Activity
Aiming for GRADE 4	Describe some safety procedures that take place during the operation of devices that produce ionising radiation.		Main
	Describe the formation of an X-ray photograph in terms of absorption or transmission.	End of chapter 4	Starter 2, Main
	State that X-ray therapy can be used to kill cancerous cells in the body.		Main
Aiming for GRADE 6	Describe the operation of an X-ray machine.	2, End of chapter 4	Main
	Explain why contrast media can be used during X-rays.	1, End of chapter 4	Main
	Describe the factors that affect the radiation doses received by people.	4	Main
Aiming for GRADE 8	Compare the operation of a CT-scanner and that of a simple X-ray device.	3	Main
	Evaluate the doses of ionising radiation received in a variety of occupations or medical treatments.	4	Main
	Explain in detail how various safety features reduce exposure to ionising radiation.	End of chapter 4	Main

Maths
Students can compare radiation dose for different occupations using the appropriate units (1a).

Literacy
Students discuss the options for medical diagnosis in terms of costs, health benefits, and risks.

Key words
contrast medium, charged-coupled device (CCD), radiation dose

Starter	Support/Extend	Resources
X-ray visions (10 min) Show a range of animal skeleton X-rays and ask students to identify the animals. At the same time, ask the students to discuss how the images were made. ***Hand mit Ringen*** (5 min) Show the very first medical X-ray image and ask the students what it shows and how it might have been made. It is an image of Wilhelm Röntgen's wife's hand with rings.	**Support:** Select simple images. **Extend:** X-rays of more complex objects can be used. **Extend:** The students can discuss whether taking this image was safe or necessary.	
Main	**Support/Extend**	**Resources**
Medical X-rays and CT scanners (40 min) Outline the process of making a medical X-ray, supporting this with some real images. Discuss the images in terms of absorption or transmission of the X-rays. Show some images that use contrast media to differentiate tissues. Recap ionisation and discuss the procedures used to reduce dose. The students should recognise the unit sievert and use it in comparisons – although they do not need to remember it. Then describe the operation of a CT scanner with a comparison to simple X-ray machines. Video clips of a CT scan can be found easily and show the advantage of 3D reconstruction. Make sure that students understand the improved soft-tissue differentiation. Link back to ionisation and the destruction of cells when discussing X-ray treatment.	**Support:** A simplified flowchart of the process can be produced. **Extend:** Students can compare photographic film, high resolution so greater image detail, with the convenience of CCD. Compare the exposure of a radiologist with that of a patient, and evaluate the relative risks. **Support:** A simplified table comparing the devices can be made for the students. **Extend:** Discuss the potential for causing new damage to cells.	**Activity:** Medical X-rays and CT scanners
Plenary	**Support/Extend**	**Resources**
Cost/benefit analysis (10 min) Interactive where students complete a paragraph to explain why all patients do not have CT scans instead of X-ray scans. They then sort statements according to whether they are benefits or disadvantages of these diagnostic technologies. **Organ identification** (5 min) Can the students identify particular organs from 3D CT scans or simple X-rays?	**Support:** Students can match up simple facts with the appropriate diagnostic technique. **Extend:** Include a comparison of ultrasound diagnosis.	**Interactive:** Cost/benefit analysis
Homework		
Students complete the WebQuest to research how X-ray and ultrasound scans work and consider their different uses and the risks associated with them. They use their research to create a short pamphlet aimed at a hospital patient who requires an X-ray or an ultrasound scan.		**WebQuest:** Ultrasound or X-ray?

kerboodle

A Kerboodle highlight for this lesson is **Working scientifically: Risks and benefits of using X-rays or gamma rays**. Refer to the **Content map** on Kerboodle for a full list of resources and assessment.

P13 The electromagnetic spectrum

Overview of P13 The electromagnetic spectrum

In this chapter the students have described the electromagnetic spectrum in terms of different regions related to wavelength. The speed of electromagnetic waves in a vacuum has been described as constant allowing the use of the wave equation to link wavelength and frequency which has then been tied to the energy carried by the wave.

Each of the regions of the electromagnetic spectrum has been described along with associated uses and students have investigated the relationship between surface colour, temperature, and the rate of emission of infra-red radiation. The use of radio waves in communications for television and mobile phones has been described along with outlining transmissions of signals through optical fibres. Higher tier students have also described the process of modulation of carrier waves to give a more complex picture of how information can be transmitted using waves.

All students have described the application of ultra violet waves in phosphorescence and the damage these waves can cause to skin and eyes before describing the uses of X-rays and gamma rays in medical applications. The process of ionisation has been outlined as well as the cause of tissue damage as a useful technique in killing bacteria or cancerous cells. Further details of the use of X-rays have been described including contrast media and detection devices such as the CCD and the concept of radiation dose. Higher tier students have compared the intensity of imaging and therapeutic X-rays.

Required practical

All students are expected to have carried out the required practical:

Practical	Topic
Investigate how the amount of infrared radiation absorbed or radiated by a surface depends on the nature of that surface.	B13.2

You can find additional support for the maths skills covered in this chapter on **MyMaths**, including recognise and use expressions in decimal form, use an appropriate number of significant figures, understand and use the symbols: $=, <, <<, >>, >, \propto, \sim$, change the subject of an equation.

For this chapter, the following assessments are available on Kerboodle:

P13 Checkpoint quiz: The electromagnetic spectrum
P13 Progress quiz: The electromagnetic spectrum 1
P13 Progress quiz: The electromagnetic spectrum 2
P13 On your marks: The electromagnetic spectrum
P13 Exam-style questions and mark scheme: The electromagnetic spectrum

Checkpoint follow up lesson

A student's route through this lesson can be determined using the Checkpoint assessment. Percentage pass marks are supplied in the Checkpoint teacher notes.

For each successive route through it is assumed that the student can perform to their current route as well as previous routes. For example, students working at Aiming for 6 are assumed to be secure in Aiming for 4 knowledge and understanding and working towards achieving all the learning outcomes for Aiming for 6.

	Aiming for 4	Aiming for 6	Aiming for 8
Learning outcomes	Recall all the main groupings of the electromagnetic spectrum and how they are different in terms of wavelength and frequency, and recall which waves our eyes detect.	Recall the electromagnetic spectrum, some of their uses and dangers, and calculate their frequencies and wavelengths.	Recall the electromagnetic spectrum, some of their uses and dangers, and calculate their frequencies and wavelengths.
	Describe some sources and detectors of electromagnetic waves and link them to their uses and dangers.	Compare the ways that we image the body with how we treat the body in terms of electromagnetic radiation.	Compare the ways that we image the body with how we treat the body in terms of electromagnetic radiation.
	Describe how we use some of the waves in medicine and in communication.	Explain what is meant by radiation dose, and how you minimise risk.	Explain what is meant by radiation dose, and how you minimise risk.
	Write down the unit of radiation dose.	Describe how radio waves are produced and detected, and how they can be changed to carry information.	Describe how radio waves are produced and detected, and how they can be changed to carry information.
Starter	**What's the use? (10 min)** Give out cards for a pairs matching game that contains the names of waves of the electromagnetic waves on blue cards, with the same number of each card in yellow with a use on it. Students put the cards face down, and pick up pairs of different colours, keeping any pairs that match. When they have completed the game they sort the pairs into those used in communication and those used in medicine. **Good or bad? (5 min)** Put a large 'Safe' sign on one side of the room and 'Dangerous' on the other. Ask students to stand in a place that shows what they think about electromagnetic radiation. Ask for some reasons for the choice of position.		
Differentiated checkpoint activity	Aiming for 4 students use the Checkpoint follow-up sheet to either create a matching game to summarise the main groupings of the electromagnetic spectrum or to produce a poster to summarise some of the uses of electromagnetic waves. Students will need access to scissors and A3 paper. The follow-up sheet is highly structured and provides simple questions to support students with consolidating their understanding from the tasks of the lesson.	Aiming for 6 students use the Checkpoint follow-up sheet to either calculate typical wavelengths and frequencies of the waves of the electromagnetic spectrum and describe how radio waves were discovered or create a poster to describe some uses of electromagnetic waves. Students will need access to large paper and a radio. The follow-up sheet provides some support and questions to consolidate students' understanding from the tasks of the lesson.	Aiming for 8 students use the Checkpoint follow-up sheet to either calculate typical wavelengths and frequencies of the waves of the electromagnetic spectrum and describe how radio waves were discovered or create a poster to describe some uses of electromagnetic waves. Students will need access to large paper and a radio. The follow-up sheet provides minimal support and more complex questions to consolidate students' understanding from the tasks of the lesson.
	Kerboodle resource P13 Checkpoint follow up: Aiming for 4, P13 Checkpoint follow up: Aiming for 6, P13 Checkpoint follow up: Aiming for 8		
Plenary	**Electromagnetic spectrum splat (5 min)** Write the names of all the electromagnetic waves on the board. Divide the class in two and have them line up on either side of the board. Read out a question about the waves of the electromagnetic spectrum, and each team member tries to find the word on the board and hit it with their hand (hence splat). Keep score to see which team wins. **Danger words (10 min)** Use an online crossword maker to make a crossword using these words: DNA, radiotherapy, cancer, damage, treatment, dose, Sievert. Either give them the clues and ask them to solve the crossword, or give them the completed crossword and ask them to write the clues. They should swap with another student to check what they have done.		
Progression	Encourage students to think about finding a way of remembering the order of the waves, and the unit of radiation dose.	Encourage students to think about the balance of risk and benefit when using electromagnetic waves in medicine.	Encourage students to think about describing the use of electromagnetic waves in term of risk and benefit, and to remember broadly the range of wavelengths of the waves.

P GCSE Physics only 14 Light

14.1 Reflection of light

AQA spec Link: 6.1.3 Waves can be reflected at the boundary between two different materials.

Waves can be absorbed or transmitted at the boundary between two different materials.

Students should be able to construct ray diagrams to illustrate the reflection of a wave at a surface.

Students should be able to describe the effects of reflection, transmission, and absorption of waves at material interfaces.

6.2.6 Reflection from a smooth surface in a single direction is called specular reflection. Reflection from a rough surface causes scattering: this is called diffuse reflection.

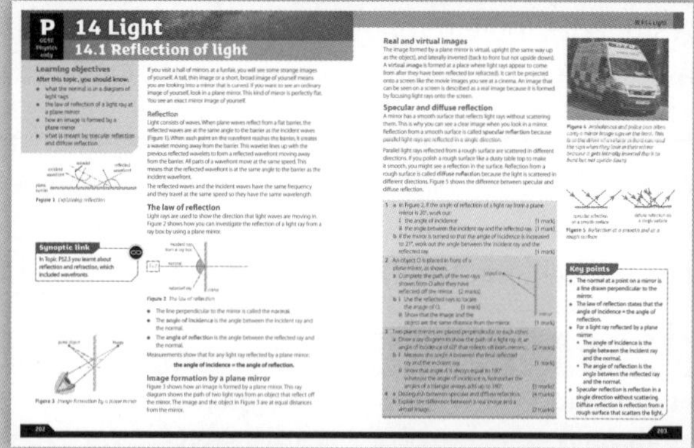
P 14 Light
14.1 Reflection of light

WS 1.2
MS 5a, 5b, 5c

Aiming for	Outcome	Checkpoint	
		Question	**Activity**
Aiming for GRADE 4	State the law of reflection.	1, End of chapter 1	Main, Plenary 2
	Describe the properties of an image in a mirror in simple terms and investigate reflection with guidance.	End of chapter 1	Main
↓	Describe how a real image can be formed on a screen but a virtual image cannot.		Starter 1, Main
Aiming for GRADE 6	Construct accurate ray diagrams showing the reflection of light rays.	3	Main, Plenary 1
	Explain why some surfaces form images during reflection but others do not.	End of chapter 3	Main
↓	Investigate the formation of images in mirrors.		Main
Aiming for GRADE 8	Draw a ray diagram showing the position of an image in a plane mirror.	2, End of chapter 1	Main
	Use ray diagrams to discuss why some surfaces form images during reflection but others do not.		Main
↓	Evaluate the data from an investigation to discuss the precision and accuracy of any results.	4	Main

Maths 

Students measure angles and construct diagrams with protractors and rulers (5a, 5b).

Literacy 

Students describe experimental results, working in teams to verify specific laws.

Key words

normal, angle of incidence, angle of reflection, virtual image, specular reflection, diffuse reflection

Practical

Title	Mirror mirror
Equipment	ray box and power supply, plane mirror, ruler, curved mirrors
Overview of method	Students observe their images in plane mirrors and describe their properties. They can also try to find a method to show that the distance the image is behind the mirror is the same as the distance from the object to the mirror. The activity can be extended by observing images in cured mirrors.
Safety considerations	Check glass mirrors for sharp edges and clean up any broken glass immediately. Ray box bulbs can become hot, allow time for cooling.

Starter	Support/Extend	Resources
Virtually real (5 min) Ask the students to give several examples of the use of the word 'virtual'. What about the word 'real'? Many will have heard of virtual reality – point out that the terms have a specific meaning in optics.	**Support:** Show a portion of a film or game with virtual reality in it.	
Lunar see (10 min) Interactive where students complete an explanation of how we are able to see the Moon. The explanations should include the concepts of a light source, reflection, and light entering our eyes.	**Extend:** The effects of the Earth's atmosphere, scattering, and refraction, should be included in students' explanation.	**Interactive:** Lunar see
Main	**Support/Extend**	**Resources**
Mirror mirror (40 min) Start by checking the students' ability to produce simple ray diagrams. Producing a ray with a ray box will help students to understand why rays are drawn to explain some of the properties of light.	**Support:** Show a ray diagram and discuss the key features. **Extend:** A curved mirror can be used to show that the law still applies.	**Practical:** Mirror mirror
Outline real and virtual images, showing the one produced by a projector as an example of a real image and that produced by a mirror as an example of a virtual image. Allow students to investigate a range of surfaces that produce clear images, blurry images, and then no image at all, then describe the surfaces in terms of 'roughness'. The students can then use a few mirrors to investigate images of objects as described in the practical task.	**Extend:** Students should draw ray paths to show the position of the image in the mirror. **Support:** Students can use the diagrams in the student book to support the explanations of specular and diffuse reflection.	
Plenary	**Support/Extend**	**Resources**
Pepper's ghost (5 min) Show students this simple but classic optical illusion and ask them to come up with an explanation of how it works. This leads to the idea of partial reflection – an effect that students often see when looking through glass.	**Extend:** The students should be challenged to draw ray diagrams explaining the effect.	
Curved mirrors (10 min) The students can examine the reflection of light in curved mirrors either practically or by constructing a ray diagram.	**Extend:** Students use ray diagrams to determine whether an image can form.	
Homework		
Students should find out about the origins of the ray model of light and the numerous scientists who contributed to its development.	**Support:** Assign particular scientists to individual students to research. **Extend:** Students can contrast the development of particle and wave theories.	

kerboodle

A Kerboodle highlight for this lesson is **Working scientifically: Modelling waves**. Refer to the **Content map** on Kerboodle for a full list of resources and assessment.

P14.2 Refraction of light

AQA spec Link: 6.2.2 (H) **Different substances may absorb, transmit, refract, or reflect electromagnetic waves in ways that vary with wavelength.**

Some effects, for example refraction, are due to the difference in velocity of the waves in different substances.

Students should be able to construct ray diagrams to illustrate the refraction of a wave at the boundary between two different media.

(H) **Students should be able to use wave front diagrams to explain refraction in terms of the change of speed that happens when a wave travels from one medium to a different medium.**

Whilst the specification point 6.2.2 is not a Physics only specification point, students will need to apply the content to the context of this topic, and have a good understanding of the content of 6.2.2 to complete the required practical.

6.1.3 Waves can be reflected at the boundary between two different materials.

Waves can be absorbed or transmitted at the boundary between two different materials.

Students should be able to construct ray diagrams to illustrate the reflection of a wave at a surface.

Students should be able to describe the effects of reflection, transmission and absorption of waves at material interfaces.

Required practical: Investigate the reflection of light by different types of surface and the refraction of light by different substances.

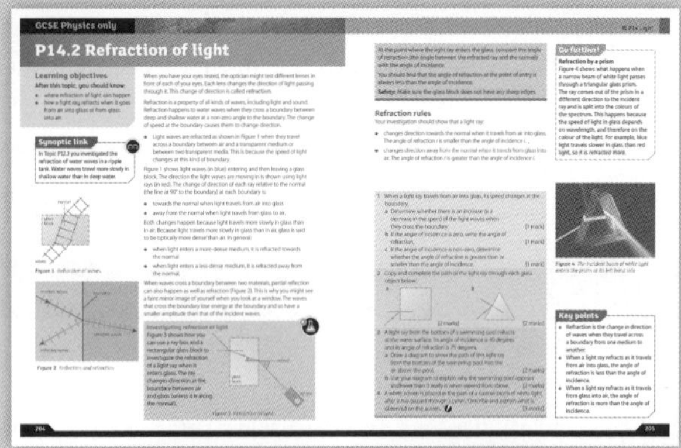

WS 1.2
MS 1a, 5a, 5c

Aiming for	Outcome	Checkpoint	
		Question	Activity
Aiming for GRADE 4	Describe how the path of a ray of light will change at a boundary between two transparent materials.	1	Main 1
	Identify the angle of incidence and angle of refraction in a ray diagram.		Main 1
	Measure the angle of incidence and angle of refraction for a simple refraction.		Main 1
Aiming for GRADE 6	Construct a ray diagram showing the refraction of a ray of light at a boundary between two different media.	2, End of chapter 2	Main 1
	Describe the dispersion of white light as it passes through a prism.	4, End of chapter 2	Main 2
	Investigate the refraction of light through a glass or Perspex block.		Main 1
Aiming for GRADE 8	Explain how the refraction of light can cause the depth of a material to appear less than it actually is.	3	Main 2
	Explain the dispersion of light as it passes through a prism in terms of different changes of speed for different wavelengths of light.	1, 4, End of chapter 2	Main 2
	Analyse the data from a refraction investigation to test different substances to determine whether it fits a suggested relationship.		Main 1

Maths
The students will measure angles with a protractor (5a). Some will calculate the sine of angles to check for a possible relationship (1a).

Literacy
Students explore the behaviour of light rays at various boundaries between different materials, and form general descriptions of this behaviour.

Key words
refraction

Required practical

Title	Investigating refraction of light
Equipment	low-voltage power supply, ray box, single slit, ray box stops, rectangular glass block, Perspex block, semi-circular glass or Perspex block, ruler, protractor, sheet of A3 paper Additional transparent materials such as ice and jelly blocks can be used.
Overview of method	The glass block should be placed in the centre of the A3 sheet of paper. It is a good idea to draw around it in case it gets knocked. The students shine rays into the block from a range of angles aiming for a fixed point on the front surface. They should draw small crosses to mark the path and then measure the angles of incidence and refraction from normal lines. Students can then test refraction with Perspex, ice, or other transparent materials and differently shaped blocks.
Safety considerations	Ray box bulbs can become hot – allow time for cooling. Check the edges of glass blocks to ensure that they are not sharp.

Starter	Support/Extend	Resources
Wave fronts (5 min) Demonstrate waves in a ripple tank passing over an object and slowing. Ask students to describe any change in direction and speed. **Stealth beaker** (10 min) Place one small Pyrex beaker inside another. Slowly fill the inner beaker with baby lotion and then the outer beaker. The inner beaker becomes invisible. Students should attempt to explain this effect by discussing how people see transparent materials.		
Main	**Support/Extend**	**Resources**
Investigating refraction of light (30 min) Show the refraction of a light ray at an air–glass boundary, identifying the angles clearly. Link this behaviour to the behaviour of waves from Topic P12.3. Students now investigate refraction at boundaries, noting that the change of direction increases when the angle of incidence does. They should then plan an investigation to test different materials to show that the difference between materials is important. This can be carried out next lesson.	**Support:** Demonstrate a technique for marking the ray paths to assist in the investigation. **Extend:** Suggest a formal relationship between the two angles ($\frac{\sin i}{\sin r}$ = constant) and see if the students can verify this from their data.	**Required practical:** Investigating refraction of light
Dispersion by a prism and refraction effects (10 min) The students can disperse a ray of light with a prism, noting which colours are refracted the most. Link this to the larger change in speed for that colour/wavelength. Demonstrate how depth can appear to change during refraction by filling a deep bucket – the effect should be obvious when observed from above.	**Support:** Students should label/colour a diagram, noting the relative changes in speed for the different colours.	
Plenary	**Support/Extend**	**Resources**
Reflect or refract? – Part 2 (10 min) This interactive builds on the interactive from Topic P12.3. Students complete an explanation on the difference between reflection and refraction, using their new understanding from this topic. They then sort a series of scenarios, identifying whether the scenario shows reflection or refraction.		**Interactive:** Reflect or refract? – Part 2
The magic penny (10 min) Place a penny at the bottom of an opaque cup so that it just about disappears from view. Pour water into the cup, and it reappears. The students should explain why by using a diagram.	**Support:** Complete the ray diagram as a class. Students then use it in their explanation.	
Homework		
Students complete the WebQuest where they research archerfish and how they use refraction to catch prey. They use their research to produce a poster.	**Extend:** The students can explain why rainbows have no 'end'.	**WebQuest:** Archerfish – masters of refraction

kerboodle

A Kerboodle highlight for this lesson is **Extension sheet: Refraction**. Refer to the **Content map** on Kerboodle for a full list of resources and assessment.

P14.3 Light and colour

AQA spec Link: 6.2.2 (H) Different substances may absorb, transmit, refract, or reflect electromagnetic waves in ways that vary with wavelength.

Whilst the specification point 6.2.2 is not a Physics only specification point, students will need to apply the content to the context of this topic, and have a good understanding of the content of 6.2.2 to complete the required practical.

6.2.6 Each colour within the visible light spectrum has its own narrow band of wavelength and frequency.

Colour filters work by absorbing certain wavelengths (and colour) and transmitting other wavelengths (and colour).

The colour of an opaque object is determined by which wavelengths of light are more strongly reflected. Wavelengths that not reflected are absorbed. If all wavelengths are reflected equally the object appears white. If all wavelengths are absorbed the objects appears black.

Objects that transmit light are either transparent or translucent.

Students should be able to explain:

- how the colour of an object is related to the differential absorption, transmission, and reflection of different wavelengths of light by the object
- the effect of viewing objects through filters or the effect on light of passing through filters
- why an opaque object has a particular colour.

6.1.3 **Required practical:** Investigate the reflection of light by different types of surface and the refraction of light by different substances.

Aiming for	Outcome	Checkpoint	
		Question	**Activity**
Aiming for GRADE 4	Describe the visible spectrum as a continuous series of colours or wavelengths.		Starter 1, Main 1
	Explain the colour of objects in white light in terms of reflection of parts of the spectrum.	1	Main 1
	Use the terms transparent and translucent accurately.		Starter 2, Main 2
Aiming for GRADE 6	Describe the colours of objects in different colours of light.	1, 2	Main 2, Plenary 2
	Describe the reflection of a ray of light from a smooth or rough surface.		Main 1
	Determine the appearance of a white object when illuminated by combinations of primary coloured light.		Main 2, Plenary 2
Aiming for GRADE 8	Explain the apparent colour of surfaces using the concept of reflection and absorption when illuminated by white light or combinations of primary colours.	2	Main 1
	Describe the effects of combinations of coloured light and filters on the appearance of a variety of coloured objects.	3	Main 2
	Determine the apparent colour of a coloured surface when illuminated by different combinations of red, green, and blue light.		Main 2

Maths 

Students can compare the colour of light to the wavelength or frequency.

Literacy 

There is plenty of opportunity for students to describe the appearance of objects in a range of light combinations and through filters, and write up their investigation into refraction by different substances.

Key words

transmitting

Required practical

Title	Surface tests
Equipment	ray box and power supply, plane mirror, white card and coloured cards, coloured filters, protractor, ruler
Overview of method	The students should firstly verify the law of reflection using plane mirror and tracing the incident and reflected rays. After this they should examine reflection from different textured surfaces and different coloured surfaces. Coloured incident rays can be produced with the filters.
Safety considerations	Check glass mirrors for sharp edges and clean up any broken glass immediately. Ray box bulbs can become hot – allow time for cooling.

Starter	Support/Extend	Resources
Rainbow (5 min) Students list the colours produced by a rainbow and then describe how they think secondary colours (such as pink) are produced.	**Support:** Demonstrate the production of a spectrum to show the absence of many colours.	
See through (10 min) Students use the interactive match up the key terms transparent, opaque, and translucent with their definitions. They then sort an example set of materials into these three groups, including some awkward materials that are just about transparent and some coloured filters.	**Support:** Students can match ray diagrams to the key words. **Extend:** Instead of giving students the categories, ask them to produce criteria and examples of their own.	**Interactive:** See through
Main	**Support/Extend**	**Resources**
Surface tests (30 min) Show a spectrum produced by dispersion of white light by a prism by projecting it onto white paper. The students should briefly discuss light sources and the concept of a spectrum before moving on to complete the required practical to investigate reflection.	**Extend:** Gas discharge tubes can be used to show specific frequencies. These can be viewed through spectroscopes. **Support:** Ensure students describe several possible scenarios for reflection of coloured light by coloured surfaces.	**Required practical:** Surface tests
Coloured light (10 min) The mixing of light can be demonstrated with overlapping coloured light sources projected onto white surfaces. Students should also observe the light sources and mixing results through filters to determine their effects. Recap transparency, translucency, and opacity if these have not already been covered in the starter.	**Extend:** Students can look at mixing light when it is projected onto coloured surfaces. **Support:** Students can match ray diagrams to the key words.	
Plenary	**Support/Extend**	**Resources**
Starlight (5 min) Show some images of stars and ask the students to rank them in order of temperature based on their colour. Include other very hot objects if time permits.	**Extend:** A temperature/colour scale can be used to estimate the actual surface temperature.	
Colour wheel (10 min) The students can observe the apparent production of a white surface during the rotation of a colour wheel. Discuss this optical process with them.	**Extend:** Further optical illusions involving colour can be discussed.	
Homework		
Students plan an investigation into combinations of filters and the proportion of light they transmit using light meters.	**Extend:** Do light meters detect all frequencies of visible light equally? Students can incorporate the idea of calibration curves.	

kerboodle

A Kerboodle highlight for this lesson is **Working scientifically: Newton the experimenter.** Refer to the **Content map** on Kerboodle for a full list of resources and assessment.

P14.4 Lenses

AQA spec Link: 6.2.5 A lens forms an image by refracting light. In a convex lens, parallel rays of light are brought to a focus at the principal focus. The distance from the lens to the principal focus is called the focal length. Ray diagrams are used to show the formation of images by convex and concave lenses.

The image produced by a convex lens can be either real or virtual. The image produced by a concave lens is always virtual.

Students should be able to construct ray diagrams to illustrate the similarities and differences between convex and concave lenses.

The magnification produced by a lens can be calculated using the equation:

$$\text{magnification} = \frac{\text{image height}}{\text{object height}}$$

Magnification is a ratio and so has no units. Image height and object height should both be measured in either mm or cm.

In ray diagrams a convex lens will be represented by:

↕

A concave lens will be represented by:

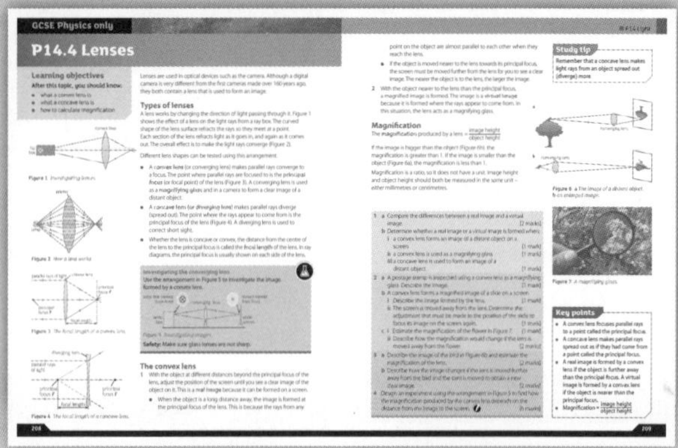

WS 1.2

MS 1c, 3b, 3c, 5a, 5b, 5c

Aiming for	Outcome	Checkpoint	
		Question	Activity
Aiming for GRADE 4	Distinguish whether a lens is converging or diverging based on a simple ray diagram.	1, 2	Main 2, Plenary 2
	Identify convex (converging) and concave (diverging) lenses from their shapes.		Starter 1, Main 1
	Form images by using a range of lenses.		Main 2
Aiming for GRADE 6	Identify real and virtual images by using ray diagrams.	1	Main 2, Plenary 2
	Calculate the magnification of a lens based on object and image size.	4	Main 2
	Investigate the image-forming properties of a converging lens.	3	Main 2
Aiming for GRADE 8	Explain ray paths through a lens in terms of refraction and the focal point.	2, 3	Main 2
	Perform calculations involving the rearrangement of the magnification equation.	4	Main 2
	Construct complete ray diagrams showing image formation by a convex lens with a variety of object positions.	End of chapter 5, 7	Main 2

Maths
Students calculate magnification based on image and object size (1c, 3b, 3c). They use careful geometrical construction techniques to form ray diagrams (5a, 5b).

Literacy
Students describe to each other the properties of lenses and the images formed by them.

Key words
convex lens, principal focus, magnifying glass, concave lens, diverging lens, focal length, real image, virtual image, magnification

Practical

Title	Investigating the converging lens
Equipment	10 cm converging lens, metre ruler, illuminated object, screen (card with graph paper)
Overview of method	The screen of card with graph paper can be used to focus the image on and measure its dimensions. The object is placed at one end of the ruler and is lit from behind. The lens is placed at a measured distance from the object and then the screen is moved until the image is in focus. The procedure is repeated by moving either the lens or the object to change the distance between them. In this way, the students can see the effect of the object's distance and the focal length of the lens on the magnification.
Safety considerations	Lamps in ray boxes can become very hot and so should be given time to cool.

Starter	Support/Extend	Resources
Sorted (5 min) Give the students a pile of different lenses and ask them to sort them into two or three lines based on criteria they make up themselves (e.g., shape). They should explain their criteria.	**Extend:** Provide ray boxes for some of the students to test the lenses.	
Top quality diagrams (10 min) Provide the students with some poorly drawn ray diagrams showing reflection, refraction, and so on and ask them to improve them.	**Support:** Provide a set of rules for the students to follow.	
Main	**Support/Extend**	**Resources**
Types of lenses (10 min) Students examine a range of lenses to see the variations, before demonstrating their effect on rays of light with ray boxes. Ensure that both converging rays and diverging rays are shown to the students, identifying the focal point.	**Support:** Limit the lenses to cylindrical types of different focal lengths.	
Investigating the converging lens (30 min) Students then investigate a converging lens as described in the practical. Plano-cylindrical lenses can make this experiment simpler to set up. After the investigation, the students should examine ray diagrams showing the ray paths through the lens, as these are crucial in later explanations. The importance of the focal points should be emphasised. The difference between a real and virtual image also needs to be clear to the students. Calculate a magnification before asking the students to try some calculations of their own, perhaps based on data collected earlier in the practical. Students then complete the Maths skills interactive for further practice in calculating magnification.	**Support:** Provide specific object distances and a results table. Provide partially completed ray diagrams and ask the students to complete them by adding the final ray paths.	**Practical:** Investigating the converging lens **Maths skills:** Light waves
Plenary	**Support/Extend**	**Resources**
Which lens? (5 min) Use the interactive to show students a range of diverging and converging lenses diagrams. Students identify which lenses are which. They then put the lenses in order of longest to shortest focal length.	**Extend:** Students should identify real and virtual images produced by the lens.	**Interactive:** Which lens?
Spot the lens (10 min) Show the students a variety of ray diagrams of optical instruments (eye, microscope, telescope, camera, projector, etc.) and ask them to spot the lenses.	**Support:** Students should categorise the lenses that they see, based on changes in the ray paths.	
Homework		
Students research and report on the development of a key optical device such as the microscope, telescope, or projector.	**Support:** Allocate particular instruments and provide some starting points for the students.	

kerboodle

A Kerboodle highlight for this lesson is **Calculation sheet: Light waves.** Refer to the **Content map** on Kerboodle for a full list of resources and assessment.

P14.5 Using lenses

AQA spec Link: 6.2.5 A lens forms an image by refracting light. In a convex lens, parallel rays of light are brought to a focus at the principal focus. The distance from the lens to the principal focus is called the focal length. Ray diagrams are used to show the formation of images by convex and concave lenses.

The image produced by a convex lens can be either real or virtual. The image produced by a concave lens is always virtual.

Students should be able to construct ray diagrams to illustrate the similarities and differences between convex and concave lenses.

The magnification produced by a lens can be calculated using the equation:

$$\text{magnification} = \frac{\text{image height}}{\text{object height}}$$

Magnification is a ratio and so has no units.

Image height and object height should both be measured in either mm or cm.

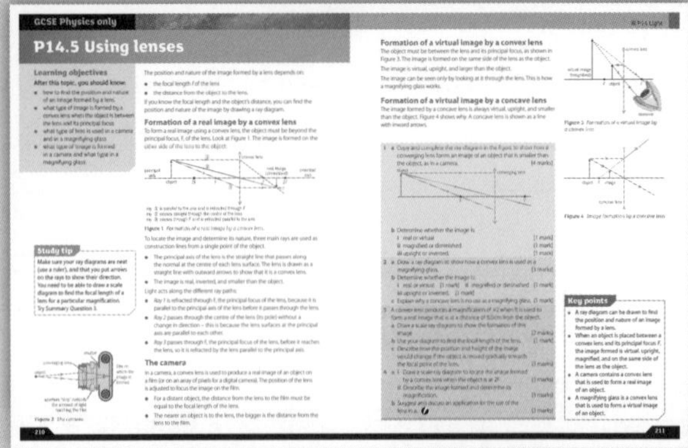
GCSE Physics only
P14.5 Using lenses

WS 1.2
MS 3b, 3c 5a, 5b, 5c

Aiming for	Outcome	Checkpoint	
		Question	Activity
Aiming for GRADE 4	Identify the optical axis and focal point for a diagram showing image formation.		Starter 1, Main 1, Plenary 2
↓	Identify the position of the image formed by a lens using pre-existing rays on a diagram.		Main 1
	Describe how a focused image can be formed by a camera lens.	1	Main 1
Aiming for GRADE 6	With support, construct ray diagrams showing the formation of images by a convex lens and a concave lens.	3	Main 1, Main 2
↓	Describe the image formed by a magnifying glass.	2, End of chapter 7	Main 2
	Describe the image formed by a camera lens.	1, End of chapter 4	Main 1
Aiming for GRADE 8	From first principles, construct ray diagrams showing the formation of images by a convex lens and a concave lens.	3, 4, End of chapter 5, 6, 7	Main 1, Main 2
↓	Fully describe the properties of an image (real, virtual, magnified, diminished, upright, and inverted) based on a ray diagram.	1, 2, End of chapter 7	Main 1, Main 2
	Use scale diagrams to determine the size of an image produced by a lens.	End of chapter 5	Main 1

Maths
Students employ geometrical techniques to produce a range of ray diagrams to determine the position and properties of an image (5a, 5b).

Literacy
Students discuss developments in technology and the application of lenses in a variety of situations.

Practical

Title	Real image from a convex lens
Equipment	converging lens (focal length approx.10 cm), metre ruler, illuminated object, screen
Overview of method	Set the screen in a fixed position at the end of the ruler or optical bench. Position the lens 10 cm in front of it, then place an illuminated object somewhere along the bench. By moving the lens, the image can be brought into focus on the screen. Reposition the object to show that further adjustment needs to be made to form a clear image again.
Safety considerations	Lamps in ray boxes can become very hot and so should be given time to cool.

Starter	Support/Extend	Resources
Magnified mystery objects (5 min) Show close-up photographs of a range of mystery objects for the students to identify. Include a fly's eye, human hairs, Velcro hooks, hairs on a gecko's feet.		
The right path (10 min) Provide students with some diagrams of sets of three parallel rays reaching to lenses, along with the description of the lens (focal length and type). Students use the interactive to identify what happens to the rays.	**Support:** Show the path of one of the three rays.	**Interactive:** The right path
Main	**Support/Extend**	**Resources**
Real image from a convex lens (20 min) The construction of this diagram is time consuming but critical to understanding image formation. Students should follow stages and construct at least one diagram showing the formation of a real image. Demonstrate the adjustment of a lens to form a clear image on the screen described in the practical. Compare this with the movement of a lens on a real camera.	**Support:** Partially completed ray diagrams can be provided. **Extend:** Students can compare this with the focusing systems in the eye.	**Activity:** Constructing ray diagrams
Virtual image from a lens (20 min) The students should follow the ray construction technique again and produce a ray diagram showing the position of the image. Discuss the difference between a real and virtual image again. Students should then look at concave lens and the images formed. Again, the students should practise construction of the appropriate diagram using the appropriate rays.	**Support:** Students should compare a few convex lenses to see which makes the best magnifying glass. **Extend:** An extension sheet is available on lenses used for different purposes, and the corresponding ray diagrams.	
Plenary	**Support/Extend**	**Resources**
Camera developments (10 min) Discuss the advantages and disadvantages of film-based technology in comparison with digital photography. Show students some important historical images and explain how the technology has developed into the pervasive technology of today.	**Support:** Show images of cameras throughout history. **Extend:** Discuss the effects of changes such as reduction in lens size.	
Know your rays (5 min) Provide the students with a ray diagram for the image formed by a convex lens, and ask them to label the important features.	**Support:** Provide the appropriate labels for the students to add.	
Homework		
The students should draw ray diagrams to locate the images formed by a variety of lenses. These can include convex and concave lenses with objects placed inside and outside the focal length.	**Support:** Provide partially completed diagrams on graph paper. **Extend:** Provide written descriptions for the students to produce diagrams from.	

kerboodle

A Kerboodle highlight for this lesson is **WebQuest: Our visions of vision.** Refer to the **Content map** on Kerboodle for a full list of resources and assessment.

P14 Light

Overview of P14 Light

The students began this chapter by looking at the reflection of light by plane mirrors using both a wave front and ray model. This led to descriptions of real and virtual images and their properties and why images are not formed by 'rough' surfaces.

Then they move on to investigate and describe refraction of light in more detail – analysing the change in direction of rays at boundaries between surfaces. The students also describe the relationship between colour and wavelength for visible light investigating the reflection of both white and coloured light from coloured or white surfaces along with the additive nature of coloured light. They described the differences between translucent and transparent media.

Students also describe the action of lenses using the ray model of light and a range of ray diagrams. This includes the behaviour of converging and diverging lenses with an investigation of image formation for a converging lens. The image properties have been described along with the concept of magnification and its calculation from image and object height. Methods used to construct ray diagrams for the convex lens for objects at a range of positions have been described alongside image formation for a concave lens.

Required practical

All students are expected to have carried out the required practical:

Practical	Topic
Investigate the reflection of light by different types of surface and the refraction of light by different substances.	P14.2 P14.3

You can find additional support for the maths skills covered in this chapter on **MyMaths**, including using an appropriate number of significant figures, understanding and using the symbols: =, <, <<, >>, >, ∝ , ~, and changing the subject of an equation.

For this chapter, the following assessments are available on Kerboodle:

P14 Checkpoint quiz: Light
P14 Progress quiz: Light 1
P14 Progress quiz: Light 2
P14 On your marks: Light
P14 Exam-style questions and mark scheme: Light

Checkpoint follow up lesson

A student's route through this lesson can be determined using the Checkpoint assessment. Percentage pass marks are supplied in the Checkpoint teacher notes.

For each successive route through it is assumed that the student can perform to their current route as well as previous routes. For example, students working at Aiming for 6 are assumed to be secure in Aiming for 4 knowledge and understanding and working towards achieving all the learning outcomes for Aiming for 6.

	Aiming for 4	Aiming for 6	Aiming for 8
Learning outcomes	State the law of reflection.	Describe how an image is formed in a mirror.	Explain the formation of an image in a mirror using the law of reflection.
	Describe how light is refracted.	Explain how and why light is refracted.	Explain how and why light is refracted in a variety of contexts.
	State the appearance of coloured objects in coloured light.	Describe what filters do and the appearance of coloured objects in coloured light.	Explain what filters do and the appearance of coloured objects in coloured light.
	Describe what convex and concave lenses do.	Explain what convex and concave lenses do.	Use your knowledge of convex lenses to analyse data from an experiment, and apply it to everyday situations.
Starter	**Seeing the invisible (10 min)** Give each group a beaker of glycerol that has two test tubes in it: one containing water and the other containing glycerol. Alternatively show an image of this demonstration. Ask groups to come up with an explanation for what they observe using ideas about reflection and refraction. Each group writes their explanation on a whiteboard to be kept for the plenary. **Your eyes deceive you! (5 min)** Project an inverted illusion such as the rotating pink dots, or union jack where the students have to stare at the image for a minute then look at a white screen. Discuss what is happening in the eye and the difference between the visible spectrum and the way that the eye works in detecting red, green and blue using cones in the retina.		
Differentiated checkpoint activity	Students use the Checkpoint follow-up sheet to complete one of three activities: • investigate reflection and refraction • prepare a leaflet to explain how coloured clothing changes under different coloured light • investigate lenses. The Aiming for 4 Checkpoint follow-up sheet provides structured support and simple questions for students to consolidate their understanding from the tasks of the lesson. The Aiming for 6 Checkpoint follow-up sheet provides some support and questions for students to consolidate their understanding from the tasks of the lesson. The Aiming for 8 Checkpoint follow-up sheet provides minimal support and questions for students to consolidate their understanding from the tasks of the lesson.		
	Kerboodle resource P14 Checkpoint follow up: Aiming for 4, P14 Checkpoint follow up: Aiming for 6, P14 Checkpoint follow up: Aiming for 8		
Plenary	**Seeing the invisible (10 min)** Students revisit their explanation of the disappearing test tube in the starter. Each group refines its explanation and the class moves around the room and puts a mark out of 10 on each board for the quality of the explanation. The winning team could get a prize. **How much bigger? (5 min)** Give students A4 dry wipe boards, pens and an eraser. Give out Perspex rods, and ask students to experiment by looking at a line of text through the rod as they hold it at different distances. Aiming at 4 students can estimate the largest magnification that is possible using the rod, and Aiming at 6/8 students should do the same, then draw a diagram to show how the image is produced.		
Progression	Encourage students to think about explaining the action of filters and the appearance of coloured objects in terms of absorption, and use ray diagrams to show what happens when light is reflected, or goes through a lens.	Encourage students to think about using ray diagrams in the explanation of how images form, or how light goes through lenses.	Encourage students to think about using ray diagrams in the explanation.

P 15 Electromagnetism

15.1 Magnetic fields

AQA spec Link: 7.1.1 The poles of a magnet are the places where the magnetic forces are strongest. When two magnets are brought close together they exert a force on each other. Two like poles repel each other. Two unlike poles attract each other. Attraction and repulsion between two magnetic poles are examples of non-contact force.

A permanent magnet produces its own magnetic field. An induced magnet is a material that becomes a magnet when it is placed in a magnetic field. Induced magnetism always causes a force of attraction. When removed from the magnetic field an induced magnet loses most/all of its magnetism quickly.

Students should be able to describe:

- the attraction and repulsion between unlike and like poles for permanent magnets
- the difference between permanent and induced magnets.

7.1.2 The region around a magnet where a force acts on another magnet or on a magnetic material (iron, steel, cobalt, and nickel) is called the magnetic field.

The force between a magnet and a magnetic material is always one of attraction.

The strength of the magnetic field depends on the distance from the magnet. The field is strongest at the poles of the magnet.

The direction of the magnetic field at any point is given by the direction of the force that would act on another north pole placed at that point. The direction of a magnetic field line is from the north (seeking) pole of a magnet to the south (seeking) pole of the magnet.

A magnetic compass contains a small bar magnet. The Earth has a magnetic field. The compass needle points in the direction of the Earth's magnetic field.

Students should be able to:

- describe how to plot the magnetic field pattern of a magnet using a compass
- draw the magnetic field pattern of a bar magnet showing how strength and direction change from one point to another
- explain how the behaviour of a magnetic compass is related to evidence that the core of the Earth must be magnetic.

WS 2.2

Aiming for	Outcome	Checkpoint	
		Question	Activity
Aiming for GRADE 4	State the names of the poles of a magnet.	1	Main 1
	Describe the interaction of magnetic poles (attraction and repulsion).	1, 2	Starter 2, Main 1
	List some magnetic and non-magnetic metals.		Main 1
Aiming for GRADE 6	Sketch the shape of a magnetic field around a bar magnet.	End of chapter 1	Main 2
	Describe how the shape of a magnetic field can be investigated.	2	Main 2
	Compare the Earth's magnetic field to that of a bar magnet.		Main 1, Homework
Aiming for GRADE 8	Describe the regions in a magnetic field where magnetic forces are greatest using the idea of field lines.	4, End of chapter 1	Main 2
	Explain in detail how magnetism can be induced in some materials.		Main 2
	Plan in detail how the strength of a magnetic field can be investigated.	4	Plenary 1

Maths
Students use graphical representations of fields (field lines).

Literacy
Students describe the interactions of magnetic poles clearly and concisely.

Key words
magnetic field

Practical

Title	Investigating bar magnets
Equipment	two bar magnets, cotton thread, retort stand and clamp
Overview of method	Suspend a bar magnet from a retort stand and clamp using string. Use a compass to identify the end of the magnet that points north, then hold the north pole of a second bar magnet near the suspended magnet. Finally hold the south pole of the second bar magnet to the suspended magnet.

Title	Plotting a magnetic field
Equipment	bar magnet, plotting compass, A4 paper
Overview of method	Place the bar magnet on an A4 sheet of paper. Mark a dot near the north pole of the bar magnet. Place the tail of the compass needle above the dot, and mark a second dot at the tip of the needle. Repeat the procedure with the tail over the new dot each time until the compass reaches the S-pole of the magnet. Draw a line through the dots and mark the direction from the N-pole to the S-pole.

Starter	Support/Extend	Resources
Force fields (10 min) Interactive where students categorise a list of the various forces they have studied into contact and non-contact forces. **Lost** (5 min) Show the students a compass (or a compass application for a mobile phone) and ask them how it works in terms of magnetic fields and poles.	**Extend:** Students should list the factors that affect the magnitude of the forces. **Extend:** Students describe other technology for finding their position and direction.	**Interactive:** Force fields
Main	**Support/Extend**	**Resources**
Investigating bar magnets (15 min) Students test the properties of magnets using the practical. Discuss the interaction of the bar magnet with the Earth's magnetic field, comparing the two. Demonstrate that only some metals are magnetic. **Plotting a magnetic field** (25 min) Demonstrate the existence of a magnetic field around a bar magnet using iron filings and then allow the students to plot the field pattern with the plotting compasses. Discuss regions where the field lines are closer together as regions where the force would be strongest. Show induced magnetism by lifting a paperclip with a strong bar magnet. A second clip will attach to the first even though the original clip was not magnetic. Explain the effect using the figure in the student book.	**Extend:** Discuss the naming of the poles of the magnets and the poles of the Earth's magnetic field. **Support:** Provide a list of the magnetic materials students are required to know from the specification. **Extend:** Use the idea of domains within the atoms in materials aligning to explain the effect.	**Practical:** Magnets and magnetic fields
Plenary	**Support/Extend**	**Resources**
Stronger fields (10 min) Show the students a horseshoe magnet and ask them to discuss the shape the field might be. **Applications** (5 min) Ask the students to list as many applications of permanent magnets as they can. Would these applications be improved if the magnetism could be turned off and on?	**Extend:** Students describe how the direction of the field lines can be found.	
Homework		
Students complete the WebQuest where they investigate the the scientific claims behind magnetic therapies, such as the magnetic healing bracelets sold by some retailers. They use their research to write a letter to a friend to recommend whether or not they should buy a product.		**WebQuest:** Magnetic therapies

kerboodle

A Kerboodle highlight for this lesson is **Bump up your grade: Magnets and magnetic fields**. Refer to the **Content map** on Kerboodle for a full list of resources and assessment.

P15.2 Magnetic fields of electric current

AQA spec Link: 7.2.1 When a current flows through a conducting wire a magnetic field is produced around the wire. The strength of the magnetic field depends on the current through the wire and the distance from the wire.

Shaping a wire to form a solenoid increases the strength of the magnetic field created by a current through the wire. The magnetic field inside a solenoid is strong and uniform.

The magnetic field around a solenoid has a similar shape to that of a bar magnet. Adding an iron core increases the strength of the magnetic field of a solenoid. An electromagnet is a solenoid with an iron core.

Students should be able to:

- describe how the magnetic effect of a current can be demonstrated
- draw the magnetic field pattern for a straight wire carrying a current and for a solenoid (showing the direction of the field)
- explain how a solenoid arrangement can increase the magnetic effect of the current.

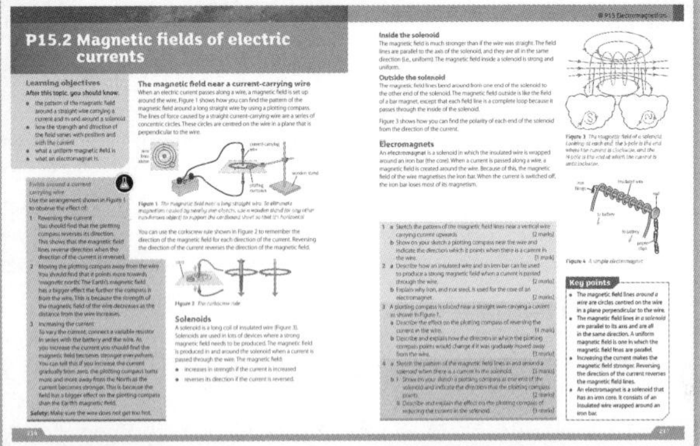

WS 2.2
MS 4a

Aiming for	Outcome	Checkpoint	
		Question	Activity
Aiming for GRADE 4	State that the magnetic field produced by a current-carrying wire is circular.	1	Main 1
	Describe the effect of increasing the current on the magnetic field around a wire.	2	Main 1
	Describe the effect of reversing the direction of the current in the wire.	2	Main 1
Aiming for GRADE 6	Use the corkscrew rule to determine the direction of the field around a current-carrying wire.	2	Main 1
	Describe the shape of the field produced by a solenoid.	3	Main 2
	Describe the factors that affect the strength or direction of the magnetic field around a wire and solenoid.		Main 2, Plenary 1
Aiming for GRADE 8	Determine the polarity of the ends of a solenoid from the direction of the current.	3	Main 2
	Sketch the shape of the field surrounding a solenoid relating this to the direction of the current through the coil.	3, 4	Main 2
	Plan a detailed investigation into the factors that affect the strength of the magnetic field around a solenoid.		Main 2, Plenary 1

Maths
Students analyse graphical data to discuss the relationship between two factors (4a).

Literacy
Students describe the operation of a variety of devices in a structured way.

Practical

Title	Fields around a current-carrying wire
Equipment	thick copper wire passing through a cardboard or Perspex sheet, power supply or battery pack, plotting compass, iron filings, variable resistor
Overview of method	Suspend the wire from a wooden stand so that it passes through the card vertically (Figure 1 in the student book). Connect the wire to a power supply and pass a current through it. A compass placed near the wire should be deflected, or iron filings should form ring patterns.
Safety considerations	Limit the current through the wire with a variable resistor.

Starter	Support/Extend	Resources
Electricity and magnetism recap (10 min) Complete the interactive with a set of electricity questions to establish the students' prior knowledge. **Current effect** (5 min) Students should describe the factors which affect the current in a wire and the physical effects a current has in, and around, the wire.	**Support:** Differentiate the questions as appropriate. **Extend:** Students should describe the nature of a current in terms of charge movement.	**Interactive:** Electricity and magnetism recap
Main	**Support/Extend**	**Resources**
Fields around a current-carrying wire (20 min) Demonstrate the magnetic effect of a wire with the practical, or let the students find it. Discuss and then test the effect of reversing the current and/or increasing it. Ensure that students can apply the corkscrew rule (also known as the right-hand grip rule) to determine the direction of the field around the wire. **Fields around a solenoid** (20 min) Show a solenoid and compare it to a bar magnet. Connect it to a power supply and show the deflection on a plotting compass as the compass is moved around the coil. Students then plan an investigation into the factors which would affect the strength of this field.	**Support:** Diagrams of the corkscrew rule for current moving 'upwards' and downwards' are useful here. **Extend:** The students can discuss the shape of the field in more depth.	**Practical:** Fields around a current-carrying wire
Plenary	**Support/Extend**	**Resources**
More power (10 min) Ask the students to outline a test to see what affects the strength of the field around a solenoid. They should choose one possible factor (current, number of loops in coil, type of core) and form a plan to see if there is a qualitative or quantitative relationship that can be determined. **Space boots** (5 min) In space, astronauts are weightless but need some way of walking around the outer surface of a space station. Can the students describe a system to do this?	**Support:** Provide methods for the students to use in the investigation.	
Homework	**Support/Extend**	**Resources**
Students start or complete their plan to test what affects the strength of the field around a solenoid (from plenary 1).		

P15.3 Electromagnets in devices

AQA spec Link: 7.2.1 Students should be able to interpret diagrams of electromagnetic devices in order to explain how they work.

WS 1.4

MS 4a

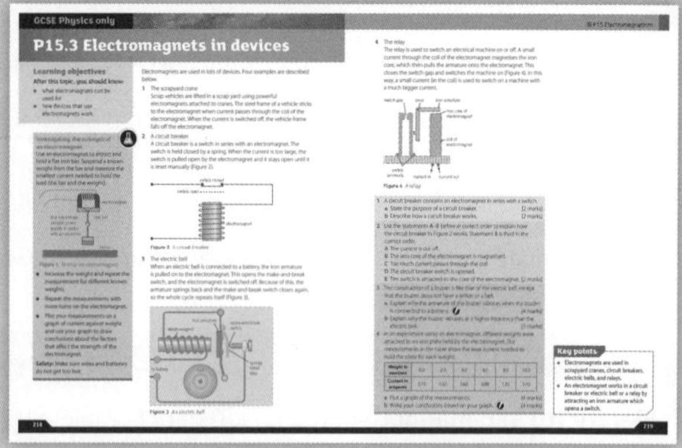

Aiming for	Outcome	Checkpoint	
		Question	Activity
Aiming for GRADE 4	List some electromagnet devices.		Main
	State some uses of electromagnets.		Main
	State the factors which increase the strength of an electromagnet.	4	Main
Aiming for GRADE 6	Describe the structure of an electromagnet in simple terms.	1	Main
	Describe the operation of simple devices that use electromagnets.	2, 3	Main
	Investigate the factors that affect the strength of an electromagnet.	4	Main
Aiming for GRADE 8	Explain the effect of an iron core on the strength of an electromagnet in terms of the magnetic field.		Main
	Describe in detail the operation of an electric bell.	3	Main
	Evaluate in detail an experiment into the factors which affect the strength of an electromagnet.		Main

Maths
Students analyse graphical data produced from an investigation to discuss the relationship between two factors (4a).

Literacy
Students describe the operation of electromagnetic devices in a structured way.

Practical

Title	Investigating electromagnets – strength
Equipment	low-voltage power supply, thick (insulated) copper wire, large iron nail, short length of wooden dowel, small iron bar
Overview of method	Set up the electromagnet so that it can hold the iron nail. Suspend a known weight from the nail and measure the smallest current needed to hold both the nail and the weight.
Safety considerations	Ensure that the current in the electromagnet is limited and that it does not become hot.

Title	Investigating electromagnets – applications
Equipment	small electromagnet, circuit breaker, lamps and low voltage power supply, electric bell, circuit with simple magnetic relay
Overview of method	**Lifting electromagnet** A lifting electromagnet can be built from a coil of wire wrapped around an iron core (large nail). Use about 30 loops of wire and connect to a low-voltage power supply set to 5 V, but make sure that the coil does not overheat. **Circuit breaker** Set a circuit breaker in a simple bulb circuit. Use a low-current one that cuts out before the bulb blows. **Electric bell** There are a variety of electric bells designed to demonstrate the function. Set these up according to the instructions and then explain the process that causes the hammer to move back and forth. **Relay** Place a relay in a simple circuit to demonstrate its operation. It is sufficient to build a low-voltage circuit including a relay and trigger it with an electromagnet or a bar magnet.
Safety considerations	Ensure that the current in the electromagnet is limited and that it does not become hot.

Starter	Support/Extend	Resources
On and off again (5 min) Use an electromagnet to lift a long chain of paperclips. Turn it off and ask the students to explain, in terms of forces, what has happened during the demonstration.		
Safety first (10 min) Students to examine the instructions for constructing and testing an electromagnet. They then use the instructions to carry out a risk assessment by matching hazards to their control measures.	**Support:** Provide a list of risks and allow the students to describe how they can be controlled.	**Interactive:** Safety first
Main	**Support/Extend**	**Resources**
Investigating electromagnets (40 min) Recap the magnetic field formed by a solenoid. Students investigate the usefulness of this field by testing the strength of electromagnets and the factors that affect it.	**Extend:** Student test the effect of changing the number of loops of wire on the electromagnet or the removal of the iron core.	**Practical:** Investigating electromagnets
Students then observe and describe the operation of a range of electromagnetic devices as listed in the practical. Students could investigate one or two of the applications, then collate their results in groups.	**Extend:** An extension sheet is available where students interpret diagrams of electromagnetic devices in order to explain how they work.	**Extension:** What does it do?
Plenary	**Support/Extend**	**Resources**
Safety last (5 min) Students review their safety notes from the starter in light of their experiences with the electromagnets.		
Magnetic levitation (10 min) Show the students how magnetic devices have been used in transport systems, such as mag-lev trains, using video clips. Discuss the advantages and disadvantages of this approach.		
Homework	**Support/Extend**	**Resources**
Students find and describe the use of as many electromagnetic devices as they can. They should note the importance of electric motors.		

kerboodle

A Kerboodle highlight for this lesson is **Bump up your grade: Electromagnetism (and the solenoid)**. Refer to the **Content map** on Kerboodle for a full list of resources and assessment.

P15.4 The motor effect

AQA spec Link: 7.2.2 When a conductor carrying a current is placed in a magnetic field the magnet producing the field and the conductor exert a force on each other. This is called the motor effect.

Students should be able to show that Fleming's left-hand rule represents the relative orientation of the force, the current in the conductor, and the magnetic field.

Students should be able to recall the factors that affect the size of the force on the conductor.

For a conductor at right angles to a magnetic field and carrying a current:

force = magnetic flux density × current × length

$[F = B\,I\,l]$

force, F, in newtons, N

magnetic flux density, B, in tesla, T

current, I, in amperes, A (amp is acceptable for ampere)

length, l, in metres, m

7.2.3 A coil of wire carrying a current in a magnetic field tends to rotate. This is the basis of an electric motor.

Students should be able to explain how the force on a conductor in a magnetic field causes the rotation of the coil in an electric motor.

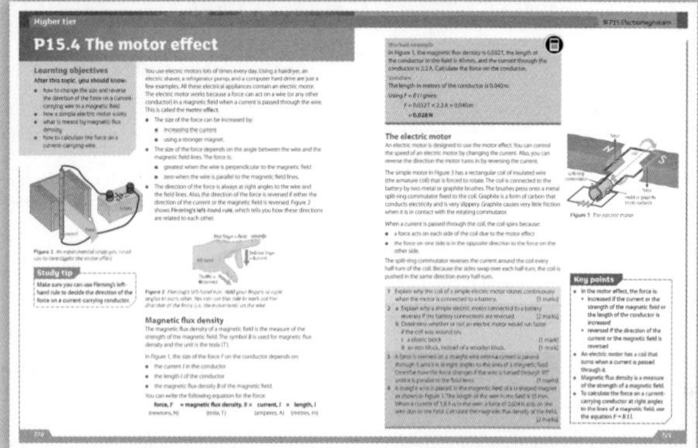
Higher tier

P15.4 The motor effect

Learning objectives

After this topic, you should know:

- how to change the size and reverse the direction of the force on a current-carrying wire in a magnetic field
- how a simple electric motor works
- what is meant by magnetic flux density
- how to calculate the force on a current-carrying wire

You use electric motors lots of times every day. Using a hairdryer, an electric shaver, a refrigerator pump and a computer hard drive are just a few examples. All these electrical appliances contain an electric motor. The electric motor works because a force can act on a wire (or any other conductor) in a magnetic field when a current is passed through the wire. This is called the **motor effect**.

- The size of the force can be increased by:
  - increasing the current
  - using a stronger magnet.
- The size of the force depends on the angle between the wire and the magnetic field lines. The force is:
  - greatest when the wire is perpendicular to the magnetic field
  - zero when the wire is parallel to the magnetic field lines.
- The direction of the force is always at right angles to the wire and the field lines. Also, the direction of the force is reversed if either the direction of the current or the magnetic field is reversed. Figure 2 shows **Fleming's left-hand rule**, which tells you how these directions are related to each other.

Study tip

Make sure you can use Fleming's left-hand rule to decide the direction of the force on a current-carrying conductor.

Magnetic flux density

The magnetic flux density of a magnetic field is the measure of the strength of the magnetic field. The symbol B is used for magnetic flux density and the unit is the tesla (T).

In Figure 1, the size of the force F on the conductor depends on:

- the current I in the conductor
- the length l of the conductor
- the magnetic flux density B of the magnetic field.

You can write the following equation for the force:

force, F (newtons, N) = magnetic flux density, B (tesla, T) × current, I (amperes, A) × length, l (metres, m)

The electric motor

An electric motor is designed to use the motor effect. You can control the speed of an electric motor by changing the current. Also, you can reverse the direction the motor turns in by reversing the current.

The simple motor in Figure 3 has a rectangular coil of insulated wire (the armature coil) that is forced to rotate. The coil is connected to the battery by two metal or graphite brushes. The brushes press onto a metal split-ring commutator fixed to the coil. Graphite is a form of carbon that conducts electricity and is very slippery. Graphite causes very little friction when it is in contact with the rotating commutator.

When a current is passed through the coil, the coil spins because:

- a force acts on each side of the coil due to the motor effect
- the force on one side is in the opposite direction to the force on the other side.

The split-ring commutator reverses the current around the coil every half-turn of the coil. Because the sides swap over each half-turn, the coil is pushed in the same direction every half-turn.

Key points

- In the motor effect, the force is:
  - increased if the current or the strength of the magnetic field or the length of the conductor is increased
  - reversed if the direction of the current or the magnetic field is reversed
- An electric motor has a coil that turns when a current is passed through it.
- Magnetic flux density is a measure of the strength of a magnetic field.
- To calculate the force on a current-carrying conductor at right angles to the lines of a magnetic field, use the equation $F = B\,I\,l$.

MS 3b, 3c

Aiming for	Outcome	Checkpoint	
		Question	Activity
Aiming for GRADE 6	Describe how the force acting on a wire due to the motor effect can be increased.	3	Main
	Apply Fleming's left-hand rule to determine the direction of the force acting on a conductor.	3	Main
	Calculate the force acting on a conductor when it is placed in a magnetic field.	4	Main
Aiming for GRADE 8	Describe and explain in detail the operation of a motor.	1, 2	Starter 2, Main, Plenary 2
	Perform calculations involving rearrangements of the equation $F = BIl$.	4	Main
	Investigate the factors that affect the rotation of an electric motor.		Main

Maths

Students calculate the force acting on a wire using the relationship $F = BIl$ (3c).

Literacy

Students describe the operation of a loudspeaker and a motor.

Key words

motor effect, Fleming's left-hand rule

Practical

Title	The motor effect
Equipment	battery, length of wire (stiff wire works best), variable resistor, leads, two magnets mounted on U frame (or a U-shaped magnet)
Overview of method	Place the wire between the two magnets and pass a small current through it. The variable resistor allows control of the current to show its effect. Alternatively, as a simple demonstration of the effect, a wider strip of foil can be used instead of the stiff wire. This will deflect or bend when a current is passed through it, demonstrating that a force is experienced.
Safety considerations	Limit the current by using a variable resistor.

Starter	Support/Extend	Resources
Magnetic magic (5 min) Some magicians use magnetic effects to levitate objects. Show some footage of this levitation and ask the students to explain the 'magic' to see if they realise there is a scientific principle behind the mystery.	**Extend:** Ask the students about the properties the levitated objects must have.	
Motor demonstration (10 min) Demonstrate an electric motor lifting a small load from the floor. Ask the students to explain what can be done to increase the force the motor can provide. They should be able to identify increasing the current.	**Extend:** Ask students to determine the power of the motor by giving them the load it lifts, the height it moves, and the time taken. Does this power match the electrical power provided ($P = VI$)? Why not?	
Main	**Support/Extend**	**Resources**
The motor effect (40 min) Demonstrate the motor effect and discuss the factors that affect the size and direction of the force. Show how Fleming's left-hand rule can be used to determine the direction of motion for the wire. Recap the idea of strong or weak magnetic fields and then introduce the equation, describing how this links to the earlier demonstration. The students should try some example calculations to embed the equation. Discuss how this force could be applied to produce continual movement. Allow the students to construct a motor or investigate the operation of one. If time permits, the students can construct small model motors from standard kits.	**Extend:** Ask the students to suggest a mathematical relationship between the factors. **Support:** Use calculation frames along with examples. **Support:** Provide constructed motors for the students to investigate. **Extend:** Discuss in detail the function of the split-ring commutator. **Extend:** Students complete the extension sheet to develop qualitative and quantitative understanding of the motor effect and some of its applications.	**Practical:** The motor effect
Plenary	**Support/Extend**	**Resources**
The motor effect (10 min) Students use the interactive to complete a paragraph to describe the motor effect. They then carry out some calculations using the equation $F = B I l$. **Motor competition** (5 min) The students should select the motor that is smoothest and most stable as the winner and give a prize.		**Interactive:** The motor effect
Homework		
Students can identify the differences in the sizes of loudspeakers used on different devices and explain why these are needed to produce a range of sounds.	**Extend:** Expect explanations in terms of mass, momentum, energy, and frequency.	

kerboodle

A Kerboodle highlight for this lesson is **Working scientifically: Current through a motor**. Refer to the **Content map** on Kerboodle for a full list of resources and assessment.

P15.5 The generator effect

AQA spec Link: 7.3.1 If an electrical conductor moves relative to a magnetic field or if there is a change in the magnetic field around a conductor, a potential difference is induced across the ends of the conductor. If the conductor is part of a complete circuit, a current is induced in the conductor. This is called the generator effect.

An induced current generates a magnetic field that opposes the original change, either the movement of the conductor or the change in magnetic field.

Students should be able to recall the factors that affect the size of the induced potential difference/induced current.

Students should be able to recall the factors that affect the direction of the induced potential difference/induced current.

Students should be able to apply the principles of the generator effect in a given context.

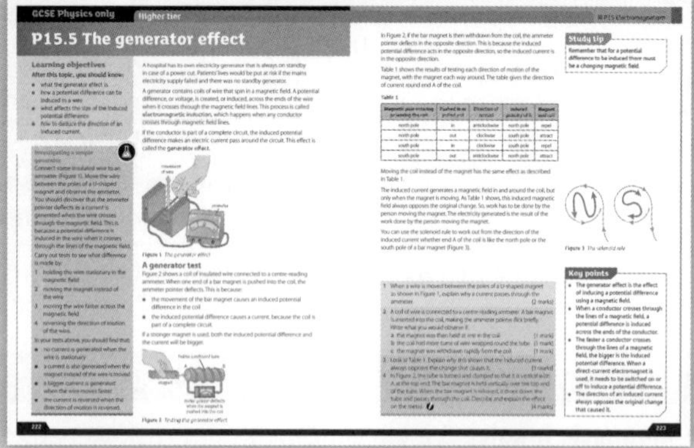

Aiming for	Outcome	Checkpoint	
		Question	**Activity**
Aiming for GRADE 6	Describe electromagnetic induction in a wire.	1	Main 1
	Identify the factors that affect the size of an induced current in a wire.	2	Main 1
	Identify the direction of current induced in a solenoid.	2, End of chapter 3	Main 2
Aiming for GRADE 8	Explain why relative movement of a wire through a magnetic field is required to cause induction.	1, 3	Main 1
	Independently investigate the magnitude and polarity of a current induced in a solenoid when a magnet is moved in it.	2	Main 2
	Describe how a changing current in one coil can be used to induce a current in another.	3	Main 2

Literacy
Students form descriptions of the complex interactions between conductors and magnets.

Key words
electromagnetic induction, generator effect

Practical

Title	Investigating a simple generator
Equipment	strong U-shaped magnet (or pair of strong magnets in U-shaped steel block), stiff wire, leads, sensitive ammeter or galvanometer
Overview of method	The students simply move the wire up and down through the magnet, cutting the magnetic field lines. The ammeter should register a small current in one direction when the wire is moving down and a small current in the opposite direction when it is moving up. The size of the current should increase if the wire is moved more quickly.

Title	Induction in a solenoid
Equipment	cardboard tube, sensitive ammeter, thin insulated wire, strong bar magnet
Overview of method	The students connect the circuit as shown in the student book and move the magnet into and out of the tube. They should try all possible polarities and movement directions.

Starter	Support/Extend	Resources
Motor recap (10 min) Show the students a motor and ask them to identify the factors that affect the power of the motor. Discuss what the students think would happen in the coils if the motor was forced to rotate. **Generate ideas** (5 min) Show footage of a large generator in operation in a power station. Ask students to list the key components and explain why it has to rotate.	**Support:** An animation that shows the forces acting on the coil can be useful here.	
Main	**Support/Extend**	**Resources**
Investigating a simple generator (20 min) Demonstrate the principle of electromagnetic induction by moving a wire connected to a galvanometer or sensitive ammeter in a magnetic field. Introduce the term induction and ask the students to discuss the factors that may affect the size of the induced p.d. The students test out the factors suggested as described in the practical, noting changes in the induced current.	**Extend:** Students should suggest their own variables to then investigate in the subsequent practical.	**Practical:** Investigating a simple generator
Induction in a solenoid (20 min) Demonstrate or allow students to test induction in a solenoid as described in the practical. They must identify all possible combinations and note that there must always be a relative movement between the wire and the magnet in order to produce the current.	**Support:** Provide a list of variables to investigate and a partial results table for students to complete.	
Plenary	**Support/Extend**	**Resources**
Conservation (10 min) Students use the interactive to explain how they know that energy is conserved in all of these generator tests by using the idea of work done by a force and work done by a current. **Coil checks** (5 min) Ask students to complete or correct a version of the summary table similar to Table 1 in the student book that has some missing or incorrect information.	**Extend:** The factors used to calculate work done in each case should be identified.	**Interactive:** Coil checks
Homework		
Students should find out who first discovered the generator effect and what was initially done with this discovery.		

kerboodle

A Kerboodle highlight for this lesson is **Bump up your grade: Induced current and EMF**. Refer to the **Content map** on Kerboodle for a full list of resources and assessment.

P15.6 The alternating-current generator

AQA spec Link: 7.2.4 Loudspeakers and headphones use the motor effect to convert variations in current in electrical circuits to the pressure variations in sound waves.

Students should be able to explain how a moving-coil loudspeaker and headphones work.

7.3.2 The generator effect is used in an alternator to generate a.c. and in a dynamo to generate d.c.

Students should be able to:

- explain how the generator effect is used in an alternator to generate a.c. and in a dynamo to generate d.c.
- draw/interpret graphs of potential difference generated in the coil against time.

7.3.3 Microphones use the generator effect to convert the pressure variations in sound waves into variations in current in electrical circuits.

Students should be able to explain how a moving-coil microphone works.

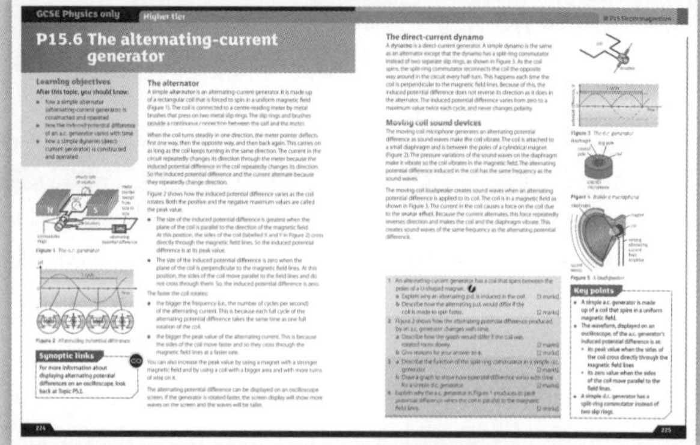
GCSE Physics only Higher tier
P15.6 The alternating-current generator

WS 1.4
MS 4a

Aiming for	Outcome	Checkpoint Question	Checkpoint Activity
Aiming for GRADE 6	Describe the operation of an alternator, moving-coil microphone and loudspeaker in simple terms.	1, 2	Main 1, 2
	Describe the operation of a d.c. generator.	3, End of chapter 4	Main 1
	Identify the period and peak output voltage for generators from an oscilloscope trace.		Main 1 Plenary 2
Aiming for GRADE 8	Describe the output of an alternator, linking this to the position of the coil to the magnetic field and the speed of rotation.	1, 2	Main 1, 2
	Explain the operation of a d.c. generator and its output.	3	Main 1
	Explain why the peak voltage of an a.c. generator is produced when the plane of the coil is parallel to the magnetic field lines.	4	Main 1

Maths
Students analyse a range of graphs to determine the period and amplitude of an a.c. signal (4a).

Literacy
Students describe the key features of oscilloscope graphs to each other, comparing the patterns.

Key words
alternator, dynamo, motor effect

Practical

Title	Alternators and generators
Equipment	a.c. generator, dynamo, oscilloscope, connecting leads
Overview of method	Connect the generators, one at a time, to the oscilloscope. Turn the generators at different speeds to display the output of each, noting the changes in period and amplitude for the waveforms.
Safety considerations	Ensure that only low-voltage generators are used.

Starter	Support/Extend	Resources
Oscilloscope recap (10 min) Show the students an oscilloscope and ask then to describe what it does. They should describe the key controls and what they will do to the waveform displayed. **Sound waves** (5 min) The students describe sound waves and their properties, particularly the frequency and amplitude.		
Main	**Support/Extend**	**Resources**
Alternators and generators (30 min) Show the students an a.c. generator and compare its construction to a motor. Ask the students what will happen if the coil is made to rotate and then demonstrate this using the practical. Describe in detail how the movement of the coil links to the output waveform. Demonstrate a generator and its output, asking the students to explain the waveform produced. Link this to the brushes and the changes of connection. Connect a bicycle dynamo to the oscilloscope to show the waveform. Students should note that this is an a.c. signal.	**Extend:** Focus in detail on the action of the commutator rings, comparing these with split-rings used in motors. **Extend:** An extension sheet is available to develop qualitative understanding of the generator effect and some of its applications.	**Activity:** Alternators and generators **Extension:** Electricity from movement
Microphones (10 min) Show a deconstructed coil microphone, linking closely to the generator effect covered previously. The microphone can be connected to the oscilloscope to link the movement to an electrical signal.	**Support:** Provide cross-sectional diagrams to annotate.	
Plenary	**Support/Extend**	**Resources**
The flywheel (10 min) Demonstrate a flywheel connected to a dynamo and lamp. Ask the students to explain how this could be useful on a bicycle or car.	**Extend:** Discuss the practicality of the flywheels in cars and bicycles. Show real applications.	
Microphones and loudspeakers (10 min) Show a deconstructed coil microphone linking its operation to the generator effect and then show a loudspeaker linking it to the motor effect studied in P15.4	**Support:** Use simple periods. **Extend:** Ask for the frequency of the signal.	**Interactive:** Signal recognition
Homework		
Students can research and report on the many different generators used in electricity production, such as those in wind turbines or wave resources.		

kerboodle

A Kerboodle highlight for this lesson is **Working scientifically: How electricity changed the world**. Refer to the **Content map** on Kerboodle for a full list of resources and assessment.

P15.7 Transformers

AQA spec Link: 7.3.4 A basic transformer consists of a primary coil and a secondary coil wound on an iron core.

Iron is used as it is easily magnetised.

Knowledge of laminations and eddy currents in the core are not required.

层压，薄板 涡流

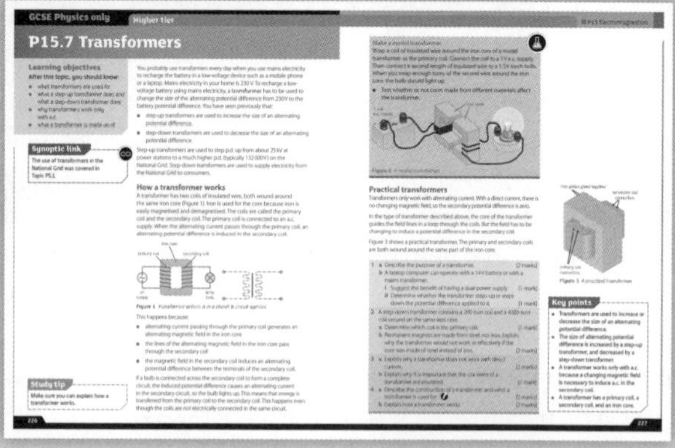
GCSE Physics only Higher tier
P15.7 Transformers

WS 1.4

Aiming for	Outcome	Checkpoint	
		Question	**Activity**
Aiming for GRADE 6	Describe the structure of a transformer.	2, 3, 3, 4	Main, Plenary 2
	Describe the operation of a transformer in simple terms.	1, 3, 4, End of chapter 4	Main
	Explain why transformers only operate with alternating currents.	3	Main
Aiming for GRADE 8	Justify the choice of materials used to construct a transformer.	2	Main
	Describe and explain the operation of a transformer in terms of induction and changes in magnetic fields.	3, 4, End of chapter 4	Main
	Investigate the effect that changing the ratio of the input and output loops on a transformer has on the change in voltage.		Main

Maths
Students discuss the frequency of a signal using SI units.

Literacy
Students describe in detail the complex operation of a transformer. They also describe the structure of the National Grid and the reasons for its design.

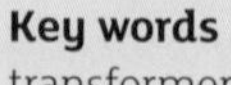

Key words
transformer

Practical

Title	Make a model transformer
Equipment	transformer C core (laminated if possible), insulated wire, low-voltage a.c. power supply, 1.5 V torch bulb, 1.5 V cell, a.c. ammeter and a.c. voltammeter (optional)
Overview of method	Use a power supply that can be locked at 1 V, so that the students cannot produce a high output p.d. with the transformer. The students should wrap about 10 loops of wire for the input coil and a maximum of about 15 for the output coil. This will produce a step-up transformer, but only up to the required 1.5 V for the bulb. Students should also determine that a transformer will only operate with an a.c. source.
Safety considerations	Use a low-voltage power supply and ensure that, even after stepping up, the voltage does not exceed 6 V.

Starter	Support/Extend	Resources
Safety first (5 min) Students complete this sentence scientifically 'If a carbon fishing rod touches a very high potential difference cable …'. The students' responses need to include ideas about high p.d. values causing high currents in conducting materials. **Supplies supplies**! (10 min) Show the students some example power supplies used for phones, laptops, and so on. They should note that although they operate from a 230 V a.c. supply, they have range of different outputs. Ask students for their ideas about what is inside these power supplies.	**Support:** Provide a list of words that the students must use, for example, p.d. resistance, and current. **Extend:** Ask the students to describe half-wave rectification.	
Main	**Support/Extend**	**Resources**
Making a model transformer (40 min) Remind students of the use of transformers in the National Grid, from Topic P5.1. Show a simplified diagram of the National Grid, pointing out the transformers. The students should remember that the transformer changes the voltage and use the terms step-up and step-down appropriately. Students then construct a transformer, if possible, and then describe its operation. They may also investigate the relationship between the coil ratio and voltage ratio. Show the students that the transformer will not operate with direct current and explain that changing magnetic fields are required for induction in the secondary coil.	**Support:** Use a real transformer as a prop and attach labels. **Support:** Students may still construct a transformer to help them to understand the design, even though they are not required to explain how it operates.	**Practical:** Making a model transformer
Plenary	**Support/Extend**	**Resources**
Compare transformers (10 min) The students produce a table that summarises the differences between large National Grid transformers and the smaller switch-mode transformers. **Transformers** (5 min) Students complete the interactive where they identify the appropriate terms to complete a summary on the use of transformers and how they work.		**Interactive:** Transformers
Homework		
Students design a controlled experiment to test which material is best for a transformer core. They need to include some way of measuring the current induced in the secondary coil.	**Support:** Provide some of the diagrams and instructions. **Extend:** Circuit diagrams must be included.	

P15.8 Transformers in action

AQA spec Link: 7.3.4 The ratio of the potential differences across the primary and secondary coils of a transformer V_p and V_s depends on the ratio of the number of turns on each coil, n_p and n_s.

$$\left[\frac{V_P}{V_S} = \frac{n_P}{n_S}\right]$$

potential difference, V_p and V_s in volts, V

In a step-up transformer $V_s > V_p$

In a step-down transformer $V_s < V_p$

If transformers were 100% efficient, the electrical power output would equal the electrical power input.

$V_s \times I_s = V_p \times I_p$

Where $V_s \times I_s$ is the power output (secondary coil) and $V_p \times I_p$ is the power input (primary coil).

power input and output, in watts, W

Students should be able to:

- explain how the effect of an alternating current in one coil in inducing a current in another is used in transformers
- explain how the ratio of the potential differences across the two coils depends on the ratio of the number of turns on each
- calculate the current drawn from the input supply to provide a particular power output
- apply the equation linking the p.d.s and number of turns in the two coils of a transformer to the currents and the power transfer involved, and relate these to the advantages of power transmission at high potential differences.

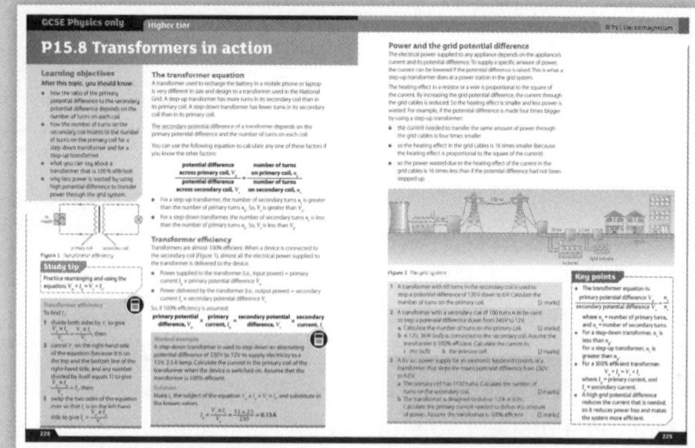

MS 1c, 3b, 3c

Aiming for	Outcome	Checkpoint	
		Question	Activity
Aiming for GRADE 6	Use the transformer equation to calculate input or output voltages for a transformer.	1	Main, Plenary 1, Plenary 2
	Calculate the secondary current in a transformer.	1, End of chapter 5, 6, 7	Main
	Measure the efficiency of a transformer.		Main
Aiming for GRADE 8	Apply the transformer equation in a wide variety of situations.	1, 2, 3	Main, Plenary 1, Plenary 2
	Use the relationship $V_P \times I_P = V_S \times I_S$ to calculate all variables.	End of chapter 5, 6, 7	Main, Plenary 2
	Measure the efficiency of a transformer and explain why this may not be 100%.		Main

Maths
Students apply the transformer equation and the transformer power relationship to solve a range of problems (1c, 3b, 3c).

Literacy
Students discuss the types of transformer used in the National Grid and the reasons they are used.

Starter	Support/Extend	Resources
Higher or lower? (5 min) Show the students a transformer arrangement and ask if the output voltage will be higher or lower than the input. Repeat a few times with different transformers.	**Extend:** Ask students to state the ratio of voltage or current changes for each transformer.	
Electrical power (10 min) Students have studied electrical power before and now need to refresh their memories by performing some simple calculations using the equation ($P = VI$).	**Extend:** Set some differentiated questions involving electrical power calculations.	
Main	**Support/Extend**	**Resources**
Transformers and efficiency (40 min) Discuss the factors that will affect transformers – the number of turns and the voltages. This leads to the transformer equation. After an example, the students will need some time to practise with this equation as there are four variables. Ensure that they try a calculation to find each variable at least once. Then discuss potential sources of energy dissipation in the transformer before noting that most transformers are nearly 100% efficient. Move on to the equation, which assumes 100% efficiency. As usual, after an example, the students need to practise with the equation. Use a diagram of the National Grid and discuss the different potential differences used. Explain the reasons for this in terms of resistance.	**Support:** The students may need additional time with the equation and multiple examples. **Extend:** Use some SI prefixes in examples, for example, 33 kV. **Extend:** Students try a calculation of power loss using the equations $V = IR$, $P = IV$, and $P = I^2R$ to support the discussion. Discuss the heating effect and the reduction in 'eddy currents' by using a laminated core. **Extend:** An extension sheet is available on power transformers and the transformer equation.	**Activity:** Transformers and efficiency **Extension:** The important role of transformers
Plenary	**Support/Extend**	**Resources**
Transformer matching (5 min) Interactive where students match up transformers with the changes in p.d.	**Support:** Provide a set of possible ratios to choose from for each transformer.	**Interactive:** Transformer matching
Combinations (10 min) Give the students a circuit with a set of four transformers in a row and ask them to find the final output p.d. Provide them with the input p.d. and the number of turns on each transformer.	**Support:** Provide a calculation template and reduce the number of transformers. **Extend:** Tell students that each transformer is only 95% efficient.	
Homework		
Additional examination-level questions involving transformer calculations should be used to reinforce learning, such as end-of-chapter Questions 5, 6, and 7 in the student book.		

kerboodle

A Kerboodle highlight for this lesson is **Maths skills: The motor effect and transformers**. Refer to the **Content map** on Kerboodle for a full list of resources and assessment.

P15 Electromagnetism

Overview of P15 Electromagnetism

Students began this chapter by reinforcing their knowledge of magnetism by looking at the magnetic fields around permanent magnets and the concept of induced magnetism in some materials. The students have been reminded of the techniques used to plot a magnetic field and the shape of the Earth's field.

Students moved on to examine the magnetic field produced by a current and investigate the factors that affect the direction and strength of this field. They compared the field shape of a solenoid to that produced by a simple bar magnet.

Building on this understanding *GCSE Physics* students investigated the factors affecting the strength of an electromagnet before moving on to describe how these devices can be used in a variety of devices.

All higher-tier students described how a current carrying wire placed in a magnetic field would experience the motor effect before going on to explain how this effect could be used to create an electric motor. The force produced on the motor was linked mathematically to the magnetic flux density of the magnetic field.

Only those studying *GCSE Physics* at higher level looked at the generator effect and the factors which affect the current induced in a wire as it is moved through a magnetic field. These concepts were applied to the design of a practical generator and the a.c. waveform produced as the coil in the generator rotates.

Higher-tier GCSE Physics students also described the operation of a transformer in terms of changes in magnetic fields before constructing a practical transformer. The transformer question was used to determine changes in potential difference along with a discussion of transformer efficiency. Finally, these students described the application of transformers in the National Grid.

You can find additional support for the maths skills covered in this chapter on **MyMaths**, including recognising and using expressions in decimal form, using an appropriate number of significant figures, understanding and using the symbols: =, <, <<, >>, >, ∝ , ~, and changing the subject of an equation.

For this chapter, the following assessments are available on Kerboodle:

P15 Checkpoint quiz: Electromagnetism
P15 Progress quiz: Electromagnetism 1
P15 Progress quiz: Electromagnetism 2
P15 On your marks: Electromagnetism
P15 Exam-style questions and mark scheme: Electromagnetism

Checkpoint follow up lesson

A student's route through this lesson can be determined using the Checkpoint assessment. Percentage pass marks are supplied in the Checkpoint teacher notes.

For each successive route through it is assumed that the student can perform to their current route as well as previous routes. For example, students working at Aiming for 6 are assumed to be secure in Aiming for 4 knowledge and understanding and working towards achieving all the learning outcomes for Aiming for 6.

	Aiming for 4	Aiming for 6	Aiming for 8
Learning outcomes	Describe how to work out the shape of the magnetic field around a magnet.	Explain how the shape of a magnetic field explains why magnets attract or repel.	Explain how to investigate the shape of magnetic fields to explain why magnets attract or repel.
		Describe what affects the magnetic field pattern near a wire, and what affects the strength of a solenoid.	Explain what factors affect the magnetic field pattern near a wire, and the strength of a solenoid.
		Describe how motors, generators, loudspeakers, and microphones work.	Explain how motors, generators, loudspeakers and microphones work
Starter	**Magnetic what? (10 min)** Give students A4 dry wipe boards, pens and an eraser. Display the word 'magnetic' on the board. Read out a description, like a crossword clue for words associated with 'magnetic', e.g. field, field lines, field strength, Earth's field, flux density. Students write the correct word or words on their white board and hold them up.		
Differentiated checkpoint activity	Aiming for 4 students use the Checkpoint follow-up sheet to complete one of three activities: • investigate magnetic fields around different magnets • suggest how to improve a plan for investigating electromagnets • describe what transformers are. The follow-up sheet is highly structured, and students could work in pairs for support. Simple questions are provided to support students with consolidating their understanding from the lesson.	Aiming for 6 students use the Checkpoint follow-up sheet to complete one of three activities: • investigate magnetic fields around different magnets • investigate electromagnets • model microphones and loudspeakers to sumamrise the concepts behind motors and generators. The follow-up sheet provides structured support, and students could work in pairs for support. Questions are provided to support students with consolidating their understanding from the lesson.	Aiming for 8 students use the Checkpoint follow-up sheet to complete one of three activities: • plot data on the strength of magnetic fields around a current carrying wire • model microphones and loudspeakers to sumamrise the concepts behind motors and generators • play a dominoes-based game on transformers. The follow-up sheet provides some support. Questions are provided to support students with consolidating their understanding from the lesson.
	Kerboodle resource P15 Checkpoint follow up: Aiming for 4, P15 Checkpoint follow up: Aiming for 6, P15 Checkpoint follow up: Aiming for 8		
Plenary	**Transformer dominos (5 min)** Aiming for 4 or 6 students could play the transformer domino game produced by the Aiming for 8 students. **Electromagnetic Venn diagrams (10 min)** Give each group a large piece of paper and a marker pen. They divide the paper in two by drawing a line. Aiming for 6/8 students make a Venn diagram of an electromagnet and a transformer, by writing the common *components* of the two things in the middle and the differences in each circle on one side of the paper, and repeat on the other side by drawing a Venn diagram about *how each works.*		
Progression	Encourage students to think about the interaction of magnetic fields when explaining attraction and repulsion.	Encourage students to think about the interaction of magnetic fields when explaining the forces on objects, such as coils in motors, and to use ratios to check calculations involving transformers.	Encourage students to think about giving explanations of forces in terms of the combination of magnetic fields, and to link these to the action of motors and loudspeakers, and of generators and microphones.

P
GCSE
Physics
only

16 Space

16.1 Formation of the Solar System

AQA spec Link: 8.1.1 Within our Solar System there is one star, the Sun, plus the eight planets and the dwarf planets that orbit around the Sun. Natural satellites, the moons that orbit planets, are also part of the Solar System.

Our Solar System is a small part of the Milky Way galaxy.

The Sun was formed from a cloud of dust and gas (nebula) pulled together by gravitational attraction.

Students should be able to explain:

- how, at the start of a star's life cycle, the dust and gas drawn together by gravity causes fusion reactions
- that fusion reactions lead to an equilibrium between the gravitational collapse of a star and the expansion of a star due to fusion energy.

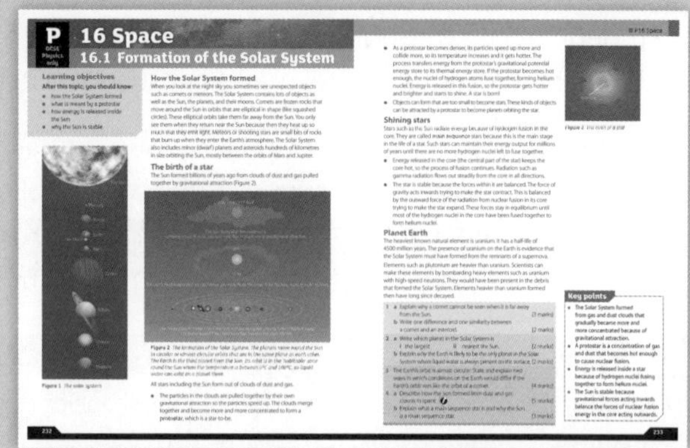

MS 1a, 1b

Aiming for	Outcome	Checkpoint	
		Question	Activity
Aiming for GRADE 4 ↓	Describe a variety of objects within the Solar System.	1	Starter 1, Plenary 2
	Use simple data to compare objects in the Solar System.	2	Main 1
	State that the material in a star is pulled together by gravitational forces.	4	Main 2
Aiming for GRADE 6 ↓	Describe the formation of a protostar and planets.	End of chapter 1	Main 2
	Explain why a star radiates light in terms of nuclear fusion.	4	Main 2
	Describe how evidence for the early Solar Sytem is gathered.		Main 2
Aiming for GRADE 8 ↓	Analyse data about the planets to compare them in terms of composition.	3	Starter 1, Main 1
	Explain why a star in its main sequence maintains a constant radius.	4, End of chapter 1	Main 2
	Discuss the methods used to gather evidence for the early Solar System and formation of stars.		Main 2

Maths
Students can compare some of the physical properties of the planets, such as mass, temperature, and orbital period (1a, 1b).

Literacy
The students discuss the possibility of extra-terrestrial life and the methods used in the search for it. They also debate whether this search is worthwhile.

Key words
protostar, main sequence

Practical

Title	From birth to the main sequence
Equipment	deep measuring cylinder, long thin tubing, glycerol or wallpaper paste
Overview of method	Fill the cylinder with the glycerol or thick paste and push one end of the tubing to the bottom. Blow a bubble through the tube and observe it as it rises. As the pressure decreases, the bubble should expand.
Safety considerations	Clean up any spills promptly.

Starter	Support/Extend	Resources
My Very Easy Method Just Speeds Up Naming (10 min) The students name all of the planets in order and describe their properties (e.g., rocky, gaseous, temperature patterns).	**Support:** Provide details and ask students to put the planets into the correct order.	
Gravity always wins (5 min) Students complete the interactive where they complete an explanation of why the planets orbit the Sun and what factors affect the size of this force.	**Extend:** Ask about the direction of the force and if there is also a force acting on the Sun.	**Interactive:** Gravity always wins
Main	**Support/Extend**	**Resources**
Solar System recap (10 min) Briefly recap the structure of the Solar System, outlining what planets, moons, comets, and asteroids are and their basic properties. Begin to discuss the origin of the materials which form these objects.		
From birth to the main sequence (30 min) Ask the students what a star is made of, and then describe the formation of a protostar. Emphasise the abundance of hydrogen in the initial nebula that forms the major part of the Sun. Discuss the increase in temperature in the core of the star and link back to nuclear fusion, which requires these high temperatures and pressures. Describe the forces in balance when a star is in its main sequence. The gravitational force is balanced by radiation pressure pushing outwards. If either of these forces change, then the star will change size. Use the practical demonstration to discuss forces in balance although the forces are different.	**Support:** Numerous animations are available online showing this process. **Extend:** Students should discuss how evidence is gathered about the early Solar System and the evolution of stars.	**Activity:** From birth to the main sequence
Plenary	**Support/Extend**	**Resources**
We come in peace (10 min) Ask the students to write a brief message describing what the Earth is like to send outwards to the universe to be transmitted to nearby stars.		
Solar System objects (5 min) Show images of some Solar System objects and ask students to identify them and describe their properties and behaviour.	**Extend:** Use more obscure images such as surface images from the Moon or Mars.	
Homework		
Students complete the WebQuest where they research the evidence that the Moon came into existence as a result of the a collision between the Earth and another planet.		**WebQuest:** The birth of the Moon

kerboodle

A Kerboodle highlight for this lesson is **WebQuest: Man on the Moon – fact of fiction?** Refer to the **Content map** on Kerboodle for a full list of resources and assessment.

P16.2 The life history of a star

AQA spec Link: 8.1.2 A star goes through a life cycle. The life cycle is determined by the size of the star.

Students should be able to describe the life cycle of a star:

- the size of the Sun
- much more massive than the Sun.

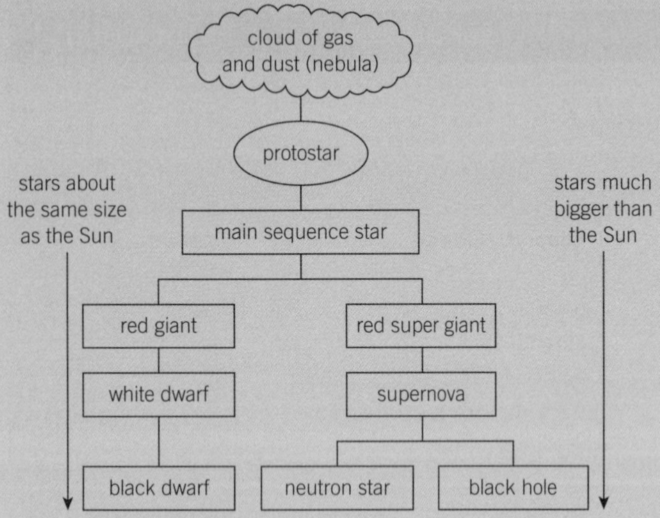

Fusion processes in stars produce all of the naturally occurring elements. Elements heavier than iron are produced in a supernova.

The explosion of a massive star (supernova) distributes the elements throughout the universe.

Students should be able to explain how fusion processes lead to the formation of new elements.

MS 1a, 1b

Aiming for	Outcome	Checkpoint	
		Question	Activity
Aiming for GRADE 4	Identify the sequence of development for a small star such as the Sun from a diagram.	1	Main 1, Plenary 2
	State that changes in the fusion processes in a star result in changes in its appearance.		Main 1
	State that the Sun is in its main sequence and is stable.	1	Main 1
Aiming for GRADE 6	Compare the life cycle of small and large stars, identifying the names of the stages.	1	Main 1, Plenary 2
	Describe the formation of 'light' elements by stars in their main sequence.	3, End of chapter 3	Starter 2, Main 2
	Describe the forces that are acting when a star is in its main sequence.	2	Main 1
Aiming for GRADE 8	Describe changes in the wavelength (colour) and quantity (brightness) of light emitted by stars during various stages of their life cycle.	2	Main 1, Plenary 2
	Explain, in terms of energy requirements, why elements heavier than iron are produced only in supernovae.	3, 4, End of chapter 2, 3	Main 2
	Describe the features of neutron stars and black holes.	End of chapter 2	Main 2

Maths
Students can compare the sizes and surface temperatures of stars (1a, 1b).

Literacy
The students need to describe the changes in a star's appearance and link these to changes in the fusion processes occurring in the star's core.

Key words
red giant, white dwarf, black dwarf, red supergiant, supernova, neutron star, black hole

Starter	Support/Extend	Resources
Star stuff (5 min) 'We are all made of stars.' What do the students think this means – is it a scientific statement? **Building blocks** (10 min) Ask: what is the meaning of the word element? Show the students a graph or chart showing the proportion of these elements found throughout the universe – this will be dominated by hydrogen and helium, with trace amounts of everything else.	**Support:** Revise the nature of elements by using models such as Lego blocks. These can be used to form molecules.	
Main	**Support/Extend**	**Resources**
Aging stars (15 min) Recap the main sequence and then ask the students what they think will happen when the star's core starts to heat up as more energy is released. They should realise that the star will expand. Discuss what will happen to the surface (its area increases dramatically and so it cools) and how this will affect its colour. Describe the final stages of a small star such as the Sun, emphasising that these changes are in the very distant future. The students can then compare these processes with the changes in a much larger star.	**Extend:** Link the temperature of a star's surface and the dominant colour of the light emitted.	**Activity:** The life history of a star
Element production (25 min) Recap the production of helium through nuclear fusion and describe how this process can continue to form elements up to iron. Explain that producing even heavier elements requires an energy input and so they cannot form in normal stars – they must be formed by the immense pressures of a supernova explosion. Show images of supernovae remnants and their nebulae. Describe the unusual objects that can be formed by the shockwave.	**Extend:** Show some example nuclear fusion equations for heavier elements. Extend the discussion about black holes to include how they may be detected.	
Plenary	**Support/Extend**	**Resources**
Stellar images (5 min) Show the students a set of images depicting stars in their various stages and ask the students to match them up with the names.		
Star sequence sort (10 min) Students use the interactive to match the stages in the life cycle of stars with their descriptions. They then put the stages in the correct order.	**Support:** Ask the students to sort the names of the stellar life stages into a diagram and then add some of the processes on top of this.	**Interactive:** Star sequence sort
Homework		
Give each student a stellar object to research in depth. Some suitable objects to find out about are the Sun, stellar nurseries, protostars, giant molecular clouds, neutron stars, black holes, pulsars, white dwarfs, black dwarfs, red giants, blue giants, and planetary nebulae.	**Support:** Select the most appropriate objects for the students.	

P16.3 Planets, satellites, and orbits

AQA spec Link: 8.1.3 Gravity provides the force that allows planets and satellites (both natural and artificial) to maintain their circular orbits.

Students should be able to describe the similarities and distinctions between the planets, their moons, and artificial satellites.

(H) Students should be able to explain qualitatively how:

- **for circular orbits, the force of gravity can lead to changing velocity but unchanged speed**
- **for a stable orbit, the radius must change if the speed changes.**

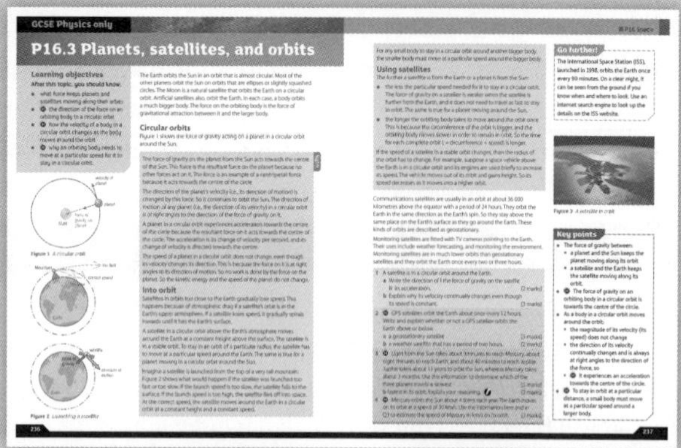
GCSE Physics only

P16.3 Planets, satellites, and orbits

MS 1a, 1b, 1c

Aiming for	Outcome	Checkpoint: Question	Checkpoint: Activity
Aiming for GRADE 4	Compare the orbits of planets, moons, and artificial satellites.	1	Main 2
	Describe how, for an object to be moving in an orbit, there must be a gravitational force acting directed at the centre of the orbit.	1	Starter 1, Main 1
	List some uses of artificial satellites.		Main 2
Aiming for GRADE 6	**(H) State that, for a greater radius of orbit, the object must travel at a slower speed and orbit in a longer period.**	2, 3	Main 1, Plenary 1
	(H) Describe the forces acting on an object that cause it to travel in a circular path.	1	Starter 1, Main 1, Plenary 1
	Describe the different orbits of a variety of satellites.	2	Main 2
Aiming for GRADE 8	**(H) Explain why a centripetal force can change the velocity of an object without changing its speed.**		Main 1
	(H) Explain why the force acting on an object travelling in a circle must be at right angles to the direction of motion and directed towards the centre of the circle.		Main 1, Plenary 1
	Explain why a geostationary satellite must be a specific distance from the centre of the Earth.	2	Main 2

Maths

Students describe the relationship between the radius of an orbit and the period of that orbit. They use numerical data to compare orbits and speeds (1a, 1b, 1c).

Literacy

The students describe the forces that cause an object to move in a circle and the factors that affect the sizes of these forces.

Key words
centripetal force

Practical

Title	Orbital forces
Equipment	ball (or rubber bung) on the end of a piece of string optional: clear plastic tube
Overview of method	The ball can be spun around in a horizontal circle whilst the inwardly acting force is discussed. Releasing the string will show that the ball will continue moving in a straight line (at a tangent to the circle) when there is no centripetal force acting on it. Thread the string through the plastic tube, with a mass on the end of the string. This can be used to show that when you choose a particular rotation rate (orbits per unit time), the radius changes in response to that.
Safety considerations	Do not use objects with a large mass. Release the string so that the ball moves away from students.

Starter	Support/Extend	Resources
Roundabout (10 min) Ask students to describe the forces acting on the children and the roundabout structure. They should describe the direction and relative size of the forces.	**Extend:** Ask the students to explain what will happen to the size of the forces when the roundabout spins faster.	
Curved paths (5 min) Show the students a video or simulation of projectile motion under gravity and ask the students to describe the forces acting throughout the flight.	**Extend:** Incorporate the effects of air resistance.	

Main	Support/Extend	Resources
Orbital forces (20 min) (H) Demonstrate that for an object to travel in a circle (or ellipse) there must be a force directed inwards. This is a centripetal force. The bump up your grade can be used to develop students' understand of centripetal force. For orbital motion, the force is gravitational. Describe the nature of orbital forces and the direction they must be acting to cause the shape of the orbits of planets and moons. Ask the students to describe the factors that affect the size of the force, ensuring that the students understand the direction of the force and acceleration.		**Bump up your grade:** Understanding circular motion **Activity:** Orbital forces and artificial satellites
Artificial satellites (20 min) (H) Discuss why a specific speed is required for each orbital distance. Link this to the speeds of the planets and their distances from the Sun (Mercury having the greatest speed, and Neptune the lowest). Describe the relationship between the distance of a satellite from the Earth's centre and its period around the Earth. Point out that there is a distance where the orbital period would be exactly 24 hours. All students can describe the uses of communications satellites that are in geostationary orbit and other, much closer, satellites.	**Support:** Use a simulation of this scenario to demonstrate the paths of projectiles. **Extend:** The students should analyse a few images taken by monitoring satellites and discuss what the images show.	

Plenary	Support/Extend	Resources
Comet motion (5 min) (H) Show the students a diagram representing the elliptical path of a comet around the Sun. They must mark the direction of the force acting on the comet and the direction of travel at four points in the motion.	**Extend:** The students should indicate changes in the size of the force and speed of the comet.	
Lunar launcher (10 min) Interactive where students complete an explanation into the differences between the launch of Apollo 11 from the Earth and the launch of the Eagle lander from the Moon.	**Support:** Provide data about gravitational field strength and the atmosphere.	**Interactive:** Lunar launcher

Homework		
Ask students to find information about some important satellites such as Sputnik, Skylab, the ISS, or a GPS system, comparing them in terms of orbital distance, mass, and so on.		

kerboodle

A Kerboodle highlight for this lesson is **Literacy sheet: Satellites and orbits**. Refer to the **Content map** on Kerboodle for a full list of resources and assessment.

P16.4 The expanding universe

AQA spec Link: 8.2 There is an observed increase in the wavelength of light from most distant galaxies. The further away the galaxies, the faster they are moving and the bigger the observed increase in wavelength. This effect is called red-shift.

The observed red-shift provides evidence that space itself (the universe) is expanding [and supports the Big Bang theory].

Students should be able to explain:

- qualitatively the red-shift of light from galaxies that are receding
- that the change of each galaxy's speed with distance is evidence of an expanding universe.

MS 1b, 2g

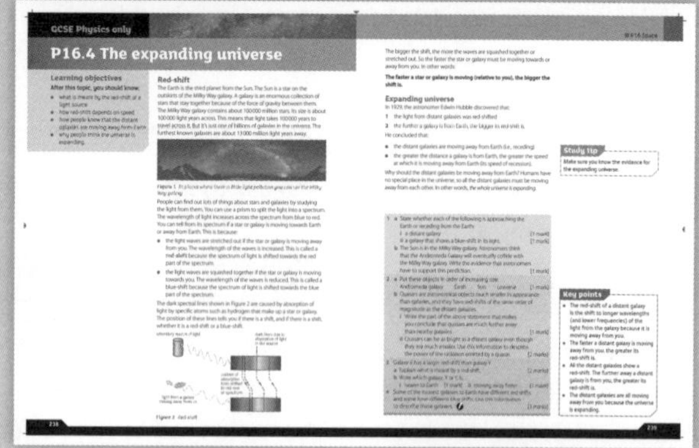

Aiming for	Outcome	Checkpoint	
		Question	Activity
Aiming for GRADE 4	State that the wavelength of a wave is changed by the movement of the source.		Main 1
	State that a galaxy showing red-shift is moving away from us.	1, 4	Main 1
	Describe the structure of a galaxy as a collection of billions of stars many light years in diameter.	2	Starter 1, Main 2, Plenary 1
Aiming for GRADE 6	Describe how the frequency or wavelength of a wave can be altered by the movement of the source through the Doppler effect.	End of chapter 5	Main 1
	Compare galaxies in terms of their red-shift and distance from us.	1, 3, 4, End of chapter 6, 7	Main 1
	State that all galaxies are moving away from each other and that this shows the universe is expanding.	End of chapter 5	Main 2
Aiming for GRADE 8	Identify red-shift or blue-shift by comparing emission spectra of objects with those of a non-moving source.		Main 1, Plenary 2
	Identify the relationship between the red-shift of a galaxy and its speed of recession from a data set or graph.	End of chapter 5, 8	Main 2
	Explain how red-shift data is used to show that the universe is expanding.	End of chapter 5	Main 2

Maths
Students use standard form to represent large numbers and interpret a graph to determine a correlation (1b, 2g).

Literacy
Students describe how evidence from observations can be used to describe the structure and behaviour of the universe.

Key words
red-shift

Practical

Title	Doppler effect and the red-shift
Equipment	1.5 m length of hosepipe (narrower tubes do not work as well) with a large funnel securely attached to one end Alternative: high pitched buzzer and string
Overview of method	Simply swing the funnel end of the hosepipe around your head (in a lasso style) whilst blowing into the other end. The pitch (and frequency and wavelength of the sound) changes as it swings towards and away from the students. When it is moving away, the wavelength is increased so the sound is lower pitched and vice versa. As an alternative a high pitched electrical buzzer can be swung around on the end of a piece of string.
Safety considerations	Ensure there is adequate space to swing the hose and that the funnel cannot become detached.

Starter	Support/Extend	Resources
How many stars? (5 min) Give the students estimates of the number of stars in a galaxy and the number of galaxies. Ask them to work out how many stars they could have each if they shared them out among the class.		
Stars, planets, and moons (10 min) Ask the students to define the properties of stars, planets, and moons.	**Support:** Provide cards describing the properties and behaviours of stars and planets, and ask students to sort them into piles corresponding to the objects.	
Main	**Support/Extend**	**Resources**
Doppler effect and the red-shift (25 min) Demonstrate the Doppler effect with sound by using the practical and the animation. The students should note the changes in pitch (frequency) during the movement. Explain how the Doppler effect applies to electromagnetic radiation – shifting the wavelength of objects moving away or towards us. Show a spectral line pattern from the Sun, identifying the positions of key dark lines in the spectrum, and then compare this to a spectrum of an object moving away. The students should identify that it shifts towards the red part of the spectrum. Ensure that students understand that the shifts become larger when the objects are moving away from us more quickly.	**Support:** Use the concept of shifts in colour to describe the changes in the electromagnetic radiation.	**Animation:** The Doppler Effect **Activity:** Doppler effect, red-shift, and the expanding Universe
The expanding universe (15 min) Show the students an example recession graph for galaxies. The pattern may not be immediately clear, so the trend may need to be pointed out. Ask the students what they think this pattern means, and then lead them towards the idea that long ago the galaxies were much closer together. The universe was much smaller and has been expanding over time.	**Extend:** An extension sheet is available where students look at some of the evidence for the Big Bang theory, analysing spectra and plotting graphs. This can lead into a discussion into how they can use distances and recession speeds to estimate how old the Universe is.	**Extension:** Small things lead to large things
Plenary	**Support/Extend**	**Resources**
Space is big (10 min) Students use the interactive to put a list of distances in order (e.g., the school to Paris, the school to New York, the Earth to the Moon, the Earth to the Sun, the Earth to Pluto, the Sun to the nearby star Alpha Centauri, the Sun to the centre of the Milky Way (or galaxy), the Milky Way to Andromeda, the Milky Way to the edge of the observable universe). They can then match these to the actual distances in kilometres.	**Extend:** Ask students to convert the numbers into standard form, and discuss why this is generally used for large numbers.	**Interactive:** Space is big
Elements in the Sun (5 min) Give the students a card showing the absorption spectrum of the Sun's atmosphere and a set of emission spectra for various elements, some of which are present in the Sun. Ask the students to work out which ones match.	**Extend:** Students can match the spectra to rapidly moving galaxies, noting the shifts.	
Homework		
The Andromeda galaxy is one of our nearest galactic neighbours and it is getting nearer all the time. Ask the students to find out whether it will 'collide' with Earth and what might happen.		

P16.5 The beginning and future of the universe

AQA spec Link: 8.2 The observed red-shift provides evidence that space itself (the universe) is expanding and supports the Big Bang theory.

The Big Bang theory suggests that the universe began from a very small region that was extremely hot and dense.

Since 1998 onwards, observations of supernovae suggest that distant galaxies are receding ever faster.

Students should be able to explain:

- qualitatively the red-shift of light from galaxies that are receding
- that the change of each galaxy's speed with distance is evidence of an expanding universe
- how red-shift provides evidence for the Big Bang model
- how scientists are able to use observations to arrive at theories such as the Big Bang theory
- that there is still much about the universe that is not understood, for example, dark mass and dark energy.

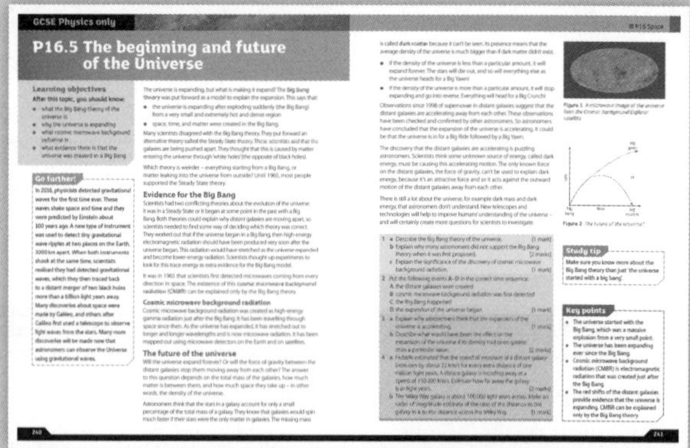

WS 1.1, 1.2, 1. 3
MS 1b

Aiming for	Outcome	Checkpoint	
		Question	Activity
Aiming for GRADE 4	State that the currently accepted model for the early universe is the Big Bang model.	1	Main 1
	Describe how red-shift provides evidence for expansion of the universe and the Big Bang model.		Main 1
	Identify the cosmic microwave background radiation (CMBR) as evidence for the Big Bang model.	End of chapter 5	Main 1
Aiming for GRADE 6	Discuss why scientists were initially reluctant to accept the Big Bang model.		Main 1, Main 2
	Describe the origin of the CMBR.	End of chapter 5	Main 1
	Describe changes in the universe from the time of the Big Bang to the present day.	2	Main 1, Plenary 1, Homework
Aiming for GRADE 8	Outline recent discoveries that have led to changes in the theories of how the universe will develop.	3	Main 2, Plenary 1
	Explain in detail how the CMBR supports the Big Bang model.	End of chapter 5	Main 1, Plenary 1
	Discuss how scientists using new evidence have changed their theories about how the universe has evolved over time and how it will change in the future.	3, End of chapter 5	Starter 1, Main 2, Plenary 1

Maths
Students can use standard form to represent vary large numbers (1b).

Literacy
The students discuss complex ideas and how theories are built upon the evidence available and so will change over time.

Key words
Big Bang Theory, cosmic microwave background radiation (CMBR), dark matter

Practical

Title	The Big Bang model
Equipment	uninflated balloon with several galaxies drawn on its surface
Overview of method	The balloon can be inflated to show that all of the galaxies drawn on its surface move away from each other when space (the rubber) stretches. This is similar to the expansion of the universe but in two (curved) dimensions.
Safety considerations	Do not overinflate the balloon.

Starter	Support/Extend	Resources
Heat death (10 min) Remind students that all energy transfers lead to energy being transferred by heating, making it more difficult for further energy transfers to take place. Ask them to describe what will happen when all of the energy the universe started with has been dissipated.		
Ultimate timeline (5 min) Draw a 14 billion year timeline on the board and mark on a few key events – start of the universe (13.8 billion years ago), formation of the Solar System (4.6 billion years ago), and first life on Earth (3.6 billion years ago).	**Extend:** Ask students when the first humans evolved and why this can't be marked on the timeline.	
Main	**Support/Extend**	**Resources**
The Big Bang model (25 min) Recap the idea that all of the observable universe was once in the same place many billions of years ago and what this would be like. All of the mass and energy would be concentrated in an unimaginably small region, which would make the temperature and density very high. Demonstrate expansion using the practical and outline the changes that occur during expansion. Remind students that hot materials radiate and so the early universe would have produced vast amounts of high energy radiation. As the universe expanded, this radiation was 'stretched', increasing in wavelength. The remnant of this process is the CMBR detected today. Discuss how the Big Bang Theory is also supported by red-shift observations that demonstrate expansion in all directions.	**Extend:** The students can discuss the slight variations in the radiation and how these may be responsible for the formation of structures seen today such as galaxies.	**Working scientifically:** Before the Big Bang
The future (15 min) If not already done so, remind students that all energy transfers lead to energy being transferred by heating and dissipated. Discuss the idea of dark matter – its presence seemed to indicate that a 'Big Crunch' would happen in the distant future as the universe would become dense enough for this to happen. But the discovery of increasing rates of expansion due to dark energy rejects the possibility of a Big Crunch. Use these ideas to show that the model of the universe is constantly evolving and that more knowledge of dark energy and dark matter is needed before people can become more certain.	**Extend:** Ensure that students can explain why scientific theories are rejected when sufficient conflicting evidence is discovered.	
Plenary	**Support/Extend**	**Resources**
Sceptic (10 min) Interactive where students summarise the evidence for the expanding universe and CMBR.		**Interactive:** Sceptic
Multiverse (5 min) Do the students believe that there could be multiple universes? What would be different in these universes when compared with ours?	**Extend:** Can a multiverse theory ever be disproved? Does this make the theory unscientific?	
Homework		
Students write a letter to summarise the evidence for the expanding universe and cosmic background microwave radiation (CMBR) so as to explain the Big Bang model to someone who is sceptical.		

kerboodle

A Kerboodle highlight for this lesson is **Maths skills: The Solar System**. Refer to the **Content map** on Kerboodle for a full list of resources and assessment.

P16 Space

Overview of P16 Space

In this chapter the students have examined the formation of the solar system from a nebula, particularly the formation of the Sun from hydrogen gas into a protostar until it reaches the main sequence. The source of materials for formation of the planets has also been described.

Students moved on from the main sequence to describe the pathways for small stars from main sequence through red giants, white dwarfs, and finally black dwarfs along with the pathway for larger stars through red supergiant, supernova and neutron star/black holes has been described. The students noted the role of supernovae in the production of heavy elements. They have also examined the orbits of planets, with higher-tier students discussing the role of centripetal force and acceleration in more detail for planets and artificial satellites.

All students have also evaluated the evidence for an expanding universe prompted by the red shift of the majority of galaxies leading to Edwin Hubble's conclusions. This, combined with the evidence provided by the cosmic microwave background radiation, was used in discussion of the Big Bang theory. Finally, these students discussed the models predicting the distant future of the universe touching on the role of dark matter and dark energy.

You can find additional support for the maths skills covered in this chapter on **MyMaths**, including using graphs and using standard form.

For this chapter, the following assessments are available on Kerboodle:

P16 Checkpoint quiz: Space
P16 Progress quiz: Space 1
P16 Progress quiz: Space 2
P16 On your marks: Space
P16 Exam-style questions and mark scheme: Space

Checkpoint follow up lesson

A student's route through this lesson can be determined using the Checkpoint assessment. Percentage pass marks are supplied in the Checkpoint teacher notes.

For each successive route through it is assumed that the student can perform to their current route as well as previous routes. For example, students working at Aiming for 6 are assumed to be secure in Aiming for 4 knowledge and understanding and working towards achieving all the learning outcomes for Aiming for 6.

	Aiming for 4	Aiming for 6	Aiming for 8
Learning outcomes	State how the Solar System formed.	Describe how the Solar System was formed.	Explain how the Solar System was formed.
	State simply why the Sun shines.	Describe the lifecycle of the Sun and more massive stars.	Explain the lifecycle of the Sun and more massive stars.
	Describe how gravity keeps objects in orbit.	Explain the effect of gravity on objects in orbit.	Explain the link between the force of gravity, the speed of an object in orbit, and the radius of the orbit.
	Describe the Big Bang model and evidence for it.	Describe the evidence for the Big Bang and evaluate models of the Universe.	Evaluate models of the Big Bang in terms of the evidence for the Big Bang.
Starter	**Stars and the Universe (5 min)** Give each group a piece of paper and ask them to divide it in two by drawing a line down the middle. On one side they write 'Sun', and on the other they write 'Universe'. Ask them to make a spider diagram of all the key words to do with each word. Groups swap diagrams and count the number of relevant words on each side. Keep the diagrams for the plenary. **What keeps them up? (5 min)** Ask students to come up with 2 situations in everyday life where what people do depends on there being a satellite in orbit. (TV, GPS). Display an image of satellites in orbit, such as from the NASA link below. Students discuss why satellites don't fall to earth, and the difference between satellites used for TV and GPS.		
Differentiated checkpoint activity	Aiming for 4 students use the Checkpoint follow-up sheet to complete one of three activities: • design an animation to show the formation of our Solar System and draw a timeline for the Sun • model gravity and analyse orbits of satellites • model the expansion of the Universe using a balloon. The follow-up sheet provides structured instructions for each task, and simple questions to consolidate their understanding.	Aiming for 6 students use the Checkpoint follow-up sheet to complete one of three activities: • design an animation to show the formation of our Solar System and the Sun • model gravity and analyse orbits of satellites • model the expansion of the Universe using a balloon. The follow-up sheet provides instructions for each task, and questions to consolidate their understanding.	Aiming for 8 students use the Checkpoint follow-up sheet to complete one of three activities: • write a series of quiz questions on the formation of the Solar system • model gravity and analyse orbits of satellites • model the expansion of the Universe using a balloon. The follow-up sheet provides minimal instructions for each task, and questions to consolidate their understanding.
	Kerboodle resource P16 Checkpoint follow up: Aiming for 4, P16 Checkpoint follow up: Aiming for 6, P16 Checkpoint follow up: Aiming for 8		
Plenary	**What's missing and how do we know? (5 min)** Give students A4 dry wipe boards, pens and an eraser. Display the stages of the lifecycle of a star like our Sun, but with one stage missing, and ask students to identify the mission stage. Then display the stages in the formation of the universe in terms of the Big Bang model, and ask them to identify the missing stage. Repeat for the evidence for the Big Bang. **String gravity (5 min)** Tell students that you are going to model a planet in orbit around the Sun. Take a bung on a piece of string and whirl it around your head, and say 'this is planet 1'. Repeat with planet 2 with a smaller orbit so that it is obviously travelling faster. Ask a series of questions about the model that students can answer on their whiteboards, such as 'what does the string represent?', 'name a pair of planets that could be 1 and 2'.		
Progression	Encourage students to think about the effect of gravity on objects with different speeds.	Encourage students to think about the gas pressure and gravity when discussing a star during its lifecycle, and how the decrease in the force of gravity with distance from the Sun affects the speed of objects in orbit.	Encourage students to think about the how to critically evaluate the evidence for the Big Bang, and the model of it that we use.

Answers

P1.1

1a loses GPE and gains KE, [1] some heat → surroundings due to air resistance [1]

b electrical energy → heat to heater element, [1] some heat → surroundings [1]

2a any two from: e.g., electric torch: chemical energy stored in battery → electric current transfers energy to lamp → light or heat energy → surroundings, [1] e.g., candle: energy from chemical reactions when candle burns → light or heat energy → surroundings [1]

b i candle [1]

ii electric torch [1]

3a energy transferred by electric current to train motor [1] → GPE to train [1]

b friction on train wheels due to brakes reduces KE of train to zero [1] → heat and sound to surroundings [1]

4 electrical energy supplied to oven used to generate microwaves, [1] microwaves → make food particles move faster so food becomes hot [1]

P1.2

1a brake pads become hot due to friction and energy transferred from brake pads to surroundings as heat, [1] braking → sound energy → surroundings [1]

b KE → GPE in roller coaster, [1] → KE in air going up, [1] GPE → KE going down [1]

2a descent: GPE → KE + heat to surroundings due to air resistance, [1] impact: KE → elastic energy of trampoline + heat to surroundings due to impact + sound, [1] ascent: elastic energy of trampoline → KE → GPE + heat to surroundings due to air resistance [1]

b less energy at top of bounce than at point of release [1]

c clamp metre ruler vertically over middle of trampoline, hold ball next to ruler with lowest point level with top of ruler, [1] release ball and observe highest level of bottom of ball after rebound, [1] repeat several times → average rebound position, [1] repeat with same ball for other two trampolines, [1] highest rebound position → bounciest [1]

3 elastic energy of rubber straps → KE of capsule, [1] KE → GPE as capsule [1]

4 rope not stretched as much so bungee jumper would not fall as far **or** rope stops jumper in shorter distance [1] so jumper experiences bigger (average) deceleration before ascent [1]

P1.3

1a i chemical energy stored in rower's muscles → KE of boat and water + heat to surroundings [1]

ii motor KE → GPE of barrier + thermal energy from friction and sound energy [1]

b 2000 N × 40 m = 80 000 J [1]

2a KE of car → brake pads by friction between brake pads and wheel discs [1] so brake pads become warm [1]

b 7000 N × 20 m = 140 000 J [1]

3a i 20 N × 4.8 m = 96 J [1]

ii 80 N × 1.2 m = 96 J [1]

b $\frac{1400\ \text{J}}{7.0\ \text{m}}$ [1] = 200 N [1]

4a 25 N × 12 m [1] = 300 J [1]

b chemical energy stored in student's muscles → KE in box, [1] when box moving KE + GPE of box does not change, [1] frictional force between box and floor transfers energy by heating from box to floor [1]

P1.4

1a descent: GPE of ball transferred by force of gravity → KE of ball, [1] + KE of air pushed aside by ball moving, [1] impact: KE of ball → elastic energy of ball + some elastic energy → KE as it rebounds, [1] after impact: KE of ball → GPE of ball as it rises → KE of air pushed aside by ball as it moves through the air [1]

b i mg = 1.4 N = 1.4 N × (2.5 m − 1.7 m) [1] = 1.1 J [1]

ii any two from: energy → surroundings due to air resistance as ball moves through air, [1] energy transfer due to heating of ball when it is deformed, [1] energy → surroundings by sound waves when ball hits floor [1]

2a 450 N × 0.20 m = 90 J [1]

b 50 × 90 J = 4500 J [1]

3a 25 kg × 10 N/kg × 1.8 m [1] = 450 J [1]

b ball falls 1.8 m − 0.3 m = 1.5 m [1]

$E_p = mgh$ = 25 kg × 10 N/kg × 1.5 m = 375 J [1]

4 energy supplied by blood system to biceps to keep muscle contracted, [1] no work done on object as it doesn't move, [1] energy supplied heats muscles → heat to surroundings [1]

P1.5

1a i 0.5 × 500 kg × (12 m/s)^2 [1] = 36 000 J [1]

ii 0.5 × 0.44 kg × (20 m/s)^2 [1] = 88 J [1]

b $E_K = \frac{1}{2}mv^2$ = 2 × 36 000 J so $\frac{1}{2}$ × 500 kg × v^2 = 72 000 J [1]

$\therefore v^2 = \frac{72\,000\ \text{J}}{0.5 \times 500\ \text{kg}}$ [1] = 288 m^2/s^2 $\therefore v$ = 17 m/s [1]

2a i work done by muscles transfer chemical energy from muscles [1] → elastic PE of catapult [1]

ii elastic PE of catapult [1] → KE of object [1]

b i 2.0 N × 5.0 m [1] = 10 J [1]

ii mass = weight $/g$ = 2.0 N ÷ 10 N/kg = 0.20 kg [1] assume all elastic energy → KE in object, $E_K = \frac{1}{2}mv^2$ = 10 J so $\frac{1}{2}$ × 0.20 kg × v^2 = 10 J [1] $\therefore v^2 = \frac{10\ \text{J}}{0.5 \times 0.20\ \text{kg}}$ [1] = 100 m^2/s^2 $\therefore v$ = 10 m/s [1]

3a work done by brakes = energy transferred from kinetic store = 360 000 J [1] using $W = Fs$ → 360 000 J = F × 100 m [1]

$\therefore F = \frac{360\,000\ \text{J}}{100\ \text{m}}$ = 3600 N [1]

b $\frac{1}{2}$ × m × (30 m/s)^2 = 360 000 J [1] ∴ 0.5 × m × 900 (m/s)^2 = 360 000 J, rearranging → $m = \frac{360\,000\ \text{J}}{0.5 \times 900\ \text{m}^2/\text{s}^2}$ [1] = 800 kg [1]

4 elastic energy $E_e = \frac{1}{2}ke^2$ = 0.5 × 250 N/m × (0.21 m)^2 [1] = 5.5 J [1]

P1.6

1a i 0.5 × 500 kg × (12 m/s)^2 [1] = 36 000 J [1]

ii 0.5 × 0.44 kg × (20 m/s)^2 [1] = 88 J [1]

b 2 × 36 000 J so $\frac{1}{2}$ × 500 kg × v^2 = 72 000 J [1]

$\therefore v^2 = \frac{72\,000\ \text{J}}{0.5 \times 500\ \text{kg}}$ [1] = 288 m^2/s^2 $\therefore v$ = 17 m/s [1]

2a i WD by muscles transfers chemical energy from muscles [1] → elastic PE of catapult [1]

ii elastic PE of catapult [1] → KE of object [1]

b i 2.0 N × 5.0 m [1] = 10 J [1]

ii mass = 2.0 N ÷ 10 N/kg = 0.20 kg [1] assume all elastic energy → KE in object, $E_K = 10\text{ J}$ so $\frac{1}{2} \times 0.20\text{ kg} \times v^2 = 10\text{ J}$ [1] $\therefore v^2 = \frac{10\text{ J}}{0.5 \times 0.20\text{ kg}}$ [1] = 100 m²/s² ∴ $v = 10\text{ m/s}$ [1]

3a work done by brakes = energy transferred from kinetic store = 360 000 J [1] $W = 360\,000\text{ J} = F \times 100\text{ m}$ [1]

$\therefore F = \frac{360\,000\text{ J}}{100\text{ m}} = 3600\text{ N}$ [1]

b $E_K = \frac{1}{2} \times m \times (30\text{ m/s})^2 = 360\,000\text{ J}$ [1] ∴ $0.5 \times m \times 900\ (\text{m/s})^2 = 360\,000\text{ J}$, rearranging → $m = \frac{360\,000\text{ J}}{0.5 \times 900\text{ m}^2/\text{s}^2}$ [1] = 800 kg [1]

4 $0.5 \times 250\text{ N/m} \times (0.21\text{ m})^2$ [1] = 5.5 J [1]

P1.6

1a wasted: sound, KE of air [1]

b useful: light and sound, wasted: heat [1]

c useful: boils water, wasted: heat lost through surfaces, sound [1]

d useful: sound, wasted: heat loss [1]

2a any two from: gear box would heat up due to energy transfer through friction between the gears,[1] the hotter the gear box, the less efficient the gears, [1] if gear box becomes very hot, stops working as oil in it burns up and gear wheels wear away [1]

b inside of shoes heat up due to energy transfer (by conduction + infrared radiation) from feet which rub, [1] feet transfer less energy as shoes warm up so feet and athlete become hotter [1]

c drill heats up due to friction between rotating drill and wood, [1] if drill becomes very hot, it burns wood creating smoke [1]

d discs heat up due to energy transfer by friction between discs and brake pads, [1] KE of car decreases [1]

3a as pendulum swings towards middle GPE decreases and KE increases, [1] as it moves from middle to highest position its KE → GPE, [1] air resistance causes some KE → heat to surroundings [1]

b as air resistance opposes motion KE from pendulum → air, [1] until pendulum stops moving and has no KE, [1] energy transferred to air dissipated to surroundings [1]

4 friction at wheel axles [1] and air resistance [1] reduces KE of cyclist and KE → heat to surroundings ,[1] sound might also be created and → energy to surroundings [1]

P1.7

1a useful energy < energy supplied [1]

b i efficiency = useful energy delivered/input energy supplied, [1] a machine never > 100% efficient because useful energy delivered never > total energy supplied [1]

ii useful energy always < total energy supplied, [1] due to electric currents in circuit wires/components [1] and friction between moving parts, [1] energy dissipated by transferring heat to surroundings [1]

2a 60 J – 24 J [1] = 36 J [1]

b $\frac{24\text{ J}}{60\text{ J}}$ (× 100%) [1] = 0.40 (or 40%) [1]

3 0.25 × total energy supplied [1] = 0.25 × 3200 J = 800 J [1]

4 electric current supplied energy to fan heater → heat air and make air move, [1] air becomes hotter and gains KE, [1] energy wasted because sound waves transfer energy to surroundings [1] and friction between moving parts heats moving parts instead of air [1]

P1.8

1a B [1]

b B [1]

c A [1]

2a WD winding clockwork spring up [1] to store energy in spring [1]

b spring drives small electric generator in radio, energy → from spring to generator by force of spring when spring unwinds, [1] current from generator → energy to radio circuits [1]

c advantage: no replacement batteries needed [1] disadvantage: spring needs to be rewound after unwinding [1]

3a heat water, [1] spray it and pump it out [1]

b hot water pumped from machine transfers energy to surroundings, [1] machine vibrations create sound waves → energy to surroundings [1]

4a 80% × 60% [1] = 48% [1]

b (100% – 48%) = 52% [1]

P1.9

1a i mains filament bulb [1]

ii 10 000 W electric cooker [1]

b 2 million × 3 kW [1] = 6 million kW [1]

2a 5000 W × 20 s [1] = 100 000 J [1]

b 12 000 J (× 100%)/100 000 J [1] = 0.12 (or 12%) [1]

3a $\frac{1500\text{ kJ}}{50\text{ s}}$ [1] = 30 kW [1]

b $\frac{30\text{ kW}}{100\text{ kW}}$ [1] = 0.30 (or 30%) [1]

4a current through heater → energy to heater raising temperature of water, [1] pump → energy to water to keep water moving enabling water to overcome resistive forces due to pipes, [1] energy → to surroundings by sound waves from pump [1]

b 12 000 W × 4800 s [1] =960 000 J [1]

P2.1

1a any two from: do not conduct by heating, [1] so handle not hot when pan hot, [1] steel handle becomes as hot as pan as steel is good conductor [1]

b felt: contains fibres that trap layers of air, [1] dry air good insulator [1]

2a felt/synthetic fur, [1] trapped air good insulator [1]

b fair test e.g., wrapping each lining round can of hot water with same volume of water, [1] time temperature change in 5 minutes from same initial temperature, [1] smallest temperature decrease indicates best insulator [1]

3 any five from: fill beaker with measured volume hot water, measure initial temperature of water, place lid on beaker and measure temperature again after 300 s, [1] stir water before measuring temperature, [1] repeat test using two identical beakers, one inside the other, using same volume hot water at same initial temperature, [1] repeat test using three or more beakers, [1] should find temperature falls less the more beakers you use, [1] plot graph of temperature decrease *vs* number of beakers used [1]

4 C: glass has lowest thermal conductivity [1] so cool end heats up slower than A or B [1]

P2.2

1 electromagnetic radiation emitted from surface of objects due to their temperature (**or** electromagnetic radiation with wavelengths in range from about 700 nm to about 1 mm) [1]

2a city hotter than rural area [1] possible more energy dissipated in urban areas [1]

b put hand near iron and see if it gets warm [1]

3a temperature increased as heated so emitted more infrared radiation, increase in radiation emitted greater at shorter wavelengths than at longer wavelengths, [1] wavelength of light decreases from red to orange to yellow (to green and blue) so at higher temperature radiation emitted was orange-red rather than dull-red [1]

b i Z hottest, [1] because more light at shorter wavelengths [1]

ii Y coolest [1] because X emits orange and yellow which have shorter wavelengths than Y which emits red [1]

P2.3

1a similarity: radiation emitted and absorbed is infrared, [1] difference: wavelengths of radiation emitted from Earth longer than wavelengths absorbed from the Sun [1]

b radiation covers continuous range of wavelengths including longer wavelengths that are absorbed by greenhouse gases in atmosphere, [1] shorter wavelengths not absorbed and on a clear night they pass through atmosphere into space [1]

2a infrared radiation from Sun passes through car windows to heat surfaces inside car, [1] hot surfaces heat air inside car so temperature in car rises, [1] inside surfaces emit more infrared as they heat up until rate emitted = rate absorbed [1]

b less infrared radiation from Sun reaches car so less infrared absorbed by surfaces inside in car, [1] ∴ surfaces not as hot as inside car not as hot [1]

3 infrared radiation emitted by Earth's surface has continuous range of wavelengths, [1] molecules of greenhouse gases in atmosphere absorb longer wavelength infrared from Earth and emit it back to surface, [1] making Earth warmer than if no greenhouse gases [1]

P2.4

1 small bucket [1] because mass of water much less than in large bucket [1]

2a lead has lower specific heat capacity, [1] for equal masses, less energy needed for a given temperature rise [1]

b i 0.20 kg × 900 J/kg °C × (40 – 15)°C [1] = 4500 J [1]

ii 0.40 kg × 4200 J/kg °C × (40 – 15) °C [1] = 42 000 J [1]

iii $\Delta E_{Al} = (mc\Delta\vartheta)_{Al}$ = 4500 J (as in **i**) [1] $\Delta E_{water} = (mc\Delta\vartheta)_{water}$ = 42 000 J (as in **ii**) [1] total energy = 4500 J + 42 000 J = 46 500 J [1]

c ΔE_{Cu} = 20 kg × 490 J/kg °C × (55 – 15)°C [1] = 392 kJ [1]
ΔE_{water} = 150 kg × 4200 J/kg °C × (55 – 15)°C [1] = 25 200 kJ [1]
total energy = 392 kJ + 25 200 kJ = 25 592 kJ = 25.6 MJ [1]

3 storage heater contains bricks/concrete heated by element, radiant heater does not, [1] storage heater gradually → heat to surroundings, radiant heater instantly [1]

4 any four from: measure mass *m* of empty beaker, fill two-thirds full with oil and measure mass of beaker and oil, calculate mass of oil, in beaker,[1] insulate beaker and use thermometer to measure initial temperature of oil, record initial joulemeter reading,[1] use heater and joulemeter to heat oil for 100 seconds then switch off power supply, [1] record final joulemeter reading, stir oil and measure its highest temperature, [1] calculate ΔE from the two joulemeter readings and temperature increase $\Delta\vartheta$ from the two temperature readings, use equation $\Delta E = mc\Delta\vartheta$ to calculate specific heat capacity of oil, [1] assuming negligible energy to heat polythene beaker [1]

P2.5

1a conducts much less energy than air, especially if air damp, [1] prevents energy transfer by radiation (and convection) across cavity [1]

b foil reflects infrared radiation from radiator [1] preventing absorption of radiation by surface of wall behind foil [1]

2a plastic = heat insulator, metal = good conductor, [1] ∴ more energy transferred through metal frame [1]

b air convects so energy transferred if space filled with air but not with vacuum [1]

3 wider gap transfers less energy, [1] air between panes insulates and the wider the air gap, the more effective the window is at reducing energy transfer through it [1]

4a 6 × £15 for the rolls + £90 to fit the insulation [1] = £180 [1]

b 6 × £10 [1] = £60 [1]

c £180 ÷ £60/year [1] = 3 years [1]

P3.1

1a i coal, oil and gas-fired power stations [1]

ii nuclear power station [1]

b nuclear fuel → radioactive waste [1] which must be stored for many years until it becomes non-radioactive [1]

2a i advantage: no radioactive waste, disadvantage: produces greenhouse gases [1]

ii advantage: starts quicker, disadvantage: gas supplies will run out before coal [1]

b 300 000 MJ ÷ 30 MJ/kg = 10 000 kg [1]

3a biofuel = any fuel obtained from living or recent organisms, [1] ethanol biofuel because obtained from fermented sugar cane [1]

b CO_2 released when burnt = C taken in as CO_2 from atmosphere [1] when it grows [1]

4 energy/person per year = 500 million million million J/6000 million [1] = 83000 MJ [1] energy/person per second = 83000 MJ/365 days × 24 × 3600) [1] =2600 J/s [1]

P3.2

1a source of energy replenished by natural processes [1] at same rate as it is used [1]

b i tidal power [1]

ii wind power [1]

2a i 1000 [1]

ii 25 km [1]

b from top: hilly or coastal areas, estuaries, coastline, mountain areas (4 = [2] 3 =[1])

3a tidal: sea water flows through turbines in barriers built across estuaries, [1] hydroelectric: involve less construction because uses rainwater trapped in upland reservoirs [1] **or** tidal: sea water trapped by tidal flow in estuary by long barrier, periodic not constant, hydroelectric use water flowing continuously from upland reservoirs, [1] hydroelectric ∴ continuous, tidal power is produced for only part of each tidal cycle [1]

b i hydroelectricity [1]

ii only possible where hilly not flat [1] with significant rainfall not dry [1]

4a HEP station that uses electricity from other power stations at off-peak time to pump water to upland reservoir, [1] when demand high, flow reversed and water in reservoir used to generate electricity [1]

b coal, oil and nuclear power stations run continuously as cannot be restarted quickly if demand rises suddenly, [1] water in reservoirs generates electricity when demand high [1]

P3.3

1a energy released by radioactive substances deep underground [1]

b solar energy not available at night whereas geothermal energy released all the time **or** output of solar panel reduced by cloud cover whereas geothermal energy unaffected [1]

2a 300 W/0.2 W per cell [1] = 1500 cells [1]

b to supply electricity when dark [1]

3a 200 kW × 48 hours [1] = 4800 kW [1]

b advantage: geothermal energy does not vary whereas wind energy depends on weather conditions, [1] disadvantage: geothermal power stations only operate where flow of geothermal energy from within the Earth is significant [1]

4a 0.010 kg/s × 4200 J/kg °C × (35 − 14)°C [1] = 880 J/s [1]

b 880 J/s = 0.017 kg/s × 4200 J/kg °C × $\Delta\theta$ [1] $\therefore \Delta\theta = \frac{880\ \text{J/s}}{0.017\ \text{kg/s} \times 4200\ \text{J/kg °C}}$ [1] = 30 °C [1] so output temperature = 44 °C [1]

P3.4

1a gas [1]

b increase of CO_2 in atmosphere, [1] acid rain [1]

c advantages: any two from: never run out, [1] do not release greenhouse gases/ CO_2 into atmosphere, [1] do not produce radioactive waste, [1] disadvantages: take up large areas, [1] affect habitats of plants and animals [1]

2a A [1]

b D [1]

c C [1]

d B [1]

3a solar, [1] wave energy, [1] wind [1]

b nuclear, [1] geothermal, [1] tidal [1]

4 discuss three types in terms of reliability (see **P3.2 to P3.4** for main points to include: each point requires an advantage and a disadvantage) [1] and environmental effects including use of land, [1] effect on natural habitats, [1] pollution, [1] and waste, [1]

P3.5

1a gas-fired [1]

b geothermal/hydroelectric/tidal [1]

c wind, solar, wave [1]

d hydroelectric [1]

2a not enough electricity at night if no wind or waves [1]

b more pumped storage schemes needed to store surplus electricity [1]

3 output power not increased quickly enough to meet sudden variations in demand [1]

4 HEP stations that use electricity at times of low demand [1] to pump water to uphill reservoir from lower level, [1] then reverse flow to generate electricity when high demand [1]

5a gas without carbon capture storage [1]

b i capital costs for wind and solar power much higher for same power output [1]

ii nuclear and coal-fired power capital costs much higher for same power output, [1] when include carbon capture storage higher overall costs for gas-fired/oil power [1]

c 4000 MW × 30 years = 4×10^6 kW × (30 × 365 × 24) = 1.05×10^{12} kW h [1] decommissioning cost per kW h = £1000 million/$1.05 \times 10^{12} \approx$ 0.1 p/kW h [1]

P4.1

1a i electrons transfer from cloth to polythene rod [1]

ii electrons transfer from perspex rod to cloth [1]

b electrons negatively charged, [1] glass loses electrons so gains positive charge [1]

2a attract [1]

b repel [1]

3a attract [1]

b attract [1]

c repel [1]

4a X and Y have same type of charge [1]

b Suspend R horizontally, rub with dry cloth to charge, charge X and hold near R, [1] if X repels R, X also negative, [1] if X attracts R, X positive, [1] Y repels X so same charge as X [1]

5a friction between soles of shoes and carpet causes you and shoes to become charged, [1] touching metal radiator gives shock because radiator earthed and you are charged at very high voltage, [1] electrons transfer between you and radiator as a spark [1]

b as you move in seat clothing rubs against car seat fabric so you become charged, [1] if metal frame of car earthed, [1] when you get out of seat you get electric shock when touch metal frame of car because charge on you creates a spark between you and car frame [1]

P4.2

1 1 = cell, 2 = switch, 3 = indicator, 4 = fuse (all correct = [2], 3 correct =[1])

2a circuit correct: diode at 2 with arrow pointing to 3 [1]

b variable resistor [1]

c 0.25 A × 60 s [1] = 15 C [1]

3a measure electric current [1]

b change current in the circuit [1]

4a circuit with bulb, wires and cell (all correct = [2] one component incorrect = [1])

b electron passing through battery gains energy from chemical reactions in battery, [1] electron transfers energy to filament bulb by colliding with atoms in filament as it passes through, [1] transfers some energy to atoms in wire in same way [1]

P4.3

1a $\frac{4.0\ \text{V}}{0.5\ \text{A}} = 8.0\ \Omega$ [1]

b suitable values read off graph and used [1] to give 10.0 Ω [1]

2 W 6.0 Ω [1] X 80 V [1] Y 2.0 A [1]

3a $\frac{12.0\ \text{V}}{0.015\ \text{A}} = 800\ \Omega$ [1]

b i 0.015 A × 1200 s = 18 C [1]

ii 18 C × 12.0 V [1] = 216 J [1]

4a suitable values read off graph and used [1] to give 10.0 Ω [1]

b i $\frac{1.6\ \text{V}}{10\ \Omega}$ [1] = 0.16 A [1]

ii 0.42 A × 10.0 Ω [1] = 4.2 V [1]

P4.4

1a i thermistor [1]

ii diode [1]

iii filament bulb [1]

b i $\frac{0.5\,\text{V}}{0.1\,\text{A}} = 5\,\Omega$ [1]

ii $\frac{2.0\,\text{V}}{0.2\,\text{A}} = 10\,\Omega$ [1]

2a $\frac{9.0\,\text{V}}{0.6\,\text{A}} = 15\,\Omega$ [1]

b ammeter reading increases, [1] because resistance of thermistor decreases, [1] so total resistance decreases [1]

3 if LDR covered current decreases [1] as LDR resistance increases [1] and p.d. still 9.0 V [1]

4a current = 0 until p.d. ≈0.7 V [1] then increases rapidly [1]

b resistance very large until ≈ 0.7 V [1] then decreases rapidly [1]

P4.5

1a 1.2 V − 0.8 V[1] = 0.4 V [1]

b $I = \frac{1.0\,\text{V}}{5.0\,\Omega} = 0.20\,\text{A}$ [1], p.d. = 1.5 V − 1.0 V = 0.5 V [1]

2a circuit with cell and 2 resistors in series correct [1]

b i 3.0 Ω + 2.0 Ω = 5.0 Ω [1]

ii $\frac{1.5\,\text{V}}{5.0\,\Omega}$ [1] = 0.3 A [1]

c total $R = \frac{1.5\,\text{V}}{0.25\,\text{A}} = 6.0\,\Omega$ [1] $R_X = 6.0\,\Omega - 2.0\,\Omega = 4.0\,\Omega$ [1]

3a i 2 Ω + 10 Ω = 12 Ω [1]

ii 2 × 1.5 V = 3.0 V [1]

b $\frac{3.0\,\text{V}}{12\,\Omega} = 0.25\,\text{A}$ [1]

c $V_P = 0.25\,\text{A} \times 2\,\Omega = 0.5\,\text{V}$ [1] $V_Q = 0.25\,\text{A} \times 10\,\Omega = 2.5\,\text{V}$ [1]

d i 2 Ω + 10 Ω + 5 Ω = 15 Ω [1]

ii $\frac{3.0\,\text{V}}{15\,\Omega}$ [1] = 0.20 A [1]

iii $V_P = 0.20\,\text{A} \times 2\,\Omega = 0.4\,\text{V}$ [1] $V_Q = 0.20\,\text{A} \times 10\,\Omega = 2.0\,\text{V}$ [1] $V_R = 0.20\,\text{A} \times 3\,\Omega = 0.6\,\text{V}$ [1]

4 any four from: same current through each resistor, [1] with additional resistor in series more resistors share total p.d. , [1] so p.d. across each resistor less, [1] current through resistors less, [1] total p.d. unchanged so total resistance (= total p.d. ÷ current) > before [1]

P4.6

1a 0.40 A − 0.10 A = 0.30 A [1]

b 3 Ω resistor [1]

c battery current = 10 A ∴ current same if *R* of single resistor = $\frac{6.0\,\text{V}}{10\,\text{A}}$ [1] = 0.60 Ω [1]

2a circuit diagram: 6.0 V battery across 12 Ω and 24 Ω resistors in parallel [1]

b i current = $\frac{6.0\,\text{V}}{12\,\Omega}$ [1] = 0.50 A [1]

ii current = $\frac{6.0\,\text{V}}{24\,\Omega}$ [1] = 0.25 A [1]

c cell current = 0.5 A + 0.25 A [1] = 0.75 A [1]

3a i $I_1 = \frac{6.0\,\text{V}}{2\,\Omega} = 3.0\,\text{A}$ [1] $I_2 = \frac{6.0\,\text{V}}{3\,\Omega} = 2.0\,\text{A}$ [1] $I_3 = \frac{6.0\,\text{V}}{6\,\Omega} = 1.0\,\text{A}$ [1]

ii 6.0 A [1]

b *I* through R_3 6.0 V/4.0 Ω = 1.5 A [1] total *I* = 3.0 A + 2.0 A + 1.5 A = 6.5 A [1]

4 *I* through 2 Ω resistor = 3.0 A [1] total *I* = sum of currents in individual resistors so > 3.0 A [1] equivalent *R* = total p.d. across resistors (i.e. 6 V) ÷ total current [1] as total current > 3.0 A, equivalent *R* < 2 Ω [1] (**or** current through 2 Ω resistor < total current [1] as all resistors contribute to total current, [1] p.d. across 2 Ω resistor = p.d. across combination, [1] so equivalent *R* < 2 Ω as total current > current through 2 Ω resistor and p.d. is the same [1])

P5.1

1a 12 V [1]

b 230 V [1]

c 1.5 V [1]

d 325 V [1]

2a no. cycles increases, [1] waves same height [1]

b no. cycles decreases [1] waves twice as high [1]

3 each centimetre →10 ms so one cycle takes 80 ms [1] so *f* = 1/0.080 s = 12.5 Hz [1]

4a d.c. in one direction only, a.c. repeatedly reverses direction [1]

b diode only allows current in one direction, (so it rectifies a.c. to d.c.) [1]

c i similar shape to P5.1, Figure 1 but when negative, current = 0 [1]

ii peaks not as high [1] horizontal spacing unchanged [1]

P5.2

1a live = brown , neutral = blue, earth = yellow and green [1]

b i so each appliance can be switched on and off [1] without affecting others [1]

ii brass doesn't oxidise but copper does, [1] brass harder than copper and doesn't deform as easily [1]

iii live wire could be exposed where cable is worn or damaged [1]

2a 1 = C, 2 = D, 3 = A, 4 = B (all correct = [2] 3 correct = [1])

b 1: flexible and insulator, [1] 2: insulator, doesn't wear and can't be squashed,[1] 3: good conductor and doesn't deteriorate, [1] 4: excellent conductor and wires bend easily [1]

3a each must be insulated to avoid dangerously large current in cable [1] due to very low resistance between live and other wires where they touch [1]

b earth is connected to terminal fixed to metal case, [1] other end of earth wire connected to earth pin, [1] so when plug connected to wall socket, metal case is connected via earth wire to the ground [1]

4a wall sockets: cables thicker so resistance lower and more current passes through them than through lighting cables [1] otherwise heating effect of current greater and cables would overheat [1]

b two-core cable has only live and neutral, three-core also has earth wire [1]

c any appliance with double-insulated plastic case can have two-core cable, [1] appliance with metal case must have three-core cable so metal case is earthed [1]

P5.3

1a 30 000 J/(8 hr × 3600 s) [1] ≈ 1 W [1]

b 5 A × 230 V [1] = 1150 W [1]

c *I* = 0.4 A (= 80 W/30 V) [1] *I* > 0.4 A would not melt 13 A fuse [1]

2a i 5 A × 12 V [1] = 60 W [1]

ii 12 A × 230 V [1] = 2760 W [1]

b i current is (50 W/12 V) = 4.2 A [1] so 5 A fuse should be used [1]

ii current is (800 W/230 V) = 3.5 A [1] so 5A fuse should be used [1]

3a in normal operation, current in oven = 3.5 A [1] so 3 A fuse would melt [1]

b i $\frac{12\,\text{V}}{4.0\,\Omega}$ [1] = 3.0 A [1]

ii 3.0 A × 12 V [1] = 36 W [1]

iii 36 W × 1200 s [1] = 43 200 J [1]

4a i $26\,A \times 0.25\,\Omega$ [1] $= 6.5\,V$ [1]

ii $26\,A \times 6.5\,V$ [1] $= 169\,W$ [1] (**or** $26^2 \times 0.25\,\Omega = 169\,W$)

b $\frac{169\,W}{6000\,W} \times 100\%)$ [1] $= 2.8\%$ [1]

P5.4

1a $3\,A \times 50\,s$ [1] $= 150\,C$ [1]

b $30\,C \times 4\,V$ [1] $= 120\,J$ [1]

c $P = 0.5^2 \times 12\,\Omega = 3.0\,W$ [1] $E = 3.0\,W \times 60\,s = 180\,J$ [1]

2a i $4\,A \times 20\,s$ [1] $= 80\,C$ [1]

ii $0.2\,A \times 3600\,s$ [1] $= 720\,C$ [1]

b i $20\,C \times 6\,V$ [1] $= 120\,J$ [1]

ii $3\,A \times 20\,s \times 5\,V$ [1] $= 300\,J$ [1]

3a $2\,A \times 60\,s$ [1] $= 120\,C$ [1]

b 12 J/C from battery [1] 9 J/C to lamp + 3 J/C to variable resistor [1]

c 1440 J from battery [1] = 1080 J to lamp + 360 J to variable resistor [1]

4a $4.0\,\Omega + 8.0\,\Omega$) [1] $= 12.0\,\Omega$ [1]

b $6.0\,V/12.0\,\Omega)$ [1] $= 0.50\,A$ [1]

c $4\,\Omega$: 2.0 V (= $0.50\,A \times 4.0\,\Omega$) [1] $8.0\,\Omega$: 4.0 V (= $0.50\,A \times 8.0\,\Omega$) [1]

d $4\,\Omega$: 60 J (= $30\,C \times 2.0\,V$) [1] $8.0\,\Omega$: 120 J (= $30 \times 4.0\,V$) [1]

e 60 J + 120 J [1] = 180 J [1]

P5.5

1.a i $5\,W \times 3000\,s$ [1] $= 15\,kJ$ [1]

ii $100\,W \times (24 \times 60 \times 60)\,s$ [1] $= 8.64\,MJ$ [1]

b i $3000\,W \times (6 \times 5 \times 60)\,s$ [1] $= 5.4\,MJ$ [1]

ii $1000\,W \times (30 \times 60)\,s$ [1] $= 1.8\,MJ$ [1]

2a i 80 J (= 20% of 100 J) [1]

ii 5 J (= 20% of 25 J) [1]

b efficiencies very different, efficiency of each LED much > efficiency of halogen lamp [1] energy per second transferred by light from halogen lamp is 25 J (= 25% of 100 W) compared to 1.8 J (= 90% of 2 W) for each LED [1] so 14 LEDs (~ 25/1.8) give same light output as one 100 W lamp [1]

3a $\frac{36\,MJ}{4 \times 3600\,s}$ [1] $= 2.5\,kW$ [1]

b $\frac{36\,MJ}{2000\,W}$ [1] $= 18\,000\,s$ **or** 5 hours [1]

4a $1.5\,A \times 230\,V$ [1] $= 345\,W$ [1]

b $345\,W \times (130 \times 60 \times 60)\,s$ [1] $= 161\,MJ$ [1]

P6.1

1a $0.024\,m^3$ (= $0.80\,m \times 0.60\,m \times 0.05\,m$) [1]

b $\frac{60\,kg}{0.024\,m^3}$ [1] $= 2500\,kg/m^3$ [1]

2a $136\,g - 48\,g$ [1] $= 88\,g$ [1]

b $\frac{88\,kg}{80\,cm^3}$ [1] $= 1.1\,g/cm^3$ [1]

3a i $0.000\,40\,m^3$ (= $0.10\,m \times 0.080\,m \times 0.05\,m$) [1]

ii $\frac{0.76\,kg}{0.000\,40\,m^3}$ [1] $= 19\,000\,kg/m^3$ [1]

b $v = \frac{0.0015\,kg}{19\,000\,kg/m^3} = 7.9 \times 10^{-8}\,m^3$ [1] thickness $t = \frac{7.9 \times 10^{-8}\,m^3}{0.15\,m \times 0.12\,m}$ [1] $= 4.4 \times 10^{-6}\,m$ **or** 0.0044 mm [1]

4 Use top pan balance to measure mass of bolt, [1] fill measuring cylinder half-full of water and measure volume of water in it, [1] tie bolt on thread and gently lower fully into water, volume of bolt given by rise in level of water in measuring cylinder, [1] use density = mass/ volume to calculate density of bolt from its mass and volume [1]

P6.2

1a i vaporisation [1]

ii freezing [1]

iii melting [1]

b same mass of ice cube and water in beaker after ice cube has melted, [1] density = mass per unit volume so if volume of ice cube > volume of melted water, density of ice < density of water [1]

2a condensation [1]

b evaporation/vaporisation [1]

c melting [1]

d freezing [1]

3a particles start to move about at random, [1] no longer in fixed positions [1]

b particles in water vapour move at random and not in contact with each other except when they collide, [1] when water vapour condenses on a cold surface, vapour particles lose energy when they collide with surface and stay on surface as a film of liquid, [1] particles in film move at random in contact with each other [1]

4 particles in gas much more energetic and move faster and spaced further apart than particles in solid or liquid, [1] for given mass of gas, particles occupy much greater volume than equal mass of same substance in liquid or solid state, [1] density = mass / volume, [1] density of gas much less than density of same substance as liquid or solid [1]

P6.3

1 boiling takes place at a certain temperature whereas evaporation occurs from a liquid at any temperature, [1] boiling takes place throughout liquid whereas evaporation from surface only, [1] evaporation can cause liquid to cool whereas boiling does not [1]

2a i graph with suitable scales, [1] correctly plotted points, [1] best fit line with flat section from 150 s to about 240 s [1]

ii 79 °C [1]

b 60 °C: solid, [1] at 79 °C: begins to melt, [1] after 90 s all melted and liquid temperature then rises to above 90 °C [1]

3 any two from: salt and water form solution which will not freeze unless temperature drops below freezing point of solution, [1] so no ice forms on road unless temperature drops below this freezing point, [1] if solution does freeze, grit provides friction between tyres and ice to help stop vehicles sliding [1]

4 particles move randomly in contact with each other as temperature falls from 80 °C to 75 °C, [1] as temperature falls particles lose energy and move more slowly until at 75 °C they stop moving around and substance changes from liquid to solid, [1] at 75 °C particles become fixed in position and vibrate, [1] once all substance has changed state, temperature falls from 75 °C to 70 °C and vibrations of particles less vigorous [1]

P6.4

1a particles in agas move at high speed in random directions, [1] colliding with each other and with internal surface of container, [1] pressure on solid surface caused by force of impacts of gas particles with surface [1]

b when solid heated to its melting point particles gain KE and vibrate more about fixed positions, [1] at melting point, particles gain enough energy to break away from each other and move about, [1] molecules that break free are in liquid state as they move about in contact with each other [1]

2a liquid: particles close together and move about, not in fixed positions [1]

b gas: particles far apart and move about [1]

c solid: particles vibrate about fixed positions and close together [1]

d does not exist: particles that vibrate about fixed positions are in solid and ∴ not far apart [1]

3 internal energy transferred to solid at its melting point gives molecules enough energy to overcome strong forces of attraction holding them together in solid structure, [1] PE increases as particles break free from each other [1]

4 heat energy transferred by heating from warm water to ice, [1] water cools and water particles move more slowly so they lose KE, [1] ice melts because it gains internal energy and particles in ice gain enough PE to break free from each other, [1] when ice melts, melted water from ice and warm water mix so molecules from the ice, on average, gain KE and molecules from warm water lose KE [1]

P6.5

1a 0.068 kg – 0.024 kg [1] = 0.044 kg

b 15 000 J/0.044 kg) [1] = 340 kJ/kg [1]

2 m_w = 0.152 kg – 0.144 kg = 0.008 kg [1]
L = 18 400 J/0.008 kg [1] = 2.3 MJ/kg [1]

3a $E_1 = 0.120 \times 4200 \times (15 - 9)$ °C [1] = 3024 J [1]

b $E_2 = 0.008 \times 4200 \times 9$ [1] = 302 J [1]

c energy transferred to melt ice = 3024 – 302 = 2722 J [1] specific latent heat of fusion of water = $\frac{2722\text{ J}}{0.008\text{ kg}}$ [1] = 340 kJ/kg [1]

4 $E = 0.100\text{ kg} \times 2.25\text{ MJ/kg} = 225\,000\text{ J}$ [1] $t = \frac{225\,000\text{ J}}{3000\text{ W}}$ [1] = 75 s [1]

P6.6

1a increases [1]

b unchanged [1]

c increases [1]

2 smoke particles move at random due to random impacts of air molecules, [1] if gas temperature increases, gas molecules move faster on average so impacts are harder and number of impacts per second increases, [1] so smoke particles move faster [1]

3 gas pressure stops increasing (or decreases) when valve opens, [1] number of gas molecules in cylinder decreases, [1] so number of impacts they make per second on cylinder's internal surface decreases and gas pressure stops increasing (or decreases) [1]

4a unless water is stirred, (hot water rises and so) temperature of water differs in beaker, [1] thermometer does not measure average temperature of water [1]

b air in flask before sealed at atmospheric pressure, [1] so pressure gauge reads atmospheric pressure before it is sealed [1]

P6.7

1 volume increases and pressure decreases [1]

2a $\frac{100\,000\text{ Pa} \times 0.000\,20\text{ m}^3}{50\,000\text{ Pa}}$ [1] = 0.000 40 m^3 [1]

b $\frac{100\,000\text{ Pa} \times 0.000\,30\text{ m}^3}{0.000\,15\text{ m}^3}$ [1] = 200 000 Pa [1]

c $\frac{100\,000\text{ Pa} \times 0.000\,60\text{ m}^3}{120\,000\text{ Pa}}$ [1] = 0.000 50 m^3 [1]

d $\frac{60\,000\text{ Pa} \times 0.000\,45\text{ m}^3}{0.000\,15\text{ m}^3}$ [1] = 180 000 Pa [1]

3 initial volume $V_1 = (100 + 20)\text{ cm}^3 = 120\text{ cm}^3$, final volume V_2 = 100 cm^3 [1] $\frac{100\,000\text{ Pa} \times 120\text{ cm}^3}{100\text{ cm}^3}$ [1] = 120 kPa [1]

4 to reduce volume of air in cylinder, force must be applied to piston to overcome force of air pressure in cylinder, [1] WD on air by applied force, [1] so internal energy of trapped air increases, temperature of air ∴ increases, [1] as compression rapid very little energy transfer to surroundings takes place [1]

P7.1

1a radiation from U consists = particles, radiation from lamp = electromagnetic waves, [1] radiation from U is ionising, radiation from lamp is non-ionising [1]

b radioactive atoms have unstable nuclei whereas atoms in lamp filament do not, [1] decay of radioactive atom cannot be stopped whereas atoms in lamp filament stop emitting radiation when filament current switched off [1]

2a i alpha [1]

ii beta or gamma [1]

b gamma [1]

3 atoms have unstable nuclei, [1] these nuclei become stable by emitting radiation [1]

4a substance emits (ionising) radiation [1] so radioactive [1]

b paper stopped most radiation from substance reaching Geiger counter, [1] paper absorbed radiation, [1] so must be alpha radiation [1]

P7.2

1 nucleus much smaller than atom, [1] nucleus positively charged, [1] mass of atom concentrated in nucleus [1] all positive charge of atom concentrated in nucleus [1]

2a B [1]

b A: attracted by nucleus [1] C: unaffected by nucleus [1]
D: repelled in wrong direction by nucleus [1]

3a i atoms not indivisible, [1] atoms contain negatively charged electrons [1]

ii any two from: nuclear: all positive charge concentrated in nucleus much smaller than atom, plum pudding: positive charge spread out throughout atom, [1] nuclear: most mass concentrated in nucleus, plum pudding: mass spread out throughout atom [1] nuclear: most atom empty space, plum pudding: no empty space [1]

b nuclear model explains why some alpha particles scattered through large angles, [1] in plum pudding model such large-angle scattering should not be observed [1]

4a similarity: proton and neutron have about same mass (**or** both found in nucleus) [1] difference: proton is charged whereas neutron has no charge [1]

b He nucleus contains 4 (neutrons + protons) whereas H nucleus only contains one = a single proton, [1] 2 protons particles in He nucleus because He nucleus has twice as much charge as H nucleus, [1] ∴other 2 particles in He nucleus are neutrons [1]

P7.3

1a 6 p + 6 n [1]

b 27 p + 33 n [1]

c 92 p + 143 n [1]

d 4 p [1] 10 n [1]

2a 92 p + 146 n [1]

b 90 p [1] + 144 n [1]

c 91 p [1] + 143 n [1]

3a $^{235}_{92}U \rightarrow {}^{231}_{90}Th + {}^{4}_{2}\alpha$ [2]

b $^{64}_{29}Cu \rightarrow {}^{64}_{30}Zn + {}^{0}_{-1}\beta$ [2]

4 $^{210}_{83}Bi$ [1] $\rightarrow {}^{210}_{84}Po$ [1] $+ {}^{0}_{-1}\beta$ [1]

P7.4

1a stops irradiation of nearby people or objects [1]

b alpha [1]

c α, β [1]

2a i gamma [1]

ii alpha [1]

iii beta [1]

b i gamma [1]

ii alpha [1]

3a can knock electrons from atoms, [1] this ionisation damages cell (**or** kills cell **or** affects genes in cell which can be passed on if cell generates more cells) [1]

b (place Geiger tube in a holder so it can be moved horizontally,) move tube so end close to source and Geiger counter detects radiation from source, [1] move tube gradually away from source until count rate decreases significantly, [1] distance from end of tube to source is range of α radiation from source [1]

4 very little γ radiation absorbed by foil, it would all pass straight through [1] so thickness of foil would not affect detector reading [1]

P7.5

1a average time for no. nuclei in sample of isotope to halve [1]

b 190 cpm [1]

2a i 4 milligrams (= 8 mg/2) [1]

ii 1 milligram (= 8 mg/2^3) [1]

b 5% of 8 mg = 0.4 mg [1] so mass < 0.5 mg (= 8 mg/2^4) after 4 half-lives, [1] time taken ∴ just over 4 half-lives → about 65 hours [1]

3a i 160 million atoms [1]

ii 1/32 (= 1/2^5) [1]

iii number remaining = 320 million/2^5 [1] = 10 million atoms [1]

b after 4 half-lives, count rate = initial count rate of 320 cpm/24 = < 37.5 cpm [1] so time taken to drop to 40 cpm from start < 180 minutes (4 half-lives) [1]

4 after 2 half-lives count rate due to wood = 25% of initial count rate, [1] ∴ the wood is 11 200 years old (= 2 × 5600 yrs) [1]

P7.6

1a beta or gamma, [1] can be detected outside body [1]

b gamma, [1] radioactive source injected into patient to enter organ to be imaged so needs to do least damage whilst in body, [1] gamma radiation passes through body tissue and detected using gamma camera [1]

2 any two from: food, drink, radon [1]

3a small 'seeds' of radioactive isotope placed in tumour, [1] radiation from isotope destroys cancer cells, [1] use isotope with half-lives not long enough to damage normal cells surrounding tumour, [1] half-life not too short or unstable nuclei decay before radiation destroys tumour [1]

b beta **or** gamma [1]

4a too short: radioactive isotope decays too much before scan completed, [1] too long: patient exposed to ionising radiation unnecessarily [1]

b too long: after scan radioisotope needs to be stored for a long time until radioactivity insignificant, [1] too short: radioactive isotope decays too much before scan completed [1]

5a any three from: emits radiation detectable outside body (e.g., gamma), [1] non-toxic, [1] short half-life (1–24 hours), [1] decays into stable isotope [1]

b stable isotope in body (or elsewhere) not dangerous [1] whereas unstable isotope harmful [1] as it emits ionising radiation harmful to body [1]

P7.7

1a nucleus splits into two fragments, [1] releases energy and several neutrons [1]

b nucleus absorbs neutron without undergoing fission, [1] forms unstable nucleus which decays [1]

2 (in order) B, A, C, D, B [1]

3a to absorb fission neutrons, [1] and keep chain reaction under control by maintaining even rate of fission [1]

b more fission neutrons absorbed so number of fission neutrons in reactor core decreases, [1] rate of release of energy due to fission ∴ decreases [1]

c thick steel withstands very high temperature and pressure in core, [1] thick concrete walls absorb ionising radiation [1] that escapes through steel walls [1]

4a A and D [1]

b undergone fission and released neutrons and energy [1]

c C and E [1]

P7.8

1a formation of nucleus when two smaller nuclei collide and fuse together [1]

b forms $^{3}_{2}He$ nucleus (with 2 protons and single neutron) [1]

2a so enough KE to overcome force of repulsion between nuclei so they fuse [1]

b energy output < energy input so does not produce any energy overall [1]

3 advantages: any two from: nuclear fusion fuel easily available [1] fusion products non-radioactive (**or** less radioactive than) fission products [1] fusion stops if plasma out of control, [1] disadvantages: any two from: very large current needed to heat plasma to start fusion [1] plasma difficult to control, [1] at present, fission reactors produce far more power than fusion reactors [1]

4a 1 p and 1 n [1]

b $^{2}_{1}H + {}^{1}_{1}p \rightarrow {}^{3}_{2}He$ [1]

c $^{3}_{2}He + {}^{3}_{2}He \rightarrow {}^{4}_{2}He + {}^{1}_{1}p + {}^{1}_{1}p$ [2]

P7.9

1a i hazardous and ∴ a danger to people and animals if it escapes [1]

ii contains radioactive isotopes with long half-lives [1]

b absorbed by surrounding tissues and could damage or kill cells in body or cause cancer, outside less dangerous as α radiation has no penetrating power [1]

2a may be more concentrated than outdoors and people could breathe it in, [1] lungs then exposed to α radiation, [1] ionising effect of α particles in tissue damages cells (**or** kills cells **or** causes cancer) [1]

b install pipes under house and pump radon gas out of ground before it seeps into house, [1] top of outlet pipe from pump needs to be high up outside house [1]

3 benefits: any two from: no greenhouse gas emissions, [1] reliable and secure electricity supplies, [1] large-scale generation from small sites compared with renewable supplies that take up much larger areas (**or** other valid points) [1] drawbacks: any two from: long-term storage of nuclear waste, [1] possible escape of radioactive substances into environment, [1] impracticality of fusion reactors, (**or** other valid points) [1]

4 any five from: total annual dose ≈2400 units/year so risk of death about 1 in 10 000 /year, [1] some such as cosmic radiation unavoidable, [1] measures reducing total dose by < 10 units/year (e.g. avoiding air travel) have negligible effect, [1] reducing food and drink unlikely to be effective, [1] may be counterproductive due to adverse effects, [1] e.g., cutting food intake by more than half only reduces annual dose by about 3% (~$0.5 \times 140/2400$) so reduce radiation risk very slightly but would harm human health in most cases, [1] could reduce risk from medical X-rays where possible by restricting use of X-rays and using MRI instead [1]

P8.1

1a size of quantity [1]

b scalar has magnitude only, vector has direction too [1]

2 between 20 and 21 km [1]

3 scale diagram with ratio B : A = 1.25 : 1 (= 15 N ÷ 12 N, arrow for B ∴ be 1.25 times the length of the arrow for A. [1]

4a depends on 48 N arrow length: e.g., 60 mm arrow → scale 10 mm ≡ 8.0 N [1]

b ratio B : A = 0.75 : 1 (= 36 N ÷ 48 N), arrow for B points downwards from object along dashed line, arrow ∴ 0.75 times length of arrow for A [1]

P8.2

1a decelerates [1]

b force equal and opposite to force road exerts on each tyre [1]

2a 50 N upwards [1]

b 200 N [1]

3a forces equal in magnitude to each other and opposite in direction [1] because book presses on table and table exerts equal and opposite force on book [1]

b forces vertically downwards but force of table on floor > force of book on floor [1] because floor supports weight of table **and** book, table only supports book [1]

4a 500 N downwards [1]

b 500 N upwards [1]

c 500N upwards [1]

P8.3

1 glider makes contact with track and stops moving along it, friction between glider and track no longer absent when glider makes contact with track so glider stops because friction opposes its motion [2]

2a opposite in direction to velocity [1]

b zero [1]

3a force of mud on car > force on car from tractor [1]

b 300 N [1]

4a weight vector downward vertical arrow with non-arrow end on car mid-way between wheels [1]

b support force vectors upward and vertical from point of contact of each wheel on road [1]

P8.4

1a i increased [1]

ii unchanged [1]

iii reduced to a quarter [1]

b 18 [1] N m [1]

2a anticlockwise [1]

b i increased [1]

ii decreased [1]

3a moment of applied force about pivot is greater the longer the handle, so greater force exerted on nail [1]

b rust on hinge increases frictional forces in hinge, [1] so greater moment so more force must be applied to door to overcome moment of frictional forces at hinge [1]

4 72 N [1]

P8.5

1 force applied to each handle of T bar acts at much greater distance from axis of T bar than force of nut on T bar so force applied to nut much > force applied to T bar, [1] as moment of forces applied to T bar must least = moment of nut on T bar to turn nut [1]

2 120 N [1]

3 uphill, climb force of wheel on road > on flat road, [1] turning effect of chain on gear wheel opposed by turning effect of frictional force of road on wheel, [1] if use larger gear wheel , turning effect of force of chain on gear wheel increases so force of wheel on road increases [1]

4 forces and fulcrum shown correctly, [1] correct direction of each force, [1] line of action of applied force 8 times further from line of action of cable force [1]

P8.6

1a and **c** centre of mass is where two diagonal lines from corners cross [2]

b centre of mass found by drawing two diametric lines at right angles, centre of mass is where the two lines cross [1]

2 centre of mass of child then directly below midpoint M of points of suspension of swing, [1] at this position, moment of child about M = 0 [1]

3 (see P8.6, Figure 4) make hole in one corner of card and suspend from rod, use plumb line to draw vertical line on card from rod, [1] repeat, hanging card from different corner, point where two lines meet is centre of mass [1]

4 in **a** resultant force = 0 because basket at rest, [1] **b** magnitude of resultant force is non-zero and acts towards wall in direction perpendicular to line between centre of mass and point of suspension [1]

P8.7

1a i 3.0 N [1]

ii 1.2 N [1]

b in both examples line of action of effort at greater perpendicular distance from pivot than corresponding distance for load, [1] smaller effort ∴ gives equal and opposite moment about pivot to load's moment [1]

2a Dawn [1]

b 340 N, 1.84 m [1]

c Dawn needs to move 0.5 × 450/340 [1] = 0.66 m towards pivot, [1] Dawn's distance from pivot = 1.84 m [1]

3 1.5 N [1]

4 20 N [1]

P8.8

1a 50 N vertically upwards [1]

b 500 N up the slope [1]

2a 5.0 N at 37° to 4.0 N force [2]

b 6.1 N at 26° to 4.0 N force [2]

c 6.5 N at 28° to 4.0 N force [2]

3 5400 N (to 2 s.f.) correct diagram [1] correct answer [1]

4a diagram shows vertical line intersected at same point P by 2 upward straight lines at 70° to vertical line [1]

b i weight vector as downward vertical arrow from P, scale shown and arrow labelled 'weight' [1]

ii resultant of two tension arrows is equal and opposite to weight vector, resultant arrow ∴ vertically upwards from P and same length as weight arrow, [1] completing parallelogram of forces gives length of the two tension arrows, [1] using scale should then give 2.9 N for each tension [1]

P8.9

1 690 N correct diagram [1] correct answer [1]

2a 130 N (to 2 s.f.) correct diagram [1] correct answer [1]

b friction on bearings of trolley wheels makes trolley harder to push **or** force exerted by student may not be parallel to slope [1]

3 not enough friction on ladder at floor [1] so weight pulls ladder down [1]

4a correct diagram [1] with parallel component = 25 N [1], perpendicular component = 43 N, [1]

b friction on box equal and opposite to parallel component of weight (25 N) [1]

P9.1

1a i does not change [1]

ii constant gradient [1]

b i $\frac{30\,000\text{ m}}{1000\text{ s}}$ [1] = 30 m/s [1]

ii 500 s [1]

iii $\frac{20\,000\text{ m}}{1500\text{ s}}$ [1] = 13.3 m/s [1]

2a $\frac{1800\text{ m}}{60\text{ s}}$ [1] = 30 m/s [1]

b 30 m/s × 3000 s [1] = 9000 m [1]

c $\frac{3300\text{ m}}{30\text{ ms}}$ [1] = 110 s [1]

3 distance = 7560 m, [1] speed = 18 m/s [1]

4a $\frac{360\,000\text{ m}}{160 \times 60\text{ s}}$ [1] = 37.5 m/s [1]

b $\frac{180\,000\text{ m}}{40\text{ m/s}}$ [1] = 4500 s = 75 minutes [1]

P9.2

1a speed is distance travelled ÷ time taken regardless of direction, velocity is speed in a given direction [1]

b distance apart = (30 m/s − 20 m/s) × 300 s [1] = 2400 m [1]

2 $\frac{28\text{ m/s} - 8\text{ m/s}}{16\text{ s}}$ [1] = 1.25 m/s² [1]

3a i as it left motorway [1]

ii when travelling at constant velocity [1]

b $a = \frac{v-u}{t}$ gives $2.0 = \frac{v-7}{10}$ [1] $v - 7 = 2.0 \times 10 = 20$ [1] ∴ $v = 27$ m/s [1]

4a $\frac{9.2\text{ m/s} - 0}{3.1\text{ s}}$ [1] = 2.97 m/s² [1]

b $\frac{100\text{ m}}{10.4\text{ s}}$ [1] = 9.6 m/s [1]

P9.3

1 i B

ii A

iii D

iv C (all correct = [2] any 3 correct = 1])

2a i A [1]

ii C [1]

b B [1]

3a 8 × 20 = 160 m [1]

b $\frac{1}{2} \times 8 \times 20$ = 80 m [1]

4a $\frac{1}{2} \times$ 4 m/s × 20 s [1] = 40 m [1]

b $\frac{1}{2} \times$ 6 m/s × 20 s [1] = 60 m [1] difference = 160 m − 60 m = 100 m [1]

P9.4

1a $\frac{120\text{ m}}{8\text{ s}}$ [1] = 15 m/s [1]

b increases gradually [1] from 0 at start [1]

2a constant acceleration from rest to 8 m/s for 40 s [1] then constant deceleration for last 20 s [1]

b i $a = \frac{8\text{ m/s} - 0\text{ m/s}}{40\text{ s}}$ [1] = 0.20 m/s² [1] $s = \frac{1}{2} \times$ 8 m/s × 40 s [1] = 160 m [1]

ii $a = \frac{0\text{ m/s} - 8\text{ m/s}}{20\text{ s}}$ [1] = −0.40 m/s² [1] $s = \frac{1}{2} \times$ 8 m/s × 20 s [1] = 80 m [1]

c $\frac{(160 + 80)\text{ m}}{60\text{ s}}$ [1] = 4.0 m/s [1]

3a suitable scales [1] correctly plotted [1] best fit line drawn [1]

b $\frac{40\text{ m/s} - 0\text{ m/s}}{20\text{ s}}$ [1] = 2.0 m/s² [1]

c i $\frac{1}{2} \times$ 40 m/s × 20 s [1] = 400 m [1]

ii 40 m/s × 10 s [1] = 400 m [1]

4 $v^2 = 0 + (2 \times 2.0\text{ m/s}^2 \times 1000\text{ m}) = 4000\text{ m}^2/\text{s}^2$ [1] v = 63 m/s [1]

P10.1

1a 640 N [1]

b 4.0 m/s² [1]

2a 16 N [1]

b 40 kg [1]

c 12 m/s² [1]

d 2.4 N [1]

e 25 000 kg [1]

3a 1500 kg × 2 m/s² [1] = 3000 N [1]

b i 600 N [1]

ii 3000 N − 600 N [1] = 2400 N [1]

4a total mass greater in 2nd case [1] and force same so acceleration is less [1]

b $F = 0.60m = 0.48(m + 0.5)$ [1] gives m = 2.0 kg [1]

P10.2

1a initial resultant force = weight [1]

b frictional force < weight [1]

c zero [1]

d zero [1]

2a 500 N [1]

b 80 N [1]

c mass = 300 N/10 N/kg = 30 kg [1] weight on Moon = 30 kg × 1.6 N/kg = 48 N [1]

3a resultant force = weight - frictional force [1] frictional force due to parachute increases with speed [1] so resultant force on parachutist decreases, [1] when frictional force = weight, resultant force = 0 and parachutist moves at terminal velocity [1]

b i 900 N [1]

ii 900 N upwards [1]

4a gradient measured at 0.10 s [1] = 5.2 m/s² [1]

b for mass m, resultant force at 0.10 s = $m \times$ acceleration a, a = 5.2 m/s² = 0.52g. Because resultant force = weight – drag force, drag force = $mg - ma$ [1] = $mg - 0.52mg$ [1] = $0.48mg \approx$ half its weight [1]

P10.3

1a braking distance [1]

b thinking distance [1]

c braking distance [1]

2a i 6.0 m [1]

ii 24.0 m [1]

iii 30.0 m [1]

b (30 m/s × 0.8 s) – (15 m/s × 0.8 s) [1] = 12 m [1]

3a i thinking distance proportional to speed [1] as reaction time is constant [1]

ii when speed doubled and braking force constant, braking time greater [1] so braking distance more than doubles (think about area under velocity–time graph) [1]

b braking distance divided by v^2 same for all three speeds [1] so braking distance proportional to v^2 [1] so claim is valid [1]

4a 312/150 [1] = 6.4 m/s² [1]

b 1500 kg × 6.4 m/s² [1] = 9600 N [1]

P10.4

1a momentum = mass × velocity, kg m/s [1]

b 40 kg × 6 m/s [1] = 240 kg m/s [1]

2a 80 kg × 5 m/s [1] = 400 kg m/s [1]

b 400 kg m/s ÷ 80 kg [1] = 0.5 m/s [1]

c 400 kg m/s ÷ 0.40 kg [1] = 1000 m/s

3a equal and opposite forces [1]

b equal and opposite momentum [1]

c v 80 kg skater = three-quarters v 60 kg skater [1] in opposite direction [1]

d total momentum = 0 [1]

4a 120 kg m/s [1]

b $80v = 60 \times 2.0$ kg m/s [1] ∴ $v = 60 \times 2.0/80$ [1] = 1.5 m/s [1]

P10.5

1a 1000 kg × 5.0 m/s =5000 kg m/s [1]

b (1000 kg × v) + (1500 kg × v) = 2500 v [1] ∴ 2500 v = 5000 [1] ∴ v = 2.0 m/s [1]

2 momentum before impact = (0.80 kg + m) × 1.1 m/s = (0.88 + 1.1 m) kg m/s [1] momentum after impact = (m + 0.80) kg × 0.70 m/s) + (0.80 kg × 0.70 m/s) [1] = 0.70 m + 1.12 [1] ∴ 0.70 m + 1.12 = 0.88 + 1.1 m [1] ∴ 0.40 m = 0.24 [1] ∴ m = 0.24/0.40 = 0.60 kg = [1]

3 a 12v = 600 × 0.5 kg m/s [1] ∴ v = 600 × 0.5/12 [1] = 25 m/s [1]

b less [1]

4 After they move apart, v_A is 1.5 × v_B [1] because mass of B is 1.5 × mass of A = 0.4 m [1] so if A travels 0.60 m, B would travel 0.4 m in same time as A travels 1.5 × faster than B. So the right hand block needs to be 0.4m from B at the start. [1].

P10.6

1a seat belt increases time taken to stop person [1] so change of momentum per second less ∴ force on person less [1]

b 0 – (0.1² kg × 18 m/s) = –216 kg m/s [1] impact force = change of momentum / time taken = (–)216 kg m/s / 0.0003 s [1] = (–)7200 N [1]

2a i Force = change of momentum / time taken 800 kg × 30 m/s / 6.0 s [1] = 4000 N [1]

ii Force = change of momentum / time taken 800 kg × 30 m/s / 30 s [1] = [1] 800 N [1]

b force = change of momentum / time taken [1] change of momentum same but time taken much less so force i much greater [1]

3a initial momentum = 2000 kg × 12 m/s = 24 000 kg m/s [1] = final momentum, [1] = total mass × the velocity after impact, ∴ = 24 000 kg m/s ÷ 12 000 kg = 2 m/s [1]

b i deceleration = change of velocity / time taken = (2 m/s – 12 m/s) / 0.3 s [1] = (–) [1] –33 m/s² [1]

ii change of momentum = final momentum – initial momentum = (2000 kg × 2 m/s) – 24000 kg m/s = [1] – 20 000 kg m/s [1]

iii force = change of momentum / time taken = –20 000 kg m/s / 0.3 s = [1] = (–) 67 000 N [1]

4 impact time on cushioned surface longer than on hard floor, [1] a given change of momentum, change of momentum per second ∴ less in fall on cushioned floor than on hard floor so impact force less [1]

P10.7

1 protects cyclist's head in collision (**or** if cyclist falls off cycle and head hits ground) because when impact occurs helmet increases time taken to decelerate head, [1] so it reduces change of momentum per second [1] and ∴ reduces impact force [1]

2a if car suddenly stopped, child would press against back of car seat spreading out force [1] and back of car seat would prevent child from being thrown forwards [1]

b it increases time taken to stop person, [1] reducing force of impact because change of momentum takes longer, [1] force spread out across chest so effect less [1]

3 reduces momentum of wearer more slowly than if no seat belt [1]

4a (2150 kg + 750 kg) × 9 m/s = 26 100 kg m/s [1]

b momentum before impact = 750 kg × v [1] ∴ 750v = 26 100 [1] which gives $v = \frac{26\,100}{750} = 35$ m/s [1]

c yes [1]

P10.8

1a limit beyond which tension no longer proportional to extension [1]

b force per unit extension as long as limit of proportionality not reached [1]

c increase in length from its original unstretched length [1]

2a does not return to original length when released [1]

b rubber band returns to original length when released whereas polythene strip does not [1]

3a i 80 mm [1]

ii 54 mm [1]

iii 10 mm [1]

b i 60 mm [1]

ii 3.0 N/0.060 m [1] = 50 N/m [1]

4a extension of spring directly proportional to force applied as long as limit of proportionality not exceeded [1]

b i 25 N/m × 0.10 m [1] = 2.5 N [1]

ii 5.0 N/25 N/m [1] = 0.20 m [1]

P11.1

1a weight unchanged, area of hands < area of feet [1] so pressure on hands during handstand > pressure on feet when standing [1]

b contact area of snowshoes much > contact area of soles of feet [1] pressure = weight/contact area so wearing snow shoes → less pressure on snow [1]

2a $\dfrac{1200\,\text{N}}{(0.60\,\text{m} \times 0.40\,\text{m})}$ [1] = 5000 Pa [1]

b $\dfrac{1200\,\text{N}}{(0.40\,\text{m} \times 0.05\,\text{m})}$ [1] = 60 000 Pa [1]

3 45 000 Pa × 0.0002 m^2 = 9.0 N [1]

4 $\dfrac{9400}{4}$ = 2350 N so contact area of each tyre = $\dfrac{2350\,\text{N}}{180\,000\,\text{Pa}}$ [1] = 0.013 m^2 [1]

P11.2

1a pressure of water greater at bottom of dam than at top, [1] so dam thicker at bottom to withstand greater force due to water pressure there [1]

b vertical distance from water tank to ground floor tap > distance to tap on higher floor, [1] water pressure increases with vertical distance below tank so water pressure at ground floor tap > pressure at higher tap [1]

2 rainwater flows along gutter to downpipe, if downpipe end higher than other end water overflows from lower end [1]

3a 0.090 m × 1000 kg/m^3 × 10 N/kg [1] = 900 Pa [1]

b 900 Pa × 0.0006 m^2 = 0.54 N [1]

4 measure volume V of tap water, measure height H of water column from same level as bottom of oil column,[1] empty U-tube and repeat test using same volumes of sea water and oil as before, [1] density of sea water/density of tap water = H_{tap}/H_{sea} [1]

P11.3

1 air sucked out → little or no air in straw → little or no pressure in it so atmospheric pressure on liquid surface outside straw pushes liquid up [1]

2 atmospheric pressure caused by air molecules colliding with each other and with surfaces, each impact causes tiny force on surface, many molecules hit surface each second so cause measurable pressure on surface, [1] decreases with height because number of molecules per unit volume decreases [1] (**or** pressure at any given altitude due to weight of air above [1] which decreases with increasing altitude so pressure decreases with increasing altitude [1])

3 100 000 Pa × 4.0 × 10^{-3} m^2 [1] = 400 N [1]

4 atmospheric pressure at 30 km ≈ 1 kPa so difference in pressure between 30 km and sea level ≈ 100 kPa, [1] assuming constant density and maximum height 30 km, $p = h\rho g$ where p = 100 kPa and g = 10 N/kg [1] $\rho = \dfrac{100\,000\,\text{Pa}}{30\,000\,\text{m} \times 10\,\text{N/kg}}$ [1] = 0.33 kg/m^3 [1]

P11.4

1a pressure of water on lower half of ball > on top half so ball experiences upthrust, [1] volume of liquid displaced by ball = volume of ball, [1] as water is much denser than air, weight of liquid displaced much > weight of ball [1] so upthrust on ball much > weight [1]

b cork doesn't absorb water and much less dense than water, [1] upthrust on cork doesn't need to be very large to support its weight [1] so cork doesn't need to be fully immersed [1]

2a upthrust acts on object in water, [1] reading on newton-meter < when in air as upthrust helps support it in water [1]

b reading changes gradually from 5.2 N in air [1] to 4.7 N when all in water [1]

3a ice less dense than water [1]

b i A has greatest density because it sinks and B and C both float, [1] A more dense than water, B and C less dense than water [1]

ii B floats higher in water than C so difference between B's density and water > C, [1] density of B < density of C so lowest density = B [1]

4a extra weight causes tube to float lower in water, [1] ∴ length of tube above water decreases (linearly) as total weight is increased [1]

b remove tube from water, add metal object (e.g., steel nail) of known weight to tube, [1] use ruler to measure length of tube (and cork) above water,[1] repeat five more times, each time adding another object of known weight, [1] record results in table, plot graph of L against W, [1] if prediction correct, graph has negative gradient [1] = straight line [1]

P12.1

1a oscillations perpendicular to direction of energy transfer in transverse wave but parallel in a longitudinal wave [1]

b i electromagnetic wave **or** waves on stretched string / wire [1]

ii sound waves [1]

c particles displaced so closer together [1]

2a transverse [1]

b i along rope from one end to the other [1]

ii oscillates in a direction perpendicular to energy transfer [1]

3 stretch slinky out, move one end at right angles to slinky for transverse waves or parallel to slinky for longitudinal waves [1]

4 ball moves up and down repeatedly on surface [1] because waves consist of successive crests and troughs moving across surface, [1] each crest pushes ball up and each trough allows it to move down [1]

P12.2

1 the number crests passing a point in one second **or** the number of cycles of waves that pass a point in one second [1]

2a i horizontally from P to next crest [1]

ii vertically from P to midpoint [1]

b P moves vertically [1] down to a minimum then back to point P [1]

3a 2.0 Hz × 3.0 m [1] = 6.0 m/s [1]

b i $\dfrac{6.0\,\text{m/s}}{1.0\,\text{Hz}}$ [1] = 6.0 m [1]

ii 6.0 m/s × 60 s [1] = 360 m [1]

4a 340 m/s × 5.0 s [1] = 1700 m [1]

b $\dfrac{340\,\text{m/s}}{3000\,\text{Hz}}$ [1] = 0.11 m to 2 s.f. [1]

P12.3

1 incident = reflected angle [1]

2 see P12.3 Figures 2 and 3: correct refraction, [1] correct directions, [1] refracted wavelength < incident wavelength [1]

3a slopes prevent reflection at sides of tank [1]

b reflected waves make it hard to see incident waves [1]

4 any four from: place sunglasses on white paper at fixed distance from light source in darkened room directly facing light source, [1] place light meter behind each lens in turn with meter as close as possible to lens without touching it, [1] mark position of meter at each lens on the paper, record each meter reading, [1] remove sunglasses without moving paper and record reading when meter at each marked position for each lens, [1] second reading – first reading for each lens → effect of lens on light: the bigger the difference the less light transmitted [1]

P12.4

1 340 m/s × 4.0 s [1] = 1360 m [1]

2a 20 000 Hz [1]

b time delay = 0.24 s (= 2.4 s /10) [1] distance to wall and back = speed × time = 340 m/s × 0.24 s = 82 m, s = 0.5 × 82 m = 41 m [1]

3a cliff face reflects sound from horn creating echo, [1] indicating cliffs nearby [1]

b distance = 340 m/s × 5.0 s/2 [1] = 850 m [1]

P12.5

1 amplitude decreases, frequency unchanged [1]

2 amplitude smaller, [1] horizontal spacing between peaks and troughs unchanged [1]

3 distance to sea bed and back = 1350 m/s × 0.36 s = 486 m [1] distance to sea bed = 0.5 × 486 m = 243 m [1]

4a vibrating tuning fork makes table surface vibrate, [1] vibrating surface creates sound waves in much greater volume of air than tips of vibrating tuning fork [1]

b switch on radio (or TV) and adjust sound to low level, go to adjacent room, close doors, [1] put ear to wall between the rooms and listen for radio, [1] sound waves from radio cause vibrations to pass through wall and send sound waves into ear [1]

P12.6

1a organs have different density to surrounding tissue, [1] so ultrasound reflected at tissue/organ boundaries [1]

b ultrasound is not ionising radiation but X-rays are, [1] X-rays harmful to living tissue, [1] ultrasound reflected at boundaries between tissues whereas X-rays are not [1]

c some energy absorbed by body tissue as waves pass through body, [1] amplitude of waves ∴ becomes smaller [1]

2a three, if last pulse is due to far side of body [1]

b i distance on oscilloscope screen between transmitted and far-side pulses = 0.6 × width of screen, [1] each far-side pulse takes 1.2×10^{-4} s to travel twice 180 mm, [1] so speed = 0.180 m/1.2×10^{-4} s = 1500 m/s [1]

ii ratio of distances on screen from transmitted pulse to nearest pulse and to far pulse is 0.54 [1] so distance from transmitter to flaw = 0.54 × 90 mm = 48 mm [1]

3 distance = 1350 m/s × 0.40 s = 540 m [1] so depth = 0.5 × 540 m = 270 m [1]

4a distance between back of lens and retina : distance between front of eye and retina = CD : AD = 0.70 [1] so distance from back of lens to retina = 0.70 × 24 mm = 17 mm [1]

b distance in **a** calculated by multiplying 24 mm by ratio of screen distances CD to AD, [1] these distances only measured to $\frac{1}{2}$ a square which limits accuracy [1]

P12.7

1a long (L), secondary (S), primary (P) [1]

b i P-wave [1]

ii S-wave [1]

c wave speed increases gradually with depth, [1] so waves refracted, gradually changing direction, [1] bending towards surface because parts of each wavefront further from surface travel faster, [1] so wavefronts <u>gradually</u> move back towards surface [1]

2a see P12.7 Figure 1: inner core, [1] outer core, [1] mantle, [1] crust [1] (correct and labelled)

b i they are transverse waves so cannot travel through liquid outer core [1]

ii speed changes at boundary, [1] because mantle is solid and outer core is liquid and seismic waves travel faster through solids than through liquids [1]

3a 5000 km/460 s = 10.9 km/s [1]

b 5000 km/(460 s + 180 s) = 7.8 km/s ∴ S-waves ≈3 km/s slower [1]

4 any six from: there is a shadow zone where no seismic waves are detected, indicating Earth has liquid core, [1] P-waves travel slower in outer core than in mantle indicating outer core is liquid whereas mantle is solid, [1] refraction at mantle/core boundary, and direction change away from boundary and from surface indicates change of state, [1] after travelling through outer core waves refract towards boundary when they travel into mantle, [1] overall effect is they refract more than waves that only just miss outer core, defining nearest part of shadow zone, [1] furthest part of shadow zone defined by waves entering core and refracted less than other waves that enter core, [1] existence of solid inner core deduced as very weak P-waves reach shadow zone [1] after entering outer core and then reaching solid inner core where refracted into shadow zone [1]

P13.1

1a radio waves [1]

b same for all electromagnetic waves [1]

c X-rays [1]

d microwaves [1]

2a radio, infrared, X-rays and gamma rays [1]

b microwaves, visible light, ultraviolet [1]

c radio, microwaves, infrared, visible light, ultraviolet X-rays, gamma rays [2]

3a $\frac{300\,000\,000 \text{ m/s}}{600\,000\,000 \text{ Hz}}$ [1] = 0.50 m [1]

b $\frac{300\,000\,000 \text{ m/s}}{0.30 \text{ m}}$ [1] = 1000 MHz [1]

4 all electromagnetic waves travel at same speed in space, [1] gamma rays and visible light travel same distance and emitted at same time so reach Earth at same time [1]

P13.2

1a i radio waves [1]

ii light [1]

b i microwaves [1]

ii radio waves [1]

2a handset signals would interfere with mobile phone signals so calls less clear [1]

b other signals might 'mask' emergency services signals [1] making vital conversations difficult to listen to [1]

3 $\frac{300\,000\,000\,\text{m/s}}{2400\,000\,000\,\text{Hz}}$ [1] = 0.125 m [1]

4a reflects microwaves from transmitter into receiver [1]

b i place receiver directly in front of transmitter and measure signal detected, [1] place metal plate between receiver and transmitter and record meter reading [1]

ii replace metal plate by cardboard and record reading again, [1] if reading not zero, microwaves can pass through [1]

P13.3

1a visible light, infrared [1]

b signals totally internally reflected so cannot escape from fibre except at receiver end, [1] radio signals travel through air so detected by any radio detector in their path [1]

2a child's skull is thinner than adult [1] so more radiation passes through more easily (and causes a greater heating effect) [1]

b light waves have a much higher frequency, [1] carry more pulses per second [1]

3 atmosphere absorbs microwaves less than radio waves [1] microwaves spread out less so suitable for satellite TV, [1] radio waves diffract more so better reception in hilly areas for terrestrial TV [1]

4a $\frac{300\,000\,000\,\text{m/s}}{105\,000\,000\,\text{Hz}}$ [1] = 2.8 m [1]

b lower frequencies not absorbed so much by atmosphere [1] → longer range so suitable for national broadcasts [1]

P13.4

1a X-rays pass through crack but not through surrounding metal, [1] X-rays passing through crack darken photographic film, [1] crack appears as break in metal object shadow [1]

b yes [1]

c metal case stops low-energy X-rays but plastic does not [1] plastic allows X-rays to reach film inside case, giving more realistic account of exposure [1]

2a penetrate skin → skin cancer, [1] damage eyes → sight defects or blindness [1]

b i absorbs most ultraviolet radiation from Sun [1]

ii ultraviolet radiation from Sun causes sunburn and skin cancer, [1] suncreams absorb UV that passes through ozone layer [1] to stop UV reaching skin [1]

3a X-rays and gamma rays [1]

b lead [1]

4a ionisation is process of making uncharged atoms become ions which are charged atoms [1] occurs when X-rays or gamma radiation pass through substances, [1] as X-rays and gamma radiation knock electrons out of uncharged atoms [1]

b i X-rays and gamma rays [1]

ii ultraviolet radiation, X-rays and gamma rays [1]

P13.5

1a absorbs X-rays, [1] otherwise X-rays pass through stomach so no details of stomach seen on X-ray film [1]

b used to destroy cancerous tissue [1]

2a dense materials such as bone absorb X-rays and stop them reaching film, [1] X-rays that do not pass through dense material darken film, [1] when film developed, clear images of bones and other absorbing materials seen as X-rays did not reach these areas [1]

b light from room would darken film [1]

c X-rays ionise substances they pass through, [1] ionisation can damage or kill cells [1] or cause cell mutation and cancerous growth, [1] shielding prevents X-rays reaching and damaging cells in parts of patient not under investigation [1]

3a X-rays used for therapy have much shorter wavelengths/greater energy [1]

b not enough energy to destroy cancerous tumours [1]

4a a measure of the damage caused by ionising radiation to a person [1]

b about 0.3 millisieverts ($\approx$ 13% of 2 mSv) [1]

P14.1

1a i 20° [1]

ii 40° [1]

b 42° [1]

2a two correctly reflected rays and normals [1] each reflected ray at same angle to the normal as incident ray [1]

b i reflected rays traced back to locate (virtual) image [1]

ii perpendicular distances from O to mirror and from the image to the mirror equal to within 2 mm [1]

3a 1st reflected ray correct [1] 2nd reflected ray correct relative to 1st [1]

b i 180° [1]

ii as two mirrors are perpendicular to each other, angle of incidence for second reflection = 90° – first angle of incidence, [1] ∴ adding both angles of incidence = 90° [1] ∴ adding both reflected rays= 90° so total = 180° [1]

4a specular: reflection of light from a smooth surface [1] so all rays reflect in same direction [1] diffuse: reflection of light from rough surface [1] scattered in all directions [1]

b real image can be focused on screen, [1] virtual image can't [1]

P14.2

1a decrease [1]

b zero [1]

c smaller [1]

2a first refractions towards normal and second away from normal, [1] rays before and after passing through b1ock parallel to each other [1]

b first refraction towards normal, [1] 2nd refraction away from normal [1]

3a both refractions drawn correctly, [1] angles correct to within 2° [1]

b as rays from bottom of pool refract away from normal at the surface, [1] they appear to travel straight from a point above the bottom [1]

4 all colours of visible spectrum from red to violet seen on screen, [1] violet furthest from original direction of beam [1] because prism refracts each light colour a different angle, refracting violet light most and red light least [1]

P14.3

1 cover appears black because blue absorbs all incident red light and reflects none, [1] title appears red because white reflects red [1]

2a black, because green absorbs blue light [1]

b silver reflects blue light so hat appears blue, dress still appears black [1]

3 light same colour as first filter passes through it, [1] first filter removes all other primary colours as only transmits light same colour as filter, [1] no light passes through second filter as it only transmits a different primary colour [1]

4. any six from: place meter facing lamp emitting white light in dark room and record reading, [1] place block so light passes at 90° through it to meter and record reading, [1] calculate ratio of these two readings, [1] rotate block 90° so light travels through a different thickness and record meter reading, [1] remove block and check first reading unchanged then calculate ratio of third reading : first reading, [1] if the two ratios differ it is because amount of absorption depends on thickness of block, [1] lower ratio corresponds to thicker block [1] as absorption greater [1]

P14.4

1a real image: formed where light rays from an object meet, [1] virtual image: formed where light rays from an object **appear** to originate from [1]
 b i real [1]
 ii virtual [1]
 iii virtual [1]
2a upright, enlarged and virtual [1]
 b i Inverted, magnified and real [1]
 ii move slide towards screen [1]
 c i $\approx \times 2$ [1]
 ii increase [1] until flower at focal point when no image seen [1]
3a real, inverted, enlarged, [1] magnification $\approx \times 3$ [1]
 b smaller [1] still inverted [1]
4 any six from: use millimetre ruler to measure diameter of object and record measurement, [1] place metre ruler alongside lens holder and screen with zero end at front of lampbox, [1] adjust lens and screen so clear image of crosswires formed on screen, [1] using set square and metre ruler, [1] measure object distance u and image distance v [1] use millimetre ruler to measure diameter of image and calculate magnification M [1] enter measurements in table, adjust positions of lens and screen and repeat for five more image distances, [1] plot graph of M against v [1] graph should be straight line with positive gradient and positive intercept on v-axis (at $v = f$) [1]

P14.5

1a [1] for each construction rays drawn correctly [1] for the image drawn correctly in the correct position
 b i real [1]
 ii diminished [1]
 iii inverted [1]
2a three construction rays drawn correctly, [1] [1] [1] image correct [1]
 b i virtual [1]
 ii magnified [1]
 iii upright [1]
 c image always smaller than the object [1]
3a diagram should show image and object correctly with image twice the height of object, [1] at least 2 construction rays drawn correctly [1]
 b 1.8 cm [1]
 c the nearer the object is to the focal point, the further the image from the lens [1] and the larger it would be, [1] no image formed at the focal point [1]
4a i scale diagram [1] at least 2 of the 3 construction rays correctly drawn, [1] object and image correctly located [1]
 ii inverted and real [1] at 2F on other side of the lens, [1] image = object height so magnification = 1 [1]
 b an inverter lens to invert image of distant object formed on screen by convex lens, [1] place inverter lens at 2F from image of distant object and move screen to distance 2F from other side of inverter lens, [1] image on screen then same way up as distant object and same size as object [1]

P15.1

1a i N
 ii S [1]
 b N-pole, [1] P repels X because it has same polarity [1]
2a i N [1]
 ii S [1]
 iii unmagnetised [1]
 b pole ofcompass nearest tip of nail induces magnetism in nail with opposite pole at tip [1] so tip of nail always attracts end of plotting compass nearest it because they have unlike poles [1]
3a X = N, Y = S [1]
 b needle would turn (anticlockwise) as N-pole end of compass follows Y [1] until X attracts the S-pole more than Y attracts the N-pole, [1] S-pole then turns towards X until adjacent to X when magnet completes the 180° rotation [1]
4 draw two straight lines crossing at middle, place plotting compass directly above where lines meet , turn paper so plotting compass points along one line, [1] place bar magnets equidistant on opposite sides of plotting compass, [1] move one magnet along the line so plotting compass points directly along the perpendicular line, magnet that is further from plotting compass must be stronger than other magnet, [1] because its effect cancels out effect of other magnet at a greater distance [1] (**or** valid alternative methods described correctly [2] and explained [2])

P15.2

1a see P15.2, Figure 1: concentric circles round wire, [1] lines of force in correct direction [1]
 b plotting compass points in same direction as nearest field line [1]
2a reverses direction plotting compass points [1]
 b gradually moves towards North, [1] magnetic field of current-carrying wire becomes weaker further from wire [1] so Earth's magnetic field has greater effect [1]
3a see P15.2, Figure 3: field lines are loops which pass through solenoid [1] and loop round outside, [1] lines in solenoid are parallel to solenoid axis [1]
 b i plotting compass points parallel to the axis [1] in a direction consistent with current direction in solenoid [1]
 ii plotting compass points turns more and more towards North [1] because field of solenoid becomes weaker so Earth's magnetic field has more effect [1]
4 similarities: field lines are continuous loops, [1] field lines reverse direction when current reverses (**or** both fields can be switched off by switching the current off) [1] differences: field lines around wire are circles whereas field lines inside solenoid are straight and parallel to solenoid, [1] field inside solenoid is uniform whereas field near wire is not [1]

P15.3

1a insulated wire wrapped in tight coils along iron bar, [1] coil connected to suitable voltage supply so current passes through coil and magnetises bar [1]

b although both can be magnetised, steel does not lose its magnetism when current is switched off, unlike iron [1] objects held on the electromagnet would not be released if the core was made of steel [1]

2 C, B, E, D, A (1st 2 correct, [1] last two correct [1])

3a current through electromagnet coil magnetises core, [1] armature is pulled on to core which opens make-and-break switch and cuts current, [1] electromagnet loses its magnetism so make-and-break switch closes and cycle repeats [1] continually so armature vibrates [1]

b buzzer has smaller mass than bell [1] so buzzer responds faster to switching on and off of electromagnet [1] which enables make-and-break switch to switch on and off at faster rate, so buzzer vibrates at higher frequency [1]

4a line graph with axes correctly labelled [1] suitable scales [1] correct points [1] best fit curve [1]

b 0.10 A current holds iron plate on the electromagnet, > 0.10 A needed to hold any weight attached to iron plate, [1] the greater the current above 0.10 A the more weight can be held, [1] but increase of weight less for equal increases of current, [1] increasing current beyond 2.5 A unlikely to enable electromagnet to hold more than about 12 N [1]

P15.4

1 any three from: when current passes through coil of motor, a force acts on each side of coil due to magnetic field of magnet in motor, [1] force on each side has turning effect on coil and because current on each side in opposite directions, forces also in opposite directions so motor turns, [1] each time coil passes position where coil perpendicular to magnetic field, split-ring commutator reverses connections to battery so current round coil reverses direction, [1] without split-ring commutator, forces would reverse and coil would turn back, vibrating, [1] action of split-ring commutator allows forces to continue to turn coil in one direction [1]

2a current in opposite direction [1] so force on each side in opposite direction, coil ∴ rotates in opposite direction [1]

b i faster (coil lighter) [1]

ii faster (field much stronger due to iron) [1]

3 force decreases [1] → zero when wire perpendicular to field lines, [1] direction of force does not change [1]

4 $\dfrac{0.024\,\text{N}}{1.8\,\text{A} \times 0.035\,\text{m}}$ [1] = 0.38 T [1]

P15.5

1a p.d. induced in wire when it cuts magnetic field lines, [1] induced p.d. causes current to pass through wire and ammeter while wire is cutting field lines [1]

2a no deflection of pointer [1]

b larger deflection [1]

c larger deflection [1]

3a induced current always creates magnetic field that opposes movement of magnet, [1] if magnet is moving, direction of induced current creates a magnetic field which repels magnetic field of coil if magnet is moving into coil [1] or attracts magnet if moving out of coil [1]

4 as magnet approaches and enters coil, pointer deflects one way briefly, [1] then deflects briefly in opposite direction as magnet moved out and away from coil, [1] second deflection bigger than first [1] because magnet accelerates as it falls through tube so its speed on leaving coil is greater on average than when it was entering coil [1]

P15.6

1a p.d. induced in coil when sides of coil cut across field lines, [1] p.d. reverses direction each time coil is at position where its sides are moving parallel to the field lines, [1] this happens every half-turn of coil so one full turn of coil corresponds to one full cycle of a.c. [1]

b voltage has greater peak value (i.e. amplitude) [1] and time period is less (or greater frequency) [1]

2a peak value smaller, [1] waves stretched more across screen [1]

b sides of coil cut more slowly across field lines so p.d. at any position of coil less than when coil spins faster, [1] waves more stretched out across screen because time for each cycle longer [1]

3a split-ring commutator reconnects coil opposite way round in circuit every half-turn, each time coil is perpendicular to magnetic field lines, [1] so induced p.d. does not reverse its polarity [1]

b correct half-wave form [1] half-wave part and zero part equal [1]

4 when coil is spinning, sides of coil cut across magnetic field lines directly when plane of coil is parallel to field lines, [1] induced voltage is peak value here because sides cross directly through field lines [1]

P15.7

1a to increase or decrease peak value (or amplitude) of an alternating voltage, [1] step-up transformer used to increase voltage, step-down transformer i used to decrease voltage [1]

b i if mains supply fails, battery takes over [1]

ii steps down [1]

2a 4000-turn coil [1]

b steel core not so easily magnetised and demagnetised, [1] when a.c. passes through primary coil, steel core would not produce as strong a magnetic field as iron core, so induced p.d. in secondary coil much smaller **or** transformer with steel core less efficient [1]

3a d.c. in primary coil does not produce alternating magnetic field [1] so no p.d. induced in secondary coil [1]

b current would short-circuit across wires instead of passing through them and cause coil to overheat or blow a fuse [1]

4a two insulated coils of wire wound on an iron core, [1] primary coil connected to a.c. supply, alternating p.d. induced in secondary coil, [1] transformer used to change amplitude (**or** peak value) of alternating p.d. [1]

b a.c. passed through primary coil creating an alternating magnetic field through secondary coil, [1] so an alternating p.d. induced in secondary coil [1]

P15.8

1 $n_p = \dfrac{120\,\text{V} \times 60}{6\,\text{V}}$ [1] = 1200 turns [1]

2a $n_p = \dfrac{240\,\text{V} \times 100}{12\,\text{V}}$ [1] = 2000 turns [1]

b i 3.0 A (= 36 W/12 V) [1]

ii 0.15 A (= 36 W/240 V) [1]

3a $n_s = \dfrac{6.0\,\text{V} \times 1150}{230\,\text{V}}$ [1] = 30 turns [1]

b $I_p = \dfrac{6\,\text{V} \times 1.0\,\text{A}}{230\,\text{V}}$ [1] = 0.026 A [1]

P16.1

1a comets follow elliptical orbits round Sun so distance from comet to Sun varies, [1] when near Sun, solar radiation heats them so much they emit light and become visible, [1] as they move away they absorb less solar radiation and stop emitting light [1]

b similarity: both orbit Sun [1] difference: orbits of comets highly elliptical whereas orbits of asteroids rounder [1]

2a i Jupiter [1]

ii Mercury [1]

b planets nearer to Sun than Earth too hot for liquid water to exist on their surface, [1] planets further than Earth too cold for liquid water to exist [1]

3 Earth would be frozen if far from Sun [1] because it would receive much less energy from Sun, [1] if close to Sun, water on its surface would evaporate [1] and atmosphere would be lost as heated so much it its particles would leave Earth and go into space [1]

4a particles in clouds of dust and gas pulled together by gravitational attraction, [1] clouds became increasingly concentrated to form a protostar, [1] as protostar became denser its particles collided more and its temperature increased [1] until it became hot enough for nuclei of hydrogen atoms to fuse together, [1] forming helium nuclei and releasing enough energy to make protostar emit light [1]

b star in which hydrogen nuclei in core fuse to form helium nuclei, [1] this is main stage in life of a star as it can maintain its energy output for millions of years until no more hydrogen nuclei left to fuse together, [1] Sun is a main sequence star because most of its core consists of hydrogen nuclei [1]

P16.2

1a B, D, C, A [1]

b i D [1]

ii fade out, go cold and become black dwarf [1]

2a i gravitational attraction acting on its mass [1]

ii radiation flowing to surface from core [1]

b white dwarf cools down, [1] when it no longer emits light it can no longer be seen → black dwarf [1]

3a i hydrogen [1]

ii uranium [1]

iii helium, iron [1]

b any two from: red giant star much larger than neutron star, [1] neutron star consists only of neutrons whereas red giant core contains helium and other light elements, [1] red giant star emits light and neutron star does not [1]

4a Sun and Solar System formed from debris of a supernova, [1] most U-238 formed from the supernova still exists because U-238 has half-life comparable with age of Earth [1]

b some Pu-239 was created in the supernova from which Sun and Solar System formed, [1] about 5000 million years ago, which is many half-lives of plutonium-239 so Pu-239 created then has decayed into other elements [1]

P16.3

1a i towards centre of the Earth [1]

ii towards centre of the circle [1]

b direction of satellite's motion is changed by force of gravity on it so it continues to circle Earth, [1] direction of its velocity always at right angles to direction of force of gravity on it, [1] no work done on it so speed does not change [1]

2a geostationary satellite orbits once every 24 hours, [1] GPS satellite orbits in half this time, [1] the larger the orbit, the longer it takes so GPS satellite in lower orbit [1]

b weather satellite takes less time to orbit than GPS satellite, [1] the larger the orbit, the longer it takes so weather satellite in lower orbit than GPS satellite [1]

3a Jupiter is slowest, [1] it is about 5 times further from the Sun than Earth because light takes 5 times longer to reach it, [1] but takes about 11 times longer to go round its orbit so its speed must be less than Earth,[1] Jupiter is about 13 times further than Mercury (as light from the Sun takes about 13 times longer to reach it) [1] but Jupiter takes about 120 times as long to orbit the Sun as Mercury , so must be slower than Mercury [1] (**or** for a circular orbit, speed of a satellite = circumference ÷ time it takes to go round once, [1] circumference of a circular orbit is proportional to its radius [1] so speed of a satellite proportional to orbit radius ÷ time satellite takes to go round once, [1] this ratio is equal to 1.6 for Mercury , 1 for Earth and 0.4 for Jupiter, [1] so Jupiter is slowest because it has the lowest ratio [1])

b Mercury is fastest: takes ≈ 0.25 years to go round its orbit although its orbit is 0.39 times size of Earth's, [1] ∴ Mercury is faster than Earth and Jupiter [1] (**or** Mercury has highest ratio in the analysis in **a** [1] so it is the fastest [1])

4 speed of satellite in circular orbit is proportional to orbit radius ÷ time satellite takes to go round once, this ratio is equal to 1.6 for Mercury and 1.0 for Earth [1] so Mercury's speed is about 1.6 times that of Earth, [1] Mercury's speed is ∴ 1.6×30 km/s which gives 48 km/s [1]

P16.4

1a i receding [1]

ii approaching [1]

b blue-shift means Andromeda must be moving towards us [1]

2a Earth, Sun, Andromeda galaxy, universe [1]

b i they have red-shifts of same order of magnitude as distant galaxies [1]

ii as brightness of a quasar seen from Earth is same as brightness of billions of stars in a distant galaxy even though a quasar is much smaller than a galaxy, [1] power output of a quasar is about same as billions of stars/a galaxy [1]

3a light from a light source (e.g. galaxy) moving away from us has increased wavelength due to motion of source, [1] this increase in wavelength called red-shift [1]

b i Y [1]

ii X [1]

4 any three from: these galaxies have different speeds because they have different red- or blue-shifts, [1] ones with red-shifts are moving away from us, [1] ones with blue-shifts are moving towards us, [1] some galaxies may be moving across but we can't tell because they are so far away [1]

P16.5

1a universe was created in a massive explosion about 13 billion years ago [1]

b no evidence for a massive explosion, [1] they could explain Hubble's finding that universe is expanding by assuming that universe has always existed and is expanding because matter is entering it and pushing galaxies apart [1]

c it provided evidence that universe was created in a massive explosion [1]

2 C D B A [1]

3a distant galaxies are accelerating away from each other [1]

b universe would stop expanding [1] and go into reverse, ending in Big Crunch [1]

4a ≈ 150 000 km/s ÷ 22 km/s) × 10^6 light years) [1] ≈ 6.8×10^9 **or** 6800 million light years [1]

b ≈70 000 [1]

MS1

1a ratio = 5.6 g : 25.2 g = 1 : 4.5 [1]

b width of strip = width of card / 4.5 [1] = 210 mm /4.5 = 47 mm [1]

2a $\frac{30}{24} = 1.25$, [1] ∴ ratio of car speed to coach speed = 1.25 : 1 [1]

b for the same time, $\frac{\text{distance travelled by car}}{\text{distance travelled by coach}} = 1.25$ [1]

∴ distance travelled by car = 1.36 × distance travelled by coach = 1.25 × 12 km = 16 km[1]

MS2

1a 1.679 s = 1.68 to 3 s.f. [1]

b 1.66 s [1]

c 1.61 s and 1.65 s [1]

2a 1 [1]

b 3 [1]

c 3 [1]

d 4 [1]

e 3 [1]

f 3 [1]

3a gas was hardly used in 1990 whereas in 2010 it was used to generate about 40% of UK electricity, [1] coal was used to generate about two-thirds of UK electricity in 1990 but in 2010 this reduced to about one third of UK electricity, [1] oil generated < 10% of UK electricity in 2010 but this is much more than in 1990, [1] nuclear power stations provided just under 20% of UK electricity in both 2010 and in 1990 [1]

b i renewable energy sources in 2010 were used to generate less than 10% of UK electricity whereas the comparable figure for fossil fuels was about 70%, [1] comparable figures for 1990 were about 5% for renewable energy and 75% for fossil fuels. [1]

ii since 1990, fossil fuel use as a percentage of total UK electricity generation down by about 5% [1] and renewable energy use up by about same amount [1]

4 speed ~ 0.1 m/s, [1] distance in 1 minute ~ 6 m [1]

MS3

1a i m [1]

ii m^3 [1]

iii kg [1]

iv N [1]

b i 7.2×10^{-2} m [1]

ii 1.6×10^{-5} m [1]

iii 3.85×10^8 m [1]

iv 5.6×10^4 [1]

2a the circumference of the Earth is much less than the circumference of the Sun [1]

b atmospheric pressure is proportional to altitude [1]

c 4.5 kJ is about the same as 4.61 kJ [1]

3a $k = \frac{F}{e}$ [1]

b unit of k is the unit of force (N) divided by the unit of distance (m) = N/m [1]

4a $e = \sqrt{\frac{2E}{k}}$ [1]

b √(J ÷ N/m) = m [1]

5a $S = \frac{v^2 - u^2}{2a}$ [1]

b 69 m [1]

MS4

1a i gradient [1]

ii y-intercept [1]

b i positive gradient straight line [1] through origin [1]

ii straight line below A with lower gradient and lower y-intercept [1]

2 $y \to F$, $x \to e$, $m \to k$ and $c \to y$-intercept [2]

3 $y \to v$, $x \to t$, $m \to a$ and $c \to u$ [2]

4 gradient of tangent at 4s [1] determined from gradient triangle [1] = 7.5 m/s (7.3 to 7.7 m/s acceptable) [1]

MS5

1a 4.4 m^2 [1]

b 0.21 m^2 [1] (both to 2 sf)

2a 3.4 m^3 [1]

b 14 m^2 [1] (both to 2 sf)

3a area of each coloured triangle is same, taking base of each triangle as 1.6 m, height of each triangle is half width of kite = 0.575 m (= 1.15 m/2), [1] area of each triangle = $\frac{1}{2}$ × height × base = 0.5 × 0.575 m × 1.60 m = 0.46 m^2 [1] so area of kite = area of both triangles = 2 × 0.46 m^2 = 0.92 m^2 [1]

Index